Contents

REPAIRS & OVERHAUL

Engine and Associated Systems

Transmission

Brakes and Suspension

Body Equipment

Wiring Diagrams

REFERENCE

Index

The Peugeot 205 was introduced in the UK in September 1983 as a five-door Hatchback with a transversely-mounted engine and transmission assembly driving the front wheels. The suspension is of front coil springs and rear transverse torsion bars.

Three engine sizes were originally available, featuring a chain driven overhead camshaft design mounted directly over the transmission. The GTi was introduced in the Spring of 1984 and was fitted with a belt-driven overhead camshaft engine with a side-mounted transmission. The GTI engine is equipped with an electronically controlled fuel injection system.

In October 1984 three-door versions became available, with an X series designation, in addition to the three-door GTI. Van versions were introduced in June 1985, together with the limited edition Lacoste, based on the GT version. In September 1985 the XT was introduced, being a three-door version of the GT, and at the same time the 954 cc XL three-door was introduced, having a higher specification than the XE. The 1580 cc Automatic was introduced in April 1986 at the same time as the Cabriolet CTI. The XS replaced the XT in July 1986, at which time the limited edition Junior, based on the XE, became available. The 1.9 GTI was introduced in August 1986, and at the same time dim-dip headlights and rear seat belts were fitted as standard. In December 1987 the new TU engines and MA transmissions were fitted to all except fuel injection, diesel and automatic models.

Latest models feature single- and multi-point fuel injection, with full emission control equipment and a sophisticated engine management system.

Peugeot 205 GTi

Peugeot 205 van

The Peugeot 205 Team

Haynes manuals are produced by dedicated and enthusiastic people working in close co-operation. The team responsible for the creation of this book included:

Authors	**Andy Legg**
	John Mead
Sub-editors	**Carole Turk**
Editor & Page Make-up	**Steve Churchill**
Workshop manager	**Paul Buckland**
Photo Scans	**John Martin**
	Paul Tanswell
Cover illustration & Line Art	**Roger Healing**
Wiring diagrams	**Matthew Marke**

We hope the book will help you to get the maximum enjoyment from your car. By carrying out routine maintenance as described you will ensure your car's reliability and preserve its resale value.

Your Peugeot 205 Manual

The aim of this manual is to help you get the best value from your vehicle. It can do so in several ways. It can help you decide what work must be done (even should you choose to get it done by a garage), provide information on routine maintenance and servicing, and give a logical course of action and diagnosis when random faults occur. However, it is hoped that you will use the manual by tackling the work yourself. On simpler jobs it may even be quicker than booking the car into a garage and going there twice, to leave and collect it. Perhaps most important, a lot of money can be saved by avoiding the costs a garage must charge to cover its labour and overheads.

The manual has drawings and descriptions to show the function of the various components so that their layout can be understood. Then the tasks are described and photographed in a clear step-by-step sequence.

Acknowledgements

Thanks are due to Champion Spark Plug, who supplied the illustrations showing spark plug condition. Certain illustrations are the copyright of Peugeot Talbot Motor Company Limited, and are used with their permission. Thanks are also due to Sykes-Pickavant Limited, who provided some of the workshop tools, and to Duckhams Oils who provided lubrication data, also to all those people at Sparkford who helped in the production of this manual.

We take great pride in the accuracy of information given in this manual, but vehicle manufacturers make alterations and design changes during the production run of a particular vehicle of which they do not inform us. No liability can be accepted by the authors or publishers for loss, damage or injury caused by any errors in, or omissions from the information given.

Working on your car can be dangerous. This page shows just some of the potential risks and hazards, with the aim of creating a safety-conscious attitude.

General hazards

Scalding

• Don't remove the radiator or expansion tank cap while the engine is hot.
• Engine oil, automatic transmission fluid or power steering fluid may also be dangerously hot if the engine has recently been running.

Burning

• Beware of burns from the exhaust system and from any part of the engine. Brake discs and drums can also be extremely hot immediately after use.

Crushing

• When working under or near a raised vehicle, always supplement the jack with axle stands, or use drive-on ramps. *Never venture under a car which is only supported by a jack.*

• Take care if loosening or tightening high-torque nuts when the vehicle is on stands. Initial loosening and final tightening should be done with the wheels on the ground.

Fire

• Fuel is highly flammable; fuel vapour is explosive.
• Don't let fuel spill onto a hot engine.
• Do not smoke or allow naked lights (including pilot lights) anywhere near a vehicle being worked on. Also beware of creating sparks (electrically or by use of tools).
• Fuel vapour is heavier than air, so don't work on the fuel system with the vehicle over an inspection pit.
• Another cause of fire is an electrical overload or short-circuit. Take care when repairing or modifying the vehicle wiring.
• Keep a fire extinguisher handy, of a type suitable for use on fuel and electrical fires.

Electric shock

• Ignition HT voltage can be dangerous, especially to people with heart problems or a pacemaker. Don't work on or near the ignition system with the engine running or the ignition switched on.

• Mains voltage is also dangerous. Make sure that any mains-operated equipment is correctly earthed. Mains power points should be protected by a residual current device (RCD) circuit breaker.

Fume or gas intoxication

• Exhaust fumes are poisonous; they often contain carbon monoxide, which is rapidly fatal if inhaled. Never run the engine in a confined space such as a garage with the doors shut.

• Fuel vapour is also poisonous, as are the vapours from some cleaning solvents and paint thinners.

Poisonous or irritant substances

• Avoid skin contact with battery acid and with any fuel, fluid or lubricant, especially antifreeze, brake hydraulic fluid and Diesel fuel. Don't syphon them by mouth. If such a substance is swallowed or gets into the eyes, seek medical advice.
• Prolonged contact with used engine oil can cause skin cancer. Wear gloves or use a barrier cream if necessary. Change out of oil-soaked clothes and do not keep oily rags in your pocket.
• Air conditioning refrigerant forms a poisonous gas if exposed to a naked flame (including a cigarette). It can also cause skin burns on contact.

Asbestos

• Asbestos dust can cause cancer if inhaled or swallowed. Asbestos may be found in gaskets and in brake and clutch linings. When dealing with such components it is safest to assume that they contain asbestos.

Special hazards

Hydrofluoric acid

• This extremely corrosive acid is formed when certain types of synthetic rubber, found in some O-rings, oil seals, fuel hoses etc, are exposed to temperatures above 400°C. The rubber changes into a charred or sticky substance containing the acid. *Once formed, the acid remains dangerous for years. If it gets onto the skin, it may be necessary to amputate the limb concerned.*
• When dealing with a vehicle which has suffered a fire, or with components salvaged from such a vehicle, wear protective gloves and discard them after use.

The battery

• Batteries contain sulphuric acid, which attacks clothing, eyes and skin. Take care when topping-up or carrying the battery.
• The hydrogen gas given off by the battery is highly explosive. Never cause a spark or allow a naked light nearby. Be careful when connecting and disconnecting battery chargers or jump leads.

Air bags

• Air bags can cause injury if they go off accidentally. Take care when removing the steering wheel and/or facia. Special storage instructions may apply.

Diesel injection equipment

• Diesel injection pumps supply fuel at very high pressure. Take care when working on the fuel injectors and fuel pipes.

⚠ *Warning: Never expose the hands, face or any other part of the body to injector spray; the fuel can penetrate the skin with potentially fatal results.*

Remember...

DO

• Do use eye protection when using power tools, and when working under the vehicle.

• Do wear gloves or use barrier cream to protect your hands when necessary.

• Do get someone to check periodically that all is well when working alone on the vehicle.

• Do keep loose clothing and long hair well out of the way of moving mechanical parts.

• Do remove rings, wristwatch etc, before working on the vehicle – especially the electrical system.

• Do ensure that any lifting or jacking equipment has a safe working load rating adequate for the job.

DON'T

• Don't attempt to lift a heavy component which may be beyond your capability – get assistance.

• Don't rush to finish a job, or take unverified short cuts.

• Don't use ill-fitting tools which may slip and cause injury.

• Don't leave tools or parts lying around where someone can trip over them. Mop up oil and fuel spills at once.

• Don't allow children or pets to play in or near a vehicle being worked on.

The following pages are intended to help in dealing with common roadside emergencies and breakdowns. You will find more detailed fault finding information at the back of the manual, and repair information in the main chapters.

If your car won't start and the starter motor doesn't turn

☐ If it's a model with automatic transmission, make sure the selector is in 'P' or 'N'.
☐ Open the bonnet and make sure that the battery terminals are clean and tight.
☐ Switch on the headlights and try to start the engine. If the headlights go very dim when you're trying to start, the battery is probably flat. Get out of trouble by jump starting (see next page) using a friend's car.

If your car won't start even though the starter motor turns as normal

☐ Is there fuel in the tank?
☐ Is there moisture on electrical components under the bonnet? Switch off the ignition, then wipe off any obvious dampness with a dry cloth. Spray a water-repellent aerosol product (WD-40 or equivalent) on ignition and fuel system electrical connectors like those shown in the photos. Pay special attention to the ignition coil wiring connector and HT leads. (Note that Diesel engines don't normally suffer from damp.)

A Check that the spark plug HT leads are securely connected by pushing them home

B Check that all ignition wiring connectors such as this at the distributor are secure and spray with water dispersant if necessary.

C Check the security of all the fuel injection system wiring connectors (where applicable).

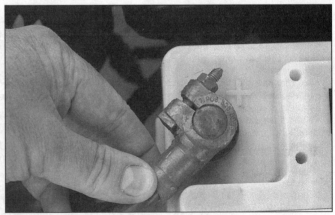

D Check the security and condition of the battery terminals.

Check that electrical connections are secure (with the ignition switched off) and spray them with a water dispersant spray like WD40 if you suspect a problem due to damp

Jump starting

HAYNES HINT *Jump starting will get you out of trouble, but you must correct whatever made the battery go flat in the first place. There are three possibilities:*

1 *The battery has been drained by repeated attempts to start, or by leaving the lights on.*

2 *The charging system is not working properly (alternator drivebelt slack or broken, alternator wiring fault or alternator itself faulty).*

3 *The battery itself is at fault (electrolyte low, or battery worn out).*

When jump-starting a car using a booster battery, observe the following precautions:

✔ Before connecting the booster battery, make sure that the ignition is switched off.

✔ Ensure that all electrical equipment (lights, heater, wipers, etc) is switched off.

✔ Make sure that the booster battery is the same voltage as the discharged one in the vehicle.

✔ If the battery is being jump-started from the battery in another vehicle, the two vehcles MUST NOT TOUCH each other.

✔ Make sure that the transmission is in neutral (or PARK, in the case of automatic transmission).

1 Connect one end of the red jump lead to the positive (+) terminal of the flat battery

2 Connect the other end of the red lead to the positive (+) terminal of the booster battery.

3 Connect one end of the black jump lead to the negative (-) terminal of the booster battery

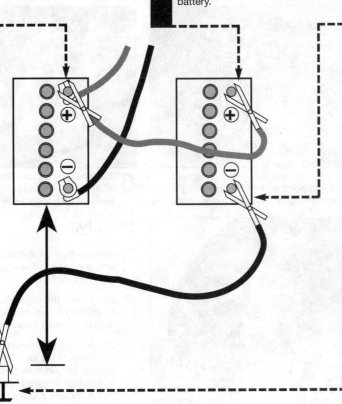

4 Connect the other end of the black jump lead to a bolt or bracket on the engine block, well away from the battery, on the vehicle to be started.

5 Make sure that the jump leads will not come into contact with the fan, drive-belts or other moving parts of the engine.

6 Start the engine using the booster battery, then with the engine running at idle speed, disconnect the jump leads in the reverse order of connection.

Wheel changing

Some of the details shown here will vary according to model. For instance, the location of the spare wheel and jack is not the same on all cars. However, the basic principles apply to all vehicles.

Preparation

□ When a puncture occurs, stop as soon as it is safe to do so.
□ Park on firm level ground, if possible, and well out of the way of other traffic.
□ Use hazard warning lights if necessary.

⚠ **Warning: Do not change a wheel in a situation where you risk being hit by other traffic. On busy roads, try to stop in a lay-by or a gateway. Be wary of passing traffic while changing the wheel – it is easy to become distracted by the job in hand.**

□ If you have one, use a warning triangle to alert other drivers of your presence.
□ Apply the handbrake and engage first or reverse gear.
□ Chock the wheel diagonally opposite the one being removed – a couple of large stones will do for this.
□ If the ground is soft, use a flat piece of wood to spread the load under the foot of the jack.

Changing the wheel

1 From inside the boot area, use the wheelbrace to lower the spare wheel cradle.

2 Slide the spare wheel out from the underside of the car.

3 For safety in the event of the jack slipping, position the spare wheel under the sill, close to the jacking point.

4 Remove the wheel trim (where fitted) then slacken each wheel bolt by a half turn.

5 Locate the jack below the reinforced jacking point and on firm ground (don't jack the car at any other point on the sill).

6 Turn the jack handle clockwise until the wheel is raised clear of the ground, remove the bolts and lift the wheel clear.

7 Position the spare wheel and fit the bolts. Tighten moderately with the wheelbrace, then lower the car to the ground.

8 Tighten the wheel bolts in the sequence shown, fit the wheel trim, and secure the punctured wheel in the spare wheel cradle.

Finally...

□ Remove the wheel chocks. Stow the jack and tools in the appropriate locations in the car.

□ Don't leave the spare wheel cradle empty and unsecured – it could drop onto the ground while the car is moving.

□ Check the tyre pressure on the wheel just fitted. If it is low, or if you don't have a pressure gauge with you, drive slowly to the nearest garage and inflate the tyre to the correct pressure. Have the damaged tyre or wheel repaired, or renew it, as soon as possible.

Identifying leaks

Puddles on the garage floor or drive, or obvious wetness under the bonnet or underneath the car, suggest a leak that needs investigating. It can sometimes be difficult to decide where the leak is coming from, especially if the engine bay is very dirty already. Leaking oil or fluid can also be blown rearwards by the passage of air under the car, giving a false impression of where the problem lies.

⚠ **Warning:** *Most automotive oils and fluids are poisonous. Wash them off skin, and change out of contaminated clothing, without delay.*

HAYNES HINT *The smell of a fluid leaking from the car may provide a clue to what's leaking. Some fluids are distinctively coloured. It may help to clean the car carefully and to park it over some clean paper overnight as an aid to locating the source of the leak.*

Remember that some leaks may only occur while the engine is running.

Sump oil

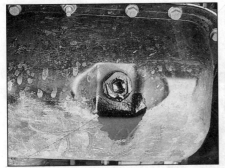

Engine oil may leak from the drain plug...

Oil from filter

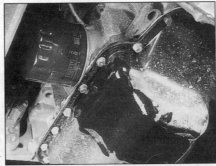

...or from the base of the oil filter.

Gearbox oil

Gearbox oil can leak from the seals at the inboard ends of the driveshafts.

Antifreeze

Leaking antifreeze often leaves a crystalline deposit like this.

Brake fluid

A leak occurring at a wheel is almost certainly brake fluid.

Power steering fluid

Power steering fluid may leak from the pipe connectors on the steering rack.

Towing

When all else fails, you may find yourself having to get a tow home – or of course you may be helping somebody else. Long-distance recovery should only be done by a garage or breakdown service. For shorter distances, DIY towing using another car is easy enough, but observe the following points:

☐ Use a proper tow-rope – they are not expensive. The vehicle being towed must display an 'ON TOW' sign in its rear window.
☐ Always turn the ignition key to the 'on' position when the vehicle is being towed, so that the steering lock is released, and that the direction indicator and brake lights will work.

☐ Only attach the tow-rope to the towing eyes provided.
☐ Before being towed, release the handbrake and select neutral on the transmission.
☐ Note that greater-than-usual pedal pressure will be required to operate the brakes, since the vacuum servo unit is only operational with the engine running.
☐ On models with power steering, greater-than-usual steering effort will also be required.
☐ The driver of the car being towed must keep the tow-rope taut at all times to avoid snatching.
☐ Make sure that both drivers know the route before setting off.

☐ Only drive at moderate speeds and keep the distance towed to a minimum. Drive smoothly and allow plenty of time for slowing down at junctions.
☐ On models with automatic transmission, special precautions apply. If in doubt, do not tow, or transmission damage may result.
☐ **Do not** tow BH type gearbox models with the front wheels on the ground for long distances, as the engine lubrication system also supplies pressure-fed oil to the gears and differential bearings Unnecessary wear may occur if the car is towed with the engine stopped.

Introduction

There are some very simple checks which need only take a few minutes to carry out, but which could save you a lot of inconvenience and expense.

These "Weekly checks" require no great skill or special tools, and the small amount of time they take to perform could prove to be very well spent, for example;

☐ Keeping an eye on tyre condition and pressures, will not only help to stop them wearing out prematurely, but could also save your life.

☐ Many breakdowns are caused by electrical problems. Battery-related faults are particularly common, and a quick check on a regular basis will often prevent the majority of these.

☐ If your car develops a brake fluid leak, the first time you might know about it is when your brakes don't work properly. Checking the level regularly will give advance warning of this kind of problem.

☐ If the oil or coolant levels run low, the cost of repairing any engine damage will be far greater than fixing the leak, for example.

Underbonnet check points

◀ TU series

Other engine similar

A *Engine oil level dipstick*
B *Engine oil filler cap*
C *Coolant expansion tank*
D *Brake fluid reservoir*
E *Screen washer fluid reservoir*
F *Battery*

Engine oil level

Before you start

✔ Make sure that your car is on level ground.
✔ Check the oil level before the car is driven, or at least 5 minutes after the engine has been switched off.

 If the oil is checked immediately after driving the vehicle, some of the oil will remain in the upper engine components, resulting in an inaccurate reading on the dipstick!

The correct oil

Modern engines place great demands on their oil. It is very important that the correct oil for your car is used (See "Lubricants, fluids and tyre pressures").

Car Care

● If you have to add oil frequently, you should check whether you have any oil leaks. Place some clean paper under the car overnight, and check for stains in the morning. If there are no leaks, the engine may be burning oil *(see "Fault Finding")*.

● Always maintain the level between the upper and lower dipstick marks (see photo 3). If the level is too low severe engine damage may occur. Oil seal failure may result if the engine is overfilled by adding too much oil.

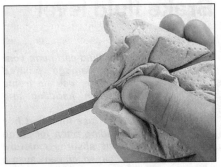

1 The dipstick top is often brightly coloured for easy identification (see *"Underbonnet check points"* on page 0•10 for exact location). Withdraw the dipstick.

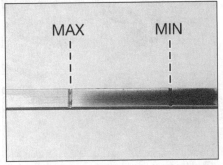

3 Note the oil level on the end of the dipstick, which should be between the upper ("MAX") mark and lower ("MIN") mark. Approximately 1.0 litre of oil will raise the level from the lower mark to the upper mark.

2 Using a clean rag or paper towel remove all oil from the dipstick. Insert the clean dipstick into the tube as far as it will go, then withdraw it again.

4 Oil is added through the filler cap. Unscrew the cap and top-up the level; a funnel may help to reduce spillage. Add the oil slowly, checking the level on the dipstick often. Don't overfill (see *"Car Care"* left).

Coolant level

⚠ **Warning: DO NOT attempt to remove the expansion tank pressure cap when the engine is hot, as there is a very great risk of scalding. Do not leave open containers of coolant about, as it is poisonous.**

Car Care

● With a sealed-type cooling system, adding coolant should not be necessary on a regular basis. If frequent topping-up is required, it is likely there is a leak. Check the radiator, all hoses and joint faces for signs of staining or wetness, and rectify as necessary.

● It is important that antifreeze is used in the cooling system all year round, not just during the winter months. Don't top-up with water alone, as the antifreeze will become too diluted.

1 The coolant level varies with engine temperature. When cold, the coolant level should be between the "MAX" and "MIN" marks. When the engine is hot, the level may rise slightly above the "MAX" mark.

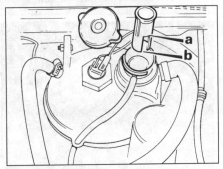

2 Where the expansion tank has a level indicator inside the expansion tank, the coolant level should be between the upper level indicator step (a) and lower step (b). On all engines, when the coolant is hot, the level may rise above the "MAX" mark or level indicator step.

3 If topping-up is necessary, turn the expansion tank cap slowly anti-clockwise and wait until any pressure in the system is released. Once any pressure is released, unscrew it fully and lift it off. Add a mixture of water and antifreeze through the filler neck until the coolant is at the correct level. Refit the cap, turning it clockwise as far as it will go to secure.

Brake fluid level

Warning:
● Brake fluid can harm your eyes and damage painted surfaces, so use extreme caution when handling and pouring it.
● Do not use fluid that has been standing open for some time, as it absorbs moisture from the air, which can cause a dangerous loss of braking effectiveness.

 HAYNES HiNT
● Make sure that your car is on level ground.
● The fluid level in the reservoir will drop slightly as the brake pads wear down, but the fluid level must never be allowed to drop below the "MIN" mark.

Safety First!

● If the reservoir requires repeated topping-up this is an indication of a fluid leak somewhere in the system, which should be investigated immediately.

● If a leak is suspected, the car should not be driven until the braking system has been checked. Never take any risks where brakes are concerned.

1 The "MAX" and "MIN" marks are indicated on the front of the reservoir. The fluid level must be kept between the marks at all times.

3 Unscrew the reservoir cap and carefully lift it out of position. Inspect the reservoir, if the fluid is dirty the hydraulic system should be drained and refilled (see Chapter 1).

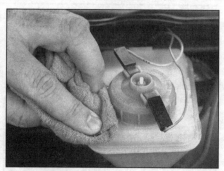

2 If topping-up is necessary, first wipe clean the area around the filler cap to prevent dirt entering the hydraulic system.

4 Carefully add fluid, taking care not to spill it onto the surrounding components. Use only the specified fluid; mixing different types can cause damage to the system. After topping-up to the correct level, securely refit the cap and wipe off any spilt fluid.

Power steering fluid level

Before you start:

✔ Park the vehicle on level ground.
✔ Set the steering wheel straight-ahead.
✔ The engine should be turned off.

 HAYNES HiNT
For the check to be accurate, the steering must not be turned once the engine has been stopped.

Safety First!

● The need for frequent topping-up indicates a leak, which should be investigated immediately.

1 The reservoir is located in the front left-hand corner of the engine compartment, next to the battery. Wipe clean the area around the reservoir filler neck and unscrew the filler cap/dipstick from the reservoir.

2 When the engine is cold, the fluid level should be between the "MAX" mark and the "MIN" mark on the reservoir or filler cap dipstick. Top-up as necessary to maintain the level between the two marks.

3 When topping-up, use the specified type of fluid and do not overfill the reservoir. When the level is correct, securely refit the cap.

Screen washer fluid level

Screenwash additives not only keep the winscreen clean during foul weather, they also prevent the washer system freezing in cold weather - which is when you are likely to need it most. Don't top up using plain water as the screenwash will become too diluted, and will freeze during cold weather. *On no account use coolant antifreeze in the washer system - this could discolour or damage paintwork.*

The screenwasher fluid is also used to clean the tailgate rear window, and on some models, the headlights

The washer fluid reservoir filler is located at the front left-hand side of the engine compartment (or right-hand side on models with headlight wash).

The washer reservoir itself is actually located under the car on some models; release the cap and observe the level in the reservoir by looking down the filler neck.

1 When topping-up the reservoir, add a screenwash additive in the quantities recommended on the bottle.

Battery

Caution: Before carrying out any work on the vehicle battery, read the precautions given in "Safety first" at the start of this manual.

✔ Make sure that the battery tray is in good condition, and that the clamp is tight. Corrosion on the tray, retaining clamp and the battery itself can be removed with a solution of water and baking soda. Thoroughly rinse all cleaned areas with water. Any metal parts damaged by corrosion should be covered with a zinc-based primer, then painted.

✔ Periodically (approximately every three months), check the charge condition of the battery as described in Chapter 5A.

✔ If the battery is flat, and you need to jump start your vehicle, see *Roadside Repairs.*

1 The battery is located on the left-hand side of the engine compartment. The exterior of the battery should be inspected periodically for damage such as a cracked case or cover.

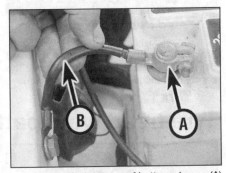

2 Check the tightness of battery clamps (A) to ensure good electrical connections. You should not be able to move them. Also check each cable (B) for cracks and frayed conductors.

HAYNES HINT

Battery corrosion can be kept to a minimum by applying a layer of petroleum jelly to the clamps and terminals after they are reconnected.

3 If corrosion (white, fluffy deposits) is evident, remove the cables from the battery terminals, clean them with a small wire brush, then refit them. Automotive stores sell a tool for cleaning the battery post . . .

4 . . . as well as the battery cable clamps

Tyre condition and pressure

It is very important that tyres are in good condition, and at the correct pressure - having a tyre failure at any speed is highly dangerous. Tyre wear is influenced by driving style - harsh braking and acceleration, or fast cornering, will all produce more rapid tyre wear. As a general rule, the front tyres wear out faster than the rears. Interchanging the tyres from front to rear ("rotating" the tyres) may result in more even wear. However, if this is completely effective, you may have the expense of replacing all four tyres at once!

Remove any nails or stones embedded in the tread before they penetrate the tyre to cause deflation. If removal of a nail does reveal that the tyre has been punctured, refit the nail so that its point of penetration is marked. Then immediately change the wheel, and have the tyre repaired by a tyre dealer.

Regularly check the tyres for damage in the form of cuts or bulges, especially in the sidewalls. Periodically remove the wheels, and clean any dirt or mud from the inside and outside surfaces. Examine the wheel rims for signs of rusting, corrosion or other damage. Light alloy wheels are easily damaged by "kerbing" whilst parking; steel wheels may also become dented or buckled. A new wheel is very often the only way to overcome severe damage.

New tyres should be balanced when they are fitted, but it may become necessary to re-balance them as they wear, or if the balance weights fitted to the wheel rim should fall off. Unbalanced tyres will wear more quickly, as will the steering and suspension components. Wheel imbalance is normally signified by vibration, particularly at a certain speed (typically around 50 mph). If this vibration is felt only through the steering, then it is likely that just the front wheels need balancing. If, however, the vibration is felt through the whole car, the rear wheels could be out of balance. Wheel balancing should be carried out by a tyre dealer or garage.

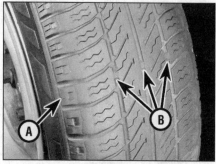

1 Tread Depth - visual check
The original tyres have tread wear safety bands (B), which will appear when the tread depth reaches approximately 1.6 mm. The band positions are indicated by a triangular mark on the tyre sidewall (A).

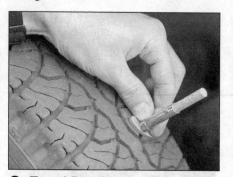

2 Tread Depth - manual check
Alternatively, tread wear can be monitored with a simple, inexpensive device known as a tread depth indicator gauge.

3 Tyre Pressure Check
Check the tyre pressures regularly with the tyres cold. Do not adjust the tyre pressures immediately after the vehicle has been used, or an inaccurate setting will result.

Tyre tread wear patterns

Shoulder Wear

Underinflation (wear on both sides)
Under-inflation will cause overheating of the tyre, because the tyre will flex too much, and the tread will not sit correctly on the road surface. This will cause a loss of grip and excessive wear, not to mention the danger of sudden tyre failure due to heat build-up.
Check and adjust pressures
Incorrect wheel camber (wear on one side)
Repair or renew suspension parts
Hard cornering
Reduce speed!

Centre Wear

Overinflation
Over-inflation will cause rapid wear of the centre part of the tyre tread, coupled with reduced grip, harsher ride, and the danger of shock damage occurring in the tyre casing.
Check and adjust pressures

If you sometimes have to inflate your car's tyres to the higher pressures specified for maximum load or sustained high speed, don't forget to reduce the pressures to normal afterwards.

Uneven Wear

Front tyres may wear unevenly as a result of wheel misalignment. Most tyre dealers and garages can check and adjust the wheel alignment (or "tracking") for a modest charge.
Incorrect camber or castor
Repair or renew suspension parts
Malfunctioning suspension
Repair or renew suspension parts
Unbalanced wheel
Balance tyres
Incorrect toe setting
Adjust front wheel alignment
Note: *The feathered edge of the tread which typifies toe wear is best checked by feel.*

Wiper blades

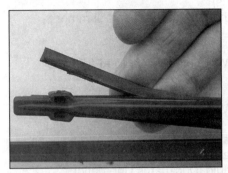

1 Check the condition of the wiper blades; if they are cracked or show any signs of deterioration, or if the glass swept area is smeared, renew them. Wiper blades should be renewed annually.

2 To remove a windscreen wiper blade, pull the arm fully away from the screen until it locks. Swivel the blade through 90°, press the locking tab with your fingers and slide the blade out of the arm's hooked end.

✔ Don't forget to check the tailgate wiper blade as well. To remove the blade, depress the retaining tab and slide the blade out of the hooked end of the arm.

Bulbs and fuses

✔ Check all external lights and the horn. Refer to the appropriate Sections of Chapter 12 for details if any of the circuits are found to be inoperative.

✔ Visually check all accessible wiring connectors, harnesses and retaining clips for security, and for signs of chafing or damage.

> **HAYNES HiNT** *If you need to check your brake lights and indicators unaided, back up to a wall or garage door and operate the lights. The reflected light should show if they are working properly.*

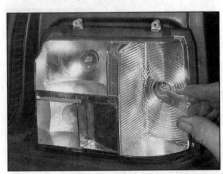

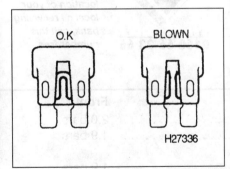

O.K   BLOWN

H27336

1 If a single indicator light, stop-light or headlight has failed, it is likely that a bulb has blown and will need to be replaced. Refer to Chapter 12 for details. If both stop-lights have failed, it is possible that the switch has failed (see Chapter 12).

2 If more than one indicator light or tail light has failed it is likely that either a fuse has blown or that there is a fault in the circuit (see Chapter 12). The fuses are located behind a panel on the bottom of the driver's side lower facia panel.

3 To replace a blown fuse, simply pull it out and fit a new fuse of the correct rating (see Chapter 12). If the fuse blows again, it is important that you find out why - a complete checking procedure is given in Chapter 12.

Lubricants and fluids

Engine	Multigrade engine oil, viscosity SAE 10W/40, or 15W/40, to API SG/CD (Duckhams QXR, QS or Hypergrade Plus)
Cooling system	Ethylene glycol-based antifreeze (Duckhams Antifreeze and Summer Coolant)
Manual transmission:	
BH3 transmission	Multigrade engine oil, viscosity SAE 10W/40 or 15W/40, to API SG/CD (Duckhams QXR or Hypergrade Plus)
BE1, and BE3 transmissions:	
Pre-August 1987	Multigrade engine oil, viscosity SAE 10W/40 or 15W/40, to API SG/CD (Duckhams QXR or Hypergrade Plus)
August 1987 onward	Gear oil, viscosity SAE 75W/80 (Duckhams Hypoid PT 75W/80W Gear oil)
MA transmission	Gear oil, viscosity SAE 75W/80 (Duckhams Hypoid PT 75W/80W Gear oil)
Automatic transmission	Dexron type II automatic transmission fluid (Duckhams Uni-Matic)
Braking system	Universal brake fluid to DOT 4 (Duckhams Universal Brake and Clutch Fluid)
Power steering	Dexron type II automatic transmission fluid (Duckhams Uni-Matic)

Choosing your engine oil

Oils perform vital tasks in all engines. The higher the engine's performance, the greater the demand on lubricants to minimise wear as well as optimise power and economy. Duckhams tailors lubricants to the highest technical standards, meeting and exceeding the demands of all modern engines.

HOW ENGINE OIL WORKS

• Beating friction

Without oil, the surfaces inside your engine which rub together will heat, fuse and quickly cause engine seizure. Oil, and its special additives, forms a molecular barrier between moving parts, to stop wear and minimise heat build-up.

• Cooling hot spots

Oil cools parts that the engine's water-based coolant cannot reach, bathing the combustion chamber and pistons, where temperatures may exceed 1000°C. The oil assists in transferring the heat to the engine cooling system. Heat in the oil is also lost by air flow over the sump, and via any auxiliary oil cooler.

• Cleaning the inner engine

Oil washes away combustion by-products (mainly carbon) on pistons and cylinders, transporting them to the oil filter, and holding the smallest particles in suspension until they are flushed out by an oil change. Duckhams oils undergo extensive tests in the laboratory, and on the road.

Note: It is antisocial and illegal to dump oil down the drain. To find the location of your local oil recycling bank, call this number free.

Tyre pressures

	Front	Rear
135 SR 13	2.0 bars	2.1 bars
145 SR 13 (Hatchback models)	1.9 bars	2.1 bars
145 SR 13 (Van models):		
Normal use	1.9 bars	2.3 bars
Fully laden	1.9 bars	2.6 bars
165/70 SR 13 (manual transmission models)	1.7 bars	1.9 bars
165/70 SR 13 (automatic transmission models)	2.0 bars	2.1 bars
185/60 HR 14 (except CTI models)	2.0 bars	2.0 bars
185/60 HR 14 (CTI models)	2.0 bars	2.1 bars
185/55 VR 15	2.0 bars	2.0 bars

Note: *Refer to the tyre pressure data sticker for the correct tyre pressures for your particular vehicle. Pressures apply only to original-equipment tyres, and may vary if other makes or type is fitted; check with the tyre manufacturer or supplier for correct pressures if necessary.*

Chapter 1
Routine maintenance and servicing

Contents

Degrees of difficulty

| Easy, suitable for novice with little experience | Fairly easy, suitable for beginner with some experience | Fairly difficult, suitable for competent DIY mechanic | Difficult, suitable for experienced DIY mechanic | Very difficult, suitable for expert DIY or professional |

Lubricants and fluids .... Refer to end of "Weekly checks"

Capacities

Engine oil

XV and XW series engines (including filter)	4.5 litres
XY and XU series engines (including filter)	5.0 litres
TU series engines (including filter)	3.5 litres

Cooling system

XV8, XW7, TU9 and TU3 series engines	5.8 litres
XY7 and XY8 engines	6.0 litres
XU engines (except automatic transmission models)	6.6 litres
XU engines (automatic transmission models)	6.7 litres
TU1 series engine (except Van models)	7.0 litres
TU1 series engine (Van models)	5.8 litres

Manual transmission .... 2.0 litres

Automatic transmission

From dry	6.2 litres
Drain and refill	2.4 litres

Fuel tank .... 50 litres

Engine

Oil filter:

XV, XW and XY series engines	Champion C204
XU and TU series engines	Champion F104

Cooling system

Antifreeze mixture:

Protection down to - 15°C (5°F)	27% antifreeze
Protection down to - 35°C (- 31°F)	50% antifreeze

Note: *Refer to Chapter 3 for further details.*

Fuel system

Air cleaner filter element:

Pre-1988 carburettor engines	Champion W138
1988 onward carburettor engines	Champion U401
Fuel injection engines	Champion W175
Fuel filter	Champion L205
Idle speed and mixture CO content	Refer to Chapter 4A, 4B and 4C Specifications

Ignition system

Spark plugs:

XV8, XW7 and XY7 engines	Champion RS9YCC or S281YC*
XY8 and XU5J engines	Champion S7YCC or S279YC*
XU51C engines (up to 1988)	Champion S9YCC or S281YC*
XU51C engines (from 1988)	Champion RC9YCC or C9YCX*
XU5JA engines (up to 1988)	Champion S7YCC or S279YC*
XU5JA (from 1988), XU5JA/K, XU9JA, XU9JA/K, XU9JA/Z and XU9JA/L engines	Champion RC7YCC or C7YCX*
TU9 series, TU1 series, TU3 and TU3A engines	Champion RC9YCC or C9YCX*
TU3S engines	Champion RC7YCC or C7YCX*

Peugeot recommendation

Spark plug electrode gap** .... 0.7 to 0.8 mm

**The spark plug electrode gap quoted is that recommended by Champion for their specified plugs listed above. If spark plugs of any other type are to be fitted, refer to their manufacturer's recommendations.*

Brakes

Front brake pad minimum lining thickness	2.0 mm
Rear brake shoe minimum lining thickness	1.0 mm
Rear brake pad minimum lining thickness	2.0 mm

Tyre pressures .... See "Weekly checks"

Torque wrench settings

	Nm	lbf ft
Spark plugs	17	13
Manual transmission drain/filler plugs		
BE1 and BE3 transmissions:		
Main gearbox drain plug	10	7
Final drive drain plug	30	22
MA transmission	25	19

The maintenance intervals in this manual are provided with the assumption that you, not the dealer, will be carrying out the work. These are the average maintenance intervals recommended for vehicles driven daily under normal conditions. Obviously some variation of these intervals may be expected depending on territory of use, and conditions encountered. If you wish to keep your vehicle in peak condition at all times, you may wish to perform some of these procedures more often. We encourage frequent maintenance because it enhances the efficiency, performance and resale value of your vehicle.

If the vehicle is driven in dusty areas, used to tow a trailer, driven frequently at slow speeds (idling in traffic) or on short journeys, more frequent maintenance intervals are recommended.

Every 250 miles (400 km) or weekly

- ☐ Refer to "Weekly checks".

Every 6000 miles (9000 km) or 6 months - whichever comes sooner

In addition to all the items listed above, carry out the following:

- ☐ Renew the engine oil and filter (Section 3)*.
- ☐ Check the condition of the front brake pads, and renew if necessary (Section 4).
- ☐ Check the automatic transmission fluid level and top-up if necessary (Section 5).

Note: *Renewal of the engine oil filter at this service interval is only necessary on models fitted with the XU9J1/L engine and automatic transmission. On all other models, oil filter renewal is recommended at every second oil change (ie 12 000 miles/12 months).*

Every 12 000 miles (18 000 km) or 12 months - whichever comes sooner

In addition to all the items listed above, carry out the following:

- ☐ Check all underbonnet components and hoses for fluid leaks (Section 6).
- ☐ Renew the spark plugs (Section 7).
- ☐ Check, adjust and lubricate the throttle and choke cables (Section 8).
- ☐ Check the condition of the auxiliary drivebelt, and renew if necessary (Section 9).
- ☐ Check the clutch pedal stroke adjustment (Section 10).
- ☐ Check the condition of the seat belts (Section 11).
- ☐ Lubricate the locks and hinges (Section 12).
- ☐ Check the condition of the rear brake shoes and renew if necessary - rear drum brake models (Section 13).
- ☐ Check the condition of the rear brake pads and renew if necessary - rear disc brake models (Section 14).
- ☐ Check the operation of the handbrake (Section 15).
- ☐ Inspect the underbody and the brake hydraulic pipes and hoses (Section 16).
- ☐ Check the condition of the fuel lines (Section 16).
- ☐ Check the condition and security of the exhaust system (Section 17).
- ☐ Check the condition of the exterior trim and paintwork (Section 18).
- ☐ Check the headlight beam alignment (Section 19).
- ☐ Check the operation of the air conditioning system (Section 20).

Every 24 000 miles (36 000 km) or 2 years - whichever comes sooner

In addition to all the items listed above, carry out the following:

- ☐ Check the manual transmission oil level, and top-up if necessary (Section 21).
- ☐ Renew the manual transmission oil (pre-1988 BE1 transmissions only) (Section 22).
- ☐ Renew the automatic transmission fluid (Section 23).
- ☐ Check the condition of the driveshaft bellows (Section 24).
- ☐ Check the steering and suspension components for condition and security (Section 25).
- ☐ Renew the air cleaner filter element (Section 26).
- ☐ Check the ignition system (Section 27).
- ☐ Check the idle speed and mixture adjustment (Section 28).
- ☐ Check the condition of the emissions control system hoses and components (Section 29).
- ☐ Carry out a road test (Section 30).

Every 36 000 miles (58 000 km) or 3 years - whichever comes sooner

In addition to all the items listed above, carry out the following:

- ☐ Renew the timing belt (Section 31).

Note: *Although the normal interval for timing belt renewal is 72 000 miles (120 000 km), It is strongly recommended that the timing belt renewal interval is halved to 36 000 miles (60 000 km) on vehicles which are subjected to intensive use, ie. mainly short journeys or a lot of stop-start driving. The actual belt renewal interval is therefore very much up to the individual owner, but bear in mind that severe engine damage will result if the belt breaks.*

Every 48 000 miles (80 000 km) or 4 years - whichever comes sooner

- ☐ Renew the fuel filter - fuel injection models (Section 32).

Every 72 000 miles (120 000 km)

In addition to all the items listed above, carry out the following:

- ☐ Renew the timing belt (Section 31).

Note: *This is the interval recommended by Peugeot, but we recommend that the belt is changed more frequently, at 36 000 miles (60 000 km) - see above*

Every 2 years (regardless of mileage)

- ☐ Renew the coolant (Section 33).
- ☐ Renew the brake fluid (Section 34).

1

Underbonnet view of a 1360 cc GT model (XY8 series engine)

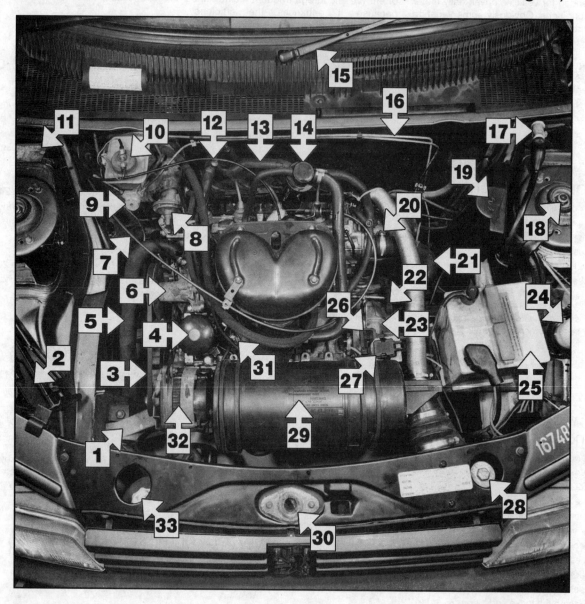

1	Right-hand front engine mounting
2	Jack
3	Drivebelt
4	Oil filter
5	Bottom hose
6	Water pump
7	Throttle cable
8	Fuel pump
9	Brake master cylinder
10	Brake fluid reservoir filler cap
11	Vehicle identification plate
12	Choke cable
13	Heater hose
14	Oil filler cap/crankcase ventilation filter
15	Windscreen wiper arm
16	Hydraulic brake lines
17	Cooling fan motor resistor
18	Front suspension shock absorber top mounting nut
19	Ignition coil cover
20	Distributor
21	Bottom hose
22	Clutch release fork
23	Clutch housing
24	Washer reservoir
25	Battery
26	Ignition timing aperture
27	Diagnostic socket
28	Radiator filler cap
29	Air cleaner
30	Bonnet lock
31	Oil pressure switch
32	Alternator
33	Cooling system expansion bottle

Underbonnet view of a 1360 cc XS model (TU series engine)

1 Brake fluid reservoir filler cap
2 Brake master cylinder
3 Brake vacuum servo unit
4 Servo vacuum hose
5 Cooling system bleed screw
6 Air cleaner cover
7 Fuel pump
8 Cooling system expansion bottle

9 Fuel filter
10 Washer fluid reservoir
11 Battery
12 Air temperature control unit
13 Auxiliary fusebox
14 Radiator filler cap
15 Ignition coil

16 Bonnet lock
17 Engine oil filler cap
18 Exhaust manifold hot air shroud
19 Alternator
20 Engine oil level dipstick
21 Inlet manifold
22 Right-hand engine mounting

1

Front underside view of a 1360 cc GT model

1 Bottom hose
2 Reverse lamp switch
3 Engine/transmission oil drain plug
4 Radiator
5 Gear linkage
6 Clutch housing and transfer gear
   assembly

7 Washer reservoir
8 Disc caliper
9 Lower suspension arm
10 Anti-roll bar
11 Track rod
12 Guide bar

13 Exhaust front pipe
14 Fuel feed and return pipes
15 Hydraulic brake lines
16 Subframe
17 Driveshaft
18 Front towing eye

Rear underside view of a 1360 cc GT model

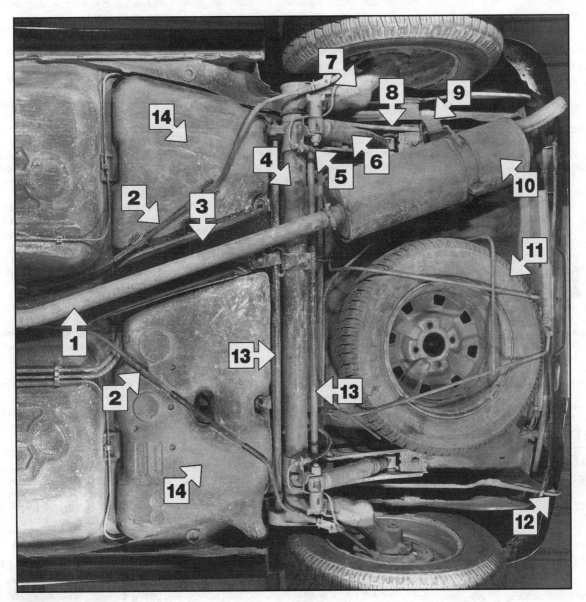

1 Exhaust front pipe
2 Handbrake cables
3 Heatshield
4 Rear suspension cross-tube
5 Brake hydraulic flexible hose

6 Rear shock absorber
7 Trailing arm
8 Side-member
9 Exhaust rubber mounting
10 Exhaust rear silencer

11 Spare wheel
12 Rear towing eye
13 Torsion bars
14 Fuel tank

1 Introduction

This Chapter is designed to help the home mechanic maintain his/her vehicle for safety, economy, long life and peak performance.

This Chapter contains a master maintenance schedule, followed by Sections dealing specifically with each task in the schedule. Visual checks, adjustments, component renewal and other helpful items are included. Refer to the accompanying illustrations of the engine compartment and the underside of the vehicle for the locations of the various components.

Servicing your vehicle in accordance with the mileage/time maintenance schedule and the following Sections will provide a planned maintenance programme, which should result in a long and reliable service life. This is a comprehensive plan, so maintaining some items but not others at the specified service intervals will not produce the same results.

As you service your vehicle, you will discover that many of the procedures can - and should - be grouped together, because of the particular procedure being performed, or because of the close proximity of two otherwise-unrelated components to one another. For example, if the vehicle is raised for any reason, the exhaust should be inspected at the same time as the suspension and steering components.

The first step of this maintenance programme is to prepare yourself before the actual work begins. Read through all the Sections relevant to the work to be carried out, then make a list and gather together all the parts and tools required. If a problem is encountered, seek advice from a parts specialist or a dealer service department.

2 Intensive maintenance

1 If, from the time the vehicle is new, the routine maintenance schedule is followed closely, and frequent checks are made of fluid levels and high-wear items, as suggested throughout this manual, the engine will be kept in relatively good running condition, and the need for additional work will be minimised.
2 It is possible that there will be some times when the engine is running poorly due to the lack of regular maintenance. This is even more likely if a used vehicle, which has not received regular and frequent maintenance checks, is purchased. In such cases, additional work may need to be carried out, outside of the regular maintenance intervals.
3 If engine wear is suspected, a compression test (refer to Chapter 2A, B or C) will provide valuable information regarding the overall performance of the main internal components. Such a test can be used as a basis to decide on the extent of the work to be carried out. If, for example, a compression test indicates serious internal engine wear, conventional maintenance as described in this Chapter will not greatly improve the performance of the engine, and may prove a waste of time and money, unless extensive overhaul work (Chapter 2D) is carried out first.
4 The following series of operations are those often required to improve the performance of a generally poor-running engine:

Primary operations

a) Clean, inspect and test the battery (See "Weekly checks").
b) Check all the engine-related fluids (See "Weekly checks").
c) Check the condition of the auxiliary drivebelt (Section 9).
d) Inspect the distributor cap, rotor arm and HT leads (Section 27).
e) Renew the spark plugs (Section 7).
f) Check the condition of the air cleaner filter element and renew if necessary (Section 26).
g) Renew the fuel filter - fuel injection models (Section 32).
h) Check the condition of all hoses, and check for fluid leaks (Section 6).

5 If the above operations do not prove fully effective, carry out the following operations:

Secondary operations

All the items listed under "Primary operations", plus the following:

a) Check the charging system (Chapter 5A).
b) Check the ignition system (Chapter 5B).
c) Check the fuel system (Chapter 4A, B and C).
d) Renew the distributor cap and rotor arm (Section 27).
e) Renew the ignition HT leads (Section 27).

Every 6000 miles or 6 months

3 Engine oil and filter renewal

Note: A suitable square-section wrench may be required to undo the sump drain plug on some models. These wrenches can be obtained from most motor factors or your Peugeot dealer.
1 Frequent oil changes are the best preventive maintenance the home mechanic can give the engine, because ageing oil becomes diluted and contaminated, which leads to premature engine wear.
2 Make sure that you have all the necessary tools before you begin this procedure. You should also have plenty of rags or newspapers handy, for mopping up any spills. The oil should preferably be changed when the engine is still fully warmed-up to normal operating temperature, just after a run; warm oil and sludge will flow out more easily. Take care, however, not to touch the exhaust or any other hot parts of the engine when working under the vehicle. To avoid any possibility of scalding, and to protect yourself from possible skin irritants and other harmful contaminants in used engine oils, it is advisable to wear gloves when carrying out this work. Access to the underside of the vehicle is greatly improved if the vehicle can be lifted on a hoist, driven onto ramps, or supported by axle stands. (see "Jacking and vehicle support"). Whichever method is chosen, make sure that the vehicle remains level, or if it is at an angle, that the drain point is at the lowest point.

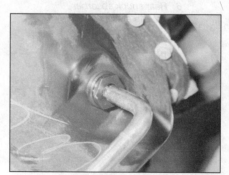

3.3 Slackening the sump drain plug with a square section wrench

3 Position the draining container under the drain plug, and unscrew the plug. On some models, a square-section wrench may be needed to slacken the plug **(see illustration)**. If possible, try to keep the plug pressed into the sump while unscrewing it by hand the last couple of turns **(see Haynes Hint)**.

Keep the drain plug pressed into the sump while unscrewing it by hand the last couple of turns. As the plug releases, move it away sharply so that the stream of oil issuing from the sump runs into the container, not up your sleeve!

3.7 Using an oil filter removal tool to slacken the filter

5.1 Withdrawing the automatic transmission fluid dipstick

4 Allow the oil to drain into the container, and check the condition of the plug's sealing washer; renew it if worn or damaged.

5 Allow some time for the old oil to drain, noting that it may be necessary to reposition the container as the oil flow slows to a trickle; when the oil has completely drained, wipe clean the drain plug and its threads in the sump and refit the plug, tightening it securely.

6 If the filter is also to be renewed, move the container into position under the oil filter, which is located on the front side of the cylinder block. On XV, XW and XY series engines, place some rag around the filter otherwise the oil that runs out as the filter is unscrewed will make a mess all over the front of the engine.

7 Using an oil filter removal tool if necessary, slacken the filter initially, then unscrew it by hand the rest of the way **(see illustration)**. Empty the oil in the old filter into the container.

8 Use a clean rag to remove all oil, dirt and sludge from the filter sealing area on the engine. Check the old filter to make sure that the rubber sealing ring hasn't stuck to the engine. If it has, carefully remove it.

9 Apply a light coating of clean engine oil to the sealing ring on the new filter, then screw it into position on the engine. Tighten the filter firmly by hand only - **do not** use any tools.

10 Remove the old oil and all tools from under the car, then lower the car to the ground (if applicable).

11 Remove the dipstick, then unscrew the oil filler cap from the rocker/cylinder head cover or oil filler/breather neck (as applicable). Fill the engine, using the correct grade and type of oil (see *"Lubricants and fluids, and capacities"*). An oil can spout or funnel may help to reduce spillage. Pour in half the specified quantity of oil first, then wait a few minutes for the oil to fall to the sump. Continue adding oil a small quantity at a time until the level is up to the lower mark on the dipstick. Adding approximately 1.5 litres will bring the level up to the upper mark on the dipstick. Refit the filler cap.

12 Start the engine and run it for a few minutes; check for leaks around the oil filter seal and the sump drain plug. Note that there may be a delay of a few seconds before the oil pressure warning light goes out when the engine is first started, as the oil circulates through the engine oil galleries and the new oil filter (if fitted) before the pressure builds up.

13 Switch off the engine, and wait a few minutes for the oil to settle in the sump once more. With the new oil circulated and the filter completely full, recheck the level on the dipstick, and add more oil as necessary.

14 Dispose of the used engine oil safely, with reference to *"General repair procedures"* in the preliminary Sections of this manual.

4 Front brake pad check

1 Jack up the front of the vehicle, and support it on axle stands (see *"Jacking and vehicle support"*).

2 For better access to the brake calipers, remove the roadwheels.

 HAYNES HiNT *For a quick check, the thickness of the friction material on each brake pad can be measured through the aperture in the caliper body*

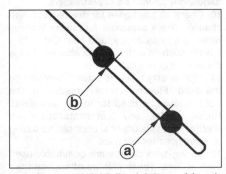

5.2 Automatic fluid dipstick lower (a) and upper (b) fluid level markings

3 If any of the pads friction material is worn to the specified thickness or less, *all four pads must be renewed* as a set.

4 For a comprehensive check, the brake pads should be removed and cleaned. The operation of the caliper can then also be checked, and the condition of the brake disc itself can be fully examined on both sides. Refer to Chapter 9 for further information.

5 Automatic transmission fluid level check

1

1 Take the vehicle on a short journey, to warm the transmission up to normal operating temperature, then park the vehicle on level ground. The fluid level is checked using the dipstick located at the front of the engine compartment, directly in front of the engine **(see illustration)**. The dipstick top is brightly-coloured for easy identification.

2 With the engine idling and the selector lever in the "P" (Park) position, withdraw the dipstick from the tube, and wipe all the fluid from its end with a clean rag or paper towel. Insert the clean dipstick back into the tube as far as it will go, then withdraw it once more. Note the fluid level on the end of the dipstick; it should be between the upper and lower marks **(see illustration)**.

3 If topping-up is necessary, add the required quantity of the specified fluid to the transmission via the dipstick tube. Use a funnel with a fine-mesh gauze, to avoid spillage, and to ensure that no foreign matter enters the transmission. **Note:** *Never overfill the transmission so that the fluid level is above the upper mark.*

4 After topping-up, take the vehicle on a short run to distribute the fresh fluid, then recheck the level again, topping-up if necessary.

5 Always maintain the level between the two dipstick marks. If the level is allowed to fall below the lower mark, fluid starvation may result, which could lead to severe transmission damage.

6 Frequent need for topping-up indicates that there is a leak, which should be found and corrected before it becomes serious.

6 Underbonnet check for fluid leaks and hose condition

⚠️ **Warning: Renewal of any air conditioning hoses (where fitted) must be left to a dealer service department or air conditioning specialist who has the equipment to depressurise the system safely. Never remove air conditioning components or hoses until the system has been depressurised.**

General

1 High temperatures in the engine compartment can cause the deterioration of the rubber and plastic hoses used for engine, accessory and emission systems operation. Periodic inspection should be made for cracks, loose clamps, material hardening and leaks.

2 Carefully check the large top and bottom radiator hoses, along with the other smaller-diameter cooling system hoses and metal pipes; do not forget the heater hoses/pipes which run from the engine to the bulkhead. Inspect each hose along its entire length, replacing any that are cracked, swollen or shows signs of deterioration. Cracks may become more apparent if the hose is squeezed **(see Haynes Hint)**.

3 Make sure that all hose connections are tight. If the spring clamps that are used to secure some of the hoses appear to be slackening, they should be renewed to prevent the possibility of leaks.

4 Some other hoses are secured to their fittings with screw type clips. Where screw type clips are used, check to be sure they haven't slackened, allowing the hose to leak. If clamps or screw type clips aren't used, make sure the hose has not expanded and/or hardened where it slips over the fitting, allowing it to leak.

5 Check all fluid reservoirs, filler caps, drain plugs and fittings etc, looking for any signs of leakage of oil, transmission and/or brake hydraulic fluid, coolant and power steering fluid. If the vehicle is regularly parked in the same place, close inspection of the ground underneath will soon show any leaks; ignore the puddle of water which will be left if the air conditioning system is in use. As soon as a leak is detected, its source must be traced and rectified. Where oil has been leaking for some time, it is usually necessary to use a steam cleaner, pressure washer or similar, to clean away the accumulated dirt, so that the exact source of the leak can be identified.

Vacuum hoses

6 It's quite common for vacuum hoses, especially those in the emissions system, to be numbered or colour-coded, or to be identified by coloured stripes moulded into them. Various systems require hoses with different wall thicknesses, collapse resistance

HAYNES HINT

A leak in the cooling system will usually show up as white or rust-coloured deposits on the area adjoining the leak

and temperature resistance. When renewing hoses, be sure the new ones are made of the same material.

7 Often the only effective way to check a hose is to remove it completely from the vehicle. If more than one hose is removed, be sure to label the hoses and fittings to ensure correct installation.

8 When checking vacuum hoses, be sure to include any plastic T-fittings in the check. Inspect the fittings for cracks, and check the hose where it fits over the fitting for distortion, which could cause leakage.

9 A small piece of vacuum hose can be used as a stethoscope to detect vacuum leaks. Hold one end of the hose to your ear, and probe around vacuum hoses and fittings, listening for the "hissing" sound characteristic of a vacuum leak.

 Warning: When probing with the vacuum hose stethoscope, be very careful not to come into contact with moving engine components such as the auxiliary drivebelt, radiator electric cooling fan, etc.

Fuel hoses

 Warning: Before carrying out the following operation, refer to the precautions given in "Safety first!" at the beginning of this manual, and follow them implicitly. Petrol is a highly dangerous and volatile liquid, and the precautions necessary when handling it cannot be overstressed.

10 Check all fuel hoses for deterioration and chafing. Check especially for cracks in areas where the hose bends, and also just before fittings, such as where a hose attaches to the carburettor or fuel rail.

11 High-quality fuel line, usually identified by the word "Fluoroelastomer" printed on the hose, should be used for fuel line renewal. Never, under any circumstances, use unreinforced vacuum line, clear plastic tubing or water hose for fuel lines.

12 Spring-type clamps are commonly used on fuel lines. These clamps often lose their tension over a period of time, and can be "sprung" during removal. Replace all spring-

type clamps with screw clips whenever a hose is replaced.

Metal lines

13 Sections of metal piping are often used for fuel line between the fuel filter and the engine. Check carefully to be sure the piping has not been bent or crimped, and that cracks have not started in the line.

14 If a section of metal fuel line must be renewed, only seamless steel piping should be used, since copper and aluminium piping don't have the strength necessary to withstand normal engine vibration.

15 Check the metal brake lines where they enter the master cylinder and ABS hydraulic unit for cracks in the lines or loose fittings. Any sign of brake fluid leakage calls for an immediate and thorough inspection of the brake system.

7 Spark plug renewal

1 The correct functioning of the spark plugs is vital for the correct running and efficiency of the engine. It is essential that the plugs fitted are appropriate for the engine (a suitable type is specified at the beginning of this Chapter). If this type is used and the engine is in good condition, the spark plugs should not need attention between scheduled replacement intervals. Spark plug cleaning is rarely necessary, and should not be attempted unless specialised equipment is available, as damage can easily be caused to the firing ends.

2 If the marks on the original-equipment spark plug (HT) leads cannot be seen, mark the leads "1" to "4", to correspond to the cylinder the lead serves (No 1 cylinder is at the transmission end of the engine). Pull the leads from the plugs by gripping the end fitting, not the lead, otherwise the lead connection may be fractured.

3 It is advisable to remove the dirt from the spark plug recesses using a clean brush, vacuum cleaner or compressed air before removing the plugs, to prevent dirt dropping into the cylinders.

4 Unscrew the plugs using a spark plug spanner, suitable box spanner or a deep socket and extension bar **(see illustration)**.

7.4 Tools required for spark plug removal, gap adjustment and refitting

7.9 Measuring the spark plug gap with a feeler blade

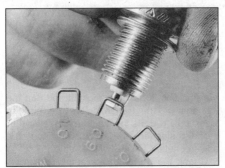

7.10 Measuring the spark plug gap with a wire gauge

Keep the socket aligned with the spark plug - if it is forcibly moved to one side, the ceramic insulator may be broken off. As each plug is removed, examine it as follows.

5 Examination of the spark plugs will give a good indication of the condition of the engine. If the insulator nose of the spark plug is clean and white, with no deposits, this is indicative of a weak mixture or too hot a plug (a hot plug transfers heat away from the electrode slowly, a cold plug transfers heat away quickly).

6 If the tip and insulator nose are covered with hard black-looking deposits, then this is indicative that the mixture is too rich. Should the plug be black and oily, then it is likely that the engine is fairly worn, as well as the mixture being too rich.

7 If the insulator nose is covered with light tan to greyish-brown deposits, then the mixture is correct and it is likely that the engine is in good condition.

8 The spark plug electrode gap is of considerable importance as, if it is too large or too small, the size of the spark and its efficiency will be seriously impaired. The gap should be set to the value given in the *Specifications* at the beginning of this Chapter.

9 To set the gap, measure it with a feeler blade, and then bend open, or closed, the outer plug electrode until the correct gap is achieved **(see illustration)**. The centre electrode should never be bent, as this may crack the insulator and cause plug failure, if nothing worse. If using feeler blades, the gap is correct when the appropriate-size blade is a firm sliding fit.

10 Special spark plug electrode gap adjusting tools are available from most motor accessory shops, or from some spark plug manufacturers **(see illustration)**.

11 Before fitting the spark plugs, check that the threaded connector sleeves are tight, and that the plug exterior surfaces and threads are clean **(see Haynes Hint)**.

12 Remove the rubber hose (if used), and tighten the plug to the specified torque using the spark plug socket and a torque wrench. Refit the remaining spark plugs in the same manner.

13 Connect the HT leads in their correct order, and refit any components removed for access.

8 Throttle and choke cable lubrication and adjustment

1 The throttle cable is connected to a spring-loaded reel which pivots on the face of the cylinder head. On certain models, the reel then operates the throttle lever on the carburettor through a plastic balljointed control rod.

2 Sparingly apply a few drops of light oil to the throttle spindles, linkage pivot points and to the cable itself. Similarly lubricate the exposed ends of the choke cable (where fitted).

3 Check that there is a small amount of slackness in the cable so that the throttle linkage closes fully with the accelerator pedal released. Also check that full throttle can be obtained with the accelerator pedal fully depressed.

4 If there is any doubt about the cable adjustment, refer to the relevant Parts of Chapter 4 for the full adjustment procedure.

9 Auxiliary drivebelt check and renewal

1 Depending on specification, either one or two auxiliary drivebelts are fitted. Where two belts are fitted, it will obviously be necessary to remove the outer belt in order to renew the inner belt.

Checking the auxiliary drivebelt condition

2 Apply the handbrake, then jack up the front of the car and support it on axle stands. Remove the right-hand front roadwheel.

3 From underneath the front of the car, prise out the retaining clips, and remove the plastic cover from the wing valance where necessary, to gain access to the crankshaft sprocket/pulley bolt.

4 Using a suitable socket and extension bar fitted to the crankshaft sprocket/pulley bolt, rotate the crankshaft so that the entire length of the drivebelt(s) can be examined. Examine the drivebelt(s) for cracks, splitting, fraying or

It is very often difficult to insert spark plugs into their holes without cross-threading them. To avoid this possibility, fit a short length of 5/16 inch internal diameter rubber hose over the end of the spark plug. The flexible hose acts as a universal joint to help align the plug with the plug hole. Should the plug begin to cross-thread, the hose will slip on the spark plug, preventing thread damage to the aluminium cylinder head

damage. Check also for signs of glazing (shiny patches) and for separation of the belt plies. Renew the belt if worn or damaged.

5 If the condition of the belt is satisfactory, check the drivebelt tension as described below.

Auxiliary drivebelt - removal, refitting and tensioning

Removal

6 If not already done, proceed as described in paragraphs 2 and 3.

7 Disconnect the battery negative lead.

8 Slacken both the alternator upper and lower mounting nuts/bolts (as applicable).

9 Push the alternator toward the engine until the belt is slack then slip the drivebelt from the pulleys. Where an adjuster bolt is fitted, back off the adjuster to relieve the tension in the drivebelt, then slip off the belt **(see illustration)**.

Refitting

10 If the belt is being renewed, ensure that the correct type is used. Fit the belt around the pulleys, and take up the slack in the belt

9.9 Slackening the alternator adjuster bolt to release the auxiliary drivebelt

1

by moving the alternator by hand, or tightening the adjuster bolt.

11 Tension the drivebelt as described in the following paragraphs.

Tensioning

12 If not already done, proceed as described in paragraphs 2 and 3.

13 Correct tensioning of the drivebelt will ensure that it has a long life. A belt which is too slack will slip and perhaps squeal. Beware, however, of overtightening, as this can cause wear in the alternator bearings.

14 The belt should be tensioned so that, under firm thumb pressure, there is approximately 5.0 mm of free movement at the mid-point between the pulleys on the longest belt run.

15 To adjust, with the upper mounting nut/bolt just holding the alternator firm, and the lower mounting nut/bolt loosened, lever the alternator away from the engine, or turn the adjuster bolt until the correct tension is achieved. Rotate the crankshaft a couple of times, recheck the tension, then securely tighten both the alternator mounting nuts/bolts. Where applicable, also tighten the bolt securing the adjuster strap to its mounting bracket.

16 Reconnect the battery negative lead.

17 Refit the plastic cover to the wing valance. Refit the roadwheel, and lower the vehicle to the ground.

10 Clutch pedal stroke adjustment

1 The clutch pedal stroke adjustment is checked by measuring the clutch pedal travel. Before doing this, settle the cable by depressing and releasing it a few times.

2 Ensure that there are no obstructions beneath the clutch pedal then measure the distance from the centre of the clutch pedal pad to the base of the steering wheel with the pedal in the at-rest position. Depress the clutch pedal fully to the floor, and measure the distance from the centre of the clutch pedal pad to the base of the steering wheel **(see illustration)**.

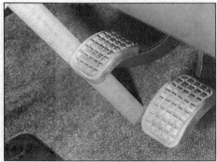

10.2 To check the clutch pedal stroke, measure the clutch pedal travel as described in the text

3 Subtract the first measurement from the second to obtain the clutch pedal travel. If this is not with the range given in the *Specifications* at the start of this Chapter, adjust the clutch as follows.

4 On models fitted with the BH3 transmission, loosen the locknut and turn the adjuster on the transmission intermediate lever pushrod as necessary. On all other models, slacken the locknut and turn the adjuster nut on the end of the cable.

5 Check the pedal stroke again and make further adjustments as necessary. When all is correct, tighten the relevant locknut.

11 Seat belt check

Check the seat belts for satisfactory operation and condition. Inspect the webbing for fraying and cuts. Check that they retract smoothly and without binding into their reels.

Check the seat belt mountings, ensuring that all the bolts are securely tightened.

12 Lock and hinge check and lubrication

1 Check that the doors, bonnet and tailgate close securely. Check that the bonnet safety catch operates correctly. Check the operation of the door check straps.

2 Lubricate the hinges, door check straps, the striker plates and the bonnet catch sparingly with a little oil or grease.

3 If any of the doors, bonnet or tailgate/boot lid do not close effectively or appear not to be flush with the surrounding panels, carry out the relevant adjustment procedures contained in Chapter 11.

13 Rear brake shoe check - models with rear drum brakes

Remove the rear brake drums, and check the brake shoes for signs of wear or contamination. At the same time, also inspect the wheel cylinders for signs of leakage, and the brake drum for signs of wear. Refer to the relevant Sections of Chapter 9 for further information.

14 Rear brake pad condition check - models with rear disc brakes

1 Chock the front wheels, then jack up the rear of the vehicle and support it on axle stands (see *"Jacking and vehicle support"*). Remove the rear roadwheels.

2 For a quick check, the thickness of friction material remaining on each brake pad can be

measured through the top of the caliper body. If any pad's friction material is worn to the specified thickness or less, all four pads must be renewed as a set.

3 For a comprehensive check, the brake pads should be removed and cleaned. This will permit the operation of the caliper to be checked, and the condition of the brake disc itself to be fully examined on both sides. Refer to Chapter 9 for further information.

15 Handbrake check and adjustment

Refer to Chapter 9.

16 Underbody and fuel/brake line check

1 With the vehicle raised and supported on axle stands (see *"Jacking and vehicle support"*), or over an inspection pit, thoroughly inspect the underbody and wheel arches for signs of damage and corrosion. In particular, examine the bottom of the side sills, and any concealed areas where mud can collect. Where corrosion and rust is evident, press and tap firmly on the panel with a screwdriver, and check for any serious corrosion which would necessitate repairs. If the panel is not seriously corroded, clean away the rust, and apply a new coating of underseal. Refer to Chapter 11 for more details of body repairs.

2 At the same time, inspect the treated lower body panels for stone damage and general condition.

3 Inspect all of the fuel and brake lines on the underbody for damage, rust, corrosion and leakage. Also make sure that they are correctly supported in their clips. Where applicable, check the PVC coating on the lines for damage.

4 Inspect the flexible brake hoses in the vicinity of the calipers, where they are subjected to most movement. Bend them between the fingers (but do not actually bend them double, or the casing may be damaged) and check that this does not reveal previously-hidden cracks, cuts or splits.

17 Exhaust system check

1 With the engine cold (at least three hours after the vehicle has been driven), check the complete exhaust system, from its starting point at the engine to the end of the tailpipe. Ideally, this should be done on a hoist, where unrestricted access is available; if a hoist is not available, raise and support the vehicle on axle stands (see *"Jacking and vehicle support"*).

2 Check the pipes and connections for evidence of leaks, severe corrosion, or damage. Make sure that all brackets and rubber mountings are in good condition, and tight; if any of the mountings are to be renewed, ensure that the replacements are of the correct type. Leakage at any of the joints or in other parts of the system will usually show up as a black sooty stain in the vicinity of the leak.

3 At the same time, inspect the underside of the body for holes, corrosion, open seams, etc. which may allow exhaust gases to enter the passenger compartment. Seal all body openings with silicone or body putty.

4 Rattles and other noises can often be traced to the exhaust system, especially the rubber mountings. Try to move the system, silencer(s) and catalytic converter. If any components can touch the body or suspension parts, secure the exhaust system with new mountings.

18 Bodywork, paint and exterior trim check

1 The best time to carry out this check is after the car has been washed so that any surface blemish or scratch will be clearly evident and not hidden by a film of dirt.

2 Starting at one front corner check the paintwork all around the car, looking for minor scratches or more serious dents. Check all the trim and make sure that it is securely attached over its entire length.

3 Check the security of all door locks, door mirrors, badges, bumpers, radiator grille and wheel trim. Anything found loose, or in need of further attention should be done with reference to the relevant Chapters of this manual.

4 Rectify any problems noticed with the paintwork or body panels as described in Chapter 11.

19 Headlight beam alignment check

Accurate adjustment of the headlight beam is only possible using optical beam-setting setting equipment, and this work should therefore be carried out by a Peugeot dealer or service station with the necessary facilities.

Basic adjustments can be carried out in an emergency, and further details are given in Chapter 12.

20 Air conditioning system check

⚠ **Warning: The air conditioning system is under high pressure. Do not loosen any fittings or remove any components until after the system has been discharged. Air conditioning refrigerant must be properly discharged into an approved type of container, at a dealer service department or an automotive air conditioning repair facility capable of handling the refrigerant safely. Always wear eye protection when disconnecting air conditioning system fittings.**

1 The following maintenance checks should be performed on a regular basis, to ensure that the system continues to operate at peak efficiency:

  a) *Check the auxiliary drivebelt. If it's worn or deteriorated, renew it.*
  b) *Check the system hoses. Look for cracks, bubbles, hard spots and deterioration. Inspect the hoses and all fittings for oil bubbles and seepage. If there's any evidence of wear, damage or leaks, renew the hose(s).*
  c) *Inspect the condenser fins for leaves, insects and other debris. Use a "fin comb" or compressed air to clean the condenser.*

⚠ **Warning: Wear eye protection when using compressed air!**

  d) *Check that the drain tube from the front of the evaporator is clear - note that it is normal to have clear fluid (water) dripping from this while the system is in operation, to the extent that quite a large puddle can be left under the vehicle when it is parked.*

2 It's a good idea to operate the system for about 30 minutes at least once a month, particularly during the winter. Long term non-use can cause hardening, and subsequent failure, of the seals.

3 Because of the complexity of the air conditioning system and the special equipment necessary to service it, in-depth repairs are not included in this manual, apart from those procedures covered in Chapter 3.

4 The most common cause of poor cooling is simply a low system refrigerant charge. If a noticeable drop in cool air output occurs, the following quick check will help you determine if the refrigerant level is low.

5 Warm the engine up to normal operating temperature.

6 Place the air conditioning temperature selector at the coldest setting, and put the blower at the highest setting. Open the doors - to make sure the air conditioning system doesn't cycle off as soon as it cools the passenger compartment.

7 With the compressor engaged - the clutch will make an audible click, and the centre of the clutch will rotate - feel the inlet and outlet pipes at the compressor. One side should be cold, and one hot. If there's no perceptible difference between the two pipes, there's something wrong with the compressor or the system. It might be a low charge - it might be something else. Take the vehicle to a dealer service department or an automotive air conditioning specialist.

1

Every 24 000 miles or 2 years

21 Manual transmission oil level check

Note: *The following procedure is only applicable to models produced after approximately October 1986. There is no provision on the transmission for fluid level checking on earlier transmissions (see Chapter 7A). Suitable square-section wrench may be required to undo the transmission filler/level plug on some models. These wrenches can be obtained from most motor factors or your Peugeot dealer.*

1 Park the car on a level surface. The oil level must be checked before the car is driven, or at least 5 minutes after the engine has been switched off. If the oil is checked immediately after driving the car, some of the oil will remain distributed around the transmission components, resulting in an inaccurate level reading.

2 Prise out the retaining clips and remove the access cover from the left-hand wheelarch liner.

3 Wipe clean the area around the filler/level plug, which is situated on the left-hand end of the transmission **(see illustration)**. Unscrew the plug and clean it; discard the sealing washer.

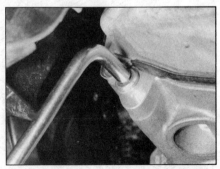

21.3 Using a square section wrench to unscrew the transmission filler/level plug (MA transmission shown)

4 The oil level should reach the lower edge of the filler/level hole. A certain amount of oil will have gathered behind the filler/level plug, and will trickle out when it is removed; this does **not** necessarily indicate that the level is correct. To ensure that a true level is established, wait until the initial trickle has stopped, then add oil as necessary until a trickle of new oil can be seen emerging **(see illustration)**. The level will be correct when the flow ceases; use only good-quality oil of the specified type (refer to *"Lubricants, fluids and capacities"*).

5 Filling the transmission with oil is an extremely awkward operation; above all, allow plenty of time for the oil level to settle properly before checking it. If a large amount is added to the transmission, and a large amount flows out on checking the level, refit the filler/level plug and take the vehicle on a short journey so that the new oil is distributed fully around the transmission components, then recheck the level when it has settled again.

6 If the transmission has been overfilled so that oil flows out as soon as the filler/level plug is removed, check that the car is completely level (front-to-rear and side-to-side), and allow the surplus to drain off into a suitable container.

7 When the level is correct, fit a new sealing washer to the filler/level plug. Refit the plug, tightening it to the specified torque wrench setting. Wash off any spilt oil then refit the access cover securing it in position with the retaining clips.

22 Manual transmission oil renewal

This service requirement is only applicable to pre-1988 BE1 transmissions. Refer to the procedures contained in Chapter 7A.

21.4 Topping-up the transmission oil level

23 Automatic transmission fluid renewal

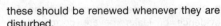

1 Take the vehicle on a short run, to warm the transmission up to normal operating temperature.

2 Park the car on level ground, then switch off the ignition and apply the handbrake firmly. For improved access, jack up the front of the car and support it securely on axle stands. Note that, when refilling and checking the fluid level, the car must be lowered to the ground, and level, to ensure accuracy.

3 Remove the dipstick, then position a suitable container under the transmission. The transmission has two drain plugs: one on the sump, and another on the bottom of the differential housing **(see illustration)**.

> ⚠ **Warning: If the fluid is hot, take precautions against scalding.**

4 Unscrew both drain plugs, and allow the fluid to drain completely into the container. Clean the drain plugs, being especially careful to wipe any metallic particles off the magnetic insert. Discard the original sealing washers;

these should be renewed whenever they are disturbed.

5 When the fluid has finished draining, clean the drain plug threads and those of the transmission casing. Fit a new sealing washer to each drain plug, and refit the plugs to the transmission, tightening each securely. If the car was raised for the draining operation, now lower it to the ground. Make sure that the car is level (front-to-rear and side-to-side).

6 Refilling the transmission is an awkward operation, adding the specified type of fluid to the transmission a little at a time via the dipstick tube. Use a funnel with a fine-mesh gauze, to avoid spillage, and to ensure that no foreign matter enters the transmission. Allow plenty of time for the fluid level to settle properly.

7 Once the level is up to the "MAX" mark on the dipstick, refit the dipstick. Start the engine, and allow it to idle for a few minutes. Switch the engine off, then recheck the level, topping-up if necessary. Take the car on a short run to fully distribute the new fluid around the transmission, then recheck the fluid level as described in Section 5.

24 Driveshaft bellows check

With the vehicle raised and securely supported on stands (see *"Jacking and vehicle support"*), turn the steering onto full lock, then slowly rotate the roadwheel. Inspect the condition of the outer constant velocity (CV) joint rubber bellows, squeezing the bellows to open out the folds **(see illustration)**. Check for signs of cracking, splits or deterioration of the rubber, which may allow the grease to escape, and lead to water and grit entry into the joint. Also check the security and condition of the retaining clips. Repeat these checks on the inner CV joints. If any damage or deterioration is found, the bellows should be renewed as described in Chapter 8.

At the same time, check the general condition of the CV joints themselves by first holding the driveshaft and attempting to rotate the wheel. Repeat this check by holding

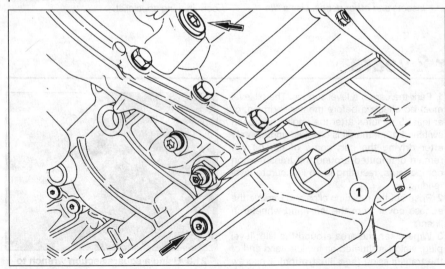

23.3 Automatic transmission fluid drain plugs (arrowed). Transmission is refilled via the dipstick tube (1)

24.1 Check the condition of the driveshaft bellows (arrowed)

the inner joint and attempting to rotate the driveshaft. Any appreciable movement indicates wear in the joints, wear in the driveshaft splines, or a loose driveshaft retaining nut.

25 Steering and suspension check

Front suspension and steering check

1 Apply the handbrake then jack up the front of the vehicle and support it on axle stands (see *"Jacking and vehicle support"*).

2 Visually inspect the balljoint dust covers and the steering gear bellows for splits, chafing or deterioration. Any wear of these components will cause loss of lubricant, together with dirt and water entry, resulting in rapid deterioration of the balljoints or steering gear.

3 Check the power steering fluid hoses (where applicable) for chafing or deterioration, and the pipe and hose unions for fluid leaks. Also check for signs of fluid leakage under pressure from the steering gear rubber bellows, which would indicate failed fluid seals within the steering gear.

4 Check for signs of fluid leakage around the suspension strut body, or from the rubber boot around the piston rod (where fitted). Should any fluid be noticed, the shock absorber is defective internally, and renewal is necessary.

26.1 On XV, XW and XY series engines, unscrew the wing nut on the air cleaner cover . . .

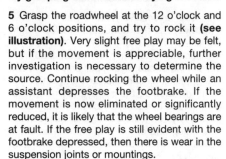

25.5 Check for wear in the hub bearings by grasping the wheel and trying to rock it

5 Grasp the roadwheel at the 12 o'clock and 6 o'clock positions, and try to rock it **(see illustration)**. Very slight free play may be felt, but if the movement is appreciable, further investigation is necessary to determine the source. Continue rocking the wheel while an assistant depresses the footbrake. If the movement is now eliminated or significantly reduced, it is likely that the wheel bearings are at fault. If the free play is still evident with the footbrake depressed, then there is wear in the suspension joints or mountings.

6 Now grasp the wheel at the 9 o'clock and 3 o'clock positions, and try to rock it as before. Any movement felt now may again be caused by wear in the wheel bearings or the steering track rod end balljoints. If the outer track rod end is worn, the visual movement will be obvious. If the inner joint is suspect, it can be felt by placing a hand over the rack-and-pinion rubber bellows, and gripping the track rod. If the wheel is now rocked, movement will be felt at the inner joint if wear has taken place.

7 Using a large screwdriver or flat bar, check for wear in the suspension mounting bushes by levering between the relevant suspension component and its attachment point. Some movement is to be expected as the mountings are made of rubber, but excessive wear should be obvious. Also check the condition of any visible rubber bushes, looking for splits, cracks or contamination of the rubber.

8 With the vehicle standing on its wheels, have an assistant turn the steering wheel back-and-forth, about an eighth of a turn each way. There should be very little, if any, lost movement between the steering wheel and

roadwheels. If this is not the case, closely observe the joints and mountings previously described, but in addition, check the steering column universal joints for wear, and also check the rack-and-pinion steering gear itself.

9 The efficiency of the shock absorber may be checked by bouncing the car at each front corner. Generally speaking, the body will return to its normal position and stop after being depressed. If it rises and returns on a rebound, the shock absorber is probably suspect. Examine also the shock absorber upper and lower mountings for any signs of wear or fluid leakage.

Rear suspension check

10 Chock the front wheels, then raise the rear of the vehicle and support it on axle stands. (see *"Jacking and vehicle support"*).

11 Check the rear hub bearings for wear, using the method described for the front hub bearings (paragraph 4).

12 Using a large screwdriver or flat bar, check for wear in the suspension mounting bushes by levering between the relevant suspension component and its attachment point. Some movement is to be expected as the mountings are made of rubber, but excessive wear should be obvious. Check the condition of the shock absorbers as described previously.

26 Air cleaner filter element renewal

XV, XW and XY series engines

1 Unscrew the wing nut on the air cleaner casing end-face **(see illustration)**.

2 Withdraw the end cover with element **(see illustration)**.

3 Discard the element and wipe the casing interior clean.

4 Fit the new element and the cover, tighten the wing nut.

XU and TU series engines

4 Disconnect the air duct from the end of the air cleaner.

5 Unscrew the nuts and remove the end (or top) cover **(see illustrations)**. On some types

1

26.2 . . . and remove the cover and filter element

26.5a On XU and TU series engines, unscrew the nuts . . .

26.5b . . . or release the spring clips . . .

26.5c ... then lift off the top, or end cover

26.6 With the cover removed, withdraw the filter element

of air cleaner, the end (or top) cover is retained by a number of spring clips.

6 Extract the element **(see illustration)**.

7 Discard the element and wipe the casing interior clean.

8 Insert the new element then refit the end cover and air duct. Ensure that the cover is correctly seated, to prevent air leaks, before fastening with the nuts or the clips.

27 Ignition system check

 Warning: Voltages produced by an electronic ignition system are considerably higher than those produced by conventional ignition systems. Extreme care must be taken when working on the system with the ignition switched on. Persons with surgically-implanted cardiac pacemaker devices should keep well clear of the ignition circuits, components and test equipment.

1 The ignition system components should be checked for damage or deterioration as described under the relevant sub-heading.

Carburettor models

General component check

2 The spark plug (HT) leads should be checked whenever new spark plugs are fitted.

3 Ensure that the leads are numbered before removing them, to avoid confusion when refitting (see Section 27). Pull the leads from the plugs by gripping the end fitting, not the lead, otherwise the lead connection may be fractured.

4 Check inside the end fitting for signs of corrosion, which will look like a white crusty powder. Push the end fitting back onto the spark plug, ensuring that it is a tight fit on the plug. If not, remove the lead again and use pliers to carefully crimp the metal connector inside the end fitting until it fits securely on the end of the spark plug.

5 Using a clean rag, wipe the entire length of the lead to remove any built-up dirt and grease. Once the lead is clean, check for burns, cracks and other damage. Do not bend

the lead excessively, nor pull the lead lengthways - the conductor inside might break.

6 Disconnect the other end of the lead from the distributor cap. Again, pull only on the end fitting. Check for corrosion and a tight fit in the same manner as the spark plug end. If an ohmmeter is available, check the resistance of the lead by connecting the meter between the spark plug end of the lead and the segment inside the distributor cap. Refit the lead securely on completion.

7 Check the remaining leads one at a time, in the same way.

8 If new spark plug (HT) leads are required, purchase a set for your specific car and engine.

9 Release the clips or unscrew its retaining screws and remove the distributor cap. Wipe it clean, and carefully inspect it inside and out for signs of cracks, black carbon tracks (tracking) and worn, burned or loose contacts; check that the cap's carbon brush is unworn, free to move against spring pressure, and making good contact with the rotor arm. Also inspect the cap seal for signs of wear or damage, and renew if necessary. Remove the rotor arm from the distributor shaft and inspect the rotor arm **(see illustration)**. It is common practice to renew the cap and rotor arm whenever new spark plug (HT) leads are fitted. When fitting a new cap, remove the leads from the old cap one at a time, and fit them to the new cap in the exact same location - do not simultaneously remove all the leads from the old cap, or firing order confusion may occur. When refitting, ensure

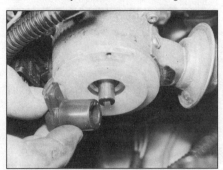

27.9 Remove the rotor arm from the distributor for inspection

that the arm is securely pressed onto the shaft, and tighten the cap retaining screws securely.

10 Even with the ignition system in first-class condition, some engines may still occasionally experience poor starting attributable to damp ignition components. To disperse moisture, a water-dispersant aerosol can be very effective.

Ignition timing - check and adjustment

11 Check the ignition timing as described in Chapter 5B.

Fuel-injected models

General component check

12 On single-point fuel injection models, carry out the checks described above in paragraphs 3 to 8 noting that on some models the HT leads are removed from the ignition module, not the distributor cap. On multi-point fuel injection models, carry out the checks described above in paragraphs 3 to 10.

Ignition timing - check and adjustment

13 Refer to Chapter 5B.

28 Idle speed and mixture check and adjustment

1 Before checking the idle speed and mixture setting, always check the following first:

a) *Check the ignition timing (Chapter 5B).*

b) *Check that the spark plugs are in good condition and correctly gapped (Section 7).*

c) *Check that the throttle cable and, on carburettor models, the choke cable (where fitted) is correctly adjusted (Section 8 and Chapter 4A, 4B or 4C).*

d) *Check that the crankcase breather hoses are secure, with no leaks or kinks (Section 29).*

e) *Check that the air cleaner filter element is clean (Section 26).*

f) *Check that the exhaust system is in good condition (Chapter 4D).*

g) *If the engine is running very roughly, check the compression pressures and valve clearances as described in Chapter 2A, 2B or 2C.*

2 Take the car on a journey of sufficient length to warm it up to normal operating temperature. Proceed as described under the relevant sub-heading. **Note:** *Adjustment should be completed within two minutes of return, without stopping the engine. If this cannot be achieved, or if the radiator electric cooling fan operates, first wait for the cooling fan to stop. Clear any excess fuel from the inlet manifold by racing the engine two or three times to between 2000 and 3000 rpm, then allow it to idle again.*

28.4a Typical idle speed adjusting screw location (A) on the Solex PBISA carburettors

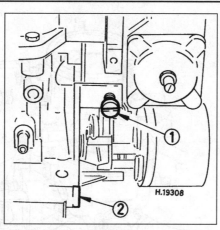

28.4b Idle speed adjusting screw (1) and mixture screw (2) location on the Solex 32-34 Z2 carburettors

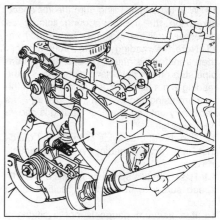

28.4c Idle speed adjusting screw location (1) on the Weber 32 IBSH carburettors

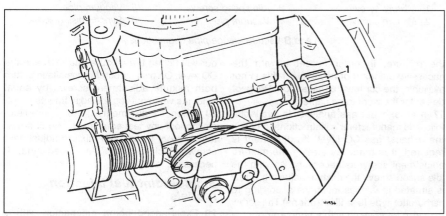

28.4d Idle speed adjusting screw location (1) on the Weber 36 TLC carburettors

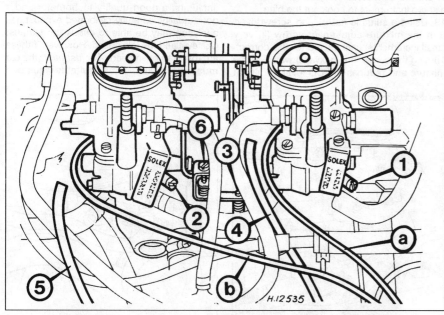

28.9a Adjustment points on the Solex twin carburettor installation

1 *Mixture screw*
2 *Mixture screw*
3 *Idle speed screw*
4 *Vacuum pipe*
5 *Vacuum pipe*
6 *Synchronising screw*
a *Vacuum gauge pipe*
b *Vacuum gauge pipe*

Carburettor models

Idle speed adjustment - single carburettor engines

3 Ensure that all electrical loads are switched off and, where applicable, the choke is pushed fully in; if the car does not have a tachometer (rev counter), connect one to the engine, following its manufacturer's instructions. Note the idle speed, and compare it with that specified.

4 The idle speed adjusting screw is situated in various locations according to carburettor type **(see illustrations)**. It may be necessary to remove a retaining clip and plastic cover to gain access to the carburettor. Using a suitable flat-bladed screwdriver, turn the idle speed screw in or out as necessary to obtain the specified idling speed as given in the *Specifications*.

5 If the idle mixture CO content is not to be adjusted, switch off the engine, disconnect any instruments and refit all disturbed components.

Idle speed adjustment - twin carburettor engines

6 On twin carburettor installations, it is necessary to balance the carburettors so that the airflow through both is the same before adjusting the idling speed. To do this a vacuum gauge or carburettor synchronising tool will be required.

7 Ensure that all electrical loads are switched off and, where applicable, the choke is pushed fully in; if the car does not have a tachometer (rev counter), connect one to the engine, following its manufacturer's instructions. Note the idle speed, and compare it with that specified.

8 Remove the air cleaner assembly as described in Chapter 4A.

9 If a vacuum gauge is being used, disconnect the vacuum pipe and connect the gauge to the vacuum pipe stub on the left-hand carburettor **(see illustrations)**.

1

10 With the engine idling, turn the idle speed screw on the interconnecting linkage as necessary until the engine speed is 1000 rpm.

11 Note the reading on the vacuum gage, then transfer the gauge pipe to the vacuum pipe stub on the right-hand carburettor. If the reading is not as previously recorded, turn the synchronising screw on the linkage as necessary until an identical reading is shown on the gauge.

12 Blip the throttle once or twice and check that both vacuum readings are as previously indicated.

13 Reset the idle speed by means of the idle speed screw to obtain the specified idling speed.

14 If a vacuum gauge is not available a carburettor synchronising tool available at most motor stores can be used instead. These instruments are basically airflow meters and should show identical readings when moved from one carburettor venturi to the other. Adjust the airflow through the carburettor, by means of the synchronising screw, until both carburettors show the same reading on the tool. When correct, reset the idling speed by means of the idle speed screw to obtain the specified speed. Note that if one of these instruments is being used, it will not be necessary to disconnect the carburettor vacuum pipes.

15 If the idle mixture CO content is not to be adjusted, switch off the engine, disconnect the instruments and refit all disturbed components.

Idle mixture CO level adjustment

16 The idle mixture (exhaust gas CO level) is set at the factory, and should require no further adjustment. If, due to a change in engine characteristics (carbon build-up, bore wear etc) or after a major carburettor overhaul, the mixture setting is lost, it can be reset. Note, however, that an exhaust gas analyser (CO meter) will be required to check

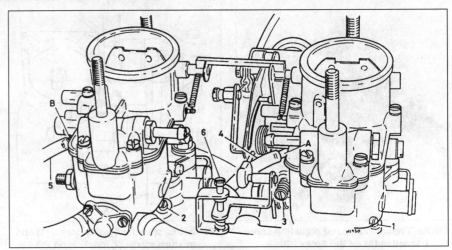

28.9b Adjustment points on the Weber twin carburettor installation

1 *Mixture screw*	3 *Idle speed screw*	5 *Vacuum pipe*
2 *Mixture screw*	4 *Vacuum pipe*	6 *Synchronising screw*

A and B Vacuum gauge pipe connections

the mixture, in order to set it with the necessary standard of accuracy; if this is not available, the car must be taken to a Peugeot dealer for the work to be carried out.

17 If an exhaust gas analyser is available, follow its manufacturer's instructions to check the exhaust gas CO level. If adjustment is required, it is made by turning the mixture adjustment screw as necessary. As with the idle speed screw, the mixture adjusting screw is situated in various locations according to carburettor type **(see illustrations)**.The screw may also be covered with a tamperproof plug to prevent unnecessary adjustment. If so, use a sharp instrument to hook out the plug.

18 Using a suitable flat-bladed screwdriver, turn the mixture adjustment screw (in very small increments) until the CO level is correct. Turning the screw in (clockwise) weakens the mixture and reduces the CO level, turning it

out will richen the mixture and increase the CO level. On twin carburettor installations turn both mixture adjustment screws by equal amounts when making the adjustments.

19 When adjustments are complete, disconnect any test equipment, and fit a new tamperproof plug to the mixture adjustment screw. Recheck the idle speed and, if necessary, readjust.

Single-point fuel injection models

20 Experienced home mechanics with a considerable amount of skill and equipment (including a good-quality tachometer and a good-quality, carefully-calibrated exhaust gas analyser) may be able to *check* the exhaust CO level and the idle speed. However, if these are found to be in need of *adjustment*, the car **must** be taken to a suitably-equipped

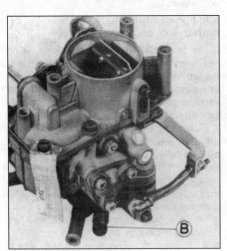

28.17a Typical idle mixture adjusting screw location (B) on the Solex PBISA carburettors

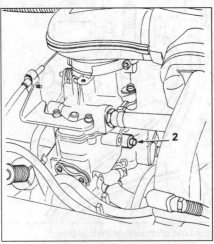

28.17b Idle mixture adjusting screw location (2) on the Weber IBSH carburettors

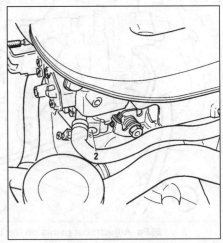

28.17c Idle mixture adjusting screw location (2) on the Weber 36 TLC carburettors

Peugeot dealer, for diagnosis. On all single-point fuel injection models, the idle speed and mixture CO content is controlled by the engine management ECU and cannot be adjusted. If the idle speed and/or CO level is incorrect, there is likely to be a fault in the engine management system (see Chapter 4B).

Multi-point fuel injection models

Idle speed adjustment

21 Ensure that all electrical loads are switched off. If the car does not have a tachometer (rev counter), connect one to the engine, following its manufacturer's instructions. Note the idle speed, and compare it with that specified.

22 If adjustment is necessary, turn the air screw (LE2-Jetronic) or idle speed adjustment screw (LU2-Jetronic and Motronic M1.3) in the throttle housing to obtain the specified idling speed **(see illustrations)**. If, on the LE2-Jetronic system, the correct speed cannot be obtained by means of the air screw, check and adjust the throttle initial position as described in Chapter 4C, Section 10.

Idle mixture CO level adjustment

Note: *Adjustment of the idle mixture CO content is only possible on the LE2-Jetronic system. On The LU2-Jetronic and Motronic M1.3 systems it is controlled by the fuel injection system ECU.*

23 The idle mixture (exhaust gas CO level) is set at the factory, and should require no further adjustment. If, due to a change in engine characteristics (carbon build-up, bore wear etc) or after a major overhaul, the mixture setting is lost, it can be reset. Note, however, that an exhaust gas analyser (CO meter) will be required to check the mixture, in order to set it with the necessary standard of accuracy; if this is not available, the car must

28.22a Idle speed air screw adjustment on the LE2-Jetronic fuel injection system

be taken to a Peugeot dealer for the work to be carried out.

24 If an exhaust gas analyser is available, follow its manufacturer's instructions to check the exhaust gas CO level. If adjustment is required, prise out the tamperproof cap on the airflow sensor and use an Allen key to adjust the mixture **(see illustration)**. Turn the screw in to richen the mixture and out to weaken it.

25 Blip the throttle two or three times and then recheck that the idle speed and mixture is correct.

26 When adjustments are complete, disconnect the test equipment, and fit a new tamperproof plug to the mixture adjustment screw.

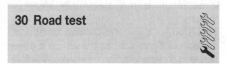

29 Emissions control systems check

1 Details of the emissions control system components are given in Chapter 4D.
2 Checking consists simply of a visual check for obvious signs of damaged or leaking hoses and joints. On engines incorporating a

breather filter in the oil filler cap, this should be removed and cleaned, or renewed if it is particularly contaminated.
3 Detailed checking and testing of the evaporative and/or exhaust emissions systems (as applicable) should be entrusted to a Peugeot dealer.

30 Road test

Instruments and electrical equipment

1 Check the operation of all instruments and electrical equipment.
2 Make sure that all instruments read correctly, and switch on all electrical equipment in turn to check that it functions properly.

Steering and suspension

3 Check for any abnormalities in the steering, suspension, handling or road "feel".
4 Drive the vehicle, and check that there are no unusual vibrations or noises.
5 Check that the steering feels positive, with no excessive "sloppiness", or roughness, and check for any suspension noises when cornering, or when driving over bumps.

Drivetrain

6 Check the performance of the engine, clutch, transmission and driveshafts.
7 Listen for any unusual noises from the engine, clutch and transmission.
8 Make sure that the engine runs smoothly when idling, and that there is no hesitation when accelerating.

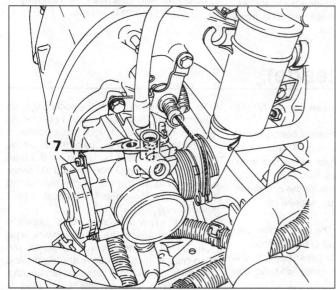

28.22b Idle speed adjustment screw (7) on the LU2-Jetronic and Motronic M1.3 fuel injection systems

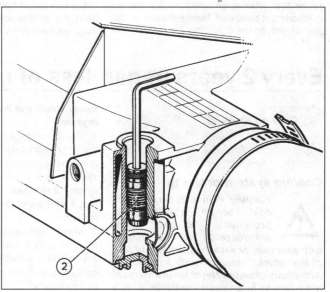

28.24 Mixture adjustment screw (2)

9 Check that the clutch action is smooth and progressive, that the drive is taken up smoothly, and that the pedal travel is not excessive. Also listen for any noises when the clutch pedal is depressed.

10 Check that all gears can be engaged smoothly, without noise, and that the gear lever action is not abnormally vague or "notchy".

11 Listen for a metallic clicking sound from the front of the vehicle, as the vehicle is driven slowly in a circle with the steering on full lock. Carry out this check in both directions. If a clicking noise is heard, this indicates wear in a driveshaft joint, in which case, the complete driveshaft must be renewed (see Chapter 8).

Check the operation and performance of the braking system

12 Make sure that the vehicle does not pull to one side when braking, and that the wheels do not lock prematurely when braking hard.

13 Check that there is no vibration through the steering when braking.

14 Check that the handbrake operates correctly, without excessive movement of the lever, and that it holds the vehicle stationary on a slope.

15 Test the operation of the brake servo unit as follows. With the engine off, depress the footbrake four or five times to exhaust the vacuum. Start the engine, holding the brake pedal depressed. As the engine starts, there should be a noticeable "give" in the brake pedal as vacuum builds up. Allow the engine to run for at least two minutes, and then switch it off. If the brake pedal is depressed now, it should be possible to detect a hiss from the servo as the pedal is depressed. After about four or five applications, no further hissing should be heard, and the pedal should feel considerably firmer.

Every 36 000 miles or 3 years

| 31 Timing belt renewal | |

Refer to Chapter 2B or 2C.

Every 48 000 miles or 4 years

| 32 Fuel filter renewal - fuel injection models | |

> ⚠ **Warning: Before carrying out the following operation, refer to the precautions given in "Safety first!" at the beginning of this manual, and follow them implicitly. Petrol is a highly-dangerous and volatile liquid, and the precautions necessary when handling it cannot be overstressed.**

1 The fuel filter is situated on the engine compartment bulkhead. Before disconnecting any of the hoses from the filter it will be necessary to depressurise the fuel system (see Chapter 4B or 4C).

2 To renew the fuel filter first disconnect the fuel hose, or unscrew the union bolt from the top of the unit then place the bolt, union and washers to one side and cover to prevent ingress of dirt **(see illustration)**. Unscrew the clamp bolt, then lift the filter and unscrew the bottom union. Dispose safely of the old filter; it will be highly inflammable, and may explode if thrown on a fire.

3 Fit the new filter using a reversal of the removal procedure; making sure that dust and dirt is prevented from entering the fuel lines. Start the engine and check the filter hose union connections for leaks.

32.2 Fuel filter fuel hose and retaining clamp locations

Every 2 years (regardless of mileage)

| 33 Coolant renewal | |

Cooling system draining

> ⚠ **Warning: Wait until the engine is cold before starting this procedure. Do not allow antifreeze to come in contact with your skin, or with the painted surfaces of the vehicle. Rinse off spills immediately with plenty of water. Never leave antifreeze lying around in an open container, or in a puddle in the driveway or on the garage floor. Children and pets are attracted by its sweet smell, but antifreeze can be fatal if ingested.**

1 With the engine completely cold, remove the expansion tank filler cap. Turn the cap anti-clockwise until it reaches the first stop. Wait until any pressure remaining in the system is released, then push the cap down, turn it anti-clockwise to the second stop, and lift it off.

2 Where fitted, unscrew the radiator filler cap from the top left-hand side of the radiator.

3 Position a suitable container beneath the coolant drain outlet at the lower left-hand side of the radiator.

4 Unscrew the drain plug and allow the coolant to drain into the container.

5 To assist draining, open the cooling system bleed screws. These are located in the heater matrix outlet hose union (to improve access, it may be located in an extension hose) on the engine compartment bulkhead, in the inlet manifold coolant hose (XV, XW and XU series engines) and on the top of the thermostat housing (TU series engines) **(see illustrations)**.

6 When the flow of coolant stops, reposition the container below the cylinder block drain plug. On all engines except TU series, the drain plug is located above the right-hand driveshaft, or driveshaft intermediate bearing. On TU series engines, the drain plug is located at the front left-hand side of the cylinder block.

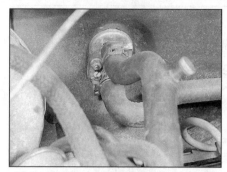

33.5a Cooling system bleed screws may be located in the heater hose . . .

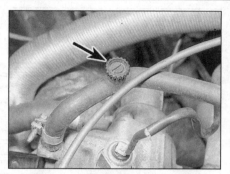

33.5b . . . in the inlet manifold coolant hose . . .

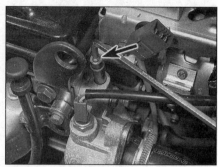

33.5c . . . or on the thermostat housing (arrowed)

7 Remove the drain plug, and allow the coolant to drain into the container.

8 If the coolant has been drained for a reason other than renewal, then provided it is clean and less than two years old, it can be re-used, though this is not recommended.

9 Refit the radiator and cylinder block drain plugs on completion of draining.

Cooling system flushing

10 If coolant renewal has been neglected, or if the antifreeze mixture has become diluted, then in time, the cooling system may gradually lose efficiency, as the coolant passages become restricted due to rust, scale deposits, and other sediment. The cooling system efficiency can be restored by flushing the system clean.

11 The radiator should be flushed independently of the engine, to avoid unnecessary contamination.

Radiator flushing

12 To flush the radiator, first tighten the radiator drain plug.

13 Disconnect the top and bottom hoses and any other relevant hoses from the radiator, with reference to Chapter 3.

14 Insert a garden hose into the radiator top

inlet. Direct a flow of clean water through the radiator, and continue flushing until clean water emerges from the radiator bottom outlet.

15 If after a reasonable period, the water still does not run clear, the radiator can be flushed with a good proprietary cleaning agent. It is important that their manufacturer's instructions are followed carefully. If the contamination is particularly bad, insert the hose in the radiator bottom outlet, and reverse-flush the radiator.

Engine flushing

16 To flush the engine, first refit the cylinder block drain plug, and tighten the cooling system bleed screws.

17 Remove the thermostat as described in Chapter 3, then temporarily refit the thermostat cover.

18 With the top and bottom hoses disconnected from the radiator, insert a garden hose into the radiator top hose. Direct a clean flow of water through the engine, and continue flushing until clean water emerges from the radiator bottom hose.

19 On completion of flushing, refit the thermostat and reconnect the hoses with reference to Chapter 3.

Cooling system filling

20 Before attempting to fill the cooling system, make sure that all hoses and clips are in good condition, and that the clips are tight. Note that an antifreeze mixture must be used all year round, to prevent corrosion of the engine components (see following sub-Section). Also check that the radiator and cylinder block drain plugs are in place and tight.

21 Remove the expansion tank filler cap.

22 Open all the cooling system bleed screws (see paragraph 4).

23 Some of the cooling system hoses are positioned at a higher level than the top of the radiator expansion tank. It is therefore necessary to use a "header tank" when refilling the cooling system, to reduce the possibility of air being trapped in the system. Although Peugeot dealers use a special header tank, the same effect can be achieved by using a suitable bottle, with a seal between the bottle and the expansion tank. On some engines, the expansion bottle/tank can be simply released from its normal location, raised as high as possible and tied to the bonnet to form the "header" tank.

24 Fit the "header tank" to the expansion tank and slowly fill the system. Where the radiator incorporates a filler cap, fill the radiator first until it is overflowing, and refit the filler cap **(see illustration)**. Now, on all models, slowly fill the "header" tank. Coolant will emerge from each of the bleed screws in turn, starting with the lowest screw. As soon as coolant free from air bubbles emerges from the lowest screw, tighten that screw, and watch the next bleed screw in the system. Repeat the procedure until the coolant is emerging from the highest bleed screw in the cooling system and all bleed screws are securely tightened.

25 If a separate bottle is being used as the "header tank", ensure it is full (at least 0.5 litres of coolant). If the vehicle expansion bottle/tank is being used as the "header" tank, ensure it is filled to the "MAX" markings **(see illustration)**. Start the engine, and run it at a fast idle speed (do not exceed 2000 rpm) until the cooling fan cuts in, and then cuts out. During this time, squeeze the top and bottom radiator hoses to allow any trapped air to rise.

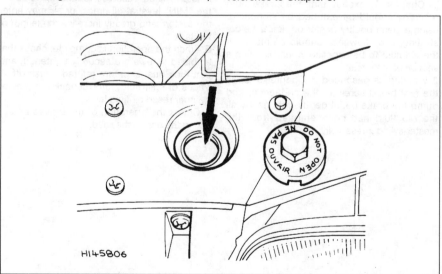

H145806

33.24 Fill the radiator through the filler (arrowed) on the left-hand side

1

Slacken and retighten the bleed screws to allow any air that has risen to escape. **Note:** *Take great care not to scald yourself with the hot coolant during this operation.*

26 Stop the engine and allow it engine to cool, then remove the "header tank" or refit the expansion bottle/tank to its original location.

27 When the engine has cooled, check the coolant level with reference to Section 3 of this Chapter. Top-up the level if necessary, and refit the expansion tank cap.

Note: *If, after draining and refilling the system, symptoms of overheating are found which did not occur previously, then the fault is almost certainly due to trapped air at some point in the system, causing an air-lock and restricting the flow of coolant; usually, the air is trapped because the system was refilled too quickly. In some cases, air-locks can be released by tapping or squeezing the various hoses. If the problem persists, stop the engine and allow it to cool down completely, before unscrewing the expansion tank filler cap, slackening the bleed screws, or disconnecting hoses to bleed out the trapped air.*

Antifreeze mixture

28 The antifreeze should always be renewed at the specified intervals. This is necessary not only to maintain the antifreeze properties, but also to prevent corrosion which would otherwise occur as the corrosion inhibitors become progressively less effective.

29 Always use an ethylene-glycol based antifreeze which is suitable for use in mixed-metal cooling systems. The quantity of antifreeze and levels of protection are indicated in the *Specifications*.

30 Before adding antifreeze, the cooling system should be completely drained, preferably flushed, and all hoses checked for condition and security.

31 After filling with antifreeze, a label should be attached to the expansion tank, stating the type and concentration of antifreeze used, and the date installed. Any subsequent topping-up should be made with the same type and concentration of antifreeze.

32 Do not use engine antifreeze in the windscreen/tailgate washer system, as it will cause damage to the vehicle paintwork. A screenwash additive should be added to the washer system in the quantities stated by the makers.

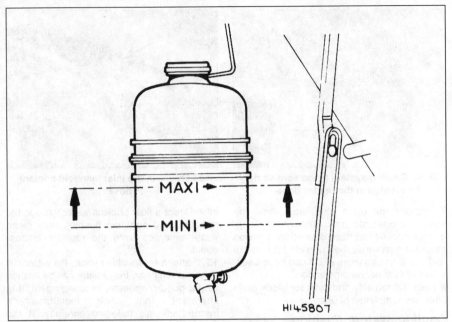

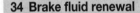

33.25 Where possible, lift out the expansion bottle, suspend it from the bonnet to form a "header" tank and fill to the "MAX" mark

---

34 Brake fluid renewal

> **Warning: Brake hydraulic fluid can harm your eyes and damage painted surfaces, so use extreme caution when handling and pouring it. Do not use fluid that has been standing open for some time, as it absorbs moisture from the air. Excess moisture can cause a dangerous loss of braking effectiveness.**

1 The procedure is similar to that for the bleeding of the hydraulic system as described in Chapter 9, except that the brake fluid reservoir should be emptied by siphoning, using a clean poultry baster or similar before starting, and allowance should be made for the old fluid to be expelled when bleeding a section of the circuit.

2 Working as described in Chapter 9, open the first bleed screw in the sequence, and pump the brake pedal gently until nearly all the old fluid has been emptied from the master cylinder reservoir.

> **HAYNES HiNT**
> *Old hydraulic fluid is invariably much darker in colour than the new, making it easy to distinguish the two.*

3 Top-up to the "MAX" level with new fluid, and continue pumping until only the new fluid remains in the reservoir, and new fluid can be seen emerging from the bleed screw. Tighten the screw, and top the reservoir level up to the "MAX" level line.

4 Work through all the remaining bleed screws in the sequence until new fluid can be seen at all of them. Be careful to keep the master cylinder reservoir topped-up to above the "MIN" level at all times, or air may enter the system and greatly increase the length of the task.

5 When the operation is complete, check that all bleed screws are securely tightened, and that their dust caps are refitted. Wash off all traces of spilt fluid, and recheck the master cylinder reservoir fluid level.

6 Check the operation of the brakes before taking the car on the road.

Chapter 2 Part A:
XV, XW and XY engines in-car repair procedures

Contents

Degrees of difficulty

Easy, suitable for novice with little experience	**Fairly easy,** suitable for beginner with some experience	**Fairly difficult,** suitable for competent DIY mechanic 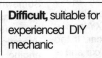	**Difficult,** suitable for experienced DIY mechanic	**Very difficult,** suitable for expert DIY or professional

Specifications

Engine general

Code and displacement:

XV8 (108C)	954 cc
XW7 (109F)	1124 cc
XY7 (150D)	1360 cc
XY8 (150B)	1360 cc

Bore:

XV8	70.0 mm
XW7	72.0 mm
XY7 and XY8	75.0 mm

Stroke:

XV8	62.0 mm
XW7	69.0 mm
XY7 and XY8	77.0 mm

Compression ratio:

XV8	9.3 : 1
XW7	9.7 : 1
XY7 and XY8	9.7 : 1

Direction of crankshaft rotation	Clockwise (viewed from right-hand side of vehicle)
Firing order	1-3-4-2 (No 1 cylinder at flywheel end of engine)

Valve clearances (engine cold)

Pre-January 1987 models:

Inlet	0.10 mm
Exhaust	0.25 mm

January 1987 on, from the following engine numbers:

XV8	28401
XW7	42460
XY7	877201
XY8	877001
Inlet	0.15 mm
Exhaust	0.30 mm

Oil pump

Endfloat	0.02 to 0.10 mm
Maximum lobe-to-body clearance	0.064 mm

2A

Torque wrench settings

	Nm	lbf ft
Engine mounting nuts	34	25
Oil pump screws	7	5
Cylinder head bolts:		
Stage 1	50	37
Stage 2	77	57
Chain tensioner bolts	7	5
Camshaft sprocket bolt	73	54
Timing chain cover bolts	7	5
Crankshaft pulley nut	88	65
Flywheel bolts	66	49
Rocker cover bolts	7	5

1 General information

How to use this Chapter

This Part of Chapter 2 describes those repair procedures that can reasonably be carried out on the XV, XW and XY series engines while they remain in the car. If the engine has been removed from the car and is being dismantled as described in Part D, any preliminary dismantling procedures can be ignored. Refer to Part B and C for information on the XU series and TU series engines.

Part D describes the removal of the engine/transmission from the vehicle, and the full overhaul procedures that can then be carried out.

Engine description

One of three different capacity engines in this series may be fitted, the difference in displacement being achieved by increasing the bore and stroke. The engine, which has four cylinders and an overhead camshaft, is mounted transversely, driving the front wheels, and it is inclined to the rear at an angle of 72° from vertical.

The manual transmission is also mounted transversely in line with and below the engine, and the final drive to the roadwheels is via the differential unit which is integral with the transmission. Drive from the engine to the transmission is by means of transfer gears which are separately encased in the clutch housing.

The crankcase, cylinder head, gearcase and clutch housing are all manufactured from aluminium alloy. Removable wet cylinder liners are fitted; the aluminium pistons each have two compression rings and one oil control ring. The valves are operated by the single overhead camshaft via rocker arms. The camshaft drives the distributor at the flywheel end. The timing sprocket, located at the other end of the camshaft, incorporates a separate eccentric lobe which actuates the fuel pump. The timing chain is driven from the crankshaft sprocket. Next to the timing chain

sprocket is the gearwheel which drives the oil pump. This is mounted low down against the crankcase face and is enclosed in the timing chain cover.

The crankshaft runs in five shell type main bearings and the endfloat is adjustable via a pair of semi-circular thrustwashers. Somewhat inconveniently, the lower half crankcase interconnects the engine with the transmission and limits the number of operations that can be carried out with the engine in the car. The engine and transmissions share the same mountings. A forced feed lubrication system is employed. The oil pump is attached to the crankcase in the lower section of the timing chest and it incorporates the pressure relief valve. The pump is driven by gears from the crankshaft.

Oil from the pump passes via an oilway to the oil filter, and thence to the crankshaft main bearings, connecting rod bearings and transmission components. Another oilway from the filter delivers oil to the overhead camshaft and rocker components. Oil from the cylinder head passes to the transfer gear housing and then back to the sump contained within the transmission housing.

Apart from the standard replaceable canister filter located on the outside of the crankcase there is a gauze filter incorporated in the oil pump suction inlet within the transmission casing.

Repair operations possible with the engine in the car

The following work can be carried out with the engine in the car:

a) Valve clearances - adjustment.
b) Compression pressure - testing.
c) Timing chain - removal and refitting.
d) Oil pump - removal, inspection and refitting.
e) Camshaft and rocker arms - removal, inspection and refitting.
f) Cylinder head - removal and refitting.
g) Cylinder head and pistons - decarbonising.
h) Crankshaft oil seals - renewal.
i) Flywheel - removal and refitting.
j) Engine mountings - inspection and renewal.

2 Valve clearances - checking and adjustment

Note: The valve clearances must be checked and adjusted only when the engine is cold.

1 The importance of having the valve clearances correctly adjusted cannot be overstressed, as they vitally affect the performance of the engine. If the clearances are too big, the engine will be noisy (characteristic rattling or tapping noises) and engine efficiency will be reduced, as the valves open too late and close too early. A more serious problem arises if the clearances are too small, however. If this is the case, the valves may not close fully when the engine is hot, resulting in serious damage to the engine (eg. burnt valve seats and/or cylinder head warping/cracking). The clearances are checked and adjusted as follows.

2 Disconnect the spark plug HT leads and remove the oil filler/crankcase ventilation cap from the rocker cover.

3 Remove the rocker cover and then turn the engine using a spanner on the crankshaft pulley nut until the valves on No 1 cylinder are rocking (ie inlet valve opening and exhaust valve closing).

HAYNES HiNT *Turning the engine will be easier if the spark plugs are removed first - see Chapter 1.*

4 The rocker arm clearances of both valves of No 4 cylinder can now be checked and, if necessary, adjusted. Remember that No 1 cylinder is at the flywheel/clutch end of the engine.

5 The feeler blade of the correct thickness is inserted between the valve stem and rocker arm. When the clearance is correctly set the feeler blade should be a smooth stiff sliding fit between the valve stem and rocker arm. The correct valve clearances are given in the *Specifications* at the start of this Chapter. The valve locations can be determined from the position of the manifolds. Note that engines manufactured from January 1987, with

bi-metal rockers consisting of an aluminium arm and steel pad, have different valve clearances than earlier engines. Ensure that the correct figures are used according to engine type.

6 If the feeler blade is a tight or loose fit then the clearance must be adjusted. To do this, loosen the locknut of the adjustment stud and screw the adjuster stud in or out until the feeler blade can be felt to drag slightly when drawn from the gap.

7 Hold the adjuster firmly in this position and tighten the locknut. Recheck the gap on completion to ensure that it has not altered when locking the nut and stud **(see illustration)**.

8 Check each valve clearance in turn in the following sequence remembering that the clearances for inlet and exhaust valves are different. The valves are numbered from the flywheel end of the engine.

Valves rocking	Valves to adjust
1 In 2 Ex	7 In 8 Ex
5 In 6 Ex	3 In 4 Ex
7 In 8 Ex	1 In 2 Ex
3 In 4 Ex	5 In 6 Ex

9 Fit the rocker cover using a new gasket, then refit the spark plugs, HT leads and oil filler/crankcase ventilation cap.

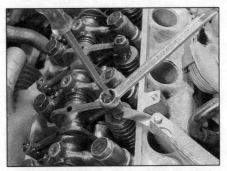

2.7 Adjusting the valve clearances

Note that the compression should build up quickly in a healthy engine; low compression on the first stroke, followed by gradually-increasing pressure on successive strokes, indicates worn piston rings. A low compression reading on the first stroke, which does not build up during successive strokes, indicates leaking valves or a blown head gasket (a cracked head could also be the cause). Deposits on the undersides of the valve heads can also cause low compression.
8 Although Peugeot do not specify exact compression pressures, as a guide, any cylinder pressure of below 10 bars can be considered as less than healthy. Refer to a Peugeot dealer or other specialist if in doubt as to whether a particular pressure reading is acceptable.

9 If the pressure in any cylinder is low, carry out the following test to isolate the cause. Introduce a teaspoonful of clean oil into that cylinder through its spark plug hole, and repeat the test.

10 If the addition of oil temporarily improves the compression pressure, this indicates that bore or piston wear is responsible for the pressure loss. No improvement suggests that leaking or burnt valves, or a blown head gasket, may be to blame.

11 A low reading from two adjacent cylinders is almost certainly due to the head gasket having blown between them; the presence of coolant in the engine oil will confirm this.

12 If one cylinder is about 20 percent lower than the others and the engine has a slightly rough idle, a worn camshaft lobe could be the cause.

13 If the compression reading is unusually high, the combustion chambers are probably coated with carbon deposits. If this is the case, the cylinder head should be removed and decarbonised.

14 On completion of the test, refit the spark plugs and reconnect the ignition system.

3 Compression test - description and interpretation

1 When engine performance is down, or if misfiring occurs which cannot be attributed to the ignition or fuel systems, a compression test can provide diagnostic clues as to the engine's condition. If the test is performed regularly, it can give warning of trouble before any other symptoms become apparent.

2 The engine must be fully warmed-up to normal operating temperature, the battery must be fully charged, and all the spark plugs must be removed (Chapter 1). The aid of an assistant will also be required.

3 Disable the ignition system by disconnecting the ignition HT coil lead from the distributor cap and earthing it on the cylinder block. Use a jumper lead or similar wire to make a good connection.

4 Fit a compression tester to the No 1 cylinder spark plug hole - the type of tester which screws into the plug thread is to be preferred.

5 Have the assistant hold the throttle wide open, and crank the engine on the starter motor; after one or two revolutions, the compression pressure should build up to a maximum figure, and then stabilise. Record the highest reading obtained.

6 Repeat the test on the remaining cylinders, recording the pressure in each.

7 All cylinders should produce very similar pressures; a difference of more than 2 bars between any two cylinders indicates a fault.

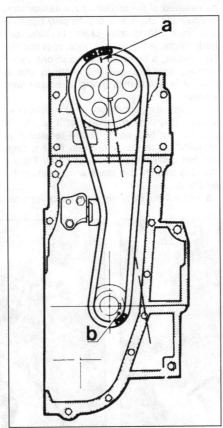

4.8 Sprocket timing marks and timing chain bright links aligned

a   Camshaft sprocket timing mark
b   Crankshaft sprocket timing mark

4 Timing chain, tensioner and sprockets - removal and refitting

2A

Removal

1 Support the engine/transmission on a trolley jack with a block of wood as an insulator.

2 Release the nuts on the right-hand flexible engine mounting at the base of the timing chain cover.

3 Raise the engine just enough to clear the side-member and anti-roll bar.

4 Remove the auxiliary drivebelt as described in Chapter 1, and the fuel pump as described in Chapter 4A.

5 Unscrew and remove the crankshaft pulley nut. To do this the crankshaft must be held against rotation by jamming the starter ring gear. Remove the starter, as described in Chapter 5A. Alternatively, if an assistant is available, apply the brakes fully with a gear engaged. Withdraw the pulley.

6 Unbolt and remove the rocker cover, and disconnect the spark plug HT leads.

7 Unscrew and remove the timing chain cover bolts. Take off the cover and extract the fuel pump operating rod.

8 Turn the crankshaft either by temporarily refitting the pulley nut or by engaging a gear and turning a front wheel (raised) until the timing marks are located in the following positions. Camshaft sprocket mark between two bright links on chain. Crankshaft sprocket mark opposite centre of single bright link **(see illustration)**.

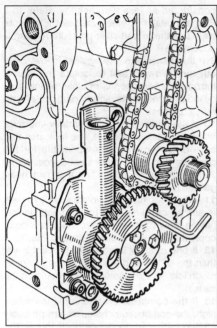

4.10a Removing oil pump screw with Allen key

9 Remove the crankshaft oil pump drivegear and its Woodruff key.

10 Unbolt the oil pump. Some socket-headed screws are accessible through the holes in the driven gear (see illustration). Lift off the pump and spacer plate (see illustration).

11 Jam the camshaft sprocket and unscrew the sprocket retaining bolt. Take off the fuel pump operating eccentric.

12 Turn the lock on the chain tensioner anti-clockwise to lock it in its retracted state (see illustration).

13 Remove the camshaft sprocket with timing chain.

14 Thoroughly clean all the removed components ensuring that all traces of old

4.10b Removing the oil pump and spacer plate

gasket are removed from the timing cover, rocker cover and engine mating faces.

15 Examine the teeth of both sprockets for wear. Each tooth on a sprocket is an inverted V-shape and wear is apparent when one side of the tooth becomes more concave in shape than the other. When badly worn, the teeth become hoop-shaped and the sprockets must be renewed. The crankshaft sprocket and oil pump drive gear are removed by sliding them off the crankshaft with their Woodruff keys.

16 If the sprockets need to be renewed then the chain will have worn also and should also be renewed. If the sprockets are satisfactory, examine the chain and look for play between the links. When the chain is held out horizontally, it should not bend appreciably. Remember, a chain is only as strong as its weakest link and, being a relatively cheap item, it is worthwhile fitting a replacement anyway.

17 Check the condition of the tensioner slipper. If it is worn, renew it; it is held in position by two bolts. If the tensioner is removed, note the fine mesh filter screen located behind the tensioner body. Ensure that it is clean and in place when refitting the tensioner.

18 Inspect the oil pump drive gears for wear

4.12 Timing chain tensioner lock (2)

Turn in direction of arrow to release slipper - turn in opposite direction to retract slipper

or damage and renew if necessary. Always fit a new timing cover oil seal (see Section 8).

Refitting

19 Check that the crankshaft is positioned correctly by observing the crankshaft sprocket keyway which should be in alignment with the crankcase joint (see illustration 4.8). Turn the crankshaft if necessary to bring it to the correct position. Temporarily fit the camshaft sprocket and rotate the camshaft until the keyway is also positioned as shown.

20 Engage the chain around the crankshaft sprocket so that the timing mark on the sprocket is in the centre of the single bright link on the chain (see illustration).

21 Now engage the upper loop of the chain over the camshaft sprocket so that the timing mark is between the two bright links on the chain (see illustration).

22 Now offer the camshaft sprocket to the shaft. Adjust the position of the camshaft so that the sprocket keyway aligns with the key.

23 Push the camshaft sprocket into position. Insert and tighten its retaining bolt with the fuel pump eccentric correctly located (see illustration).

4.20 Timing chain bright link (arrowed) positioned over crankshaft sprocket timing mark

4.21 Camshaft sprocket timing mark positioned between two bright links (arrowed) on chain

4.23 Tightening the camshaft sprocket retaining bolt

4.24 Releasing the timing chain tensioner

4.27 Timing cover bolt next to coolant pump pulley in place prior to fitting cover

24 Using a very thin screwdriver blade, turn the lock on the chain tensioner fully clockwise to release the slipper **(see illustration)**.

25 Check that the locating dowel is in position and fit the oil pump with spacer plate. If the pump driven sprocket is hard to turn, release the pump mounting bolts and turn the pump slightly on its locating dowel. Re-tighten the bolts.

26 Fit the oil pump drivegear to the crankshaft.

27 Bolt on the timing chain cover using a new gasket. The bolt nearest the coolant pump pulley must be located in the cover before offering it up, otherwise the pulley will prevent the bolt entering its cover hole **(see illustration)**. Do not tighten the cover bolts until the crankshaft pulley has been pushed into place to centralise the cover. Fit the coolant hose safety rod under its cover bolts. This rod prevents the coolant hose being cut by the rim of the coolant pump pulley should the hose sag.

28 Fit the fuel pump operating rod and fuel pump with reference to Chapter 4A, if necessary.

29 Tighten the timing chain cover bolts to the specified torque and then trim the upper ends of the gasket flush. Fit the rocker cover using a new gasket. Do not overtighten the securing bolts.

30 Tighten the crankshaft pulley nut to the specified torque, again jamming the flywheel to prevent the crankshaft rotating.

31 Refit the starter, if removed (Chapter 5A).

32 Refit and tension the auxiliary drivebelt (Chapter 1).

33 Lower the engine, reconnect the mounting.

5 Oil pump - removal, inspection and refitting

Removal

1 Carry out the operations described in Section 4, paragraphs 1 to 10.

Inspection

2 The oil pump gears are exposed once the spacer plate is removed.

3 Side movement of the gear spindles will indicate wear in the bushes and the pump should be renewed complete.

4 Worn or chipped gear teeth must be rectified by renewal of the gear.

5 Check the endfloat of the gears using a straight-edge and feeler blades **(see illustration)**.

6 Check the clearance between the tip of the gear lobes and the oil pump body **(see illustration)**.

7 If any of these clearances exceed the specified limit, renew the pump.

8 Remove the retaining pin from the relief valve housing and withdraw the cup, spring, guide and piston. Renew any worn components **(see illustration)**.

9 Check that the locating dowel is in position and fit the oil pump with spacer plate. If the pump driven sprocket is hard to turn, release

the pump mounting bolts and turn the pump slightly on its locating dowel. Re-tighten the bolts.

Refitting

10 Carry out the operations described in Section 4, paragraphs 24 to 33.

6 Camshaft and rocker arms - removal, inspection and refitting

General information

1 The rocker arm assembly is secured to the top of the cylinder head by the cylinder head bolts. Although in theory it is possible to undo the head bolts and remove the rocker arm assembly without removing the head, in practice, this is not recommended. Once the bolts have been removed, the head gasket will be disturbed, and the gasket will almost certainly leak or blow after refitting. For this reason, removal of the rocker arm assembly cannot be done without removing the cylinder head and renewing the head gasket.

2 The camshaft is slid out of the right-hand end of the cylinder head, and it therefore cannot be removed without first removing the cylinder head, due to a lack of clearance.

Removal

Rocker arm assembly

3 Remove the cylinder head as described in Section 7.

5.5 Checking oil pump gear endfloat

5.6 Checking oil pump gear to body clearance

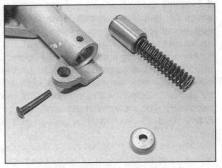

5.8 Oil pump pressure relief valve components

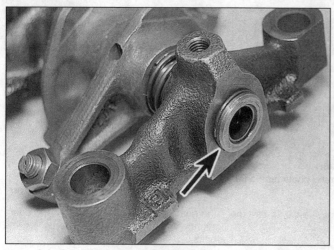

6.4a Prise off the circlip (arrowed) from the end of the rocker shaft . . .

6.4b . . . and slide the components off the shaft

4 To dismantle the rocker arm assembly, carefully prise off the circlip from the end of the rocker shaft; retain the rocker pedestal, to prevent it being sprung off the end of the shaft. Slide the various components off the end of the shaft, keeping all components in their correct fitted order **(see illustrations)**. Make a note of each component's correct fitted position and orientation as it is removed, to ensure it is fitted correctly on reassembly.

5 To separate the remaining pedestal and shaft, first unscrew the rocker cover retaining stud from the top of the pedestal; this can be achieved using a stud extractor, or two nuts locked together. With the stud removed, unscrew the grub screw from the top of the pedestal, and withdraw the rocker shaft.

Camshaft

6 Remove the cylinder head as described in Section 7.

7 Undo the retaining bolt, and remove the camshaft retaining thrust plate from the cylinder head **(see illustration)**.

8 Withdraw the camshaft taking care not to scratch the bearing journals with the edges of the cam lobes **(see illustration)**.

Inspection

Rocker arm assembly

9 Examine the rocker arm bearing surfaces which contact the camshaft lobes for wear ridges and scoring. Renew any rocker arms on which these conditions are apparent. If a rocker arm bearing surface is badly scored, also examine the corresponding lobe on the camshaft for wear, as it is likely that both will be worn. Renew worn components as necessary. The rocker arm assembly can be dismantled as described in paragraphs 4 and 5.

10 Inspect the ends of the (valve clearance) adjusting screws for signs of wear or damage, and renew as required.

11 If the rocker arm assembly has been

dismantled, examine the rocker arm and shaft bearing surfaces for wear ridges and scoring. If there are obvious signs of wear, the relevant rocker arm(s) and/or the shaft must be renewed.

Camshaft

12 Examine the camshaft bearing surfaces and cam lobes for signs of wear ridges and scoring. Renew the camshaft if any of these conditions are apparent. Examine the condition of the bearing surfaces, both on the camshaft journals and in the cylinder head. If the head bearing surfaces are worn excessively, the cylinder head will need to be renewed. If the necessary measuring equipment is available, camshaft bearing journal wear can be checked by direct measurement, noting that No 1 journal is at the transmission end of the head.

13 Examine the thrust plate for signs of wear or scoring, and renew as necessary.

Refitting

Camshaft

14 Ensure that the cylinder head and camshaft bearing surfaces are clean, then liberally oil the camshaft bearings and lobes. Slide the camshaft back into position in the cylinder head.

15 Locate the thrust plate in position, refit the plate retaining bolt, tightening it to the specified torque setting.

Rocker arm assembly

16 If the rocker arm assembly was dismantled, refit the rocker shaft to the pedestal, aligning its locating hole with the pedestal threaded hole. Refit the grub screw, and tighten it securely. With the grub screw in position, refit the rocker cover mounting stud to the pedestal, and tighten it securely. Apply a smear of clean engine oil to the shaft, then slide on all removed components, ensuring each is correctly fitted in its original position. Once all components are in position on the shaft, compress the remaining pedestal and refit the circlip. Ensure that the circlip is correctly located in its groove on the shaft.

17 Refit the cylinder head and rocker arm assembly as described in Section 7.

7 Cylinder head - removal and refitting

Note: If the crankshaft is to be rotated after removal of the cylinder head (for cleaning the pistons) it will be necessary to use the Peugeot special tool to hold the camshaft

6.7 Camshaft retaining thrust plate

6.8 Removing the camshaft

7.17 Right-hand rear engine mounting bolts

7.18 Lever up the engine and support it on a wooden block

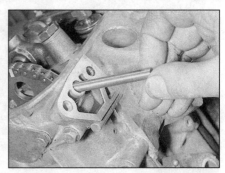

7.21 Removing the fuel pump plunger

sprocket, or fabricate a suitable alternative. If it will not be necessary to rotate the crankshaft, the home-made tool described in the text will suffice.

Removal

1 Disconnect and remove the battery, as described in Chapter 5A.
2 Remove the air cleaner, complete with mounting brackets, hot air hose and inlet hose, with reference to Chapter 4A. Also remove the inlet cowl.
3 Drain the cooling system, as described in Chapter 1.
4 Remove the engine oil filler/crankcase ventilation cap and disconnect the hoses from the inlet cowl and carburettor.
5 Chock the rear wheels then jack up the front of the car and support it on axle stands (see *"Jacking and vehicle support"*).
6 Disconnect the gearchange selector and

7.23 Unscrew and remove the camshaft sprocket bolt

7.24 Loosen the bolts securing the timing cover to the cylinder head

engagement rods with reference to Chapter 7A. Unscrew the engagement rod nut. Make sure that the gears are in neutral.
7 Unscrew the bolt and nuts, and disconnect the exhaust downpipe from the exhaust manifold.
8 Loosen the left-hand engine mounting nuts beneath the battery tray so that the mounting is lowered by approximately 4.0 mm.
9 Disconnect the heater hoses from the bulkhead, water pump and cylinder head outlet.
10 Remove the fuel pump, as described in Chapter 4A.
11 Disconnect the top hose from the thermostat housing.
12 Disconnect the temperature sender wiring.
13 Remove the distributor, as described in Chapter 5B.
14 Disconnect the spark plug HT leads and remove them from the rocker cover.
15 Disconnect the throttle and choke cables, as described in Chapter 4A.
16 Disconnect the brake servo vacuum hose from the inlet manifold (if applicable) and place to one side.
17 Unscrew and remove the two bolts securing the right-hand rear engine mounting to the subframe **(see illustration)**.
18 Using a suitable long bar inserted through the right-hand rear engine mounting bracket,

lever up the rear of the engine as far as possible, without damaging the radiator, and support with a block of wood **(see illustration)**. If necessary, loosen the left-hand engine mounting to gain extra height. Make sure that the right-hand front mounting is not damaged by excessive twisting.
19 Unbolt the rocker cover and remove the gasket.
20 Turn the engine on the crankshaft pulley nut until the key slot in the camshaft is facing upwards, then remove the ignition timing aperture cover and turn the engine as necessary until the mark on the flywheel is aligned with the TDC mark on the timing plate (refer to Chapter 5B if necessary). Pistons No 2 and 3 will be at TDC.
21 Extract the fuel pump plunger from the timing cover **(see illustration)**.
22 Unbolt the access plate from the top of the timing cover.
23 Unscrew and remove the camshaft sprocket retaining bolt from the end of the camshaft using an Allen key (retain the sprocket with a suitable bar) **(see illustration)**.
24 Loosen the four bolts securing the timing cover to the cylinder head **(see illustration)**.
25 Progressively unscrew the cylinder head bolts in the order shown **(see illustration)**, and recover the nuts from their channels in the crankcase.

2A

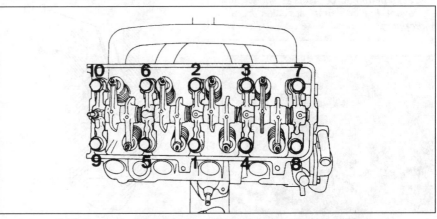

7.25 Sequence for tightening or loosening the cylinder head bolts

7.26 Removing the rocker shaft assembly

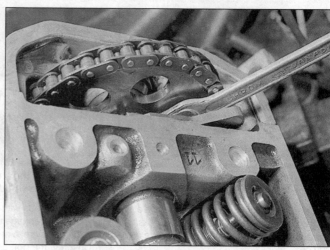

7.27 Loosening the camshaft thrust plate bolt

26 Remove the head bolts and lift off the rocker shaft assembly **(see illustration)**. It may be necessary to leave one or two bolts in the assembly if they foul the bulkhead due to insufficient engine height.

27 Loosen the camshaft thrust plate bolt, pull out the plate and temporarily retighten the bolt **(see illustration)**.

28 The camshaft sprocket must now be supported in its normal position while the

TOOL TiP

In the absence of the Peugeot tool, a nut and bolt used together with the access plate can be used as shown to prevent the camshaft sprocket from dropping.

cylinder head is removed. If it is allowed to drop it will not be possible to lift it again without releasing the timing chain tensioner which will necessitate removal of the timing cover. Peugeot dealers use a special mandrel, tool number 70132, but as this is unlikely to be available to the home mechanic it is suggested that a plate and bolt are used, together with the access plate **(see Tool Tip)**.

29 Slide the camshaft from the fuel pump eccentric and camshaft sprocket and let it rest in the cylinder head **(see illustration)**.

30 Before removing the cylinder head the following must be noted. The cylinder head is positioned during assembly by means of two dowels. When removing the cylinder head it is most important not to lift it directly from the cylinder block; it must be twisted slightly. This action prevents the cylinder liners from sticking to the cylinder head face and being lifted with it, thus breaking their bottom seals. Before the cylinder head can be twisted, the dowel at the flywheel end must be tapped down flush with the top of the cylinder block, using a drift **(see illustration)**.

31 Remove the four timing cover-to-cylinder head bolts then move the flywheel end of the cylinder head sideways slightly to release the gasket.

32 Lift the cylinder head from the block and remove the gasket without disturbing the liners. Do not turn the engine over as this also will break the liner bottom seals. If further work is to be carried out on the engine, such as cleaning the tops of the cylinder liners, they should be clamped in position using two cylinder head bolts, metal tubing, and large washers **(see illustration)**.

Preparation for refitting

Note: *As mentioned at the beginning of this Section, the camshaft sprocket must be supported in such a way that it will be allowed to rotate as the crankshaft is turned to clean the pistons. The Peugeot special tool locates through the sprocket retaining bolt hole and is bolted to the front of the timing cover. If this tool cannot be obtained, a suitable alternative can be easily fabricated.*

33 With the camshaft sprocket supported so as to allow rotation, commence the cleaning operation as follows.

34 The mating faces of the cylinder head and cylinder block/crankcase must be perfectly clean before refitting the head. Use a hard

7.29 Slide the camshaft from the fuel pump eccentric (arrowed)

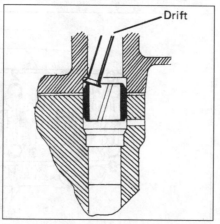

Drift

7.30 Driving the cylinder head dowel down flush with the block face

7.32 Using washers, tubing and the cylinder head bolts to clamp the liners in position

7.38 Using rubber tubing to hold the cylinder head nuts in position

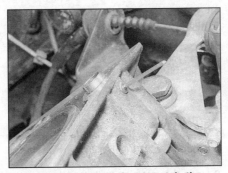

7.39 Using a pop rivet to retain the cylinder head location dowel

7.41 Applying sealing compound to the timing cover

plastic or wood scraper to remove all traces of gasket and carbon; also clean the piston crowns. Refer to paragraph 32 before turning the crankshaft. Take particular care during the cleaning operations, as aluminium alloy is easily damaged. Also, make sure that the carbon is not allowed to enter the oil and water passages - this is particularly important for the lubrication system, as carbon could block the oil supply to the engine's components. Using adhesive tape and paper, seal the water, oil and bolt holes in the cylinder block/crankcase. To prevent carbon entering the gap between the pistons and bores, smear a little grease in the gap. After cleaning each piston, use a small brush to remove all traces of grease and carbon from the gap, then wipe away the remainder with a clean rag. Clean all the pistons in the same way.

35 Check the mating surfaces of the cylinder block/crankcase and the cylinder head for nicks, deep scratches and other damage. If slight, they may be removed carefully with a file, but if excessive, machining may be the only alternative to renewal.

36 If warpage of the cylinder head gasket surface is suspected, use a straight-edge to check it for distortion. Refer to Part D of this Chapter if necessary.

37 Check the condition of the cylinder head bolts, and particularly their threads, whenever they are removed. Wash the bolts in suitable solvent, and wipe them dry. Check each for any sign of visible wear or damage, renewing any bolt if necessary. Measure the length of each bolt, to check for stretching (although this is not a conclusive test, in the event that all ten bolts have stretched by the same amount). Although Peugeot do not actually specify that the bolts must be renewed, it is strongly recommended that the bolts should be renewed as a complete set whenever they are disturbed.

38 Before refitting the head, the nuts must be retained in their channels. The use of rubber or plastic tubing is very effective, or wooden wedges may be used **(see illustration)**.

Refitting

39 Commence refitting by lifting the location dowel (paragraph 30) and retaining it by inserting a short pin in the hole provided -

leaving room for the bolt to pass through **(see illustration)**.

40 Locate a new cylinder head gasket on the cylinder block, making sure that all the holes are aligned.

41 Apply a silicone sealing compound to the timing cover mating surface **(see illustration)**.

42 Lower the cylinder head into position over the dowels.

43 Fit the four timing cover-to-cylinder head bolts finger tight.

44 Slide the camshaft into the sprocket and fuel pump eccentric. Slight rotation of the eccentric may be necessary in order to align its key with the camshaft slot.

45 Push the thrust plate fully into the camshaft groove then tighten the bolt.

46 Unbolt and remove the sprocket retaining tool.

47 Insert the sprocket retaining bolt and tighten it with an Allen key while holding the sprocket with a bar through one of the holes resting on packing pieces.

48 Apply a silicone sealing compound to the access plate then refit it and tighten the bolts.

49 Refit the rocker shaft assembly with the two location pegs towards the front.

50 Insert the head bolts (threads and heads oiled) and tighten them in two stages to the specified torques and in the sequence shown **(see illustration 7.25)**. Note that washers must be fitted beneath the bolt heads on XY7 and XY8 engines.

51 Remove the nut retainers from the cylinder block.

52 Tighten the four timing cover-to-cylinder head bolts.

53 Insert the fuel pump plunger in the timing cover.

54 Adjust the valve clearances (Section 2).

55 Refit the rocker cover with a new gasket.

56 Remove the block of wood and lower the engine to its normal position.

57 Insert and tighten the right-hand rear engine mounting bolts, also tighten the left-hand mounting bolts.

58 Reconnect the brake servo vacuum hose to the inlet manifold (if applicable).

59 Reconnect the throttle and choke cables (Chapter 4A).

60 Refit the distributor and spark plug HT leads (Chapter 5B).

61 Reconnect the temperature sender wiring.

62 Refit the top hose to the thermostat housing.

63 Refit the fuel pump (Chapter 4A).

64 Reconnect the heater hoses.

65 Refit the exhaust downpipe to the exhaust manifold.

66 Reconnect the gearchange rods (Chapter 7A).

67 Lower the car to the ground.

68 Refit the oil filler/crankcase ventilation cap and hoses.

69 Refill the cooling system (Chapter 1).

70 Refit the air cleaner, inlet cowl and inlet hoses.

71 Refit the battery.

72 After the engine has been started and run to full operating temperature, it should be switched off and allowed to cool for at least two hours. Remove the rocker cover.

73 Unscrew the first cylinder head bolt one half a turn and then retighten it to the Stage 2 torque. Repeat the operation on the remaining bolts, one at a time in the sequence specified **(see illustration 7.25)**.

74 Check the valve clearances again and readjust if necessary.

8 Crankshaft oil seals - renewal

Right-hand (front) oil seal

1 Support the engine/transmission on a trolley jack with a block of wood as an insulator.

2 Release the nuts on the right-hand flexible engine mounting at the base of the timing chain cover.

3 Raise the engine just enough to clear the side-member and anti-roll bar.

4 Remove the auxiliary drivebelt as described in Chapter 1, and the fuel pump as described in Chapter 4A.

5 Unscrew and remove the crankshaft pulley nut. To do this the crankshaft must be held against rotation by jamming the starter ring gear. Remove the starter, as described in Chapter 5A. Alternatively, if an assistant is available, apply the brakes fully with a gear engaged. Withdraw the pulley.

2A

6 Note the fitted depth of the seal as a guide to refitting the new seal, then punch or drill two small holes opposite each other in the seal. Screw a self-tapping screw into each, and pull on the screws with pliers to extract the seal. Alternatively, the seal can be levered out of position using a suitable flat-bladed screwdriver, taking great care not to damage the crankshaft shoulder or timing cover.

7 Clean the timing cover, and polish off any burrs or raised edges, which may have caused the seal to fail in the first place.

8 Lubricate the lips of the new seal with clean engine oil, and carefully locate the seal on the end of crankshaft. Note that its sealing lip must face inwards. Take care not to damage the seal lips during fitting.

9 Using a suitable tubular drift (such as a socket) which bears only on the hard outer edge of the seal, tap the seal into position, to the same depth in the timing cover as the original was prior to removal.

10 Wash off any traces of oil, then refit the crankshaft pulley and nut. Tighten the crankshaft pulley nut to the specified torque, again jamming the flywheel to prevent the crankshaft rotating.

11 Refit the starter, if removed (Chapter 5A).

12 Refit and tension the auxiliary drivebelt (Chapter 1).

13 Lower the engine, reconnect the mounting.

Left-hand oil seal

14 Remove the flywheel as described in Section 9.

15 Make a note of the correct fitted depth of the seal in its housing. Punch or drill two small holes opposite each other in the seal. Screw a self-tapping screw into each, and pull on the screws with pliers to extract the seal.

16 Clean the seal housing, and polish off any burrs or raised edges, which may have caused the seal to fail in the first place.

17 Lubricate the lips of the new seal with clean engine oil, and carefully locate the seal on the end of the crankshaft.

18 Using a suitable tubular drift, which bears only on the hard outer edge of the seal, drive the seal into position, to the same depth in the housing as the original was prior to removal.

19 Wash off any traces of oil, then refit the flywheel as described in Section 9.

9 Flywheel - removal, inspection and refitting

Removal

1 Remove the clutch assembly as described for models with the BH 3 transmission in Chapter 6.

2 Undo the retaining bolts and remove the flywheel from the crankshaft. If necessary hold the flywheel stationary using a screwdriver engaged with the starter ring gear.

Inspection

3 If the flywheel's clutch mating surface is deeply scored, cracked or otherwise damaged, the flywheel must be renewed. However, it may be possible to have it surface-ground; seek the advice of a Peugeot dealer or engine reconditioning specialist.

4 If the ring gear is badly worn or has missing teeth, it must be renewed. This job is best left to a Peugeot dealer or engine reconditioning specialist. The temperature to which the new ring gear must be heated for installation is critical and, if not done accurately, the hardness of the teeth will be destroyed.

Refitting

5 Clean the mating surfaces of the flywheel and crankshaft. Remove any remaining locking compound from the threads of the bolts and crankshaft holes, using the correct-size tap, if available.

 HAYNES HINT *If a suitable tap is not available, cut two slots into the threads of an old bolt of suitable size and use the bolt to remove the locking compound from the threads.*

6 Fit the flywheel to the crankshaft. The flywheel holes are offset so it will only go onto the crankshaft flange in one position. Apply thread locking compound to clean threads, screw in the flywheel bolts and tighten to the specified torque.

7 Refit the clutch assembly as described in Chapter 6.

10 Engine/transmission mountings - inspection and renewal

Inspection

1 The engine/transmission is supported by three mountings, two at the timing chain end and one at the transfer gear end.

2 If improved access is required, raise the front of the car and support it securely on axle stands (see *"Jacking and vehicle support"*).

3 Check the mounting rubber to see if it is cracked, hardened or separated from the metal at any point; renew the mounting if any such damage or deterioration is evident.

4 Check that all the mounting's fasteners are securely tightened; use a torque wrench to check if possible.

5 Using a large screwdriver or a crowbar, check for wear in the mounting by carefully levering against it to check for free play. Where this is not possible, enlist the aid of an assistant to move the engine/transmission back and forth, or from side to side, while you watch the mounting. While some free play is to be expected even from new components, excessive wear should be obvious. If excessive free play is found, check first that the fasteners are correctly secured, then renew any worn components.

Renewal

6 It is recommended that one mounting is renewed at a time after the weight of the unit has been taken on a jack with a block of wood as an insulator. Removal and refitting of the relevant mountings is straightforward once access has been gained.

7 The battery and tray must be removed when renewing the left-hand mounting.

8 Tighten the bolts to the specified torque after renewing the mountings.

Chapter 2 Part B:
XU series engine in-car repair procedures

Contents

Degrees of difficulty

Easy, suitable for novice with little experience	**Fairly easy,** suitable for beginner with some experience	**Fairly difficult,** suitable for competent DIY mechanic 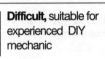	**Difficult,** suitable for experienced DIY mechanic	**Very difficult,** suitable for expert DIY or professional

Specifications

Engine general

Code and displacement:

XU5J (180A)	1580 cc
XU5JA (B6D)	1580 cc
XU5JA/K (B6E)	1580 cc
XU51C (B1A/A)	1580 cc
XU51C/K (B1F)	1580 cc
XU5M2/Z, XU5M3/Z, XU5M3/L (BDY)	1580 cc
XU9JA, XU9JA/K (D6B)	1905 cc
XU9JA/Z, XU9JA/L (DKZ)	1905 cc
XU9J1/Z, XU9J1/L (DFZ)	1905 cc
Bore	83.0 mm

Stroke:

1580 cc engines	73.0 mm
1905 cc engines	88.0 mm

Compression ratio:

XU5J, XU5JA	9.8 : 1
XU5JA/K	9.25 : 1
XU51C, XU51C/K	9.35 : 1
XU5M2/Z, XU5M3/Z, XU5M3/L	8.95 : 1
XU9JA, XU9JA/K	9.6 : 1
XU9JA/Z, XU9JA/L	9.2 : 1
XU9J1/Z, XU9J1/L	8.4 : 1
Direction of crankshaft rotation	Clockwise (viewed from right-hand side of vehicle)
Firing order	1-3-4-2 (No 1 cylinder at flywheel end of engine)

Valve clearances (engine cold)

Inlet	0.15 to 0.25 mm
Exhaust	0.35 to 0.45 mm

Camshaft

Drive	Toothed belt
Endfloat (not adjustable)	0.07 to 0.16 mm

Lubrication system

Oil pump type	Gear type, chain driven from crankshaft
Oil pressure	3.5 bar at 4000 rpm
Oil pressure warning light switch operating pressure	0.44 to 0.58 bar

2B

Torque wrench settings

	Nm	lbf ft
Camshaft cover bolts	10	7
Camshaft bearing caps	15	11
Camshaft sprocket bolt (M10)	40	30
Camshaft sprocket bolt (M12)	80	59
Crankshaft pulley bolt	109	80
Sump bolts	20	15
Sump spacer plate bolt	10	7
Flywheel bolts (renew bolts and use thread locking compound)	49	36
Cylinder head bolts (see text):		
Hexagon head bolts:		
Stage 1	58	43
Stage 2 (after slackening)	20	15
Stage 3	Tighten through a further 120°	
Torx type bolts:		
Stage 1	60	44
Stage 2 (after slackening)	20	15
Stage 3	Tighten through a further 300°	
Oil pump-to-block bolts	20	15
Oil seal carrier plate bolts	15	11
Oil cooler union nuts (remotely mounted oil cooler)	20	15
Oil filter mounting stub	60	44
Timing belt tensioner nuts (spring-loaded type tensioner)	15	11
Timing belt tensioner roller bolt (eccentric roller type tensioner)	20	15
Engine mounting bracket bolts:		
M8	34	25
M10	45	33
Engine mountings:		
RH nut	27	20
LH nut	35	26
Battery tray/bracket	18	13
Lower mounting centre bolt	34	25
Lower mounting to subframe	45	33

---

1 General information

How to use this Chapter

This Part of Chapter 2 describes those repair procedures that can reasonably be carried out on the XU series engine while it remains in the car. If the engine has been removed from the car and is being dismantled as described in Part D, any preliminary dismantling procedures can be ignored. Refer to Part A and C for information on the XV, XW and XY series and TU series engines.

Part D describes the removal of the engine/transmission from the vehicle, and the full overhaul procedures that can then be carried out.

Engine description

The engine has four cylinders and an overhead camshaft, is mounted transversely, driving the front wheels, and it is inclined to the rear at an angle of 30° from vertical. The XU series engines are of 1580 cc (XU5) or 1905 cc (XU9), the difference in displacement being achieved by increasing the stroke.

The transmission is also mounted transversely in line with and on the left-hand end of the engine. The final drive unit is integral with the transmission and transmits drive to the front wheels via driveshafts.

The engine has four wet liner cylinders, a five-bearing crankshaft and an overhead camshaft.

The connecting rods rotate on horizontally-split bearing shells at their big-ends. The pistons are attached to the connecting rods by gudgeon pins. The gudgeon pins are an interference fit in the connecting rod small-end eyes. The aluminium alloy pistons are fitted with three piston rings - two compression rings and an oil control ring.

Camshaft drive is by a toothed timing belt. The belt is tensioned by a spring loaded, or eccentric roller tensioner assembly and also drives the coolant pump. The camshaft operates directly on bucket tappets; valve clearance adjustment is by shims inserted between the tappet and the valve stem. The distributor is driven directly from the left-hand end of the camshaft.

The oil pump is located in the sump and is chain driven from the crankshaft. A forced feed lubrication system is employed. Oil from the pump passes to the oil filter then to the oil gallery, crankshaft and camshaft. The valve stems are lubricated by oil returning from the camshaft to the sump. The oil pump chain and sprockets are lubricated by oil in the sump. On certain models an oil cooler may be fitted, either on the engine between the cylinder block and oil filter, or mounted remotely in front of the radiator.

Repair operations possible with the engine in the car

The following work can be carried out with the engine in the car:

a) Valve clearances - adjustment.
b) Compression pressure - testing.
c) Timing belt - removal, refitting and adjustment.
d) Timing belt tensioner and sprockets - removal, inspection and refitting.
e) Camshaft oil seal - renewal.
f) Camshaft and followers - removal, inspection and refitting.
g) Cylinder head - removal and refitting.
h) Cylinder head and pistons - decarbonising.
i) Sump - removal and refitting.
j) Oil pump - removal, inspection and refitting.
k) Crankshaft oil seals - renewal.
l) Flywheel/driveplate - removal and refitting.
m) Engine mountings - inspection and renewal.

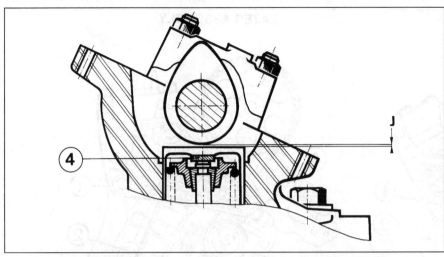

2.6 Valve clearance is measured at point J and altered by shim (4)

2 Valve clearances - checking and adjustment

Note: *The valve clearances must be checked and adjusted only when the engine is cold.*

1 The importance of having the valve clearances correctly adjusted cannot be overstressed, as they vitally affect the performance of the engine. If the clearances are too big, the engine will be noisy (characteristic rattling or tapping noises) and engine efficiency will be reduced, as the valves open too late and close too early. A more serious problem arises if the clearances are too small, however. If this is the case, the valves may not close fully when the engine is hot, resulting in serious damage to the engine (eg. burnt valve seats and/or cylinder head warping/cracking).

Checking

2 Remove the air cleaner and ducts as described in the relevant Part of Chapter 4.
3 Disconnect the brake servo vacuum hose.
4 Remove the camshaft cover, trying not to damage the gasket.
5 Have ready a pencil and paper to record the measured clearances.
6 Turn the crankshaft using a spanner on the crankshaft pulley bolt until the cam lobe nearest the flywheel end of the engine is pointing vertically upwards **(see illustration)**.

> **HAYNES HiNT** *Turning the engine will be easier if the spark plugs are removed first - see Chapter 1.*

7 Using feeler blades, measure the clearance between the base of the cam and the cam follower **(see illustration)**. Record the clearance.
8 Repeat the measurement for the other seven valves, turning the crankshaft as necessary so that the cam lobe in question is always vertically upwards.
9 Calculate the difference between each measured clearance and the desired value (see *Specifications*). Note that the value for inlet valves is different from that for exhaust. Counting from either end of the engine, the valve sequence is:
Exhaust - Inlet - Inlet - Exhaust - Exhaust - Inlet - Inlet - Exhaust.
10 If any clearance measured is outside the specified tolerance, adjustment must be carried out as described below. If all clearances are within tolerance, refit the camshaft cover, using a new gasket if necessary. Note the diagnostic socket and copper washer under the bolt at the timing belt end on certain engines.

Adjustment

11 To adjust the clearances remove the camshaft as described in Section 7.
12 Lift off a cam follower and its shim. Be careful that the shim does not fall out of the follower. Clean the shim and measure its thickness with a micrometer **(see illustrations)**.
13 Refer to the clearance recorded for the valve concerned. If the clearance was larger than specified, a thicker shim must be fitted; if the clearance was too small, a thinner shim must be fitted.

Sample calculation - clearance too large:

Desired clearance (A) 0.20 mm
Measured clearance (B) 0.28 mm
Difference (B - A) = + 0.08 mm
Original shim thickness 2.62 mm
Req'd shim thickness 2.62 + 0.08 = 2.70 mm

Sample calculation - clearance too small:

Desired clearance (A) 0.40 mm
Measured clearance (B) 0.23 mm
Difference (B-A) = -0.17 mm
Original shim thickness 2.86 mm
Req'd shim thickness 2.86 - 0.17 = 2.69 mm

14 Shims are available in thicknesses from 1.650 to 4.000 mm, in steps of 0.025 mm in the middle of the range and at the ends in steps of 0.075 mm. Clean new shims before measuring or fitting them.
15 Repeat the operations on the other cam followers and shims, keeping each follower identified so that it can be refitted in the same position.
16 When reassembling, oil the shim and fit it on the valve stem, then oil the cam follower and lower it smoothly into position. If the follower is raised at any stage the shim may be dislodged.
17 When all the followers are in position with their shims, refit the camshaft. Check the valve clearances before refitting the timing belt in case a mistake has been made and the camshaft has to be removed again. With the timing belt disconnected the camshaft will not be moved by rotation of the crankshaft. Before rotating the camshaft alone, position all the pistons halfway down the bores to avoid piston-to-valve contact.

2B

2.7 Using feeler blades to measure a valve clearance

2.12a Lift off the cam follower and shim . . .

2.12b . . . then measure the shim thickness with a micrometer

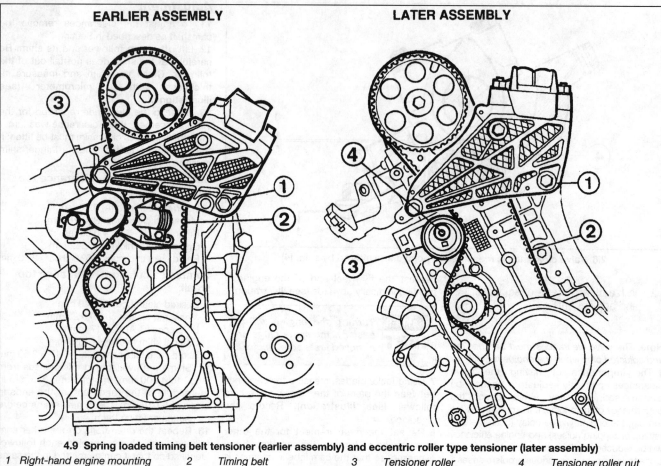

EARLIER ASSEMBLY   **LATER ASSEMBLY**

4.9 Spring loaded timing belt tensioner (earlier assembly) and eccentric roller type tensioner (later assembly)

1	*Right-hand engine mounting*	*2*	*Timing belt*	*3*	*Tensioner roller*	*4*	*Tensioner roller nut*

3 Compression test -
description and interpretation

Refer to Part A, Section 3 but on engines with a static distributorless ignition system, disable the ignition by depressing the retaining clip and disconnecting the wiring connector from the ignition module.

4 Timing belt - general
information, removal and refitting

General information

1 The timing belt drives the camshaft and coolant pump from a toothed sprocket on the front of the crankshaft. If the belt breaks or slips in service, the pistons are likely to hit the valve heads, resulting in extensive (and expensive) damage.
2 The timing belt should be renewed at the specified intervals (see Chapter 1), or earlier if it is contaminated with oil, or if it is at all noisy in operation (a "scraping" noise due to uneven wear).
3 If the timing belt is being removed, it is a wise precaution to check the condition of the coolant pump at the same time (check for signs of coolant leakage). This may avoid the need to remove the timing belt again at a later stage, should the coolant pump fail.

Removal

4 Disconnect the battery negative lead.
5 Remove the auxiliary drivebelt as described in Chapter 1.
6 Remove the inner shield from the right-hand wheel arch and wedge the radiator bottom hose under the sump.
7 Remove the shield from the camshaft sprocket.

4.10 Crankshaft and camshaft sprockets locked with timing dowels

8 Remove the plastic covers from the front of the timing belt. Note the location of the various bolts.
9 Observe the timing belt tensioner assembly and ascertain whether it is of the spring-loaded type or the later eccentric roller type **(see illustration)**. Proceed as follows under the appropriate sub-heading according to type fitted.

Models with spring-loaded tensioner

10 Turn the crankshaft using a spanner on the pulley bolt until the dowel hole in the pulley is at about 12 o'clock and the hole in the camshaft sprocket is at about 7 o'clock. In this position a 10 mm dowel should pass through each hole and into the timing recess behind. Verify this and then remove the dowels **(see illustration)**.
11 Remove the clutch bottom shield. Have an assistant jam the starter ring gear while the crankshaft pulley bolt is undone. This bolt is very tight. Do not jam the pulley by means of the timing dowel: damage will result. Remove the bolt and washer.
12 Check that the 10 mm dowels will still enter the timing holes: adjust the crankshaft position if necessary by means of the starter ring gear. Remove the crankshaft pulley, retrieving the Woodruff key if it is loose.

4.13a Slacken the two nuts at the front of the timing belt tensioner . . .

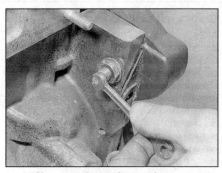

4.13b . . . and turn the tensioner cam spindle to the horizontal position

4.19 Timing line on belt aligned with mark on camshaft sprocket

13 Slacken the two nuts on the front of the timing belt tensioner and the single nut at the rear. Use a spanner on the square end of the tensioner cam spindle to turn the cam to the horizontal position and so compress the tensioner spring **(see illustrations)**. Tighten the cam locknut.

14 Remove the timing belt, taking care not to kink it or contaminate it with oil if it is to be re-used. Draw an arrow on the belt using chalk to mark the running direction unless a new belt is to be fitted.

15 Check the timing belt carefully for any signs of uneven wear, splitting, or oil contamination. Pay particular attention to the roots of the teeth. Renew it if there is the slightest doubt about its condition. If the engine is undergoing an overhaul, and has covered more than 36 000 miles (60 000 km) with the existing belt fitted, renew the belt as a matter of course, regardless of its apparent condition. The cost of a new belt is nothing compared with the cost of repairs, should the belt break in service. If signs of oil contamination are found, trace the source of the oil leak and rectify it. Wash down the engine timing belt area and all related components, to remove all traces of oil. If the timing belt is to be renewed, ensure that the correct belt type is obtained - the timing belt used with the earlier spring-loaded tensioner is not interchangeable with the later type.

Models with eccentric roller tensioner

Note: *Peugeot specify the use of special tool (SEEM C. TRONIC type 105 or 105.5 belt tension measuring equipment) to correctly set the belt tension. If this equipment cannot be obtained, an approximate setting can be achieved using the method described below. If the method described here is used, the tension must be checked using the special equipment at the earliest opportunity. Do not drive the vehicle over large distances, or use high engine speeds until the belt tension is known to be correct. Refer to a Peugeot dealer for advice.*

16 Proceed as described in paragraphs 10 to 12, noting that the crankshaft pulley timing dowel must be of 10 mm diameter, stepped down to 8 mm at one end to engage with the smaller hole in the timing recess.

17 Slacken the tensioner roller bolt to relieve the belt tension, then withdraw the belt, noting the direction of fitting and the markings. Take care not to kink it or contaminate it with oil if it is to be re-used. Draw an arrow on the belt using chalk to mark the running direction unless a new belt is to be fitted.

18 Examine the belt carefully with reference to paragraph 15.

Refitting

Models with spring-loaded tensioner

19 Commence refitting by positioning the belt on the crankshaft sprocket, then refitting the pulley and verifying the correct position of the crankshaft by means of the dowel. Observe the arrows on the belt showing the direction of rotation, and the timing lines which align with marks on the crankshaft and camshaft sprockets **(see illustration)**.

20 Fit the belt to the camshaft sprocket, round the tensioner and to the coolant pump sprocket.

21 Release the tensioner cam locknut and turn the cam downwards to release the spring. Tighten the locknut and the tensioner front nuts.

22 Remove the timing dowels and turn the crankshaft through two full turns in the normal direction of rotation. Turn the crankshaft further to bring No 1 piston to TDC on the firing stroke.

23 Slacken the tensioner front nuts and the cam locknut, then retighten them.

24 Turn the crankshaft further and make sure that the timing dowels can still be inserted. If not, remove the drivebelt and start again.

25 If a new belt has been fitted, it must be run in and retensioned, as follows.

26 Tighten the crankshaft pulley bolt to the specified torque, then refit and tension the auxiliary drivebelt (see Chapter 1). Temporarily refit the camshaft sprocket cover.

27 Run the engine up to operating temperature, indicated by the cooling fan operating, then stop it and allow it to cool for at least two hours.

28 Rotate the crankshaft to the TDC position, No 1 cylinder firing, then slacken and retighten the tensioner nuts once more.

29 Remove the auxiliary drivebelt and the crankshaft pulley. Refit and secure the plastic covers, then refit the pulley and tighten its bolts to the specified torque. Refit and tension the auxiliary drivebelt.

30 Check the ignition timing and adjust if necessary (Chapter 5B).

Models with eccentric roller tensioner

31 Commence refitting by slipping the belt over the camshaft sprocket, followed by the crankshaft sprocket, the coolant pump sprocket, and finally over the tensioner roller. Observe the arrows on the belt indicating the direction of rotation, and the timing lines which align with corresponding marks on the crankshaft and camshaft sprockets.

32 With the camshaft timing dowel fitted, rotate the tensioner roller anti-clockwise by hand as far as possible to take up any slack in the belt, then tighten the tensioner roller bolt sufficiently to hold the roller in position. If the special belt tension measuring equipment is available, it should be fitted to the tensioned run of the belt, and the tensioner roller should be moved to give a reading of 30 ± 2 units. Tighten the roller bolt to the specified torque, taking care not to move the roller as the bolt is tightened.

33 Check that the crankshaft and camshaft are still positioned correctly by temporarily refitting the crankshaft pulley and re-inserting the timing dowel.

34 Remove the timing dowels, temporarily refit the crankshaft pulley, and turn the crankshaft through two full turns in the normal direction of rotation. Check that both timing dowels can still be inserted. If not, remove the drivebelt and start again. Never turn the crankshaft backwards during this procedure.

35 If all is well, remove the dowels, and turn the crankshaft through two further turns in the normal direction of rotation.

36 Refit the camshaft timing dowel, and check that the belt can just be twisted through 90° (using moderate pressure from the forefinger and thumb) at the midpoint of the longest belt run between the camshaft and crankshaft sprockets. If in doubt about this setting, it is better to err on the tight side until the tension can be checked by a Peugeot dealer; if the belt is too slack, it may jump on the sprockets, which could cause serious engine damage. If the special belt tension measuring equipment

2B

is available, it should be refitted to the tensioned run of the belt. The reading should now be between 42 and 46 units.

37 If the tension is not as specified, repeat the tensioning operation.

38 Refit the belt covers and the crankshaft pulley. Apply thread locking compound to the crankshaft pulley bolt threads, and tighten the bolt to the specified torque.

39 On completion, refit all disturbed components, and tension the auxiliary drivebelt, as described in Chapter 1.

---

5 Timing belt tensioner and sprockets - removal, inspection and refitting

Removal

Camshaft sprocket

1 Remove the timing belt as described in Section 4.

2 Remove the locking pin from the camshaft sprocket, slacken the sprocket retaining bolt and remove it, along with its washer. To prevent the camshaft rotating as the bolt is slackened, restrain the sprocket with a suitable tool through the holes in the sprocket face **(see Tool Tip)**. *Do not* attempt to use the sprocket locking pin to prevent the sprocket from rotating whilst the bolt is slackened.

3 With the retaining bolt removed, slide the sprocket off the end of the camshaft. If the locating peg is a loose fit in the rear of the sprocket, remove it for safe-keeping. Examine the camshaft oil seal for signs of oil leakage and, if necessary, renew it as described in Section 6.

To make a camshaft sprocket holding tool, obtain two lengths of steel strip about 6 mm thick by 30 mm wide or similar, one 600 mm long, the other 200 mm long (all dimensions approximate). Bolt the two strips together to form a forked end, leaving the bolt slack so that the shorter strip can pivot freely. At the end of each 'prong' of the fork, secure a bolt with a nut and a locknut, to act as the fulcrums; these will engage with the cut-outs in the sprocket, and should protrude by about 30 mm

Crankshaft sprocket

4 Remove the timing belt as described in Section 4.

5 Slide the sprocket off the end of the crankshaft. Remove the Woodruff key from the crankshaft, and store it with the sprocket for safe-keeping. Where necessary, also slide the spacer (where fitted) off the end of the crankshaft.

6 Examine the crankshaft oil seal for signs of oil leakage and, if necessary, renew it as described in Section 12.

Tensioner assembly (models with spring-loaded tensioner)

7 Remove the timing belt as described in Section 4.

8 Undo the two bolts at the front and single nut at the rear and withdraw the spring housing spring and tensioner pulley. Take care to keep the spring under control as the bolts are undone to prevent it flying out.

Tensioner assembly (models with eccentric roller tensioner)

9 Remove the timing belt as described in Section 4.

10 Slacken and remove the timing belt tensioner pulley retaining bolt, and slide the pulley off its mounting stud. Examine the mounting stud for signs of damage and if necessary, renew it.

Inspection

11 Clean the camshaft/crankshaft sprockets thoroughly, and renew any that show signs of wear, damage or cracks.

12 Clean the tensioner assembly, but do not use any strong solvent which may enter the pulley bearing. Check that the pulley rotates freely on the backplate, with no sign of stiffness or free play **(see illustration)**. Renew the assembly if there is any doubt about its condition, or if there are any obvious signs of wear or damage.

Refitting

Camshaft sprocket

13 Refit the locating peg (where removed) to the rear of the sprocket. Locate the sprocket on the end of the camshaft, ensuring that the locating peg is correctly engaged with the cut-out in the camshaft end.

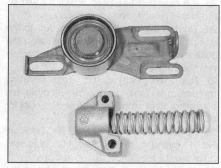

5.12 Spring loaded timing belt tensioner components

14 Refit the sprocket retaining bolt and washer, and tighten it to the specified torque. Retain the sprocket with the tool used on removal. Note that on early models the sprocket is secured with an M12 bolt whereas this has been reduced to M10 on later engines. Ensure that the correct torque wrench setting is used according to bolt type.

15 Realign the hole in the camshaft sprocket with the corresponding hole in the cylinder head, and refit the locking pin. Check that the crankshaft pulley locking pin is still in position.

16 Refit the timing belt (Section 4).

Crankshaft sprocket

17 Slide the spacer (where fitted) into position, taking great care not to damage the crankshaft oil seal, and refit the Woodruff key to its slot in the crankshaft end.

18 Slide on the crankshaft sprocket, aligning its slot with the Woodruff key.

19 Refit the timing belt (Section 4).

Tensioner assembly (models with spring-loaded tensioner)

20 Assemble the tensioner spring, spring housing and pulley then locate the assembly on the engine.

21 Fit the front bolts and rear locknut finger tight only. Use a spanner on the square end of the tensioner cam spindle to turn the cam to the horizontal position and so compress the tensioner spring. Tighten the cam locknut.

22 Refit the timing belt (Section 4).

Tensioner assembly (models with eccentric roller tensioner)

23 Refit the tensioner pulley to its mounting stud, and fit the retaining bolt.

24 Refit the timing belt (Section 4).

---

6 Camshaft oil seal - renewal

1 Remove the camshaft sprocket as described in Section 5. Remove the rear cover plate behind the sprocket.

2 Punch or drill two small holes opposite each other in the oil seal. Screw a self-tapping screw into each, and pull on the screws with pliers to extract the seal.

3 Clean the seal housing, and polish off any burrs or raised edges, which may have caused the seal to fail in the first place.

4 Lubricate the lips of the new seal with clean engine oil, and drive it into position until it seats on its locating shoulder. Use a suitable tubular drift, such as a socket, which bears only on the hard outer edge of the seal. Take care not to damage the seal lips during fitting. Note that the seal lips should face inwards.

5 Refit the sprocket rear cover plate, locate it correctly with a 10 mm dowel and tighten its fastenings.

6 Refit the camshaft sprocket as described in Section 5.

7.5a Removing the camshaft thrust plate bolt . . .

7.5b . . . followed by the thrust plate

7 Camshaft and followers - removal, inspection and refitting

Removal

1 Remove the camshaft sprocket as described in Section 5. Remove the rear cover plate behind the sprocket.

2 Remove the camshaft cover. For ease of access, remove the distributor cap and HT leads, air cleaner assembly and brake servo vacuum hose.

3 Remove the distributor as described in Chapter 5B.

4 Carefully ease the oil supply pipe out from the top of the camshaft bearing caps, and remove it. Note the O-ring seals fitted to each of the pipe unions on later models.

5 Where fitted undo the bolt and remove the camshaft thrust plate **(see illustrations)**.

6 The camshaft bearing caps should be numbered 1 to 5, number 1 being at the transmission end of the engine. If not, make identification marks on the caps, using white paint or a suitable marker pen. Also mark each cap in some way to indicate its correct fitted orientation. This will avoid the possibility of installing the caps the wrong way around on refitting.

7 Evenly and progressively slacken the camshaft bearing cap retaining nuts by one turn at a time. This will relieve the valve spring pressure on the bearing caps gradually and evenly. Once the pressure has been relieved,

the nuts can be fully unscrewed and removed **(see illustration)**.

8 Note the correct fitted orientation of the bearing caps, then remove them from the cylinder head **(see illustration)**.

9 Lift the camshaft away from the cylinder head, and slide the oil seal off the camshaft end **(see illustration)**.

10 Obtain eight small, clean plastic containers, and number them 1 to 8; alternatively, divide a larger container into eight compartments. Using a rubber sucker, withdraw each follower in turn, and place it in its respective container. Do not interchange the cam followers, or the rate of wear will be much-increased. If necessary, also remove the shim from the top of the valve stem, and store it with its respective follower. Note that the shim may stick to the inside of the follower as it is withdrawn. If this happens, take care not to allow it to drop out as the follower is removed.

Inspection

11 Examine the camshaft bearing surfaces and cam lobes for signs of wear ridges and scoring. Renew the camshaft if any of these conditions are apparent. Examine the condition of the bearing surfaces, both on the camshaft journals and in the cylinder head/bearing caps. If the head bearing surfaces are worn excessively, the cylinder head will need to be renewed.

12 Examine the cam follower bearing surfaces which contact the camshaft lobes for wear ridges and scoring. Renew any follower

on which these conditions are apparent. If a follower bearing surface is badly scored, also examine the corresponding lobe on the camshaft for wear, as it is likely that both will be worn. Renew worn components as necessary.

Refitting

13 Where removed, refit each shim to the top of its original valve stem. *Do not* interchange the shims, as this will upset the valve clearances (see Section 2).

14 Liberally oil the cylinder head cam follower bores and the followers. Carefully refit the followers to the cylinder head, ensuring that each follower is refitted to its original bore. Some care will be required to enter the followers squarely into their bores.

15 Liberally oil the camshaft bearings and lobes, then refit the camshaft to the cylinder head. Temporarily refit the sprocket to the end of the shaft, and position it so that the sprocket timing hole is aligned with the corresponding cut-out in the cylinder head. Also ensure that the crankshaft is still locked in the timing position (see Section 4).

16 Ensure that the bearing cap and head mating surfaces are completely clean, unmarked, and free from oil. Refit all the caps, using the identification marks noted on removal to ensure that each is installed correctly and in its original location.

17 Evenly and progressively tighten the camshaft bearing cap nuts by one turn at a time until the caps touch the cylinder head. Then go round again and tighten all the nuts to the specified torque setting. Work only as described, to impose the pressure of the valve springs gradually and evenly on the bearing caps.

18 Where applicable, refit the camshaft thrust plate and secure with its retaining bolt.

19 Examine the oil supply pipe union O-rings (where fitted) for signs of damage or deterioration, and renew as necessary. Apply a smear of clean engine oil to the O-rings. Ease the pipe into position in the top of the bearing caps, taking great care not to displace the O-rings.

20 Refit the distributor as described in Chapter 5B.

2B

7.7 Progressively unscrew the camshaft bearing cap nuts . . .

7.8 . . . and remove the caps

7.9 Lift the camshaft from the cylinder head

7.21 Align the camshaft sprocket cover plate using a dowel or twist drill

21 Fit a new camshaft oil seal, using the information given in Section 6, then refit the sprocket rear cover plate. Align the cover plate using a 10 mm dowel or drill bit then secure with the retaining bolt **(see illustration)**.

22 Refit the camshaft sprocket as described in Section 5.

23 Check the valve clearances as described in Section 2.

24 Refit the camshaft cover, HT leads and distributor cap, air cleaner, and brake servo vacuum hose.

25 Reconnect the battery negative terminal.

8 Cylinder head - removal and refitting

Removal

1 Drain the cooling system as described in Chapter 1.

2 Remove the timing belt as described in Section 4.

3 Slacken, but do not remove, the engine lower mounting rubber centre nut and bolt **(see illustration)**.

4 Remove the air cleaner assembly, inlet ducts and pipes with reference to the relevant Part of Chapter 4.

5 Remove the crankcase breather and its pipes.

6 Remove the nut which secures the engine right-hand mounting rubber to the cylinder head bracket **(see illustration)**.

7 Carefully raise the engine 60 to 80 mm using a hoist or a well-protected jack. Remove the two bolts which secure the right-hand mounting bracket to the cylinder head, then lower the engine back into position.

8 Remove the inlet manifold and associated fuel system components with reference to the relevant Part of Chapter 4.

9 Make suitable notes as an aid to refitting then disconnect all coolant and vacuum hoses and electrical leads from the cylinder head.

10 Disconnect the exhaust downpipe(s) at the manifold flange.

11 Remove the coolant pipe from the pump inlet housing. Also remove the diagnostic socket from its bracket.

12 Remove the camshaft cover, at the same time removing the distributor cap and HT leads. If the cylinder head is to be dismantled for overhaul, remove the distributor or, on models with static distributorless ignition systems, the ignition module, as described in Chapter 5B.

13 Working in the *reverse* of the sequence shown in illustration 8.27, progressively slacken the cylinder head bolts by half a turn at a time, until all bolts can be unscrewed by hand. Remove the bolts along with their washers, noting the correct location of the spacer fitted to the front right-hand bolt.

14 With all the cylinder head bolts removed, the joint between the cylinder head and gasket and the cylinder block/crankcase must now be broken without disturbing the wet liners. Although these liners are better-located and sealed than some wet-liner engines, there is still a risk of coolant and foreign matter leaking into the sump if the cylinder head is lifted carelessly. If care is not taken and the liners are moved, there is also a possibility of the bottom seals being disturbed, causing leakage after refitting the head.

15 To break the joint, obtain two L-shaped metal bars which fit into the cylinder head bolt holes, and gently "rock" the cylinder head free towards the front of the car. *Do not* try to swivel the head on the cylinder block/crankcase; it is located by dowels, as well as by the tops of the liners.

16 When the joint is broken, lift the cylinder head away. Remove the gasket from the top of the block, noting the two locating dowels. If the locating dowels are a loose fit, remove them and store them with the head for safe-keeping.

17 *Do not* attempt to turn the crankshaft with the cylinder head removed, otherwise the wet liners may be displaced. Operations that require the crankshaft to be turned (eg cleaning the piston crowns), should only be carried out once the cylinder liners are firmly clamped in position. In the absence of the special Peugeot liner clamps, the liners can be clamped in position as follows. Use large flat washers positioned underneath suitable-length bolts, or temporarily refit the original head bolts, with suitable spacers fitted to their shanks **(see illustration)**.

18 If the cylinder head is to be dismantled for overhaul, remove the camshaft and cam followers as described in Section 7, then refer to Part D of this Chapter.

Preparation for refitting

19 The mating faces of the cylinder head and cylinder block/crankcase must be perfectly clean before refitting the head. Use a hard plastic or wood scraper to remove all traces of gasket and carbon; also clean the piston crowns. Refer to paragraph 17 before turning the crankshaft. Take particular care during the cleaning operations, as aluminium alloy is easily damaged. Also, make sure that the carbon is not allowed to enter the oil and water passages - this is particularly important for the lubrication system, as carbon could block the oil supply to the engine's components. Using adhesive tape and paper, seal the water, oil and bolt holes in the cylinder block/crankcase. To prevent carbon entering the gap between the pistons and bores, smear a little grease in the gap. After cleaning each piston, use a small brush to remove all traces of grease and carbon from the gap, then wipe away the remainder with a clean rag. Clean all the pistons in the same way.

20 Check the mating surfaces of the cylinder block/crankcase and the cylinder head for nicks, deep scratches and other damage. If slight, they may be removed carefully with a file, but if excessive, machining may be the only alternative to renewal.

8.3 Engine lower mounting

8.6 Right-hand engine mounting and cylinder head bracket

8.17 Cylinder liners clamped with washers and bolts

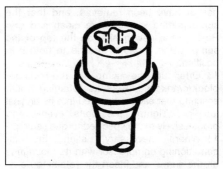

8.23 Torx type cylinder head bolts fitted to later models

8.24 Using a nail to hold the cylinder block dowel in the raised position

21 If warpage of the cylinder head gasket surface is suspected, use a straight-edge to check it for distortion. Refer to Part D of this Chapter if necessary.

22 Check the condition of the cylinder head bolts, and particularly their threads, whenever they are removed. Wash the bolts in suitable solvent, and wipe them dry. Check each for any sign of visible wear or damage, renewing any bolt if necessary. Measure the length of each bolt, to check for stretching (although this is not a conclusive test, in the event that all ten bolts have stretched by the same amount). Although Peugeot do not actually specify that the bolts must be renewed, it is strongly recommended that the bolts should be renewed as a complete set whenever they are disturbed.

23 Note that as from early 1987, the cylinder head bolts are of No 55 Torx type and 8 mm thick washers are fitted to these bolts, whereas 3 mm thick washers fitted to the earlier type hexagon head bolts **(see illustration)**. The spacer fitted to the bolt at the timing belt end is 25 mm thick, (previously 23 mm), and is identified by a groove around its perimeter. A modified cylinder head gasket is also fitted to engines with Torx type cylinder head bolts, so it is important to quote the engine number accurately when obtaining a new one.

Refitting

24 Commence refitting by fitting the dowels to the cylinder block. Keep the flywheel-end dowel raised by inserting a 5 mm punch or large nail through the hole in the front of the block **(see illustration)**. Remove the liner clamps.

25 Fit the new gasket, dry, with the tab at the flywheel end. Lower the cylinder head into position, making sure that it mates with the dowels. Remove the punch or nail.

26 Fit the cylinder head bolts, their threads clean and lightly oiled. Remember to fit the spacer to the bolt at the timing belt end. When fitting the Torx type cylinder head bolts, apply a little molybdenum disulphide grease to their heads, and to the contact surface of their heads.

27 Progressively tighten the bolts in the order shown to the Stage 1 specified torque setting **(see illustration)**. Note that the torque settings are different for the two cylinder head bolt types; ensure that the correct setting is being used according to bolt type.

28 Raise the engine slightly and refit the two bolts which secure the right-hand mounting bracket to the cylinder head. Tighten these bolts and slacken the one which holds the same bracket to the engine block. Lower the engine and tighten the right-hand mounting nut and the lower mounting rubber nut and bolt.

Engines with hexagon head type cylinder head bolts

29 Slacken cylinder head bolt No 1, then immediately retighten it to the Stage 2 specified torque. Tighten further by the angle specified for Stage 3 using a socket and extension bar. It is recommended that an angle-measuring gauge is used during this stage of tightening, to ensure accuracy **(see illustration)**. Repeat for all the bolts, following the tightening sequence.

30 Check the valve clearances and adjust, if necessary (see Section 2).

31 Refit the remaining components in the reverse order of removal. Make sure that the correct inlet manifold gasket is fitted. A gasket for carburettor versions is included in the gasket overhaul set which is not the same as the one for fuel injection models.

32 Refill and bleed the cooling system (Chapter 1).

33 Start the engine and warm it up until the cooling fan cuts in, then switch off and allow it to cool for at least two hours.

34 Retighten the cylinder head bolts, as described in paragraph 29, then recheck the valve clearances.

35 If a new timing belt has been fitted, refer to Section 4 and retension it if necessary.

36 Tighten the engine mounting bracket bolt.

Engines with Torx type cylinder head bolts

37 Fully slacken all the head bolts, working in the reverse of the tightening sequence. Once the bolts are loose, tighten all bolts to their Stage 2 specified torque setting, again following the specified sequence.

38 With all the bolts tightened to their Stage 2 setting, working again in the specified sequence, angle-tighten the bolts through the specified Stage 3 angle, using a socket and extension bar. It is recommended that an angle-measuring gauge is used during this stage of tightening, to ensure accuracy. Note that no further tightening of the Torx type head bolts is necessary.

2B

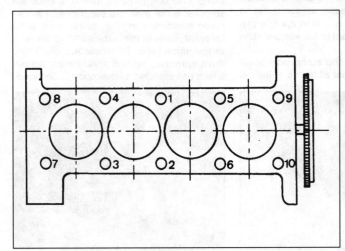

8.27 Cylinder head bolt tightening sequence

8.29 Home-made torque angle measuring gauge. Disc is fixed and pointer rotates

39 Check the valve clearances and adjust, if necessary (see Section 2).

40 Refit the remaining components in the reverse order of removal and with reference to the relevant Sections and Chapters of this manual as applicable. Make sure that the correct inlet manifold gasket is fitted. A gasket for carburettor versions is included in the gasket overhaul set which is not the same as the one for fuel injection models.

41 Refill and bleed the cooling system (Chapter 1).

42 If a new timing belt has been fitted, refer to Section 4 and retension it if necessary.

43 Tighten the engine mounting bracket bolt.

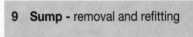

9 Sump - removal and refitting

Removal

1 Disconnect the battery negative lead.

2 Drain the engine oil, then clean and refit the engine oil drain plug, tightening it securely. If the engine is nearing its service interval when the oil and filter are due for renewal, it is recommended that the filter is also removed, and a new one then fitted. After reassembly, the engine can then be refilled with fresh oil. Refer to Chapter 1 for further information.

3 Chock the rear wheels then jack up the front of the car and support it on axle stands (see *"Jacking and vehicle support"*).

4 On models with air conditioning, where the compressor is mounted onto the side of the sump, remove the drivebelt as described in Chapter 1. Unbolt the compressor, and position it clear of the sump. Support the weight of the compressor by tying it to the vehicle, to prevent any excess strain being placed on the compressor lines. *Do not disconnect the refrigerant lines from the compressor (refer to the warnings given in Chapter 3).*

5 Disconnect the wiring to the oil level sensor and the hose to the crankcase ventilation system suction drain pipe on models so equipped.

6 Progressively slacken and remove all the sump retaining bolts. Since the sump bolts vary in length and type, remove each bolt in turn, and store it in its correct fitted order by pushing it through a clearly-marked cardboard template. This will avoid the possibility of installing the bolts in the wrong locations on refitting.

7 Break the joint by striking the sump with the palm of your hand. Lower the sump, and withdraw it from underneath the vehicle. Remove the gasket (where fitted), and discard it; a new one must be used on refitting. While the sump is removed, take the opportunity to check the oil pump pick-up/strainer for signs of clogging or splitting. If necessary, remove the pump as described in Section 10, and clean or renew the strainer.

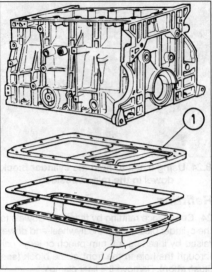

9.8 Sump spacer plate (1) fitted to certain models

8 On some models, a large spacer plate is fitted between the sump and the base of the cylinder block/crankcase (see illustration). If this plate is fitted, undo the two retaining screws from diagonally-opposite corners of the plate. Remove the plate from the base of the engine, noting which way round it is fitted.

Refitting

9 Clean all traces of sealant/gasket from the mating surfaces of the cylinder block/crankcase and sump, then use a clean rag to wipe out the sump and the engine's interior.

10 Where a spacer plate is fitted, remove all traces of sealant/gasket from the spacer plate, then apply a thin coating of silicone sealant to the plate upper mating surface. Offer up the plate to the base of the cylinder block/crankcase, and securely tighten its retaining screws (see illustration).

11 On models where the sump was fitted without a gasket, ensure that the sump mating surfaces are clean and dry, then apply a thin coating of suitable sealant to the sump mating surface.

12 On models where the sump was fitted with a gasket, ensure that all traces of the old

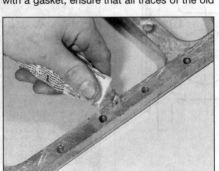

9.10 Applying sealant to the sump spacer plate upper surface

gasket have been removed, and that the sump mating surfaces are clean and dry. Position the new gasket on the top of the sump, using a dab of grease to hold it in position.

13 Offer up the sump to the cylinder block/crankcase. Refit its retaining bolts, ensuring that each is screwed into its original location. Tighten the bolts evenly and progressively to the specified torque setting.

14 Where necessary, align the air conditioning compressor with its mountings on the sump, and insert the retaining bolts. Securely tighten the compressor retaining bolts, then refit the drivebelt as described in Chapter 1.

15 Reconnect the wiring connector to the oil level sensor (where fitted).

16 Lower the vehicle to the ground, then refill the engine with oil as described in Chapter 1.

10 Oil pump - removal, inspection and refitting

Removal

1 Remove the sump as described in Section 9.

2 Where necessary, undo the two retaining screws, and slide the sprocket cover off the front of the oil pump.

3 Slacken and remove the three bolts securing the oil pump to the base of the cylinder block/crankcase. Disengage the pump sprocket from the chain, and remove the oil pump (see illustration). Where necessary, also remove the spacer plate which is fitted behind the oil pump on some engines.

Inspection

4 Examine the oil pump sprocket for signs of damage and wear, such as chipped or missing teeth. If the sprocket is worn, the pump assembly must be renewed, since the sprocket is not available separately. It is also recommended that the chain and drive sprocket, fitted to the crankshaft, be renewed at the same time. To renew the chain and drive sprocket, first remove the crankshaft timing belt sprocket as described in Section 5.

10.3 Removing the oil pump

10.5a Lift off the pump strainer cover . . .

10.5b . . . and take out the relief valve piston and spring

Unbolt the oil seal carrier from the cylinder block. The sprocket, spacer (where fitted) and chain can then be slid off the end of the crankshaft.

5 Slacken and remove the bolts (along with the baffle plate, where fitted) securing the strainer cover to the pump body. Lift off the strainer cover, and take out the relief valve piston and spring, noting which way round they are fitted **(see illustrations)**.

6 Examine the pump rotors and body for signs of wear ridges or scoring. If worn, the complete pump assembly must be renewed.

7 Examine the relief valve piston for signs of wear or damage, and renew if necessary. The condition of the relief valve spring can only be

measured by comparing it with a new one; if there is any doubt about its condition, it should also be renewed. Both the piston and spring are available individually.

8 Thoroughly clean the oil pump strainer with a suitable solvent, and check it for signs of clogging or splitting. If the strainer is damaged, the strainer and cover assembly must be renewed.

9 Locate the relief valve spring and piston in the strainer cover. Refit the cover to the pump body, aligning the relief valve piston with its bore in the pump. Refit the baffle plate (where fitted) and the cover retaining bolts, and tighten them securely.

Refitting

10 Offer up the spacer plate (where fitted), then locate the pump sprocket with its drive chain. Seat the pump on the base of the cylinder block/crankcase. Refit the pump retaining bolts, and tighten them to the specified torque setting.

11 Where necessary, slide the sprocket cover into position on the pump. Refit its retaining bolts, tightening them securely.

12 Refit the sump as described in Section 9.

11 Oil cooler - removal and refitting

Cylinder block-mounted oil cooler

Removal

1 Certain models may be fitted with an oil cooler mounted between the cylinder block and the oil filter.

2 To prevent the oil cooler from being unscrewed as the oil filter is removed, on later models, a retaining lug is provided on the cylinder block, which engages with a fork on the oil cooler.

3 To remove the oil cooler, first remove the oil filter and partially drain the cooling system as described in Chapter 1.

4 Disconnect the coolant hoses from the filter. Be prepared for coolant spillage, and plug the open ends of the hoses to prevent dirt ingress and further coolant loss.

5 Unscrew the oil filter mounting stub, then withdraw the oil cooler from the engine **(see illustration)**.

Refitting

6 Refitting is a reversal of removal, bearing in mind the following points.
  a) When refitting the oil cooler, where applicable, ensure that the fork on the cooler engages with the lug on the cylinder block.
  b) Before refitting the oil filter mounting stub, thoroughly clean the threads, and coat them with thread-locking compound.
  c) Tighten the mounting stub to the specified torque.
  d) Fit a new oil filter and fill the engine with oil as described in Chapter 1.
  e) On completion, refill the coolant level as described in or Chapter 1.

Remotely mounted oil cooler

Removal

7 On models with a remotely mounted oil cooler, this is located in front of the radiator.

8 Remove the radiator grille and front bumper as described in Chapter 11.

9 Unbolt the engine compartment front crossmember, and position it to one side, leaving the bonnet release cable still attached.

10 Remove the air inlet hose.

11 Remove the stone guard from the front cowling.

12 Unscrew the retaining bolts, then release the clips and move the front cowling forwards for access to the oil cooler.

13 Place rags or a container beneath the oil cooler to collect any spilled oil. Unscrew the union nuts while holding the connection stubs stationary. Plug the stubs, or tie them to one side.

14 Unscrew the nuts, release the oil cooler from the front cowling, and remove it from the car **(see illustration)**.

2B

11.5 Cylinder block mounted oil cooler mounting stub (A) and locating notch (B)

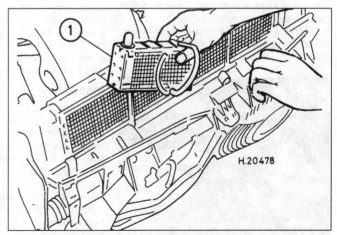

H.20478

11.14 Removing the remotely mounted oil cooler (1)

Refitting

15 Refitting is a reversal of removal, but tighten the union nuts carefully to the specified torque while holding the connection stubs stationary. Check and if necessary top-up the engine oil as described in *"Weekly checks"*.

12 Crankshaft oil seals - renewal

Right-hand oil seal

1 Remove the crankshaft sprocket and, where fitted, the spacer as described in Section 5.

2 Punch or drill two small holes opposite each other in the seal. Screw a self-tapping screw into each, and pull on the screws with pliers to extract the seal. Alternatively, the seal can be levered out of position. Use a flat-bladed screwdriver, and take great care not to damage the crankshaft shoulder or seal housing.

3 Clean the seal housing, and polish off any burrs or raised edges, which may have caused the seal to fail in the first place.

4 Lubricate the lips of the new seal with clean engine oil, and carefully locate the seal on the end of crankshaft. Note that its sealing lip must be facing inwards. Take care not to damage the seal lips during fitting.

5 Fit the new seal using a suitable tubular drift, such as a socket, which bears only on the hard outer edge of the seal. Tap the seal into position, to the same depth in the housing as the original was prior to removal.

6 Wash off any traces of oil, then refit the crankshaft sprocket as described in Section 5.

Left-hand oil seal

7 Remove the flywheel/driveplate as described in Section 13. Make a note of the correct fitted depth of the seal in its housing.

8 Punch or drill two small holes opposite each other in the seal. Screw a self-tapping screw into each, and pull on the screws with pliers to extract the seal.

9 Clean the seal housing, and polish off any burrs or raised edges, which may have caused the seal to fail in the first place.

13.10 Apply thread locking compound to the flywheel bolts if not already pre-coated

10 Lubricate the lips of the new seal with clean engine oil, and carefully locate the seal on the end of the crankshaft.

11 Fit the new seal using a suitable tubular drift, which bears only on the hard outer edge of the seal. Drive the seal into position, to the same depth in the housing as the original was prior to removal.

12 Wash off any traces of oil, then refit the flywheel/driveplate as described in Section 13.

13 Flywheel/driveplate - removal, inspection and refitting

Removal

Flywheel (models with manual transmission)

1 Remove the transmission as described in Chapter 7A, then remove the clutch assembly as described in Chapter 6.

2 Prevent the flywheel from turning by locking the ring gear teeth with a screwdriver or similar tool.

3 Slacken and remove the flywheel retaining bolts, and remove the flywheel from the end of the crankshaft. Be careful not to drop it; it is heavy. If the flywheel locating dowel is a loose fit in the crankshaft end, remove it and store it with the flywheel for safe-keeping. Discard the flywheel bolts; new ones must be used on refitting.

Driveplate (models with automatic transmission)

4 Remove the transmission as described in Chapter 7B. Lock the driveplate as described in paragraph 2. Mark the relationship between the torque converter plate and the driveplate, and slacken all the driveplate retaining bolts.

5 Remove the retaining bolts, along with the torque converter plate and the two shims (where fitted). Note that the shims are of different thickness, the thicker one being on the outside of the torque converter plate. Discard the driveplate retaining bolts; new ones must be used on refitting.

6 Remove the driveplate from the end of the crankshaft. If the locating dowel is a loose fit in the crankshaft end, remove it and store it with the driveplate for safe-keeping.

Inspection

7 On models with manual transmission, examine the flywheel for scoring of the clutch face, and for wear or chipping of the ring gear teeth. If the clutch face is scored, the flywheel may be surface-ground, but renewal is preferable. Seek the advice of a Peugeot dealer or engine reconditioning specialist to see if machining is possible. If the ring gear is worn or damaged, the flywheel must be renewed, as it is not possible to renew the ring gear separately.

8 On models with automatic transmission, check the torque converter driveplate

carefully for signs of distortion. Look for any hairline cracks around the bolt holes or radiating outwards from the centre, and inspect the ring gear teeth for signs of wear or chipping. If any sign of wear or damage is found, the driveplate must be renewed.

Refitting

Flywheel - models with manual transmission

9 Clean the mating surfaces of the flywheel and crankshaft. Remove any remaining locking compound from the threads of the crankshaft holes, using the correct-size tap, if available.

10 If the new flywheel retaining bolts are not supplied with their threads already pre-coated, apply a suitable thread-locking compound to the threads of each bolt **(see illustration)**.

11 Ensure that the locating dowel is in position. Offer up the flywheel, locating it on the dowel, and fit the new retaining bolts.

12 Lock the flywheel using the method employed on dismantling, and tighten the retaining bolts to the specified torque.

13 Refit the clutch as described in Chapter 6, and refit the transmission as described in Chapter 7A.

Driveplate - models with automatic transmission

14 Carry out the operations described above in paragraphs 9 and 10, substituting "driveplate" for all references to the flywheel.

15 Locate the driveplate on its locating dowel.

16 Offer up the torque converter plate, with the thinner shim positioned behind the plate and the thicker shim on the outside, and align the marks made prior to removal.

17 Fit the new retaining bolts, then lock the driveplate using the method employed on dismantling. Tighten the retaining bolts to the specified torque wrench setting.

18 Refit the transmission as described in Chapter 7B.

14 Engine/transmission mountings - inspection and renewal

Refer to Part A, Section 10 but note that on early models, shims are fitted between the right-hand mounting rubber buffers and the mounting top plate. These should be added or removed as necessary to provide a clearance of 1.0 mm between the buffers and top plate. On later models, the shims have been deleted and the rubber buffers are increased in thickness to compensate. To prevent scuffing noises from the buffers, it is recommended that the inner surfaces which contact the engine bracket are lubricated with rubber grease.

Chapter 2 Part C:
TU series engine in-car repair procedures

Contents

Degrees of difficulty

Easy, suitable for novice with little experience	**Fairly easy,** suitable for beginner with some experience	**Fairly difficult,** suitable for competent DIY mechanic 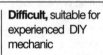	**Difficult,** suitable for experienced DIY mechanic	**Very difficult,** suitable for expert DIY or professional

Specifications

Engine general

Code and displacement:

TU9	954 cc
TU1	1124 cc
TU1M/L	1124 cc
TU1M/Z	1124 cc
TU3	1360 cc
TU3A	1360 cc
TU3A/K	1360 cc
TU3M/Z	1360 cc
TU3FM/L	1360 cc
TU3S	1360 cc
TU3S/K	1360 cc

Bore:

TU9 series	70.0 mm
TU1 series	72.0 mm
TU3 series	75.0 mm

Stroke:

TU9 series	62.0 mm
TU1 series	69.0 mm
TU3 series	77.0 mm

Compression ratio:

TU9 and TU1 series	9.4 : 1
TU3 series	9.3 : 1
Direction of crankshaft rotation	Clockwise (viewed from right-hand side of vehicle)
Firing order	1-3-4-2 (No 1 cylinder at flywheel end of engine)

Valve clearances (engine cold)

Inlet	0.15 to 0.25 mm
Exhaust	0.35 to 0.45 mm

Lubrication system

Oil pump type	Gear-type, chain-driven off the crankshaft
Minimum oil pressure at 90°C	4 bars at 4000 rpm
Oil pressure warning switch operating pressure	0.8 bars

Torque wrench settings

	Nm	lbf ft
Camshaft sprocket retaining bolt	80	59
Camshaft thrust fork retaining bolt	16	12
Crankshaft pulley retaining bolts	8	6
Crankshaft sprocket retaining bolt	110	81
Cylinder head bolts (aluminium block engine):		
Stage 1	20	15
Stage 2	Tighten through a further 240°	
Cylinder head bolts (cast-iron block engine):		
Stage 1	20	15
Stage 2	Tighten through a further 120°	
Stage 3	Tighten through a further 120°	
Cylinder head cover nuts	16	12
Flywheel retaining nuts and bolts	65	48
Engine-to-transmission bolts	35	26
Engine/transmission left-hand mounting:		
Mounting bracket-to-transmission nuts	20	15
Mounting bracket-to-body bolts	25	18
Mounting rubber nuts	20	15
Centre nut	65	48
Engine/transmission rear mounting:		
Mounting-to-cylinder block bolts	40	30
Mounting link-to-mounting bolt	70	52
Mounting link-to-body bolt	50	37
Engine/transmission right-hand mounting bracket nuts	45	33
Oil pump retaining bolts	8	6
Sump retaining nuts and bolts	8	6
Timing belt cover bolts	8	6
Timing belt tensioner pulley nut	23	17

---

1 General information

How to use this Chapter

This Part of Chapter 2 describes those repair procedures that can reasonably be carried out on the TU series engine while it remains in the car. If the engine has been removed from the car and is being dismantled as described in Part D, any preliminary dismantling procedures can be ignored. Refer to Part A and B for information on the XV, XW and XY series and XU series engines.

Part D describes the removal of the engine/transmission from the vehicle, and the full overhaul procedures that can then be carried out.

Engine description

The engine is of the in-line four-cylinder, overhead camshaft type, mounted transversely at the front of the car and inclined forward by 6°. The clutch and transmission are attached to its left-hand end. The 205 range is fitted with 954 cc (TU9), 1124 cc (TU1), and 1360 cc (TU3) versions of the engine in either carburettor or fuel-injected configuration.

The crankshaft runs in five main bearings. Thrustwashers are fitted to No 2 main bearing (upper half) to control crankshaft endfloat.

The connecting rods rotate on horizontally-split bearing shells at their big-ends. The pistons are attached to the connecting rods by gudgeon pins, which are an interference fit in the connecting rod small-end eyes. The aluminium-alloy pistons are fitted with three piston rings - two compression rings and an oil control ring.

On all except TU3FM engines, the cylinder block is made of aluminium, and replaceable wet liners are fitted to the cylinder bores. Sealing O-rings are fitted at the base of each liner, to prevent the escape of coolant into the sump.

On TU3FM engines, the cylinder block is made from cast-iron, and the cylinder bores are an integral part of the cylinder block. On this type of engine, the cylinder bores are sometimes referred to as having dry liners.

The inlet and exhaust valves are each closed by coil springs, and operate in guides pressed into the cylinder head; the valve seat inserts are also pressed into the cylinder head, and can be renewed separately if worn.

The camshaft is driven by a toothed timing belt, and operates the eight valves via rocker arms. Valve clearances are adjusted by a screw-and-locknut arrangement. The camshaft rotates directly in the cylinder head. The timing belt also drives the coolant pump.

Lubrication is by means of an oil pump, which is driven (via a chain and sprocket) off the right-hand end of the crankshaft. It draws oil through a strainer located in the sump, and then forces it through an externally-mounted filter into galleries in the cylinder block/crankcase. From there, the oil is distributed to the crankshaft (main bearings) and camshaft. The big-end bearings are supplied with oil via internal drillings in the crankshaft, while the camshaft bearings also receive a pressurised supply. The camshaft lobes and valves are lubricated by splash, as are all other engine components.

Repair operations possible with the engine in the car

The following work can be carried out with the engine in the car:

a) Compression pressure - testing.
b) Cylinder head cover - removal and refitting.
c) Valve clearances - adjustment.
d) Timing belt covers - removal and refitting.
e) Timing belt - removal, refitting and adjustment.
f) Timing belt tensioner and sprockets - removal, inspection and refitting.
g) Camshaft oil seal - renewal.
h) Camshaft and rocker arms - removal, inspection and refitting.
i) Cylinder head - removal and refitting.
j) Cylinder head and pistons - decarbonising.
k) Sump - removal and refitting.
l) Oil pump - removal, inspection and refitting.
m) Crankshaft oil seals - renewal.
n) Flywheel - removal, inspection and refitting.
o) Engine/transmission mountings - inspection and renewal.

3.4 Insert a 6 mm bolt (arrowed) through hole in cylinder block flange and into timing hole in flywheel . . .

3.5 . . . then insert a 10 mm bolt through the camshaft sprocket timing hole, and locate it in the cylinder head

2 Compression test -
description and interpretation

Refer to Part A, Section 3 but on engines with a static distributorless ignition system, disable the ignition by depressing the retaining clip and disconnecting the wiring connector from the ignition module.

3 Engine assembly/valve
timing holes - general information and usage

Note: *Do not attempt to rotate the engine whilst the crankshaft/camshaft are locked in position. If the engine is to be left in this state for a long period of time, it is a good idea to place warning notices inside the vehicle, and in the engine compartment. This will reduce the possibility of the engine being accidentally cranked on the starter motor, which is likely to cause damage with the locking pins in place.*

1 On all models, timing holes are drilled in the camshaft sprocket and in the rear of the flywheel. The holes are used to ensure that the crankshaft and camshaft are correctly positioned when assembling the engine (to

prevent the valves contacting the pistons when refitting the cylinder head), or refitting the timing belt. When the timing holes are aligned with access holes in the cylinder head and the front of the cylinder block, suitable diameter pins can be inserted to lock both the camshaft and crankshaft in position, preventing them from rotating. Proceed as follows.

2 Remove the timing belt upper cover as described in Section 6.

3 The crankshaft must now be turned until the timing hole in the camshaft sprocket is aligned with the corresponding hole in the cylinder head. The holes are aligned when the camshaft sprocket hole is in the 2 o'clock position, when viewed from the right-hand end of the engine. The crankshaft can be turned by using a spanner on the crankshaft sprocket bolt, noting that it should always be rotated in a clockwise direction (viewed from the right-hand end of the engine).

4 With the camshaft sprocket hole correctly positioned, insert a 6 mm diameter bolt or drill through the hole in the front, left-hand flange of the cylinder block, and locate it in the timing hole in the rear of the flywheel **(see illustration)**. Note that it may be necessary to rotate the crankshaft slightly, to get the holes to align.

5 With the flywheel correctly positioned, insert a 10 mm diameter bolt or a drill through

the timing hole in the camshaft sprocket, and locate it in the hole in the cylinder head **(see illustration)**.

6 The crankshaft and camshaft are now locked in position, preventing unnecessary rotation.

4 Cylinder head cover -
removal and refitting

Removal

1 Disconnect the battery negative lead.

2 Where necessary, undo the bolts securing the HT lead retaining clips to the rear of the cylinder head cover, and position the clips clear of the cover.

3 Slacken the retaining clip, and disconnect the breather hose from the left-hand end of the cylinder head cover **(see illustration)**. Where the original crimped-type Peugeot hose clip is still fitted, cut it off and discard it. Use a standard worm-drive clip on refitting.

4 Undo the two retaining nuts, and remove the washer from each of the cylinder head cover studs **(see illustration)**.

5 Lift off the cylinder head cover, and remove it along with its rubber seal **(see illustration)**.

2C

4.3 Disconnect the breather hose from the cylinder head cover . . .

4.4 . . . then slacken and remove the cover retaining nuts and washers (arrowed) . . .

4.5 . . . and lift off the cylinder head cover

4.6a Lift off the spacers (second one arrowed) . . .

4.6b . . . and remove the oil baffle plate

4.8 Ensure the rubber seal is correctly located on the cover when refitting

---

Examine the seal for signs of damage and deterioration, and if necessary, renew it.

6 Remove the spacer from each stud, and lift off the oil baffle plate (see illustrations).

Refitting

7 Carefully clean the cylinder head and cover mating surfaces, and remove all traces of oil.

8 Fit the rubber seal over the edge of the cylinder head cover, ensuring that it is correctly located along its entire length (see illustration).

9 Refit the oil baffle plate to the engine, and locate the spacers in their recesses in the baffle plate.

10 Carefully refit the cylinder head cover to the engine, taking great care not to displace the rubber seal.

11 Check that the seal is correctly located, then refit the washers and cover retaining nuts, and tighten them to the specified torque.

12 Where necessary, refit the HT lead clips to the rear of the head cover, and securely tighten their retaining bolts.

13 Reconnect the breather hose to the cylinder head cover, securely tightening its retaining clip, and reconnect the battery negative lead.

---

5 Valve clearances - checking and adjustment

Note: *The valve clearances must be checked and adjusted only when the engine is cold.*

1 The importance of having the valve clearances correctly adjusted cannot be overstressed, as they vitally affect the performance of the engine. If the clearances are too big, the engine will be noisy (characteristic rattling or tapping noises) and engine efficiency will be reduced, as the valves open too late and close too early. A more serious problem arises if the clearances are too small, however. If this is the case, the valves may not close fully when the engine is hot, resulting in serious damage to the engine (eg. burnt valve seats and/or cylinder head warping/cracking). The clearances are checked and adjusted as follows.

2 Remove the cylinder head cover as described in Section 4.

3 The engine can now be turned using a suitable socket and extension bar fitted to the crankshaft sprocket/pulley bolt.

> **HAYNES HINT** *Turning the engine will be easier if the spark plugs are removed first - see Chapter 1.*

4 It is important that the clearance of each valve is checked and adjusted only when the valve is fully closed, with the rocker arm resting on the heel of the cam (directly opposite the peak). This can be ensured by carrying out the adjustments in the following sequence, noting that No 1 cylinder is at the transmission end of the engine. The correct valve clearances are given in the *Specifications* at the start of this Chapter. The valve locations can be determined from the position of the manifolds.

Valve fully open	Adjust valves
No 1 exhaust	*No 3 inlet, No 4 exhaust*
No 3 exhaust	*No 4 inlet, No 2 exhaust*
No 4 exhaust	*No 2 inlet, No 1 exhaust*
No 2 exhaust	*No 1 inlet, No 3 exhaust*

5 With the relevant valve fully open, check the clearances of the two valves specified. The clearances are checked by inserting a feeler blade of the correct thickness between the valve stem and the rocker arm adjusting screw (see illustration). The feeler blade should be a light, sliding fit. If adjustment is necessary, slacken the adjusting screw locknut, and turn the screw as necessary. Once the correct clearance is obtained, hold the adjusting screw and securely tighten the locknut. Recheck the valve clearance, and adjust again if necessary.

6 Rotate the crankshaft until the next valve in the sequence is fully open, and check the clearances of the next two specified valves.

7 Repeat the procedure until all eight valve clearances have been checked (and if necessary, adjusted), then refit the cylinder head cover as described in Section 4.

---

6 Timing belt covers - removal and refitting

Removal

Upper cover

1 Slacken and remove the two retaining bolts (one at the front and one at the rear), and remove the upper timing cover from the cylinder head (see illustrations).

5.5 Valve clearance adjustment

6.1a Undo the two retaining bolts (arrowed) . . .

6.1b . . . and remove the timing belt upper cover

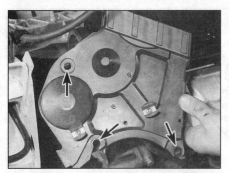

6.3 . . . then undo the three bolts (locations arrowed) and remove the centre cover

6.6a Undo the three bolts (arrowed) . . .

6.6b . . . and remove the crankshaft pulley

Centre cover

2 Remove the upper cover as described in paragraph 1, then free the wiring from its retaining clips on the centre cover.

3 Slacken and remove the three retaining bolts (one at the rear of the cover, beneath the engine mounting plate, and two directly above the crankshaft pulley), and manoeuvre the centre cover out from the engine compartment **(see illustration)**.

Lower cover

4 Remove the auxiliary drivebelt as described in Chapter 1.

5 Remove the upper and centre covers as described in paragraphs 1 to 3.

6 Undo the three crankshaft pulley retaining bolts and remove the pulley, noting which way round it is fitted **(see illustrations)**.

7 Slacken and remove the single retaining bolt, and slide the lower cover off the end of the crankshaft **(see illustration)**.

Refitting

Upper cover

8 Refit the cover, ensuring it is correctly located with the centre cover, and tighten its retaining bolts.

Centre cover

9 Manoeuvre the centre cover back into position, ensuring it is correctly located with the lower cover, and tighten its retaining bolts.

10 Clip the wiring loom into its retaining clips on the front of the centre cover, then refit the upper cover as described in paragraph 8.

6.7 Undo the retaining bolt and remove the timing belt lower cover

Lower cover

11 Locate the lower cover over the timing belt sprocket, and tighten its retaining bolt.

12 Fit the pulley to the end of the crankshaft, ensuring it is fitted the correct way round, and tighten its retaining bolts to the specified torque.

13 Refit the centre and upper covers as described above, then refit and tension the auxiliary drivebelt as described in Chapter 1.

7 Timing belt - general information, removal and refitting

Note: *Peugeot specify the use of a special electronic tool (SEEM C.TRONIC type 105 belt tensioning measuring tool) to correctly set the timing belt tension. If access to this equipment cannot be obtained, an approximate setting can be achieved using the method described below. If the method described is used, the tension must be checked using the special electronic tool at the earliest possible opportunity. Do not drive the vehicle over large distances, or use high engine speeds, until the belt tension is known to be correct. Refer to a Peugeot dealer for advice.*

General information

1 The timing belt drives the camshaft and coolant pump from a toothed sprocket on the front of the crankshaft. If the belt breaks or slips in service, the pistons are likely to hit the valve heads, resulting in extensive (and expensive) damage.

2 The timing belt should be renewed at the specified intervals (see Chapter 1), or earlier if it is contaminated with oil, or if it is at all noisy in operation (a "scraping" noise due to uneven wear).

3 If the timing belt is being removed, it is a wise precaution to check the condition of the coolant pump at the same time (check for signs of coolant leakage). This may avoid the need to remove the timing belt again at a later stage, should the coolant pump fail.

Removal

4 Disconnect the battery negative lead.

5 Align the engine assembly/valve timing

holes as described in Section 3, and lock both the camshaft sprocket and the flywheel in position. *Do not* attempt to rotate the engine whilst the locking tools are in position.

6 Remove the timing belt centre and lower covers as described in Section 6.

7 Loosen the timing belt tensioner pulley retaining nut. Pivot the pulley in a clockwise direction, using a square-section key fitted to the hole in the pulley hub, then retighten the retaining nut.

8 If the timing belt is to be re-used, use white paint or similar to mark the direction of rotation on the belt (if markings do not already exist) **(see illustration)**. Slip the belt off the sprockets.

9 Check the timing belt carefully for any signs of uneven wear, splitting, or oil contamination. Pay particular attention to the roots of the teeth. Renew the belt if there is the slightest doubt about its condition. If the engine is undergoing an overhaul, and has covered more than 36 000 miles (60 000 km) with the existing belt fitted, renew the belt as a matter of course, regardless of its apparent condition. The cost of a new belt is nothing when compared to the cost of repairs, should the belt break in service. If signs of oil contamination are found, trace the source of the oil leak, and rectify it. Wash down the engine timing belt area and all related components, to remove all traces of oil.

Refitting

10 Prior to refitting, thoroughly clean the timing belt sprockets. Check that the tensioner

7.8 Mark the direction of rotation on the belt if it is to be re-used

2C

pulley rotates freely, without any sign of roughness. If necessary, renew the tensioner pulley as described in Section 8. Make sure that the locking tools are still in place, as described in Section 3.

11 Manoeuvre the timing belt into position, ensuring that the arrows on the belt are pointing in the direction of rotation (clockwise, when viewed from the right-hand end of the engine).

12 Do not twist the timing belt sharply while refitting it. Fit the belt over the crankshaft and camshaft sprockets. Make sure that the "front run" of the belt is taut - ie, ensure that any slack is on the tensioner pulley side of the belt. Fit the belt over the coolant pump sprocket and tensioner pulley. Ensure that the belt teeth are seated centrally in the sprockets.

13 Loosen the tensioner pulley retaining nut. Pivot the pulley anti-clockwise to remove all free play from the timing belt, then retighten the nut. Tension the timing belt as described under the relevant sub-heading.

Tensioning without the special electronic measuring tool

Note: *If this method is used, ensure that the belt tension is checked by a Peugeot dealer at the earliest possible opportunity.*

14 Peugeot dealers use a special tool to tension the timing belt. A similar tool may be fabricated using a suitable square-section bar attached to an arm made from a metal strip; a hole should be drilled in the strip at a distance of 80 mm from the centre of the square-section bar. Fit the tool to the hole in the tensioner pulley, keeping the tool arm as close to the horizontal as possible, and hang a 1.5 kg (3.3 lb) weight from the hole in the tool **(see illustration)**. In the absence of an object of the specified weight, a spring balance can be used to exert the required force, ensuring that the spring balance is held at 90° to the tool arm. Slacken the pulley retaining nut, allowing the weight or force exerted (as applicable) to push the tensioner pulley against the belt, then retighten the pulley nut.

15 If this special tool is not available, an approximate setting may be achieved by pivoting the tensioner pulley anti-clockwise until it is just possible to twist the timing belt through 90° by finger and thumb, midway between the crankshaft and camshaft sprockets. The deflection of the belt at the mid-point between the sprockets should be approximately 6.0 mm.

16 Remove the locking tools from the camshaft sprocket and flywheel.

17 Using a suitable socket and extension bar on the crankshaft sprocket bolt, rotate the crankshaft through four complete rotations in a clockwise direction (viewed from the right-hand end of the engine). *Do not* at any time rotate the crankshaft anti-clockwise.

18 Slacken the tensioner pulley nut, re-tension the belt as described in paragraph 14 or 15, then tighten the tensioner pulley nut to the specified torque.

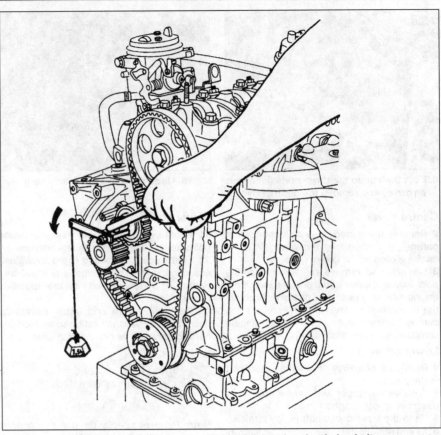

7.14 Using the Peugeot special tool to tension the timing belt

19 Rotate the crankshaft through a further two turns clockwise, and check that both the camshaft sprocket and flywheel timing holes are still correctly aligned.

20 If all is well, refit the timing belt covers as described in Section 6, and reconnect the battery negative lead.

Tensioning using the special electronic measuring tool

21 Fit the special belt tensioning measuring equipment to the "front run" of the timing belt, approximately midway between the camshaft and crankshaft sprockets. Position the tensioner pulley so that the belt is tensioned to a setting of 45 units, then retighten its retaining nut.

22 Remove the locking tools from the camshaft sprocket and flywheel, and remove the measuring tool from the belt.

23 Using a suitable socket and extension bar on the crankshaft sprocket bolt, rotate crankshaft through four complete rotations in a clockwise direction (viewed from the right-hand end of the engine). *Do not* at any time rotate the crankshaft anti-clockwise.

24 Slacken the tensioner pulley retaining nut, and refit the measuring tool to the belt. If a "new" belt is being fitted, tension it to a setting of 40 units. If an "old" belt is being re-used, tighten it to a setting of 36 units. **Note:** *Peugeot state that a belt becomes "old" after*

1 hour's use. With the belt correctly tensioned, tighten the pulley retaining nut to the specified torque.

25 Remove the measuring tool from the belt, then rotate the crankshaft through another two complete rotations in a clockwise direction, so that both the camshaft sprocket and flywheel timing holes are realigned. *Do not* at any time rotate the crankshaft anti-clockwise. Fit the measuring tool to the belt, and check the belt tension. A "new" belt should give a reading of 51 ± 3 units; an "old" belt should be 45 ± 3 units.

26 If the belt tension is incorrect, repeat the procedures in paragraphs 24 and 25.

27 With the belt tension correctly set, refit the timing belt covers as described in Section 5, and reconnect the battery negative lead.

8 Timing belt tensioner and sprockets - removal, inspection and refitting

Note: *This Section describes the removal and refitting of the components concerned as individual operations. If more than one of them is to be removed at the same time, start by removing the timing belt as described in Section 7; remove the actual component as described below, ignoring the preliminary dismantling steps.*

Removal

1 Disconnect the battery negative lead.
2 Position the engine assembly/valve timing holes as described in Section 3, and lock both the camshaft sprocket and flywheel in position. *Do not* attempt to rotate the engine whilst the pins are in position.

Camshaft sprocket

3 Remove the centre timing belt cover as described in Section 6.
4 Loosen the timing belt tensioner pulley retaining nut. Rotate the pulley in a clockwise direction, using a suitable square-section key fitted to the hole in the pulley hub, then retighten the retaining nut.
5 Disengage the timing belt from the sprocket, and move the belt clear, taking care not to bend or twist it sharply. Remove the locking pin from the camshaft sprocket.
6 Slacken the camshaft sprocket retaining bolt and remove it, along with its washer. To prevent the camshaft rotating as the bolt is slackened, restrain the sprocket with a suitable tool through the holes in the sprocket face (**see Tool Tip**). *Do not* attempt to use the sprocket locking pin to prevent the sprocket from rotating whilst the bolt is slackened.
7 With the retaining bolt removed, slide the sprocket off the end of the camshaft. If the locating peg is a loose fit in the rear of the sprocket, remove it for safe-keeping. Examine the camshaft oil seal for signs of oil leakage and, if necessary, renew it as described in Section 9.

8.10 Use the tool shown to lock the flywheel ring gear and prevent the crankshaft rotating

To make a camshaft sprocket holding tool, obtain two lengths of steel strip about 6 mm thick by 30 mm wide or similar, one 600 mm long, the other 200 mm long (all dimensions approximate). Bolt the two strips together to form a forked end, leaving the bolt slack so that the shorter strip can pivot freely. At the end of each 'prong' of the fork, secure a bolt with a nut and a locknut, to act as the fulcrums; these will engage with the cut-outs in the sprocket, and should protrude by about 30 mm

Crankshaft sprocket

8 Remove the centre and lower timing belt covers as described in Section 6.
9 Loosen the timing belt tensioner pulley retaining nut. Rotate the pulley in a clockwise direction, using a suitable square-section key fitted to the hole in the pulley hub, then retighten the retaining nut.
10 To prevent crankshaft rotation whilst the sprocket retaining bolt is slackened, select top gear, and have an assistant apply the brakes firmly. If the engine has been removed from the vehicle, lock the flywheel ring gear, using an arrangement similar to that shown (**see illustration**). *Do not* be tempted to use the flywheel locking pin to prevent the crankshaft from rotating; temporarily remove the locking pin from the rear of the flywheel prior to slackening the pulley bolt, then refit it once the bolt has been slackened.
11 Unscrew the retaining bolt and washer, then slide the sprocket off the end of the crankshaft (**see illustrations**). Refit the locating

pin to the rear of the timing hole in the rear of the flywheel.
12 If the Woodruff key is a loose fit in the crankshaft, remove it and store it with the sprocket for safe-keeping. If necessary, also slide the flanged spacer off the end of the crankshaft (**see illustration**). Examine the crankshaft oil seal for signs oil leakage and, if necessary, renew as described in Section 14.

Tensioner pulley

13 Remove the centre timing belt cover as described in Section 6.
14 Slacken and remove the timing belt tensioner pulley retaining nut, and slide the pulley off its mounting stud. Examine the mounting stud for signs of damage and, if necessary, renew it.

Inspection

15 Clean the sprockets thoroughly, and renew any that show signs of wear, damage or cracks.
16 Clean the tensioner assembly, but do not use any strong solvent which may enter the pulley bearing. Check that the pulley rotates freely about its hub, with no sign of stiffness or of free play. Renew the tensioner pulley if there is any doubt about its condition, or if there are any obvious signs of wear or damage.

Refitting

Camshaft sprocket

17 Refit the locating peg (where removed) to the rear of the sprocket, then locate the sprocket on the end of the camshaft. Ensure that the locating peg is correctly engaged with the cut-out in the camshaft end.
18 Refit the sprocket retaining bolt and washer. Tighten the bolt to the specified torque, whilst retaining the sprocket with the tool used on removal.
19 Realign the timing hole in the camshaft sprocket (see Section 3) with the corresponding hole in the cylinder head, and refit the locking pin.
20 Refit the timing belt to the camshaft sprocket. Ensure that the "front run" of the belt is taut - ie, ensure that any slack is on the tensioner pulley side of the belt. Do not twist the belt sharply while refitting it, and ensure that the belt teeth are seated centrally in the sprockets.

2C

8.11a Remove the crankshaft sprocket bolt . . .

8.11b . . . then slide off the sprocket

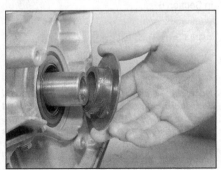

8.12 Remove the flanged spacer if necessary

21 Loosen the tensioner pulley retaining nut. Rotate the pulley anti-clockwise to remove all free play from the timing belt, then retighten the nut.

22 Tension the belt as described in paragraphs 14 to 19 of Section 7.

23 Refit the timing belt covers as described in Section 6.

Crankshaft sprocket

24 Where removed, locate the Woodruff key in the crankshaft end, then slide on the flanged spacer, aligning its slot with the Woodruff key.

25 Align the crankshaft sprocket slot with the Woodruff key, and slide it onto the end of the crankshaft.

26 Temporarily remove the locking pin from the rear of the flywheel, then refit the crankshaft sprocket retaining bolt and washer. Tighten the bolt to the specified torque, whilst preventing crankshaft rotation using the method employed on removal. Refit the locking pin to the rear of the flywheel.

27 Relocate the timing belt on the crankshaft sprocket. Ensure that the "front run" of the belt is taut - ie, ensure that any slack is on the tensioner pulley side of the belt. Do not twist the belt sharply while refitting it, and ensure that the belt teeth are seated centrally in the sprockets.

28 Loosen the tensioner pulley retaining nut. Rotate the pulley anti-clockwise to remove all free play from the timing belt, then retighten the nut.

29 Tension the belt as described in paragraphs 14 to 19 of Section 7.

30 Refit the timing belt covers as described in Section 6.

Tensioner pulley

31 Refit the tensioner pulley to its mounting stud, and fit the retaining nut.

32 Ensure that the "front run" of the belt is taut - ie, ensure that any slack is on the pulley side of the belt. Check that the belt is centrally located on all its sprockets. Rotate the pulley anti-clockwise to remove all free play from the timing belt, then tighten the pulley retaining nut securely.

33 Tension the belt as described in paragraphs 14 to 19 of Section 7.

34 Refit the timing belt covers as described in Section 6.

9 Camshaft oil seal - renewal

Note: If the camshaft oil seal is to be renewed with the timing belt still in place, check first that the belt is free from oil contamination. (Renew the belt as a matter of course if signs of oil contamination are found; see Section 7). Cover the belt to protect it from oil contamination while work is in progress. Ensure that all traces of oil are removed from the area before the belt is refitted.

1 Remove the camshaft sprocket as described in Section 8.

2 Punch or drill two small holes opposite each other in the oil seal. Screw a self-tapping screw into each, and pull on the screws with pliers to extract the seal.

3 Clean the seal housing, and polish off any burrs or raised edges, which may have caused the seal to fail in the first place.

4 Lubricate the lips of the new seal with clean engine oil, and drive it into position until it seats on its locating shoulder. Use a suitable tubular drift, such as a socket, which bears only on the hard outer edge of the seal. Take care not to damage the seal lips during fitting. Note that the seal lips should face inwards.

5 Refit the camshaft sprocket as described in Section 8.

10 Camshaft and rocker arms - removal, inspection and refitting

General information

1 The rocker arm assembly is secured to the top of the cylinder head by the cylinder head bolts. Although in theory it is possible to undo the head bolts and remove the rocker arm assembly without removing the head, in practice, this is not recommended. Once the bolts have been removed, the head gasket will be disturbed, and the gasket will almost certainly leak or blow after refitting. For this reason, removal of the rocker arm assembly cannot be done without removing the cylinder head and renewing the head gasket.

2 The camshaft is slid out of the right-hand end of the cylinder head, and it therefore cannot be removed without first removing the cylinder head, due to a lack of clearance.

Removal

Rocker arm assembly

3 Remove the cylinder head as described in Section 11.

4 To dismantle the rocker arm assembly, carefully prise off the circlip from the right-hand end of the rocker shaft; retain the rocker pedestal, to prevent it being sprung off the

10.4 Remove the circlip, and slide the components off the end of the rocker shaft

end of the shaft. Slide the various components off the end of the shaft, keeping all components in their correct fitted order **(see illustration)**. Make a note of each component's correct fitted position and orientation as it is removed, to ensure it is fitted correctly on reassembly.

5 To separate the left-hand pedestal and shaft, first unscrew the cylinder head cover retaining stud from the top of the pedestal; this can be achieved using a stud extractor, or two nuts locked together. With the stud removed, unscrew the grub screw from the top of the pedestal, and withdraw the rocker shaft **(see illustrations)**.

Camshaft

6 Remove the cylinder head as described in Section 11.

7 With the head on a bench, remove the locking pin, then remove the camshaft sprocket as described in paragraphs 6 and 7 of Section 8.

8 Unbolt the housing from the left-hand end of the cylinder head, then undo the retaining bolt, and remove the camshaft thrust fork from the cylinder head **(see illustration)**.

9 Using a large flat-bladed screwdriver, carefully prise the oil seal out of the right-hand end of the cylinder head, then slide out the camshaft **(see illustrations)**. Discard the seal - a new one must be used on refitting.

Inspection

Rocker arm assembly

10 Examine the rocker arm bearing surfaces

10.5a To remove the left-hand pedestal, lock two nuts together and unscrew the stud . . .

10.5b . . . then remove the grub screw

10.8 Undo the retaining bolt and remove the camshaft thrust fork (arrowed) . . .

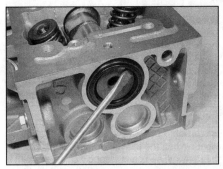

10.9a . . . prise out the oil seal . . .

10.9b . . . and slide out the camshaft

which contact the camshaft lobes for wear ridges and scoring. Renew any rocker arms on which these conditions are apparent. If a rocker arm bearing surface is badly scored, also examine the corresponding lobe on the camshaft for wear, as it is likely that both will be worn. Renew worn components as necessary. The rocker arm assembly can be dismantled as described in paragraphs 4 and 5.

11 Inspect the ends of the (valve clearance) adjusting screws for signs of wear or damage, and renew as required.

12 If the rocker arm assembly has been dismantled, examine the rocker arm and shaft bearing surfaces for wear ridges and scoring. If there are obvious signs of wear, the relevant rocker arm(s) and/or the shaft must be renewed.

Camshaft

13 Examine the camshaft bearing surfaces and cam lobes for signs of wear ridges and scoring. Renew the camshaft if any of these conditions are apparent. Examine the condition of the bearing surfaces, both on the camshaft journals and in the cylinder head. If the head bearing surfaces are worn excessively, the cylinder head will need to be renewed. If the necessary measuring equipment is available, camshaft bearing journal wear can be checked by direct measurement, noting that No 1 journal is at the transmission end of the head.

14 Examine the thrust fork for signs of wear or scoring, and renew as necessary.

Refitting

Rocker arm assembly

15 If the rocker arm assembly was dismantled, refit the rocker shaft to the left-hand pedestal, aligning its locating hole with the pedestal threaded hole. Refit the grub screw, and tighten it securely. With the grub screw in position, refit the cylinder head cover mounting stud to the pedestal, and tighten it securely. Apply a smear of clean engine oil to the shaft, then slide on all removed components, ensuring each is correctly fitted in its original position. Once all components are in position on the shaft, compress the right-hand pedestal and refit the circlip. Ensure that the circlip is correctly located in its groove on the shaft.

16 Refit the cylinder head and rocker arm assembly as described in Section 11.

Camshaft

17 Ensure that the cylinder head and camshaft bearing surfaces are clean, then liberally oil the camshaft bearings and lobes. Slide the camshaft back into position in the cylinder head. On carburettor engines, take care that the fuel pump operating lever is not trapped by the camshaft as it is slid into position. To prevent this, remove the fuel pump before refitting the camshaft, then refit it afterwards.

18 Locate the thrust fork with the left-hand end of the camshaft. Refit the fork retaining bolt, tightening it to the specified torque setting.

19 Ensure that the housing and cylinder head mating surfaces are clean and dry, then apply a smear of sealant to the housing mating surface. Refit the housing to the left-hand end of the head, and securely tighten its retaining bolts.

20 Lubricate the lips of the new seal with clean engine oil, then drive it into position until it seats on its locating shoulder. Use a suitable tubular drift, such as a socket, which bears only on the hard outer edge of the seal. Take care not to damage the seal lips during fitting. Note that the seal lips should face inwards.

21 Refit the camshaft sprocket as described in paragraphs 17 to 19 of Section 8.

22 Refit the cylinder head as described in Section 11.

---

11 Cylinder head - removal and refitting

Removal

1 Disconnect the battery negative lead.

2 Drain the cooling system as described in Chapter 1.

3 Remove the cylinder head cover as described in Section 4.

4 Align the engine assembly/valve timing holes as described in Section 3, and lock both the camshaft sprocket and flywheel in position. *Do not* attempt to rotate the engine whilst the tools are in position.

5 Note that the following text assumes that the cylinder head will be removed with both inlet and exhaust manifolds attached; this is easier, but makes it a bulky and heavy assembly to handle. If it is wished to remove the manifolds first, proceed as described in the relevant Part of Chapter 4.

6 Working as described in the relevant Part of Chapter 4, disconnect the exhaust system front pipe from the manifold. Where fitted, disconnect or release the oxygen sensor wiring, so that it is not strained by the weight of the exhaust.

7 Remove the air cleaner assembly and inlet ducts as described in Chapter 4.

8 On carburettor engines, disconnect the following from the carburettor and inlet manifold as described in Chapter 4A:

a) *Fuel feed and return hoses (plug all openings, to prevent loss of fuel and the entry of dirt into the system).*

b) *Throttle cable.*

c) *Choke cable (where applicable).*

d) *Carburettor idle fuel cut-off solenoid wiring connector(s).*

e) *Vacuum servo unit vacuum hose, coolant hose and all other relevant breather/vacuum hoses from the manifold.*

9 On fuel-injected engines, carry out the following operations as described in Chapter 4B:

a) *Depressurise the fuel system, and disconnect the fuel feed and return hoses from the throttle body (plug all openings, to prevent loss of fuel and entry of dirt into the fuel system).*

b) *Disconnect the throttle cable.*

c) *Disconnect the relevant electrical connectors from the throttle body.*

d) *Disconnect the vacuum servo unit hose, coolant hose(s) and all the other relevant/breather hoses from the manifold.*

10 Remove the centre and upper timing belt covers as described in Section 6.

11 Loosen the timing belt tensioner pulley retaining nut. Pivot the pulley in a clockwise direction, using a suitable square-section key fitted to the hole in the pulley hub, then retighten the retaining nut.

2C

12 Disengage the timing belt from the camshaft sprocket, and position the belt clear of the sprocket. Ensure that the belt is not bent or twisted sharply.

13 Slacken the retaining clips, and disconnect the coolant hoses from the thermostat housing (on the left-hand end of the cylinder head).

14 Depress the retaining clip(s), and disconnect the wiring connector(s) from the electrical switch and/or sensor(s) which are screwed into the thermostat housing/cylinder head (as appropriate). Also where necessary release the TDC sensor connector from its support on the distributor bracket on the left-hand end of the cylinder head.

Carburettor models

15 Disconnect the LT wiring connectors from the distributor and HT coil. Release the TDC sensor wiring connector from the side of the coil mounting bracket, and disconnect the vacuum pipe from the distributor vacuum diaphragm unit. If the cylinder head is to be dismantled for overhaul, remove the distributor and ignition HT coil as described in Chapter 5B. If the cylinder numbers are not already marked on the HT leads, number each lead, to avoid the possibility of the leads being incorrectly connected on refitting. Disconnect the HT leads from the spark plugs, and remove the distributor cap and lead assembly.

Fuel-injected models

16 Disconnect the wiring connector from the ignition module. If the cylinder head is to be dismantled for overhaul, remove the ignition module as described in Chapter 5B. If the cylinder numbers are not already marked on the HT leads, number each lead, to avoid the possibility of the leads being incorrectly connected on refitting. Note that the HT leads should be disconnected from the spark plugs instead of the coil, and the coil and leads removed as an assembly.

All models

17 Slacken and remove the bolt securing the engine oil dipstick tube to the cylinder head.

18 Working in the *reverse* of the sequence shown in **illustration 11.38**, progressively slacken the ten cylinder head bolts by half a turn at a time, until all bolts can be unscrewed by hand.

19 With all the cylinder head bolts removed, lift the rocker arm assembly off the cylinder head. Note the locating pins which are fitted to the base of each rocker arm pedestal. If any pin is a loose fit in the head or pedestal, remove it for safe-keeping.

20 On engines with a cast-iron cylinder block, lift the cylinder head away; seek assistance if possible, as it is a heavy assembly, especially if it is being removed complete with the manifolds.

21 On engines with an aluminium cylinder block, the joint between the cylinder head and gasket and the cylinder block/crankcase must

now be broken without disturbing the wet liners. To break the joint, obtain two L-shaped metal bars which fit into the cylinder head bolt holes. Gently "rock" the cylinder head free towards the front of the car **(see illustration)**. Do not try to swivel the head on the cylinder block/crankcase; it is located by dowels, as well as by the tops of the liners. **Note:** *If care is not taken and the liners are moved, there is also a possibility of the bottom seals being disturbed, causing leakage after refitting the head.* When the joint is broken, lift the cylinder head away; seek assistance if possible, as it is a heavy assembly, especially if it is being removed complete with the manifolds.

22 On all models, remove the gasket from the top of the block, noting the two locating dowels. If the locating dowels are a loose fit, remove them and store them with the head for safe-keeping. Do not discard the gasket - on some models it will be needed for identification purposes (see paragraphs 28 and 29).

Caution: On aluminium block engines, Do not attempt to rotate the crankshaft with the cylinder head removed, otherwise the wet liners may be displaced. Operations that require the rotation of the crankshaft (eg cleaning the piston crowns), should only be carried out once the cylinder liners are firmly clamped in position. In the absence of the special Peugeot liner clamps, the liners can be clamped in position using large flat washers positioned underneath suitable-length bolts. Alternatively, the original head bolts could be temporarily refitted, with suitable spacers fitted to their shanks.

23 If the cylinder head is to be dismantled for overhaul, remove the camshaft as described in Section 10, then refer to Part D of this Chapter.

Preparation for refitting

24 The mating faces of the cylinder head and cylinder block/crankcase must be perfectly clean before refitting the head. Use a hard plastic or wood scraper to remove all traces of gasket and carbon; also clean the piston crowns. Refer to paragraph 23 before turning the crankshaft on aluminium block engines. Take particular care during the cleaning operations, as aluminium alloy is easily damaged. Also, make sure that the carbon is not allowed to enter the oil and water passages - this is particularly important for the lubrication system, as carbon could block the oil supply to the engine's components. Using adhesive tape and paper, seal the water, oil and bolt holes in the cylinder block/crankcase. To prevent carbon entering the gap between the pistons and bores, smear a little grease in the gap. After cleaning each piston, use a small brush to remove all traces of grease and carbon from the gap, then wipe away the remainder with a clean rag. Clean all the pistons in the same way.

25 Check the mating surfaces of the cylinder block/crankcase and the cylinder head for nicks, deep scratches and other damage. If slight, they may be removed carefully with a file, but if excessive, machining may be the only alternative to renewal.

26 If warpage of the cylinder head gasket surface is suspected, use a straight-edge to check it for distortion. Refer to Part D of this Chapter if necessary.

27 When purchasing a new cylinder head gasket, it is essential that a gasket of the correct thickness is obtained. On some models only one thickness of gasket is available, so this is not a problem. However on other models, there are two different thicknesses available - the standard gasket

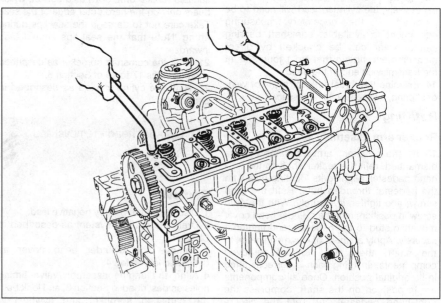

11.21 Using two angled metal rods to free the cylinder head from the block

which is fitted at the factory, and a slightly thicker "repair" gasket (+ 0.2 mm), for use once the head gasket face has been machined. If the cylinder head has been machined, it should have the letter "R" stamped adjacent to the No 3 exhaust port, and the gasket should also have the letter "R" stamped adjacent to No 3 cylinder on its front upper face. The gaskets can also be identified as described in the following paragraph, using the cut-outs on the left-hand end of the gasket.

28 With the gasket fitted the correct way up on the cylinder block, there will be a single cut-out, or no cut-out at all, at the rear of the left-hand side of the gasket identifying the engine type (ie. TU engine). In the centre of the gasket there may be another series of between 0 and 4 cut-outs, identifying the manufacturer of the gasket and whether or not it contains asbestos (these cut-outs are of little importance). The important cut-out location is at the front of the gasket; on the standard gasket there will be no cut-out in this position, whereas on the thicker "repair" gasket there will be a single cut-out (see illustration). Identify the gasket type, and ensure that the new gasket obtained is of the correct thickness. If there is any doubt as to which gasket is fitted, take the old gasket along to your Peugeot dealer, and have him confirm the gasket type.

29 Check the condition of the cylinder head bolts, and particularly their threads, whenever they are removed. Wash the bolts in suitable solvent, and wipe them dry. Check each for any sign of visible wear or damage, renewing any bolt if necessary. Measure the length of each bolt, to check for stretching (although this is not a conclusive test, in the event that all ten bolts have stretched by the same amount). Although Peugeot do not actually specify that the bolts must be renewed, it is strongly recommended that the bolts should be renewed as a complete set whenever they are disturbed.

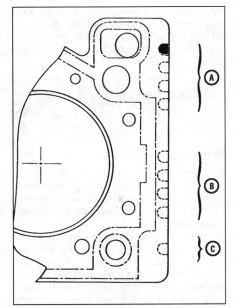

11.28 Cylinder head gasket markings

A Engine type identification cut-outs
B Gasket manufacturer identification cut-outs
C Gasket thickness identification cut-out

30 On aluminium block engines, prior to refitting the cylinder head, check the cylinder liner protrusion as described in Part D of this Chapter.

Refitting

31 Wipe clean the mating surfaces of the cylinder head and cylinder block/crankcase. Check that the two locating dowels are in position at each end of the cylinder block/crankcase surface and, if necessary, remove the cylinder liner clamps.

32 Position a new gasket on the cylinder block/crankcase surface, ensuring that its identification cut-outs are at the left-hand end of the gasket.

33 Check that the flywheel and camshaft sprocket are still correctly locked in position with their respective tools then, with the aid of an assistant, carefully refit the cylinder head assembly to the block, aligning it with the locating dowels.

34 Ensure that the locating pins are in position in the base of each rocker pedestal, then refit the rocker arm assembly to the cylinder head.

35 Apply a smear of grease to the threads, and to the underside of the heads, of the cylinder head bolts. Peugeot recommend the use of Molykote G Rapid Plus grease (available from your Peugeot dealer - a sachet is supplied with the top-end gasket set); in the absence of the specified grease, a good-quality high-melting-point grease may be used.

36 Carefully enter each bolt into its relevant hole (do not drop them in) and screw in, by hand only, until finger-tight.

37 Working progressively and in the sequence shown, tighten the cylinder head bolts to their Stage 1 torque setting, using a torque wrench and suitable socket (see illustrations).

38 Once all the bolts have been tightened to their Stage 1 setting, working again in the given sequence, angle-tighten the bolts through the specified Stage 2 angle, using a socket and extension bar. It is recommended that an angle-measuring gauge is used during this stage of the tightening, to ensure accuracy (see illustration). If a gauge is not available, use white paint to make alignment marks between the bolt head and cylinder head prior to tightening; the marks can then be used to check that the bolt has been rotated through the correct angle during tightening.

39 On cast-iron block engines, it will then be necessary to tighten the bolts through the specified Stage 3 angle setting.

40 With the cylinder head bolts correctly tightened, refit the dipstick tube retaining bolt and tighten it securely.

2C

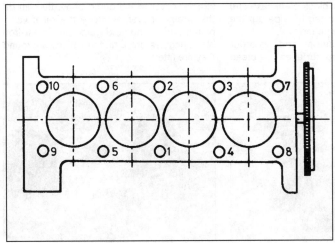

11.37a Cylinder head bolt tightening sequence

11.37b Working in the sequence, tighten the head bolts first with a torque wrench . . .

11.38 . . . then with an angle tightening gauge

41 Refit the timing belt to the camshaft sprocket. Ensure that the "front run" of the belt is taut - ie, ensure that any slack is on the tensioner pulley side of the belt. Do not twist the belt sharply while refitting it, and ensure that the belt teeth are seated centrally in the sprockets.

42 Loosen the tensioner pulley retaining nut. Pivot the pulley anti-clockwise to remove all free play from the timing belt, then retighten the nut.

43 Tension the belt as described under the relevant sub-heading in Section 7, then refit the centre and upper timing belt covers as described in Section 6.

Carburettor models

44 If the head was stripped for overhaul, refit the distributor and HT coil as described in Chapter 5B, ensuring that the HT leads are correctly reconnected. If the head was not stripped, reconnect the wiring connector and vacuum pipe to the distributor, and the HT lead to the coil; clip the TDC sensor wiring connector onto the coil bracket.

Fuel-injected models

45 If the head was stripped for overhaul, refit the ignition module and leads as described in Chapter 5B, ensuring that the leads are correctly reconnected. If the head was not stripped, simply reconnect the wiring connector to the module.

All models

46 Reconnect the wiring connector(s) to the coolant switch/sensor(s) on the left-hand end of the head.

47 Reconnect the coolant hoses to the thermostat housing, securely tightening their retaining clips.

48 Working as described in the relevant Part of Chapter 4, carry out the following tasks:
 a) Refit all disturbed wiring, hoses and control cable(s) to the inlet manifold and fuel system components.
 b) Reconnect and adjust the choke and throttle cables as applicable.
 d) Reconnect the exhaust system front pipe to the manifold. Where applicable, reconnect the oxygen sensor wiring connector.
 e) Refit the air cleaner assembly and ducting.

49 Check and, if necessary, adjust the valve clearances as described in Section 5.

50 On completion, reconnect the battery, and refill the cooling system as described in Chapter 1.

12 Sump - removal and refitting

Removal

1 Chock the rear wheels then jack up the front of the car and support it on axle stands (see *"Jacking and vehicle support"*). Remove the front roadwheels. Disconnect the battery negative lead.

2 Drain the engine oil, then clean and refit the engine oil drain plug, tightening it to the specified torque. If the engine is nearing its service interval when the oil and filter are due for renewal, it is recommended that the filter is also removed, and a new one fitted. After reassembly, the engine can then be refilled with fresh oil. Refer to Chapter 1 for further information.

3 Remove the exhaust system front pipe as described in the relevant Part of Chapter 4.

4 Progressively slacken and remove all the sump retaining nuts and bolts. On cast-iron block engines, it may be necessary to unbolt the flywheel cover plate from the transmission to gain access to the left-hand sump fasteners.

5 Break the joint by striking the sump with the palm of your hand, then lower the sump and withdraw it from underneath the vehicle **(see illustration)**.

6 While the sump is removed, take the opportunity to check the oil pump pick-up/strainer for signs of clogging or splitting. If necessary, remove the pump as described in Section 13, and clean or renew the strainer.

Refitting

7 Clean all traces of sealant from the mating surfaces of the cylinder block/crankcase and sump, then use a clean rag to wipe out the sump and the engine's interior.

8 Ensure that the sump and cylinder block/crankcase mating surfaces are clean

and dry, then apply a coating of suitable sealant to the sump mating surface.

9 Offer up the sump, locating it on its retaining studs, and refit its retaining nuts and bolts. Tighten the nuts and bolts evenly and progressively to the specified torque.

10 Refit the exhaust front pipe as described in the relevant Part of Chapter 4.

11 Replenish the engine oil as described in Chapter 1.

13 Oil pump - removal, inspection and refitting

Removal

1 Remove the sump as described in Section 12.

2 Slacken and remove the three bolts securing the oil pump in position **(see illustration)**. Disengage the pump sprocket from the chain, and remove the oil pump. If the pump locating dowel is a loose fit, remove and store it with the retaining bolts for safe-keeping.

Inspection

3 Examine the oil pump sprocket for signs of damage and wear, such as chipped or missing teeth. If the sprocket is worn, the pump assembly must be renewed, as the sprocket is not available separately. It is also recommended that the chain and drive sprocket, fitted to the crankshaft, is renewed at the same time. On aluminium block engines, renewal of the chain and drive sprocket is an involved operation requiring the removal of the main bearing ladder, and therefore cannot be carried out with the engine still fitted to the vehicle. On cast-iron block engines, the oil pump drive sprocket and chain can be removed with the engine in situ, once the crankshaft sprocket has been removed and the crankshaft oil seal housing has been unbolted. Refer to Part D for further information.

4 Slacken and remove the bolts securing the strainer cover to the pump body, then lift off the strainer cover. Remove the relief valve piston and spring (and guide pin - cast-iron block engines only), noting which way round they are fitted.

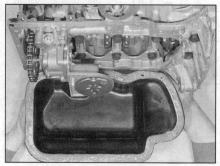

12.5 Slacken and remove the sump nuts and bolts, then remove the sump

13.2 The oil pump is retained by three bolts

5 Examine the pump rotors and body for signs of wear ridges and scoring. If worn, the complete pump assembly must be renewed.

6 Examine the relief valve piston for signs of wear or damage, and renew if necessary. The condition of the relief valve spring can only be measured by comparing it with a new one; if there is any doubt about its condition, it should also be renewed. Both the piston and spring are available individually.

7 Thoroughly clean the oil pump strainer with a suitable solvent, and check it for signs of clogging or splitting. If the strainer is damaged, the strainer and cover assembly must be renewed.

8 Locate the relief valve spring, piston and (where fitted) the guide pin in the strainer cover, then refit the cover to the pump body. Align the relief valve piston with its bore in the pump. Refit the cover retaining bolts, tightening them securely.

Refitting

9 Ensure that the locating dowel is in position, then engage the pump sprocket with its drive chain. Locate the pump on its dowel, and refit the pump retaining bolts, tightening them to the specified torque setting.

10 Refit the sump as described in Section 12.

14 Crankshaft oil seals - renewal

Right-hand oil seal

1 Remove the crankshaft sprocket and flanged spacer as described in Section 8. Secure the timing belt clear of the working area, so that it cannot be contaminated with oil. Make a note of the correct fitted depth of the seal in its housing.

2 Punch or drill two small holes opposite each other in the seal. Screw a self-tapping screw into each, and pull on the screws with pliers to extract the seal. Alternatively, the seal can be levered out of position using a suitable flat-bladed screwdriver, taking great care not to damage the crankshaft shoulder or seal housing **(see illustration)**.

3 Clean the seal housing, and polish off any

14.2 Using a screwdriver to lever out the crankshaft front oil seal

burrs or raised edges, which may have caused the seal to fail in the first place.

4 Lubricate the lips of the new seal with clean engine oil, and carefully locate the seal on the end of crankshaft. Note that its sealing lip must face inwards. Take care not to damage the seal lips during fitting.

5 Using a suitable tubular drift (such as a socket) which bears only on the hard outer edge of the seal, tap the seal into position, to the same depth in the housing as the original was prior to removal. The inner face of the seal must end up flush with the inner wall of the crankcase.

6 Wash off any traces of oil, then refit the crankshaft sprocket as described in Section 8.

Left-hand oil seal

7 Remove the flywheel as described in Section 15.

8 Make a note of the correct fitted depth of the seal in its housing. Punch or drill two small holes opposite each other in the seal. Screw a self-tapping screw into each, and pull on the screws with pliers to extract the seal.

9 Clean the seal housing, and polish off any burrs or raised edges, which may have caused the seal to fail in the first place.

10 Lubricate the lips of the new seal with clean engine oil, and carefully locate the seal on the end of the crankshaft.

11 Using a suitable tubular drift, which bears only on the hard outer edge of the seal, drive the seal into position, to the same depth in the housing as the original was prior to removal.

12 Wash off any traces of oil, then refit the flywheel as described in Section 15.

15 Flywheel - removal, inspection and refitting

Removal

1 Remove the transmission as described in Chapter 7A, then remove the clutch assembly as described in Chapter 6.

2 Prevent the flywheel from turning by locking the ring gear teeth with a screwdriver or a similar arrangement to that shown in **illustration 8.10**. Alternatively, bolt a strap between the flywheel and the cylinder block/crankcase. Do not attempt to lock the flywheel in position using the locking pin described in Section 3.

3 Slacken and remove the flywheel retaining bolts, and discard them; they must be renewed whenever they are disturbed.

4 Remove the flywheel. Do not drop it, as it is very heavy. If the locating dowel is a loose fit in the crankshaft end, remove and store it with the flywheel for safe-keeping.

Inspection

5 If the flywheel's clutch mating surface is deeply scored, cracked or otherwise

damaged, the flywheel must be renewed. However, it may be possible to have it surface-ground; seek the advice of a Peugeot dealer or engine reconditioning specialist.

6 If the ring gear is badly worn or has missing teeth, it must be renewed. This job is best left to a Peugeot dealer or engine reconditioning specialist. The temperature to which the new ring gear must be heated for installation is critical and, if not done accurately, the hardness of the teeth will be destroyed.

Refitting

7 Clean the mating surfaces of the flywheel and crankshaft. Remove any remaining locking compound from the threads of the crankshaft holes, using the correct-size tap, if available.

> **HAYNES HiNT** *If a suitable tap is not available, cut two slots into the threads of one of the old flywheel bolts and use the bolt to remove the locking compound from the threads.*

8 If the new flywheel retaining bolts are not supplied with their threads already pre-coated, apply a suitable thread-locking compound to the threads of each bolt.

9 Ensure that the locating dowel is in position. Offer up the flywheel, locating it on the dowel, and fit the new retaining bolts.

10 Lock the flywheel using the method employed on dismantling, and tighten the retaining bolts to the specified torque.

11 Refit the clutch as described in Chapter 6. Remove the locking tool, and refit the transmission as described in Chapter 7A.

16 Engine/transmission mountings - inspection and renewal

Inspection

1 If improved access is required, raise the front of the car and support it securely on axle stands (see "Jacking and vehicle support").

2 Check the mounting rubber to see if it is cracked, hardened or separated from the metal at any point; renew the mounting if any such damage or deterioration is evident.

3 Check that all the mounting's fasteners are securely tightened; use a torque wrench to check if possible.

4 Using a large screwdriver or a crowbar, check for wear in the mounting by carefully levering against it to check for free play. Where this is not possible, enlist the aid of an assistant to move the engine/transmission back and forth, or from side to side, while you watch the mounting. While some free play is to be expected even from new components, excessive wear should be obvious. If excessive free play is found, check first that the fasteners are correctly secured, then renew any worn components as described below.

2C

Renewal

Right-hand mounting

5 Disconnect the battery negative lead.

6 Place a jack beneath the engine, with a block of wood on the jack head. Raise the jack until it is supporting the weight of the engine.

7 Slacken and remove the three nuts securing the right-hand engine mounting upper bracket to the bracket on the cylinder block. Remove the nut securing the bracket to the mounting rubber, and lift off the bracket.

8 Lift the buffer plate off the mounting rubber stud, then unscrew the mounting rubber from the body.

9 Check carefully for signs of wear or damage on all components, and renew them where necessary.

10 On reassembly, securely tighten the mounting rubber in the body.

11 Refit the buffer plate (where fitted) to the mounting rubber stud, then install the mounting bracket.

12 Tighten the mounting bracket retaining nuts to the specified torque setting.

13 Remove the jack from underneath the engine, and reconnect the battery negative lead.

Left-hand mounting

14 Remove the battery and tray as described in Chapter 5A.

15 Place a jack beneath the transmission, with a block of wood on the jack head. Raise the jack until it is supporting the weight of the transmission.

16 Slacken and remove the mounting rubber's centre nut, and two retaining nuts and remove the mounting from the engine compartment.

17 If necessary, undo the two retaining bolts and remove the mounting bracket from the body. Disconnect the clutch cable from the transmission (see Chapter 6) then unscrew the retaining nuts and remove the bracket from the top of the transmission.

18 Check carefully for signs of wear or damage on all components, and renew them where necessary.

19 Refit the bracket to the transmission, tightening its mounting nuts to the specified torque. Reconnect the clutch cable and adjust as described in Chapter 6. Refit the mounting bracket to the vehicle body and tighten its bolts to the specified torque.

20 Fit the mounting rubber to the bracket and tighten its retaining nuts to the specified torque. Refit the mounting centre nut, and tighten it to the specified torque.

21 Remove the jack from underneath the transmission, then refit the battery as described in Chapter 5.

Rear mounting

22 If not already done, firmly apply the handbrake, then jack up the front of the vehicle and support it securely on axle stands (see "*Jacking and vehicle support*").

23 Unscrew and remove the bolt securing the rear mounting link to the mounting on the rear of the cylinder block.

24 Remove the bolt securing the rear mounting link to the bracket on the underbody. Withdraw the link.

25 To remove the mounting assembly it will first be necessary to remove the right-hand driveshaft as described in Chapter 8.

26 With the driveshaft removed, undo the retaining bolts and remove the mounting from the rear of the cylinder block.

27 Check carefully for signs of wear or damage on all components, and renew them where necessary.

28 On reassembly, fit the rear mounting assembly to the rear of the cylinder block, and tighten its retaining bolts to the specified torque. Refit the driveshaft as described in Chapter 8.

29 Refit the rear mounting link, and tighten both its bolts to their specified torque settings.

30 Lower the vehicle to the ground.

Chapter 2 Part D:
Engine removal and overhaul procedures

Contents

Degrees of difficulty

Easy, suitable for novice with little experience	**Fairly easy,** suitable for beginner with some experience	**Fairly difficult,** suitable for competent DIY mechanic 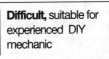	**Difficult,** suitable for experienced DIY mechanic	**Very difficult,** suitable for expert DIY or professional 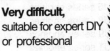

Specifications

Note: *At the time of writing, many specifications for certain engines were not available. Where the relevant specifications are not given here, refer to your Peugeot dealer for further information.*

Cylinder head

Maximum gasket face distortion	0.05 mm
Cylinder head height::	
XV, XW and XY series engines	Not available
XU series engines	141.0 ± 0.05 mm
TU series engines	111.2 ± 0.08 mm

Valves

Valve head diameter:	
Inlet:	
XV8 engines	34.8 mm
XW7, XY7 and XY8 engines	37.0 mm
XU5J engines	40.0 mm
All other XU series engines	41.6 mm
TU9 series engines	34.8 mm
TU1 series engines	36.8 mm
TU3, TU3A, TU3M and TU3S engines	36.8 mm
TU3FM engines	39.5 mm
Exhaust:	
XV8 engines	27.8 mm
XW7, XY7 and XY8 engines	29.5 mm
XU5J engines:	
Early models	32.0 mm
Later models	32.95 mm
All other XU series engines	34.5 mm
TU9 series engines	27.9 mm
TU1 series engines	29.4 mm
TU3, TU3A, TU3M and TU3S engines	29.4 mm
TU3FM engines	31.4 mm
Valve stem diameter:	
Inlet:	
XV, XW and XY series engines	8.0 mm
XU51 and XU5M series engines	7.30 mm
All other XU series engines	7.98 mm
TU series engines	6.99 mm

2D

Valve stem diameter (continued):
   Exhaust:
      XV, XW and XY series engines .... 8.0 mm
      XU5J series engines .... 7.96 mm
      XU5JA and XU9J series engines .... 7.98 mm
      XU51 and XU5M series engines .... 7.30 mm
      TU series engines .... 6.97 mm
Overall length:
   Inlet:
      XV, XW and XY series engines .... Not available
      XU series engines .... 109.29 mm
      TU series engines .... 110.76 mm
   Exhaust:
      XV, XW and XY series engines .... Not available
      XU series engines .... 108.79 mm
      TU series engines .... 110.60 mm

Cylinder block

Cylinder bore/liner diameter (nominal in three grades):
   XV series engines .... 70.0 mm
   XW series engines .... 72.0 mm
   XY series engines .... 75.0 mm
   XU5 series engines .... 83.0 mm
   XU9 series engines .... 83.0 mm
   TU9 series engines .... 70.0 mm
   TU1 series engines .... 72.0 mm
   TU3 series engines .... 75.0 mm
Maximum cylinder bore/liner taper* .... 0.10 mm
Maximum cylinder bore/liner ovality* .... 0.10 mm
Liner protrusion above block mating surface:
   XV, XW and XY series engines:
      With paper type base seals .... 0.11 to 0.18 mm
      With O-ring type base seals .... 0.10 to 0.17 mm
   XU series engines:
      Pre-1987 models .... 0.08 to 0.15 mm
      1987 models onward .... 0.03 to 0.10 mm
   TU series (aluminium block) engines .... 0.03 to 0.10 mm
Maximum difference between any two liners:
   XV, XW and XY series engines with paper type base seals .... 0.04 mm
   All other engines .... 0.05 mm
*These are suggested figures, typical for this type of engine - no exact values are stated by Peugeot.

Pistons

Piston to bore clearance:
   XV, XW, and XY series engines .... 0.07 to 0.09 mm
   XU series engines .... Not available
   TU series engines .... 0.03 to 0.05 mm

Piston rings

End gaps* .... 0.3 to 0.5 mm
*These are suggested figures, typical for this type of engine - no exact values are stated by Peugeot.

Crankshaft

Endfloat:
   XV, XW and XY series engines .... 0.07 to 0.27 mm
   All other engines .... 0.07 to 0.32 mm
Main bearing journal diameter:
   XV, XW and XY series engines:
      Standard .... 49.965 to 49.981 mm
      Undersize .... 49.665 to 49.681 mm
   XU series engines:
      Standard .... 59.981 to 60.000 mm
      Undersize .... 59.681 to 59.700 mm
   TU series engines:
      Standard .... 49.965 to 49.981 mm
      Undersize .... 49.665 to 49.681 mm

Big-end bearing journal diameter:
   XV, XW and XY series engines:
      Standard . . . . 44.975 to 44.991 mm
      Undersize . . . . 44.675 to 44.691 mm
   XU5 series engines:
      Standard . . . . 44.971 to 44.990 mm
      Undersize . . . . 44.671 to 44.690 mm
   XU9 series engines:
      Standard . . . . 49.680 to 50.000 mm
      Undersize . . . . 49.380 to 49.700 mm
   TU9 series engines:
      Standard . . . . 37.992 to 38.008 mm
      Undersize . . . . 37.692 to 37.708 mm
   TU1 and TU3 series engines:
      Standard . . . . 44.975 to 44.991 mm
      Undersize . . . . 44.675 to 44.691 mm
Maximum bearing journal out-of-round (all models) . . . . 0.007 mm
Main bearing running clearance:
   XV, XW and XY series engines* . . . . 0.023 to 0.048 mm
   XU series engines:**
      Models up to mid-1994 . . . . 0.034 to 0.075 mm
      Mid-1994 onwards models . . . . 0.025 to 0.062 mm
   TU series (aluminium block) engines:**
      Models up to mid-1993 . . . . 0.023 to 0.083 mm
      Mid-1993 onwards models . . . . 0.010 to 0.034 mm
   TU series (cast-iron block) engines . . . . 0.023 to 0.048 mm
Big-end bearing running clearance - all models* . . . . 0.025 to 0.050 mm

*These are suggested figures, typical for this type of engine - no exact values are stated by Peugeot.
**On XU series engines and TU series (aluminium block) engines the bearing clearance was modified on later models - see text for further information.

Torque wrench settings

	Nm	lbf ft
XV, XW and XY series engines		
Main bearing (crankcase housing) bolts:		
Stage 1	36	27
Stage 2	51	38
Big-end cap nuts	36	27
Engine/transmission connecting bolts	9	7
Engine mounting nuts	34	25
XU series engines		
Main bearing cap nuts and bolts	49	36
Main bearing cap side bolts	24	18
Big-end cap nuts:		
Stage 1	40	30
Fully slacken all nuts, then tighten to:		
Stage 2	20	15
Stage 3	Tighten through a further 70°	
Oil seal carrier plate bolts	15	11
Oil pressure switch	24	18
Engine-to-transmission bolts	45	33
Engine mounting bracket bolts:		
M8	34	25
M10	45	33
Engine mountings:		
RH nut	27	20
LH nut	35	26
Battery tray/bracket	18	13
Lower mounting centre bolt	34	25
Lower mounting to subframe	45	33
TU series engines		
Big-end bearing cap	37.5	28
Main bearing ladder casting - aluminium block engines (models with plain No 5 main bearing half-shell fitted to cylinder block - see text):		
11 mm bolts:		
Stage 1	20	15
Stage 2	Tighten through a further 45°	
6 mm bolts	8	6

2D

Torque wrench settings (continued)

	Nm	lbf ft
Main bearing ladder casting - aluminium block engines (models with grooved No 5 main bearing half-shell fitted to cylinder block - see text):		
11 mm bolts:		
Stage 1	20	15
Stage 2	Tighten through a further 55°	
Fully slacken bolt, then tighten to:		
Stage 3	20	15
Stage 4	Tighten through a further 45°	
6 mm bolts	8	6
Main bearing cap bolts (cast-iron block engine):		
Stage 1	20	15
Stage 2	Tighten through a further 45°	
Oil pressure switch	28	21
Engine-to-transmission bolts	35	26
Engine/transmission left-hand mounting:		
Mounting bracket-to-transmission nuts	20	15
Mounting bracket-to-body bolts	25	18
Mounting rubber nuts	20	15
Centre nut	65	48
Engine/transmission rear mounting:		
Mounting-to-cylinder block bolts	40	30
Mounting link-to-mounting bolt	70	52
Mounting link-to-body bolt	50	37
Engine/transmission right-hand mounting bracket nuts	45	33

1 General information

Included in this Part of Chapter 2 are details of removing the engine/transmission from the car and general overhaul procedures for the cylinder head, cylinder block/crankcase and all other engine internal components.

The information given ranges from advice concerning preparation for an overhaul and the purchase of replacement parts, to detailed step-by-step procedures covering removal, inspection, renovation and refitting of engine internal components.

After Section 5, all instructions are based on the assumption that the engine has been removed from the car. For information concerning in-car engine repair, as well as the removal and refitting of those external components necessary for full overhaul, refer to Part A, B or C of this Chapter (as applicable) and to Section 5. Ignore any preliminary dismantling operations described in Part A, B or C that are no longer relevant once the engine has been removed from the car.

2 Engine/transmission removal - preparation and precautions

If you have decided that an engine must be removed for overhaul or major repair work, several preliminary steps should be taken.

Locating a suitable place to work is extremely important. Adequate work space, along with storage space for the car, will be needed. If a workshop or garage is not available, at the very least, a flat, level, clean work surface is required.

If possible, clear some shelving close to the work area and use it to store the engine components and ancillaries as they are removed and dismantled. In this manner the components stand a better chance of staying clean and undamaged during the overhaul. Laying out components in groups together with their fixing bolts, screws etc will save time and avoid confusion when the engine is refitted.

Clean the engine compartment and engine/transmission before beginning the removal procedure; this will help visibility and help to keep tools clean.

The help of an assistant should be available; there are certain instances when one person cannot safely perform all of the operations required to remove the engine from the vehicle. Safety is of primary importance, considering the potential hazards involved in this kind of operation. A second person should always be in attendance to offer help in an emergency. If this is the first time you have removed an engine, advice and aid from someone more experienced would also be beneficial.

Plan the operation ahead of time. Before starting work, obtain (or arrange for the hire of) all of the tools and equipment you will need. Access to the following items will allow the task of removing and refitting the engine/transmission to be completed safely and with relative ease: an engine hoist - rated in excess of the combined weight of the engine/transmission, a heavy-duty trolley jack, complete sets of spanners and sockets as described at the rear this manual, wooden blocks, and plenty of rags and cleaning solvent for mopping up spilled oil, coolant and fuel. A selection of different sized plastic storage bins will also prove useful for keeping dismantled components grouped together. If any of the equipment must be hired, make sure that you arrange for it in advance, and perform all of the operations possible without it beforehand; this may save you time and money.

Plan on the vehicle being out of use for quite a while, especially if you intend to carry out an engine overhaul. Read through the whole of this Section and work out a strategy based on your own experience and the tools, time and workspace available to you. Some of the overhaul processes may have to be carried out by a Peugeot dealer or an engineering works - these establishments often have busy schedules, so it would be prudent to consult them before removing or dismantling the engine, to get an idea of the amount of time required to carry out the work.

When removing the engine from the vehicle, be methodical about the disconnection of external components. Labelling cables and hoses as they removed will greatly assist the refitting process.

Always be extremely careful when lifting the engine/transmission assembly from the engine bay. Serious injury can result from careless actions. If help is required, it is better to wait until it is available rather than risk personal injury and/or damage to components by continuing alone. By planning ahead and taking your time, a job of this nature, although major, can be accomplished successfully and without incident.

On all models covered by this manual, the engine and transmission are removed as a complete assembly, upwards and out of the engine bay. The engine and transmission are then separated with the assembly on the bench.

3 Engine/manual transmission - removal, separation, reconnection and refitting

Removal

Note: *The engine can be removed from the car only as a complete unit with the transmission; the two are then separated for overhaul.*

1 Park the vehicle on firm, level ground. Chock the rear wheels, then firmly apply the handbrake. Jack up the front of the vehicle, and securely support it on axle stands (see *"Jacking and vehicle support"*). Remove the front roadwheels.

2 Set the bonnet in the upright position, and remove the battery and tray as described in Chapter 5A.

3 Remove the complete air cleaner assembly and all inlet ducting, as described in the relevant Part of Chapter 4.

4 If the engine is to be dismantled, working as described in Chapter 1, first drain the oil and remove the oil filter. Clean and refit the drain plug, tightening it securely.

5 On XU and TU series engines, drain the transmission oil as described in Chapter 7A. Refit the drain and filler plugs (as applicable), and tighten them to their specified torque settings.

6 Remove the alternator as described in Chapter 5A.

7 Where applicable, remove the power steering pump as described in Chapter 10. Where possible, unbolt the pump and move it aside without disconnecting the fluid hoses.

8 On models with air conditioning, unbolt the compressor, and position it clear of the engine. Support the weight of the compressor by tying it to the vehicle body, to prevent any excess strain being placed on the compressor lines whilst the engine is removed. Do not disconnect the refrigerant lines from the compressor (refer to the warnings given in Chapter 3).

9 Drain the cooling system as described in Chapter 1 then remove the radiator as described in Chapter 3. Note that it is not strictly necessary to remove the radiator, but it does improve clearance, and removes the risk of damaging the radiator as the engine is removed. If the radiator is to be left in position, disconnect the top and bottom radiator hoses at both ends and remove them completely. It is also a good idea to place a sheet of cardboard (or preferably plywood) between the engine and radiator as protection against any accidental contact.

10 On carburettor models, carry out the following operations, using the information given in the relevant Part of Chapter 4:
a) *Disconnect the fuel feed and return hoses.*
b) *Disconnect the throttle and where applicable the choke cables from the carburettor.*
c) *Where fitted, disconnect the braking system servo vacuum hose from the inlet manifold.*

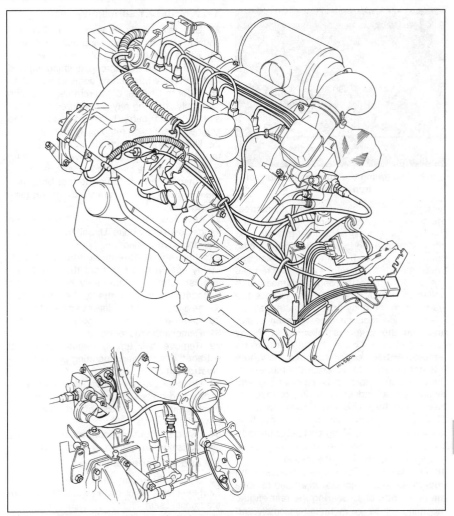

3.16 Typical engine wiring harness connections (XU series fuel injected engine shown)

d) *Disconnect the exhaust system downpipe from the exhaust manifold and remove the support brackets or clamps securing it to the engine or transmission.*

11 On fuel injection models, carry out the following operations, using the information given in the relevant Part of Chapter 4:
a) *Depressurise the fuel system, and disconnect the fuel feed and return hoses.*
b) *Disconnect the throttle cable.*
c) *Disconnect the fuel system wiring connectors.*
d) *Disconnect all vacuum hoses from the inlet manifold.*
e) *Disconnect the exhaust system downpipe from the exhaust manifold and remove the support brackets or clamps securing it to the engine or transmission.*

12 Referring to Chapter 3, release the retaining clip and disconnect the heater matrix hoses from their connection on the engine compartment bulkhead.

13 Working as described in Chapter 6, disconnect the clutch cable from the transmission, and position it clear of the working area.

14 Carry out the following operations, using the information given in Chapter 7A:
a) *Disconnect the gearchange selector rod/link rods (as applicable) from the transmission.*
b) *Disconnect the speedometer cable from the speedometer drive.*
c) *Where applicable, release the power steering pipe from the underside of the transmission.*
d) *Disconnect the wiring connector(s) from the reversing light switch and speedometer drive (as applicable).*

15 Remove both driveshafts as described in Chapter 8.

16 On some models it will be possible to remove the engine/transmission complete with the engine wiring harness left in position. This saves having to disconnect each individual wire from its relevant connection and its retaining clips. Unfortunately this will not be possible on all models, but where it is, trace the wiring harness back from the engine to the wiring connector(s) in the front, left-hand corner of the engine compartment **(see illustration)**. Release the locking ring(s) by

2D

3.21 Removing the engine and manual transmission

twisting them anti-clockwise and disconnect the connectors. Also, where applicable, trace the harness lead(s) back to the relay box, situated beside the battery. Unclip the wiring connector plate from the front of the relay box cover, then undo the retaining nut and remove the cover. Lift up the engine harness lead cover; then undo the nut(s) and release the lead(s) from the relay box. Check that all the relevant connectors have been disconnected, and that the wiring is released from any relevant clips or ties, so that it is free to be removed with the engine/transmission. Where it is not possible to separate the harness at the main connectors, make careful notes and disconnect all individual wiring connectors attached to the engine and transmission.

17 Manoeuvre the engine hoist into position, and attach it to the lifting brackets bolted to the engine. Raise the hoist until it is supporting the weight of the engine.

18 On XU and TU series engines from underneath the vehicle, slacken and remove the nuts and bolts securing the rear engine mounting link to the mounting assembly and subframe, and remove the link. On all models, undo the nuts/bolts securing the left-hand and right-hand engine mounting brackets to the engine and mountings, and remove the brackets and mountings as necessary.

19 Make a final check that any components which would prevent the removal of the engine/transmission from the car have been removed or disconnected. Ensure that components such as the gearchange selector rod are secured so that they cannot be damaged on removal.

20 Slowly and methodically lift the engine/transmission out of the car, ensuring that nothing is trapped or damaged. Enlist the help of an assistant during this procedure, as it will be necessary to tilt the assembly slightly to clear the body panels.

21 Once the engine is high enough, lift it out over the front of the body, and lower the unit to the ground **(see illustration)**.

Separation

22 With the engine/transmission assembly removed, support the assembly on suitable blocks of wood, on a workbench (or failing that, on a clean area of the workshop floor).

XV, XW and XY series engines

23 Unscrew and remove the flywheel housing-to-engine connecting bolts and nuts.

24 There are thirteen bolts and two nuts altogether. Note that an engine lifting lug and earth strap are fitted under some of the bolts.

25 Refer to Chapter 6 and remove the clutch assembly, ignoring any procedures that have already been carried out as part of the engine/transmission removal sequence.

26 Unbolt and remove the flywheel (Chapter 2A), then slacken and remove the retaining bolts, and remove the starter motor.

27 Unscrew and remove the two bolts and the nut close to the crankshaft oil seal **(see illustration)**.

28 Unscrew the engine-to-transmission flange connecting bolts. Unbolt the right-hand rear engine mounting.

29 Unscrew and remove the crankshaft pulley nut. In order to hold the crankshaft against rotation, temporarily screw in two bolts into the holes in the flywheel mounting flange and place a long lever between them.

30 Remove the crankshaft pulley.

31 Remove the rocker cover.

32 Remove the timing chain cover and extract the fuel pump operating plunger **(see illustration)**.

33 Unscrew and remove the remaining connecting bolts and nuts which are located on the final drive casing side near the driveshaft oil seals.

34 Using a length of wood, prise the engine and transmission apart **(see illustration)**.

XU and TU series engines

35 Undo the retaining bolts, and remove the flywheel lower cover plate (where fitted) from the transmission.

36 Slacken and remove the retaining bolts, and remove the starter motor from the transmission.

37 Ensure that both engine and transmission are adequately supported, then slacken and remove the remaining bolts securing the transmission housing to the engine. Note the correct fitted positions of each bolt (and the relevant brackets) as they are removed, to use as a reference on refitting.

38 Carefully withdraw the transmission from the engine, ensuring that the weight of the

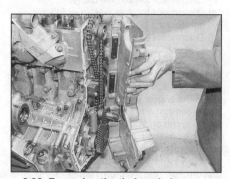

3.32 Removing the timing chain cover

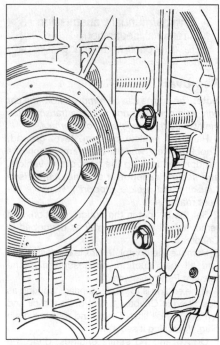

3.27 Remove the two bolts and nut close to the crankshaft oil seal - XV, XW and XY series engines

transmission is not allowed to hang on the input shaft while it is engaged with the clutch friction plate.

39 If they are loose, remove the locating dowels from the engine or transmission, and keep them in a safe place.

Reconnection

XV, XW and XY series engines

40 If removed, check that the oil pump pick-up strainer is in position within the transmission casing.

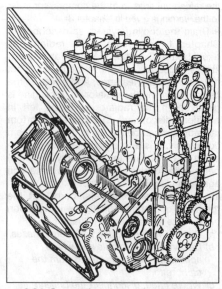

3.34 Separating the engine from the transmission

3.45 Locate a new O-ring oil seal on the transmission casing

41 Fit the sump cover to the transmission using a new gasket.

42 Tighten the tighten the cover bolts and drain plug to the specified torque.

43 Fit the protective cover plate to the sump cover.

44 Apply jointing compound to the mating surfaces on the engine and transmission.

45 On the transmission, locate a new O-ring seal and check that the locating dowels and the studs are in position **(see illustration)**.

46 Offer the transmission to the engine, screw in the connecting bolts and nuts and tighten to the specified torque.

47 With the fuel pump operating rod in place, locate the timing chain cover using a new gasket. The bolt nearest the coolant pump pulley must be located in the cover before offering it up, otherwise the pulley will prevent the bolt entering its cover hole. Use the crankshaft pulley to centralise the timing chain cover and refit the remaining cover bolts. Note that the coolant hose safety rod must be fitted under its cover bolts. This rod prevents the coolant hose being cut by the rim of the coolant pump pulley should the hose sag.

48 Tighten the timing chain cover bolts to the specified torque and then trim the upper ends of the gasket flush. Fit the rocker cover using a new gasket. Do not overtighten the securing bolts.

49 Tighten the crankshaft pulley nut to the specified torque.

50 Refit the flywheel (Chapter 2A) and the clutch and transfer gear assembly (Chapter 6).

51 If they were removed, bolt the engine mountings to the flywheel housing.

52 Fit the starter motor. Tighten the bolts and nuts in the following order:
   a) *Starter drive end flange to flywheel housing*
   b) *Brush end bracket to engine crankcase*
   c) *Brush end bracket to starter motor*

XU and TU series engines

53 Apply a smear of high-melting-point grease (Peugeot recommend the use of Molykote BR2 plus - available from your Peugeot dealer) to the splines of the transmission input shaft. Do not apply too much, otherwise there is a possibility of the grease contaminating the clutch friction plate.

54 Ensure that the locating dowels are correctly positioned in the engine or transmission.

55 Carefully offer the transmission to the engine, until the locating dowels are engaged. Ensure that the weight of the transmission is not allowed to hang on the input shaft as it is engaged with the clutch friction disc.

56 Refit the transmission housing-to-engine bolts, ensuring that all the necessary brackets are correctly positioned, and tighten them securely.

57 Refit the starter motor, and securely tighten its retaining bolts.

58 Where necessary, refit the lower flywheel cover plate to the transmission, and securely tighten its retaining bolts.

Refitting

59 Reconnect the hoist and lifting tackle to the engine lifting brackets. With the aid of an assistant, lift the assembly over the engine compartment.

60 The assembly should be tilted as necessary to clear the surrounding components, as during removal; lower the assembly into position in the engine compartment, manipulating the hoist and lifting tackle as necessary.

61 With the engine/transmission in position, and centralised over its mountings, refit the engine/transmission mountings using a reverse of the removal operations, but only tighten the mounting nuts/bolts finger tight at this stage.

62 Where applicable, from underneath the vehicle, refit the rear mounting link and install both its bolts.

63 Rock the engine to settle it on its mountings, then go around and tighten all the mounting nuts and bolts to their specified torque settings. The hoist can then be detached from the engine and removed.

64 The remainder of the refitting procedure is a direct reversal of the removal sequence, noting the following points:
   a) *Ensure that the wiring loom is correctly routed and retained by all the relevant retaining clips; all connectors should be correctly and securely reconnected.*
   b) *Prior to refitting the driveshafts to the transmission, renew the driveshaft oil seals as described in Chapter 7A.*
   c) *Ensure that all coolant hoses are correctly reconnected, and securely retained by their retaining clips.*
   d) *Reconnect the clutch cable as described in Chapter 6.*
   e) *Adjust the choke cable and/or throttle cable (as applicable) as described in the relevant Part of Chapter 4.*
   f) *Refill the engine and transmission with the correct quantity and type of lubricant, as described in Chapter 1 and 7A.*
   g) *Refill the cooling system as described in Chapter 1.*

4 Engine/automatic transmission - removal, separation, reconnection and refitting

Removal

Note: *The engine can be removed from the car only as a complete unit with the transmission; the two are then separated for overhaul.*

1 Carry out the operations described in paragraphs 1 to 12 of Section 3, noting that the transmission oil draining procedure is given in Chapter 1.

2 Carry out the following operations, using the information given in Chapter 7B:
   a) *Remove the transmission dipstick tube.*
   b) *Disconnect the wiring from the starter inhibitor/reversing light switch and the speedometer drive housing. Release the earth strap(s) from the top of the transmission housing.*
   c) *Disconnect the selector cable.*
   d) *Release the power steering pipe from the transmission.*
   e) *Disconnect the speedometer cable.*

3 Remove the engine/transmission as described in paragraphs 15 to 21 of Section 3.

Separation

4 With the engine/transmission assembly removed, support the assembly on suitable blocks of wood, on a workbench (or failing that, on a clean area of the workshop floor).

5 Detach the kickdown cable from the throttle cam. Work back along the cable, freeing it from any retaining clips, and noting its correct routing.

6 Undo the retaining bolts and remove the driveplate lower cover plate from the transmission, to gain access to the torque converter retaining bolts. Slacken and remove the visible bolt. Rotate the crankshaft using a socket and extension bar on the pulley bolt, and undo the remaining bolts securing the torque converter to the driveplate as they become accessible.

7 Slacken and remove the retaining bolts, and remove the starter motor from the transmission.

8 To ensure that the torque converter does not fall out as the transmission is removed, secure it in position using a length of metal strip bolted to one of the starter motor bolt holes.

9 Ensure that both the engine and transmission are adequately supported, then slacken and remove the remaining bolts securing the transmission housing to the engine. Note the correct fitted positions of each bolt (and any relevant brackets) as they are removed, to use as a reference on refitting.

10 Carefully withdraw the transmission from the engine. If the locating dowels are a loose fit in the engine/transmission, remove them and keep them in a safe place.

2D

Reconnection

11 Ensure that the bush fitted to the centre of the crankshaft is in good condition. Apply a little Molykote G1 grease (available from your Peugeot dealer) to the torque converter centring pin. Do not apply too much, otherwise there is a possibility of the grease contaminating the torque converter.

12 Ensure that the locating dowels are correctly positioned in the engine or transmission.

13 Carefully offer the transmission to the engine, until the locating dowels are engaged.

14 Refit the transmission housing-to-engine bolts, ensuring that all the necessary brackets are correctly positioned, and tighten them to the specified torque setting.

15 Remove the torque converter retaining strap installed prior to removal. Align the torque converter threaded holes with the retaining plate, and refit the three retaining bolts.

16 Tighten the torque converter retaining bolts to the specified torque setting, then refit the driveplate lower cover.

17 Refit the starter motor, and securely tighten its retaining bolts.

Refitting

18 Refit the engine/transmission to the vehicle as described in paragraphs 59 to 63 of Section 3.

19 The remainder of the refitting procedure is a reversal of the removal sequence, noting the following points:

a) Ensure that the wiring loom is correctly routed, and retained by all the relevant retaining clips; all connectors should be correctly and securely reconnected.

b) Prior to refitting the driveshafts to the transmission, renew the driveshaft oil seals (see Chapter 7).

c) Ensure that all coolant hoses are correctly reconnected, and securely retained by their retaining clips.

d) Adjust the selector cable and kickdown cable as described in Chapter 7B.

e) Adjust the throttle cable as described in Chapter 4.

f) Refill the engine and transmission with correct quantity and type of lubricant, as described in Chapter 1.

g) Refill the cooling system as described in Chapter 1.

---

5 Engine overhaul - preliminary information

It is much easier to dismantle and work on the engine if it is mounted on a portable engine stand. These stands can often be hired from a tool hire shop. Before the engine is mounted on a stand, the flywheel/driveplate should be removed so that the stand bolts can be tightened into the end of the cylinder block/crankcase.

If a stand is not available, it is possible to dismantle the engine with it suitably supported on a sturdy, workbench or on the floor. Be careful not to tip or drop the engine when working without a stand.

If you intend to obtain a reconditioned engine, all ancillaries must be removed first, to be transferred to the replacement engine (just as they will if you are doing a complete engine overhaul yourself). These components include the following:

a) Alternator mounting brackets.

b) Engine mountings and brackets (Part A, B or C of this Chapter).

c) The ignition system and HT components including all sensors, distributor cap and rotor arm, ignition module, HT leads and spark plugs (Chapters 1 and 5).

d) Power steering pump and air conditioning compressor brackets (where fitted).

e) Thermostat and housing, coolant pump, coolant outlet chamber/elbow (Chapter 3).

f) Dipstick tube.

g) Carburettor/fuel system components (Chapter 4).

h) All electrical switches and sensors.

i) Inlet and exhaust manifolds (Chapter 4).

j) Oil filter (Chapter 1).

k) Fuel pump - carburettor engines only (Chapter 4).

l) Flywheel/driveplate (Part A, B or C of this Chapter).

Note: When removing the external components from the engine, pay close attention to details that may be helpful or important during refitting. Note the fitting positions of gaskets, seals, washers, bolts and other small items.

If you are obtaining a "short" engine (cylinder block/crankcase, crankshaft, pistons and connecting rods all assembled), then the cylinder head, timing chain/belt (together with tensioner, tensioner and idler pulleys and covers) sump and oil pump will have to be removed also.

If a complete overhaul is planned, the engine can be dismantled in the order given below, referring to Part A, B or C of this Chapter unless otherwise stated.

a) Inlet and exhaust manifolds (Chapter 4).

b) Timing chain, sprockets, tensioner and oil pump - XV, XW and XY series engines.

c) Timing belt, sprockets and tensioner - XU and TU series engines.

d) Cylinder head.

e) Flywheel/driveplate - XU and TU series engines.

f) Sump - XU and TU series engines.

g) Oil pump - XU and TU series engines.

h) Piston/connecting rod assemblies (Section 7).

i) Crankshaft (Section 8).

---

6 Cylinder head - dismantling, cleaning, inspection and reassembly

Note: New and reconditioned cylinder heads are available from the manufacturer, and from engine overhaul specialists. Be aware that some specialist tools are required for the dismantling and inspection procedures, and new components may not be readily available. It may therefore be more practical and economical for the home mechanic to purchase a reconditioned head, rather than dismantle, inspect and recondition the original head.

Dismantling

1 Remove the cylinder head as described in Part A, B or C of this Chapter (as applicable).

2 If not already done, remove the inlet and exhaust manifolds with reference to the relevant Part of Chapter 4.

3 Remove the camshaft, followers and shims (as applicable) as described in Part A, B or C of this Chapter.

4 Using a valve spring compressor, compress each valve spring in turn until the split collets can be removed. Release the compressor, and lift off the spring retainer, spring and spring seat. Using a pair of pliers, carefully extract the valve stem oil seal from the top of the guide **(see illustrations)**.

5 If, when the valve spring compressor is screwed down, the spring retainer refuses to free and expose the split collets, gently tap the top of the tool, directly over the retainer, with a light hammer. This will free the retainer.

6 Withdraw the valve through the combustion chamber **(see illustration)**.

6.4a Compress the valve spring with a compressor and remove the split collets . . .

6.4b . . . Release the compressor and remove the spring retainer . . .

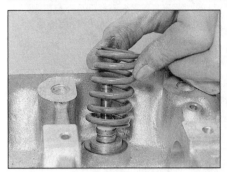

6.4c . . . spring . . .

6.4d . . . spring seat and valve stem oil seal

6.6 Withdraw the valve through the combustion chamber

7 It is essential that each valve is stored together with its collets, retainer, spring, and spring seat. The valves should also be kept in their correct sequence, unless they are so badly worn that they are to be renewed. If they are going to be kept and used again, place each valve assembly in a labelled polythene bag or similar small container **(see illustration)**. Note that No 1 valve is nearest to the transmission (flywheel/driveplate) end of the engine.

Cleaning

8 Thoroughly clean all traces of old gasket material and sealing compound from the cylinder head upper and lower mating surfaces. Use a suitable cleaning agent together with a soft putty knife; do not use a metal scraper or the faces will be damaged.

9 Remove the carbon from the combustion chambers and ports, then clean all traces of oil and other deposits from the cylinder head, paying particular attention to the bearing journals, cam follower bores (where applicable), valve guides and oilways.

10 Wash the head thoroughly with paraffin or a suitable solvent. Take plenty of time and do a thorough job. Be sure to clean all oil holes and galleries very thoroughly, dry the head completely and coat all machined surfaces with light oil.

11 Scrape off any heavy carbon deposits that may have formed on the valves, then use a power-operated wire brush to remove deposits from the valve heads and stems.

Inspection

Note: *Be sure to perform all the following inspection procedures before concluding that*

the services of an engineering works are required. Make a list of all items that require attention.

Cylinder head

12 Inspect the head very carefully for cracks, evidence of coolant leakage, and other damage. If cracks are found, a new cylinder head should be obtained.

13 Use a straight-edge and feeler blade to check that the cylinder head gasket surface is not distorted. If it is, it may be possible to have it machined. Seek the advice of a Peugeot dealer or engine overhaul specialist if distortion is suspected.

14 Examine the valve seats in each of the combustion chambers. If they are severely pitted, cracked, or burned, they will need to be renewed or re-cut by an engine overhaul specialist. If they are only slightly pitted, this can be removed by grinding-in the valve heads and seats with fine valve-grinding compound, as described below.

15 Check the valve guides for wear by inserting the relevant valve, and checking for side-to-side motion of the valve. A very small amount of movement is acceptable. If the movement seems excessive, remove the valve. Measure the valve stem diameter (see below), and renew the valve if it is worn. If the valve stem is not worn, the wear must be in the valve guide, and the guide must be renewed. The renewal of valve guides is best carried out by a Peugeot dealer or engine overhaul specialist, who will have the necessary tools available.

16 If renewing the valve guides, the valve seats should be re-cut or re-ground only *after* the guides have been fitted.

Valves

17 Examine the head of each valve for pitting, burning, cracks, and general wear. Check the valve stem for scoring and wear ridges. Rotate the valve, and check for any obvious indication that it is bent. Look for pits or excessive wear on the tip of each valve stem. Renew any valve that shows any such signs of wear or damage.

18 If the valve appears satisfactory at this stage, measure the valve stem diameter at several points using a micrometer **(see illustration)**. Any significant difference in the readings obtained indicates wear of the valve stem. Should any of these conditions be apparent, the valve(s) must be renewed.

19 If the valves are in satisfactory condition, they should be ground (lapped) into their respective seats, to ensure a smooth, gas-tight seal. If the seat is only lightly pitted, or if it has been re-cut, fine grinding compound *only* should be used to produce the required finish. Coarse valve-grinding compound should *not* be used, unless a seat is badly burned or deeply pitted. If this is the case, the cylinder head and valves should be inspected by an expert, to decide whether seat re-cutting, or even the renewal of the valve or seat insert (where possible) is required.

20 Valve grinding is carried out as follows. Place the cylinder head upside-down on a bench.

21 Smear a trace of (the appropriate grade of) valve-grinding compound on the seat face, and press a suction grinding tool onto the valve head **(see illustration)**. With a semi-rotary action, grind the valve head to its seat,

6.7 Place each valve and its associated components in a labelled polythene bag

6.18 Measuring the valve stem diameter

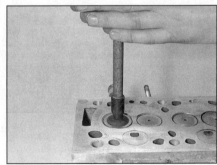

6.21 Grinding-in a valve

2D

lifting the valve occasionally to redistribute the grinding compound. A light spring placed under the valve head will greatly ease this operation.

22 If coarse grinding compound is being used, work only until a dull, matt even surface is produced on both the valve seat and the valve, then wipe off the used compound, and repeat the process with fine compound. When a smooth unbroken ring of light grey matt finish is produced on both the valve and seat, the grinding operation is complete. *Do not* grind-in the valves any further than absolutely necessary, or the seat will be prematurely sunk into the cylinder head.

23 When all the valves have been ground-in, carefully wash off *all* traces of grinding compound using paraffin or a suitable solvent, before reassembling the cylinder head.

Valve components

24 Examine the valve springs for signs of damage and discoloration. No minimum free length is specified by Peugeot, so the only way of judging valve spring wear is by comparison with a new component.

25 Stand each spring on a flat surface, and check it for squareness. If any of the springs are damaged, distorted or have lost their tension, obtain a complete new set of springs. It is normal to renew the valve springs as a matter of course if a major overhaul is being carried out.

26 Renew the valve stem oil seals regardless of their apparent condition.

Reassembly

27 Lubricate the stems of the valves, and insert the valves into their original locations **(see illustration)**. If new valves are being fitted, insert them into the locations to which they have been ground.

28 Refit the spring seat then, working on the first valve, dip the new valve stem seal in fresh engine oil. Carefully locate it over the valve and onto the guide. Take care not to damage the seal as it is passed over the valve stem. Use a suitable socket or metal tube to press the seal firmly onto the guide **(see illustration)**.

29 Locate the valve spring on top of its seat, then refit the spring retainer.

6.27 Lubricate the valve stems prior to refitting

30 Compress the valve spring, and locate the split collets in the recess in the valve stem. Release the compressor, then repeat the procedure on the remaining valves.

 HAYNES HiNT *Use a little dab of grease to hold the collets in position on the valve stem while the spring compressor is released.*

31 With all the valves installed, place the cylinder head face down on blocks on the bench and, using a hammer and interposed block of wood, tap the end of each valve stem to settle the components.

32 Refit the camshaft, followers and shims (as applicable) as described in Part A, B or C of this Chapter.

33 The cylinder head can then be refitted as described in Part A, B or C of this Chapter.

7 Piston/connecting rod assembly - removal and inspection

Removal

XV, XW and XY series engines

1 With the cylinder head removed, unscrew and remove the bolts which hold the crankcase half sections together. Split the crankcase and keep the main bearing shells with their crankcase web recesses if the shells are to be used again **(see illustration)**.

6.28 Fitting a valve stem oil seal using a socket

2 Remove the crankshaft oil seal.

3 Mark the rim of the cylinder liners in respect of their position and orientation in the block. Note that No 1 cylinder liner is at the transmission (flywheel) end of the engine.

4 Mark the big-end caps and the connecting rods so that they can be refitted in their original sequence and the correct way round. A centre punch or hacksaw blade is useful for this purpose.

5 Unscrew the big-end nuts and remove the caps **(see illustration)**. If the bearing shells are to be used again, keep them taped to their respective cap.

6 Using a hammer handle, push the piston up through the bore, and remove it from the top of the cylinder liner. Recover the bearing shell, and tape it to the connecting rod for safe-keeping.

7 Loosely refit the big-end cap to the connecting rod, and secure with the nuts - this will help to keep the components in their correct order.

XU and TU series engines

8 Remove the cylinder head, sump and oil pump as described in Part B or C of this Chapter (as applicable).

9 Using a hammer and centre-punch, paint or similar, mark each connecting rod and big-end bearing cap with its respective cylinder number on the flat machined surface provided; if the engine has been dismantled before, note carefully any identifying marks made previously **(see illustration)**. Note that No 1 cylinder is at the transmission (flywheel) end of the engine.

7.1 Undo the bolts and split the crankcase half sections - XV, XW and XY series engines

7.5 Remove the big-end bearing caps

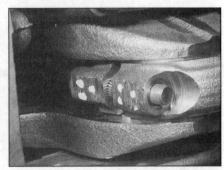

7.9 Marks made on connecting rod and bearing cap - XU and TU series engines

10 Turn the crankshaft to bring pistons 1 and 4 to BDC (bottom dead centre).

11 Unscrew the nuts from No 1 piston big-end bearing cap. Take off the cap, and recover the bottom half bearing shell **(see illustration)**. If the bearing shells are to be re-used, tape the cap and the shell together.

12 To prevent the possibility of damage to the crankshaft bearing journals, tape over the connecting rod stud threads.

13 Using a hammer handle, push the piston up through the bore, and remove it from the top of the cylinder block/liner. Recover the bearing shell, and tape it to the connecting rod for safe-keeping.

14 Loosely refit the big-end cap to the connecting rod, and secure with the nuts - this will help to keep the components in their correct order.

15 Remove No 4 piston assembly in the same way.

16 Turn the crankshaft through 180° to bring pistons 2 and 3 to BDC (bottom dead centre), and remove them in the same way.

Inspection

17 Before the inspection process can begin, the piston/connecting rod assemblies must be cleaned, and the original piston rings removed from the pistons.

18 Carefully expand the old rings over the top of the pistons. The use of two or three old feeler blades will be helpful in preventing the rings dropping into empty grooves **(see illustration)**. Be careful not to scratch the piston with the ends of the ring. The rings are brittle, and will snap if they are spread too far. They are also very sharp - protect your hands and fingers. Note that the third ring may incorporate an expander. Always remove the rings from the top of the piston. Keep each set of rings with its piston if the old rings are to be re-used.

19 Scrape away all traces of carbon from the top of the piston. A hand-held wire brush (or a piece of fine emery cloth) can be used, once the majority of the deposits have been scraped away.

20 Remove the carbon from the ring grooves in the piston, using an old ring. Break the ring in half to do this (be careful not to cut your fingers - piston rings are sharp). Be careful to remove only the carbon deposits - do not remove any metal, and do not nick or scratch the sides of the ring grooves.

21 Once the deposits have been removed, clean the piston/connecting rod assembly with paraffin or a suitable solvent, and dry thoroughly. Make sure that the oil return holes in the ring grooves are clear.

22 If the pistons and cylinder liners/bores are not damaged or worn excessively, the original pistons can be refitted. Normal piston wear shows up as even vertical wear on the piston thrust surfaces, and slight looseness of the top ring in its groove. New piston rings should always be used when the engine is reassembled.

7.11 Removing a big-end bearing cap and shell

23 Carefully inspect each piston for cracks around the skirt, around the gudgeon pin holes, and at the piston ring "lands" (between the ring grooves).

24 Look for scoring and scuffing on the piston skirt, holes in the piston crown, and burned areas at the edge of the crown. If the skirt is scored or scuffed, the engine may have been suffering from overheating, and/or abnormal combustion which caused excessively high operating temperatures. The cooling and lubrication systems should be checked thoroughly. Scorch marks on the sides of the pistons show that blow-by has occurred. A hole in the piston crown, or burned areas at the edge of the piston crown, indicates that abnormal combustion (pre-ignition, knocking, or detonation) has been occurring. If any of the above problems exist, the causes must be investigated and corrected, or the damage will occur again. The causes may include incorrect ignition timing, or a carburettor or fuel injection system fault.

25 Corrosion of the piston, in the form of pitting, indicates that coolant has been leaking into the combustion chamber and/or the crankcase. Again, the cause must be corrected, or the problem may persist in the rebuilt engine.

26 On aluminium-block engines with wet liners, it is not possible to renew the pistons separately; pistons are only supplied with piston rings and a liner, as part of a matched assembly (see Section 9). On cast-iron block engines, pistons can be purchased from a Peugeot dealer.

27 Examine each connecting rod carefully for signs of damage, such as cracks around the big-end and small-end bearings. Check that the rod is not bent or distorted. Damage is highly unlikely, unless the engine has been seized or badly overheated. Detailed checking of the connecting rod assembly can only be carried out by a Peugeot dealer or engine repair specialist with the necessary equipment.

28 On XU series engines, due to the tightening procedure for the connecting rod big-end cap retaining nuts, it is highly recommended that the big-end cap nuts and bolts are renewed as a complete set prior to refitting.

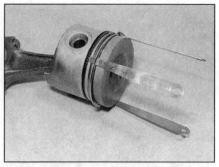

7.18 Using old feeler blades to assist removal of the piston rings

29 On all engines, the gudgeon pins are an interference fit in the connecting rod small-end bearing. Therefore, piston and/or connecting rod renewal should be entrusted to a Peugeot dealer or engine repair specialist, who will have the necessary tooling to remove and install the gudgeon pins.

8 Crankshaft - removal and inspection

Removal

Note: *If no work is to be done on the pistons and connecting rods, then removal of the cylinder head and pistons will not be necessary. Instead, the pistons need only be pushed far enough up the bores so that they are positioned clear of the crankpins.*

1 With reference to Part A, B or C of this Chapter, and earlier Sections of this Part as applicable, carry out the following:
  a) *Separate the engine from the transmission.*
  b) *Remove the timing chain/belt and crankshaft sprocket.*
  c) *Remove the sump - XU and TU series engines.*
  d) *Remove the oil pump.*
  e) *Remove the clutch components and flywheel/driveplate.*

XV, XW and XY series engines

2 Unscrew and remove the bolts which hold the crankcase half sections together. Split the crankcase and keep the main bearing shells with their crankcase web recesses if the shells are to be used again.

3 Remove the crankshaft oil seal.

4 If the piston/connecting rod assemblies are to be left in place, mark the big-end caps and the connecting rods so that they can be refitted in their original sequence and the correct way round. Note that No 1 cylinder liner is at the transmission (flywheel) end of the engine.

5 Unscrew the big-end nuts and remove the caps and lower big-end bearing shells.

6 Before removing the crankshaft it is advisable to check the endfloat using a dial gauge in contact with the end of the crankshaft. Push the crankshaft fully one way,

2D

8.7 Checking crankshaft endfloat using feeler blades

8.11 Removing the oil seal carrier from the front of the block - XU series engines

8.12a Slide off the oil pump drive sprocket . . .

and then zero the gauge. Push the crankshaft fully the other way, and check the endfloat. The result can be compared with the specified amount, and will give an indication as to whether new thrustwashers are required.

7 If a dial gauge is not available, feeler blades can be used. First push the crankshaft fully towards the flywheel end of the engine, then use feeler blades to measure the gap between the web of the crankpin and the thrustwasher **(see illustration)**.

8 Lift the crankshaft from its crankcase half section, keep the shell bearings in their original web recesses if they are to be used again and retrieve the semi-circular thrust-washers from either side of No 2 bearing web.

9 Loosely refit the big-end caps to the connecting rods, and secure with the nuts - this will help to keep the components in their correct order.

XU series engines

10 Remove the pistons and connecting rods as described in Section 7. (Refer to the Note at the beginning of this Section).

11 Slacken and remove the retaining bolts, and remove the oil seal carrier from the front (timing belt) end of the cylinder block, along with its gasket (where fitted) **(see illustration)**.

12 Remove the oil pump drive chain, and slide the drive sprocket and spacer (where fitted) off the end of the crankshaft. Remove the Woodruff key, and store it with the sprocket for safe-keeping **(see illustrations)**.

13 Before removing the crankshaft it is advisable to check the endfloat as described in paragraphs 6 and 7.

14 The main bearing caps should be numbered 1 to 5, starting from the transmission (flywheel/driveplate) end of the engine **(see illustration)**. If not, mark them accordingly using a centre-punch. Also note the correct fitted depth of the rear crankshaft oil seal in the bearing cap.

15 Undo the two bolts (one at the front of the block, and one at the rear) securing the centre main bearing cap to the block. Remove the bolts, along with their sealing washers.

16 Slacken and remove the main bearing cap retaining bolts/nuts, and lift off each bearing cap. Recover the lower bearing shells, and tape them to their respective caps for safe-keeping. Also recover the lower thrustwasher halves from the side of No 2 main bearing cap **(see illustration)**. Remove the rubber sealing strips from the sides of No 1 main bearing cap, and discard them.

17 Lift out the crankshaft, and discard the rear oil seal.

18 Recover the upper bearing shells from the cylinder block, and tape them to their respective caps for safe-keeping. Remove the upper thrustwasher halves from the side of No 2 main bearing, and store them with the lower halves.

TU series aluminium block engines

19 Remove the pistons and connecting rods as described in Section 7. (Refer to the Note at the beginning of this Section).

20 Before removing the crankshaft it is advisable to check the endfloat as described in paragraphs 6 and 7.

21 Work around the outside of the cylinder block, and unscrew all the small (6 mm) bolts securing the main bearing ladder to the base of the cylinder block. Note the correct fitted depth of both the left- and right-hand crankshaft oil seals in the cylinder block/main bearing ladder.

22 Working in a diagonal sequence, evenly and progressively slacken the ten large (11 mm) main bearing ladder retaining bolts by a turn at a time. Once all the bolts are loose, remove them from the ladder.

23 With all the retaining bolts removed, carefully lift the main bearing ladder casting away from the base of the cylinder block. Recover the lower main bearing shells, and tape them to their respective locations in the casting. If the two locating dowels are a loose fit, remove them and store them with the casting for safe-keeping.

24 Lift out the crankshaft, and discard both the oil seals. Remove the oil pump drive chain from the end of the crankshaft. Where necessary, slide off the drive sprocket, and recover the Woodruff key.

25 Recover the upper main bearing shells, and store them along with the relevant lower bearing shell. Also recover the two thrustwashers (one fitted either side of No 2 main bearing) from the cylinder block.

TU series cast-iron block engines

26 Remove the pistons and connecting rods as described in Section 7. (Refer to the Note at the beginning of this Section).

8.12b . . . and remove the Woodruff key

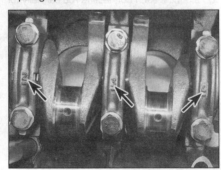

8.14 Main bearing cap identification markings (arrowed)

8.16 Removing the main bearing cap and thrustwashers (arrowed)

27 Before removing the crankshaft it is advisable to check the endfloat as described in paragraphs 6 and 7.

28 Unbolt and remove the crankshaft left- and right-hand oil seal housings from each end of the cylinder block, noting the correct fitted locations of the locating dowels. If the locating dowels are a loose fit, remove them and store them with the housings for safe-keeping.

29 Remove the oil pump drive chain, and slide the drive sprocket off the end of the crankshaft. Remove the Woodruff key, and store it with the sprocket for safe-keeping.

30 The main bearing caps should be numbered 1 to 5 from the transmission (flywheel) end of the engine. If not, mark them accordingly using a centre-punch or paint.

31 Unscrew and remove the main bearing cap retaining bolts, and withdraw the caps. Recover the lower main bearing shells, and tape them to their respective caps for safe-keeping.

32 Carefully lift out the crankshaft, taking care not to displace the upper main bearing shell.

33 Recover the upper bearing shells from the cylinder block, and tape them to their respective caps for safe-keeping. Remove the thrustwasher halves from the side of No 2 main bearing, and store them with the bearing cap.

Inspection

34 Clean the crankshaft using paraffin or a suitable solvent, and dry it, preferably with compressed air if available. Be sure to clean the oil holes with a pipe cleaner or similar probe, to ensure that they are not obstructed.

 Warning: Wear eye protection when using compressed air!

35 Check the main and big-end bearing journals for uneven wear, scoring, pitting and cracking.

36 Big-end bearing wear is accompanied by distinct metallic knocking when the engine is running (particularly noticeable when the engine is pulling from low speed) and some loss of oil pressure.

37 Main bearing wear is accompanied by severe engine vibration and rumble - getting progressively worse as engine speed increases - and again by loss of oil pressure.

38 Check the bearing journal for roughness by running a finger lightly over the bearing surface. Any roughness (which will be accompanied by obvious bearing wear) indicates that the crankshaft requires regrinding (where possible) or renewal.

39 If the crankshaft has been reground, check for burrs around the crankshaft oil holes (the holes are usually chamfered, so burrs should not be a problem unless regrinding has been carried out carelessly). Remove any burrs with a fine file or scraper, and thoroughly clean the oil holes as described previously.

8.40 Measuring a crankshaft big-end journal diameter

40 Using a micrometer, measure the diameter of the main and big-end bearing journals, and compare the results with the *Specifications* **(see illustration)**. By measuring the diameter at a number of points around each journal's circumference, you will be able to determine whether or not the journal is out-of-round. Take the measurement at each end of the journal, near the webs, to determine if the journal is tapered. Compare the results obtained with those given in the *Specifications*.

41 Check the oil seal contact surfaces at each end of the crankshaft for wear and damage. If the seal has worn a deep groove in the surface of the crankshaft, consult an engine overhaul specialist; repair may be possible, but otherwise a new crankshaft will be required.

42 At the time of writing, it was not clear whether Peugeot produce oversize bearing shells for all of these engines. On some engines, if the crankshaft journals have not already been reground, it may be possible to have the crankshaft reconditioned, and to fit oversize shells (see Section 13). If no oversize shells are available and the crankshaft has worn beyond the specified limits, it will have to be renewed. Consult your Peugeot dealer or engine specialist for further information on parts availability.

9 Cylinder block/crankcase - cleaning and inspection

Cleaning

1 Remove all external components and electrical switches/sensors from the block.

2 On aluminium block engines with wet liners, remove the liners as described in paragraph 11.

3 Scrape all traces of gasket from the cylinder block/crankcase, and from the main bearing ladder (where fitted), taking care not to damage the gasket/sealing surfaces.

4 Remove all oil gallery plugs (where fitted). The plugs are usually very tight - they may have to be drilled out, and the holes re-tapped. Use new plugs when the engine is reassembled.

5 If any of the castings are extremely dirty, all should be steam-cleaned.

6 After the castings are returned, clean all oil holes and oil galleries one more time. Flush all internal passages with warm water until the water runs clear. Dry thoroughly, and apply a light film of oil to all mating surfaces, to prevent rusting. On cast-iron block engines, also oil the cylinder bores. If you have access to compressed air, use it to speed up the drying process, and to blow out all the oil holes and galleries.

 Warning: Wear eye protection when using compressed air!

7 If the castings are not very dirty, you can do an adequate cleaning job with hot (as hot as you can stand!), soapy water and a stiff brush. Take plenty of time, and do a thorough job. Regardless of the cleaning method used, be sure to clean all oil holes and galleries very thoroughly, and to dry all components well. On cast-iron block engines, protect the cylinder bores as described above, to prevent rusting.

8 All threaded holes must be clean, to ensure accurate torque readings during reassembly. To clean the threads, run the correct-size tap into each of the holes to remove rust, corrosion, thread sealant or sludge, and to restore damaged threads **(see illustration)**. If possible, use compressed air to clear the holes of debris produced by this operation.

Warning: Wear eye protection when cleaning out these holes in this way!

9 Apply suitable sealant to the new oil gallery plugs, and insert them into the holes in the block. Tighten them securely.

10 If the engine is not going to be reassembled right away, cover it with a large plastic bag to keep it clean; protect all mating surfaces and the cylinder bores as described above, to prevent rusting.

Inspection (aluminium cylinder block with wet liners)

11 Remove the liner clamps (where used), then use a hard wood drift to tap out each liner from the inside of the cylinder block.

9.8 Cleaning a cylinder block threaded hole using a suitable tap

2D

9.11 Cylinder liner with paper base seal

When all the liners are released, tip the cylinder block/crankcase on its side and remove each liner from the top of the block. As each liner is removed, stick masking tape on its left-hand (transmission side) face, and write the cylinder number on the tape. No 1 cylinder is at the transmission (flywheel/driveplate) end of the engine. Remove the paper base seal or O-ring from the base of each liner, and discard **(see illustration)**.

12 Check each cylinder liner for scuffing and scoring. Check for signs of a wear ridge at the top of the liner, indicating that the bore is excessively worn.

13 If the necessary measuring equipment is available, measure the bore diameter of each cylinder liner at the top (just under the wear ridge), centre, and bottom of the cylinder bore, parallel to the crankshaft axis.

14 Next, measure the bore diameter at the same three locations, at right-angles to the crankshaft axis.

15 Repeat the procedure for the remaining cylinder liners.

16 If the liner wear is excessive at any point, or if the cylinder liner walls are badly scored or scuffed, then renewal of the relevant liner assembly will be necessary. If there is any doubt about the condition of the cylinder bores, seek the advice of a Peugeot dealer or engine reconditioning specialist.

17 If renewal is necessary, new liners, complete with pistons and piston rings, can be purchased from a Peugeot dealer. Note that it is not possible to buy liners individually - they are supplied only as a matched assembly complete with piston and rings.

18 To allow for manufacturing tolerances, pistons and liners are separated into three size groups. The size group of each piston is indicated by a letter (A, B or C) stamped onto its crown, and the size group of each liner is indicated by a series of 1 to 3 notches on the upper lip of the liner **(see illustration)**; a single notch for group A, two notches for group B, and three notches for group C (on some engines the actual letters A, B, C may also appear on the liners instead of the notches). Ensure that each piston and its respective liner are both of the same size group. It is permissible to have different size group piston and liner assemblies fitted to the same engine, but never fit a piston of one size group to a liner in a different group.

19 Prior to installing the liners it is necessary to check the liner protrusion above the top of the cylinder block as follows.

XV, XW and XY series engines with paper type base seals

20 If the cylinder liners had paper type base seals, the liner protrusion must be measured and seals of the correct thickness selected.

21 Paper base seals are available in four different thicknesses:

Blue	0.087 mm
White	0.102 mm
Red	1.122 mm
Yellow	0.147 mm

22 The correct protrusion for each liner above the surface of the cylinder block is given in the *Specifications* and it is preferable to aim for the greater protrusion when selecting new seals.

23 Fit the liners without the seals into their original locations. If new liners are being fitted, they of course can be fitted in any order.

24 Using a dial indicator or feeler blades and a straight-edge, measure the protrusion of each liner above the top of the cylinder block **(see illustration)**.

25 It is now a simple matter to select a paper base seal which, when its thickness is added to the recorded protrusion will equal the specified protrusion.

26 Make sure that the difference in protrusion between adjacent liners does not exceed 0.04 mm. If it does, reduce the seal thickness on the greater protruding liner.

27 If new liners are being fitted, the protrusion differences can be eliminated by changing the position of the liner in the block or by twisting it on its base.

28 Prior to installing the liners, thoroughly clean the liner mating surfaces in the cylinder block, and use fine abrasive paper to polish away any burrs or sharp edges which might damage the liner base seals. Clean the liners and wipe dry, then fit the selected paper seals to the base of each liner so that their tabs are diametrically opposite to the liner rim marks. To aid installation, apply a smear of oil to the base of the liner.

29 Insert each liner into its correct location in the block then, using a hammer and a block of wood, tap each liner lightly but fully onto its locating shoulder. Wipe clean, then lightly oil, all exposed liner surfaces, to prevent rusting.

XV, XW and XY series engines with O-ring type seals

30 If the original liners are being refitted then the projection should be correct once new O-ring seals have been fitted.

31 If new liners are being fitted, then measure the protrusion of each liner without its seal as described in paragraph 24 and compare the figures obtained with those given in the *Specifications*.

32 If the difference between adjacent liners exceeds 0.05 mm, rotate the liners through half a turn or interchange the liner position in the block.

9.18 Cylinder liner size group marking

9.24 Measuring cylinder liner protrusion

9.36 Fitting a liner to the cylinder block

33 Prior to installing the liners, thoroughly clean the liner mating surfaces in the cylinder block, and use fine abrasive paper to polish away any burrs or sharp edges which might damage the liner base seals. Clean the liners and wipe dry, then fit the O-ring seals to the base of each liner. To aid installation, apply a smear of oil to the base of the liner.

34 Insert each liner into its correct location in the block then, using a hammer and a block of wood, tap each liner lightly but fully onto its locating shoulder. Wipe clean, then lightly oil, all exposed liner surfaces, to prevent rusting.

XU and TU series engines

35 Prior to installing the liners, thoroughly clean the liner mating surfaces in the cylinder block, and use fine abrasive paper to polish away any burrs or sharp edges which might damage the liner base seals. Clean the liners and wipe dry, then fit a new O-ring to the base of each liner. To aid installation, apply a smear of oil to each O-ring and to the base of the liner.

36 If the original liners are being refitted, use the marks made on removal to ensure that each is refitted the correct way round, and is inserted into its original bore. Insert each liner into the cylinder block, taking care not to damage the O-ring, and press it home as far as possible by hand **(see illustration)**. Using a hammer and a block of wood, tap each liner lightly but fully onto its locating shoulder. Wipe clean, then lightly oil, all exposed liner surfaces, to prevent rusting.

37 With all four liners correctly installed, use a dial gauge (or a straight-edge and feeler blade) to check that the protrusion of each liner above the upper surface of the cylinder block is within the limits given in the *Specifications*. The maximum difference between any two liners must not be exceeded. Note that the liner protrusion figures are different for later XU series engines.

38 If new liners are being fitted, it is permissible to interchange them to bring the difference in protrusion within limits. Remember to keep each piston with its respective liner.

39 If liner protrusion cannot be brought within limits, seek the advice of a Peugeot dealer or engine reconditioning specialist before proceeding with the engine rebuild.

Inspection (cast-iron cylinder block)

40 Visually check the castings for cracks and corrosion. Look for stripped threads in the threaded holes. If there has been any history of internal water leakage, it may be worthwhile having an engine overhaul specialist check the cylinder block/crankcase with special equipment. If defects are found, have them repaired if possible, or renew the assembly.

41 Check each cylinder bore for scuffing and scoring. Check for signs of a wear ridge at the top of the cylinder, indicating that the bore is excessively worn.

42 If the necessary measuring equipment is available, measure the bore diameter of each cylinder liner at the top (just under the wear ridge), centre, and bottom of the cylinder bore, parallel to the crankshaft axis.

43 Next, measure the bore diameter at the same three locations, at right-angles to the crankshaft axis. As no tolerance figures are actually stated by Peugeot, if there is any doubt about the condition of the cylinder bores, seek the advice of a Peugeot dealer or suitable engine reconditioning specialist.

44 At the time of writing, it was not clear whether oversize pistons were available for all models. Consult your Peugeot dealer for the latest information on piston availability. If oversize pistons are available, then it may be possible to have the cylinder bores rebored and fit the oversize pistons. If oversize pistons are not available, and the bores are worn, renewal of the block seems to be the only option.

10 Main and big-end bearings - inspection

Inspection

1 Even though the main and big-end bearing shells should be renewed during the engine overhaul, the old shells should be retained for close examination, as they may reveal valuable information about the condition of the engine.

2 Bearing failure occurs because of lack of lubrication, the presence of dirt or other foreign particles, overloading the engine, and corrosion **(see illustration)**. Regardless of the cause of bearing failure, the cause must be corrected (where applicable) before the engine is reassembled, to prevent it from happening again.

3 When examining the bearing shells, remove them from the cylinder block/crankcase and main bearing caps, and from the connecting rods and the big-end bearing caps, then lay them out on a clean surface in the same general position as their location in the engine. This will enable you to match any bearing problems with the corresponding crankshaft journal. *Do not* touch any shell's bearing surface with your fingers while checking it, or the delicate surface may be scratched.

4 Dirt or other foreign matter gets into the engine in a variety of ways. It may be left in the engine during assembly, or it may pass through filters or the crankcase ventilation system. It may get into the oil, and from there into the bearings. Metal chips from machining operations and normal engine wear are often present. Abrasives are sometimes left in engine components after reconditioning, especially when parts are not thoroughly cleaned using the proper cleaning methods. Whatever the source, these foreign objects often end up embedded in the soft bearing material, and are easily recognised. Large particles will not embed in the material, and will score or gouge the shell and journal. The best prevention for this cause of bearing failure is to clean all parts thoroughly, and to keep everything spotlessly-clean during engine assembly. Frequent and regular engine oil and filter changes are also recommended.

5 Lack of lubrication (or lubrication breakdown) has a number of inter-related causes. Excessive heat (which thins the oil), overloading (which squeezes the oil from the bearing face) and oil

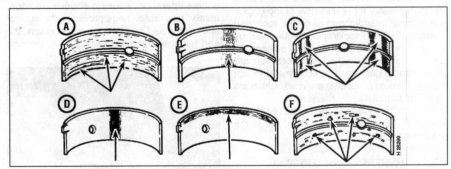

10.2 Typical bearing failures

A Scratched by dirt; dirt embedded in bearing material
B Lack of oil; overlay wiped out
C Improper seating; bright (polished sections)

D Tapered journal; overlay gone from entire surface
E Radius ride
F Fatigue failure; craters or pockets

leakage (from excessive bearing clearances, worn oil pump or high engine speeds) all contribute to lubrication breakdown. Blocked oil passages, which usually are the result of misaligned oil holes in a bearing shell, will also starve a bearing of oil, and destroy it. When lack of lubrication is the cause of bearing failure, the bearing material is wiped or extruded from the shell's steel backing. Temperatures may increase to the point where the steel backing turns blue from overheating.

6 Driving habits can have a definite effect on bearing life. Full-throttle, low-speed operation (labouring the engine) puts very high loads on bearings, which tends to squeeze out the oil film. These loads cause the shells to flex, which produces fine cracks in the bearing face (fatigue failure). Eventually, the bearing material will loosen in pieces, and tear away from the steel backing.

7 Short-distance driving leads to corrosion of bearings, because insufficient engine heat is produced to drive off condensed water and corrosive gases. These products collect in the engine oil, forming acid and sludge. As the oil is carried to the engine bearings, the acid attacks and corrodes the bearing material.

8 Incorrect shell refitting during engine assembly will lead to bearing failure as well. Tight-fitting shells leave insufficient bearing running clearance, and will result in oil starvation. Dirt or foreign particles trapped behind a bearing shell result in high spots on the bearing, which lead to failure.

9 Do not touch any shell's bearing surface with your fingers during reassembly; there is a risk of scratching the delicate surface, or of depositing particles of dirt on it.

11 Engine overhaul - reassembly sequence

1 Before reassembly begins, ensure that all new parts have been obtained, and that all necessary tools are available. Read through the entire procedure to familiarise yourself with the work involved, and to ensure that all items necessary for reassembly of the engine are at hand. In addition to all normal tools and materials, thread-locking compound will be needed. A suitable tube of liquid sealant will also be required for the joint faces that are fitted without gaskets. It is recommended that Peugeot's own product(s) are used, which are specially formulated for this purpose.

2 In order to save time and avoid problems, engine reassembly can be carried out in the following order:
   a) Crankshaft (Section 13)*.
   b) Piston/connecting rod assemblies (Section 14)*.
   c) Oil pump - XU and TU series engines.
   d) Sump - XU and TU series engines (See Part B or C as applicable).
   e) Flywheel (See Part A, B or C as applicable).
   f) Cylinder head (See Part A, B or C - as applicable).

g) Timing chain/belt, sprockets and tensioner (See Part A, B, or C as applicable).
h) Oil pump - XV, XW and XY series engines.
i) Engine external components.
*On XV XW and XY series engines the piston connecting rod assemblies must be fitted before the crankshaft due to the arrangement of the split crankcase.

3 At this stage, all engine components should be absolutely clean and dry, with all faults repaired. The components should be laid out (or in individual containers) on a completely clean work surface.

12 Piston rings - refitting

1 Before fitting new piston rings, the ring end gaps must be checked as follows.

2 Lay out the piston/connecting rod assemblies and the new piston ring sets, so that the ring sets will be matched with the same piston and cylinder during the end gap measurement and subsequent engine reassembly.

3 Insert the top ring into the first cylinder, and push it down the bore using the top of the piston. This will ensure that the ring remains square with the cylinder walls. Position the ring near the bottom of the cylinder bore, at the lower limit of ring travel. Note that the top and second compression rings are different. The second ring is easily identified by the step on its lower surface, and by the fact that its outer face is tapered.

4 Measure the end gap using feeler blades.

5 Repeat the procedure with the ring at the top of the cylinder bore, at the upper limit of its travel **(see illustration)**, and compare the measurements with the figures given in the Specifications. Where no figures are given, seek the advice of a Peugeot dealer or engine reconditioning specialist.

6 If the gap is too small (unlikely if genuine Peugeot parts are used), it must be enlarged, or the ring ends may contact each other during engine operation, causing serious damage. Ideally, new piston rings providing the correct end gap should be fitted. As a last resort, the end gap can be increased by filing the ring

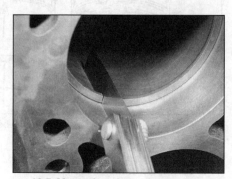

12.5 Measuring piston ring end gap

ends very carefully with a fine file. Mount the file in a vice equipped with soft jaws, slip the ring over the file with the ends contacting the file face, and slowly move the ring to remove material from the ends. Take care, as piston rings are sharp, and are easily broken.

7 With new piston rings, it is unlikely that the end gap will be too large. If the gaps are too large, check that you have the correct rings for your engine and for the particular cylinder bore size.

8 Repeat the checking procedure for each ring in the first cylinder, and then for the rings in the remaining cylinders. Remember to keep rings, pistons and cylinders matched up.

9 Once the ring end gaps have been checked and if necessary corrected, the rings can be fitted to the pistons.

10 Fit the piston rings using the same technique as for removal. Fit the bottom (oil control) ring first, and work up. When fitting a three piece oil control ring, first insert the expander and position its gap in line with the centre of the gudgeon pin. Fit the scraper rings with their gaps positioned 20 to 30 mm either side of the expander gap. Where the oil control scraper is of one-piece type, position its gap 180° from the expander gap. Ensure that the second compression ring is fitted the correct way up, with its identification mark (either a dot of paint or the word "TOP" or "TOPC" stamped on the ring surface) at the top, and the stepped surface at the bottom **(see illustration)**. Arrange the gaps of the top and second compression rings 120° either side of the oil control expander gap. **Note:** Always follow any instructions supplied with the new piston ring sets - different manufacturers may specify different procedures. Do not mix up the top and second compression rings, as they have different cross-sections.

13 Crankshaft - refitting and main bearing running clearance check

Main bearing shell selection

XV, XW and XY series engines

1 Bearing shells on these engines are not graded and are supplied in one standard size or one oversize only, to match the dimensions of the respective journal. As the manufacturer's do not specify an actual running clearance dimension for the bearings, the only safe course of action is to fit new shells whenever an overhaul is being undertaken. Assuming that the relevant crankshaft journals are all within tolerance, the running clearances will then be correct.

2 Note also that from early 1986, the locating tabs of the main bearing shells are offset, and it is not possible to fit the earlier type of main bearing shell to later models with this modification. Seek the advice of a Peugeot dealer or engine overhaul specialist when selecting bearing shells.

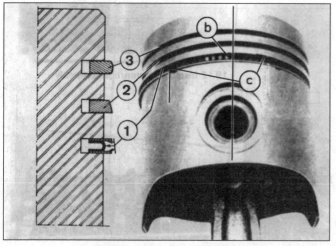

12.10 Piston ring identification

1 Oil control ring
2 Second compression ring
3 First compression ring

b Oil control expander ring
  gap
c Oil control scraper ring gaps

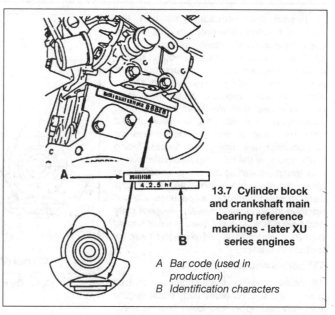

13.7 Cylinder block and crankshaft main bearing reference markings - later XU series engines

A Bar code (used in production)
B Identification characters

XU series engines

3 On some early engines, both the upper and lower bearing shells were of the same thickness.

4 However, on later engines the main bearing running clearance was significantly reduced. To enable this to be done, four different grades of bearing shell were introduced. The grades are indicated by a colour-coding marked on the edge of each shell, which denotes the shell's thickness, as listed in the following table. The upper shell on all bearings is of the same size, and the running clearance is controlled by fitting a lower bearing shell of the required thickness. This arrangement has been fitted to all engines produced since mid-1994 and, if possible, should also be fitted to earlier engines during overhaul (see paragraph 11).

Bearing colour code	Thickness (mm)	
	Standard	Undersize
Upper bearing:		
Yellow	1.856	2.006
Lower bearing:		
Blue (Class A)	1.836	1.986
Black (Class B)	1.848	1.998
Green (Class C)	1.859	2.009
Red (Class D)	1.870	2.020

Note: On later engines, upper shells are easily distinguished from lower shells, by their grooved bearing surface; the lower shells have a plain surface.

5 On early engines, the correct size of bearing shell must be selected by measuring the running clearance as described under the sub-heading below.

6 On engines produced since mid-1994, when the new bearing shell sizes were introduced, the crankshaft and cylinder block/crankcase have had reference marks on them to identify the size of the journals and bearing bores.

7 The cylinder block reference marks are on the left-hand (transmission) end of the block. The crankshaft reference marks are on the left-hand (transmission) end of the crankshaft, on the left-hand web of No 1 crankpin **(see illustration)**. These marks can be used to select bearing shells of the required thickness as follows.

8 On both the crankshaft and block, there are two lines of identification, a bar code, which is used by Peugeot during production, and a row of five characters (letters and numbers). The first character in the sequence refers to the relevant size of No 1 bearing (at the flywheel/driveplate end) and the last letter in the sequence refers to the relevant size of No 5 main bearing. These marks can be used to select the required bearing shell grade as follows.

9 Obtain the identification character of both the relevant crankshaft journal and the cylinder block bearing bore. Note that the crankshaft characters are listed across the top of the chart, and the cylinder block characters down the side **(see illustration)**. Trace a vertical line down from the relevant crankshaft character, and a horizontal line across from the relevant cylinder block character, and find the point at which both lines cross. This crossover point will indicate the grade of lower bearing shell required to give the correct main bearing running clearance. For example, the illustration shows cylinder block reference H, and crankshaft reference 6, crossing at a point within the area of Class D, indicating that a Red (Class D) lower bearing shell is required to give the correct main bearing running clearance.

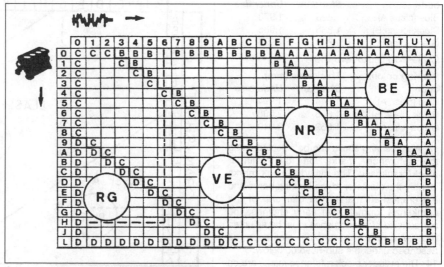

	0	1	2	3	4	5	6	7	8	9	A	B	C	D	E	F	G	H	J	L	N	P	R	T	U	Y
0	C	C	C	B	B	B		B	B	B	B	B	B	B	A	A	A	A	A	A	A	A	A	A	A	A
1	C			C	B									B	A											A
2	C				C	B									B	A										A
3	C					C										B	A									A
4	C							C	B								B	A								A
5	C								C	B								B	A							A
6	C									C	B								B	A						A
7	C										C	B								B	A					A
8	C											C	B								B	A				A
9	D	C											C	B								B	A			A
A	D	D	C											C	B								B	A		A
B	D		D	C											C	B								B	A	A
C	D			D	C											C	B								B	B
D	D				D	C											C	B								B
E	D					D	C											C	B							B
F	D						D	C											C	B						B
G	D							D	C											C	B					B
H	D								D	C											C	B				B
J	D									D	C											C	B			B
L	D	D	D	D	D	D	D	D	D	D	D	D	C	C	C	C	C	C	C	C	C	C	B	B	B	B

13.9 Main bearing shell selection chart - later XU series engines

BE Blue (Class A)   NR Black (Class B)   VE Green (Class C)   RG Red (Class D)

2D

10 Repeat this procedure so that the required bearing shell grade is obtained for each of the five main bearing journals.

11 Seek the advice of your Peugeot dealer on parts availability, and on the best course of action when ordering new bearing shells. **Note**: *On early models, at overhaul it is recommended that the later bearing shell arrangement is fitted. This, however, should only be done if the lubrication system components are upgraded (necessitating replacement of the oil pump relief valve piston and spring, as well as the pump sprocket and drive chain) at the same time. If the new bearing arrangement is to be used without uprating the lubrication system, Peugeot state that Blue (Class A) lower bearing shells should be fitted. Refer to your Peugeot dealer for further information.*

TU series engines

12 As with the XU series engines described previously, the TU aluminium block engine originally had upper and lower bearing shells of the same thickness, with only two sets of bearing shell sizes available; standard and oversize. On aluminium block engines from mid-1993 onwards, and all cast-iron block engines, to ensure that the main bearing running clearance can be accurately set, there are three different grades of bearing shell. The grades are indicated by a colour-coding marked on the edge of each shell, which denotes the shell's thickness, as listed in the following table. The upper shell on all bearings is of the same size (class B, colour code black), and the running clearance is controlled by fitting a lower bearing shell of the required thickness. This later arrangement should also, if possible, be fitted to earlier engines during overhaul.

Aluminium block engine

Bearing colour code	Thickness (mm)	
	Standard	*Undersize*
Blue (class A)	1.823	1.973
Black (class B)	1.835	1.985
Green (class C)	1.848	1.998

Cast-iron block engine

Bearing colour code	Thickness (mm)	
	Standard	*Undersize*
Blue (class A)	1.844	1.994
Black (class B)	1.858	2.008
Green (class C)	1.869	2.019

13 New bearing shells can be selected using the reference marks on the cylinder block/crankcase. The cylinder block marks identify the diameter of the bearing bores and the crankshaft marks, the diameter of the crankshaft journals. On early engines, the correct size of bearing shell must be selected by measuring the running clearance as described under the sub-heading below.

14 The cylinder block reference marks are on the right-hand (timing belt) end of the block, and the crankshaft reference marks are on the right-hand (timing belt) end of the crankshaft,

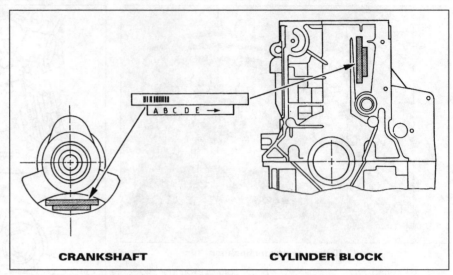

CRANKSHAFT   **CYLINDER BLOCK**

13.14 Cylinder block and crankshaft main bearing reference markings - TU series engines

on the right-hand web of No 4 crankpin **(see illustration)**. These marks can be used to select bearing shells of the required thickness as follows.

15 On both the crankshaft and block there are two lines of identification: a bar code, which is used by Peugeot during production, and a row of five letters. The first letter in the sequence refers to the size of No 1 bearing (at the flywheel/driveplate end). The last letter in the sequence (which is followed by an arrow) refers to the size of No 5 main bearing. These marks can be used to select the required bearing shell grade as follows.

16 Obtain the identification letter of both the relevant crankshaft journal and the cylinder block bearing bore. Noting that the cylinder block letters are listed across the top of the chart, and the crankshaft letters down the side, trace a vertical line down from the relevant cylinder block letter, and a horizontal line across from the relevant crankshaft letter, and find the point at which both lines cross. This crossover point will indicate the grade of lower bearing shell required to give the correct main bearing running clearance. For example, the illustration shows cylinder block reference G, and crankshaft reference T, crossing at a point within the area of Class A, indicating that a blue-coded (Class A) lower bearing shell is required to give the correct main bearing running clearance **(see illustration)**.

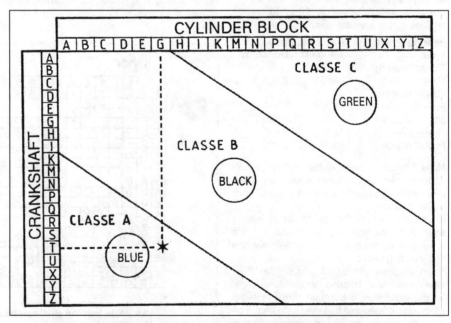

13.16 Main bearing shell selection chart - TU series engines

13.26 Plastigage in place on a crankshaft main bearing journal

13.29 Measure the width of the deformed Plastigage using the scale on the card

17 Repeat this procedure so that the required bearing shell grade is obtained for each of the five main bearing journals.

18 Seek the advice of your Peugeot dealer for the latest information on parts availability when ordering new bearing shells.

Main bearing running clearance check

XU series engines

19 On early engines, if the modified bearing shells are to be fitted, obtain a set of new (Yellow) upper bearing shells and new Blue (Class A) lower bearing shells. On later (mid-1994 on) engines where the modified bearing shells are already fitted, the running clearance check can be carried out using the original bearing shells, although it is preferable to use a new set, since the results obtained will be a lot more conclusive.

20 Clean the backs of the bearing shells, and the bearing locations, in both the cylinder block/crankcase and the main bearing caps.

21 Press the bearing shells into their locations, ensuring that the tab on each shell engages in the notch in the cylinder block/crankcase or bearing cap, and taking care not to touch any shell's bearing surface with your fingers. There is conflicting information from the manufacturer on the exact placement of the grooved and plain bearing shells, which appears to vary according to engine code and model year. Also, the bearing arrangement on the project cars dismantled in the preparation of this manual did not conform to the expected placement, but no harm seemed to have resulted. As a general recommendation, if the old bearing shells are being used they must be positioned in their original locations. If new bearing shells are being used on early models, fit the plain shells in all locations that had a plain shell on removal, and likewise for the grooved shells. From mid-1994 onwards, all upper bearing shells are grooved, whereas all lower shells are plain.

22 The running clearance can be checked in either of two ways.

23 One method (which will be difficult to achieve without a range of internal micrometers or internal/external expanding calipers) is to refit the main bearing caps to the cylinder block/crankcase, with bearing shells in place. With the cap retaining bolts tightened to the specified torque, measure the internal diameter of each assembled pair of bearing shells. If the diameter of each corresponding crankshaft journal is measured and then subtracted from the bearing internal diameter, the result will be the main bearing running clearance.

24 The second (and more accurate) method is to use a product known as Plastigage. This consists of a fine thread of perfectly round plastic, which is then compressed between the bearing shell and the journal. When the shell is removed, the plastic is deformed, and can be measured with a specified card gauge supplied with the kit. The running clearance is determined from this gauge. Plastigage should be available from your Peugeot dealer, otherwise, enquiries at one of the larger specialist quality motor factors should produce the name of a stockist in your area. The procedure for using Plastigage is as follows.

25 With the main bearing upper shells in place, carefully lay the crankshaft in position. Do not use any lubricant; the crankshaft journals and bearing shells must be perfectly clean and dry.

26 Cut several lengths of the appropriate-size Plastigage (they should be slightly shorter than the width of the main bearings), and place one length on each crankshaft journal axis **(see illustration)**.

27 With the main bearing lower shells in position, refit the main bearing caps and tighten their retaining bolts to the specified torque. Take care not to disturb the Plastigage, and do not rotate the crankshaft at any time during this operation.

28 Remove the main bearing caps again, taking great care not to disturb the Plastigage, nor to rotate the crankshaft.

29 Compare the width of the crushed Plastigage on each journal to the scale printed on the Plastigage envelope, to obtain the main bearing running clearance **(see illustration)**. Compare the clearance measured with that given in the *Specifications* at the start of this Chapter.

30 If the clearance is significantly different from that expected, the bearing shells may be the wrong size (or excessively worn, if the original shells are being re-used). Before deciding that different size shells are required, make sure that no dirt or oil was trapped between the bearing shells and the caps or block when the clearance was measured. If the Plastigage was wider at one end than at the other, the crankshaft journal may be tapered.

31 If the clearance is not as specified, use the reading obtained, along with the shell thicknesses quoted above, to calculate the necessary grade of bearing shells required. When calculating the bearing clearance required, bear in mind that it is always better to have the running clearance towards the lower end of the specified range, to allow for wear in use.

32 Where necessary, obtain the required grades of bearing shell, and repeat the running clearance checking procedure as described above.

33 On completion, carefully scrape away all traces of the Plastigage material from the crankshaft and bearing shells, using a fingernail or other object which is unlikely to score the bearing surfaces.

TU series aluminium block engines

34 The procedure is similar to that described in paragraphs 20 to 33, except that the lower shells are fitted to the main bearing ladder instead of the individual bearing caps. On early engines, if the modified bearing shells are to

2D

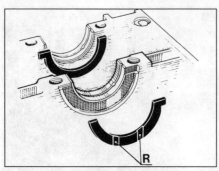

**13.38 Crankshaft thrustwashers -
XV, XW and XY series engines**

R Oil grooves

13.39 Lowering the crankshaft into place

13.41 Crankcase flange O-ring seal

**13.45 Tightening the main bearing/casing
bolts**

be fitted, obtain a set of new Black (Class B) upper bearing shells and new Blue (Class A) lower bearing shells. On later (mid-1993 on) engines where the modified bearing shells are already fitted, the running clearance check can be carried out using the original bearing shells, although it is preferable to use a new set as described above, since the results obtained will be a lot more conclusive. Note that on most models, all the bearing shells are plain except those fitted to journals 2 and 4 which are grooved. Some engines, however, may have a grooved bearing shell fitted to the upper (cylinder block) location of No 5 main bearing. Fit the ladder, tighten the bolts to the specified torque and carry out the running clearance check.

TU series cast-iron block engines

35 The procedure is similar to that described in paragraphs 20 to 33 except that all the bearing shells are plain except those fitted to journals 2 and 4 which are grooved.

Final crankshaft refitting

XV, XW and XY series engines

36 Due to the arrangement of the split crankcase it is necessary to have the pistons, and connecting rods in place in the block before refitting the crankshaft. Carry out the operations described in Section 14, then proceed as follows.
37 Place the bearing shells in their locations as described earlier. If new shells are being

fitted, ensure that all traces of protective grease are cleaned off using paraffin. Wipe dry the shells with a lint-free cloth. Liberally lubricate each bearing shell in the cylinder block/crankcase with clean engine oil.
38 Fit the semi-circular thrustwashers which control crankshaft endfloat. The oil grooves of the thrustwashers must be against the machined face of the crankshaft **(see illustration)**.
39 Oil the shell bearings and lower the crankshaft into position **(see illustration)**.
40 Reconnect the connecting rods to the crankshaft as described in Section 14.
41 Fit a new O-ring seal to the crankcase flange and check that the locating dowels are in position **(see illustration)**.
42 Apply jointing compound to the flange.
43 Clean the recesses in the remaining crankcase housing section and fit the main bearing shells. Note that the grooved shells are located in positions 2 and 4.
44 Locate the housing, taking care not to displace the bearing shells.
45 Screw in the ten main bearing/casing bolts with flat washers; noting that the two longer bolts are at the flywheel housing end and the very long one at the crankshaft pulley end on the oil pump side **(see illustration)**.
46 Tighten the bolts in the sequence given in two stages to the specified torque **(see illustration)**.
47 Now screw in and tighten the seven casing flange bolts with their spring washers **(see illustration)**.

48 Fit a new crankshaft rear oil seal as described in Part A of this Chapter.
49 Where removed, fit the cylinder head, as described in Part A.

XU series engines

50 Carefully lift the crankshaft out of the cylinder block once more.
51 Using a little grease, stick the upper thrustwashers to each side of the No 2 main bearing upper location. Ensure that the oilway grooves on each thrustwasher face outwards (away from the cylinder block) **(see illustration)**.
52 Place the bearing shells in their locations as described earlier. If new shells are being fitted, ensure that all traces of protective grease are cleaned off using paraffin. Wipe dry the shells and connecting rods with a lint-free cloth. Liberally lubricate each bearing shell in the cylinder block/crankcase and cap with clean engine oil.

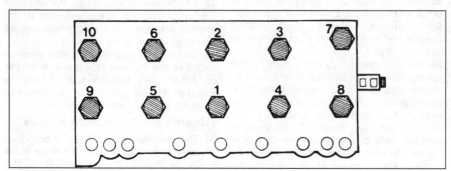

13.46 Main bearing/casing bolt tightening sequence - XV, XW and XY series engines

**13.47 Refit the casing flange bolts and
washers**

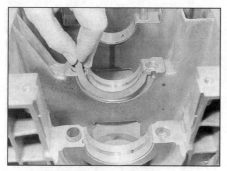

13.51 Fitting the thrustwasher upper segments - XU series engines

13.56 Applying sealant to the cylinder block No 1 main bearing cap mating face

13.57 Fitting a sealing strip to No 1 main bearing cap

13.58 Using feeler blades to protect the sealing strips as the cap is fitted

2D

53 Lower the crankshaft into position so that Nos 2 and 3 cylinder crankpins are at TDC; Nos 1 and 4 cylinder crankpins will be at BDC, ready for fitting No 1 piston.

54 Lubricate the lower bearing shells in the main bearing caps with clean engine oil. Make sure that the locating lugs on the shells engage with the corresponding recesses in the caps.

55 Fit main bearing caps Nos 2 to 5 to their correct locations, ensuring that they are fitted the correct way round (the bearing shell tab recesses in the block and caps must be on the same side). Insert the bolts/nuts, tightening them only loosely at this stage.

56 Apply a small amount of sealant to the No 1 main bearing cap mating face on the cylinder block, around the sealing strip holes **(see illustration)**.

57 Locate the tab of each sealing strip over the pins on the base of No 1 bearing cap, and press the strips into the bearing cap grooves **(see illustration)**. It is now necessary to obtain two thin metal strips, of 0.25 mm thickness or less, in order to prevent the strips moving when the cap is being fitted. Peugeot garages use a special tool, which acts as a clamp. Metal strips (such as old feeler blades) can be used, provided all burrs which may damage the sealing strips are first removed.

58 Where applicable, oil both sides of the metal strips, and hold them on the sealing strips. Fit the No 1 main bearing cap, insert the bolts loosely, then carefully pull out the metal strips in a horizontal direction, using a pair of pliers if necessary **(see illustration)**.

59 Tighten all the main bearing cap bolts/nuts evenly to the specified torque. Using a sharp knife, trim off the ends of the No 1 bearing cap sealing strips, so that they protrude above the cylinder block/crankcase mating surface by approximately 1 mm

60 Refit the centre main bearing side retaining bolts and sealing washers (one at the front of the block, and one at the rear) and tighten them both to the specified torque **(see illustration)**.

61 Fit a new crankshaft rear oil seal as described in Part B of this Chapter.

62 Refit the piston/connecting rod assemblies to the crankshaft as described in Section 14.

63 Refit the Woodruff key, then slide on the oil pump drive sprocket and spacer (where fitted), and locate the drive chain on the sprocket.

64 Ensure that the mating surfaces of the front oil seal carrier and cylinder block are clean and dry. Note the correct fitted depth of the oil seal then, using a large flat-bladed screwdriver, lever the old seal out of the housing.

65 Apply a smear of suitable sealant to the oil seal carrier mating surface. Ensure that the locating dowels are in position, then slide the carrier over the end of the crankshaft and into position on the cylinder block. Tighten the carrier retaining bolts to the specified torque.

66 Fit a new crankshaft front oil seal as described in Part B of this Chapter.

67 Ensuring that the drive chain is correctly located on the sprocket, refit the oil pump and

sump as described in Part B of this Chapter.

68 Where removed, refit the cylinder head as described in Part B.

TU series aluminium block engines

69 Carefully lift the crankshaft out of the cylinder block once more.

70 Using a little grease, stick the upper thrustwashers to each side of the No 2 main bearing upper location; ensure that the oilway grooves on each thrustwasher face outwards (away from the cylinder block) **(see illustration)**.

71 Place the bearing shells in their locations as described earlier. If new shells are being fitted, ensure that all traces of protective grease are cleaned off using paraffin. Wipe dry the shells and connecting rods with a lint-free cloth. Liberally lubricate each bearing shell in the cylinder block/crankcase with clean engine oil **(see illustration)**.

13.60 Refit and tighten the centre main bearing side bolts

13.70 Refitting a crankshaft thrustwasher - TU series aluminium block engine

13.71 Ensure each bearing shell tab (arrowed) is correctly located and apply clean oil

13.72 Refitting the oil pump drive chain and sprocket

13.73 Apply a thin film of sealant to the cylinder block/crankcase mating face . . .

13.74 . . . then lower the main bearing ladder into position

72 Refit the Woodruff key, then slide on the oil pump drive sprocket, and locate the drive chain on the sprocket **(see illustration)**. Lower the crankshaft into position so that Nos 2 and 3 cylinder crankpins are at TDC; Nos 1 and 4 cylinder crankpins will be at BDC, ready for fitting No 1 piston.

73 Thoroughly degrease the mating surfaces of the cylinder block/crankcase and the main bearing ladder. Apply a thin bead of suitable sealant to the cylinder block/crankcase mating surface of the main bearing ladder casting, then spread to an even film **(see illustration)**.

74 Lubricate the lower bearing shells with clean engine oil, then refit the main bearing ladder, ensuring that the shells are not displaced, and that the locating dowels engage correctly **(see illustration)**.

75 Install the ten 11 mm main bearing ladder retaining bolts, and tighten them all by hand only. Working progressively outwards from the centre bolts, tighten the ten bolts, by a turn at a time, to the specified Stage 1 torque wrench setting. Once all the bolts have been tightened to the Stage 1 setting, angle-tighten the bolts through the specified Stage 2 angle using a socket and extension bar. It is recommended that an angle-measuring gauge is used during this stage of the tightening, to ensure accuracy **(see illustrations)**. If a gauge is not available, use a dab of white paint to make alignment marks between the bolt head and casting prior to tightening; the marks can then be used to check that the bolt has been rotated sufficiently during tightening.

76 Refit all the 6 mm bolts securing the main

bearing ladder to the base of the cylinder block, and tighten them to the specified torque. Check that the crankshaft rotates freely. On engines with a grooved bearing shell fitted to the upper (cylinder block) location of No 5 main bearing, working on one bolt at a time starting with the centre and working progressively outwards, loosen the 11 mm main bearing ladder retaining bolts, and then tighten to the Stage 3 and then Stage 4 torque wrench settings.

77 Refit the piston/connecting rod assemblies to the crankshaft as described in Section 14.

78 Ensuring that the drive chain is correctly located on the sprocket, refit the oil pump and sump as described in Part A of this Chapter.

79 Fit two new crankshaft oil seals as described in Part A.

80 Refit the flywheel as described in Part A of this Chapter.

81 Where removed, refit the cylinder head as described in Part A. Also refit the crankshaft sprocket and timing belt as described in Part A.

TU series cast-iron block engines

82 Carefully lift the crankshaft out of the cylinder block once more.

83 Using a little grease, stick the upper thrustwashers to each side of the No 2 main bearing upper location. Ensure that the oilway grooves on each thrustwasher face outwards (away from the cylinder block) **(see illustration)**.

84 Place the bearing shells in their locations as described earlier **(see illustration)**. If new shells are being fitted, ensure that all traces of protective grease are cleaned off using paraffin. Wipe dry the shells and connecting rods with a lint-free cloth. Liberally lubricate each bearing shell in the cylinder block/crankcase and cap with clean engine oil.

85 Lower the crankshaft into position so that Nos 2 and 3 cylinder crankpins are at TDC; Nos 1 and 4 cylinder crankpins will be at BDC, ready for fitting No 1 piston.

86 Lubricate the lower bearing shells in the main bearing caps with clean engine oil. Make sure that the locating lugs on the shells engage with the corresponding recesses in the caps.

13.75a Tighten the 11 mm main bearing bolts to the Stage 1 torque setting . . .

13.75b . . . then angle-tighten them through the specified Stage 2 angle

13.83 Fitting a thrustwasher to No 2 main bearing upper location - TU series cast iron block engines

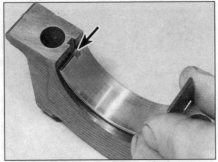

13.84 Ensure that the tab (arrowed) is correctly located in the cap when fitting the bearing shells

87 Fit the main bearing caps to their correct locations, ensuring that they are fitted the correct way round (the bearing shell lug recesses in the block and caps must be on the same side). Insert the bolts loosely.

88 Tighten the main bearing cap bolts to the specified Stage 1 torque wrench setting. Once all the bolts have been tightened to the Stage 1 setting, angle-tighten the bolts through the specified Stage 2 angle, using a socket and extension bar. It is recommended that an angle-measuring gauge is used during this stage of the tightening, to ensure accuracy. If a gauge is not available, use a dab of white paint to make alignment marks between the bolt head and casting prior to tightening; the marks can then be used to check that the bolt has been rotated sufficiently during tightening.

89 Check that the crankshaft rotates freely.

90 Refit the piston/connecting rod assemblies to the crankshaft as described in Section 14.

91 Refit the Woodruff key to the crankshaft groove, and slide on the oil pump drive sprocket. Locate the drive chain on the sprocket.

92 Ensure that the mating surfaces of front oil seal housing and cylinder block are clean and dry. Note the correct fitted depth of the front oil seal then, using a large flat-bladed screwdriver, lever the seal out of the housing.

93 Apply a smear of suitable sealant to the oil seal housing mating surface, and make sure that the locating dowels are in position. Slide the housing over the end of the crankshaft, and into position on the cylinder block. Tighten the housing retaining bolts securely.

94 Repeat the operations in paragraphs 92 and 93, and fit the rear oil seal housing.

95 Fit a new front and rear crankshaft oil seal as described in Part C of this Chapter.

96 Ensuring that the chain is correctly located on the drive sprocket, refit the oil pump and sump as described in Part C of this Chapter.

97 Refit the flywheel as described in Part C of this Chapter.

98 Where removed, refit the cylinder head and install the crankshaft sprocket and timing belt as described in the relevant Sections of Part C.

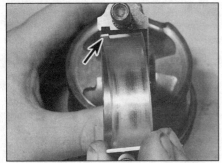

14.5 Ensure that the tab (arrowed) is correctly located in the connecting rod when fitting the bearing shells

14 Piston/connecting rod assembly - refitting and big-end bearing clearance check

Selection of bearing shells

1 On most engines, there are two sizes of big-end bearing shell produced by Peugeot; a standard size for use with the standard crankshaft, and an oversize for use once the crankshaft journals have been reground.

2 Consult your Peugeot dealer for the latest information on parts availability. To be safe, always quote the diameter of the crankshaft big-end crankpins when ordering bearing shells.

3 Prior to refitting the piston/connecting rod assemblies, it is recommended that the big-end bearing running clearance is checked as follows.

Big-end bearing running clearance check

4 Clean the backs of the bearing shells, and the bearing locations in both the connecting rod and bearing cap.

5 Press the bearing shells into their locations, ensuring that the tab on each shell engages in the notch in the connecting rod and cap. Take care not to touch any shell's bearing surface with your fingers (see illustration). If the original bearing shells are being used for the check, ensure that they are refitted in their original locations. The clearance can be checked in either of two ways.

6 One method is to refit the big-end bearing cap to the connecting rod, ensuring that they are fitted the correct way around (see paragraph 21), with the bearing shells in place. With the cap retaining nuts correctly tightened, use an internal micrometer or vernier caliper to measure the internal diameter of each assembled pair of bearing shells. If the diameter of each corresponding crankshaft journal is measured and then subtracted from the bearing internal diameter, the result will be the big-end bearing running clearance.

7 The second, and more accurate method is to use Plastigage (see Section 13).

8 Ensure that the bearing shells are correctly fitted. Place a strand of Plastigage on each (cleaned) crankpin journal.

9 Refit the (clean) piston/connecting rod assemblies to the crankshaft, and refit the big-end bearing caps, using the marks made or noted on removal to ensure that they are fitted the correct way around.

10 Tighten the bearing cap nuts as described below in paragraph 22 or 23 (as applicable). Take care not to disturb the Plastigage, nor rotate the connecting rod during the tightening sequence.

11 Dismantle the assemblies without rotating the connecting rods. Use the scale printed on the Plastigage envelope to obtain the big-end bearing running clearance.

12 If the clearance is significantly different from that expected, the bearing shells may be the wrong size (or excessively worn, if the original shells are being re-used). Make sure that no dirt or oil was trapped between the bearing shells and the caps or block when the clearance was measured. If the Plastigage was wider at one end than at the other, the crankshaft journal may be tapered.

13 Note that Peugeot do not specify a recommended big-end bearing running clearance. The figure given in the *Specifications* is a guide figure, which is typical for this type of engine. Before condemning the components concerned, refer to your Peugeot dealer or engine reconditioning specialist for further information on the specified running clearance. Their advice on the best course of action to be taken can then also be obtained.

14 On completion, carefully scrape away all traces of the Plastigage material from the crankshaft and bearing shells. Use your fingernail, or some other object which is unlikely to score the bearing surfaces.

Final piston/connecting rod refitting

15 Note that the following procedure assumes that the cylinder liners (where fitted) are in position in the cylinder block/crankcase as described in Section 9, and that on XU and TU series engines, the crankshaft and main bearing ladder/caps are in place (see Section 13). On XV, XW and XY series engines, do not fit the crankshaft until all the piston/connecting rod assemblies have been inserted.

16 Ensure that the bearing shells are correctly fitted as described earlier. If new shells are being fitted, ensure that all traces of the protective grease are cleaned off using paraffin. Wipe dry the shells and connecting rods with a lint-free cloth.

17 Lubricate the cylinder bores, the pistons, and piston rings, then lay out each piston/connecting rod assembly in its respective position.

18 Start with assembly No 1. Make sure that the piston rings are still spaced as described in Section 12, then clamp them in position with a piston ring compressor.

19 Insert the piston/connecting rod assembly into the top of cylinder/liner No 1. Ensure that the arrow on the piston crown is pointing towards the timing chain/belt end of the engine. Using a block of wood or hammer handle against the piston crown, tap the assembly into the cylinder/liner until the piston crown is flush with the top of the cylinder/liner (see illustration).

20 On XV, XW and XY series engines, refit the remaining three piston/connecting rod assemblies in the same way. The crankshaft should then be placed in position in the crankcase as described in Section 13.

21 Ensure that the bearing shell is still correctly installed. Liberally lubricate the

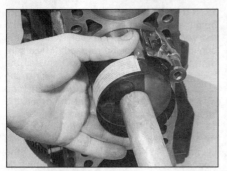

14.19 Tap the piston into the bore using a hammer handle

14.22 Tightening a big-end bearing cap nut using a torque wrench . . .

14.23 . . . and further, on XU series engines, through the specified angle using an angle tightening gauge

crankpin and both bearing shells. Taking care not to mark the cylinder/liner bores, pull the piston/connecting rod assembly down the bore and onto the crankpin. Refit the big-end bearing cap, tightening its retaining nuts finger-tight at first. Note that the faces with the identification marks must match (which means that the bearing shell locating tabs abut each other).

22 On XV, XW, XY and TU series engines, tighten the bearing cap retaining nuts evenly and progressively to the specified torque setting **(see illustration)**.

23 On XU series engines, tighten the bearing cap retaining nuts evenly and progressively to the Stage 1 torque setting. Fully slacken both nuts, then tighten them to the Stage 2 torque setting. Once both nuts have been tightened to the Stage 2 setting, angle-tighten them through the specified Stage 3 angle, using a socket and extension bar. It is recommended that an angle-measuring gauge is used during this stage of the tightening, to ensure accuracy **(see illustration)**. If a gauge is not available, use a dab of white paint to make alignment marks between the nut and bearing cap prior to tightening; the marks can then be used to check that the nut has been rotated sufficiently during tightening.

24 On XU and TU series engines, once the bearing cap retaining nuts have been correctly tightened, rotate the crankshaft. Check that it turns freely; some stiffness is to be expected if new components have been fitted, but there should be no signs of binding or tight spots.

25 On XU and TU series engines, refit the

remaining three piston/connecting rod assemblies in the same way.

26 On XV, XW and XY series engines, continue the crankshaft refitting procedure described in Section 13. On all other engines, refit the cylinder head and oil pump as described in Part B or C of this Chapter (as applicable).

15 Engine - initial start-up after overhaul

1 With the engine refitted in the vehicle, double-check the engine oil and coolant levels. Make a final check that everything has been reconnected, and that there are no tools or rags left in the engine compartment.

2 Remove the spark plugs. On models with a distributor, disable the ignition system by disconnecting the ignition HT coil lead from the distributor cap, and earthing it on the cylinder block. Use a jumper lead or similar wire to make a good connection. On models with a static (distributorless) ignition system, disable the ignition system by disconnecting the LT wiring connector from the ignition module, referring to Chapter 5B for further information.

3 Turn the engine on the starter until the oil pressure warning light goes out. Refit the spark plugs, and reconnect the spark plug (HT) leads, referring to Chapter 1 for further information. Reconnect any HT leads or wiring which was disconnected in paragraph 2.

4 Start the engine, noting that this may take a little longer than usual, due to the fuel system components having been disturbed.

5 While the engine is idling, check for fuel, water and oil leaks. Don't be alarmed if there are some odd smells and smoke from parts getting hot and burning off oil deposits.

6 Assuming all is well, keep the engine idling until hot water is felt circulating through the top hose, then switch off the engine.

7 Check the ignition timing and the idle speed settings (as appropriate), then switch the engine off.

8 After a few minutes, recheck the oil and coolant levels as described in Chapter 1, and top-up as necessary.

9 On XV, XW and XY series engines, and XU series engines with hexagon type cylinder head bolts, it will be necessary to re-tighten the head bolts after the engine has been run up to normal working temperature then switched off and allowed to cool (see Part A and B of this Chapter, as applicable). On all other engines, if they were tightened as described, there is no need to re-tighten the cylinder head bolts once the engine has first run after reassembly.

10 If new pistons, rings or crankshaft bearings have been fitted, the engine must be treated as new, and run-in for the first 500 miles (800 km). *Do not* operate the engine at full-throttle, or allow it to labour at low engine speeds in any gear. It is recommended that the oil and filter be changed at the end of this period.

Chapter 3
Cooling, heating and air conditioning systems

Contents

Degrees of difficulty

Easy, suitable for novice with little experience	Fairly easy, suitable for beginner with some experience	Fairly difficult, suitable for competent DIY mechanic	Difficult, suitable for experienced DIY mechanic	Very difficult, suitable for expert DIY or professional

Specifications

General

System type .... Pressurised with expansion tank/bottle and front-mounted radiator, electric cooling fan, coolant pump and thermostat

Pressure cap setting .... 0.8 or 1.0 bar (according to engine)

Thermostat

Start-to-open temperature:
XV, XW and XY series engines .... 79° to 82°C
XU series engines .... 82°C
TU9 series, TU3 series and TU1 series (Van) engines .... 88°C
TU1 series (except Van) engines .... 83°C
Fully-open temperature:
XU, XV, XW and XY series engines .... 93°C
TU9 series, TU3 series and TU1 series (Van) engines .... 102°C
TU1 series (except Van) engines .... 96°C

Torque wrench settings

	Nm	lbf ft
Coolant pump attachments:		
XV, XW, and XY series engines	13	10
XU series engines	15	11
TU series engines:		
Housing inlet elbow (aluminium block engines)	8	6
Housing bolts (aluminium block engines):		
Small bolts	30	22
Large bolts	50	37
Coolant pump bolts (cast-iron block engines):	15	11

1 General information and precautions

The cooling system is of pressurised type incorporating an expansion bottle or expansion tank according to model. The system includes a front-mounted cross-flow radiator, thermoswitch controlled electric cooling fan, coolant pump and thermostat. The car interior heater matrix is incorporated into the coolant circuit with the interior air supply and distribution being controlled by air flaps.

On XU and TU Series engines the coolant pump is driven by the engine timing belt, but on all other engines it is driven by the auxiliary (alternator) drivebelt.

The cooling system functions in the following way. After a cold start the thermostat valve is shut and coolant circulation is restricted to the engine and heater matrix. When the coolant reaches the normal engine operating temperature the thermostat starts to open and coolant circulation also flows through the radiator. The engine temperature is then controlled by the thermostat and the electric cooling fan located on the front of the radiator.

Air conditioning is available as an option on certain models and is described in Section 10.

Precautions

Warning: Do not attempt to remove the expansion tank filler cap, or to disturb any part of the cooling system, while it or the engine is hot, as there is a very great risk of scalding. If the expansion tank filler cap must be removed before the engine and radiator have fully cooled down (even though this is not recommended) the pressure in the cooling system must first be released. Cover the cap with a thick layer of cloth, to avoid scalding, and slowly unscrew the filler cap until a hissing sound can be heard. When the hissing has stopped, showing that pressure is released, slowly unscrew the filler cap further until it can be removed; if more hissing sounds are heard, wait until they have stopped before unscrewing the cap completely. At all times, keep well away from the filler opening.

Warning: Do not allow antifreeze to come in contact with your skin, or with the painted surfaces of the vehicle. Rinse off spills immediately with plenty of water. Never leave antifreeze lying around in an open container, or in a puddle in the driveway or on the garage floor. Children and pets are attracted by its sweet smell, but antifreeze is fatal if ingested.

Warning: Refer to Section 10 for precautions to be observed when working on vehicles equipped with air conditioning.

2 Cooling system hoses - disconnection and renewal

Note: Refer to the warnings given in Section 1 of this Chapter before proceeding. Hoses should only be disconnected once the engine has cooled sufficiently to avoid scalding.

1 If the checks described in Chapter 1 reveal a faulty hose, it must be renewed as follows.
2 First drain the cooling system (Chapter 1); if the antifreeze is not due for renewal, the drained coolant may be re-used, if it is collected in a clean container.

Models with conventional hose connections

3 To disconnect any hose, use a pair of pliers to release the spring clamps (or a screwdriver to slacken screw-type clamps), then move them along the hose clear of the union. Carefully work the hose off its stubs. The hoses can be removed with relative ease when new - on an older vehicle, they may have stuck.
4 If a hose proves to be difficult to remove, try to release it by rotating it on its unions before attempting to work it off. Gently prise the end of the hose with a blunt instrument (such as a flat-bladed screwdriver), but do not apply too much force, and take care not to damage the pipe stubs or hoses. Note in particular that the radiator hose unions are fragile; do not use excessive force when attempting to remove the hoses.

If all else fails, cut the hose with a sharp knife, then slit it so that it can be peeled off in two pieces. Although this may prove expensive if the hose is otherwise undamaged, it is preferable to buying a new radiator.

5 When refitting a hose, first slide the clamps onto the hose, then engage the hose with its unions. Work the hose into position, then check that the hose is settled correctly and is properly routed. Slide each clip along the hose until it is behind the union flared end, before tightening it securely.

If the hose is stiff, use a little soapy water as a lubricant, or soften the hose by soaking it in hot water. Do not use oil or grease, which may attack the rubber.

Models with CONRAD "click-on" radiator hose connections

6 Some TU3FM engine models may be fitted with pre-production "click-on" radiator hose connections. These fittings were only fitted to a limited number of vehicles, and have now been discontinued in favour of conventional hose clips.

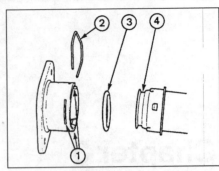

2.7 CONRAD "click-on" type radiator hose connection

1 Radiator fitting
2 Retaining clip
3 O-ring
4 Hose end fitting

7 The hose end fitting is retained by a large circlip, which must be extracted before pulling the hose out **(see illustration)**.
8 When refitting, first fit the circlip into the radiator fitting, placing the flat part in position first, and bringing the ends into position one at a time.
9 Ensure that the O-ring is in good condition, and securely located in the hose end fitting. It should not be necessary to lubricate the O-ring to fit it, but if any form of lubrication is used, the radiator must be refilled with fresh coolant, to avoid contamination.
10 Align the hose end fitting with the three lugs in the radiator connection, push firmly into place, and check that the hose is secure by pulling back on it.

All models

11 Refill the system with coolant (see Chapter 1).
12 Check carefully for leaks as soon as possible after disturbing any part of the cooling system.

3 Antifreeze - general information

Note: Refer to the warnings given in Section 1 of this Chapter before proceeding.
1 The cooling system should be filled with a water/ethylene glycol-based antifreeze solution, of a strength which will prevent freezing down to at least -25°C, or lower if the local climate requires it. Antifreeze also provides protection against corrosion, and increases the coolant boiling point. As with all engines of aluminium construction, the corrosion protection properties of the antifreeze are critical. Only a top quality antifreeze should be used in the system and should never be mixed with different antifreeze types.
2 The cooling system should be maintained according to the schedule described in Chapter 1. If antifreeze is used that is not to Peugeot's specification, old or contaminated

coolant mixtures are likely to cause damage, and encourage the formation of corrosion and scale in the system.

3 Before adding antifreeze, check all hoses and hose connections, because antifreeze tends to leak through very small openings. Engines don't normally consume coolant, so if the level goes down, find the cause and correct it.

4 Ideally, a 50% mixture of antifreeze and clean soft water (by volume) should be used to maintain maximum protection against freezing and corrosion. Mix the required quantity in a clean container and then fill the system as described in Chapter 1, and "Weekly checks". Save any surplus mixture for topping-up.

4 Thermostat - removal, testing and refitting

Note: *Refer to the warnings given in Section 1 of this Chapter before proceeding.*

Removal

1 The thermostat housing is located on the cylinder head adjacent to the distributor.
2 Drain the cooling system as described in Chapter 1.
3 Disconnect the radiator top hose from the thermostat housing. Where necessary for access, also remove the air inlet duct from the air cleaner.
4 Unscrew and remove the two thermostat housing cover bolts and remove the cover.

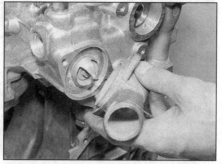

4.4 Removing the thermostat housing cover on XV, XW and XY series engines

This may need a little persuasion with a wooden or plastic-faced hammer **(see illustration)**.
5 Remove the thermostat. If it is stuck, do not lever it out under its bridge piece, but cut around its edge with a sharp knife.
6 Remove the rubber ring(s) and clean the mating faces of the housing and cover.

Testing

7 If the thermostat is suspected of being faulty, suspend it in a container of water which is being heated. Using a thermometer, check that the thermostat starts to open at the specified temperature and is fully open also at the specified temperature.
8 Remove the thermostat from the water and allow it to cool. The valve plate should close smoothly.
9 If the unit fails to operate as described or is stuck open or shut, renew it with one of similar temperature rating **(see illustration)**.

4.9 Thermostat temperature rating (arrowed) stamped on base

Refitting

10 Refitting is a reversal of removal but use new rubber sealing ring(s). Refill the cooling system as described in Chapter 1 on completion.

5 Radiator - removal and refitting

Note: *Refer to the warnings given in Section 1 of this Chapter before proceeding.*

> **HAYNES HINT** *If leakage is the reason for wanting to remove the radiator, bear in mind that minor leaks can often be cured using a radiator sealant with the radiator in situ.*

Removal

1 Drain the cooling system, as described in Chapter 1.
2 Remove the front grille (see Chapter 11) then unbolt the engine compartment front crossmember **(see illustration)**.
3 Disconnect the top and bottom hoses from the radiator and, where applicable, disconnect and unclip the vent hose for the expansion tank **(see illustration)**.
4 Disconnect the wiring from the cooling fan, the thermo-switch and, where applicable, the low level sensor. On TU series engines, remove the cooling fan relay from the clip on the top of the radiator **(see illustrations)**.

5.2 Undo the bolts (arrowed) on each side and lift off the front crossmember

5.3 Expansion tank vent hose connection on the radiator

5.4a Disconnect the thermo-switch (arrowed) . . .

5.4b . . . and low coolant level sensor wiring

5.4c On TU series engines, remove the cooling fan relay (arrowed)

3

5 Disconnect the top mountings, as applicable, then lift the radiator, complete with cooling fan, from the car - taking care not to damage the matrix **(see illustration)**. The base of the radiator incorporates pins which locate in rubber mountings.

6 If necessary separate the cooling fan, with reference to Section 6.

Refitting

7 Refitting is a reversal of removal; fill the cooling system as described in Chapter 1 on completion.

6 Radiator cooling fan - removal and refitting

Removal

The radiator cooling fan may be removed with the radiator, as described in the preceding Section, and then separated. Alternatively it may be unbolted or unclipped (as applicable) from the radiator after having removed the front grille and crossmember, and disconnected the wiring. The motor can be unbolted from the frame and then the fan removed from the motor **(see illustrations)**. No spare parts are available for the motor.

Refitting

Refitting is a reversal of removal.

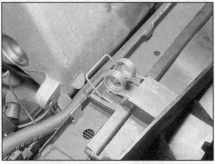

6.1a Radiator cooling fan retaining clip

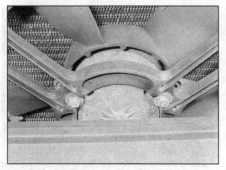

6.1b Radiator cooling fan to frame mounting bolts

5.5 Disconnect the top mountings and lift out the radiator

7 Cooling system electrical switches and sensors - removal and refitting

Radiator cooling fan thermoswitch

Removal

1 The thermostatically controlled switch for the cooling fan is screwed into the radiator side tank.

2 Drain the cooling system as described in Chapter 1.

3 Disconnect the switch wiring and unscrew the switch from its location.

Refitting

4 Refitting is a reversal of removal, but use a new sealing washer if necessary. Fill the cooling system as described in Chapter 1 on completion.

Coolant temperature sensor

Removal

5 The coolant temperature sensor may be located in the left-hand end of the cylinder head, on or beneath the thermostat housing, or below the distributor, according to engine type **(see illustration)**. On some engines, two sensors may be fitted, one for the temperature gauge and another for the engine management system. Testing should be carried out by an auto-electrician or by substitution with a known good unit.

7.5 Coolant temperature sensor location on XV, XW and XY series engines

6 Partially drain the cooling system (see Chapter 1) to below the level of the sensor unit.

7 Disconnect the wiring from the sensor and unscrew it from its location.

Refitting

8 Screw in the new unit, using a smear of sealant on the threads or a new sealing washer, as applicable. Reconnect the wiring.

9 Top-up the coolant level (see Chapter 1 and *"Weekly checks"*).

Coolant level sensor

Removal

10 The coolant level sensor is located in the radiator right-hand side tank on XV, XW and XY series engines and in the expansion tank on all other engines **(see illustration)**. The switch is float-operated and actuates a warning lamp in the event of a low coolant level.

11 The sensor is removed by unscrewing it from its location after disconnecting the wiring.

Refitting

12 Refitting is a reversal of removal using a new sealing washer where necessary.

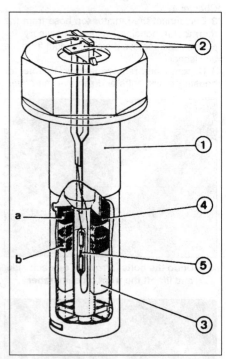

7.10 Cutaway diagram of the coolant level sensor

1	Body	3	Float
2	Terminal connections	4	Magnet
		5	Reed contact

a *Off position (float lifts magnet above reed contact)*

b *On position (magnet field switches on reed contact)*

8.2 Radiator and heater hose connections on the coolant pump - XV, XW and XY series engines

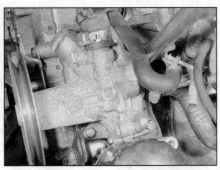

8.3a Undo the mounting bolts . . .

8.3b . . . withdraw the pump from the cylinder block . . .

8.3c . . . and recover the O-ring - arrowed (XV, XW and XY series engines

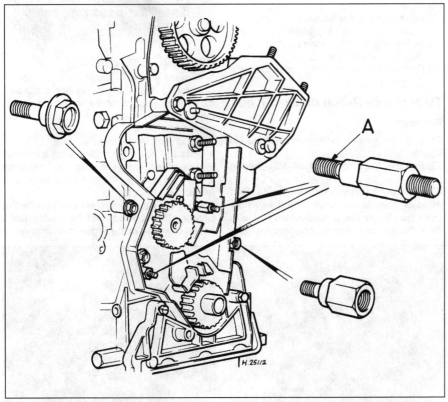

8.8 Timing belt inner plastic shield and special bolt locations on early XU series engines

Apply sealant to bolt threads A

8 Coolant pump - removal and refitting

Note: *Refer to the warnings given in Section 1 of this Chapter before proceeding.*

XV, XW, and XY series engines

Removal

1 Drain the cooling system and remove the auxiliary drivebelt as described in Chapter 1.

2 Disconnect the radiator bottom hose, heater return hose, and inlet manifold return hose from the coolant pump **(see illustration)**. For better access, remove the air cleaner and inlet cowl, with reference to the relevant Part of Chapter 4.

3 Unscrew the mounting bolts and remove the coolant pump from the cylinder block. Remove the O-ring **(see illustrations)**.

4 If the coolant pump is worn, noisy or leaks coolant it must be renewed, as repair is not possible. However, if either of the half casings is individually damaged it may be renewed, together with the central gasket.

Refitting

5 Refitting is a reversal of removal, bearing in mind the following points:

 a) *Renew the pump O-ring.*
 b) *Refit the auxiliary drivebelt and refill the cooling system as described in Chapter 1.*

XU series engines

Removal

6 Drain the cooling system (Chapter 1).

7 Remove the timing belt and tensioner, as described in Chapter 2B.

8 Remove the plastic shield, noting the locations of the different types of bolt **(see illustration)**.

9 Unscrew the five mounting bolts and remove the coolant pump from the cylinder block. Remove the gasket **(see illustration)**.

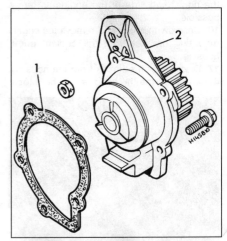

8.9 Coolant pump assembly fitted to XU series engines

1 *Gasket* 2 *Coolant pump*

3

8.17a On TU series aluminium block engines, disconnect the hoses (arrowed) from the coolant pump housing

8.17b ... then undo the bolts (arrowed) and remove the housing from the block

10 If the coolant pump is worn, noisy or leaks coolant it must be renewed, as repair is not possible.

Refitting

11 Refitting is a reversal of removal, bearing in mind the following points:
a) Thoroughly clean the mating faces and use a new gasket.
c) Refit and tension the timing belt as described in Chapter 2B.
d) Refill the cooling system (Chapter 1).

TU series aluminium block engines

Removal

12 Drain the cooling system as described in Chapter 1.
13 Remove the timing belt as described in Chapter 2C.
14 Unscrew the nut from the right-hand engine mounting.
15 Using a trolley jack and block of wood, lift the right-hand side of the engine as far as possible.
16 Unscrew the nuts and remove the engine mounting bracket from the coolant pump housing.
17 Disconnect the hoses from the housing, then unbolt the housing from the block.

Remove the O-ring seal **(see illustrations)**.
18 Unbolt the coolant pump from the housing, and remove the O-ring **(see illustrations)**. If necessary, similarly remove the inlet elbow.
19 If the coolant pump is worn, noisy or leaks coolant it must be renewed, as repair is not possible.

Refitting

20 Refitting is a reversal of removal, bearing in mind the following points:
a) Renew the O-rings.
b) Make sure that the housing-to-block location dowels are in position.
c) Refit and tension the timing belt as described in Chapter 2C.
d) Refill the cooling system as described in Chapter 1.

TU series cast-iron block engines

Removal

21 Drain the cooling system as described in Chapter 1.
22 Remove the timing belt as described in Chapter 2C.
23 Unscrew the two securing bolts, and withdraw the coolant pump from the cylinder block **(see illustration)**. Recover the O-ring.
24 If the coolant pump is worn, noisy or leaks

coolant it must be renewed, as repair is not possible.

Refitting

25 Refitting is a reversal of removal, bearing in mind the following points.
a) Renew the pump O-ring.
b) Refit and tension the timing belt, as described in Chapter 2C.
c) Refill the cooling system (Chapter 1).

---

9 Heater assembly - removal, dismantling, reassembly and refitting

Removal

1 Remove the facia panel, as described in Chapter 11. On later models this procedure also covers removal of the vents and control panel. If further dismantling is necessary proceed as follows.
2 Disconnect the lower air vents.
3 Note the position of the wiring loom and switches then remove the clips and move the wiring clear. Lower the fuse board with reference to Chapter 12.
4 Drain the cooling system as described in Chapter 1, and disconnect the heater hoses on the bulkhead in the engine compartment.

8.18a With the housing removed, undo the bolts and remove the coolant pump ...

8.18b ... then recover the O-ring seal (arrowed)

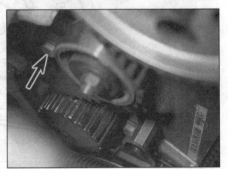

8.23 Coolant pump securing bolt (arrowed) on TU series cast iron block engines

9.6a **Remove the heater matrix mounting screws and pipe clip (arrowed) . . .**

9.6b **. . . then withdraw the matrix from the heater casing**

9.7 **Removing the heater blower motor**

5 Unscrew the heater assembly mounting nuts and withdraw it from the car.

Dismantling

6 To remove the matrix, disconnect the pipe clip and unscrew the mounting screws then slide the matrix from the casing **(see illustrations)**. If necessary the pipes can be removed by unscrewing the flange screws. Use water from a hose to clean both the inside and outside of accumulated debris.

7 To remove the heater blower, unscrew the mounting screws and lift the unit from the casing **(see illustration)**.

8 If necessary remove the heater control panel and cable.

Reassembly and refitting

9 Reassembly and refitting is a reversal of removal and dismantling, but fill the cooling system as described in Chapter 1 on completion.

10 Air conditioning system - general information and precautions

General information

1 Air conditioning is available as an option on later models. In conjunction with the heater, the system enables any reasonable air temperature to be achieved inside the car. It also reduces the humidity of the incoming air, aiding demisting even when cooling is not required **(see illustration)**.

3

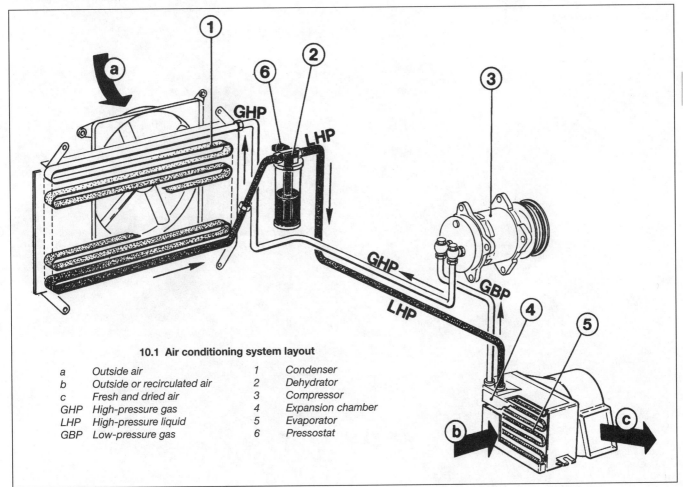

10.1 Air conditioning system layout

a	Outside air	1	Condenser
b	Outside or recirculated air	2	Dehydrator
c	Fresh and dried air	3	Compressor
GHP	High-pressure gas	4	Expansion chamber
LHP	High-pressure liquid	5	Evaporator
GBP	Low-pressure gas	6	Pressostat

2 The refrigeration side of the air conditioning system functions in a similar way to a domestic refrigerator. A compressor, belt-driven from the crankshaft pulley, draws refrigerant in its gaseous phase from an evaporator. The compound refrigerant passes through a condenser where it loses heat and enters its liquid phase. After dehydration the refrigerant returns to the evaporator where it absorbs heat from air passing over the evaporator fins. The refrigerant becomes a gas again and the cycle is repeated.

3 Various subsidiary controls and sensors protect the system against excessive temperature and pressures. Additionally, engine idle speed is increased when the system is in use to compensate for the additional load imposed by the compressor.

Precautions

4 When an air conditioning system is fitted, it is necessary to observe special precautions whenever dealing with any part of the system, or its associated components. If for any reason the system must be discharged, entrust this task to your Peugeot dealer or air conditioning specialist.

 Warning: The refrigeration circuit may contain a liquid refrigerant (Freon), and it is therefore dangerous to disconnect any part of the system without specialised knowledge and equipment.

5 The refrigerant is potentially dangerous, and should only be handled by qualified persons. If it is splashed onto the skin, it can cause frostbite. It is not itself poisonous, but in the presence of a naked flame (including a cigarette) it forms a poisonous gas. Uncontrolled discharging of the refrigerant is dangerous, and potentially damaging to the environment.

6 Components of the air conditioning system may obstruct work being undertaken in other areas on or around the engine. In many instances, it may be possible to unbolt and move these components aside, within the limits of their flexible connecting pipes, to gain the necessary access. Apart from this, complete removal and refitting or fault diagnosis, of any air conditioning system components, must be left to a specialist.

Chapter 4 Part A:
Fuel system - carburettor engines

Contents

Degrees of difficulty

Easy, suitable for novice with little experience	Fairly easy, suitable for beginner with some experience	Fairly difficult, suitable for competent DIY mechanic	Difficult, suitable for experienced DIY mechanic	Very difficult, suitable for expert DIY or professional

Specifications

General
System type . . . .   Rear-mounted fuel tank, mechanical or electric fuel pump, single or twin carburettor

Carburettor
Type . . . .   Fixed jet, downdraught

Application:

XV8 (954 cc)	Solex 32 PBISA
XW7 (1124 cc)	Solex 32 PBISA
XY7 (1360 cc)	Solex 34 PBISA
XY8 (1360 cc)	Solex 35 PBISA 8 or Weber 35 IBSH
XU51C (1580 cc)	Weber 36 TLC
TU1 (1124 cc)	Solex 32 PBISA 16, Weber 32 IBS 15 or Weber 32 IBSH 17
TU3 (1360 cc)	Weber 34 TLP3
TU3A (1360 cc)	Solex 34 PBISA 17
TU3A/K (1360 cc)	Solex 34 PBISA 17
TU3S (1360 cc)	Solex 32-34 Z2
TU3S/K (1360 cc)	Solex 32-34 Z2
TU9 (954 cc)	Solex 32 PBISA 16 or Weber 32 IBSH 16

Carburettor data

Calibrations and settings:	XV8	XW7	XY7
Venturi diameter	25 mm	25 mm	26 mm
Main jet	120 ± 5	125 ± 5	130 ± 25
Air correction jet	155 ± 20	175 ± 20	160 ± 20
Idling fuel jet	44 ± 5	42 ± 5	45 ± 5
Acceleration pump injector	35 ± 5	32 ± 5	40 ± 5
Enriched calibration	55 ± 20	60 ± 20	75 ± 20
Needle valve	1.6 mm	1.6 mm	1.6 mm
Initial throttle opening	20°40' ± 30'	20°40' ± 30'	20°40' ± 30'
Idling speed	650 ± 50 rpm	650 ± 50 rpm	650 ± 50 rpm
CO%	1.5 ± 0.5	1.5 ± 0.5	1.5 ± 0.5

4A

Carburettor data (continued)

Calibrations and settings:

	XY8 Solex	XY8 Weber	XU51C
Venturi diameter	28 mm	26 mm	28 mm
Main jet	145 ± 10	130 ± 5	137/42
Air correction jet	175 ± 10	165 ± 15	150 ± 10
Idling fuel jet	47 ± 5	45 ± 5	48 ± 1
Emulsion tube	-	F104	F80
Acceleration pump injector	40 ± 10	45 ± 5	40
Needle valve	1.5 mm*		
Initial throttle opening	15°		
Normal idling position	7°45'		
Choke opening after starting	2.5 mm ± 0.3	3.25 mm	-
Float level	-	9.0 mm	28.0 mm
Idling speed	950 to 1000 rpm**	975 ± 25 rpm	750 rpm
CO%	2.0 ± 0.5	2.0 ± 0.5	1.5 ± 0.5

*1.2 mm from serial number 5043526
**850 to 900 rpm from serial number 5043526

	TU9 Weber	TU9 Solex
Venturi diameter	25	25
Main jet	122	127.5 ± 2.5
Air correction jet	135	155 ± 10
Emulsion tube	F112	31
Enrichener drilling	30	-
Idling fuel jet	45	47 ± 4
Idling air jet	150	135 ± 10
Accelerator pump injector	40	40 ± 5
Fuel inlet needle valve	1.5	1.6
Float setting	8.0 mm	-
Idling speed	700 rpm	700 rpm
CO%	1.5	1.5 ± 0.5

	TU1 Weber 32IBS15	TU1 Weber 32IBSH17	TU1 Solex
Venturi diameter	26	25	25
Main jet	140 ± 5	132	127.5 ± 2.5
Air correction jet	180 ± 15	165	175 ± 10
Emulsion tube	F102	F100 EM	-
Enrichener drilling	50 ± 10	50	35 ± 5
Idling fuel jet	45 ± 5	45	46 ± 4
Idling air jet	-	170	165 ± 10
Accelerator pump injector	45 ± 10	40	40 ± 10
Fuel inlet needle valve	1.5	1.5	1.6
Float setting	8.0 mm	-	-
Idling speed	700 rpm	700 rpm	700 rpm
CO%	1.0	1.5 ± 0.5	1.5 ± 0.5

	TU3	TU3A and TU3A/K	TU3S and TU3S/K
Venturi diameter	26	26	24/27
Main jet	132 (127)*	132	117/130
Air correction jet	145	155	145/170 (155/175)*
Emulsion tube	F80 (F115)*	EC	27/AZ
Enrichener drilling	40	55	-
Idling fuel jet	43 (45)*	44 ± 2	44/80 (44/100)*
Idling air jet	140(130)*	140	190/150
Accelerator pump injector	40	40	35/35
Fuel inlet needle valve	1.5	1.6	1.8
Float setting	28.0 mm	28.0 mm	-
Idling speed	700 rpm	750 rpm	750 rpm
CO%	1.5 ± 0.5	1.0	1.5 ± 0.5

*1988 models onward

Recommended fuel

Minimum octane rating (see text Section 8) .... 97 RON leaded or 95 RON unleaded

Torque wrench settings

	Nm	lbf ft
Carburettor nuts	18	13
Fuel pump	18	13

2.2 On all engines except TU series, release the air cleaner rubber straps from the mounting brackets

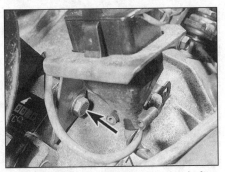

2.4a Air cleaner mounting bracket bolt (arrowed) . . .

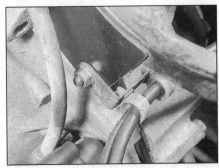

2.4b . . . and cable retaining bracket

1 General information and precautions

General information

The fuel system consists of a fuel tank mounted under the rear of the car, a mechanical fuel pump, and a single or twin downdraught carburettor.

On manual transmission and early automatic transmission models, the fuel pump is operated by an eccentric on the camshaft, and is mounted on the rear of the cylinder head. On automatic transmission models manufactured from November 1986, an electric fuel pump submerged in the fuel tank is fitted instead of the previous mechanical type. The two relays which supply the pump are located on the side of the heater. One relay incorporates a safety feature, in that its primary windings are short-circuited to earth via the engine oil pressure switch. When the engine is stationary, this relay will not operate the fuel pump, but as soon as the engine is running it will supply current to the pump. The other relay operates in conjunction with the starter motor to operate the fuel pump for starting.

A number of different Solex and Weber carburettors may be encountered and their type and engine applications are shown in the *Specifications*. All carburettors are of the fixed jet downdraught type with either manual or automatic choke arrangements. XY8 engine models utilise a twin carburettor configuration.

The air cleaner contains a disposable paper filter element, and on certain models incorporates a flap valve air temperature control system; this allows cold air from the outside of the car, and warm air from the exhaust manifold, to enter the air cleaner in the correct proportions.

Precautions

 Warning: Petrol is extremely flammable - great care must be taken when working on any part of the fuel system. Do not smoke or allow any naked flames or uncovered light bulbs near the work area. Note that gas powered domestic appliances with pilot flames, such as heaters, boilers and tumble dryers, also present a fire hazard - bear this in mind if you are working in an area where such appliances are present. Always keep a suitable fire extinguisher close to the work area and familiarise yourself with its operation before starting work. Wear eye protection when working on fuel systems and wash off any fuel spilt on bare skin immediately with soap and water. Note that fuel vapour is just as dangerous as liquid fuel; a vessel that has just been emptied of liquid fuel will still contain vapour and can be potentially explosive. Petrol is a highly dangerous and volatile liquid, and the precautions necessary when handling it cannot be overstressed.

Many of the operations described in this Chapter involve the disconnection of fuel lines, which may cause an amount of fuel

spillage. Before commencing work, refer to the above Warning and the information in "Safety first" at the beginning of this manual.

When working with fuel system components, pay particular attention to cleanliness - dirt entering the fuel system may cause blockages which will lead to poor running.

2 Air cleaner assembly - removal and refitting

Removal

All engines except TU series

1 Disconnect the inlet and warm air hoses.
2 Release the rubber straps from the mounting brackets **(see illustration)**.
3 Lift the air cleaner from the brackets then disconnect the outlet hose and where fitted, the crankcase ventilation hose.
4 If necessary, unbolt the mounting brackets - noting the location of the diagnostic socket and cable retaining brackets **(see illustrations)**.

TU series engines

5 Loosen the screw and release the air cleaner ducting from the carburettor **(see illustration)**.
6 Disconnect the crankcase ventilation hose **(see illustrations)** from the valve cover and inlet manifold.

4A

2.5 On TU series engines, slacken the air cleaner and release the ducting from the carburettor

2.6a Disconnect the crankcase ventilation hose from the valve cover . . .

2.6b . . . and inlet manifold

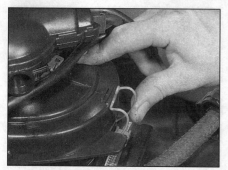

2.7a Release the spring clips . . .

2.7b . . . and remove the air cleaner ducting and element from the body

2.9 Disconnect the hose from the vacuum motor

7 Release the spring clips, and lift the element and ducting from the air cleaner body **(see illustrations)**.
8 Disconnect the fuel pump inlet hose, and release it from the clip on the ducting.
9 Disconnect the hose from the vacuum motor **(see illustration)**.
10 Disconnect the inlet and warm air hoses.
11 Remove the special clip, then lift the air cleaner and ducting from the mounting on the starter motor.

Refitting

All engines

12 Refitting is a reversal of removal.

3 Throttle cable - removal and refitting

Removal

1 The throttle cable is connected to a spring-loaded reel which pivots on the face of the cylinder head. On certain models, the reel then operates the throttle lever on the carburettor through a plastic balljointed control rod.
2 Extract the spring clip from the adjustment ferrule at the cable bracket on the cylinder head. Release the cable end fitting from the linkage.
3 Working inside the car, disconnect the cable end fitting from the top of the

accelerator pedal arm.
4 Release the cable from the engine bracket.
5 Withdraw the throttle cable through the bulkhead grommet.

Refitting

6 Refitting is a reversal of removal, but adjust the cable at the ferrule to remove all but the slightest amount of play. Check that full throttle can be obtained with the accelerator pedal fully depressed.

4 Choke cable - removal and refitting

Removal

1 Remove the carburettor inlet cowl.
2 Unscrew the pinch bolts and disconnect the inner and outer cables from the lever and bracket **(see illustration)**.
3 Release the cable from the clips in the engine compartment.
4 Working inside the car, disconnect the warning lamp wiring and detach the cable from the support bracket.

Refitting

5 Refitting is a reversal of removal, but adjust the cable at the carburettor end so that, when the control knob is pushed fully in, the choke valve plate is fully open.

5 Fuel pump - removal, overhaul and refitting

Note: *Observe the precautions in Section 1 before working on any component in the fuel system.*

Mechanical fuel pump

Removal

1 Disconnect the battery negative lead.
2 Where necessary for improved access, remove the air cleaner assembly as described in Section 2.
3 Disconnect the fuel hoses from the pump. Plug the inlet hose.
4 Unscrew the pump mounting bolts and lift the pump away **(see illustrations)**.
5 Remove the gasket.
6 Once the pump is removed on XV, XW and XY series engines, the pushrod may be withdrawn.
7 If the pump is to be dismantled, remove the cover, gasket and filter screen **(see illustrations)**. Note that dismantling can only be undertaken on the pump fitted to XV, XW and XY series engines; The TU series engine pump is a sealed assembly and no repair or overhaul is possible.

Overhaul

8 Scribe a mark across the edges of the upper and lower body flanges and extract the flange screws.

4.2 Disconnect the choke inner and outer cables from the lever and bracket - twin carburettor installation shown

5.4a Removing the fuel pump on TU series engines . . .

5.4b . . . and XV, XW and XY series engines

5.7a Removing the fuel pump cover . . .

5.7b . . . and filter

9 Unscrew the mounting and safety strap bolts and nuts, then lower the tank - at the same time disconnecting the filler, breather and supply hoses.

10 If the tank is contaminated with sediment or water, remove the fuel gauge sender unit as described previously and swill the tank out with clean fuel. The tank is moulded from a synthetic material and if damaged, it should be renewed. However, in certain cases it may be possible to have small leaks or minor damage repaired. Seek the advice of a dealer or suitable specialist concerning tank repair.

Refitting

11 Refitting is a reversal of removal.

9 Remove the upper body.
10 Drive out the operating arm pivot pin, withdraw the arm and lift out the diaphragm.
11 Obtain a repair kit which will contain a new diaphragm and the necessary gaskets.
12 If the valves are damaged, reassemble the pump and obtain a new one complete.
13 If the valves are in good condition, locate the diaphragm, push the operating arm into position so that its forked end engages with the groove in the end of the diaphragm rod, with the coil springs in position.
14 Fit the pivot pin and stake around the holes to secure both ends of the pin.
15 Fit the upper body so that the alignment marks are opposite and then fit the screws and tighten evenly.
16 Fit the filter screen and cover with gasket.

Refitting

17 Refitting to the cylinder head is a reversal of removal, but fit a new gasket.

Electric fuel pump

18 Refer to the procedures contained in Part B, Section 5.

6 Fuel gauge sender unit - removal and refitting

Note: Observe the precautions in Section 1 before working on any component in the fuel system.

Removal

1 Disconnect the battery negative lead.
2 Raise the rear seat cushion.
3 Remove the circular plastic cover to expose the sender unit **(see illustrations)**.
4 Disconnect the electrical lead.
5 Using a suitable tool, unscrew the sender unit mounting plate to release it from the securing tabs.
6 Withdraw the sender unit, taking care not to damage the float as it passes through the hole in the tank.

Refitting

7 Refitting is a reversal of removal, but use a new sealing ring if there is any doubt about the condition of the original one.

7 Fuel tank - removal and refitting

Note: Observe the precautions in Section 1 before working on any component in the fuel system.

Removal

1 Before the tank can be removed, it must be drained of as much fuel as possible. To avoid the dangers and complications of fuel handling and storage, it is advisable to carry out this operation with the tank almost empty. Any fuel remaining can be drained as follows.
2 Disconnect the battery negative lead.
3 Using a hand pump or syphon inserted through the filler neck, remove any remaining fuel from the bottom of the tank.
4 Chock the front wheels then jack up the rear of the car and support it on axle stands (see "Jacking and vehicle support").
5 Either remove the complete exhaust system or, on later models, release the support band on the silencer, and lower the system using a jack under the tailpipe.
6 Release the handbrake cables from their fuel tank and other guide sleeves - there is no need to disconnect the cables.
7 Unbolt and remove the heat shield.
8 Disconnect the wiring from the fuel gauge sender unit.

8 Unleaded petrol - general information and usage

Note: The information given in this Chapter is correct at the time of writing. If updated information is thought to be required, check with a Peugeot dealer. If travelling abroad, consult one of the motoring organisations (or a similar authority) for advice on the fuel available.

The fuel recommended by Peugeot is given in the *Specifications* Section of this Chapter.

Only the following models may be operated on unleaded fuel, and where applicable, the ignition timing **must** be retarded as shown with reference to Chapter 5B:

Engine	Code	Retard ignition by
XY7 from engine No 598051	150D	3°
TU9	C1A	None
TU9/K	C1A	None
TU9A	C1A	None
TU1	H1A	None
TU1/K	H1A	None
TU3	K1A	4°
TU3A	K1G	4°
TU3A/K	K1G	4°
TU3S	K2A	4°
TU3S/K	K2A	None
TU3.2/K	K2D	None
XU51C/K	B1F	None

4A

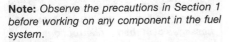

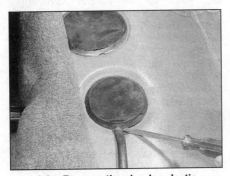

6.3a Remove the circular plastic covers . . .

6.3b . . . for access to the sender unit and fuel supply and return pipes

9 Carburettor - removal and refitting

Note: *Observe the precautions in Section 1 before working on any component in the fuel system.*

Removal

1 Remove the air cleaner assembly, as described in Section 2.

2 Unscrew the bolts or nuts and remove the air inlet duct from the top of the carburettor(s).

3 Disconnect the throttle cable or ball-jointed throttle control rod from the carburettor(s) with reference to Section 3 **(see illustration)**.

4 Disconnect the choke cable with reference to Section 4.

5 Where fitted, remove the short hose which runs between the oil filler cap and the carburettor.

6 Disconnect the wiring connector from the idle cut-off solenoid as applicable.

7 Slacken the retaining clip, and disconnect the fuel feed hose from the carburettor. Place wads of rag around the union to catch any spilled fuel, and plug the hose as soon as it is disconnected, to minimise fuel loss.

8 Make a note of the correct fitted positions of all the relevant vacuum pipes and breather hoses, to ensure that they are correctly positioned on refitting, then release the retaining clips (where fitted) and disconnect them from the carburettor.

9 Disconnect and plug the carburettor coolant hose(s). Plug the hoses immediately to prevent coolant loss.

10 Unscrew the nuts and washers securing the carburettor(s) to the inlet manifold. Remove the carburettor assembly from the car. Remove the insulating spacer and/or gasket(s). Discard the gasket(s); new ones must be used on refitting. Plug the inlet manifold port with a wad of clean cloth, to prevent the possible entry of foreign matter.

Refitting

11 Refitting is the reverse of the removal procedure, noting the following points:

a) *Ensure that the carburettor and inlet manifold sealing faces are clean and flat. Fit a new gasket, and securely tighten the carburettor retaining nuts.*

b) *Use the notes made on dismantling to ensure that all hoses are refitted to their original positions and, where necessary, are securely held by their retaining clips.*

c) *Where the original crimped-type Peugeot hose clips were fitted, discard them; use standard worm-drive hose clips when refitting.*

d) *Refit and adjust the throttle cable and choke cable (where applicable) as described in Sections 3 and 4.*

e) *Refit the air cleaner assembly as described in Section 2.*

f) *Top-up the cooling system as described in "Weekly checks".*

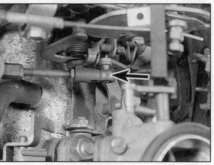

9.3 Ball-jointed throttle control rod (arrowed)

g) *On completion, check and, if necessary, adjust the idle speed and mixture settings as described in Chapter 1.*

10 Carburettor - fault diagnosis, overhaul and adjustments

Fault diagnosis

1 If a carburettor fault is suspected, always check first that the ignition timing is correctly set, that the spark plugs are in good condition and correctly gapped, that the throttle and choke cables are correctly adjusted, and that the air cleaner filter element is clean; refer to the relevant Sections of Chapter 1, Chapter 5 or this Chapter. If the engine is running very roughly, first check the valve clearances as described in Chapter 1, then check the compression pressures as described in Chapter 2.

2 If careful checking of all the above produces no improvement, the carburettor must be removed for cleaning and overhaul.

3 Prior to overhaul, check the availability of component parts before starting work; note that most sealing washers, screws and gaskets are available in kits, as are some of the major sub-assemblies. In most cases, it will be sufficient to dismantle the carburettor and to clean the jets and passages.

Overhaul

Note: *Refer to the warning note in Section 1 before proceeding. The following procedures are typical for the various carburettors encountered on 205 models. Refer to the accompanying illustrations for details of specific carburettor types and component locations.*

4 Remove the carburettor from the car as described in Section 9.

5 Unscrew the idle cut-off solenoid (where fitted) from the carburettor body, and remove it along with its plunger and spring. To test the solenoid, connect a 12-volt battery to it (positive terminal to the solenoid terminal, negative terminal to the solenoid body), and check that the plunger is retracted fully into the body. Disconnect the battery, and check that the plunger is pushed out by spring

pressure. If the valve does not perform as expected, and cleaning does not improve the situation, the solenoid valve must be renewed.

6 Remove the screws and lift off the carburettor upper body.

7 Tap out the float pivot pin and remove the float assembly, needle valve, and float chamber gasket. Check that the needle valve anti-vibration ball is free in the valve end, then examine the needle valve tip and seat for wear or damage. Examine the float assembly and pivot pin for signs of wear and damage. The float assembly must be renewed if it appears to be leaking - shake the float to detect the presence of fuel inside.

8 Unscrew the fuel inlet union and inspect the fuel filter. Clean the filter housing of debris and dirt, and renew the filter if it is blocked.

9 Undo the screws and remove the various diaphragm covers and diaphragms. Remove the diaphragm(s) and spring(s), noting which way around all the parts are fitted. Examine the diaphragm(s) for signs of damage and deterioration, and renew if necessary.

10 Unscrew the jets from the upper body and main body making notes as to their location and arrangement.

11 Remove the idle mixture adjustment screw tamperproof cap if fitted. Screw the screw in until it seats lightly, counting the exact number of turns required to do this, then unscrew it. On refitting, screw the screw in until it seats lightly, then back the screw off by the number of turns noted on removal, to return the screw to its original position.

12 Clean the jets, carburettor body assemblies, float chamber and internal drillings. An air line may be used to clear the internal passages once the carburettor is fully dismantled.

Caution: If high pressure air is directed into drillings and passages where a diaphragm is fitted, the diaphragm is likely to be damaged.

> **HAYNES HINT** *Aerosol cans of carburettor cleaner are widely available and can prove very useful in helping to clear internal passages of stubborn obstructions.*

13 Use a straight edge to check all carburettor body assembly mating surfaces for distortion.

14 On reassembly renew any worn components and fit a complete set of new gaskets and seals. A jet kit and a gasket and seal kit are available from your Peugeot dealer.

15 Reassembly is a reversal of the dismantling procedure. Ensure that all jets are securely locked in position, but take great care not to overtighten them. Ensure that all mating surfaces are clean and dry, and that all body sections are correctly assembled with their fuel and air passages correctly aligned. Prior to refitting the carburettor to the car, carry out all the applicable adjustments, according to carburettor type as described below.

Solex 32 and 34 PBISA adjustments

Idle speed and mixture

16 Refer to Chapter 1.

Fast idle setting

17 To adjust this accurately it will be necessary to measure the angular movement of the throttle valve. The use of a piece of card with the angle drawn on it will provide the necessary setting.

18 Fully close the choke valve then check that the throttle valve has opened by 20° 40' ± 30'.

19 If necessary turn the fast idle adjustment screw as required.

Solex 35 PBISA 8 adjustments

Idle speed and mixture

20 Refer to Chapter 1.

Initial throttle opening

21 To adjust the initial throttle valve opening, fully unscrew the adjustment screw then, using a piece of card as described in paragraph 17, turn the screw until the valve is opened by 7° 45'.

Fast idle setting

22 The fast idle setting is only made on the left-hand carburettor with the reference number 346. First close the choke valve then check that the throttle valve has opened by 15°. If not, turn the adjustment screw as required.

Choke opening after starting

23 To adjust the choke opening after starting, first close the choke then pull the vacuum opener rod and, using a suitable twist drill, check that the gap between the bottom edge of the throttle valve and the carburettor wall is 2.5 ± 0.3 mm. If not, turn the nut on the end of the vacuum opener as required.

Solex 32 PBISA 16 adjustments

Idle speed and mixture

24 Refer to Chapter 1.

Fast idle setting

25 With the carburettor removed, invert it then pull the choke lever fully on.

26 Using a twist drill, check that the gap between the throttle valve and barrel is 0.8 mm. If not, turn the adjustment screw.

Choke opening after starting

27 Close the choke flap, then fully operate the pneumatic opener either manually or by vacuum.

28 Using a twist drill, check that the gap between the choke flap and barrel is 3.0 mm. If not, turn the adjusting screw in the end of the opener.

Throttle damper

29 Certain models may have a throttle damper assembly, fitted to the carburettor on a modified throttle cable support bracket, to prevent engine stalling during gearchanges.

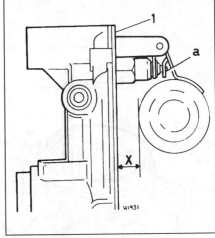

10.35 Checking float level dimension "X" on the Weber 35 IBSH carburettor

1   Gasket
a   Adjustment tongue

30 The assembly should not require any adjustment, but if the throttle is held open by the damper excessively during gearchanges, adjustment can be made by loosening the locknut, and altering the position of the damper in the bracket as necessary. Tighten the locknut on completion of adjustment.

Solex 32-34 Z2 adjustments

Idle speed and mixture

31 Refer to Chapter 1.

Additional adjustments

32 At the time of writing, not further information was available relating to any further adjustment of these carburettors.

Weber 35 IBSH adjustments

Idle speed and mixture

33 Refer to Chapter 1.

Float level

34 Hold the cover vertical with the float arm touching, but not depressing, the spring-tensioned ball on the needle valve.

35 Using vernier calipers, measure the dimension between the float and the fitted gasket **(see illustration)**. If it is not 9.0 mm, bend the tongue on the arm as necessary.

Throttle normal idling position

36 This adjustment is made after overhauling the carburettors, and is necessary to enable the engine to be started and to prevent the throttle valve sticking in the closed position. The idle speed screw must be adjusted to set the throttle valve 6° open, using a piece of card as described in paragraph 17.

Fast idle setting

37 With the choke fully closed, the throttle valve should be open by 14°. Adjust the fast idle screw on the throttle lever to achieve the desired setting **(see illustration)**.

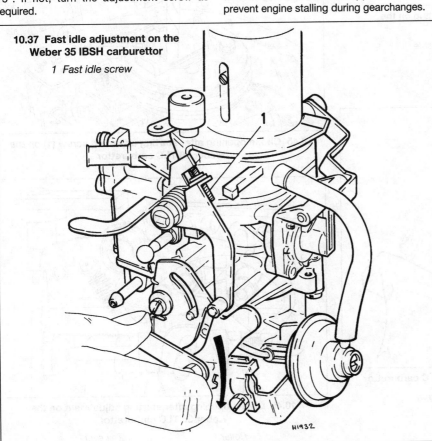

10.37 Fast idle adjustment on the Weber 35 IBSH carburettor

1 Fast idle screw

4A

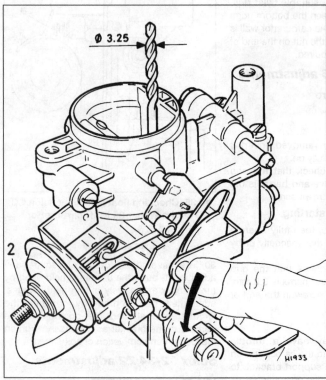

10.39 Checking the choke opening setting on the Weber 35 IBSH carburettor

2 Adjustment screw on vacuum capsule

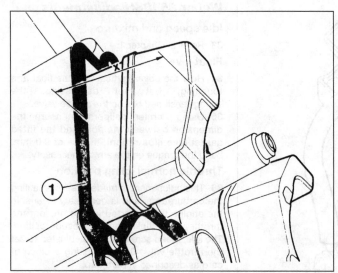

10.42 Float level setting on the Weber 36 TLC carburettor

1 Gasket   *x = 28.0 mm*

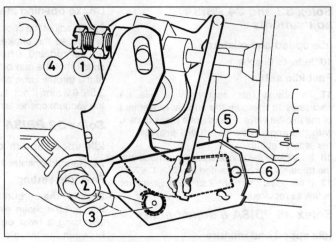

10.44 Choke opening after starting adjustment on the Weber 36 TLC carburettor

1	Locknut	4	Adjusting screw
2	Hole	5	Can
3	Roller	6	Peg on special tool

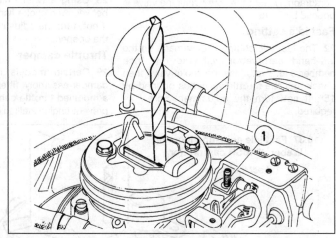

10.45 Choke opening after starting adjusting screw (1) on the Weber 36 TLC carburettor

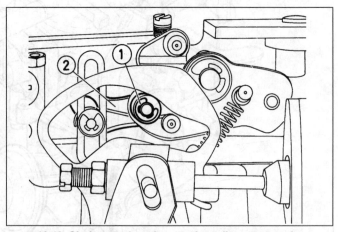

10.46 Choke opening after starting adjustment on the Weber 36 TLC carburettor

1 Roller   *2 Lever*

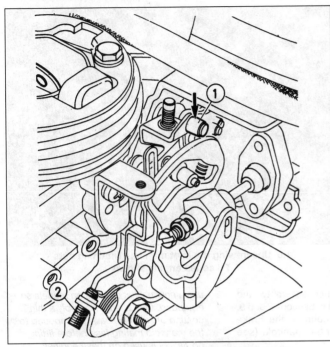

10.47 Positive throttle opening adjustment on the Weber 36 TLC carburettor

1 Roller	*2 Adjusting screw*

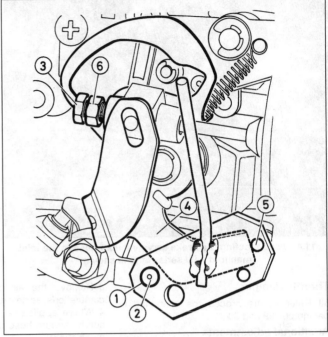

10.48 Choke cam adjustment on the Weber 36 TLC carburettor

1 Hole	*4 Cam*
2 Roller	*5 Peg on special tool*
3 Adjusting screw	*6 Locknut*

Choke opening setting

38 This adjustment can be made with the carburettor removed using a vacuum pump, or with the carburettor fitted and the engine running.

39 Turn the choke lever so that the choke is fully closed **(see illustration)**.

40 With the engine running or vacuum applied, check that the gap between the lower edge of the choke valve and the barrel is 3.25 mm. Use a twist drill to make the check, and if adjustment is necessary, turn the screw located in the end of the vacuum capsule.

Weber 36 TLC adjustments

Idle speed and mixture

41 Refer to Chapter 1.

Float level

42 To check the float level, hold the cover vertically with the gasket in place. Check that the dimension is as specified **(see illustration)**, and if necessary bend the tongue on the float arm to correct it.

Choke opening after starting

43 To adjust the cold start device choke opening after starting, Peugeot tool No 0.145G is essential. The carburettor must be fitted and the engine must be at normal operating temperature and idling at the specified idle speed (the cooling fan should have cut in and out at least twice). The air cleaner hose and the cold start device cover must be removed, and the transmission selector lever should be in the Park (P) position.

44 Fit the tool, then slacken the locknut and turn the adjusting screw to bring the end of the cam just into contact with the peg on the tool **(see illustration)**.

45 Using a 9.5 mm twist drill, check that the choke flap has opened by 9.5 mm - if not, adjust by means of the adjusting screw **(see illustration)**.

46 Disconnect and plug the diaphragm vacuum hose, and using a 5.5 mm twist drill,

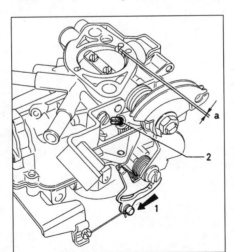

10.52 Fast idle adjustment on Weber IBS, IBSH and TLP carburettors

1	*Choke lever fully on*
2	*Adjustment screw*
	a = 0.8 mm

check that the choke flap has opened by 5.5 mm if not, loosen the clamp screw then hold the roller against the top of the cam, and adjust the lever until the drill will just pass **(see illustration)**. Tighten the screw and reconnect the hose on completion.

Positive throttle opening

47 With the choke opening after starting adjusted as described previously, press the roller to open the choke flap and check that the engine speed is 2000 rpm with the cooling fan stopped. If necessary, adjust the screw to obtain the specified speed **(see illustration)**.

48 To adjust the choke cam, Peugeot tool No 0.145G must again be used. Fit the tool, loosen the locknut, and adjust the screw until the cam contacts peg **(see illustration)**. Tighten the locknut on completion.

49 With the adjustments completed, stop the engine and refit the cold start device cover and the air cleaner hose.

Weber 32 IBS 15, 32 IBSH 16/17 and 34 TLP 3 adjustments

Idle speed and mixture

50 Refer to Chapter 1.

Fast idle setting

51 With the carburettor removed, invert it then pull the choke lever fully on.

52 Using a twist drill, check that the gap between the throttle valve and barrel is 0.8 mm. If not, turn the adjustment screw **(see illustration)**.

4A

11.4 Disconnecting the brake servo vacuum hose at the inlet manifold - TU series engine shown

11.6 Unscrewing the inlet manifold retaining nuts - TU series engine shown

Throttle damper

53 Refer to the procedures contained in paragraphs 29 and 30

Additional adjustments

54 At the time of writing, not further information was available relating to any further adjustment of these carburettors.

11 Inlet manifold - removal and refitting

Removal

1 Disconnect the battery negative lead.
2 Drain the cooling system as described in Chapter 1.

3 Remove the air cleaner assembly and carburettor(s) as described in Sections 2 and 9.
4 Where applicable, disconnect the brake servo vacuum hose from the manifold **(see illustration)**.
5 Disconnect the coolant hoses from the manifold together with any cable clips and support brackets.
6 Unbolt the manifold, releasing any additional attachments as necessary and remove it from the cylinder head **(see illustration)**. Where fitted, recover the gasket or seals.

Refitting

7 Refitting is a reversal of removal, bearing in mind the following points:

a) *Ensure that the manifold and cylinder head mating faces are perfectly clean and*

use a new gasket or seals on models so equipped. On TU engines apply a thin coating of suitable sealing compound to the manifold mating face before fitting - no gasket is used on these engines.
b) *Ensure that all hoses are reconnected to their original positions and are securely held by their retaining clips.*
c) *Refit the carburettor(s) and air cleaner assembly as described in Sections 9 and 2.*
d) *On completion, refill the cooling system as described in Chapter 1.*

Chapter 4 Part B:
Fuel system - single-point fuel injection engines

Contents

Degrees of difficulty

Easy, suitable for novice with little experience	**Fairly easy,** suitable for beginner with some experience	**Fairly difficult,** suitable for competent DIY mechanic 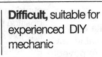	**Difficult,** suitable for experienced DIY mechanic 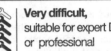	**Very difficult,** suitable for expert DIY or professional

Specifications

General

System type . . . . Rear-mounted fuel tank, electric fuel pump, single-point fuel injection system

System application:
TU1M/Z, TU3M/Z and TU3FM/L engines. . . . . Bosch Mono-Jetronic A2.2
XU5M2/Z engines . . . . MMFD Mono-point G5
TU1M/L, XU5M3/Z and XU5M3/L engines . . . . MMFD Mono-point G6

Fuel system data

Idling speed* . . . . 850 ± 50 rpm
Idle mixture CO content* . . . . Less than 1.0 %
*Not adjustable, controlled by ECU - data given for reference purposes only

Recommended fuel

Minimum octane rating (see text Section 8) . . . . 95 RON unleaded. Leaded fuel must not be used

---

1 General information and precautions

General information

The fuel system consists of a fuel tank (which is mounted under the rear of the car, with an electric fuel pump immersed in it), a fuel filter, fuel feed and return lines, and the throttle body assembly (which incorporates the single fuel injector and the fuel pressure regulator). In addition, there is an Electronic Control Unit (ECU) and various sensors, electrical components and related wiring. The air cleaner contains a disposable paper filter element, and incorporates a flap valve air temperature control system. This allows cold air from the outside of the car and warm air from around the exhaust manifold to enter the air cleaner in the correct proportions.

Refer to Section 9 for further information on the operation of each fuel injection system.

Precautions

 Warning: Petrol is extremely flammable - great care must be taken when working on any part of the fuel system. Do not smoke or allow any naked flames or uncovered light bulbs near the work area. Note that gas powered domestic appliances with pilot flames, such as heaters, boilers and tumble dryers, also present a fire hazard - bear this in mind if you are working in an area where such appliances are present. Always keep a suitable fire extinguisher close to the work area and familiarise yourself with its operation before starting work. Wear eye protection when working on fuel systems and wash off any fuel spilt on bare skin immediately with soap and water. Note that fuel vapour is just as dangerous as liquid fuel; a vessel that has just been emptied of liquid fuel will still contain vapour and can be potentially explosive. Petrol is a highly dangerous and volatile liquid, and the precautions necessary when handling it cannot be overstressed.

Many of the operations described in this Chapter involve the disconnection of fuel lines, which may cause an amount of fuel spillage. Before commencing work, refer to the above Warning and the information in "Safety first" at the beginning of this manual.

When working with fuel system components, pay particular attention to cleanliness - dirt entering the fuel system may cause blockages which will lead to poor running.

Note: *Residual pressure will remain in the fuel lines long after the vehicle was last used. When disconnecting any fuel line, first depressurise the fuel system as described in Section 4.*

2 Air cleaner assembly - removal and refitting

Refer to the procedures in Chapter 4A, Section 2, substituting "throttle body" for all references to the carburettor.

3 Throttle cable - removal, refitting and adjustment

Removal and refitting

1 Refer to Chapter 4A, Section 3 substituting "throttle body" for all references to the carburettor. Adjust the cable as described below.

Adjustment

2 Remove the spring clip from the adjustment ferrule then, ensuring that the throttle cam is fully against its stop, gently pull the cable out of its grommet until all free play is removed from the inner cable.

3 With the cable held in this position, ensure that the flat washer is pressed securely against the grommet, then fit the spring clip to the third ferrule groove visible in front of the rubber grommet and washer **(see illustration)**. This will leave a fair amount of freeplay in the inner cable which is necessary to ensure correct operation of the idle speed control motor.

4 Have an assistant depress the accelerator pedal and check that the throttle cam opens fully and returns smoothly to its stop.

4 Fuel system - depressurisation

Note: Refer to the warning note in Section 1 before proceeding.

 Warning: The following procedure will merely relieve the pressure in the fuel system - remember that fuel will still be present in the system components, and take precautions accordingly before disconnecting any of them.

1 The fuel system referred to in this Section is defined as the tank-mounted fuel pump, the fuel filter, the fuel injector and the pressure regulator in the injector housing, and the metal pipes and flexible hoses of the fuel lines between these components. All these contain fuel which will be under pressure while the engine is running, and/or while the ignition is switched on. The pressure will remain for some time after the ignition has been switched off, and it must be relieved in a controlled fashion when any of these components are disturbed for servicing work.

2 Disconnect the battery negative lead.

3.3 Adjust the throttle cable as described in text

3 If possible, place a suitable container beneath the connection or union to be disconnected, and have a large rag ready to soak up any escaping fuel not being caught by the container.

4 Slowly loosen the connection or union nut to avoid a sudden release of pressure, and position the rag around the connection, to catch any fuel spray which may be expelled. Once the pressure is released, disconnect the fuel line. Plug the pipe ends, to minimise fuel loss and prevent the entry of dirt into the fuel system.

5 Fuel pump - removal and refitting

Note: Observe the precautions in Section 1 before working on any component in the fuel system.

Removal

1 Disconnect the battery negative lead.

2 Raise the rear seat cushion.

3 Prise up the right-hand plastic cover from the floor then disconnect the wiring, and the fuel supply and return pipes, noting their location **(see illustration)**.

4 Unscrew the retaining screws and lift the fuel pump housing from the fuel tank. Note that in some cases, the hole in the floor may not be aligned with the pump, in which case the fuel tank may need to be lowered for access (refer to Section 7 for details).

5 Release the filter from the bottom of the housing, then the collar **(see illustration)**.

5.3 Fuel pump locations and connections

6 Disconnect the wiring and release the fuel pump from the upper collar.

Refitting

7 Refitting is a reversal of removal, but fit new collars and make sure that the wiring terminals are positioned away from the pump terminals. Always fit a new gasket between the pump housing and fuel tank.

6 Fuel gauge sender unit - removal and refitting

Refer to Part A, Section 6.

7 Fuel tank - removal and refitting

Refer to Part A, Section 7, noting that it will be necessary to depressurise the fuel system as the feed and return hoses are disconnected from the fuel pump (see Section 5). It will also be necessary to disconnect the wiring connector from the fuel pump before lowering the tank out of position.

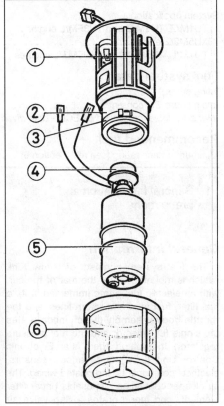

5.5 Fuel pump components

1	Bleed tube	4	Collar
2	Bracket	5	Fuel pump
3	Collar	6	Filter

8 Unleaded petrol - general information and usage

Note: *The information given in this Chapter is correct at the time of writing. If updated information is thought to be required, check with a Peugeot dealer. If travelling abroad, consult one of the motoring organisations (or a similar authority) for advice on the fuel available.*

All Peugeot 205 single-point fuel injection models are designed to run on fuel with a minimum octane rating of 95 (RON). All models are equipped with catalytic converters, and therefore must be run on unleaded fuel **only**. Under no circumstances should leaded fuel be used, as this may damage the catalytic converter.

Super unleaded petrol (97/98 RON) can also be used in all models if wished, though there is no advantage in doing so.

9 Fuel injection systems - general information

Bosch Mono-Jetronic A2.2 system

The Mono-Jetronic A2.2 system is a single-point fuel injection system incorporating a catalytic converter in the exhaust system.

The fuel pump, located in the fuel tank, pumps the fuel through a filter to the single fuel injector. The electronic control unit (ECU), which is triggered by the ignition circuit, sends impulses to the injector, which sprays fuel upstream of the throttle valve. A constant fuel pressure is maintained by a fuel pressure regulator, which returns excess fuel to the fuel tank. The ECU also receives information from various sensors to determine engine temperature, speed and load, and the quality of air entering the engine. The sensors inform the ECU of throttle position, inlet air temperature, coolant temperature, and exhaust gas oxygen content. Engine speed and crankshaft position information is provided by the ignition circuit. All the information supplied to the ECU is computed and compared with pre-set values stored in the ECU memory, to determine the required period of injection. The injector operates four times per engine cycle, and the injector opening duration is varied to control the quantity of fuel delivered.

The ECU constantly varies the fuel mixture and engine idle speed to provide optimum engine efficiency under all operating conditions, and to reduce exhaust gas emissions. The mixture strength is accurately controlled to maintain it within the operating limits of the catalytic converter.

MMFD Mono-point G5 and G6 systems

The Mono-point G5 and G6 systems are single-point fuel injection systems also incorporating a catalytic converter in the exhaust system. The only difference between the two systems is that the idle speed is controlled via a control valve on the G5 system, and via a control motor on the G6 system. The system operation is as described above for the Mono-Jetronic system and is under the overall control of an electronic control until (ECU), which also controls the ignition system.

10 Fuel injection system - testing and adjustment

Testing

1 If a fault appears in the fuel injection system, first ensure that all the system wiring connectors are securely connected and free of corrosion. Ensure that the fault is not due to poor maintenance; ie, check that the air cleaner filter element is clean, the spark plugs are in good condition and correctly gapped, the valve clearances are correctly adjusted, the cylinder compression pressures are correct, the ignition timing is correct (where adjustable), and that the engine breather hoses are clear and undamaged, referring to Chapters 1, 2 and 5 for further information.
2 If these checks fail to reveal the cause of the problem, the vehicle should be taken to a suitably-equipped Peugeot dealer for testing. A wiring block connector is incorporated in the engine management circuit, into which a special electronic diagnostic tester can be plugged. The tester will locate the fault quickly and simply, alleviating the need to test all the system components individually, which is a time-consuming operation that also carries a risk of damaging the ECU.

Adjustment

3 Experienced home mechanics with a considerable amount of skill and equipment (including a tachometer and an accurately

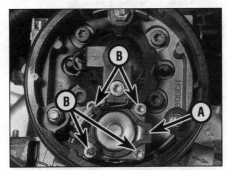

11.1 Fuel injector wiring clip (A), and fuel pressure regulator securing screws (B) - Mono-Jetronic A2.2 system

calibrated exhaust gas analyser) may be able to check the exhaust CO level and the idle speed. However, if these are found to be in need of adjustment, the car *must* be taken to a suitably-equipped Peugeot dealer for further testing.
4 On both single-point fuel injection systems, no adjustment of the CO level and idle speed is possible, these being under the complete control of the ECU. Should the idle speed or exhaust gas CO level be incorrect, then a fault is likely to be present in the fuel injection system.

11 Mono-Jetronic A2.2 system components - removal and refitting

Note: *Check the availability of individual components with your Peugeot dealer before dismantling.*

Fuel pressure regulator

Note: *Refer to the warning note in Section 1 before proceeding.*

1 The fuel pressure regulator (consisting of a valve operated by a spring-loaded diaphragm and a metal cover) is secured by four screws to the top of the throttle body **(see illustration)**. Although the unit can be dismantled for cleaning, if required (once the air inlet trunking and the fuel injector wiring clip have been removed for access), it should not be disturbed unless absolutely necessary.
2 Note that the regulator assembly is only available as part of the complete throttle body assembly; no individual components can be renewed separately.
3 If the regulator cover is removed, note its orientation on the throttle body before removal, to ensure correct refitting.

Fuel injector

Note: *Refer to the warning note in Section 1 before proceeding. If a faulty injector is suspected, before condemning the injector, it is worth trying the effect of one of the proprietary injector-cleaning treatments.*

4 Disconnect the battery negative lead.
5 Remove the air inlet trunking from the top of the throttle body.
6 Remove the Torx screws securing the injector wiring connector to the top of the throttle body, then carefully lift off the connector **(see illustrations)**.
7 Withdraw the injector **(see illustration)**. Recover and discard the injector sealing rings.
8 Refitting is the reverse of the removal procedure, noting the following points.
   a) *Always renew both sealing rings: apply a smear of grease to each ring, to ease injector refitting.*
   b) *Ensure that the injector is refitted so that its connector pins align with the connector when the connector is correctly located on the top of the throttle body.*

4B

11.6a Remove the Torx screw . . .

11.6b . . . and lift off the wiring connector

11.7 Withdrawing the fuel injector

c) *Before refitting the injector securing screw, apply a few drops of a suitable thread-locking compound to the threads.*
d) *On completion, switch on the ignition and check carefully for signs of fuel leaks; if*

11.11a Remove the sealing ring . . .

any signs of leakage are detected the problem must be rectified before the engine is started.

Inlet air temperature sensor

9 The sensor is located in the fuel injector wiring connector, and is available only as part of the connector assembly. To remove the connector assembly, proceed as follows.
10 Disconnect the battery negative lead.
11 Remove the air trunking from the top of the throttle body, then unscrew the three securing nuts, and remove the sealing ring. Recover the O-ring **(see illustrations)**.
12 Release the securing clips, separate the two halves of the fuel injector wiring connector, then release the wiring from the clip on the top of the throttle body **(see illustrations)**.
13 Remove the Torx screw securing the fuel

injector wiring connector to the top of the throttle body, then carefully lift off the connector **(see illustration)**.

Idle speed control motor

14 Disconnect the battery negative lead.
15 Release the securing clip, and disconnect the wiring plug from the motor **(see illustration)**.
16 Unscrew the securing screws, and withdraw the motor from the throttle body assembly **(see illustration)**.
17 Refitting is the reverse of the removal procedure. Note that the motor will reset itself as soon as the engine is restarted.

Throttle switch

18 The throttle switch is accurately matched on the throttle valve during manufacture - it is not adjustable and must not be disturbed.

11.11b . . . and recover the O-ring

11.12a Separate the two halves of fuel injector wiring connector . . .

11.12b . . . then release wiring from clip

11.13 Intake air temperature sensor (arrowed)

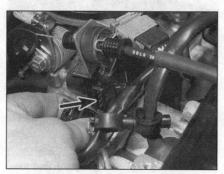

11.15 Disconnecting wiring plug from idle speed control motor (arrowed)

11.16 Unscrewing an idle speed control motor securing screw

11.23a Disconnecting the wiring plug from the fuel injector . . .

11.23b . . . and the throttle switch

11.25 Vacuum hose connection to throttle body (arrowed)

19 Do not attempt to adjust the throttle switch setting or that of the stop screw on the throttle valve external linkage; if the accurately matched relationship between these components is lost, the components must be replaced. At the time of writing this means renewing the entire throttle body assembly.

Throttle body

Note: *Refer to the warning note in Section 1 before proceeding.*

20 Disconnect the battery negative lead.

21 Remove the air inlet trunking from the top of the throttle body.

22 Disconnect the throttle cable (see Section 3).

23 Release the securing clips, and disconnect the wiring plugs from the fuel injector, the idle speed control motor, and the throttle switch (**see illustrations**).

24 Disconnect the fuel hoses from the unions on the throttle body (refer to Section 4). Plug the open ends of the hoses, to prevent dirt ingress and further fuel loss. Take note of the connections, and label them to ensure correct refitting.

25 Disconnect the vacuum hoses and pipes from the throttle body unions (**see illustration**). Label the hoses and pipes so that they can be correctly reconnected on refitting.

26 Remove the screws securing the throttle body to the inlet manifold, then withdraw the assembly (**see illustration**). Recover the gasket, and discard it.

27 If desired, the throttle body upper and lower sections may be separated by removing the securing screws. Note that a new gasket must be fitted on reassembly. As noted previously, do not disturb the throttle switch. The fuel inlet and return unions may be unscrewed from the throttle body, and the vacuum hose unions may be detached, but note that new sealing rings must be fitted on reassembly.

28 Refitting is the reverse of the removal procedure, noting the following points.

a) *Renew all gaskets and seals, and use suitable thread-locking compound where applicable.*

b) *Check the throttle cable operation and adjustment (Section 3).*

c) *Ensure that all vacuum hoses and pipes are correctly reconnected, as noted before removal.*

d) *Ensure that the fuel hoses are correctly reconnected. The direction of fuel flow is indicated by arrows cast into the throttle body next to each union.*

e) *On completion, switch on the ignition, and check for signs of fuel leaks from all disturbed unions. If any signs of leakage are detected, the problem must be rectified before the engine is started.*

Coolant temperature sensor

Refer to Chapter 3, Section 7.

Electronic control unit (ECU)

29 The ECU is located behind the facia, to the right of the steering column.

30 Disconnect the battery negative lead.

31 For improved access, remove the driver's side lower facia panel. The panel is secured by four screws, and a single bolt.

32 Remove the nuts securing the ECU bracket to the facia, then lower the assembly. Withdraw the ECU from the bracket (**see illustration**).

33 Release the securing clip, or remove the securing screws, as applicable, and disconnect the wiring plug (**see illustration**).

34 Refitting is a reversal of removal, but ensure that the wiring plug is securely reconnected, and where applicable, ensure that the ECU locates correctly in the bracket.

Fuel injection system fuses and relays

35 The relays are generally mounted on the left-hand side of the engine compartment bulkhead. The relays may be mounted on individual brackets, or on later models, in a plastic box.

36 Most of the fuses are located in the main fusebox inside the car, although on certain models, additional fuses may be located in a small fusebox mounted at the front left-hand corner of the engine compartment.

37 The number and type of fuses and relays fitted will depend on engine type and exact vehicle specification.

4B

11.26 Throttle body securing screws (arrowed)

11.32 Removing the ECU from its bracket. Note securing lug (arrowed)

11.33 Disconnecting the ECU wiring plug

12.1 Fuel pressure regulator (A) and fuel injector wiring plug (B)

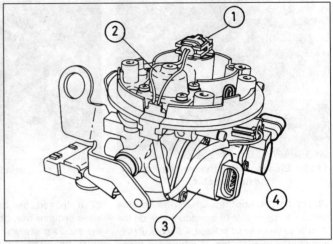

12.4 MMFD G6 fuel injection system throttle body assembly

1 Fuel injector wiring connector   3 Idle speed control motor
2 Fuel pressure regulator   4 Throttle switch

12 MMFD Mono-point G5 and G6 system components - removal and refitting

Note: *Check the availability of individual components with your Peugeot dealer before dismantling.*

Fuel pressure regulator

1 Refer to Section 11, Paragraphs 1 to 3 noting the revised component arrangement **(see illustration).**

Fuel injector

Note: *Refer to the warning note in Section 1 before proceeding. If a faulty injector is suspected, before condemning the injector, it is worth trying the effect of one of the proprietary injector-cleaning treatments. Note that at the time of writing, the injector does not appear to be available separately from the throttle body upper section assembly.*
2 Disconnect the battery negative lead.
3 Remove the air inlet trunking from the top of the throttle body.
4 Release the securing clip, and disconnect the injector wiring plug **(see illustration).**
5 Remove the Torx screw securing the injector retainer plate to the top of the throttle body **(see illustration)**, lift off the retainer, then withdraw the injector. Recover and discard the injector sealing rings (check to ensure that new sealing rings can be obtained before discarding the old ones).
6 Refitting is the reverse of the removal procedure, noting the following points.
  a) *Always renew both sealing rings; apply a smear of grease to each, to ease injector refitting.*
  b) *Refit the injector so that its wiring terminals point towards the front of the vehicle, and locate the edge of the*

retainer securely in the groove at the top of the injector.
  c) *Before refitting the injector securing screw, apply a few drops of a suitable thread-locking compound to the threads.*
  d) *On completion, switch on the ignition, and check carefully for signs of fuel leaks; if any signs of leakage are detected, the problem must be rectified before the engine is started.*

Throttle switch

7 Disconnect the battery negative lead.
8 Disconnect the wiring plug, and disconnect the wiring plug from the switch.
9 Remove the two securing screws and withdraw the switch.
10 Refitting is a reversal of removal, noting the following points.
  a) *Before refitting the switch, ensure that the throttle valve is fully closed.*
  b) *Ensure that the switch wiper engages correctly with the throttle shaft.*

Idle speed control valve (MMFD G5 system)

11 For improved access, remove the air cleaner trunking.

12.5 Fuel injector retaining plate securing screw (arrowed)

12 Disconnect the battery negative lead.
13 Release the securing clip, and disconnect the wiring plug from the valve.
14 Loosen the securing clamps, and disconnect the air hoses from the valve. Note the locations of the hoses to ensure correct refitting.
15 Remove the securing screws, and withdraw the valve.
16 Refitting is a reversal of removal, noting that the arrows cast on the valve unions indicate the direction of airflow through the valve. Ensure that the hoses are securely refitted, to prevent air leaks.

Idle speed control motor (MMFD G6 system)

Note: *At the time of writing, it was not clear whether the motor is available separately from the throttle body assembly. It is advisable to seek the advice of a Peugeot dealer before deciding on the course of action to be followed if the motor is thought to be faulty.*
17 For improved access, remove the air inlet trunking.
18 Disconnect the battery negative lead.
19 Release the securing clip, and disconnect the wiring plug from the motor.
20 Remove the two securing screws, then withdraw the motor. Recover and discard the sealing ring (check to ensure that a new sealing ring can be obtained before discarding the old one).
21 Refitting is a reversal of removal bearing in mind the following points.
  a) *Always fit a new sealing ring, greasing it lightly to ease installation.*
  b) *The control motor will be reset by the ECU as soon as the engine is restarted.*
  c) *Apply suitable thread-locking compound to the securing screw threads before refitting.*

Inlet air temperature sensor

22 The sensor is screwed into the top of the inlet manifold.

23 Disconnect the battery negative lead.

24 Release the securing clip, and disconnect the wiring plug from the sensor.

25 Unscrew the sensor and withdraw it.

26 Refitting is a reversal of removal.

Throttle body

Note: *Refer to the warning note in Section 1 before proceeding.*

27 Disconnect the battery negative lead.

28 Remove the air inlet trunking from the top of the throttle body.

29 Disconnect the throttle cable (see Section 3).

30 Release the securing clips, then disconnect the wiring plugs from the fuel injector (remove the rubber throttle body/trunking seals to release the wiring), throttle switch, and the idle speed control motor (MMFD G6 system only).

31 Disconnect the fuel hoses from the unions on the throttle body, labelling the hoses to ensure correct refitting. Plug the open ends of the hoses, to prevent dirt ingress and further loss of fuel.

32 Disconnect the vacuum pipes and hoses from the throttle body unions. Label the hoses so that they can be correctly reconnected.

33 Unscrew the studs securing the throttle body to the inlet manifold, and withdraw the assembly. Recover and discard the gasket.

34 If desired, the two halves of the throttle body (upper and lower) can be separated by removing the securing screws. Note that in this case, a new gasket must be used on reassembly.

35 Refitting is a reversal of removal, bearing in mind the following points.

a) *Renew all disturbed gaskets and seals, and use suitable thread locking compound where necessary.*

b) *Check the throttle cable operation and adjustment (Section 3).*

c) *Ensure that all vacuum hoses and pipes are correctly reconnected as noted before removal.*

d) *When reconnecting the manifold absolute pressure sensor hose, ensure that it is routed so that it falls steadily from the sensor to the throttle body. This is necessary to prevent any fuel droplets from entering the sensor (no fuel vapour trap is fitted), allowing them to drain into the throttle body instead.*

e) *Ensure that the fuel hoses are correctly reconnected, as noted before removal.*

f) *On completion, switch on the ignition, and check carefully for signs of fuel leakage from all disturbed unions. If any signs of leakage are detected the problem must be rectified before the engine is started.*

Manifold absolute pressure sensor

36 Disconnect the battery negative lead.

37 Release the securing clip, and disconnect the wiring plug from the idle speed control motor (MMFD G6 systems only).

38 Slacken the clamp (if fitted), and disconnect the vacuum hose from the sensor.

39 Remove the securing screws and withdraw the sensor, complete with bracket, from the body front panel (or wing panel, as applicable).

40 Refitting is a reversal of removal, but note the following. When reconnecting the vacuum hose to the sensor ensure that the hose is routed so that it falls steadily from the sensor to the throttle body. This is necessary to prevent any fuel droplets from entering the sensor (no fuel vapour trap is fitted), allowing them to drain into the throttle body instead.

Coolant temperature sensor

Refer to Chapter 3, Section 7.

Electronic control unit (ECU)

Refer to Section 11, paragraphs 29 to 34.

Fuel injection system fuses and relays

Refer to Section 11, paragraphs 35 to 37.

13 Inlet manifold - removal and refitting

The procedure is essentially as described in Part A, Section 11, but remove the throttle body as described in Section 11 or 12 of this Part and ignore any references to carburettor.

Chapter 4 Part C:
Fuel system - multi-point fuel injection engines

Contents

Degrees of difficulty

Easy, suitable for novice with little experience	**Fairly easy,** suitable for beginner with some experience	**Fairly difficult,** suitable for competent DIY mechanic 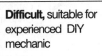	**Difficult,** suitable for experienced DIY mechanic	**Very difficult,** suitable for expert DIY or professional

Specifications

General

System type . . . . Rear-mounted fuel tank, electric fuel pump, multi-point fuel injection system

System application:
XU5J, XU5JA, XU5JA/K, XU51C/K, XU9JA, XU9JA/K . . . . Bosch LE2-Jetronic
XU9J1/Z, XU9J1/L . . . . Bosch LU2-Jetronic
XU9JA/Z, XU9JA/L . . . . Bosch Motronic M1.3

Fuel system data

Regulated fuel pressure . . . . 2.9 to 3.1 bar
Fuel pump delivery . . . . 540 cc/15 sec
Idling speed . . . . 900 ± 50 rpm
Idle mixture CO content* . . . . 1.0 to 2.0 %
Adjustable on LE2-Jetronic system only - controlled by ECU on all other systems

Recommended fuel

Minimum octane rating (see text Section 8) . . . . 95 RON unleaded or 97/98 RON unleaded*
* **Note:** *The XU9JA engine should not be operated on 95 RON unleaded petrol*

---

1 General information and precautions

General information

The fuel supply system consists of a fuel tank (which is mounted under the rear of the car, with an electric fuel pump immersed in it), a fuel filter, fuel feed and return lines. The fuel pump supplies fuel to the fuel rail, which acts as a reservoir for the four fuel injectors which inject fuel into the inlet tracts. The fuel filter incorporated in the feed line from the pump to the fuel rail ensures that the fuel supplied to the injectors is clean.

Refer to Section 9 for further information on the operation of each fuel injection system.

Precautions

 Warning: Petrol is extremely flammable - great care must be taken when working on any part of the fuel system. Do not smoke or allow any naked flames or uncovered light bulbs near the work area. Note that gas powered domestic appliances with pilot flames, such as heaters, boilers and tumble dryers, also present a fire hazard - bear this in mind if you are working in an area where such appliances are present. Always keep a suitable fire extinguisher close to the work area and familiarise yourself with its operation before starting work. Wear eye protection when working on fuel systems and wash off any fuel spilt on bare skin immediately with soap and water. Note that fuel vapour is just as dangerous as liquid fuel; a vessel that has just been emptied of liquid fuel will still contain vapour and can be potentially explosive. Petrol is a highly dangerous and volatile liquid, and the precautions necessary when handling it cannot be overstressed.

Many of the operations described in this Chapter involve the disconnection of fuel lines, which may cause an amount of fuel spillage. Before commencing work, refer to the above Warning and the information in "Safety first" at the beginning of this manual.

When working with fuel system components, pay particular attention to cleanliness - dirt entering the fuel system may cause blockages which will lead to poor running.

4C

Note: *Residual pressure will remain in the fuel lines long after the vehicle was last used. When disconnecting any fuel line, first depressurise the fuel system as described in Section 4.*

2 Air cleaner assembly - removal and refitting

Removal

1 Disconnect the inlet and outlet ducts.
2 Unscrew the mounting bolts and lift the air cleaner from the engine.

Refitting

3 Refitting is a reversal of removal.

3 Throttle cable - removal, refitting and adjustment

Removal

1 Extract the spring clip from the adjustment ferrule located beneath the inlet manifold. Release the cable end fitting from the linkage the outer cable from the support bracket.
2 Working inside the car, disconnect the cable end fitting from the top of the accelerator pedal arm.
3 Withdraw the throttle cable through the bulkhead grommet.

Refitting and adjustment

4 Refitting is a reversal of removal, but adjust the cable as follows.
5 Remove the spring clip from the adjustment ferrule then, ensuring that the throttle cam is fully against its stop, gently pull the cable out of its grommet until all free play is removed from the inner cable.
6 With the cable held in this position, ensure that the flat washer is pressed securely against the grommet, then fit the spring clip to the third ferrule groove visible in front of the rubber grommet and washer.
7 Have an assistant depress the accelerator pedal and check that the throttle cam opens fully and returns smoothly to its stop.

4 Fuel system - depressurisation

Note: *Refer to the warning note in Section 1 before proceeding.*

 Warning: The following procedure will merely relieve the pressure in the fuel system - remember that fuel will still be present in the system components, and take precautions accordingly before disconnecting any of them.

1 The fuel system referred to in this Section is defined as the tank-mounted fuel pump, the fuel filter, the fuel injectors, the fuel rail and the pressure regulator, and the metal pipes and flexible hoses of the fuel lines between these components. All these contain fuel which will be under pressure while the engine is running, and/or while the ignition is switched on. The pressure will remain for some time after the ignition has been switched off, and must be relieved in a controlled fashion when any of these components are disturbed for servicing work.
2 Disconnect the battery negative lead.
3 Where possible, place a container beneath the connection/union to be disconnected, and have a large rag ready to soak up any escaping fuel not being caught by the container.
4 Slowly loosen the connection or union nut to avoid a sudden release of pressure, and position the rag around the connection, to catch any fuel spray which may be expelled. Once the pressure is released, disconnect the fuel line. Plug the pipe ends, to minimise fuel loss and prevent the entry of dirt into the fuel system.

5 Fuel pump - removal and refitting

Refer to Part B, Section 5.

6 Fuel gauge sender unit - removal and refitting

Refer to Part A, Section 6.

7 Fuel tank - removal and refitting

Refer to Part A, Section 7, noting that it will be necessary to depressurise the fuel system as the feed and return hoses are disconnected from the fuel pump which is located inside the tank. It will also be necessary to disconnect the wiring connector from the fuel pump before lowering the tank out of position.

8 Unleaded petrol - general information and usage

Note: *The information given in this Chapter is correct at the time of writing. If updated information is thought to be required, check with a Peugeot dealer. If travelling abroad, consult one of the motoring organisations (or a similar authority) for advice on the fuel available.*

1 With the exception of the XU9JA engine (fitted to 1.9 GTI models without a catalytic converter), all engines can be operated on 95 RON unleaded petrol. The XU9JA engine should not be operated on 95 RON unleaded petrol.
2 No adjustments to the ignition timing are necessary in order to operate engines on 95 RON unleaded petrol, with the exception of the XU5J and XU5JA engines, which must both have the ignition timing retarded by 2°. Refer to Chapter 5B for details of ignition timing adjustment.
3 Do not operate an engine equipped with a catalytic converter on leaded petrol. If a catalytic converter is fitted, unleaded petrol must be used at all times.

Engine	Code	Retard ignition by
XU5J	180A	2° (95 or 97/98 RON unleaded)
XU5JA	B6D	2° (95 or 97/98 RON unleaded)
XU5JA/K	B6E	None (95 or 97/98 RON unleaded)
XU9JA/K	D6B	None (97/98 RON leaded or unleaded)
XU9JA/Z	DKZ	None (95 or 97/98 RON unleaded)
XU9JA/L	DKZ	None (95 or 97/98 RON unleaded)
XU9J1/Z	DFZ	None (95 or 97/98 RON unleaded)
XU9J1/L	DFZ	None (95 or 97/98 RON unleaded)

9 Fuel injection systems - general information

Bosch LE2-Jetronic system

A roller type electric pump located in the fuel tank pumps fuel through the filter to the injectors via a fuel distribution rail. The electronic control unit (ECU) which is triggered by the ignition circuit sends impulses to the injectors which operate simultaneously and inject fuel in the vicinity of the inlet valves. The electronic control unit is provided with sensors to determine engine temperature, speed and load, and the quantity of air entering the engine. This information is computed to determine the period of injection.

For cold starting, additional fuel is provided and, to compensate for this, additional air is provided by a supplementary air device.

Bosch LU2-Jetronic system

The principle of operation of the LU2-Jetronic system is similar to that described above for the LE2-Jetronic system, the only significant difference is that the LU2-Jetronic system incorporates an oxygen sensor in the exhaust system. This enables the ECU to carry out fine fuel mixture adjustment, to allow the use of a catalytic converter.

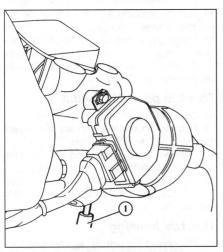

10.5 To check the throttle initial position, connect a vacuum gauge to the test point (1)

Bosch Motronic M1.3 system

The Bosch Motronic fuel injection system is designed to meet stringent emission control legislation whilst still providing excellent engine performance and fuel economy. The system is under the overall control of the Motronic M1.3 engine management system, which also controls the ignition timing.

The principle of operation of the system is similar to that described above for the LE2-Jetronic system, noting the following differences.

a) A double-barrel throttle housing is used with two throttle valves operating simultaneously.

b) An oxygen sensor is fitted to the exhaust system which allows fine mixture adjustment to enable the use of a catalytic converter.

c) A TDC sensor is used to provide the ECU with information on crankshaft speed and position.

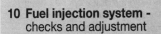

10 Fuel injection system - checks and adjustment

General information

1 If a fault appears in the fuel injection system, first ensure that all the system wiring connectors are securely connected and free of corrosion. Ensure that the fault is not due to poor maintenance; ie, check that the air cleaner filter element is clean, the spark plugs are in good condition and correctly gapped, the valve clearances are correctly adjusted, the cylinder compression pressures are correct, the ignition timing is correct (where adjustable), and that the engine breather hoses are clear and undamaged, referring to Chapters 1, 2 and 5 for further information.

2 If these checks fail to reveal the cause of the problem, carry out the checks and

adjustments described in the following sub-sections which represent the limit of work that can be done without sophisticated test equipment. If problems still exist, the vehicle should be taken to a suitably-equipped Peugeot dealer for testing. A wiring block connector is incorporated in the engine management circuit, into which a special electronic diagnostic tester can be plugged. The tester will locate the fault quickly and simply, alleviating the need to test all the system components individually, which is a time-consuming operation that also carries a risk of damaging the ECU.

Checks and adjustment

Idle speed and mixture CO content

3 Refer to Chapter 1.

Throttle initial position - LE2-Jetronic system

4 Run the engine to normal operating temperature - indicated when the electric cooling fan has cut in and out twice. The ignition timing must be correctly adjusted, as described in Chapter 5B.

5 Connect a vacuum gauge to the test point in the distributor vacuum advance line **(see illustration)**.

6 Check that the throttle movement is smooth.

7 With the engine stopped turn the air screw fully in **(see illustration)**.

8 Prise the tamperproof cap from the throttle stop screw **(see illustration)**.

9 Unscrew the throttle stop screw then retighten it until it just touches the throttle lever. Tighten the screw a further four complete turns.

10 Start the engine and allow it to idle. Turn the throttle stop screw to obtain an idle speed of 650 rpm (XU5J engines) or 600 rpm (XU5JA and XU9JA engines). Check that the vacuum reading shown on the gauge does not exceed 50 mm Hg (65 mbar) and if necessary adjust the throttle stop screw.

11 Now turn the air screw in the throttle housing as necessary to obtain the specified idling speed.

12 Stop the engine and adjust the throttle switch, as described below.

10.7 Turn the air screw fully in

Throttle initial position - LU2-Jetronic and Motronic M1.3 systems

13 The throttle initial position is set in production, and will not normally require adjustment unless the throttle housing has been tampered with. Adjustment should be entrusted to a Peugeot dealer.

Throttle switch - LE2-Jetronic system

14 Pull the connector from the throttle switch **(see illustration)**.

15 Connect a voltmeter between the middle terminal on the connector and earth.

16 Pull the connector from the ignition amplifier (see Chapter 5B), then operate the starter motor and check that there is a reading of at least 9 volts.

17 Disconnect the air hose from the throttle housing.

18 On all engines except XU5JA and XU9JA, position a 0.30 mm feeler blade between the throttle stop screw and the throttle lever.

19 Loosen the two throttle switch screws.

20 Connect an ohmmeter between terminals 18 and 2 on the throttle switch, then rotate the switch until the internal contacts close and the reading is zero ohms. Tighten the screws with the switch in this position.

21 Remove the feeler blade (where applicable) and on all engines, insert in its place a 0.70 mm feeler blade. The internal contacts should now be separated and the reading on the ohmmeter infinity. If not, repeat the procedure in paragraph 19.

22 Remove the feeler blade.

4C

10.8 Prise the tamperproof cap from the throttle stop screw (arrowed) and adjust as described in text

10.14 Removing the throttle switch connector

23 Check the full throttle operation by connecting an ohmmeter between terminals 18 and 3, then fully opening the throttle so that dimension X is 4.0 mm (see illustration). The internal contacts should close and the ohmmeter reading be zero.
24 If the switch does not operate correctly it should be renewed.

Throttle switch - LU2-Jetronic and Motronic M1.3 systems

25 The throttle initial position must be correct before attempting to adjust the throttle switch.
26 Slacken the throttle switch securing screws.
27 Turn the switch unit fully clockwise, then turn it slowly back until the idling contacts are heard to close.
28 Tighten the securing screws.
29 Pull the wiring from the switch, then connect an ohmmeter between terminals 2 and 18 in the switch (see illustration). The ohmmeter should read zero.
30 Operate the throttle linkage, and the ohmmeter should read infinity.
31 If the readings are not correct, repeat the procedure described in paragraphs 26 to 30 inclusive.
32 Connect the ohmmeter between switch terminals 3 and 18. The ohmmeter should read infinity.
33 Fully open the throttle, and the ohmmeter should read zero.
34 If the specified readings cannot be obtained, renew the switch.
35 Reconnect the switch wiring plug on completion.

11 Fuel injection system components - removal and refitting

Note: *Although some of the components may differ slightly in detail, the following procedures are applicable to all three multi-point fuel injection systems. It is advisable to check the availability of individual components with your Peugeot dealer before dismantling.*

Fuel injectors

Note: *Refer to the warning note in Section 1 before proceeding. Ensure that the working area is clean before removing the injectors, and ensure that no dirt is allowed to enter the system during the procedure. No attempt should be made to overhaul the injectors. If a fault or contamination is suspected, seek specialist advice.*
1 Disconnect the battery negative lead.
2 Disconnect the wiring plugs from the fuel injectors, labelling them if necessary to ensure correct refitting.
3 Disconnect the vacuum hose from the top of the fuel pressure regulator.
4 Unscrew the four bolts securing the fuel rail to the inlet manifold (two upper bolts, and two bolts at the right-hand end of the rail), then

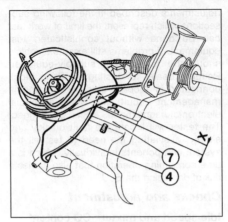

10.23 Full throttle dimension "X"

4   *Throttle lever*
7   *Throttle housing*
      X = 4.0 mm

carefully lift the rail, complete with pressure regulator and fuel injectors, from the inlet manifold, taking care not to strain any of the hoses or pipes.
5 To remove a fuel injector from the fuel rail, carefully remove the metal securing clip, then pull the injector from the rail. Be prepared for fuel spillage, and take adequate precautions.
6 Refitting is a reversal of removal, but fit new injector O-rings.

Fuel pressure regulator

Note: Refer to the warning note in Section 1 before proceeding. Ensure that the working area is clean and that no dirt is allowed to enter the system during the procedure.
7 For improved access to the lower pressure regulator securing nut, proceed as described in paragraphs 3 and 4.
8 If not already done, disconnect the vacuum hose from the top of the pressure regulator.
9 Slacken the hose clip, and disconnect the fuel return hose from the bottom of the pressure regulator. Be prepared for fuel spillage, and take adequate precautions.
10 Unscrew the two bolts securing the pressure regulator to the fuel rail bracket assembly, whilst counter holding the nuts. Note that on some models, a hose bracket is secured by the upper bolt.

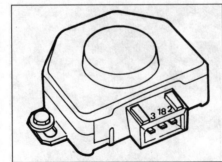

10.29 Throttle switch terminal identification - LU2-Jetronic and Motronic M1.3 systems

11 Pull the regulator from the end of the fuel rail, and recover the O-ring.
12 Refitting is a reversal of removal, but use a new O-ring when refitting the pressure regulator to the fuel rail, and where applicable, use new injector O-rings.

Throttle position switch

13 Disconnect the battery negative lead.
14 Release the securing clip and disconnect the wiring plug from the switch.
15 Remove the two securing screws, then withdraw the switch from the throttle body.
16 Refitting is a reversal of removal, but on completion, adjust the switch as described in Section 10.

Throttle housing

17 Disconnect the battery negative lead.
18 Release the securing clip, and disconnect the wiring plug from the throttle position switch.
19 Loosen the securing clamp, and disconnect the air trunking from the front of the throttle housing.
20 Disconnect the throttle cable, with reference to Section 3.
21 Disconnect the vacuum and/or breather hoses from the throttle housing, noting their locations to ensure correct refitting.
22 Unscrew the three throttle housing securing nuts, and recover the washers. Remove the throttle cable bracket from the top throttle housing securing stud, noting its orientation.
23 Withdraw the throttle housing from the inlet manifold.
24 Refitting is a reversal of removal, bearing in mind the following points.
  a) *Ensure that the vacuum and/or breather hoses are correctly reconnected, as noted before removal.*
  b) *After refitting the throttle housing, check the adjustment of the throttle cable, as described in Section 3.*
  c) *On completion, if any work has been carried out on the housing, check the adjustment of the throttle switch, as described in Section 10.*

Supplementary air (cold start) device

25 Remove the battery as described in Chapter 5A.
26 Disconnect the air hoses then unbolt the airflow sensor and bracket. Disconnect the wiring.
27 Unscrew the supplementary air device bracket nuts and disconnect the wiring.
28 Tilt the assembly and coolant outlet housing (without disconnecting the coolant hoses) and remove the concealed mounting bolt.
29 Disconnect the air hoses, then remove the remaining mounting bolt and withdraw the unit.
30 Refitting is a reversal of removal.

Coolant temperature sensor

31 Refer to Chapter 3, Section 7.

Electronic control unit (ECU)

32 Refer to Part B, Section 11.

Fuel injection system fuses and relays

33 Refer to Part B, Section 11.

---

12 Inlet manifold - removal and refitting

Note: *The following procedure is applicable to all three multi-point fuel injection systems, but slight differences in component layout may be encountered.*

Removal

1 Disconnect the battery negative lead.
2 Slacken the retaining clip, then disconnect the inlet duct from the throttle housing and recover the sealing ring.

3 Disconnect the throttle inner cable from the throttle cam, then withdraw the outer cable from the mounting bracket, along with its flat washer and spring clip.
4 Depress the retaining clip and disconnect the wiring connector from the throttle position switch.
5 Release the retaining clips (where fitted) and disconnect all the relevant vacuum and breather hoses from the manifold. Make identification marks on the hoses to ensure that they are connected correctly on refitting.
6 Bearing in mind the information given in Section 4, slacken the retaining clips and disconnect the fuel feed and return hoses from the fuel rail.
7 Depress the retaining tangs and disconnect the wiring connectors from the four injectors. Free the wiring from any relevant retaining clips and position it clear of the manifold.
8 Where necessary, undo the retaining bolts and remove the support bracket from the underside of the manifold.
9 Undo the manifold retaining nuts and withdraw the manifold from the engine compartment. Recover the four manifold seals and discard them; new ones must be used on refitting.

Refitting

10 Refitting is a reverse of the relevant removal procedure, noting the following points:
  a) *Ensure that the manifold and cylinder head mating surfaces are clean and dry, then locate the new seals in their recesses in the manifold.*
  b) *Ensure that all relevant hoses are reconnected to their original positions and are securely held (where necessary) by the retaining clips.*
  c) *Adjust the throttle cable as described in Section 3.*

4C

Notes

Chapter 4 Part D:
Exhaust and emission control systems

Contents

Degrees of difficulty

Easy, suitable for novice with little experience	Fairly easy, suitable for beginner with some experience	Fairly difficult, suitable for competent DIY mechanic	Difficult, suitable for experienced DIY mechanic	Very difficult, suitable for expert DIY or professional

1 General information

Exhaust system

1 The exhaust system consists of front, intermediate and rear sections, the number varying according to model. The system is suspended from the underbody on rubber mountings, and bolted to the exhaust manifold at the front. Flanged joints incorporating gasket seals or pipe clamps are used to secure the sections. The front section downpipe is of twin, or "siamesed" type and is attached to the manifold by a flanged joint incorporating compression springs or by a single spherical joint. On TU series engines, a ball-and-socket type joint is provided between the front downpipe and intermediate pipes, to allow for engine movement.

2 Later fuel-injected models are equipped with a catalytic converter as part of the exhaust emission control system.

Emission control systems

3 Various systems may be fitted to reduce the emission of unburned hydrocarbons and harmful exhaust gases into the atmosphere. Basically, these systems can be divided as follows:

a) Air inlet heating system.
b) Crankcase ventilation system.
c) Electro-pneumatic ignition timing
   retarding system.
d) Catalytic converter.
e) Fuel vapour recirculation system.

4 The operation of the systems is described briefly in the following paragraphs.

Air inlet heating system

5 This system is fitted to certain carburettor and all single-point fuel injection models, and assists the vaporisation of the fuel, providing more complete combustion of the fuel/air mixture **(see illustration)**. This is achieved by controlling the temperature of the air entering the engine.

6 The air drawn through the air inlet pipe from the engine compartment is mixed with hot air drawn from a shroud around the exhaust manifold. The proportions of hot and cold air are controlled by the position of a flap valve, which in turn is controlled by a wax thermostat and a vacuum capsule (connected to the inlet manifold).

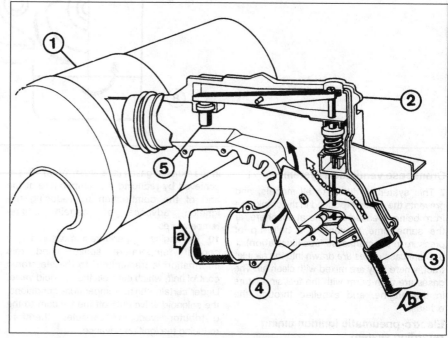

1.5 Typical air intake heating system

1	Air cleaner	3	Exhaust manifold	4	Flap valve	a	Cold air
2	Air ducting		hot air duct	5	Wax thermostat	b	Hot air

4D

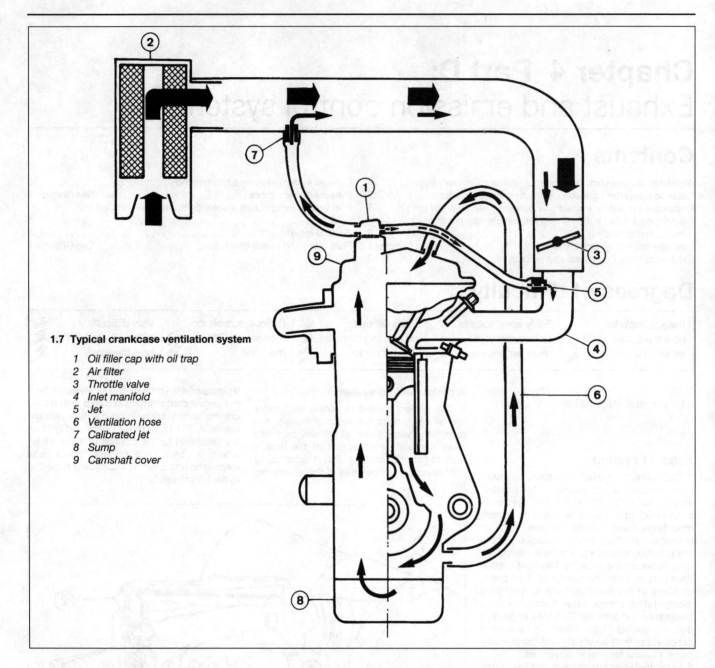

1.7 Typical crankcase ventilation system

1 Oil filler cap with oil trap
2 Air filter
3 Throttle valve
4 Inlet manifold
5 Jet
6 Ventilation hose
7 Calibrated jet
8 Sump
9 Camshaft cover

Crankcase ventilation system

7 This system is fitted to all models, and prevents the gases produced in the crankcase from being released into the atmosphere, at the same time preventing a build-up of pressure in the crankcase **(see illustration).**

8 Crankcase gases are drawn into the air inlet tract, where they are mixed with clean air. The gases are then burnt with the fuel/air mixture in the engine, and expelled through the exhaust.

Electro-pneumatic ignition timing retarding system

9 This system is used on models fitted with the Mono-Jetronic A2.2 fuel injection system, and reduces the nitrous oxide (NOx) content

in the exhaust gases **(see illustration).** This is achieved by reducing the temperature at the end of the combustion by reducing the ignition advance at certain engine temperatures.

10 The engine temperature is measured by a coolant temperature sensor, and this information is transmitted to the electronic control unit, which controls the solenoid valve. Under certain engine temperature conditions, the solenoid valve cuts off the vacuum to the distributor vacuum capsule, therefore reducing the ignition advance.

Catalytic converter

11 Catalytic converters have been introduced progressively on all models in the

range, to meet emissions regulations.

12 The catalytic converter is located in the exhaust system, and operates in conjunction with an exhaust gas oxygen sensor to reduce exhaust gas emissions. The catalytic converter effectively cleans the exhaust gases by speeding up their decomposition.

13 In order for a catalytic converter to operate effectively, the air/fuel mixture must be very accurately controlled, and this is achieved by measuring the oxygen content of the exhaust gas. The oxygen sensor transmits information on the exhaust gas oxygen content to the electronic control unit, which adjusts the air/fuel mixture strength accordingly.

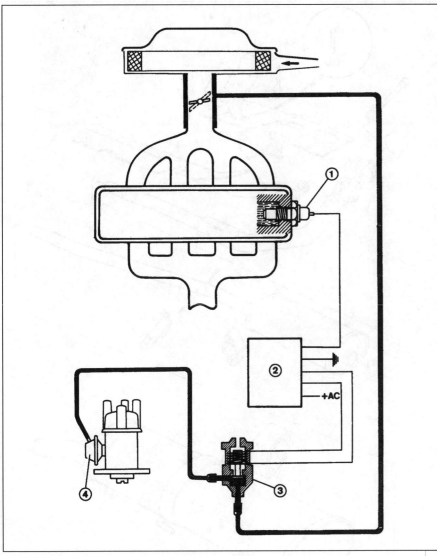

1.9 Electro-pneumatic ignition timing retarding system

1 *Coolant temperature sensor*
2 *Electronic control unit*
3 *Solenoid valve*
4 *Distributor vacuum capsule*

Fuel vapour recirculation system

14 This system has been introduced progressively on all fuel injection models, and prevents fuel vapour from the fuel tank from being ejected into the atmosphere **(see illustration)**.

15 The fuel filler cap is sealed, and the fuel vapours from the tank pass into a carbon canister, via a calibrated orifice and a pipe. The fuel vapour is absorbed by the carbon filling in the canister.

16 When the engine is running, it draws a proportion of its inlet air through the carbon canister, and this air picks up the fuel vapour contained in the carbon canister.

17 A solenoid valve mounted in the pipe between the canister and the inlet manifold prevents the system from operating when the engine is cold. The solenoid valve is controlled by the electronic control unit, on the basis of information received from the coolant temperature sensor.

2 Exhaust system - removal and refitting

Removal

1 Details of exhaust system routing and mounting will vary with model and year, but the principles of removal and refitting remain the same **(see illustration)**.

4D

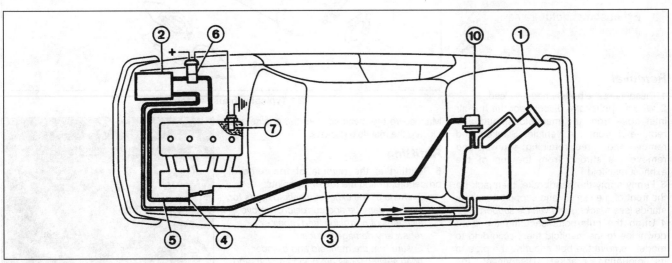

1.14 Fuel vapour recirculation system

1 *Fuel filler cap*
2 *Charcoal canister*
3 *Hose*
4 *Calibrated orifice*
5 *Hose*
6 *Solenoid valve*
7 *Coolant temperature sensor*
10 *Safety valve*

2 In many cases it will be found easier to remove the complete system from the car and then to renew individual sections on the bench.

3 To remove the complete system, raise and support the vehicle at a convenient working height (see *"Jacking and vehicle support"*). Apply penetrating oil to the nuts, bolts and clamps which will have to be undone.

4 Where applicable, disconnect the oxygen sensor wiring plug is disconnected before removing the downpipe.

5 Unbolt the flanged joint at the union of the exhaust system with the downpipe or at the manifold connection. According to model, unbolt the additional support brackets at the transmission.

6 With the aid of an assistant, unhook the system from its mountings and remove it.

7 With the system removed, undo the retaining clamp bolts and separate the various sections as required.

Refitting

8 Refitting is a reversal of removal, noting the following points:

a) *Ensure that all traces of corrosion have been removed from the flanges and renew all necessary gaskets.*

b) *Inspect the rubber mountings for signs of damage or deterioration, and renew as necessary.*

c) *When tightening a spring loaded flange joint, tighten the flange mounting nuts evenly so that the special springs are compressed equally; approximately four threads of the bolt should be visible and the springs should be compressed to approximately 22.0 mm.*

d) *Prior to tightening the exhaust system fasteners, ensure that all rubber mountings are correctly located, and that there is adequate clearance between the exhaust system and vehicle underbody.*

---

3 Exhaust manifold - removal and refitting

Removal

1 Disconnect the battery negative lead.

2 Where applicable, disconnect the hot-air inlet hose from the manifold shroud and remove it from the vehicle. Slacken and remove the three retaining screws, and remove the shroud from the top of the exhaust manifold

3 Firmly apply the handbrake, then jack up the front of the vehicle and support it on axle stands (see *"Jacking and vehicle support"*).

4 Undo the nuts/bolts securing the front downpipe to the manifold then, according to model, remove the bolt securing the pipe to its mounting bracket. Disconnect the downpipe from the manifold.

5 Undo the retaining nuts securing the manifold to the cylinder head **(see illustration)**.

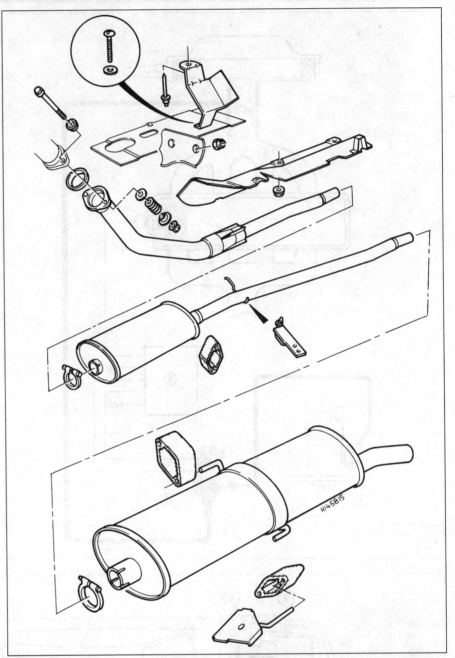

2.1 Typical exhaust system layout

Manoeuvre the manifold from the engine and discard the manifold gaskets.

Refitting

6 Refitting is the reverse of the removal procedure, noting the following points:

a) *Examine all the exhaust manifold studs for signs of damage and corrosion; remove all traces of corrosion, and repair or renew any damaged studs.*

b) *Ensure that the manifold and cylinder head sealing faces are clean and flat, and fit the new manifold gaskets.*

c) *Reconnect the downpipe to the manifold using the information given in Section 2.*

3.5 Exhaust manifold upper retaining nuts (arrowed)

4 Air inlet heating system components - removal and refitting

Note: *The components of the system vary slightly according to engine type. The following procedures depict one of the more common systems, but all are similar.*

Vacuum switch

Removal

1 Remove the air cleaner housing-to-carburettor inlet duct.
2 Bend up the tangs on the switch retaining clip, then remove the clip, along with its seal, and withdraw the switch from inside the duct. Examine the seal for signs of damage or deterioration, and renew if necessary.

Refitting

3 On refitting, ensure that the switch and duct mating surfaces are clean and dry, and position the switch inside the duct.
4 Fit the seal over the switch unions, and refit the retaining clip. Ensure that the switch is pressed firmly against the duct, and secure it in position by bending down the retaining clip tangs. Refit the duct.

Air temperature control valve

Removal

5 Disconnect the vacuum pipe from the air temperature control valve, then slacken the retaining clips securing the inlet ducts to the valve.
6 Disconnect both inlet ducts and the hot-air inlet hose from the control valve assembly, and remove it from the vehicle.

Refitting

7 Refitting is the reverse of the removal procedure, noting that the air temperature control valve assembly can only be renewed as a complete unit.

5 Crankcase ventilation system components - removal and refitting

The crankcase ventilation system consists simply of a number of ventilation hoses, and a wire mesh filter in the engine oil filler cap on certain models. Removal and refitting is self-explanatory, but it may be necessary to detach surrounding components for improved access. Refer to the various Chapters of this manual as necessary if problems are encountered.

6.2 Disconnecting wiring plug from ignition retarding system solenoid valve

6 Electro-pneumatic ignition retarding system components - removal and refitting

Solenoid valve

Removal

1 The valve is located on a bracket at the rear of the engine compartment. To remove the valve, proceed as follows.
2 Disconnect the battery negative lead, then disconnect the wiring plug from the valve **(see illustration)**.
3 Note the orientation of the valve, then disconnect the hoses from the valve, and pull the valve from its bracket.

Refitting

4 Refitting is a reversal of removal, ensuring that the valve is correctly orientated, as noted before removal.

Coolant temperature sensor

Removal

5 The sensor is located in the left-hand end of the cylinder head, below the engine coolant temperature sensor for the fuel injection system.
6 To remove the sensor, partially drain the cooling system (see Chapter 1), then disconnect the wiring, and unscrew and remove the sensor.

Refitting

7 When refitting the sensor, ensure that the seal is in good condition, and take care not to overtighten the switch. Refill the cooling system on completion as described in Chapter 1 and *"Weekly checks"*.

7 Catalytic converter - general information and precautions

The catalytic converter is a reliable and simple device, which needs no maintenance in itself, but there are some facts of which an owner should be aware if the converter is to function properly for its full service life.

a) DO NOT use leaded petrol in a vehicle equipped with a catalytic converter - the lead will coat the precious metals, reducing their converting efficiency, and will eventually destroy the converter.
b) Always keep the ignition and fuel systems well-maintained in accordance with the manufacturer's schedule (see Chapter 1).
c) If the engine develops a misfire, do not drive the vehicle at all (or at least as little as possible) until the fault is cured.
d) DO NOT push - or tow-start the vehicle - this will soak the catalytic converter in unburned fuel, causing it to overheat when the engine does start.
e) DO NOT switch off the ignition at high engine speeds, ie do not "blip" the throttle immediately before switching off.
f) DO NOT use fuel or engine oil additives - these may contain substances harmful to the catalytic converter.
g) DO NOT continue to use the vehicle if the engine burns oil to the extent of leaving a visible trail of blue smoke.
h) Remember that the catalytic converter operates at very high temperatures. DO NOT, therefore, park the vehicle in dry undergrowth, over long grass or piles of dead leaves, after a long run.
l) Remember that the catalytic converter is FRAGILE. Do not strike it with tools during servicing work.
j) In some cases, a sulphurous smell (like that of rotten eggs) may be noticed from the exhaust. This is common to many catalytic converter-equipped vehicles. Once the vehicle has covered a few thousand miles, the problem should disappear - in the meantime, try changing the brand of petrol used.
k) The catalytic converter used on a well-maintained and well-driven vehicle should last for between 50 000 and 100 000 miles. If the converter is no longer effective, it must be renewed.

8 Fuel vapour recirculation system components - removal and refitting

4D

Carbon canister

Removal

1 The carbon canister is located at the rear left-hand corner of the engine compartment **(see illustration)**.
2 To remove the canister, first disconnect the hoses, noting their locations to ensure correct refitting.

8.1 Fuel vapour recirculation system carbon canister (A) and solenoid valve (B)

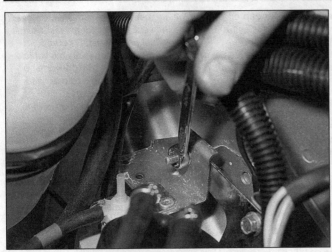

8.7a Unscrew the securing nut . . .

8.7b . . . and withdraw the solenoid bracket

3 Unscrew the clamp bolt, and lift the canister from its clamp on the body panel.

Refitting

4 Refitting is a reversal of removal, but ensure that the hoses are correctly reconnected, as noted before removal.

Solenoid valve

Removal

5 The solenoid valve is mounted on a bracket next to the carbon canister, at the rear left-hand corner of the engine compartment.
6 To remove the valve, first disconnect the battery negative lead.
7 Unbolt the bracket from the body panel, then disconnect the wiring plug **(see illustrations)**.

8 Disconnect the hoses from the valve, noting their locations to ensure correct refitting, then withdraw the valve.

Refitting

9 Refitting is a reversal of removal, ensuring that the hoses are correctly reconnected, as noted before removal.

Chapter 5 Part A:
Starting and charging systems

Contents

Degrees of difficulty

Easy, suitable for novice with little experience		**Fairly easy,** suitable for beginner with some experience		**Fairly difficult,** suitable for competent DIY mechanic		**Difficult,** suitable for experienced DIY mechanic		**Very difficult,** suitable for expert DIY or professional	

Specifications

System type .... 12-volt, negative earth

Battery

Type	Low maintenance or "maintenance-free" sealed for life
Capacity	25 to 33 Ah (depending on model)
Charge condition:	
Poor	12.5 volts
Normal	12.6 volts
Good	12.7 volts

1 General information and precautions

General information

The engine electrical system consists mainly of the charging and starting systems. Because of their engine-related functions, these components are covered separately from the body electrical devices such as the lights, instruments, etc (which are covered in Chapter 12). Information on the ignition system is covered in Part B of this Chapter.

The electrical system is of the 12-volt negative earth type.

The battery is of the low maintenance or "maintenance-free" (sealed for life) type and is charged by the alternator, which is belt-driven from the crankshaft pulley.

The starter motor is of the pre-engaged type incorporating an integral solenoid. On starting, the solenoid moves the drive pinion into engagement with the flywheel ring gear before the starter motor is energised. Once the engine has started, a one-way clutch prevents the motor armature being driven by the engine until the pinion disengages from the flywheel.

Precautions

Further details of the various systems are given in the relevant Sections of this Chapter. While some repair procedures are given, the usual course of action is to renew the component concerned. The owner whose interest extends beyond mere component renewal should obtain a copy of the *"Automobile Electrical & Electronic Systems Manual"*, available from the publishers of this manual.

It is necessary to take extra care when working on the electrical system to avoid damage to semi-conductor devices (diodes and transistors), and to avoid the risk of personal injury. In addition to the precautions given in *"Safety first!"* at the beginning of this manual, observe the following when working on the system:

Always remove rings, watches, etc before working on the electrical system. Even with the battery disconnected, capacitive discharge could occur if a component's live terminal is earthed through a metal object. This could cause a shock or nasty burn.

Do not reverse the battery connections. Components such as the alternator, electronic control units, or any other components having semi-conductor circuitry could be irreparably damaged.

If the engine is being started using jump leads and a slave battery, connect the batteries *positive-to-positive* and *negative-to-negative* (see *"Booster battery (jump) starting"*). This also applies when connecting a battery charger.

Never disconnect the battery terminals, the alternator, any electrical wiring or any test instruments when the engine is running.

Do not allow the engine to turn the alternator when the alternator is not connected.

Never "test" for alternator output by "flashing" the output lead to earth.

Never use an ohmmeter of the type incorporating a hand-cranked generator for circuit or continuity testing.

Always ensure that the battery negative lead is disconnected when working on the electrical system.

Before using electric-arc welding equipment on the car, disconnect the battery, alternator and components such as the fuel injection/ignition electronic control unit to protect them from the risk of damage.

The radio/cassette units fitted as standard or optional equipment may be equipped with a built-in security code to deter thieves. If the power source to the unit is cut, the anti-theft system will activate. Even if the power source is immediately reconnected, the radio/cassette unit will not function until the correct security code has been entered. Therefore, if you do not know the correct security code for the radio/cassette unit **do not** disconnect the negative terminal of the battery or remove the radio/cassette unit from the car. Refer to the Owner's Manual, or your Peugeot dealer for further information on security codes.

2 Electrical fault finding - general information

Refer to Chapter 12.

3 Battery - testing and charging

Standard and low maintenance battery - testing

1 If the vehicle covers a small annual mileage, it is worthwhile checking the specific gravity of the electrolyte every three months to determine the state of charge of the battery. Use a hydrometer to make the check and compare the results with the following table.

	Above 25°C (77°F)	Below 25°C (77°F)
Fully-charged	1.210 to 1.230	1.270 to 1.290
70% charged	1.170 to 1.190	1.230 to 1.250
Discharged	1.050 to 1.070	1.110 to 1.130

Note that the specific gravity readings assume an electrolyte temperature of 15°C (60°F); for every 10°C (50°F) below 15°C (60°F) subtract 0.007. For every 10°C (50°F) above 15°C (60°F) add 0.007.

2 If the battery condition is suspect, first check the specific gravity of electrolyte in each cell. A variation of 0.040 or more between any cells indicates loss of electrolyte or deterioration of the internal plates.

3 If the specific gravity variation is 0.040 or more, the battery should be renewed. If the cell variation is satisfactory but the battery is discharged, it should be charged as described later in this Section.

Maintenance-free battery - testing

4 In cases where a "sealed for life" maintenance-free battery is fitted, topping-up and testing of the electrolyte in each cell is not possible. The condition of the battery can therefore only be tested using a battery condition indicator or a voltmeter.

5 If testing the battery using a voltmeter, connect the voltmeter across the battery and compare the result with those given in the Specifications under "charge condition". The test is only accurate if the battery has not been subjected to any kind of charge for the previous six hours. If this is not the case, switch on the headlights for 30 seconds, then wait four to five minutes before testing the battery after switching off the headlights. All other electrical circuits must be switched off, so check that the doors and tailgate are fully shut when making the test.

6 If the voltage reading is less than 12.2 volts, then the battery is discharged, whilst a reading of 12.2 to 12.4 volts indicates a partially discharged condition.

7 If the battery is to be charged, remove it from the vehicle (Section 4) and charge it as described later in this Section.

Standard and low maintenance battery - charging

Note: *The following is intended as a guide only. Always refer to the manufacturer's recommendations (often printed on a label attached to the battery) before charging a battery.*

8 Charge the battery at a rate of 3.5 to 4 amps and continue to charge the battery at this rate until no further rise in specific gravity is noted over a four hour period.

9 Alternatively, a trickle charger charging at the rate of 1.5 amps can safely be used overnight.

10 Specially rapid "boost" charges which are claimed to restore the power of the battery in 1 to 2 hours are not recommended, as they can cause serious damage to the battery plates through overheating.

11 While charging the battery, note that the temperature of the electrolyte should never exceed 37.8°C (100°F).

Maintenance-free battery - charging

Note: *The following is intended as a guide only. Always refer to the manufacturer's recommendations (often printed on a label attached to the battery) before charging a battery.*

12 This battery type takes considerably longer to fully recharge than the standard type, the time taken being dependent on the extent of discharge, but it can take anything up to three days.

13 A constant voltage type charger is required, to be set, when connected, to 13.9 to 14.9 volts with a charger current below 25 amps. Using this method, the battery should

be usable within three hours, giving a voltage reading of 12.5 volts, but this is for a partially discharged battery and, as mentioned, full charging can take considerably longer.

14 If the battery is to be charged from a fully discharged state (condition reading less than 12.2 volts), have it recharged by your Peugeot dealer or local automotive electrician, as the charge rate is higher and constant supervision during charging is necessary.

4 Battery - removal and refitting

Note: *Make sure that you have a copy of the radio/cassette unit security code number (where applicable) before disconnecting the battery.*

Removal

1 The battery is located in the front left-hand corner of the engine compartment.

2 Slacken the clamp bolts and disconnect the clamp from the battery negative (earth) terminal.

3 Remove the insulation cover (where fitted) and disconnect the positive terminal lead(s) in the same way.

4 Release the battery clamp and lift the battery carefully from the engine compartment.

5 If required, the battery tray can be removed after undoing the retaining bolts.

Refitting

6 Refitting is a reversal of removal, but smear petroleum jelly on the terminals when reconnecting the leads, and always reconnect the positive lead first, and the negative lead last.

5 Charging system - testing

Note: *Refer to the warnings given in "Safety first!" and in Section 1 of this Chapter before starting work.*

1 If the ignition warning light fails to illuminate when the ignition is switched on, first check the alternator wiring connections for security. If satisfactory, check that the warning light bulb has not blown, and that the bulbholder is secure in its location in the instrument panel. If the light still fails to illuminate, check the continuity of the warning light feed wire from the alternator to the bulbholder. If all is satisfactory, the alternator is at fault and should be renewed or taken to an auto-electrician for testing and repair.

2 If the ignition warning light illuminates when the engine is running, stop the engine and check that the drivebelt is correctly tensioned (see Chapter 1) and that the alternator connections are secure. If all is so far satisfactory, have the alternator checked by an auto-electrician for testing and repair.

3 If the alternator output is suspect even though the warning light functions correctly, the regulated voltage may be checked as follows.

4 Connect a voltmeter across the battery terminals and start the engine.

5 Increase the engine speed until the voltmeter reading remains steady; the reading should be approximately 12 to 13 volts, and no more than 14 volts.

6 Switch on as many electrical accessories (eg, the headlights, heated rear window and heater blower) as possible, and check that the alternator maintains the regulated voltage at around 13 to 14 volts.

7 If the regulated voltage is not as stated, the fault may be due to worn brushes, weak brush springs, a faulty voltage regulator, a faulty diode, a severed phase winding or worn or damaged slip rings. The alternator should be renewed or taken to an auto-electrician for testing and repair.

6 Alternator - removal and refitting

Removal

1 Disconnect the battery negative lead.

2 Remove the auxiliary drivebelt as described in Chapter 1.

3 Where necessary, refer to Chapter 4 and move the relevant air cleaner components to one side for increased access.

4 Disconnect the wiring from the alternator **(see illustration)**.

5 Unscrew the pivot and adjustment bolts and lift the alternator from the engine. On certain models note that the alternator front bracket is slotted to allow the pivot bolt to remain in the bracket on the engine.

Refitting

6 Refitting is a reversal of removal, but tension the drivebelt, as described in Chapter 1.

7 Alternator - testing and overhaul

If the alternator is thought to be suspect, it should be removed from the vehicle and taken to an auto-electrician for testing. Most auto-electricians will be able to supply and fit brushes at a reasonable cost. However, check on the cost of repairs before proceeding as it may prove more economical to obtain a new or exchange alternator.

8 Starting system - testing

Note: *Refer to the precautions given in "Safety first!" and in Section 1 of this Chapter before starting work.*

1 If the starter motor fails to operate when the ignition key is turned to the appropriate position, the following possible causes may be to blame.

  a) *The battery is faulty.*
  b) *The electrical connections between the switch, solenoid, battery and starter motor are somewhere failing to pass the necessary current from the battery through the starter to earth.*
  c) *The solenoid is faulty.*
  d) *The starter motor is mechanically or electrically defective.*

2 To check the battery, switch on the headlights. If they dim after a few seconds, this indicates that the battery is discharged - recharge (see Section 3) or renew the battery. If the headlights glow brightly, operate the ignition switch and observe the lights. If they dim, then this indicates that current is reaching the starter motor, therefore the fault must lie in the starter motor. If the lights continue to glow brightly (and no clicking sound can be heard from the starter motor solenoid), this indicates that there is a fault in the circuit or solenoid - see following paragraphs. If the starter motor turns slowly when operated, but the battery is in good condition, then this indicates that either the starter motor is faulty, or there is considerable resistance somewhere in the circuit.

3 If a fault in the circuit is suspected, disconnect the battery leads (including the earth connection to the body), the starter/solenoid wiring and the engine/transmission earth strap. Thoroughly clean the connections, and reconnect the leads and wiring, then use a voltmeter or test lamp to check that full battery voltage is available at the battery positive lead connection to the solenoid, and that the earth is sound. Smear petroleum jelly around the battery terminals to prevent corrosion - corroded connections are amongst the most frequent causes of electrical system faults.

4 If the battery and all connections are in good condition, check the circuit by disconnecting the wire from the solenoid blade terminal. Connect a voltmeter or test lamp between the wire end and a good earth (such as the battery negative terminal), and check that the wire is live when the ignition switch is turned to the "start" position. If it is, then the circuit is sound - if not the circuit wiring can be checked as described in Chapter 12.

5 The solenoid contacts can be checked by connecting a voltmeter or test lamp between the battery positive feed connection on the starter side of the solenoid, and earth. When the ignition switch is turned to the "start" position, there should be a reading or lighted bulb, as applicable. If there is no reading or lighted bulb, the solenoid is faulty and should be renewed.

6 If the circuit and solenoid are proved sound, the fault must lie in the starter motor. In this event, it may be possible to have the starter motor overhauled by a specialist, but check on the cost of spares before proceeding, as it may prove more economical to obtain a new or exchange motor.

9 Starter motor - removal and refitting

Removal

1 Disconnect the battery negative lead.

2 Where necessary, refer to Chapter 4 and move the relevant air cleaner components to one side for increased access.

3 On GTI models, remove the inlet manifold, with reference to the relevant Part of Chapter 4.

4 Disconnect the wiring from the solenoid **(see illustration)**.

5 Unscrew the bolts securing the brush end bracket to the engine **(see illustration)**.

6 Unscrew the mounting bolts at the flywheel end **(see illustration)**.

7 Withdraw the starter motor from the engine.

5A

6.4 Alternator wiring connections

9.4 Starter motor solenoid wiring

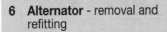

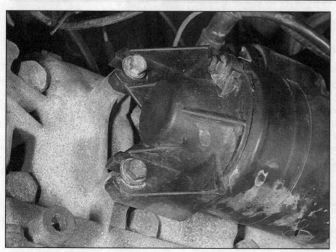

9.5 Starter motor brush end bracket retaining bolts on XV, XW and XY series engines

9.6 Removing the starter motor mounting bolts on XV, XW and XY series engines

Refitting

8 Refitting is a reversal of removal, but first insert all mounting bolts finger tight, then tighten the flywheel end bolts followed by the brush end bolts.

10 Starter motor - testing and overhaul

If the starter motor is thought to be suspect, it should be removed from the vehicle and taken to an auto-electrician for testing. Most auto-electricians will be able to supply and fit brushes at a reasonable cost. However, check on the cost of repairs before proceeding as it may prove more economical to obtain a new or exchange motor.

11 Ignition switch - removal and refitting

The ignition switch is integral with the steering column lock, and can be removed as described in Chapter 10.

12 Oil pressure warning light switch - removal and refitting

Removal

1 The switch is located at the front of the cylinder block, above the oil filter mounting. Note that on some models access to the switch may be improved if the vehicle is jacked up and supported on axle stands so that the switch can be reached from underneath (see "Jacking and vehicle support").
2 Disconnect the battery negative lead.
3 Remove the protective sleeve from the wiring plug (where applicable), then disconnect the wiring from the switch.
4 Unscrew the switch from the cylinder block, and recover the sealing washer. Be prepared for oil spillage, and if the switch is to be left removed from the engine for any length of time, plug the hole in the cylinder block.

Refitting

5 Examine the sealing washer for signs of damage or deterioration and if necessary renew.
6 Refit the switch, complete with washer, and tighten it securely. Reconnect the wiring connector.
7 Lower the vehicle to the ground then check and, if necessary, top-up the engine oil as described in "Weekly checks".

13 Electronic oil level sensor - general information

1 Some 1985 XU series engine models have an oil level sensor fitted to the engine sump, together with a warning lamp on the instrument panel. The system was only fitted on the 1985 model year, and has been deleted from later models.
2 The sensor incorporates a high-resistance wire, which varies in conductivity depending on whether it is immersed in or above the oil. An electronic control unit mounted under the right-hand side of the facia monitors the conductivity, and operates the warning lamp when necessary.
3 It should be noted that the system only functions accurately if the car is on a level surface. When the ignition is initially switched on, the warning lamp should light for two seconds. If the oil level is correct, the lamp will then go out, but if it starts to flash the oil level is low.
4 To prevent the system functioning unnecessarily after the engine has started, the control unit is earthed through the oil pressure switch. The level check is made before starting the engine. Some early models are not earthed through the oil pressure switch and on these, the warning lamp may flash if for instance the engine is temporarily stalled and the oil has not returned to the sump.

Chapter 5 Part B:
Ignition system

Contents

Degrees of difficulty

Easy, suitable for novice with little experience	Fairly easy, suitable for beginner with some experience	Fairly difficult, suitable for competent DIY mechanic	Difficult, suitable for experienced DIY mechanic	Very difficult, suitable for expert DIY or professional

Specifications

System type
All engines except XU5M2/Z, XU5M3/Z, XU5M3/L and TU1M/L ...... Electronic breakerless ignition system
XU5M2/Z, XU5M3/Z, XU5M3/L and TU1M/L engines .... Static distributorless ignition system

Distributor
Rotor arm rotation .... Anti-clockwise
Firing order .... 1 - 3 - 4 - 2 (No 1 cylinder at flywheel end of engine)

Ignition timing (vacuum hose disconnected)
XV8 and XW7 engines .... 6° BTDC at 650 rpm
XY7 engines .... 8°BTDC at 650 rpm
XY8 engines:
  Early models with M152E advance curve .... 0° BTDC at 950 rpm
  Later models with M159E advance curve .... 8° BTDC at 850 to 950 rpm
XU5J engines (up to VIN 5520364) .... 30° BTDC at 3500 rpm or 6° BTDC at 700 rpm
XU5J engines (from VIN 5520364) .... 10° BTDC at 850 ± 50 rpm
XU5JA and XU5JA/K engines .... 10° BTDC at 900 rpm
XU51C and XU51C/K engines .... 10° BTDC at 750 rpm
XU5M2/Z, XU5M3/Z and XU5M3/L engines .... Not adjustable, controlled by MMFD Mono-point G5/6 engine management system
XU9JA and XU9JA/K engines .... 5° BTDC at 700 rpm
XU9JA/Z and XU9JA/L engines .... Not adjustable, controlled by Motronic M1.3 engine management system
XU9J1/Z and XU9J1/L engines .... 10° BTDC at 900 rpm
TU series engines (except TU1M/L) .... 8° BTDC at idling speed (see Chapter 4)
TU1M/L engines .... Not adjustable, controlled by MMFD Mono-point G6 engine management system

Ignition coil
Ignition HT coil resistances:*
  Electronic breakerless ignition systems:
    Primary windings .... 0.8 ohms
    Secondary windings .... 6.5 K ohms
  Static distributorless ignition systems:
    Primary windings .... 0.5 to 0.8 ohms
    Secondary windings - Bosch coil .... 14.6 K ohms
    Secondary windings - Valeo coil .... 8.6 K ohms
*The above results are approximate values and are accurate only when the coil is at 20°C. See text for further information
Spark plugs .... See Chapter 1 Specifications

1 General information

Electronic breakerless ignition system

A number of different breakerless ignition systems are used on 205 models according to engine type and fuel system fitted. Some are simple self-contained systems and some work in conjunction with the fuel system to form an integrated engine management package.

In order that the engine may run correctly it is necessary for an electrical spark to ignite the fuel/air mixture in the combustion chamber at exactly the right moment in relation to engine speed and load.

Basically the ignition system functions as follows. Low tension voltage from the battery is fed to the ignition coil, where it is converted into high tension voltage. The high tension voltage is powerful enough to jump the spark plug gap in the cylinder many times a second under high compression pressure, providing that the ignition system is in good working order.

The distributor contains a reluctor mounted onto its shaft and a magnet and stator fixed to its body. An ignition amplifier unit is mounted either remotely, adjacent to the ignition coil, or on the side of the distributor body.

When the ignition is switched on but the engine is stationary the transistors in the amplifier unit prevent current flowing through the ignition system primary (LT) circuit.

As the crankshaft rotates, the reluctor moves through the magnetic field created by the stator. When the reluctor teeth are in alignment with the stator projections a small AC voltage is created. The amplifier unit uses this voltage to switch the transistors in the unit and complete the ignition system primary (LT) circuit.

As the reluctor teeth move out of alignment with the stator projections the AC voltage changes and the transistors in the amplifier unit are switched again to interrupt the primary (LT) circuit. This causes a high voltage to be induced in the coil secondary (HT) windings which then travels down the HT lead to the distributor and onto the relevant spark plug.

The ignition is advanced and retarded automatically by centrifugal weights and a vacuum capsule or by the engine management electronic control unit to ensure that the spark occurs at the correct instant in relation to engine speed and load.

Static distributorless ignition system

A static ignition system is used on models with MMFD Mono-point G5 and G6 engine management systems. The system is integrated with the fuel injection system, and is controlled by the MMFD electronic control unit (ECU). The ECU receives information from various sensors, and using this information, the optimum ignition advance for the prevailing engine conditions is selected from a series of "mapped" values stored in the ECU memory (see Chapter 4B for further information).

The single ignition module replaces the amplifier unit, HT coil and distributor in a conventional system. The ignition module incorporates a double coil, with four high-tension outputs to the spark plugs, which dispenses with the requirement for a conventional distributor and rotor arm.

Each coil is controlled by the MMFD electronic control unit. Each time one of the coil primary circuits is switched, two sparks are provided, one to a cylinder on the compression stroke, and one to a cylinder on the exhaust stroke. The spark to the cylinder on the exhaust stroke is effectively a "wasted spark", but has no detrimental effect on the performance of the engine.

2 Ignition system - testing

> **Warning: Voltages produced by an electronic ignition system are considerably higher than those produced by conventional ignition systems. Extreme care must be taken when working on the system with the ignition switched on. Persons with surgically-implanted cardiac pacemaker devices should keep well clear of the ignition circuits, components and test equipment.**

Models with electronic breakerless ignition systems

Note: *Refer to the warning given in Section 1 of Part A of this Chapter before starting work. Always switch off the ignition before disconnecting or connecting any component and when using a multi-meter to check resistances.*

General

1 The components of electronic ignition systems are normally very reliable; most faults are far more likely to be due to loose or dirty connections or to "tracking" of HT voltage due to dirt, dampness or damaged insulation than to the failure of any of the system's components. **Always** check all wiring thoroughly before condemning an electrical component and work methodically to eliminate all other possibilities before deciding that a particular component is faulty.

2 The old practice of checking for a spark by holding the live end of an HT lead a short distance away from the engine is not recommended; not only is there a high risk of a powerful electric shock, but the HT coil or amplifier unit will be damaged. Similarly, **never** try to "diagnose" misfires by pulling off one HT lead at a time.

Engine will not start

3 If the engine either will not turn over at all, or only turns very slowly, check the battery and starter motor. Connect a voltmeter across the battery terminals (meter positive probe to battery positive terminal), disconnect the ignition coil HT lead from the distributor cap and earth it, then note the voltage reading obtained while turning over the engine on the starter for (no more than) ten seconds. If the reading obtained is less than approximately 9.5 volts, first check the battery, starter motor and charging system as described in Part A of this Chapter.

4 If the engine turns over at normal speed but will not start, check the HT circuit by connecting a timing light (following the manufacturer's instructions) and turning the engine over on the starter motor; if the light flashes, voltage is reaching the spark plugs, so these should be checked first. If the light does not flash, check the HT leads themselves followed by the distributor cap, carbon brush and rotor arm using the information given in Chapter 1.

5 If there is a spark, check the fuel system for faults referring to the relevant part of Chapter 4 for further information.

6 If there is still no spark, check the voltage at the ignition HT coil "+" terminal; it should be the same as the battery voltage (ie, at least 11.7 volts). If the voltage at the coil is more than 1 volt less than that at the battery, check the feed back through the fusebox and ignition switch to the battery and its earth until the fault is found.

7 If the feed to the HT coil is sound, check the coil's primary and secondary winding resistance as described later in this Chapter; renew the coil if faulty, but be careful to check carefully the condition of the LT connections themselves before doing so, to ensure that the fault is not due to dirty or poorly-fastened connectors.

8 If the HT coil is in good condition, the fault is probably within the amplifier unit or distributor stator assembly. Testing of these components should be entrusted to a Peugeot dealer.

Engine misfires

9 An irregular misfire suggests either a loose connection or intermittent fault on the primary circuit, or an HT fault on the coil side of the rotor arm.

10 With the ignition switched off, check carefully through the system ensuring that all connections are clean and securely fastened. If the equipment is available, check the LT circuit as described above.

11 Check that the HT coil, the distributor cap and the HT leads are clean and dry. Check the leads themselves and the spark plugs (by substitution, if necessary), then check the distributor cap, carbon brush and rotor arm as described in Chapter 1.

12 Regular misfiring is almost certainly due to a fault in the distributor cap, HT leads or spark plugs. Use a timing light (paragraph 4 above) to check whether HT voltage is present at all leads.

13 If HT voltage is not present on any particular lead, the fault will be in that lead or in the distributor cap. If HT is present on all leads, the fault will be in the spark plugs; check and renew them if there is any doubt about their condition.

14 If no HT is present, check the HT coil; its secondary windings may be breaking down under load.

Models with static distributorless ignition systems

15 If a fault appears in the engine management (fuel injection/ignition) system first ensure that the fault is not due to a poor electrical connection or poor maintenance; ie, check that the air cleaner filter element is clean, the spark plugs are in good condition and correctly gapped, that the engine breather hoses are clear and undamaged, referring to Chapter 1 for further information. Also check that the throttle cable is correctly adjusted as described in the relevant part of Chapter 4. If the engine is running very roughly, check the compression pressures and the valve clearances as described in Chapter 2B or 2C.

16 If these checks fail to reveal the cause of the problem the vehicle should be taken to a suitably equipped Peugeot dealer for testing. A wiring block connector is incorporated in the engine management circuit into which a special electronic diagnostic tester can be plugged. The tester will locate the fault quickly and simply alleviating the need to test all the system components individually which is a time consuming operation that carries a high risk of damaging the ECU.

17 The only ignition system checks which can be carried out by the home mechanic are those described in Chapter 1, relating to the spark plugs, and the ignition coil test described in this Chapter. If necessary, the system wiring and wiring connectors can be checked as described in Chapter 12 ensuring that the ECU wiring connector(s) have first been disconnected.

---

3 Ignition HT coil - removal, testing and refitting

Note: *On models with static distributorless ignition systems, the ignition HT coil is an integral part of the ignition module. Refer to Section 6 for removal and refitting procedures.*

Removal

All engines except TU series

1 The ignition HT coil is located at the left-hand side of the engine compartment mounted on the side of the suspension strut tower.

2 Disconnect the battery negative lead.

3.3 On all engines except TU series, access to the coil and ignition module is gained after sliding up the protective cover

3 Slide the cover off the coil and adjacent ignition module **(see illustration)**.

4 Disconnect the wiring at the coil LT terminals, and the HT lead at the coil centre terminal.

5 Release the coil mounting clamp and remove the coil.

TU series engines

6 The ignition HT coil is mounted on the left-hand end of the cylinder head, above the distributor.

7 Disconnect the battery negative lead.

8 Refer to the relevant Part of Chapter 4 and remove the air cleaner assembly. Once the air cleaner is removed, move aside any pipes, hoses or wiring as necessary for improved access.

9 Where applicable, disconnect the wiring connector from the capacitor mounted on the coil mounting bracket and release the TDC sensor wiring connector from the bracket.

10 Disconnect the HT lead from the coil then depress the retaining clip and disconnect the coil wiring connector **(see illustration)**.

11 Slacken and remove the two retaining bolts and remove the coil and mounting bracket from the cylinder head. Where necessary, slacken and remove the four screws and nuts and separate the HT coil and mounting bracket.

Testing

12 Testing of the coil consists of using a multimeter set to its resistance function, to check the primary (LT "+'" to "-" terminals) and secondary (LT "+" to HT lead terminal) windings for continuity, bearing in mind that on the four output, static type HT coil there are two sets of each windings. Compare the results obtained to those given in the *Specifications* at the start of this Chapter. Note the resistance of the coil windings will vary slightly according to the coil temperature, the results in the *Specifications* are approximate values for when the coil is at 20°C.

13 Check that there is no continuity between the HT lead terminal and the coil body/mounting bracket.

14 If the coil is thought to be faulty, have your findings confirmed by a Peugeot dealer before renewing the coil.

3.10 Disconnecting the coil wiring connector (arrowed) on TU series engines

Refitting (all models)

15 Refitting is a reversal of the relevant removal procedure ensuring that the wiring connectors are securely reconnected and, where necessary, the HT leads are correctly connected.

---

4 Distributor (breakerless ignition systems) - removal and refitting

Removal

All engines except TU series

1 Disconnect the battery negative lead.

2 Remove the air cleaner and/or inlet duct, as necessary for access, with reference to the relevant Part of Chapter 4.

3 Identify the HT leads for position then disconnect them from the spark plugs.

4 Slide off the ignition coil cover and disconnect the HT lead from the coil.

5 Pull back the plastic cover then unclip and remove the distributor cap **(see illustration)**. Note that on certain later models the cap is retained by two screws instead of clips.

6 Disconnect the wiring at the connector, where necessary pulling out the spring clip first.

7 Pull the hose from the vacuum advance unit.

8 Mark the distributor mounting flange in relation to the cylinder head or thermostat housing as applicable.

4.5 Pull back the plastic cover then unclip and remove the distributor cap

4.9a On non-TU series engines, unscrew the mounting nuts . . .

4.9b . . . and remove the distributor

4.15 Disconnect the distributor wiring connector on TU series engines

9 Unscrew the mounting nuts, remove the small plates, and withdraw the distributor **(see illustrations)**.

10 Check the condition of the O-ring on the mounting flange and renew it if necessary.

TU series engines

11 Remove the ignition HT coil (Section 3).
12 Identify the HT leads for position, then disconnect them from the spark plugs.
13 Unbolt the HT lead support from the cylinder head.
14 Pull back the plastic cover, then extract the screws and remove the distributor cap.
15 Disconnect the wiring at the connector **(see illustration)**.
16 Pull the hose from the vacuum advance unit.
17 Mark the distributor mounting flange in relation to the distributor/fuel pump housing **(see illustration)**.
18 Unscrew the mounting nuts, remove the small plates, and withdraw the distributor **(see illustration)**.
19 Check the condition of the O-ring on the mounting flange, and renew it if necessary.

Refitting

All engines

20 Refitting is a reversal of removal, but turn the rotor arm as required to align the lugs with the offset slot in the camshaft. If the old distributor is being refitted, align the previously made marks before tightening the mounting nuts. If fitting a new distributor, initially set the distributor in the middle of the

4.17 Mark the distributor and housing . . .

slotted holes or follow the procedure given in Section 8, then finally adjust the ignition timing (Section 8).

5 Ignition amplifier (breakerless ignition systems) - removal and refitting

Removal

All engines except TU series

1 The ignition amplifier unit is located at the left-hand side of the engine compartment mounted on the side of the suspension strut tower.
2 Disconnect the battery negative lead.
3 Slide the cover off the ignition HT coil and amplifier.
4 Disconnect the amplifier wiring harness.
5 Remove the screws and withdraw the amplifier from the mounting plate.

TU series engines

6 The amplifier unit is attached to the side of the distributor.
7 Disconnect the battery negative lead.
8 Disconnect the amplifier wiring at the connector.
9 Remove the two screws and withdraw the amplifier from the distributor, taking care not to bend the terminals **(see illustration)**.
10 Do not wipe away the special heat-conductive grease, as this protects the semi-conductor components within the amplifier. If necessary, obtain new grease from a Peugeot dealer.

4.18 . . . then remove the distributor

Refitting

All engines

11 Refitting is a reversal of removal. On TU series engines, make sure that the special grease is spread evenly over the mating surfaces of both the distributor and amplifier unit.

6 Ignition module (distributorless ignition systems) - removal and refitting

Removal

1 The ignition module is mounted on the left-hand end of the cylinder head.
2 Disconnect the battery negative lead.
3 Where necessary, remove the air cleaner ducting for improved access.

6.5 HT lead connections on the static distributorless ignition module

5.9 Removing the ignition amplifier on TU series engines

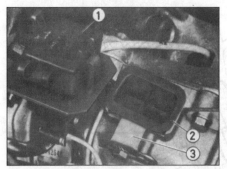

7.1 Timing plate components on XV, XW and XY series engines

1 Diagnostic socket 3 Timing plate
2 Cover

4 Depress the retaining clip and disconnect the wiring connector from the module.

5 Make a note of the correct fitted positions of the HT leads then disconnect them from the module terminals **(see illustration)**.

6 Undo the four retaining screws securing the module to its mounting bracket and remove it from the engine.

Refitting

7 Refitting is a reversal of removal.

7 Timing plate (breakerless ignition systems) - adjustment

Note: *Timing plate adjustment is only possible on models fitted with XV, XW and XY series engines. Peugeot special tool 80133 or a suitable alternative will be required for the adjustment procedure.*

1 The timing plate which is located in the aperture under the plastic cover at the top of the flywheel housing can be moved within the limits of its elongated slot **(see illustration)**.

2 The plate is set during production and should not be disturbed unless a new flywheel, flywheel housing or other associated components have been fitted.

3 To adjust the timing plate, carry out the following operations.

4 Remove the plastic cover.

5 Using the crankshaft pulley nut, turn the crankshaft until the mark on the flywheel is at the start of the timing plate.

6 Remove the plug from behind the crankshaft pulley using an Allen key. Note that if the hole in the pulley is not over the plug, the crankshaft should be turned exactly half a turn. This is because there are two diametrically opposite timing marks on the flywheel, and the mark corresponding to TDC on No 2 and 3 cylinders must be used to bring the slot in the crankshaft counterbalance in line with the plug hole.

7 Insert the crankshaft locking tool (Peugeot special tool 80133) into the plug hole and turn the crankshaft until the tool is felt to drop into the cut-out in the counterbalance weight of the crankshaft.

TOOL TIP

A crankshaft locking tool can be made from a 100 mm length of 8.0 mm dowel rod.

8 If the special tool is not available, a suitable alternative can be used **(see Tool Tip)**.

9 With the tool or dowel rod inserted, pistons 2 and 3 are now located at TDC.

10 Release the timing plate bolt and move the plate to align the flywheel, and 0 (TDC) mark on the plate. Tighten the bolt to the specified torque. Apply a blob of paint on the edge of the bolt so that any subsequent movement can be recognised.

11 Withdraw the tool, fit a new sealing ring to the plug and tighten securely.

8 Ignition timing - checking and adjustment

Note: *On engines equipped with MMFD Mono-point G5/6 or Motronic M1.3 engine management systems the ignition timing is controlled by the system ECU and cannot be adjusted.*

XV, XW and XY series engines

1 To set the ignition timing statically so that the engine can be started first remove No 2 spark plug and turn the engine in the normal rotational direction until pressure is felt - indicating that the piston is commencing the compression stroke. The pressure can be felt using a suitable wooden rod or a piece of cork placed over the spark plug hole.

2 Remove the plastic cover from the timing aperture then continue turning the crankshaft

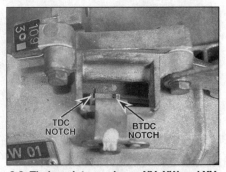

8.2 Timing plate marks on XV, XW and XY series engines

until the mark on the flywheel is opposite the BTDC mark on the timing plate **(see illustration)**.

3 Check that the distributor rotor arm is facing the No 2 HT lead segment position in the distributor cap. To do this, remove the cap and mark the outside in line with the segment, then put it back on the distributor noting which way the rotor arm is facing.

4 If necessary, loosen the mounting nuts and turn the distributor body to bring the segment and rotor arm in line, then tighten the nuts. Refit No 2 spark plug.

5 Run the engine to normal operating temperature then stop it and connect a tachometer and stroboscopic timing light as described in the instrument manufacturer's instructions. If the HT pick-up lead of the timing light is connected to the HT lead on the ignition coil it is possible to detect any discrepancy between the firing of Nos 1 and 4 and Nos 2 and 3 cylinders since there are two diametrically opposite timing marks on the flywheel. However, the pick-up lead may be connected to any one of the spark plug HT leads, in which case only one of the flywheel timing marks will be used.

6 Disconnect and plug the vacuum pipe at the distributor vacuum advance unit.

7 Run the engine at the specified speed and point the timing light into the timing aperture. The single mark on the flywheel should be aligned with the BTDC mark on the timing plate **(see illustration)**. If the ignition coil HT lead has been used (see paragraph 5), and there is wear in the distributor, there will be two marks visible on the flywheel close to each other. In this case the mid-point between the two marks should be aligned with the BTDC mark on the timing plate.

8 If adjustment is necessary, loosen the distributor mounting nuts and rotate the distributor body as required. Tighten the nuts on completion.

9 The operation of the centrifugal advance weights in the distributor can be checked by increasing the engine speed with the timing light pointing in the timing aperture and observing that the mark on the flywheel advances from its initial position.

5B

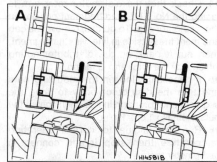

8.7 Ignition timing adjustment on XV, XW and XY series engines

A Using spark plug HT lead
B Using ignition coil HT lead

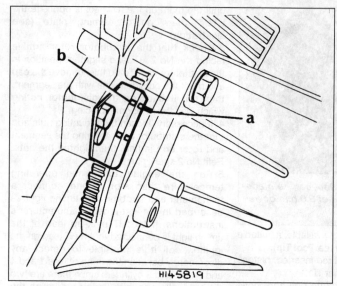

8.13 Initial static ignition timing on XU series engines

a Single flywheel mark   b BTDC mark on timing plate

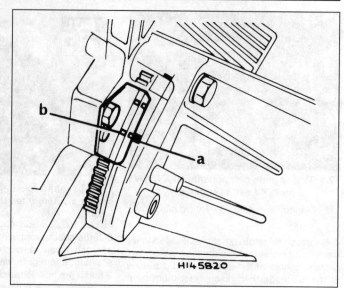

8.19 Dynamic ignition timing on XU series engines

a Double flywheel mark   b TDC mark on timing plate

10 To check the vacuum advance unit, run the engine at a fast idle speed and reconnect the vacuum pipe. The flywheel mark should again advance.

11 Stop the engine, disconnect the tachometer and timing light and reconnect the vacuum pipe. Refit the timing aperture cover.

XU series engines

12 To set the ignition timing statically so that the engine can be started, first remove No 1 spark plug (nearest the flywheel) and turn the engine in the normal rotational direction until pressure is felt - indicating that the piston is commencing the compression stroke. The pressure can be felt using a suitable wooden rod or piece of cork placed over the spark plug hole.

13 While looking into the timing aperture in the clutch housing/transmission casing, continue turning the crankshaft until the single mark on the flywheel is opposite the BTDC mark on the timing plate **(see illustration)**.

14 Check that the distributor rotor arm is facing the No 1 HT lead segment position in the distributor cap. To do this, remove the cap and mark the outside in line with the segment, then put it back on the distributor noting which way the rotor arm is facing.

15 If necessary, loosen the mounting nuts and turn the distributor body to bring the segment and rotor arm in line, then tighten the nuts. Refit No 1 spark plug.

16 Run the engine to normal operating temperature then stop it and connect a tachometer to it.

17 Disconnect and plug the vacuum pipe at the distributor vacuum advance unit.

18 Disconnect and remove the air cleaner inlet duct then connect a stroboscopic timing light to the engine as described in the timing light manufacturer's instructions, and with the HT pick-up lead connected to No 1 spark plug HT lead.

19 On early models, run the engine at 3500 rpm and point the timing light into the timing aperture. The double mark on the flywheel should be aligned with the TDC mark on the timing plate; indicating that the ignition is advanced by 30° **(see illustration)**. On engines without double timing marks, refer to the *Specifications* for the relevant ignition timing setting and engine speed, then check that the single mark on the flywheel is aligned with the appropriate mark on the timing plate.

20 If adjustment is necessary, loosen the distributor mounting nuts and rotate the distributor body as required. Tighten the nuts on completion.

21 Check the centrifugal and vacuum advance characteristics of the distributor, as described in paragraphs 9 and 10.

22 Stop the engine, disconnect the tachometer and timing light then reconnect the vacuum pipe and air cleaner inlet duct.

TU series engines

23 To set the ignition timing statically so that the engine can be started, refer to the procedures contained in paragraphs 12 to 15 above.

24 To check the ignition timing, a stroboscopic timing light will be required. It is also recommended that the flywheel timing mark is highlighted as follows.

25 Remove the plug from the aperture on the front of the transmission clutch housing. Using a socket and suitable extension bar on the crankshaft pulley bolt, slowly turn the engine over until the timing mark (a straight line) scribed on the edge of the flywheel appears in the aperture. Highlight the line with quick-drying white paint - typist's correction fluid is ideal **(see illustrations)**.

26 Start the engine, allow it to warm up to normal operating temperature, and then stop it.

27 Disconnect the vacuum hose from the distributor diaphragm, and plug the hose end.

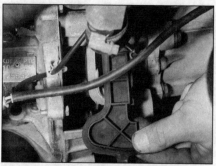

8.25a On TU series engines, remove the plug from the transmission housing . . .

8.25b . . . to reveal the timing plate and flywheel timing mark (arrowed)

28 Connect the timing light to No 1 cylinder spark plug lead (No 1 cylinder is at the transmission end of the engine) as described in the timing light manufacturer's instructions.
29 Start the engine, allowing it to idle at the specified speed, and point the timing light at the transmission housing aperture. The flywheel timing mark should be aligned with the appropriate notch on the timing plate. The numbers on the plate indicate degrees Before Top Dead Centre (BTDC).
30 If adjustment is necessary, slacken the two distributor mounting nuts, then slowly rotate the distributor body as required until the flywheel mark and the timing plate notch are brought into alignment. Once the marks are correctly aligned, hold the distributor stationary and tighten its mounting nuts. Recheck that the timing marks are still correctly aligned and, if necessary, repeat the adjustment procedure.
31 When the timing is correctly set, increase the engine speed, and check that the flywheel mark advances to beyond the beginning of the timing plate reference marks, returning to the specified mark when the engine is allowed to idle. This shows that the centrifugal

advance mechanism is functioning. Reconnect the vacuum hose to the distributor, and repeat the check. The rate of advance should significantly increase if the vacuum diaphragm is functioning correctly.
32 When the ignition timing is correct, stop the engine and disconnect the timing light.

9 TDC sensor - removal and refitting

Removal

1 Depending on engine type, the TDC sensor is for use with the diagnostic socket located on the clutch housing, or for the provision of information on crankshaft position to the engine management system ECU. When used in conjunction with the diagnostic socket, a special instrument and adapter are required and therefore it will normally be used only by a Peugeot garage.
2 To remove the sensor, unscrew the mounting screw or release the clamp as applicable.

3 Where the sensor forms part of the diagnostic socket assembly, if it is to be completely removed, the socket must be unclipped from its bracket and the remaining wiring and earth leads disconnected.

Refitting

4 Refitting is a reversal of removal, but the adjustment procedure for new and used sensors differs. New sensors have three extensions on the inner face and the unit should be inserted through the clamp until the extensions just touch the flywheel. The clamp screw is then tightened and clearance is provided as the flywheel rotates and wears the ends of the extensions. This method should not be used when refitting a used sensor. In this case, cut off the extensions completely then temporarily insert the sensor until it touches the flywheel, remove it and reposition it in the clamp 1.0 mm further out.

5B

Chapter 6
Clutch

Contents

Degrees of difficulty

Easy, suitable for novice with little experience	Fairly easy, suitable for beginner with some experience	Fairly difficult, suitable for competent DIY mechanic	Difficult, suitable for experienced DIY mechanic	Very difficult, suitable for expert DIY or professional

Specifications

General

Type	Diaphragm spring, single dry plate, cable operation

Driven plate diameter:

XV, XW and XY series engines - BH3 transmission	180.0 mm
XU series engines - BE1, BE3 transmission	200.0 mm
TU series engines - MA transmission	180.0 mm

Torque wrench settings	Nm	lbf ft
Pressure plate to flywheel bolts	10	7
Clutch housing bolts (BH 3 transmission)	12	9

1 General information

The clutch is of diaphragm spring, single dry plate type with cable actuation.

The clutch pedal pivots in a bracket mounted under the facia and operates a cable to the clutch release arm (or fork). The release lever operates a thrust bearing (clutch release bearing) which bears on the diaphragm spring of the pressure plate, and releases the clutch driven plate from the flywheel. The driven plate (or disc) is splined to a shaft which transmits the drive to the transmission. On models with XV, XW and XY series engines, the shaft is part of the transmission transfer gear assembly; on all other models, the shaft is the transmission input shaft.

The clutch release mechanism consists of a fork and bearing which are in permanent contact with release fingers on the pressure plate assembly. The fork pushes the release bearing forwards to bear against the release fingers, so moving the centre of the diaphragm spring inwards. The spring is sandwiched between two rings which act as fulcrum points. As the centre of the spring is pushed in, the outside of the spring is pushed out, so moving the pressure plate backwards and disengaging it from the clutch driven plate.

When the clutch pedal is released, the diaphragm spring forces the pressure plate into contact with the friction linings on the driven plate and at the same time pushes the driven plate fractionally forwards on its splines so engaging it with the flywheel. The driven plate is now firmly sandwiched between the pressure plate and the flywheel, so the drive is taken up.

As wear takes place on the driven plate friction linings the diaphragm fingers move outwards and the pedal stroke decreases; the cable mechanism incorporates an adjustment to compensate for this wear.

6

2 Clutch cable - removal and refitting

Removal

1 On models fitted with the BH3 transmission, loosen the locknut and slacken the adjuster on the transmission intermediate lever pushrod. On all other models, slacken the locknut and adjuster nut on the end of the cable.

2 Release the cable end fitting from the intermediate lever and recover the pushrod.

3 Working inside the car, remove the lower facia panel from under the steering column.

4 Pull off the spring clip and remove the clevis pin from the top of the clutch pedal to disconnect the cable end.

5 Release the cable from the bulkhead and withdraw it into the engine compartment.

Refitting

6 Refitting is a reversal of removal. On completion, adjust the clutch pedal stroke as described in Chapter 1.

3 Clutch pedal - removal and refitting

Removal

1 On models fitted with the BH3

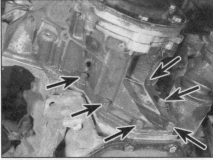

4.13a Lower clutch housing mounting bolts (arrowed) (BH3 transmission)

transmission, loosen the locknut and slacken the adjuster on the transmission intermediate lever pushrod. On all other models, slacken the locknut and adjuster nut on the end of the cable.

2 Working inside the car, remove the lower facia panel from the steering column.

3 Pull off the spring clip and remove the clevis pin from the top of the pedal to disconnect the cable end.

4 Unhook the cable tension spring from the pedal.

5 Unscrew the nut from the pivot bolt, pull out the bolt and lower the clutch pedal from the bracket.

6 Examine the pedal bushes for wear and renew them if necessary.

Refitting

7 Refitting is a reversal of removal, but lightly grease the bushes and clevis pin. On completion, adjust the clutch pedal stroke as described in Chapter 1.

4 Clutch assembly - removal, inspection and refitting

 Warning: Dust created by clutch wear and deposited on the clutch components may contain asbestos which is a health hazard. DO NOT blow it out with compressed air or inhale any of it. DO NOT use petrol or petroleum-based solvents to clean off the dust. Brake system cleaner or methylated spirit should be used to flush the dust into a suitable receptacle. After the clutch components are wiped clean with rags, dispose of the contaminated rags and cleaner in a sealed, marked container.

Removal

Models with BH3 transmission

1 Remove the battery and starter motor, as described in Chapter 5A.

2 Apply the handbrake then jack up the front of the car and securely support it on axle stands (see "Jacking and vehicle support").

4.10 Unscrew the two nuts securing the left-hand engine mounting to the bottom of the battery tray (BH3 transmission)

Drain the engine/transmission oil as described in Chapter 1.

3 Disconnect the gear selector rod with reference to Chapter 7A.

4 Disconnect the bonnet stay from the right-hand suspension tower and use suitable U-brackets in the bonnet hinge holes to hold the bonnet in a vertical position.

5 Remove the complete air cleaner and brackets, as described in Chapter 4A.

6 Disconnect the vacuum advance pipe from the distributor.

7 Disconnect the clutch cable at the transmission end with reference to Section 2.

8 Working through the hole in the battery tray, unscrew and remove the top nut from the left-hand engine mounting. If necessary remove the splash guard from the wheel housing.

9 Using a trolley jack and block of wood, support the left-hand side of the engine beneath the transmission.

10 Unscrew the two nuts securing the left-hand engine mounting to the bottom of the battery tray **(see illustration)**. Remove the mounting.

11 Lower the engine and transmission until the left-hand driveshaft rests on the subframe.

12 Unclip the starter motor wiring from the clutch housing.

13 Unscrew the bolts securing the clutch housing and transfer gear assembly to the transmission and engine noting the location of the lifting eye and earth cable. Do not forget to remove the bolt located in the bottom recess of the housing **(see illustrations)**.

4.13b Engine lifting eye (BH3 transmission)

4.13c Earth cable location (BH3 transmission)

4.13d Mounting bolt located in the clutch housing recess (arrowed) (BH3 transmission)

4.15a Remove the clutch housing and transfer gear assembly (BH3 transmission) . . .

4.15b . . . and the gasket (BH3 transmission)

4.18 Removing the clutch pressure plate assembly and driven plate

14 If necessary for additional working room, unbolt and remove the battery tray.

15 Withdraw the clutch housing and transfer gear assembly from the engine and transmission. Remove the gasket **(see illustrations)**.

Models with BE1, BE3 and MA transmissions

16 Remove the transmission from the engine, as described in Chapter 7A.

All models

17 Mark the clutch pressure plate in relation to the flywheel then progressively loosen the bolts. If necessary hold the flywheel stationary using a screwdriver engaged with the starter ring gear.

18 With all the bolts removed lift the pressure plate assembly from the location dowels followed by the driven plate **(see illustration)**.

Inspection

19 With the clutch assembly removed, clean off all traces of asbestos dust using a dry cloth. This is best done outside or in a well ventilated area; asbestos dust is harmful, and must not be inhaled

20 Examine the linings of the driven plate for wear and loose rivets, and the rim for distortion, cracks, broken torsion springs and worn splines. The surface of the friction linings may be highly glazed but, as long as the friction material pattern can be clearly seen, this is satisfactory. If there is any sign of oil contamination, indicated by a continuous or patchy, shiny black discoloration, the plate must be renewed and the source of the contamination traced and rectified. The driven plate must also be renewed if the lining thickness has worn down to, or just above, the level of the rivet heads.

21 Check the machined faces of the flywheel and pressure plate. If either is grooved, or heavily scored, renewal is necessary. The pressure plate must also be renewed if any cracks are apparent, if the diaphragm spring is damaged or its pressure suspect, or if there is excessive warpage of the pressure plate face.

22 With the transmission removed, check the condition of the release bearing, as described in Section 5.

Refitting

23 Locate the driven plate on the flywheel with the cushioning spring hub facing outwards. Place the pressure plate assembly over it with the dowels and holes correctly aligned, and fit the bolts finger tight.

24 It is now necessary to align the centre of the driven plate with that of the flywheel. To do this, use a commercially available clutch aligning tool, obtainable from most accessory shops, engaged with the flywheel spigot bearing, or alternatively a suitable diameter bar or wooden dowel can be used.

25 With the driven plate centralised, the pressure plate bolts should be tightened diagonally and evenly to the specified torque. Ideally new spring washers should be used each time a replacement clutch is fitted. When the bolts are tight remove the centralising tool.

26 Lubricate the clutch shaft splines, release bearing guide tube and the release fork ball-stud and fingers with a molybdenum disulphide-based grease.

Models with BE1, BE3 and MA transmissions

27 Refit the transmission as described in Chapter 7A.

Models with BH3 transmission

28 Clean the mating surfaces, then locate a new gasket on the dowels on the cylinder block.

29 Refit the clutch housing and transfer gear assembly to the engine and transmission. If the splines on the shafts do not line up correctly move the flywheel fractionally. Make sure that the clutch cable intermediate lever is in its working position.

30 Insert the bolts, together with the lifting eye and earth cable, and tighten them progressively to the specified torque.

31 If removed, refit the battery tray and tighten the bolts.

32 Clip the starter motor wiring to the clutch housing.

33 Using a trolley jack and block of wood, raise the engine and gearbox, locate the left-hand mounting and tighten the two nuts on the bottom of the battery tray.

34 Refit and tighten the mounting top nut.

35 Refer to Section 2 and reconnect the clutch cable, then adjust the pedal stroke as described in Chapter 1.

36 Reconnect the distributor vacuum advance pipe.

37 Refit the air cleaner, with reference to Chapter 4A, and refit the bonnet stay.

38 Reconnect the gear selector rod and lower the car to the ground.

39 Refit the starter motor and battery, with reference to Chapter 5A.

40 Refill the engine/transmission assembly with oil as described in Chapter 1.

5 Clutch release mechanism - overhaul

Note: *Refer to the warning at the beginning of Section 4 before proceeding.*

Models with BH3 transmission

1 Remove the clutch housing and transfer gear assembly, as described in Section 4.

2 Release the spring clips and slide the release bearing from the guide sleeve **(see illustration)**.

3 Remove the foam ring.

4 Withdraw the release fork from the ball-stud **(see illustration)**.

5 Check the release bearing for smoothness of operation and renew it if there is any roughness or harshness as it is spun. It is a good idea to renew the bearing as a matter of

6

5.2 Release spring clips and slide the release bearing from the guide sleeve (BH3 transmission)

5.4 Withdraw the release fork from the ball-stud (BH3 transmission)

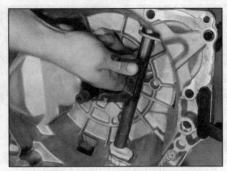

5.26 Manipulate the release lever pivot shaft from the bellhousing (BE3 transmission shown)

course during clutch overhaul, regardless of its apparent condition.

6 Inspect the fork retaining ball-stud and, if obviously distorted or worn, renew it. Drift the ball-stud from the housing using a suitable diameter drift. Fit the new one, together with a new rubber cup, by driving it carefully into position using a soft-faced hammer. Support the housing during this operation to prevent it from being damaged.

7 Before reassembly, check the output (clutch) shaft oil seal. If it is leaking then the complete guide sleeve/seal assembly must be renewed as the seal is not supplied separately.

8 Press the guide sleeve out of the clutch housing.

9 Press the new sleeve/seal assembly fully into its recess so that it seats firmly.

10 Any wear in the spigot bush which is located in the centre of the crankshaft rear flange (flywheel mounting) and supports the output shaft can be rectified by renewal of the bush, as described in Chapter 2A.

11 Refit the components using a reversal of the removal procedure. Lubricate the ball-stud and guide sleeve with a molybdenum disulphide-based grease. When fitting the release fork, locate the spring blade under the rubber cap.

Models with BE1 transmission

12 Remove the transmission, as described in Chapter 7A.

13 Release the spring clips and slide the bearing from the guide sleeve.

14 Withdraw the release fork from the ball-stud.

15 Check the release bearing for smoothness of operation and renew it if there is any roughness or harshness as it is spun. It is a good idea to renew the bearing as a matter of course during clutch overhaul, regardless of its apparent condition.

16 Where applicable, the pivot bush may be removed as follows. First drill out the rivets which secure the old bush. Remove the bush and discard it. Position the new bush on the fork and pass its rivets through the holes. Heat the rivets with a cigarette lighter or a low powered blowlamp, then peen over their heads while they are still hot.

17 Lightly coat the bush with grease, then refit the release fork. Press it onto the ball-stud until it snaps home.

18 If the ball-stud requires renewal, remove it with a slide hammer having a suitable claw. Support the casing and drive in the new stud using a soft metal drift.

19 Refit the remaining components using a reversal of the removal procedure. Lubricate the clutch shaft splines, guide sleeve, ball-stud and fingers with a molybdenum disulphide-based grease.

20 Refit the transmission, as described in Chapter 7A.

Models with BE3 and MA transmissions

21 Remove the transmission, as described in Chapter 7A.

22 Pull the clutch release bearing from the guide sleeve, then release the spring clips from the fork ends.

23 Check the release bearing for smoothness of operation and renew it if there is any roughness or harshness as it is spun. It is a good idea to renew the bearing as a matter of course during clutch overhaul, regardless of its apparent condition.

24 Using a suitable punch, drive out the roll-pin securing the release lever to the pivot shaft, then withdraw the release lever.

25 Prise the upper pivot shaft bush from the bellhousing.

26 Lift the lower end of the release lever pivot shaft from the lower bush in the bellhousing, then lower the pivot shaft into the bellhousing, and manipulate it as necessary to enable removal **(see illustration)**.

27 If desired, the lower pivot bush can be prised from the bellhousing.

28 Reassembly is a reversal of dismantling, but ensure that the pivot bushes are correctly located in the bellhousing.

29 Refit the transmission, as described in Chapter 7A.

Chapter 7 Part A:
Manual transmission

Contents

Degrees of difficulty

Easy, suitable for novice with little experience	**Fairly easy,** suitable for beginner with some experience	**Fairly difficult,** suitable for competent DIY mechanic	**Difficult,** suitable for experienced DIY mechanic	**Very difficult,** suitable for expert DIY or professional

Specifications

General

Type	Four or five forward speeds all with synchromesh, and one reverse
Application:	
XV, XW and XY series engines	BH3 transmission
XU series engines	BE1 and BE3 transmissions
TU series engines	MA transmission

Lubrication

Lubricant type:	
BH3 transmission	Multigrade engine oil, viscosity SAE 10W/40 or 15W/40
BE1, and BE3 transmissions:	
Pre-August 1987	Multigrade engine oil, viscosity SAE 10W/40 or 15W/40
August 1987 onward	Gear oil, viscosity SAE 75W/80
MA transmission	Gear oil, viscosity SAE 75W/80
Lubricant capacity	See "Weekly checks"

Torque wrench settings

	Nm	lbf ft
BH3 transmission		
Drain plug	27	20
Selector lever bolt	13	10
Reversing light switch	25	18
BE1 and BE3 transmissions		
Clutch release bearing guide sleeve bolts	12	9
Engine-to-transmission fixing bolts	45	33
Left-hand engine/transmission mountings:		
LH nut	35	26
Battery tray/bracket	18	13
Lower mounting centre bolt	34	25
Lower mounting to subframe	45	33
Drain plug (gearbox)	10	7
Drain plug (final drive)	35	26
Oil filler/level plug	22	16
Reversing light switch	25	18

Torque wrench settings (continued)

	Nm	lbf ft
MA transmission		
Clutch release bearing guide sleeve bolts	12	9
Engine-to-transmission fixing bolts	35	26
Engine/transmission left-hand mounting:		
Mounting bracket-to-transmission nuts	20	15
Mounting bracket-to-body bolts	25	18
Mounting rubber nuts	20	15
Centre nut	65	48
Engine/transmission rear mounting:		
Mounting-to-cylinder block bolts	40	30
Mounting link-to-mounting bolt	70	52
Mounting link-to-body bolt	50	37
Drain and filler plugs	25	19
Reversing light switch	25	18

1 General information

BH3 transmission

The BH3 transmission is fitted to models with XV, XW and XY series engines. The unit is mounted transversely directly under and to the rear of the engine with which it shares a common lubrication system.

The transmission casing is constructed in light alloy and incorporates the final drive and differential.

Power from the engine crankshaft is transmitted through the output shaft then the transfer gears to the transmission input shaft.

Drive to the front roadwheels is transmitted through open driveshafts from the differential side gears.

The transmission may be of four or five-speed type, depending upon the vehicle model. Both types are similar except for the 5th gear located on the ends of the primary and secondary shafts.

The transmission is of conventional two shaft constant-mesh layout. There are four pairs of gears, one for each forward speed. The gears on the primary shaft are fixed to the shaft, while those on the secondary or pinion shaft float, each being locked to the shaft when engaged by the synchromesh unit. The reverse idler gear is on a third shaft.

On five-speed units, the 5th gears are of fixed type with an extra synchromesh assembly.

The gear selector forks engage in the synchromesh unit; these slide axially along the shaft to engage the appropriate gear. The forks are mounted on selector shafts which are located in the base of the transmission.

The helical gear on the end of the pinion shaft drives directly onto the crownwheel mounted on the differential unit. The latter differs from normal practice in that it runs in shell bearings and the end thrust is taken up by thrustwashers in a similar manner to the engine crankshaft.

BE1 transmission

The BE1 transmission is fitted to early models with XU series engines. The unit is mounted on the left-hand side of the engine and may be removed separately leaving the engine in the car.

The transmission has five forward gears, all with synchromesh, and one reverse. As is common practice in five-speed units, the 5th gear components are on the far side of an intermediate plate which carries one pair of shaft bearings. Gear selection is by forks and synchromesh units as described for the BH transmission.

The differential (final drive) unit is contained in its own housing which is bolted to the transmission casing The transmission and differential share the same lubricant.

BE3 transmission

The BE3 transmission is a refined development of the BE1 unit, and was introduced in 1989 to progressively replace its predecessor. The two transmission types are virtually identical in appearance and construction although many of the BE3 internal components have been modified.

BE3 transmission can be identified by the revised gearchange pattern, with reverse positioned opposite 5th gear.

MA transmission

The MA transmission is fitted to models with TU series engines. The unit is mounted on the left-hand side of the engine, and may be removed separately, leaving the engine in the car. It has either four or five forward gears depending on model, all with synchromesh, and one reverse gear. All the synchromesh units are located on the output shaft, and the differential unit is located in the main transmission casing.

2 Manual transmission oil - draining and refilling

Note: *A suitable square section wrench may be required to undo the transmission filler/level and drain plugs on some models. These wrenches can be obtained from most motor factors or your Peugeot dealer.*

BH3 transmission

1 On the BH3 transmission, the engine and transmission share the same lubricating oil - refer to the engine oil and filter renewal procedures contained in Chapter 1.

BE1 transmission

Draining

Note: *On pre-1986 models, two drain plugs are provided; one for the main gearbox, the other for the final drive differential. On later models, the gearbox drain plug has been deleted and the complete transmission is now drained through the final drive drain plug.*

2 This operation is much quicker and more efficient if the car is first taken on a journey of sufficient length to warm the engine/transmission up to normal operating temperature.

3 Park the car on level ground, switch off the ignition and apply the handbrake firmly. For improved access, jack up the front of the car and support it securely on axle stands (see *"Jacking and vehicle support"*). Note that the car must be lowered to the ground and level, to ensure accuracy, when refilling and checking the oil level.

4 Position a suitable container beneath the transmission then remove the final drive drain plug **(see illustration)**.

5 Allow the oil to drain completely into the container. If the oil is hot, take precautions against scalding. When all the oil has drained, clean the drain plug, refit with a new sealing washer and tighten to the specified torque.

6 On pre-1986 models, repeat the procedure on the main gearbox drain plug.

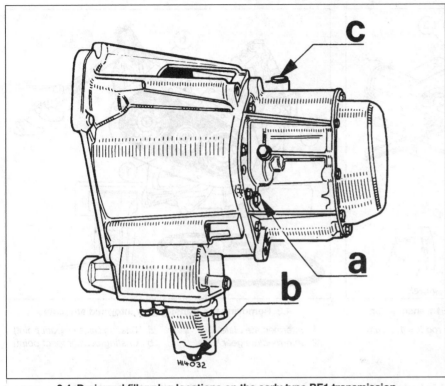

2.4 Drain and filler plug locations on the early type BE1 transmission

a *Main gearbox drain plug*
b *Final drive drain plug*

c *Filler/breather plug (depending on model)*

Refilling

7 The transmission is filled via the top filler/breather plug aperture (depending on model). Note, however, that some models have a cable-actuated reverse gear stop, with the cable entering the top of the transmission at the point where the breather was previously fitted. In order to fill these transmissions, the reverse gear stop cable must be unscrewed from the adapter on the gearbox casing.

8 From approximately October 1986, a gearbox/final drive level plug was fitted to the gearbox end cover **(see illustration)**. The plug is fitted with a copper washer, which should be cleaned and checked for condition before refitting. The oil level should reach the bottom of the level plug aperture.

9 Having identified the transmission type being worked on, remove the filler/breather plug, reverse gear stop cable or gearbox/final drive level plug as applicable.

10 As there is no provision for checking the oil level on pre-1986 transmissions, the correct oil quantity must be measured out first. It is therefore most important to ensure that the old oil has completely drained.

11 Fill the transmission with the measured quantity of the specified oil type, through the relevant aperture. On models from October 1986 onward, fill the transmission until the oil flows out of the filler, then refit and tighten the filler plug on completion. Note that the type of oil used in the transmission differs according to year; ensure that the correct oil is used (see Specifications).

BE3 and MA transmissions

Draining

12 Carry out the operations described in paragraphs 2 and 3 above

13 Wipe clean the area around the filler/level plug, which is situated on the left-hand end of the transmission, next to the end cover. Unscrew the filler/level plug from the transmission and recover the sealing washer **(see illustration)**.

14 Position a suitable container under the drain plug and unscrew the plug. On the MA transmission, the plug is on the left-hand side of the differential housing; on the BE3 transmission, it is on the base of the differential housing **(see illustration)**.

15 Allow the oil to drain completely into the container. If the oil is hot, take precautions against scalding. Clean both the filler/level and the drain plugs, being especially careful to wipe any metallic particles off the magnetic inserts. Discard the original sealing washers; they should be renewed whenever they are disturbed.

16 When the oil has finished draining, clean the drain plug threads and those of the transmission casing, fit a new sealing washer and refit the drain plug, tightening it to the specified torque wrench setting. If the car was raised for the draining operation, now lower it to the ground.

Refilling

17 Refill the transmission through the filler/level plug hole with the exact amount of the specified type of oil until the oil runs out of the filler/level hole. To ensure that a true level is established, wait until the initial trickle has stopped, then add oil as necessary until a trickle of new oil can be seen emerging. The level will be correct when the flow ceases. If the correct amount was poured into the transmission and a large amount flows out before the full quantity has been added, allow time for the level to settle then try adding more oil. If it still flows out, refit the filler/level plug and take the car on a short journey so that the new oil is distributed fully around the transmission components, then check the level again on your return as described in Chapter 1.

7A

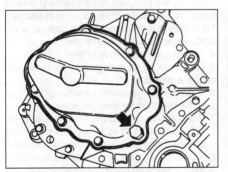

2.8 Location of level plug (arrowed) on later BE1 transmissions

2.13 Filler/level plug (arrowed) on the MA transmission

2.14 Drain plug (arrowed) on the MA transmission

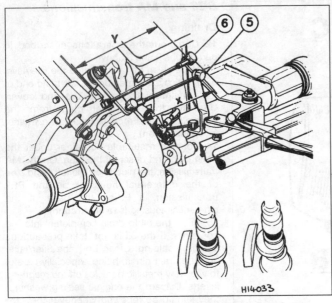

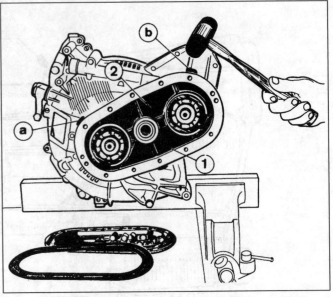

3.10 Gearchange linkage adjustment - BE1 transmission

6 Engagement rod Y = 284 mm   5 Selection rod X = 122 mm

4.3 Removing the transfer gear intermediate plate

1 Intermediate plate
2 Intermediate gear

a Casting boss (impact point)
b Casting boss (impact point)

3 Gearchange linkage - general information and adjustment

General information

1 If a stiff, sloppy or imprecise gearchange leads you to suspect that a fault exists within the linkage, first check the condition of all the link rods and their respective balljoints and bushes. Renew any components that are excessively worn and apply a smear of grease when reassembling.

2 If this does not cure the fault, the car should be examined by a dealer, as the fault may lie within the transmission itself. There is no adjustment as such in the linkage.

3 On early models equipped with the BE1 transmission, note that while the length of the link rods can be adjusted as described below, this is for initial setting-up only, and is not intended to provide a form of compensation for wear. On other models, although there is a provision for adjustment, in that the link rods have threaded balljoints whose positions on the rods can be altered, no setting data is provided by the manufacturer. Should it be necessary to renew the rods on these transmissions, check that the length of the new rod supplied is the same as the old rod removed. If necessary, alter the rod length by loosening the locknut and turning the balljoint as required. Note the relative alignment of the balljoints before making any changes, as incorrect positioning can lead to premature wear

Linkage adjustment - early BE1 transmission models

Note: *From mid-1985, the reverse gear stop is actuated by a cable acting on the transmission selector mechanism, instead of an eccentric cam at the base of the gear lever. The following procedure is therefore applicable to early transmissions that are not fitted with the reverse gear stop cable.*

4 Place the gear lever in neutral, then move it gently to the left until the commencement of resistance is felt.

5 Position a ruler against the gear knob with the zero marking aligned with the 1/2 mark on the knob.

6 Push the gear lever as far as possible to the left without moving the ruler and note the distance travelled by the knob. Repeat the operation two or three times. The desired travel is 36 to 40 mm.

7 If adjustment is necessary, unclip the gaiter from the surround and pull it up the gear lever.

8 If fitted, remove and discard the O-ring from the bottom of the gear lever.

9 Extract the spring clip and lift the plastic cam off its splines, then reposition the cam on the splines to give the correct lever movement described in paragraphs 4 to 6. Refit the spring clip on completion.

10 If the correct adjustment cannot be achieved due to the cam's being at its minimum or maximum position, the selection rod should be lengthened by 6.0 mm to provide extra movement or shortened by 6.0 mm to provide less movement. The normal initial length of the selection rod is shown **(see illustration)**. Adjust the cam position again after altering the selection rod length.

11 Also check the length of the engagement rod and adjust if necessary.

12 Apply a little grease to the gear lever stop, and refit the gear lever gaiter.

4 Transfer gears (BH3 transmission) - removal and refitting

Removal

1 The transfer gears are located under a cover plate at the end of the clutch/flywheel housing. Their purpose is to transmit power from the engine crankshaft and clutch to the transmission input shaft which lies below the engine.

2 Remove the clutch housing and transfer gear assembly, as described in Chapter 6.

3 Unbolt the cover plate then unbolt and remove the transfer gear intermediate plate. The plate will probably require tapping off with a plastic-faced hammer **(see illustration)**. Take care that the intermediate gear does not drop out as the plate is removed.

4 Remove the intermediate gear.

5 Clean away all old gasket material and obtain a new one.

6 Examine the gearteeth for wear or damage, and the bearings for wear or "shake".

7 If a ball-bearing is to be renewed, use a pair of circlips pliers to fully expand the circlip before pressing the shaft out of the bearing or the shaft/bearing out of the intermediate plate.

8 When reassembling, remember that the shorter shaft is located at the narrower end of the intermediate plate. Always use new circlips and support the plate adequately during the pressing operation.

9 Always use a new Belleville washer under the circlip so that its concave face is towards the bearing.

10 If the intermediate gear needle race is to be renewed in the intermediate plate, press the old one out and use the intermediate gear as an installation tool, but make sure that the gearteeth do not lock with those of the other gears during the pressing operation.

Refitting

11 Lubricate the bearings and fit the intermediate gear.

12 Offer the transfer gears with intermediate plate to the clutch housing. No gasket is used.

13 Locate the cover plate and its gasket **(see illustration)**.

14 Fit and tighten the cover plate bolts.

15 Refit the clutch housing and transfer gear assembly, as described in Chapter 6.

5 Oil seals - renewal

Driveshaft oil seals

1 Chock the rear wheels, apply the handbrake, then jack up the front of the car and support it on axle stands (see *"Jacking and vehicle support"*). Remove the appropriate front roadwheel.

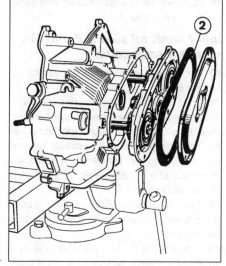

4.13 Assembling the transfer gears and cover plate

2 Gasket

2 Drain the transmission oil as described in Section 2.

3 Unscrew the clamp bolt securing the front suspension lower balljoint to the bottom of the hub carrier then pull the lower suspension arm down from the carrier. Proceed as described under the relevant sub-heading.

Right-hand seal

4 On BE and MA transmission models, loosen the two driveshaft intermediate bearing retaining bolt nuts, then rotate the bolts through 90° so that their offset heads are clear of the bearing outer race.

5 Carefully pull the hub carrier assembly outwards, and pull on the inner end of the driveshaft to free the intermediate bearing from its mounting bracket.

6 Once the driveshaft end is free from the transmission, slide the dust seal (where fitted) off the inner end of the shaft, noting which way around it is fitted, and support the inner end of the driveshaft to avoid damaging the constant velocity joints.

7 Carefully prise the oil seal out of the transmission, using a large flat-bladed screwdriver **(see illustration)**.

8 Remove all traces of dirt from the area around the oil seal aperture, then apply a smear of grease to the outer lip of the new oil seal. Fit the new seal into its aperture, and drive it squarely into position using a suitable tubular drift (such as a socket) which bears only on the hard outer edge of the seal, until it abuts its locating shoulder. If working on a post-1988 BE1 transmission, do not drive the seal fully home, as the seal inner lip may fail to contact the driveshaft, causing oil leaks. Instead position it as shown. On all models, if the seal was supplied with a plastic protector sleeve, leave this in position until the driveshaft has been refitted **(see illustrations)**.

5.7 Use a large flat bladed screwdriver to prise out the driveshaft oil seals

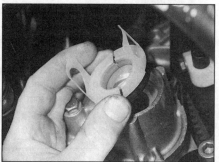

5.8a Fit the new seal to the transmission, noting the plastic seal protector . . .

5.8b . . . and tap it into position using a tubular drift

7A

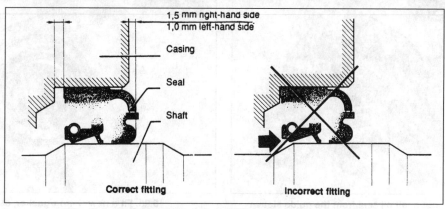

5.8c Correct fitting of oil seal on 1988 onwards BE1 transmissions

9 Thoroughly clean the driveshaft splines, then apply a thin film of grease to the oil seal lips and to the driveshaft inner end splines.

10 Where fitted, slide the dust seal into position on the end of the shaft, ensuring that its flat surface is facing the transmission.

11 Carefully locate the inner driveshaft splines with those of the differential sun gear, taking care not to damage the oil seal, then align the intermediate bearing with its mounting bracket, and push the driveshaft fully into position. If necessary, use a soft-faced mallet to tap the outer race of the bearing into position in the mounting bracket.

12 Ensure that the intermediate bearing is correctly seated, then rotate its retaining bolts back through 90° so that their offset heads are resting against the bearing outer race, and tighten the retaining nuts. Remove the plastic seal protector (where supplied), and slide the dust seal tight up against the oil seal.

13 Engage the balljoint with the hub carrier and refit and tighten the clamp bolt.

14 Refit the roadwheel, then lower the vehicle to the ground and tighten the roadwheel bolts to the specified torque.

15 Refill the transmission as described in Chapter 2.

Left-hand seal

16 Pull the hub carrier assembly outwards and withdraw the driveshaft inner constant velocity joint from the transmission, taking care not to damage the driveshaft oil seal. Support the driveshaft, to avoid damaging the constant velocity joints.

17 Renew the oil seal as described above in paragraphs 7 to 9.

18 Carefully locate the inner constant velocity joint splines with those of the differential sun gear, taking care not to damage the oil seal, and push the driveshaft fully into position. Where fitted, remove the plastic protector from the oil seal.

19 Carry out the operations described above in paragraphs 13 to 15.

Input shaft oil seal (BE and MA type transmissions)

20 Remove the transmission as described in Section 6.

21 Undo the three bolts securing the clutch release bearing guide sleeve in position, and slide the guide off the input shaft, along with its O-ring or gasket (as applicable). Recover any shims or thrustwashers which have stuck to the rear of the guide sleeve, and refit them to the input shaft.

22 Carefully lever the oil seal out of the guide using a suitable flat-bladed screwdriver **(see illustration)**.

23 Before fitting a new seal, check the input shaft's seal rubbing surface for signs of burrs, scratches or other damage, which may have caused the seal to fail in the first place. It may be possible to polish away minor faults of this sort using fine abrasive paper; however, more serious defects will require the renewal of the input shaft. Ensure that the input shaft is clean and greased, to protect the seal lips on refitting.

24 Dip the new seal in clean oil, and fit it to the guide sleeve.

25 Fit a new O-ring or gasket (as applicable) to the rear of the guide sleeve, then carefully slide the sleeve into position over the input shaft. Refit the retaining bolts and tighten them to the specified torque setting **(see illustration)**.

26 Take the opportunity to inspect the clutch components if not already done (Chapter 6). Finally, refit the transmission as described in Section 6.

6 Transmission - removal and refitting

BH3 transmission

1 The engine and transmission are removed from the car as a complete assembly and the two units are then separated after removal. Details of removal, separation, reconnection and refitting are given in Chapter 2D.

BE1 and BE3 transmissions

Removal

2 The BE1 and BE3 transmissions can be removed independently of the engine using the following procedure.

3 Disconnect the bonnet stay from the right-hand suspension tower and use suitable U-brackets in the bonnet hinge holes to hold the bonnet in a vertical position.

4 Remove the starter, as described in Chapter 5A, but it is not necessary to disconnect the wiring as the unit may be placed to one side.

5 Remove the air cleaner assembly and inlet ducts as described in the relevant Part of Chapter 4.

6 Remove the battery, as described in Chapter 5A.

7 Disconnect the clutch cable and remove the pushrod and intermediate lever, as described in Chapter 6.

8 Chock the rear wheels then jack up the front of the car and support it on axle stands (see "Jacking and vehicle support"). Remove the front roadwheels.

9 Drain the transmission oil as described in Section 2. Clean and refit the drain plug(s) on completion.

10 Unscrew the clamp bolts securing both front suspension lower balljoints to the bottom of the hub carriers.

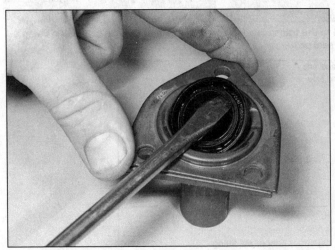

5.22 Remove the input shaft oil seal from the guide sleeve

5.25 Fit a new O-ring/gasket, as applicable

11 Loosen the two nuts retaining the right-hand driveshaft intermediate bearing in the bracket bolted to the rear of the cylinder block, then turn the bolts so that their heads move through 90°.

12 Unbolt the right-hand rear engine mounting link from the subframe, loosen the front bolt, and let the link hang free.

13 Disconnect all three gearchange control rods.

14 Turn the steering to full right-hand lock then pull the left-hand lower suspension arm down and release the balljoint from the hub carrier.

15 Pull the hub carrier outwards, and at the same time withdraw the inner end of the driveshaft from the final drive unit. Refer to Chapter 8 and fit a suitable tool to the differential side gear in order to prevent it from falling into the final drive housing.

16 Withdraw the right-hand driveshaft from the final drive unit using the procedure described in paragraphs 14 and 15 with the steering on full left-hand lock.

17 Disconnect the wiring from the reversing light switch, which is screwed into the top of the transmission housing. Tie it up out of the way.

18 Disconnect the speedometer cable, as described in Chapter 12.

19 Using a hoist, take the weight of the engine then unscrew and remove the top nut from the left-hand engine mounting.

20 Unbolt and remove the battery tray.

21 Lower the engine until the timing cover touches the body at the same time pull the unit forwards to prevent the final drive housing fouling the subframe.

22 Temporarily reconnect the right-hand rear engine mounting link to the subframe.

23 Support the transmission with a trolley jack then remove the clutch housing-to-engine mounting bolts and remove the cover plate.

24 Withdraw the transmission from the engine until the input shaft is clear of the clutch, then lower it through the engine compartment and remove from under the car.

Refitting

25 Refitting is a reversal of removal, but note the following points:
a) *It is recommended that the driveshaft oil seals in the final drive housing are renewed, as described in Section 5.*
b) *Tighten all nuts and bolts to the specified torque.*
c) *Refill the transmission with oil as described in Section 2.*
d) *Reconnect the clutch cable as described in Chapter 6.*

MA Transmission

Removal

26 Disconnect the bonnet stay from the right-hand suspension tower, and use suitable U-brackets in the bonnet hinge holes to hold the bonnet in a vertical position.

27 Remove the battery as described in Chapter 5A.

28 Remove the air cleaner assembly and inlet ducts as described in the relevant Part of Chapter 4.

29 Unscrew the nut, and detach the battery negative cable from the transmission.

30 Disconnect the wiring from the reversing light switch.

31 Pull out the rubber cotter, and remove the speedometer cable from the transmission.

32 Prise the two gearchange control rods from the transmission levers. A small open-ended spanner may be used to good effect.

33 Disconnect the clutch cable at the transmission end as described in Chapter 6.

34 Release the heater hose from the clips.

35 Unbolt the starter motor and air cleaner bracket, and support them to one side. There is no need to disconnect the wiring.

36 Chock the rear wheels then jack up the front of the car and support it on axle stands (see *"Jacking and vehicle support"*). Remove the front roadwheels.

37 Drain the transmission as described in Section 2.

38 Unscrew the clamp bolts securing both front suspension lower balljoints to the bottom of the hub carriers.

39 Loosen the two nuts retaining the right-hand driveshaft intermediate bearing in the bracket bolted to the rear of the cylinder block, then turn the bolts so that their heads move through 90°.

40 Unbolt the right-hand rear engine mounting link from the subframe, loosen the front bolt, and let the link hang free.

41 Turn the steering to full right-hand lock then pull the left-hand lower suspension arm down and release the balljoint from the hub carrier.

42 Pull the hub carrier outwards, and at the same time withdraw the inner end of the driveshaft from the final drive unit.

43 Withdraw the right-hand driveshaft from the final drive unit using the procedure described in paragraphs 41 and 42 with the steering on full left-hand lock.

44 Unscrew and remove the lower rear bolt securing the transmission to the engine, noting that the exhaust front pipe bracket is located on the bolt.

45 Support the left-hand side of the engine, using a hoist on the left-hand lifting eye, or a trolley jack and block of wood beneath the sump.

46 Unscrew the left-hand mounting nuts, including the nut on the centre stud, and remove the mounting.

47 Unbolt the battery tray.

48 Unscrew the nuts, and remove the left-hand mounting bracket from the transmission.

49 Lower the engine until the exhaust front pipe contacts the front suspension crossmember.

50 Unscrew the remaining bolts securing the transmission to the engine.

51 Support the transmission with a trolley jack or suitable sling, then withdraw it from the engine until clear of the clutch, and lower it to the ground.

Refitting

52 Refitting is a reversal of removal, but note the following points:
a) *It is recommended that the driveshaft oil seals in the final drive housing are renewed, as described in Section 5.*
b) *Tighten all nuts and bolts to the specified torque.*
c) *Lubricate the input shaft splines, clutch release bearing sleeve and fork fingers with molybdenum disulphide grease.*
d) *Refill the transmission with oil as described in Section 2.*
e) *Adjust the clutch pedal stroke with reference to Chapter 1.*

7 Transmission overhaul - general

No work can be carried out to the transmission until the engine/transmission has been removed from the car and cleaned externally.

Overhauling a manual transmission is a difficult and involved job for the DIY home mechanic. In addition to dismantling and reassembling many small parts, clearances must be precisely measured and, if necessary, changed by selecting shims and spacers. Internal transmission components are also often difficult to obtain, and in many instances, are extremely expensive. Because of this, if the transmission develops a fault or becomes noisy, the best course of action is to have the unit overhauled by a specialist repairer, or to obtain an exchange reconditioned unit.

Nevertheless, it is not impossible for the more experienced mechanic to overhaul the transmission, provided the special tools are available, and that the job is done in a deliberate step-by-step manner so that nothing is overlooked.

The tools necessary for an overhaul may include internal and external circlip pliers, bearing pullers, a slide hammer, a set of pin punches, a dial test indicator, and possibly a hydraulic press. In addition, a large, sturdy workbench and a vice will be required.

During dismantling of the transmission, make careful notes of how each component is fitted, to make reassembly easier and accurate.

Before dismantling the transmission, it will help if you have some idea which area is malfunctioning. Certain problems can be closely related to specific areas in the transmission, which can make component examination and replacement easier.

7A

Notes

Chapter 7 Part B:
Automatic transmission

Contents

Degrees of difficulty

Easy, suitable for novice with little experience	**Fairly easy,** suitable for beginner with some experience	**Fairly difficult,** suitable for competent DIY mechanic	**Difficult,** suitable for experienced DIY mechanic	**Very difficult,** suitable for expert DIY or professional

Specifications

General

Type	Automatic, four forward speeds and reverse
Designation	ZF4 HP 14

Lubrication

Recommended fluid and capacities	See "Weekly checks"

Torque wrench settings

	Nm	lbf ft
Dipstick tube-to-sump union nut	45	33
Engine-to-transmission securing bolts	45	33
Fluid cooler centre bolt	50	36
LH transmission mounting to transmission	35	26
LH transmission mounting to body	18	13
Selector cable fixings:		
Outer cable locknuts	10	7
Mounting bracket-to-transmission bolts	20	15
Cable-to-mounting bracket screws	10	7
Selector lever retaining nuts	7	5
Torque converter-to-driveplate bolts	35	26
Transmission selector lever retaining nut	30	22

1 General information

Some models covered in this manual have a four-speed fully-automatic transmission, consisting of a torque converter, an epicyclic geartrain, and hydraulically-operated clutches and brakes **(see illustration)**.

The torque converter provides a fluid coupling between engine and transmission, which acts as an automatic clutch, and also provides a degree of torque multiplication when accelerating.

The epicyclic geartrain provides either of the four forward or one reverse gear ratios, according to which of its component parts are held stationary or allowed to turn. The components of the geartrain are held or released by brakes and clutches which are activated by a hydraulic control unit. A fluid pump within the transmission provides the necessary hydraulic pressure to operate the brakes and clutches.

Driver control of the transmission is by a seven-position selector lever. The transmission has a "drive" position, and a "hold" facility on the first three gear ratios. The "drive" position "D" provides automatic

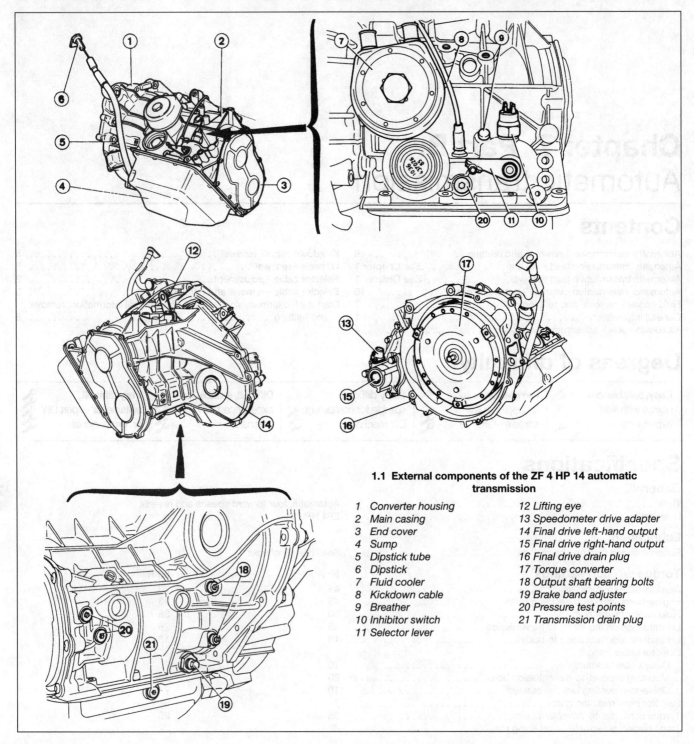

1.1 External components of the ZF 4 HP 14 automatic transmission

1 Converter housing	12 Lifting eye
2 Main casing	13 Speedometer drive adapter
3 End cover	14 Final drive left-hand output
4 Sump	15 Final drive right-hand output
5 Dipstick tube	16 Final drive drain plug
6 Dipstick	17 Torque converter
7 Fluid cooler	18 Output shaft bearing bolts
8 Kickdown cable	19 Brake band adjuster
9 Breather	20 Pressure test points
10 Inhibitor switch	21 Transmission drain plug
11 Selector lever	

changing throughout the range of all four gear ratios, and is the one to select for normal driving. An automatic kickdown facility shifts the transmission down a gear if the accelerator pedal is fully depressed. The "hold" facility is very similar, but limits the number of gear ratios available - ie when the selector lever is in the "3" position, only the first three ratios can be selected; in the "2" position, only the first two can be selected, and so on. The lower ratio "hold" is useful for providing engine braking when travelling down steep gradients, or for preventing unwanted selection of top gear on twisty roads. Note, however, that the transmission should *never* be shifted down a position if the engine speed exceeds 4000 rpm.

Due to the complexity of the automatic transmission, any repair or overhaul work must be left to a Peugeot dealer with the necessary special equipment for fault diagnosis and repair. The contents of the following Sections are therefore confined to supplying general information, and any service information and instructions that can be used by the owner.

2 Selector cable - adjustment

1 Position the selector lever firmly against its detent in the "N" (neutral) position.
2 To improve access to the transmission end of the selector cable, remove the battery and battery tray as described in Chapter 5A. To further improve access, it may also be necessary to remove the air inlet duct(s) as described in Chapter 4 (depending on model).
3 Using a large flat-bladed screwdriver, carefully lever the selector cable end fitting off the transmission selector lever balljoint, whilst ensuring that the lever does not move.
4 First ensure that the cable end fitting is screwed onto at least 5 mm of the inner cable thread.
5 With both the selector levers in the "P" position, the selector cable end fitting should be correctly aligned with the transmission lever balljoint, so that the cable can be connected to the lever without the balljoint moving. If necessary, adjust the position of the end fitting by screwing or unscrewing it (as applicable) on the cable thread, bearing in mind the point made above in paragraph 4 **(see illustration)**. If this proves impossible, further adjustments can be made by repositioning the outer cable in its mounting bracket. Reposition the nuts as required until the end fitting and balljoint are correctly aligned, then tighten the nuts.
6 Once the end fitting is correctly positioned, press it firmly onto the balljoint, and check that it is securely retained.
7 Refit any components removed to improve access.

3 Selector cable - removal and refitting

Removal

1 Firmly apply the handbrake, then jack up the front of the vehicle and support it on axle stands (see *"Jacking and vehicle support"*). Position the selector lever in the "P" position.
2 Remove the battery and battery tray as described in Chapter 5A.
3 Where necessary, remove the exhaust system heat shield(s) to gain access to the base of the selector lever assembly (see Chapter 4). On some models, it may also be necessary to remove the air inlet duct(s) as described in Chapter 4.
4 Working on the transmission end of the cable, release the outer cable mounting plate or undo the two screws securing the outer cable to its retaining bracket, and carefully lever the inner cable end fitting off its balljoint on the transmission selector lever. Note that the transmission selector lever must not be disturbed until the cable is refitted. As a precaution, mark the position of the lever in relation to the transmission housing.
5 Work back along the selector cable, releasing it from any relevant retaining clips, and noting its correct routing.
6 Disconnect the cable at the lever as described in the following paragraphs. Note that this procedure is applicable to one type of selector lever assembly; others may be encountered according to model.
7 Working from inside the vehicle, carefully prise the selector lever trim panel out from the centre console. Slacken and remove the screws securing the handle to the shaft of the selector lever. Depress the selector lever handle detent knob, then rotate the handle through 90° anti-clockwise, lift the assembly

up, and rotate it back 90° clockwise to release the detent button from the selector lever pushrod. With the handle removed, withdraw the detent button and spring from the handle.
8 Undo the four nuts securing the selector lever to the floor.
9 Working underneath the vehicle, disengage the selector lever assembly from the body, and remove the lever and cable assembly, noting the correct routing of the cable.
10 With the assembly on the bench, prise the rubber dust cover from the base of the lever, and slide it along the cable.
11 Slacken the outer cable retaining nut, then remove the retaining clip. Carefully prise the selector cable end fitting off its balljoint on the base of the selector lever, and separate the cable and lever assembly.
12 Examine the cable, looking for worn end fittings or a damaged outer casing, and for signs of fraying of the inner cable. Check the cable's operation; the inner cable should move smoothly and easily through the outer casing. Remember that a cable that appears serviceable when tested off the car may well be much heavier in operation when compressed into its working position. Renew the cable if it shows any signs of excessive wear or any damage.

Refitting

13 Apply a smear of the special grease (Mobil Temp G9, available from your Peugeot dealer) to the exposed sections of the inner cable and balljoints, and to the detent mechanism of the selector lever. In the absence of the specified grease, a good-quality molybdenum disulphide grease can be used.
14 Insert the selector cable into the selector lever housing, ensuring that the outer cable flange holes are correctly located on the pegs on the housing. Secure the cable in position with the retaining clip, ensuring that the outer

7B

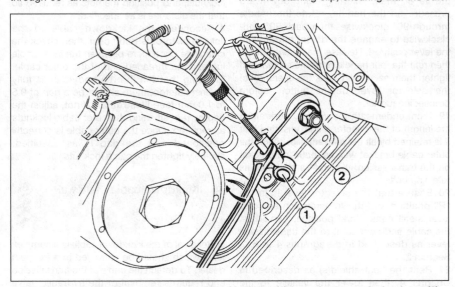

2.5 Disconnecting the selector control rod balljoint (1) from the transmission lever (2)

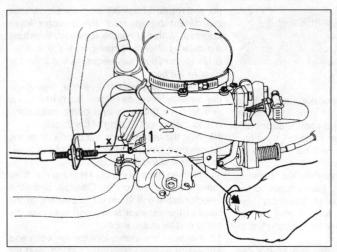

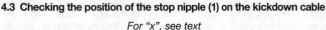

4.3 Checking the position of the stop nipple (1) on the kickdown cable

For "x", see text

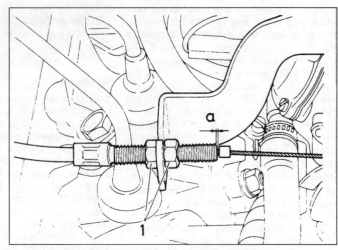

4.4 Checking idle clearance (a) on the kickdown cable

1 Adjustment nuts

ends of the clip are correctly located in the slots in the lever housing, and the inner ends are correctly hooked over the base of the housing. Tighten the outer cable retaining nut.

15 Press the inner cable end fitting firmly onto the lever balljoint. Check that the balljoint connection is securely made, then slide the rubber dust cover back into position over the selector lever base.

16 Ensuring that the cable is correctly routed, manoeuvre the lever and cable assembly back into position from underneath the vehicle.

17 From inside the vehicle, pull the lever up into position, and tighten all four selector lever retaining nuts.

18 Refit the spring and detent button to the selector lever handle, and press the button fully into the handle. Keeping the button depressed, slide the handle assembly onto the lever then, exerting light downward pressure on the handle, rotate the handle through 90° clockwise, then back 90° anti-clockwise to engage the detent button with the lever pushrod. Release the detent button, then refit the four handle retaining screws and tighten them securely. Check the operation of the selector lever detent button before proceeding further.

19 From underneath the vehicle, work along the length of the selector cable, ensuring that it is retained by all the relevant clips. Align the outer cable bracket with its mounting bracket on the transmission, then refit and tighten its retaining bolts.

20 Ensure that the selector lever is in the "P" position and the transmission selector lever is still in the "Park" position, then adjust the cable and connect it to the transmission lever as described in paragraphs 4 to 6 of Section 2.

21 Refit the heat shield(s) as described in Chapter 4, then lower the vehicle to the ground.

22 Refit all components removed for access.

4 Kickdown cable - adjustment

1 Warm the engine up to its normal operating temperature, then check that the engine idle speed is correctly set. If necessary, adjust the idle speed as described in Chapter 4.

2 Detach the kickdown inner cable from the linkage or throttle body cam then, referring to Chapter 4, check that the accelerator cable is correctly adjusted.

3 Pull the kickdown inner cable out of its outer cable until resistance is felt (indicating the start of kickdown), and measure the distance between the end of the lug on the inner cable and the threaded end of the outer cable **(see illustration)**. This should be approximately 39 mm. If necessary, slacken the two outer cable locknuts, and position the nuts as required so that the distance is as specified.

4 Reconnect the kickdown cable to the linkage or throttle body cam, then check the clearance once more between the inner cable lug and the threaded end of the outer cable. Ensuring that the throttle body cam is fully against its stop, there should be a gap of 0.5 to 1.0 mm **(see illustration)**. If not, adjust the gap by repositioning the outer cable locknuts as required. Once the outer cable is correctly positioned and the gap is as specified, securely tighten the cable locknuts.

5 Kickdown cable - renewal

Renewal of the kickdown cable is a complex task, which should be entrusted to a Peugeot dealer. To detach the cable at the transmission end requires removal of the hydraulic valve block, which is a task that should not be undertaken by the home mechanic.

6 Oil seals - renewal

Driveshaft oil seals

1 Refer to Part A of this Chapter.

Selector shaft oil seal

2 Position the selector lever firmly against its detent mechanism in the "N" position.

3 To improve access to the transmission end of the selector cable, remove the battery and battery tray as described in Chapter 5A. To further improve access, it may also be necessary to remove the inlet duct(s) as described in Chapter 4 (depending on model).

4 Undo the two screws securing the outer cable to its retaining bracket, and carefully lever the inner cable end fitting off its balljoint on the transmission selector lever. Note the transmission selector shaft must not be disturbed until the cable is refitted. As a precaution, mark the position of the lever in relation to the transmission housing.

5 Undo the retaining nut, and remove the lever from the transmission selector shaft.

6 Punch or drill two small holes opposite each other in the seal. Screw a self-tapping screw into each, and pull on the screws with pliers to extract the seal.

7 Clean the seal housing, and polish off any burrs or raised edges, which may have caused the seal to fail in the first place. Small imperfections can be removed using emery paper, but larger defects will require the renewal of the selector shaft.

8 Lubricate the lips of the new seal with clean engine oil, and carefully ease the seal into position over the end of the shaft, taking great care not to damage its sealing lip. Tap the seal into position until it is flush with the transmission casing, using a suitable tubular drift (such as a socket) which bears only on the hard outer edge of the seal. Note that the seal lips should face inwards.

9 Refit the selector lever to the shaft and tighten its retaining nut.

10 Align the outer cable bracket with its mounting bracket on the transmission, then refit and tighten its retaining bolts.

11 Ensure that the selector lever is in the "N" position and the transmission selector lever is still in the neutral position, then adjust the cable and connect it to the transmission lever as described in paragraphs 4 to 6 of Section 2.

7 Fluid cooler - removal and refitting

Removal

1 The fluid cooler is mounted on the top of the transmission housing. To gain access to the fluid cooler, remove the air inlet duct(s) as described in Chapter 4 (depending on model). Slacken and remove the bolts securing the hose retaining bracket in position, and position the bracket clear of the fluid cooler.

2 Using a hose clamp or similar, clamp both the fluid cooler coolant hoses to minimise coolant loss during subsequent operations.

3 Slacken the retaining clips, and disconnect both coolant hoses from the fluid cooler - be prepared for some coolant spillage. Wash off any spilt coolant immediately with cold water, and dry the surrounding area before proceeding further.

4 Slacken and remove the fluid cooler centre bolt, and remove the cooler from the transmission. Remove the seal from the centre bolt, and the two seals fitted to the base of the cooler, and discard them; new ones must be used on refitting.

Refitting

5 Lubricate the new seals with clean automatic transmission fluid, then fit the two new seals to the base of the fluid cooler, and a new seal to the centre bolt.

6 Locate the fluid cooler on the top of transmission housing, ensuring its flat edge is parallel to the mating surface of the transmission/driveplate housing. Refit the centre bolt, and tighten it to the specified torque setting.

7 Reconnect the coolant hoses to the fluid cooler, and securely tighten their retaining clips. Remove the hose clamp.

8 Refit the disturbed inlet duct/air cleaner housing components (as applicable) as described in Chapter 4.

9 On completion, top-up the cooling system and check the automatic transmission fluid level as described in "Weekly checks" and Chapter 1.

8 Starter inhibitor/reversing light switch - information, removal and refitting

General information

1 The starter inhibitor/reversing light switch is a dual-function switch which is screwed into the top of the transmission housing. The inhibitor function of the switch ensures that the engine can only be started with the selector lever in either the "N" or "P" positions, therefore preventing the engine being started with the transmission in gear. This is achieved by the switch cutting the supply to the starter motor solenoid. If at any time it is noted that the engine can be started with the selector lever in any position other than "P" or "N", then it is likely that the inhibitor function of the switch is faulty. The switch also performs the function of the reversing light switch, illuminating the reversing lights whenever the selector lever is in the "R" position. If either function of the switch is faulty, the complete switch must be renewed as a unit.

Removal

2 To improve access to the switch, remove the battery and battery tray as described in Chapter 5A.

3 Trace the wiring back from the switch, and disconnect it at the wiring connector.

4 Unscrew the switch, and remove it from the top of the transmission housing, along with its sealing ring.

Refitting

5 Fit a new sealing ring to the switch, screw it back into the transmission, and tighten it securely.

6 Reconnect the switch wiring, then refit the support tray and securely tighten its retaining bolts.

7 Where necessary, refit the battery as described in Chapter 5A, and test the operation of the switch.

9 Automatic transmission - removal and refitting

Removal

1 Chock the rear wheels, apply the handbrake, and place the selector lever in the "N" (neutral) position. Jack up the front of the vehicle, and securely support it on axle stands (see "Jacking and vehicle support"). Remove both front roadwheels.

2 Drain the transmission fluid as described in Chapter 1, then refit the drain plugs, tightening them securely.

3 Remove the battery, battery tray and mounting plate as described in Chapter 5A.

4 Remove the starter motor as described in Chapter 5A.

5 Remove the air inlet duct(s) as described in Chapter 4.

6 Undo the union nut securing the dipstick tube to the transmission sump, then undo the bolt securing the tube to the transmission housing, and remove the dipstick from the transmission **(see illustration)**.

7 Disconnect the wiring connector from the starter inhibitor/reversing light switch and, where necessary, the speedometer drive housing. Undo the retaining nut/bolt(s) and disconnect the earth strap(s) from the top of the transmission housing.

8 Using a hose clamp or similar, clamp both the fluid cooler coolant hoses to minimise coolant loss. Slacken the retaining clips and disconnect both coolant hoses from the fluid cooler - be prepared for some coolant spillage. Wash off any spilt coolant immediately with cold water.

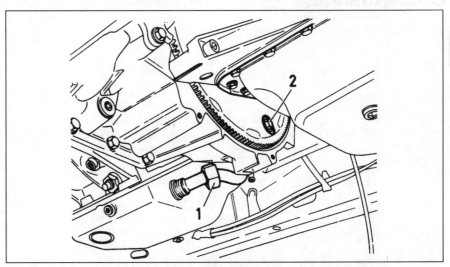

9.6 Unscrew the dipstick tube nut (1) and torque converter bolts (2)

9 Release the mounting plate or undo the two screws securing the outer selector cable to its retaining bracket, and carefully lever the inner cable end fitting off its balljoint on the transmission selector lever. Note that the transmission selector lever must not be disturbed until the cable is refitted. As a precaution, mark the position of the lever in relation to the transmission housing. Work back along the selector cable, releasing it from any relevant retaining clips, and position it clear of the transmission.

10 Detach the kickdown inner cable from the linkage or throttle body cam, then slacken the outer cable locknuts and free the cable from its mounting bracket. Release the kickdown cable from any relevant retaining clips, so that it is free to be removed with the transmission.

11 On models with power steering, undo the nut/release the retaining clips (as necessary) and free the power steering pipe from the transmission.

12 Undo the retaining bolts and remove the lower driveplate cover plate from the transmission, to gain access to the torque converter retaining bolts. Slacken and remove the visible bolt then, using a socket and extension bar to rotate the crankshaft pulley, undo the remaining bolts securing the torque converter to the driveplate as they become accessible. There are three bolts in total.

13 To ensure that the torque converter does not fall out as the transmission is removed, secure it in position using a length of metal strip bolted to one of the starter motor bolt holes.

14 Withdraw the rubber retaining pin, disconnect the speedometer cable from the drive, and free it from any retaining clips.

15 Remove the driveshafts as described in Chapter 8.

16 Place a jack with a block of wood beneath the engine, to take the weight of the engine. Alternatively, attach a couple of lifting eyes to the engine, and fit a hoist or support bar to take the weight of the engine.

17 Place a jack and block of wood beneath the transmission, and raise the jack to take the weight of the transmission.

18 Slacken and remove the centre nut and washer from the left-hand engine/transmission mounting. Undo the two nuts and washers securing the mounting rubber in position and remove it from the engine compartment.

19 Slide the spacer (where fitted) off the mounting stud, then unscrew the stud from the top of the transmission housing and remove it along with its washer. If the mounting stud is tight, a universal stud extractor can be used to unscrew it.

20 With the jack positioned beneath the transmission taking the weight, slacken and remove the remaining bolts securing the transmission housing to the engine. Note the correct fitted positions of each bolt as it is removed, to use as a reference on refitting. Make a final check that all necessary components have been disconnected, and positioned clear of the transmission so that they will not hinder the removal procedure.

21 With the bolts removed, move the trolley jack and transmission to the left, to free it from its locating dowels.

22 Once the transmission is free, lower the jack and manoeuvre the unit out from under the car. If they are loose, remove the locating dowels from the transmission or engine, and keep them in a safe place.

Refitting

23 The transmission is refitted by a reversal of the removal procedure, bearing in mind the following points:

a) *Ensure that the bush fitted to the centre of the crankshaft is in good condition, and apply a little Molykote G1 grease to the torque converter centring pin. Do not apply too much, otherwise there is a possibility of the grease contaminating the torque converter.*

b) *Ensure that the engine/transmission locating dowels are correctly positioned prior to installation.*

c) *Once the transmission and engine are correctly joined, refit the securing bolts, tightening them to the specified torque setting, then remove the metal strip used to retain the torque converter.*

d) *Apply thread-locking fluid to the left-hand engine/transmission mounting stud threads prior to refitting it to the transmission. Tighten the stud to the specified torque.*

e) *Tighten all nuts and bolts to the specified torque (where given).*

f) *Renew the driveshaft oil seals and refit the driveshafts to the transmission, using the information given in Chapter 7A.*

g) *Adjust the selector cable and kickdown cable as described in Sections 2 and 4.*

h) *On completion, top-up the cooling system, then refill the transmission with the specified type and quantity of fluid as described in "Weekly checks" and Chapter 1.*

10 Automatic transmission overhaul - general information

In the event of a fault occurring with the transmission, it is first necessary to determine whether it is of an electrical, mechanical or hydraulic nature, and to do this, special test equipment is required. It is therefore essential to have the work carried out by a Peugeot dealer if a transmission fault is suspected.

Do not remove the transmission from the car for possible repair before professional fault diagnosis has been carried out, since most tests require the transmission to be in the vehicle.

Chapter 8
Driveshafts

Contents

Degrees of difficulty

Easy, suitable for novice with little experience	**Fairly easy,** suitable for beginner with some experience	**Fairly difficult,** suitable for competent DIY mechanic	**Difficult,** suitable for experienced DIY mechanic	**Very difficult,** suitable for expert DIY or professional

Specifications

Type	Open, with constant velocity joint at each end: solid or tubular, according to model
Driveshaft CV joint lubricant type	Special lubricant supplied in repair kit

Torque wrench settings	Nm	lbf ft
Hub carrier to strut clamp bolt	58	43
Hub nut:		
Non-GTI models	250	185
GTI models	260	192
Automatic transmission models	265	196
Suspension strut top mounting nuts	12	9
Front suspension lower balljoint	35	26
Intermediate bearing bolts	18	13

1 General information

Drive to the front wheels is transmitted from the final drive unit to the front hubs by two solid or tubular driveshafts. The driveshafts incorporate inner and outer constant velocity (CV) joints to accommodate suspension and steering angular movement. An intermediate bearing is used to support the right-hand driveshaft on XU and TU series engine models.

The inner CV joint ends are splined to the final drive/differential side gears, and the outer CV joint ends are splined to the front hubs.

2 Driveshaft - removal and refitting

Removal

1 Fully apply the handbrake then, where possible, remove the front wheel centre trim. Tap up the staking securing the hub nut to the driveshaft groove or, on later models, extract the R-clip and withdraw the locking collar. Using a socket and a long extension bar, slacken the hub nut. On models without a centre trim, the hub nut must be loosened after removing the front wheel. Do not apply the footbrake when loosening the nut as damage can occur to the brake disc retaining screws.

2 Chock the rear wheels then jack up the front of the car and support it on axle stands (see *"Jacking and vehicle support"*). Remove the front roadwheel.

3 If the hub nut has yet to be loosened, fabricate a tool from two lengths of steel strip (one long, one short) and a nut and bolt; the nut and bolt form the pivot of a forked tool. Bolt the tool to the hub flange using two wheel bolts, and hold the tool to prevent the hub from rotating **(see Tool Tip)**. Slacken the hub nut using a socket and a long extension bar.

4 Drain the transmission oil as described in Chapter 7A or 7B as applicable.

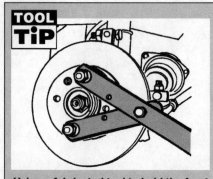

TOOL TiP

Using a fabricated tool to hold the front hub stationary whilst the hub nut is slackened

5 Unscrew the clamp bolt securing the front suspension lower balljoint to the bottom of the hub carrier then pull the lower suspension arm down from the carrier **(see illustrations)**.

6 Recover the balljoint guard plate, where fitted.

7 If working on the right-hand driveshaft on models equipped with a driveshaft intermediate bearing, loosen the two nuts retaining the intermediate bearing in the bracket bolted to the rear of the cylinder block. Turn the bolts so that their heads move through 90°.

8 Turn the front wheels to full right-hand lock (left-hand driveshaft), or full left-hand lock (right-hand driveshaft) and remove the hub nut and, where fitted, the washer. Note that a new hub nut will be required for refitting.

9 Pull the hub carrier outwards and at the same time withdraw the outer end of the driveshaft from the hub.

10 Withdraw the inner end of the driveshaft

2.5a Remove the clamp bolt (arrowed) . . .

from the final drive unit and, if working on the right-hand driveshaft, guide it through the intermediate bearing bracket on models so equipped.

11 Note that on pre-1985 models the design of the differential unit is such that if both driveshafts are removed, the differential side gears will fall down into the final drive housing. It is therefore important to retain the side gears using Peugeot tool 80317 (M and N), or alternatively re-insert the inner end of one driveshaft before removing the other. Another possibility is to improvise using a length of wooden dowel 25 mm in diameter, ground down slightly at one end to enter the splines in the side gear.

12 Note also that the weight of the car must not be taken by the front wheels with the driveshaft(s) removed otherwise damage may occur to the hub bearings.

Refitting

13 Refitting is a reversal of removal, bearing in mind the following points:

 a) When refitting the right-hand driveshaft,

2.5b . . . and pull the lower suspension arm down from the hub carrier

make sure that the lugs on the intermediate bearing bolt heads are located over the bearing outer track.

 b) Use a new hub nut to secure the driveshaft and apply a smear of multi-purpose grease to its threads and rear face. Use new self-locking nuts if the locking portion is in any way damaged.

 c) Tighten all nuts and bolts to their specified torque.

 d) After tightening the hub nut on early models secure the nut in position by staking it into the driveshaft groove. On later models, align one of the slots in the locking collar with the hole in the driveshaft and insert the R-clip to secure.

 e) Refill the transmission with oil as described in Chapter 7A or 7B on completion.

3 Driveshaft joint bellows - renewal

Note: *A number of different constant velocity joint types may be fitted to these models of which there is minimal documentation from the manufacturer. The following procedure depicts one of the common types; others may be encountered.*

Inboard joint

1 With the driveshaft removed from the car, prise back the lip of the cover and then tap the cover off to expose the tulip yoke **(see illustrations)**.

2 Remove the tulip yoke, spring and thrust cup **(see illustration)**

3 Wipe away as much of the original grease as possible.

4 If retaining circlips are not fitted, wind adhesive tape around the spider bearings to retain their needle rollers.

5 If it is now possible, borrow or make up a guide tool similar to the one shown **(see illustration)**. The defective bellows can be cut off and the new ones slid up the tool (well greased) so that they will expand sufficiently to ride over the joint and locate on the shaft.

6 Where such a tool cannot be obtained, proceed in the following way.

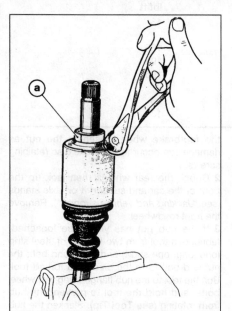

3.1a Prising back driveshaft joint cover lip

 a Oil seal rubbing surface

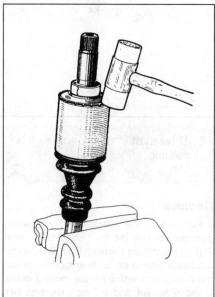

3.1b Tapping off driveshaft joint cover

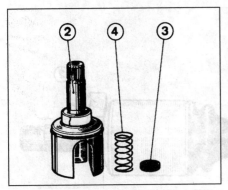

3.2 Driveshaft inboard joint components

2 Tulip   3 Thrust cap   4 Spring

7 Mark the relative position of the spider to the shaft.

8 Remove the spider retaining circlip **(see illustration)**.

9 Either support the spider and press the shaft from it, or use a suitable puller to draw it from the shaft **(see illustration)**.

10 Remove the bellows/cover and the small rubber retaining ring **(see illustration)**.

11 Commence reassembly by smearing the inside of the cover with grease, fit the spacer to the new bellows which are supplied as a repair kit complete with grease sachet.

12 Insert the spacer/gaiter into the cover.

13 Slide the small rubber ring onto the shaft followed by the bellows/cover assembly.

14 Using a piece of tubing as a drift, align the marks made before dismantling and drive the spider onto the shaft **(see illustration)**. Note that the chamfered side of the spider should go onto the shaft first.

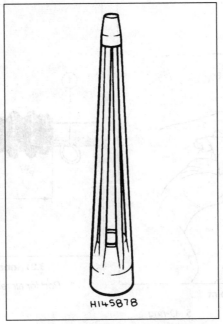

H145878

3.5 Suitable tool for fitting a new bellows

15 Fit a new spider retaining circlip.

16 Remove the bearing retaining tape.

17 Draw the cover over the spider and apply grease from the sachet to all components **(see illustration)**. Refit the tulip yoke with spring and thrust cap. Use a new O-ring seal.

18 Peen the rim of the cover evenly all around the yoke.

19 Engage the rubber retaining ring over the narrow end of the bellows.

20 Carefully insert a thin rod under the narrow end of the bellows and released trapped air.

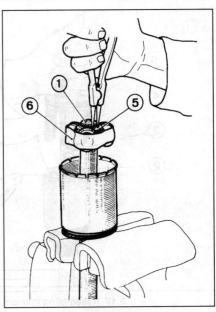

3.8 Extracting spider circlip

1 Shaft   6 Taped needle
5 Needle roller cage   rollers

21 Set the dimension as shown in the diagram by sliding the bellows or cover **(see illustration)**.

Outboard joint

22 If the guide tool mentioned in paragraph 5 is available, it is possible to cut the defective bellows from the shaft and fit the new bellows without dismantling the shaft. Where such a tool is not available, proceed in the following way.

23 With the driveshaft removed from the car and the inboard joint dismantled, as

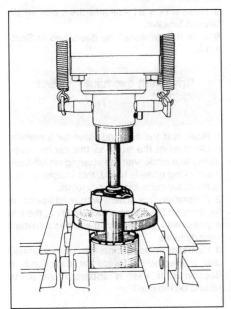

3.9 Pressing shaft out of spider

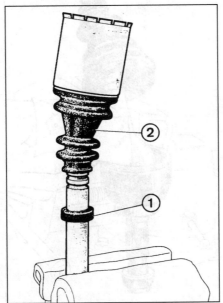

3.10 Driveshaft inboard joint

1 Rubber ring   2 Bellows

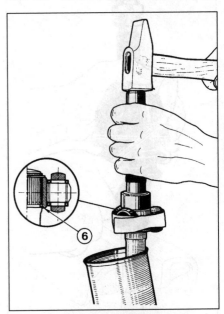

3.14 Driving spider onto shaft

6 Chamfered side

8

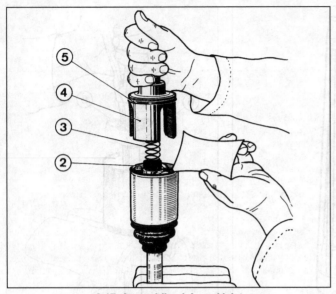

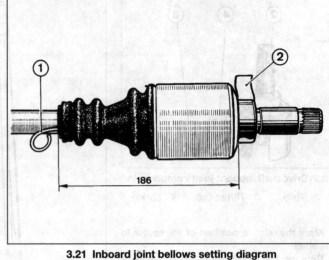

3.17 Assembling inboard joint

3.21 Inboard joint bellows setting diagram

2 *Thrust cap*   3 *Spring*   4 *Tulip*   5 *O-ring*

1 Rod for air release   *2 Protective tape*

Measurement in mm

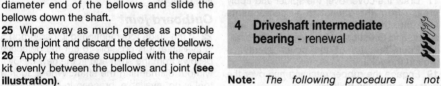

previously described, take off the spring clip which retains the larger diameter end of the bellows **(see illustration)**.

24 Prise off the rubber ring from the smaller diameter end of the bellows and slide the bellows down the shaft.

25 Wipe away as much grease as possible from the joint and discard the defective bellows.

26 Apply the grease supplied with the repair kit evenly between the bellows and joint **(see illustration)**.

27 Locate the new bellows, clip and rubber ring.

28 Insert a thin rod under the narrow end of the bellows to release any trapped air.

29 Refit the inboard joint, as previously described.

---

4 Driveshaft intermediate bearing - renewal

Note: *The following procedure is not applicable to XV, XW and XY series engine models.*

1 Remove the right-hand driveshaft, as described in Section 2.

2 Place the bearing and driveshaft in a vice with the inner track resting on the vice, then use a soft-faced mallet to drive out the driveshaft. Remove the end cover and oil seal from the driveshaft and intermediate bearing bracket. If the bearing has remained in the bracket when the driveshaft was removed use a metal tube on the inner track to drift it out.

3 Clean the bearing recess in the bracket.

4 Locate a new end cover on the driveshaft then use a metal tube on the inner track to drive the new bearing onto the special shoulder.

5 Press a new oil seal into the intermediate bearing bracket.

6 Refit the driveshaft as described in Section 2.

---

5 Driveshaft overhaul - general information

1 Road test the car, and listen for a metallic clicking from the front as the car is driven slowly in a circle with the steering on full-lock. If a clicking noise is heard, this indicates wear in the outer constant velocity joints.

2 If vibration, consistent with road speed, is felt through the car when accelerating, there is a possibility of wear in the inner constant velocity joints.

3 Constant velocity joints can be dismantled and inspected for wear as described in Section 3. If wear is apparent, the joints should be renewed.

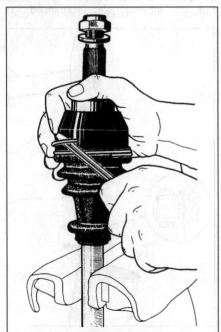

3.23 Removing bellows clip from driveshaft outboard joint

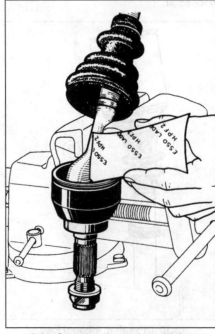

3.26 Greasing the outboard joint

Chapter 9
Braking system

Contents

Degrees of difficulty

| **Easy,** suitable for novice with little experience | | **Fairly easy,** suitable for beginner with some experience | | **Fairly difficult,** suitable for competent DIY mechanic | | **Difficult,** suitable for experienced DIY mechanic | | **Very difficult,** suitable for expert DIY or professional | |

Specifications

System type:

Footbrake	Dual-circuit hydraulic with servo assistance on all non-basic models. Anti-lock braking (ABS) optional on certain later models.
Handbrake	Mechanical by cables to rear brakes

Front brakes

Type	Solid or ventilated disc, with single piston sliding calipers
Brake pad minimum lining thickness	2.0 mm
Disc diameter	247 mm
Disc thickness:	
New:	
Non-ventilated disc	10.0 mm
Ventilated disc	20.4 mm
Minimum after resurfacing:	
Non-ventilated disc	8.5 mm
Ventilated disc	18.9 mm
Maximum disc run out	0.07 mm

Rear drum brakes

Type	Self-adjusting drum with leading and trailing shoes
Brake shoe minimum lining thickness	1.0 mm
Drum internal diameter:	
New	180.0 mm
Maximum after resurfacing	181.0 mm
Drum out-of-round (maximum)	0.10 mm

Rear disc brakes

Type	Disc, with single piston sliding calipers
Brake pad minimum lining thickness	2.0 mm
Disc diameter	247 mm
Disc thickness:	
New	8.0 mm
Minimum after resurfacing	7.0 mm
Maximum disc run out	0.07 mm

Torque wrench settings

	Nm	lbf ft
Girling front caliper mounting bolts:		
All models except 1.9 GTI	97	72
1.9 GTI models	100	74
Girling front caliper guide bolts (1.9 GTI models)	35	26
DBA Bendix front caliper mounting bolts	120	89
Rear caliper mounting bolts	120	89
Rear backplate	37	27
Rear hub nut	215	159

1 General information

The braking system is of hydraulic type with the front disc brakes and rear drum brakes on all except 1.9 GTI models. On these vehicles disc brakes are also fitted at the rear. On all models, the handbrake is cable-operated on the rear wheels.

The hydraulic system is split into two circuits, so that in the event of failure of one circuit, the other will still provide adequate braking power (although pedal travel and effort may increase). The hydraulic circuits are split either diagonally or front-to-rear according to model. In the diagonally split system, each hydraulic circuit supplies one front, and one diagonally opposite rear brake. In the front-to-rear arrangement, one circuit serves the front brakes and the other circuit the rear brakes.

A compensating valve (or valves) reduces the hydraulic pressure to the rear brakes under heavy applications of the brake pedal in order to prevent rear wheel lock-up.

A vacuum servo unit is fitted to all non-basic models.

From 1991, the Bendix anti-lock braking system (ABS) is available as an option on certain models and is described in further detail in Section 19.

Note: *When servicing any part of the system, work carefully and methodically; also observe scrupulous cleanliness when overhauling any part of the hydraulic system. Always renew components (in axle sets, where applicable) if in doubt about their condition, and use only genuine Peugeot replacement parts, or at least those of known good quality. Note the warnings given in "Safety first" and at relevant points in this Chapter concerning the dangers of asbestos dust and hydraulic fluid.*

2 Hydraulic system - bleeding

⚠️ **Warning: Hydraulic fluid is poisonous; wash off immediately and thoroughly in the case of skin contact, and seek immediate medical advice if any fluid is swallowed or gets into the eyes. Certain types of hydraulic fluid are inflammable,** *and may ignite when allowed into contact with hot components; when servicing any hydraulic system, it is safest to assume that the fluid IS inflammable, and to take precautions against the risk of fire as though it is petrol that is being handled. Hydraulic fluid is also an effective paint stripper, and will attack plastics; if any is spilt, it should be washed off immediately, using copious quantities of clean water. Finally, it is hygroscopic (it absorbs moisture from the air). The more moisture is absorbed by the fluid, the lower its boiling point becomes, leading to a dangerous loss of braking under hard use. Old fluid may be contaminated and unfit for further use. When topping-up or renewing the fluid, always use the recommended type, and ensure that it comes from a freshly-opened sealed container.*

General

1 The correct functioning of the brake hydraulic system is only possible after removing all air from the components and circuit; this is achieved by bleeding the system.

2 During the bleeding procedure, add only clean, fresh hydraulic fluid of the specified type; never re-use fluid that has already been bled from the system. Ensure that sufficient fluid is available before starting work.

3 If there is any possibility of incorrect fluid being used in the system, the brake lines and components must be completely flushed with uncontaminated fluid and new seals fitted to the components.

4 If brake fluid has been lost from the master cylinder due to a leak in the system, ensure that the cause is traced and rectified before proceeding further.

5 Park the car on level ground, switch off the ignition and select first gear (manual transmission) or Park (automatic transmission) then chock the wheels and release the handbrake.

6 Check that all pipes and hoses are secure, unions tight, and bleed screws closed. Remove the dust caps and clean any dirt from around the bleed screws.

7 Unscrew the master cylinder reservoir cap, and top-up the reservoir to the "MAX" level line. Refit the cap loosely, and remember to maintain the fluid level at least above the "MIN" level line throughout the procedure, otherwise there is a risk of further air entering the system.

8 There are a number of one-man, do-it-yourself, brake bleeding kits currently available from motor accessory shops. It is recommended that one of these kits is used wherever possible, as they greatly simplify the bleeding operation, and also reduce the risk of expelled air and fluid being drawn back into the system. If such a kit is not available, the basic (two-man) method must be used, which is described in detail below.

9 If a kit is to be used, prepare the car as described previously, and follow the kit manufacturer's instructions, as the procedure may vary slightly according to the type being used; generally, they are as outlined below in the relevant sub-section.

10 Whichever method is used, the same sequence must be followed (paragraphs 11 and 12) to ensure the removal of all air from the system.

Bleeding sequence

11 If the hydraulic system has only been partially disconnected and suitable precautions were taken to minimise fluid loss, it should only be necessary to bleed that part of the system (ie the primary or secondary circuit).

12 If the complete system is to be bled, then it should be done in the following sequence:

Non-ABS models:

Diagonally split system - all models except 1.6 GTI:
  RH rear wheel
  LH front wheel
  LH rear wheel
  RH front wheel
Front-to-rear split system - 1.6 GTI models:
  LH rear wheel and inertia compensator
  RH rear wheel
  LH front wheel
  RH front wheel

ABS models:

Note: *Before carrying out any bleeding, the battery negative lead must be disconnected, and the brown three-way, brown five-way and green five-way wiring connectors must be disconnected from the regulator unit to prevent the possibility of air entering the system. The connectors must not be reconnected until the hydraulic system has been bled.*

  LH rear wheel
  RH rear wheel
  LH front wheel
  RH front wheel
  ABS regulator unit (see illustration)

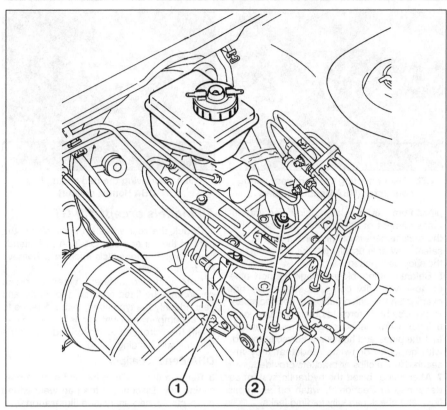

2.12 Bleed screws (1 and 2) on ABS regulator unit

Bleeding - basic (two-man) method

13 Collect a clean glass jar of reasonable size and a suitable length of plastic or rubber tubing, which is a tight fit over the bleed screw, and a ring spanner to fit the screws. The help of an assistant will also be required.

14 If not already done, remove the dust cap from the bleed screw of the first wheel to be bled and fit the spanner and bleed tube to the screw **(see illustration)**. Place the other end of the tube in the jar, and pour in sufficient fluid to cover the end of the tube.

15 Ensure that the master cylinder reservoir fluid level is maintained at least above the "MIN" level line throughout the procedure.

16 Have the assistant fully depress the brake pedal several times to build up pressure, then maintain it on the final downstroke.

17 While pedal pressure is maintained, unscrew the bleed screw (approximately one turn) and allow the compressed fluid and air to flow into the jar. The assistant should maintain pedal pressure, following it down to the floor if necessary, and should not release it until instructed to do so. When the flow stops, tighten the bleed screw again have the assistant release the pedal slowly, and recheck the reservoir fluid level.

18 Repeat the steps given in paragraphs 16 and 17 until the fluid emerging from the bleed screw is free from air bubbles. If the master cylinder has been drained and refilled, and air is being bled from the first screw in the sequence, allow approximately five seconds between cycles for the master cylinder passages to refill.

19 On 1.6 GTI models only it is now important to dislodge air trapped in the inertia compensator. To do this, open the bleed screw again and have your assistant fully depress and release the brake pedal rapidly 4 or 5 times, finally keeping the pedal depressed before tightening the bleed screw.

20 When no more air bubbles appear, tighten the bleed screw securely, remove the tube and spanner and refit the dust cap. Do not overtighten the bleed screw.

21 Repeat these procedures on the remaining brakes in sequence until all air is removed from the system and the brake pedal feels firm again.

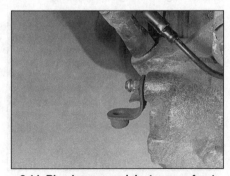

2.14 Bleed screw and dust cap on front brake caliper

Bleeding - using a one-way valve kit

22 As their name implies, these kits consist of a length of tubing with a one-way valve fitted, to prevent expelled air and fluid being drawn back into the system; some kits include a translucent container, which can be positioned so that the air bubbles can be more easily seen flowing from the end of the tube.

23 The kit is connected to the bleed screw, which is then opened. The user returns to the driver's seat, depresses the brake pedal with a smooth steady stroke, and slowly releases it; this is repeated until the expelled fluid is clear of air bubbles. When using one of these kits on 1.6 GTI models, remember to carry out the procedure described in paragraph 19 after bleeding the first brake in the sequence.

24 Note that these kits simplify work so much that it is easy to forget the master cylinder fluid level; ensure that this is maintained at least above the "MIN" level line at all times.

Bleeding - using a pressure-bleeding kit

25 These kits are usually operated by the reserve of pressurised air contained in the spare tyre. However, note that it will probably be necessary to reduce the pressure to a lower level than normal; refer to the instructions supplied with the kit.

26 By connecting a pressurised, fluid-filled container to the master cylinder reservoir, bleeding is then carried out by simply opening each bleed screw in turn (in the specified sequence) and allowing the fluid to run out, until no more air bubbles can be seen in the expelled fluid. When using one of these kits on 1.6 GTI models, remember to carry out the procedure described in paragraph 19 after bleeding the first brake in the sequence.

27 This method has the advantage that the large reservoir of fluid provides an additional safeguard against air being drawn into the system during bleeding.

28 Pressure bleeding is particularly effective when bleeding "difficult" systems, or when bleeding the complete system at the time of routine fluid renewal.

All methods

29 When bleeding is complete, and firm pedal feel is restored, wash off any spilt fluid, tighten the bleed screws securely, and refit their dust caps.

30 Check the hydraulic fluid level in the master cylinder reservoir and top-up if necessary.

31 Discard any hydraulic fluid that has been bled from the system; it will not be fit for re-use.

32 Check the feel of the brake pedal. If it feels at all spongy, air must still be present in the system, and further bleeding is required. Failure to bleed satisfactorily after a reasonable repetition of the bleeding operations may be due to worn master cylinder seals.

33 On models with ABS, reconnect the wiring connectors to the regulator unit and reconnect the battery.

9

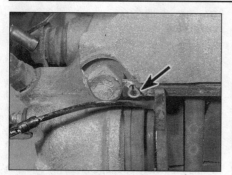

4.3a Pad sliding key clip - arrowed (DBA Bendix caliper)

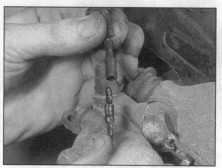

4.3b Disconnecting the pad wear wiring connector (DBA Bendix caliper)

4.4 Removing the pad sliding key (DBA Bendix caliper)

3 Hydraulic pipes and hoses - renewal

Note: Before starting work, refer to the warning at the beginning of Section 2 concerning the dangers of hydraulic fluid.

1 If any pipe or hose is to be renewed, minimise hydraulic fluid loss by removing the master cylinder reservoir cap, placing a piece of plastic film over the reservoir and sealing it with an elastic band. Alternatively, flexible hoses can be sealed, if required, using a proprietary brake hose clamp; metal brake pipe unions can be plugged (if care is taken not to allow dirt into the system) or capped immediately they are disconnected. Place a wad of rag under any union that is to be disconnected, to catch any spilt fluid.

2 If a flexible hose is to be disconnected, unscrew the brake pipe union nut before removing the spring clip which secures the hose to its mounting. Depending upon the make of the particular caliper, the other end of the hose may be connected simply by screwing it into its tapped hole or by using a hollow bolt with banjo end fitting. Use a new copper sealing washer on each side of the banjo union.

3 To unscrew the union nuts, it is preferable to obtain a brake pipe spanner of the correct size; these are available from most large motor accessory shops. Failing this, a close-fitting open-ended spanner will be required, though if the nuts are tight or corroded, their flats may be rounded-off if the spanner slips. In such a case, a self-locking wrench is often the only way to unscrew a stubborn union, but it follows that the pipe and the damaged nuts must be renewed on reassembly. Always clean a union and surrounding area before disconnecting it. If disconnecting a component with more than one union, make a careful note of the connections before disturbing any of them.

4 If a brake pipe is to be renewed, it can be obtained, cut to length and with the union nuts and end flares in place, from Peugeot dealers. All that is then necessary is to bend it to shape, following the line of the original, before fitting it to the car. Alternatively, most motor accessory shops can make up brake

pipes from kits, but this requires very careful measurement of the original, to ensure that the replacement is of the correct length. The safest answer is usually to take the original to the shop as a pattern.

5 Before refitting, blow through the new pipe or hose with dry compressed air. Do not overtighten the union nuts. It is not necessary to exercise brute force to obtain a sound joint.

6 If flexible rubber hoses are renewed, ensure that the pipes and hoses are correctly routed, with no kinks or twists, and that they are secured in the clips or brackets provided.

7 After fitting, bleed the hydraulic system as described in Section 2, wash off any spilt fluid, and check carefully for fluid leaks.

4 Front brake pads - renewal

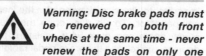

⚠️ *Warning: Disc brake pads must be renewed on both front wheels at the same time - never renew the pads on only one wheel as uneven braking may result. Dust created by wear of the pads may contain asbestos, which is a health hazard. Never blow it out with compressed air and do not inhale any of it. DO NOT use petroleum-based solvents to clean brake parts. Use brake cleaner or methylated spirit only. DO NOT allow any brake fluid, oil or grease to contact the brake pads or disc. Also refer to the warning at the start of Section 2 concerning the dangers of hydraulic fluid.*

All models except 1.9 GTI

1 Chock the rear wheels then jack up the front of the car and support it on axle stands (see *"Jacking and vehicle support"*). Remove the front roadwheels.

2 Note that two different types of brake caliper may be fitted according to model and year. Identify the type fitted, with reference to the accompanying illustrations or the caliper itself, then proceed as described under the relevant sub-heading.

DBA Bendix caliper

3 Remove the clip from the end of the upper sliding key. Disconnect the pad wear wiring connector as necessary **(see illustrations)**.

4 Pull out the upper sliding key **(see illustration)**.

5 Using a lever against the front suspension strut, push the cylinder towards the brake disc so that the outer pad can be withdrawn from the caliper **(see illustration)**.

6 Push back the caliper and withdraw the inner pad **(see illustration)**. Make a note of the correct fitted position of the anti-rattle springs and remove the spring from each pad.

7 Clean away all dust and dirt from the caliper. Check for brake fluid leakage around the piston dust seal and, if evident, overhaul the caliper, as described later in this Chapter. Check the brake disc for wear and also check that the rubber bellows on the cylinder sliding rods are in good condition.

8 Clean the backs of the brake pads and apply a little anti-squeal brake grease. Also apply the grease to the lower pad locating lip of the caliper.

4.5 Removing the outer pad (DBA Bendix caliper)

4.6 Removing the inner pad (DBA Bendix caliper)

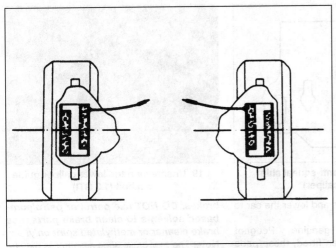

4.9 Correct orientation of offset brake pads viewed from front of vehicle (DBA Bendix caliper)

4.10 Fitted position of the anti-rattle springs on the brake pads (DBA Bendix caliper)

9 With the caliper pushed inwards, insert the inner pad then push the caliper outwards and insert the outer pad. If offset pads are fitted, it is important to fit these pads in the correct positions as shown **(see illustration)**. The inner pads with pad wear wires must be located at the top of the caliper.

10 Check that the pads are correctly positioned on the caliper lip and with the anti-rattle springs in place **(see illustration)** then tap in the upper sliding key to lock them. Fit the sliding key clip.

Girling caliper

11 Extract the spring clips and tap out the pad retaining pins. Disconnect the pad wear wiring as necessary **(see illustration)**.

12 Lever the cylinder outwards and withdraw the outer pad then push in the caliper and withdraw the inner pad. Recover the anti-squeal shims (if fitted) noting their positioning with regards to the pad retaining pins - refer to paragraph 14.

13 Clean and check the caliper, as described in paragraph 7, then clean the backs of the pads and apply a little anti-squeal brake grease. Note that, as from early 1985, a special spring is fitted to the inner pads to prevent pad knock within the caliper. The spring (obtainable from Peugeot dealers) may be fitted to earlier models by tapping the inner pad control rivet through the backing plate so that the clip may be located on both sides **(see illustration)**.

14 With the caliper pushed inwards, insert the inner pad then push the caliper outwards and insert the outer pad. Note that from chassis no 5 600 000, an anti-squeal shim was fitted between the inner pads and the caliper pistons, being located on both upper and lower pad retaining pins. However, as from chassis no 5 957 000, the shim was modified, being located only on the lower pad retaining pin **(see illustrations)**. When fitting the anti-squeal shims, the arrow cut-out must face downwards (ie in the forward rotational direction of the disc).

15 Tap in the pad retaining pins and fit the spring clips.

16 Where fitted, hook the anti-knock spring on the lower pad retaining pin.

1.9 GTI models

17 Chock the rear wheels then jack up the front of the car and support it on axle stands (see *"Jacking and vehicle support"*). Remove the front roadwheels.

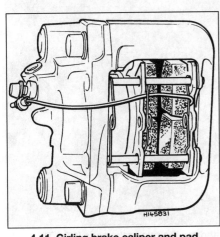

4.11 Girling brake caliper and pad arrangement

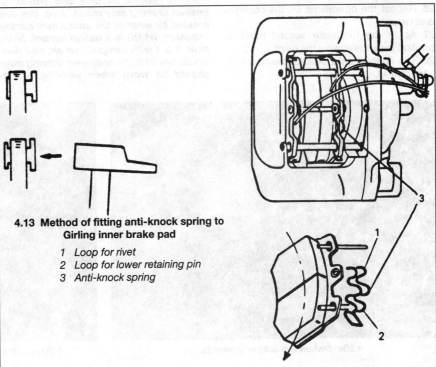

4.13 Method of fitting anti-knock spring to Girling inner brake pad

1 Loop for rivet
2 Loop for lower retaining pin
3 Anti-knock spring

9

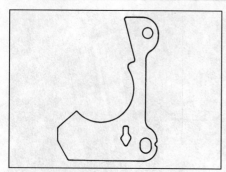

4.14a Early type anti-squeal shim (Girling caliper)

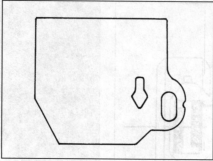

4.14b Later type anti-squeal shim (Girling caliper)

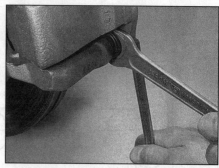

4.19 Unscrewing the lower caliper guide pin bolt (1.9 GTI)

18 Disconnect the wire for the pad wear warning light.

19 Hold the lower guide stationary with one spanner, then unscrew the bolt **(see illustration)**.

20 Swivel the caliper upwards, then withdraw the two brake pads from the caliper bracket **(see illustrations)**.

21 Clean and check the caliper, as described in paragraph 7.

22 Push the piston fully into the cylinder.

23 Clean the backs of the pads, and apply a little anti-squeal brake grease. Refit the inner pad (with the pad wear warning wire), then the outer pad.

24 Lower the caliper. Apply locking fluid to the lower guide bolt, insert it, and tighten to the specified torque while holding the guide stationary with another spanner.

25 Reconnect the pad wear warning light wire.

All calipers

26 Repeat the operations on the opposite disc caliper.

27 Apply the footbrake several times to position the pads against the discs.

28 Top-up the master cylinder reservoir to its correct level.

29 Refit the roadwheels and lower the car to the ground.

30 Note that if genuine Peugeot replacements have been fitted, these pads have a thin coating of abrasive material, which cleans the disc during the initial applications of the brakes. This coating also removes any disc imperfections which would cause steering vibration. After fitting these pads, the brakes must be applied lightly and intermittently for the first 3 miles (5 km), then "bedded-in" for 120 miles (200 km), avoiding heavy or prolonged braking wherever possible.

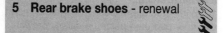

5 Rear brake shoes - renewal

⚠ *Warning: Brake shoes must be renewed on both rear wheels at the same time - never renew the shoes on only one wheel, as uneven braking may result. Also, the dust created by wear of the shoes may contain asbestos, which is a health hazard. Never blow it out with compressed air, and don't inhale any of it. An approved filtering mask should be worn when working on the*

brakes. DO NOT use petrol or petroleum-based solvents to clean brake parts; use brake cleaner or methylated spirit only.

Note: *The rear brake shoe assemblies may be of either DBA Bendix or Girling manufacture, according to model and year. The components may vary in detail, but the principles described in the following paragraphs are equally applicable to both types. Make a careful note of the fitted positions of all components before dismantling.*

1 Remove the relevant hub/drum as described in Section 11.

2 Brush the dust and dirt from the shoes, backplate and drum.

3 Note the position of each shoe and the location of the return and steady springs **(see illustrations)**.

4 Unhook and remove the upper return spring **(see illustration)**.

5 Remove the steady springs using pliers to depress the outer cups and turn them through 90° **(see illustration)**. Remove the pins from the backplate.

6 Move the serrated automatic adjuster lever quadrant against spring tension **(see illustration)**, move the lever forwards and release the strut from the top of the shoes (DBA Bendix type only).

4.20a Swivel the caliper upwards . . .

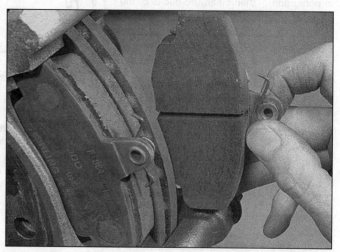

4.20b . . . then withdraw the two brake pads (1.9 GTI)

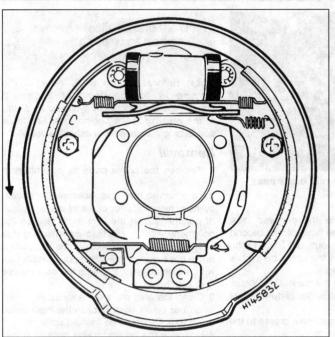

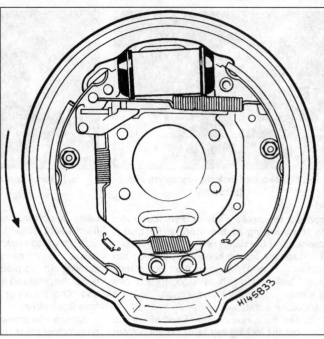

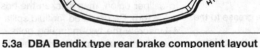

5.3a DBA Bendix type rear brake component layout

5.3b Girling type rear brake component layout

7 Expand the shoes over the wheel cylinder then release them from the bottom anchor.

8 Unhook the lever return spring and the handbrake cable.

9 If necessary, position a rubber band over the wheel cylinder to prevent the pistons coming out. Should there be evidence of brake fluid leakage from the wheel cylinder, renew it or overhaul it, as described in Section 10.

10 Transfer the handbrake and automatic adjuster levers to the new shoes as required. Note that the levers and strut on each rear wheel are different, and that the leading and trailing shoes are fitted with different grade linings.

11 Place the shoes on the bench in their correct location and fit the lower return spring.

12 Apply brake grease sparingly to the metal contact points of the shoes, then position them on the backplate and reconnect the handbrake cable. Locate the shoe ends on the bottom anchor.

13 Engage the strut with the slots at the top of the shoes, making sure it is located correctly on the automatic adjuster lever. Engage the upper shoe ends on the wheel cylinder pistons.

14 Insert the steady spring pins in the backplate and through the shoe webs, then fit the springs and outer cups.

15 Fit the upper return spring.

16 Move the serrated automatic adjuster lever quadrant against the spring tension to set the shoes at their minimum diameter.

17 Check that the handbrake lever on the rear brake shoe is positioned with the lug on the edge of the shoe web and not behind the shoe.

18 Refit the hub/drum as described in Section 11, but do not lower the car to the ground at this stage.

19 Apply the footbrake several times to set the shoes in their adjusted position.

20 Adjust the handbrake, as described in Section 15.

21 Repeat all the operations on the opposite rear brake then refit the roadwheels and lower the car to the ground.

6 Rear brake pads (1.9 GTI models) - renewal

Warning: Disc brake pads must be renewed on both rear wheels at the same time - never renew the pads on only one wheel as uneven braking may result. Dust created by wear of the pads may contain asbestos, which is a health hazard. Never blow it out with compressed air and do not inhale any of it. DO NOT use petroleum-based solvents to clean brake parts. Use brake cleaner or methylated spirit only. DO NOT allow any brake fluid, oil or grease to

9

5.4 Upper return spring location (DBA Bendix type)

5.5 Shoe steady springs - arrowed (DBA Bendix type)

5.6 Automatic adjuster lever - arrowed (DBA Bendix type)

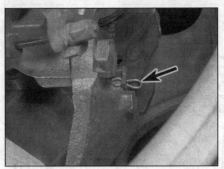

6.2 Brake pad locking key spring clip (arrowed)

6.3 Removing the rear brake pads

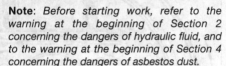

7 Front brake caliper - removal, overhaul and refitting

contact the brake pads or disc. Also refer to the warning at the start of Section 2 concerning the dangers of hydraulic fluid.

1 Chock the front wheels then jack up the rear of the car and support it on axle stands (see *"Jacking and vehicle support"*). Remove the rear roadwheels and ensure that the handbrake is released.

2 Extract the spring clip **(see illustration)** and slide out the locking key retaining the bottom of the pads.

3 Withdraw the brake pads using pliers, while pressing down on the upper locating ears **(see illustration)**.

4 Clean away all dust and dirt. Check for brake fluid leakage around the piston dust seal, and if evident, overhaul the caliper using the basic procedure described in Section 7. Check the brake disc for wear, and also check that the rubber bellows on the guides are in good condition.

5 The automatic handbrake adjustment must now be retracted, in order to accommodate the new disc pads. To do this, turn the piston

using a screwdriver in the grooves **(see illustration)**, at the same time using a second screwdriver to apply an outward force to the caliper. Do not damage the brake disc while carrying out this procedure.

6 Set the piston so that the mark is horizontal, and either above or below the piston groove **(see illustration)**.

7 Apply a little anti-squeal brake grease to the pad contact areas on the caliper.

8 Locate the two brake pads in the caliper, pressing the upper ears fully into position.

9 Slide the locking key into the caliper, and secure with the spring clip.

10 Fully depress the brake pedal several times to set the automatic adjuster and position the brake pads in their normal position.

11 Repeat the operations on the opposite disc caliper.

12 Check the fluid level in the master cylinder reservoir, and top-up if necessary.

13 Refit the roadwheels and lower the car to the ground.

Note: *Before starting work, refer to the warning at the beginning of Section 2 concerning the dangers of hydraulic fluid, and to the warning at the beginning of Section 4 concerning the dangers of asbestos dust.*

Removal

1 Remove the brake pads as described in Section 4.

2 To minimise fluid loss, unscrew the master cylinder reservoir filler cap and place a piece of polythene over the filler neck. Secure the polythene with an elastic band ensuring that an airtight seal is obtained. Alternatively, use a brake hose clamp, a G-clamp, or a similar tool with protected jaws, to clamp the front flexible hydraulic hose.

3 Clean the area around the hydraulic hose-to-caliper union, then slacken the hose union half a turn. Be prepared for fluid spillage.

4 Unscrew the two mounting bolts or upper guide bolt, as applicable, withdraw the caliper from the disc then unscrew the caliper from the flexible hose **(see illustration)**. Plug the hose to prevent loss of fluid.

5 Clean the exterior of the caliper.

6 On the Bendix type, unbolt the caliper frame from the cylinder.

Overhaul

7 Prise the dust cover and ring from the end of the piston **(see illustrations)**.

8 Withdraw the piston from the cylinder. If necessary use air pressure from a foot pump in the fluid inlet to force the piston out.

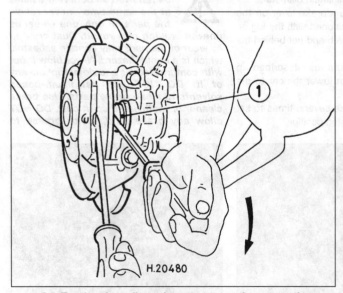

6.5 Turning the caliper piston to retract the automatic handbrake adjuster

1 Piston

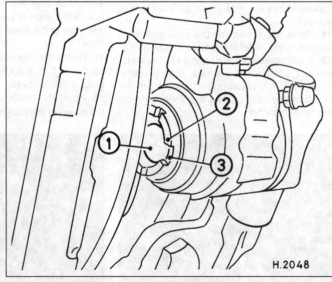

6.6 Correct final position of caliper piston

1 Piston   2 Mark   3 Groove

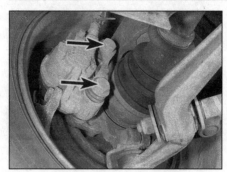

7.4 Brake caliper mounting bolts - arrowed (DBA Bendix type)

9 Prise the seal from inside the cylinder, taking care not to damage the cylinder wall.

10 If required, dismantle the sliding guides. On the Bendix type unbolt the endplate from the guides and remove the rubber dust covers. Keep the guides identified for location.

11 Clean all the components using methylated spirit or clean brake fluid then examine them for wear and damage. Check the piston and cylinder surfaces for scoring, excessive wear and corrosion, and if evident renew the complete caliper assembly. Similarly check the sliding guides. If the components are in good condition obtain a repair kit which will contain all the necessary rubber seals and other renewable items.

12 Dip the new seal in fresh brake fluid then locate it in the cylinder groove using the fingers only to manipulate it.

13 Dip the piston in brake fluid and insert it in the cylinder, twisting it as necessary to locate it in the seal.

14 Fit the dust cover and ring over the end of the piston and cylinder.

15 Lubricate the sliding guides with the grease supplied and refit them, together with the new seals. On the Bendix type refit the endplate and tighten the bolts.

16 On the Bendix type, refit the caliper frame and tighten the bolts.

Refitting

17 To refit the caliper, first screw it onto the flexible hose and locate it over the brake disc so that the hose is not twisted.

18 Clean the mounting bolt threads and apply locking fluid. Insert the mounting bolts or upper guide bolt and tighten to the specified torque.

19 Tighten the flexible hose union on the caliper. Check that the hose is clear of the strut and surrounding components and, if necessary, loosen the rigid pipe union on the body bracket, reposition the hose and retighten the union.

20 Refit the brake pads, as described in Section 4.

21 Remove the brake hose clamp or polythene sheeting and bleed the hydraulic system, as described in Section 2.

7.7a DBA Bendix type brake caliper components

1 Mounting bolt
2 Caliper assembly
3 Sliding key kit
4 Bleed screw
5 Retaining plate
6 Sliding guide kit with grease
7 Repair kit with grease

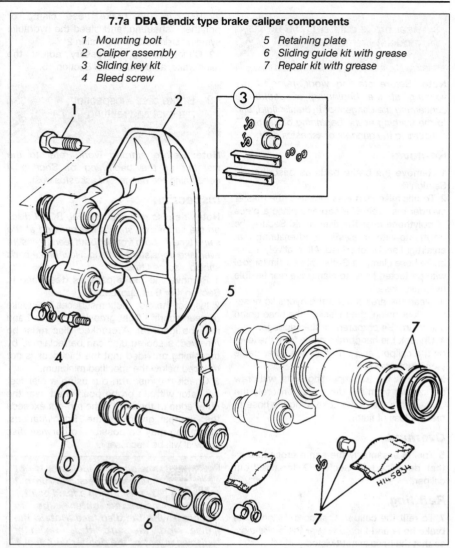

7.7b Girling type brake caliper components

1 Mounting bolt
2 Caliper assembly
3 Pad retaining pin and spring
4 Bleed screw
5 Repair kit

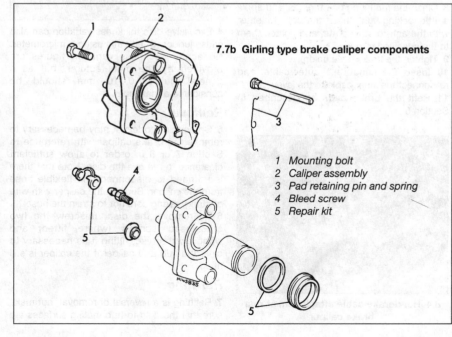

9

8 Rear brake caliper (1.9 GTI models) - removal, overhaul and refitting

Note: *Before starting work, refer to the warning at the beginning of Section 2 concerning the dangers of hydraulic fluid, and to the warning at the beginning of Section 6 concerning the dangers of asbestos dust.*

Removal

1 Remove the brake pads as described in Section 6.

2 To minimise fluid loss, unscrew the master cylinder reservoir filler cap and place a piece of polythene over the filler neck. Secure the polythene with an elastic band ensuring that an airtight seal is obtained. Alternatively, use a brake hose clamp, a G-clamp, or a similar tool with protected jaws, to clamp the rear flexible hydraulic hose.

3 Clean the area around the hydraulic hose-to-caliper union, then slacken the hose union half a turn. Be prepared for fluid spillage.

4 Unhook the handbrake cable from the lever on the caliper, and withdraw the outer cable **(see illustration)**.

5 Unscrew the two mounting bolts, withdraw the caliper from the disc, then unscrew the caliper from the brake hose. Plug the hose to prevent loss of fluid.

Overhaul

6 This is essentially the same procedure as that described in Section 7 for the front caliper.

Refitting

7 To refit the caliper, first screw it onto the brake hose and locate it over the brake disc, so that the hose is not twisted.

8 Clean the mounting bolt threads, and apply a little locking fluid. Insert the bolts together with the anti-rotation plate, and tighten them to the specified torque.

9 Tighten the brake hose union.

10 Insert the handbrake outer cable, and re-connect the inner cable to the lever.

11 Refit the brake pads as described in Section 6.

8.4 Handbrake cable attachment at rear brake caliper

12 Remove the brake hose clamp or polythene sheeting, and bleed the hydraulic system as described in Section 2.

13 Check and if necessary adjust the handbrake, as described in Section 15.

9 Brake disc - inspection, removal and refitting

Note: *Before starting work, refer to the warning at the beginning of Section 4 concerning the dangers of asbestos dust.*

Inspection

Note: *If a disc requires renewal, BOTH discs on the same axle should be renewed at the same time (ie both front or both rear) to ensure even and consistent braking. New brake pads should also be fitted.*

1 Remove the brake pads as described in Section 4 or 6 as applicable.

2 Inspect the disc friction surfaces for cracks or deep scoring (light grooving is normal and may be ignored). A cracked disc must be renewed; a scored disc can be reclaimed by machining provided that the thickness is not reduced below the specified minimum.

3 Check the disc run-out using a dial test indicator with its probe positioned near the outer edge of the disc. If the run-out exceeds the figures given in the *Specifications*, machining may be possible, otherwise disc renewal will be necessary.

> **HAYNES HiNT**
>
> *If a dial test indicator is not available, check the run-out by positioning a fixed pointer near the outer edge, in contact with the disc face. Rotate the disc and measure the maximum displacement of the pointer with feeler blades.*

4 Excessive disc thickness variation can also cause judder. Check this using a micrometer. No actual thickness variation figures are provided by the manufacturer, but as a general guide, 0.010 mm should be considered a maximum.

Removal

5 On certain models, it may be necessary to remove the brake caliper with reference to Section 7 or 8 in order to allow sufficient clearance to remove the disc. Note that there is no need to disconnect the flexible hose from the caliper. Support the caliper with wire or string, taking care not to strain the hose.

6 To remove the disc, unscrew the two cross-head screws (where fitted) and withdraw the disc, tilting it as necessary to clear the hub and caliper if the caliper is still fitted.

Refitting

7 Refitting is a reversal of removal, but make sure that the disc-to-hub mating surfaces are

clean and that the securing screws are tightened fully. If the caliper has been removed, coat the caliper mounting bolt threads with locking fluid on refitting. Refer to Section 4 or 6 when refitting the disc pads.

10 Rear wheel cylinder - removal, overhaul and refitting

Note: *Before starting work, refer to the warning at the beginning of Section 2 concerning the dangers of hydraulic fluid, and to the warning at the beginning of Section 5 concerning the dangers of asbestos dust.*

Removal

1 Chock the front wheels then jack up the rear of the car and support it on axle stands (see *"Jacking and vehicle support"*). Remove the rear roadwheels and ensure that the handbrake is released.

2 Remove the hub/drum, as described in Section 11.

3 Note the location of the brake shoe upper return spring then unhook and remove it.

4 Pull the handbrake lever on the rear shoe fully forwards so that the upper ends of the shoes are clear of the wheel cylinder. Wedge the lever in this position using a block of wood.

5 To minimise fluid loss, unscrew the master cylinder reservoir filler cap and place a piece of polythene over the filler neck. Secure the polythene with an elastic band ensuring that an airtight seal is obtained. Alternatively, use a brake hose clamp, a G-clamp, or a similar tool with protected jaws, to clamp the flexible hydraulic hose supplying the rear brakes **(see illustration)**.

6 Unscrew the hydraulic pipe union nut from the rear of the wheel cylinder.

7 Unscrew the two mounting bolts and withdraw the wheel cylinder from the backplate **(see illustration)**. Take care not to spill any brake fluid on the brake shoe linings.

8 Clean the exterior of the wheel cylinder. Note that on all models with a diagonally split hydraulic circuit the rear wheel cylinders incorporate compensators which **must not** be dismantled.

10.5 To minimise fluid loss, fit a brake hose clamp to the flexible hose

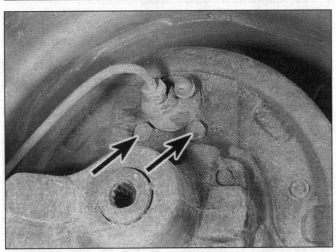

10.7 Rear wheel cylinder mounting bolts (arrowed)

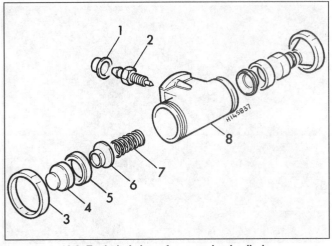

10.9 Exploded view of a rear wheel cylinder

1 Cap	4 Piston	7 Spring
2 Bleed screw	5 Seal	8 Body
3 Dust excluder	6 Spring seat	

Overhaul

9 Pull off the dust excluders **(see illustration)**.

10 Extract the pistons, seals and return spring; keeping each component identified for location.

11 Check the surfaces of the cylinder bore and pistons for scoring and corrosion and, if evident, renew the complete wheel cylinder. If the components are in good condition discard the seals and obtain a repair kit which will contain all the necessary renewable components.

12 Clean the pistons and cylinder with methylated spirit or clean brake fluid then dip each component in fresh brake fluid and reassemble in reverse order; making sure that the lips of the seals face into the cylinder. When completed, wipe clean the outer surfaces of the dust excluders.

Refitting

13 Clean the backplate and refit the wheel cylinder using a reversal of the removal procedure. Refer to Section 11 when refitting the hub/drum.

14 Make sure that the brake hose clamp or polythene sheeting is removed then bleed the hydraulic system, as described in Section 2.

11 Rear brake hub/drum - removal, inspection and refitting

Note: *Before starting work, refer to the warning at the beginning of Section 5 concerning the dangers of asbestos dust.*

Removal

1 Chock the front wheels then jack up the rear of the car and support it on axle stands (see *"Jacking and vehicle support"*). Remove the rear roadwheels and ensure that the handbrake is released.

2 Tap off the grease cap, taking care not to damage its outer lip, then relieve the staking on the rear hub nut, using a suitable drift or chisel. Unscrew the nut and recover the washer **(see illustrations)**. Should the stub axle rotate within the trailing arm, hold it stationary with a suitable Allen key on the inner. Note that a new rear hub nut will be required for refitting.

3 Withdraw the hub/drum from the stub axle. If difficulty is experienced, due to the shoes wearing grooves in the drum, insert a screwdriver through one of the wheel bolt holes and depress the handbrake lever on the rear brake shoe so that it slides back behind the shoe. This will retract the shoes and allow the hub/drum to be removed.

11.2a Unscrew the rear hub nut . . .

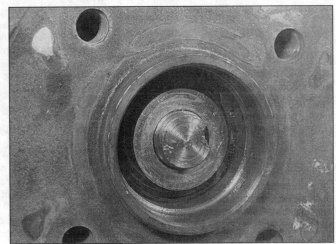

11.2b . . . and remove the washer

11.9 Lock the hub nut by staking the nut flange into the groove on the stub axle

13.1 Rear brake compensator fitted to 1.6 GTI models

Inspection

4 Brush the dust and dirt from the brake drum and carefully inspect the drum interior.

5 If the drum is grooved, owing to failure to renew worn brake shoes or after a very high mileage has been covered, then it may be possible to regrind it, provided the maximum internal diameter is not exceeded.

6 Even if only one drum is in need of grinding both drums must be reground to the same size in order to maintain even braking characteristics.

7 Judder or a springy pedal felt when the brakes are applied can be caused by a distorted (out-of-round) drum. Here again it may be possible to regrind the drums, otherwise a new drum will be required.

Refitting

8 Fit the hub/drum on the stub axle and retain with the washer and new hub nut.

9 Tighten the nut to the specified torque then lock it by staking the nut flange into the groove on the stub axle (see illustration).

10 Tap the grease cap into the hub/drum.

11 Refit the roadwheels and lower the car to the ground.

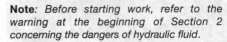

12 Master cylinder - removal, overhaul and refitting

Note: Before starting work, refer to the warning at the beginning of Section 2 concerning the dangers of hydraulic fluid.

Removal

1 Unscrew the filler cap from the master cylinder fluid reservoir and drain off the fluid.

HAYNES HiNT An ideal way to remove fluid from the master cylinder reservoir is to use a clean syringe or an old poultry baster.

2 Prise the reservoir from the master cylinder and remove the seals.

3 Unscrew the union nuts securing the rigid brake lines to the master cylinder and pull out the lines. Cap the pipe ends to prevent loss of fluid.

4 Unscrew the mounting nuts and withdraw the master cylinder from the bulkhead or servo unit, as applicable. Remove the gasket on non-servo models.

Overhaul

5 Clean the exterior of the master cylinder. It is not possible to overhaul the master cylinder fitted to non-servo models, therefore if it is known to be leaking or damaged the complete master cylinder must be renewed. On servo models proceed as follows.

6 Using circlip pliers, extract the circlip from the mouth of the cylinder.

7 Remove the primary and secondary piston components noting their locations. If necessary tap the cylinder on a block of wood.

8 Clean all the components in methylated spirit. Check the surfaces of the cylinder bore and pistons for scoring and corrosion, and if evident renew the complete master cylinder. If the components are in good condition remove and discard the seals and obtain a repair kit which will contain all the necessary renewable components.

9 Dip the new seals in fresh brake fluid and fit them to the pistons using the fingers only to manipulate them.

10 Reassemble the master cylinder in reverse order to dismantling and make sure that the circlip is fully engaged with the groove in the mouth of the cylinder.

11 On non-servo models check that the brake pedal pushrod protrudes from the bulkhead by between 9.0 and 9.6 mm. If not, loosen the locknuts and adjust the position of the stop light switch inside the car on the pedal bracket.

Refitting

12 Refitting is a reversal of removal, but fit a new gasket on non-servo models. Finally bleed the complete hydraulic system, as described in Section 2.

13 Rear brake compensator (GTI models) - information, removal and refitting

Note: Before starting work, refer to the warning at the beginning of Section 2 concerning the dangers of hydraulic fluid.

1.6 GTI models

General information

1 On 1.6 GTI models the brake hydraulic circuit is split front-to-rear, and an inertia type compensator is incorporated in the rear brake circuit to prevent rear wheel lock-up during hard braking. The compensator is located in the engine compartment on the lower left-hand side panel (see illustration), and incorporates a steel ball which stops fluid entry to the rear circuit at a preset deceleration.

Removal

2 To minimise fluid loss, unscrew the master cylinder reservoir filler cap and place a piece of polythene over the filler neck. Secure the polythene with an elastic band ensuring that an airtight seal is obtained.

3 Chock the rear wheels then jack up the front of the car and support it on axle stands (see "Jacking and vehicle support"). Remove the relevant front roadwheel.

4 Unscrew the union nuts and disconnect the rigid hydraulic lines from each end of the unit while holding the unit on the flats provided.

5 Unbolt the clamp and withdraw the compensator.

Refitting

6 Refitting is a reversal of removal, but note that the nose of the unit must face forwards and be inclined upwards at an angle of 22° to the horizontal. Provided that the mounting bracket is undamaged, this angle will automatically be achieved. Finally bleed the rear hydraulic circuit, as described in Section 2.

1.9 GTI models

General information

7 On 1.9 GTI models, the hydraulic circuit is split diagonally and two compensators are fitted. Each compensator is located in the rear circuit near the rear wheel **(see illustration)**. They are of fixed calibration, and not load-sensitive.

Removal

8 To minimise fluid loss, unscrew the master cylinder reservoir filler cap and place a piece of polythene over the filler neck. Secure the polythene with an elastic band ensuring that an airtight seal is obtained.

9 Chock the front wheels then jack up the rear of the car and support it on axle stands (see *"Jacking and vehicle support"*).

10 Unscrew the union nuts and disconnect the rigid hydraulic lines from each end of the unit while holding the unit on the flats provided. Ease out the pipes and remove the compensator from under the car.

11 Note that from December 1988, modified compensators have been fitted. The modified components can be identified by the letter on the compensator body. Early components have the identifying letter "F", while later components have the identifying letter "E". The later components can be used to replace the early components, but both compensators must be of the same type.

Refitting

12 Refitting is a reversal of removal. Bleed the relevant hydraulic circuit, as described in Section 2 on completion.

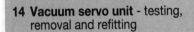

14 Vacuum servo unit - testing, removal and refitting

Testing

1 With the engine switched off, depress the brake pedal several times. The distance by which the pedal moves should now alter over all applications.

2 Depress the brake pedal fully and hold it down then start the engine. The pedal should be felt to move downward slightly.

3 Hold the pedal depressed with the engine running, switch off the ignition and continue to hold the pedal depressed for 30 seconds during which period the pedal should neither rise nor drop.

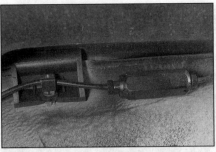

13.7 Rear brake compensator fitted to 1.9 GTI models

4 Start the engine whilst the brake pedal is released, run it for a minute and switch off. Give several applications of the brake pedal. The pedal travel should decrease with each application.

5 Failure of the brake pedal to act in the way described will indicate a fault in the servo unit.

6 The servo unit should not be serviced or overhauled beyond the operations described in this Section and in the event of a fault developing, renew the servo complete.

7 Periodically check the condition of the vacuum hose and security of the clips.

8 Renew the hose if necessary.

9 If the servo hose right-angled non-return valve is loose in its sealing grommet, or if the grommet shows evidence of cracking or perishing, renew it. Apply some hydraulic fluid to the rubber to facilitate fitting.

Air filter renewal

10 Although not a specified operation, the air filter through which the pushrod passes at the rear of the servo can become clogged after a high mileage. Disconnect the rod from the pedal, cut the filter diagonally having slipped the dust excluder off the rod. Fit the new filter.

Servo unit removal

11 Remove the master cylinder, as described in Section 12. Disconnect the servo vacuum hose.

12 Working inside the car, disconnect the pushrod from the brake pedal; noting that it is on the lower hole.

13 Unscrew the mounting nuts behind the pedal bracket then withdraw the servo unit into the engine compartment. Remove the gasket.

Servo unit refitting

14 Before fitting a servo unit, check the pushrod dimensions and adjust where possible **(see illustration)**.

15 Refitting is a reversal of removal, but fit a new gasket and fully tighten the mounting nuts. Note that the pushrod is fitted to the lower hole of the two on the brake pedal. Refer to Section 12 when refitting the master cylinder. Finally, with the brake pedal released, check that the clearance between the stop light switch threaded shank and pedal is 3.5 mm. If necessary loosen the locknuts, adjust the switch and tighten the locknuts.

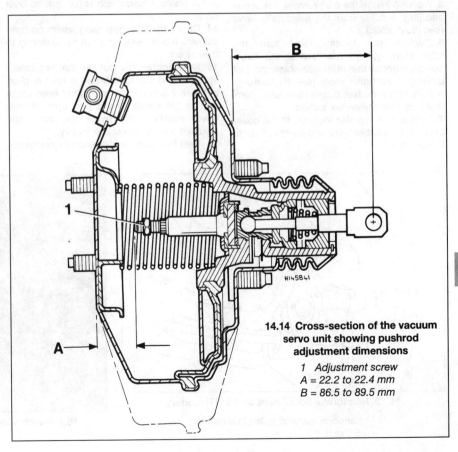

14.14 Cross-section of the vacuum servo unit showing pushrod adjustment dimensions

1 Adjustment screw
A = 22.2 to 22.4 mm
B = 86.5 to 89.5 mm

9

15.4 Remove the screw and lift the cover from the handbrake lever

15.5 Handbrake adjustment nut and locknut (arrowed)

15 Handbrake - adjustment

All models except 1.9 GTI

1 The handbrake is normally kept adjusted by the action of the automatic adjusters on the rear brake shoes. However, in due course, the cables will stretch and will have to be adjusted in order to fully apply the handbrake.

2 To adjust, first place the handbrake lever onto the seventh notch.

3 Chock the front wheels then jack up the rear of the car and support it on axle stands (see "Jacking and vehicle support").

4 Working inside the car, remove the screw and lift the cover from the handbrake lever (see illustration).

5 Slacken the locknut and turn the adjustment nut on the rear of the cable compensator so that both rear wheels are just binding on the brake shoes (see illustration).

6 Fully apply the handbrake lever and check that both rear wheels are locked.

7 Tighten the adjuster locknut, fit the cover over the handbrake lever and lower the car to the ground.

8 Over-adjustment will prevent the automatic adjusters operating correctly so make sure that the handbrake is fully applied after being pulled up between 7 and 9 notches, no fewer.

1.9 GTI models

9 Chock the wheels and fully release the handbrake.

10 Apply the brake pedal hard several times.

11 Working inside the car, remove the screw and lift the cover from the handbrake lever.

12 Working beneath the rear of the car, measure the distance between the operating levers on the calipers and the end stops on the inner cables (see illustration).

13 Inside the car, loosen the nut on the handbrake lever until the distance measured in the previous paragraph is 5.0 mm on both sides.

14 Check that the operating levers on both calipers move freely and return positively to their stops.

15 Now tighten the nut on the handbrake lever so that the handbrake is fully applied between 7 and 9 notches. Do not over-adjust so that the handbrake is fully applied over fewer notches, otherwise the automatic adjusters will not operate correctly.

16 Refit the cover over the handbrake lever.

16 Handbrake cables - renewal

All models except 1.9 GTI

1 Remove the rear brake shoes, as described in Section 5.

2 Working inside the car, remove the screw and lift the cover from the handbrake lever.

3 Unhook the cable(s) from the compensator.

4 Release the cable(s) from the retaining clips, the floor, the fuel tank, and the rear brake backplate(s) and withdraw from under the car (see illustration).

5 Fit the new cable(s) using a reversal of the removal procedure with reference also to Section 5. Finally adjust the handbrake as described in Section 15.

1.9 GTI models

6 Working inside the car, remove the screw and lift the cover from the handbrake lever.

7 Unhook the cable from the compensator.

8 Chock the front wheels then jack up the rear of the car and support it on axle stands (see "Jacking and vehicle support").

9 Release the cable(s) from the retaining clips, the floor, the fuel tank, the bracket(s), and the caliper lever(s), and withdraw from under the car.

10 Fit the new cable(s) using a reversal of the removal procedure. Finally adjust the handbrake as described in Section 15.

17 Brake pedal - removal and refitting

Removal

1 Remove the lower facia panel from the steering column in order to gain access to the pedal bracket.

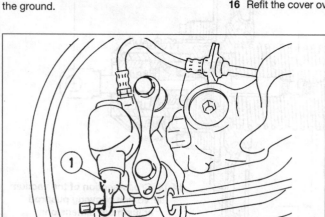

15.12 Handbrake adjustment on 1.9 GTI models

1 Handbrake operating lever on caliper
a = 5.0 mm

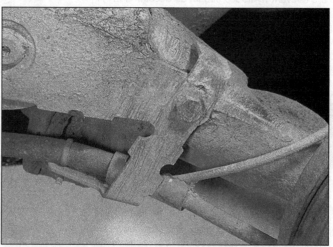

16.4 Handbrake cable clip and bracket located on rear suspension arm

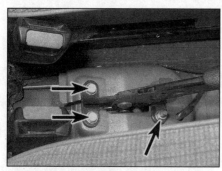

18.3 Handbrake lever mounting bolts (arrowed)

2 Remove the clevis pin and disconnect the pushrod from the brake pedal. Note that on models with a vacuum servo unit the pushrod is on the lower hole, whereas the upper hole is used for models without a servo unit.

3 Unscrew the self-locking nut from the pivot bolt, pull out the bolt and lower the brake pedal. Note that on non-servo models a return spring is also fitted to the pedal.

4 Examine the pedal bushes for wear and renew them if necessary.

Refitting

5 Refitting is a reversal of removal, but lightly grease the bushes and clevis pin and renew the self-locking nut.

18 Handbrake lever - removal and refitting

Removal

1 Move the front seats fully forward then remove the screw and lift the cover from the handbrake lever.

2 Fully release the handbrake then unscrew the adjustment nut on the rear of the cable compensator until both cables can be unhooked.

3 Unbolt and remove the handbrake lever assembly from the floor **(see illustration)**.

Refitting

4 Refitting is a reversal of removal, but adjust the handbrake, as described in Section 15 on completion.

19 Anti-lock braking system (ABS) - general information

From 1991, the Bendix anti-lock braking system is available as an option on certain models.

The system is fail-safe, and is fitted in conjunction with the conventional braking system, which allows the vehicle to retain conventional braking In the event of a failure in the ABS system.

To prevent wheel locking, the system provides pressure modulation in the brake circuits. To achieve this, sensors mounted at each front wheel monitor the rotational speeds of the wheels, and are thus able to detect when there is a risk of wheel locking (low rotational speed). Solenoid valves are positioned in the brake circuits to all four wheels and the solenoid valves are incorporated in the regulator unit, which is controlled by an electronic control unit. The electronic control unit controls modulation of the braking effort applied to each wheel, according to the information supplied by the wheel sensors.

Should a fault develop in the system, a self-diagnostic facility is incorporated in the electronic control unit, which can be used in conjunction with specialist diagnostic equipment available to a Peugeot dealer to determine the nature of the fault.

The brake components used on models fitted with ABS are similar to those used on models with a conventional braking system. Rear disc brakes are fitted to all ABS-equipped models, and all procedures for the rear brake and handbrake components are as described for 1.9 GTI models in the relevant Sections of this Chapter.

20 Anti-lock braking system (ABS) components - removal and refitting

 Warning: It is strongly recommended that any work involving components of the braking system on a vehicle equipped with ABS is entrusted to a Peugeot dealer, who will have the necessary specialist knowledge and equipment to carry out the work safely and effectively.

Regulator unit

1 At the time of writing, no information was available regarding removal and refitting of the regulator unit.

Wheel sensor

Removal

2 The wheel sensors are mounted in the rear of the hub carriers. To remove a wheel sensor, proceed as follows.

3 Disconnect the battery negative lead.

4 Chock the rear wheels then jack up the front of the car and support it on axle stands (see *"Jacking and vehicle support"*). Remove the roadwheel.

5 Carefully pull the sensor wiring from its retaining clips, and working under the wing, disconnect the sensor wiring connector.

6 Unscrew the securing bolt, and withdraw the sensor from the hub carrier.

Refitting

7 Refitting is a reversal of removal, but ensure that the front face of the sensor is perfectly clean, and ensure that the wiring is correctly routed. Clean the sensor securing bolt threads, then apply suitable thread-locking fluid and tighten the bolt securely.

Electronic control unit

Removal

8 The electronic control unit is located on the left-hand side of the luggage compartment. To remove the control unit, proceed as follows.

9 Disconnect the battery negative lead.

10 Open the tailgate, and carefully pull the trim from the left-hand side of the luggage compartment to reveal the control unit.

11 Unscrew the securing nuts, and withdraw the cover from the control unit.

12 Disconnect the control unit wiring plug.

13 Unscrew the securing nuts, and withdraw the control unit from its mounting bracket.

Refitting

14 Refitting is reversal of removal.

Notes

Chapter 10
Suspension and steering

Contents

Degrees of difficulty

| Easy, suitable for novice with little experience | Fairly easy, suitable for beginner with some experience | Fairly difficult, suitable for competent DIY mechanic 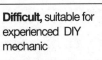 | Difficult, suitable for experienced DIY mechanic 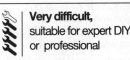 | Very difficult, suitable for expert DIY or professional |

Specifications

Front suspension
Type . . . . Independent, MacPherson struts, coil springs, anti-roll bar

Rear suspension
Type . . . . Independent, cross-tube with trailing arms, torsion bars, inclined shock absorbers, anti-roll bar

Steering
Type . . . . Rack-and-pinion. Power-assistance optional on certain models
Power steering fluid type . . . . See "Weekly checks"

Wheel alignment and steering angles
Front wheel toe setting:
All models, except GTI and automatic transmission - up to 1988 . . . 3.0 ± 1.0 mm toe-in
1.6 GTI models - up to 1988 . . . . 2.0 ± 1.0 mm toe-in
1.9 GTI models - up to 1988 . . . . 2.5 ± 1.0 mm toe-in
Automatic transmission models - up to 1988 . . . . 3.5 ± 1.0 mm toe-in
All models from 1988 onward . . . . 1.0 ± 0.5 mm toe-in

Roadwheels
Type . . . . Pressed-steel or aluminium alloy (depending on model)
Size . . . . 4.5 B x 13, 4.5J x 13, 5 B x 13, 5.5J x 14 or 6.6J x 15 (depending on model)

Tyres
Size . . . . 135 SR 13, 145 SR 13, 165/70 SR 13, 185/60 HR 14 or 185/55 VR 15 (depending on model)
Tyre pressures . . . . See "Weekly checks"

10

Torque wrench settings

	Nm	lbf ft
Front suspension		
Driveshaft/hub nut:		
Non-GTI models	250	185
GTI models	260	192
Automatic transmission models	265	196
Strut top mounting	12	9
Shock absorber piston rod nut:		
Self-locking type	45	33
Crimped type	70	52
Strut clamp bolt	58	43
Anti-roll bar clamp	35	26
Anti-roll bar end (non-GTI models)	75	55
Lower balljoint clamp bolt:		
Manual transmission models	35	26
Automatic transmission models	45	33
Anti-roll bar guide bar	30	22
Lower suspension arm pivot bolt	35	26
Anti-roll bar end (GTI models)	58	43
Lower suspension arm rear pivot bolt (GTI models)	78	58
Rear suspension		
Shock absorber upper mounting	75	55
Shock absorber lower mounting	118	87
Anti-roll bar arm	35	26
Torsion bar plug	20	15
Suspension top mountings	45	33
Suspension front mounting pivot bolt	80	59
Steering		
Steering gear mounting bolts	35	26
Power steering fluid pipe unions	23	17
Column-to-pinion clamp bolt	15	11
Track rod end balljoint nut	35	26
Track rod inner joint	50	37
Steering wheel nut	30	22
Roadwheels		
Roadwheel bolts (all wheel types)*	85	63

On alloy wheels, oil the ends of the bolt threads over a maximum length of 10 mm before fitting.

1 General information

The front suspension is of independent type; incorporating MacPherson struts with coil springs and integral shock absorbers. On non-GTI models the lower suspension arm movement is controlled by the anti-roll bar, but on GTI models the arm has two inner pivot points and the anti-roll bar operates separately on the struts.

The rear suspension is also of independent type; incorporating a cross-tube with trailing arms set in each end and supported on needle or plain bearings. Torsion bars are fitted to the trailing arms and, on certain models, an anti-roll bar located inside the cross-tube stabilises the car when cornering. The telescopic shock absorbers are inclined with their top mountings attached to the suspension side-members.

The steering system is of rack and pinion type with side track rods connected to the hub carriers by track rod end balljoints.

Further balljoints on the inner ends of the track rods are screwed into the rack. Power-assisted steering is available as an option on later models. Power assistance is derived from a hydraulic pump, belt-driven from the crankshaft pulley.

The steering column incorporates a single universal joint at its lower end connected to an intermediate shaft which also incorporates a universal joint at its connection to the pinion on the steering gear. The steering column is angled to prevent direct movement into the passenger compartment in the event of a front end impact.

2 Front suspension hub carrier - removal and refitting

Removal

1 Fully apply the handbrake then, where possible, remove the front wheel centre trim. Tap up the staking securing the hub nut to the driveshaft groove or, on later models, extract the R-clip and withdraw the locking collar

(see illustration). Using a socket and a long extension bar, slacken the hub nut. On models without a centre trim, the hub nut must be loosened after removing the front wheel. Do not apply the footbrake when loosening the nut as damage can occur to the brake disc retaining screws.

2 Chock the rear wheels then jack up the front of the car and support it on axle stands (see *"Jacking and vehicle support"*). Remove the front roadwheel.

2.1 R-clip and locking collar fitted to hub nut on later models

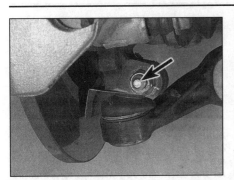

2.4a Unscrew the lower balljoint clamp bolt . . .

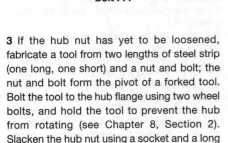

2.4b . . . and pull the suspension arm down from the hub carrier

2.11 Unscrew the clamp bolt securing the lower end of the suspension strut to the hub carrier

3 If the hub nut has yet to be loosened, fabricate a tool from two lengths of steel strip (one long, one short) and a nut and bolt; the nut and bolt form the pivot of a forked tool. Bolt the tool to the hub flange using two wheel bolts, and hold the tool to prevent the hub from rotating (see Chapter 8, Section 2). Slacken the hub nut using a socket and a long extension bar.

4 Unscrew the clamp bolt securing the front suspension lower balljoint to the bottom of the hub carrier then pull the lower suspension arm down from the carrier **(see illustrations)**.

5 Recover the balljoint guard plate, where fitted.

6 Turn the front wheels to full right-hand lock (left-hand hub carrier), or full left-hand lock (right-hand hub carrier) and remove the hub nut and, where fitted, the washer. Note that a new hub nut will be required for refitting.

7 Pull the hub carrier outwards and at the same time withdraw the outer end of the driveshaft from the hub. Suitably support or tie up the driveshaft in a near horizontal position to avoid damage to the inner CV joints.

8 Unbolt the disc brake caliper from the hub carrier and either place it on a stand or tie it to one side.

9 Remove the two screws and withdraw the brake disc.

10 Unscrew the nut and use a balljoint removal tool to separate the track rod end balljoint from the hub carrier steering arm.

11 Unscrew the clamp bolt securing the lower end of the suspension strut to the hub carrier **(see illustration)**. Spread the slot on the hub carrier using a screwdriver or suitable wedge and slide the carrier from the bottom of the strut. Remove the hub carrier from the car.

Refitting

12 Refitting is a reversal of removal, but refer to Chapters 8 and 9 respectively when refitting the driveshaft and disc brake caliper.

3 Front hub bearings - renewal

Note: *The bearing is a sealed, pre-adjusted and pre-lubricated, double-row ball type, and is intended to last the car's entire service life without maintenance or attention. Never overtighten the driveshaft nut beyond the specified torque wrench setting in an attempt to "adjust" the bearing.*

Note: *A press will be required to dismantle and rebuild the assembly; if such a tool is not available, a large bench vice and spacers (such as large sockets) will serve as an adequate substitute. The bearing's inner races are an interference fit on the hub; if the inner race remains on the hub when it is pressed out of the hub carrier, a knife-edged bearing puller will be required to remove it. A new bearing retaining circlip must be used on refitting.*

1 Remove the hub carrier assembly as described in Section 2.

2 Support the hub carrier securely on blocks or in a vice. Using a tubular spacer which bears only on the inner end of the hub flange, press the hub flange out of the bearing. If the bearing's outboard inner race remains on the hub, remove it using a bearing puller (see note above).

3 Extract the bearing retaining circlip from the inner end of the hub carrier assembly **(see illustration)**.

3.3 Front hub bearing retaining circlip (arrowed)

4 Where necessary, refit the inner race back in position over the ball cage, and securely support the inner face of the hub carrier. Using a tubular spacer which bears only on the inner race, press the complete bearing assembly out of the hub carrier.

5 Thoroughly clean the hub and hub carrier, removing all traces of dirt and grease, and polish away any burrs or raised edges which might hinder reassembly. Check both for cracks or any other signs of wear or damage, and renew them if necessary. Renew the circlip, regardless of its apparent condition.

6 On reassembly, apply a light film of oil to the bearing outer race and hub flange shaft, to aid installation of the bearing.

7 Securely support the hub carrier, and locate the bearing in the hub. Press the bearing fully into position, ensuring that it enters the hub squarely, using a tubular spacer which bears only on the bearing outer race.

8 Once the bearing is correctly seated, secure the bearing in position with the new circlip, ensuring that it is correctly located in the groove in the hub carrier.

9 Securely support the outer face of the hub flange, and locate the hub carrier bearing inner race over the end of the hub flange. Press the bearing onto the hub, using a tubular spacer which bears only on the inner race of the hub bearing, until it seats against the hub shoulder. Check that the hub flange rotates freely, and wipe off any excess oil or grease.

10 Refit the hub carrier assembly as described in Section 2.

4 Front suspension strut - removal and refitting

Removal

1 Before raising the car it is recommended that a retaining tool is fitted to the coil spring to hold the spring in a semi-compressed state. This will provide sufficient clearance to enable the strut to be withdrawn from the hub carrier. Peugeot garages use two special cables inserted through the holes at the top of

10

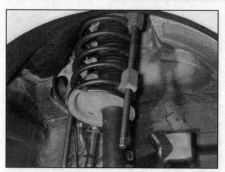

4.1 Coil spring compressors fitted to strut spring

4.2 Front suspension top mounting nuts

5 Front suspension strut - overhaul

the front suspension tower and engaged with further holes in the bottom coil spring seat. If available use these, otherwise fit universal coil spring compressors **(see illustration)**. **Do not** attempt to use any makeshift tool, as considerable damage could occur if the spring breaks free. To fit either type of tool it will be necessary to turn the front wheel to full lock in alternate directions.

2 Loosen, but do not remove, the three strut top mounting nuts **(see illustration)**.

3 Chock the rear wheels then jack up the front of the car and support it on axle stands (see *"Jacking and vehicle support"*). Remove the relevant front roadwheel.

4 On GTI models, unscrew the nut and disconnect the anti-roll bar link from the strut.

5 Unscrew the clamp bolt securing the lower end of the strut to the hub carrier. Spread the slot on the hub carrier using a screwdriver or suitable wedge, push the suspension arm down, and slide the carrier from the bottom of the strut.

6 Support the strut then unscrew the top mounting nuts and withdraw it from under the wheel arch. Recover the washers.

Refitting

7 Refitting is a reversal of removal but ensure that the strut fully enters the hub carrier. If there is any doubt about this, loosen the clamp bolt with the full weight of the car on the suspension, and the strut will be forced fully home. Retighten the bolt to the specified torque.

Warning: Before attempting to dismantle the suspension strut, a suitable tool to hold the coil spring in compression must be obtained. Adjustable coil spring compressors which can be positively secured to the spring coils are readily available, and are recommended for this operation. Any attempt to dismantle the strut without such a tool is likely to result in damage or personal injury.

1 Remove the strut from the car as described in Section 4.

2 Clean away all external dirt from the strut and coil spring.

3 Fit the spring compressors to the coils of the spring. Ensure that the compressors used are of a type that incorporate a method for positively locking them to the spring (usually by a small clamp bolt). Any other type may slip off or slide round the spring as they are tightened. Tighten the compressors until the load is taken off the spring seats. If applicable, remove the Peugeot cables.

4 Unscrew the piston rod nut, counterholding the piston rod with a 7 mm Allen key **(see illustration)**. Note that a new nut will be required for reassembly.

5 Remove the washer and top mounting, followed by the coil spring. The spring may remain in the compressed state ready for refitting to the strut. If the spring is to be renewed, release the compressors very gently and evenly until they can be removed and fitted to the new spring.

6 If necessary, remove the gaiter and bump stop from the piston rod. Note the location of each component to ensure correct refitting.

7 Check the strut for signs of fluid seepage at the piston rod seal. Temporarily refit the upper mounting to the piston rod and, with the bottom of the strut gripped in a vice, fully extend and retract the piston rod. If the resistance is not firm and even in both directions, or if there are signs of leakage or damage, the strut must be renewed.

8 Reassemble the strut using the reverse of the dismantling procedure but note that the bump stop must be fitted with the largest diameter uppermost. Use a new piston rod nut and tighten it to the specified torque. Refit the strut to the car as described in Section 4 on completion.

6 Front lower suspension arm - removal and refitting

Removal

1 Chock the rear wheels then jack up the front of the car and support it on axle stands (see *"Jacking and vehicle support"*). Remove the relevant front roadwheel.

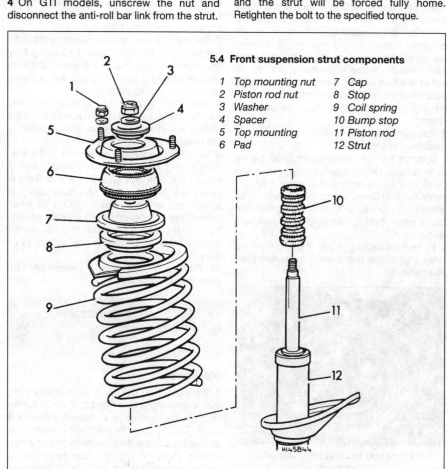

5.4 Front suspension strut components

1 *Top mounting nut*	7 *Cap*
2 *Piston rod nut*	8 *Stop*
3 *Washer*	9 *Coil spring*
4 *Spacer*	10 *Bump stop*
5 *Top mounting*	11 *Piston rod*
6 *Pad*	12 *Strut*

H145844

6.2 Anti-roll bar attachment to lower suspension arm on non-GTI models

6.4a Front lower suspension arm inner pivot bolt (arrowed) on non-GTI models

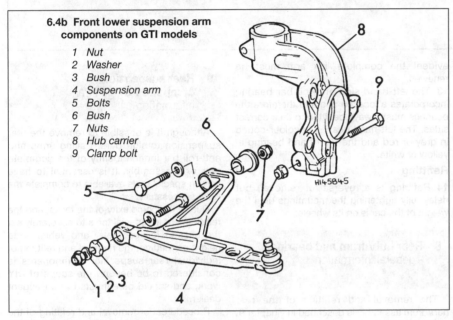

6.4b Front lower suspension arm components on GTI models

1 Nut
2 Washer
3 Bush
4 Suspension arm
5 Bolts
6 Bush
7 Nuts
8 Hub carrier
9 Clamp bolt

H145845

2 On non-GTI models, unscrew the nut securing the anti-roll bar to the suspension arm and remove the washer **(see illustration)**.
3 Unscrew the clamp bolt securing the front suspension lower balljoint to the bottom of the

hub carrier then pull the lower suspension arm down from the carrier. Recover the balljoint guard plate, where fitted.
4 Unscrew and remove the inner pivot bolt(s), noting their fitted direction **(see illustrations)**.

5 Lever down the anti-roll bar where necessary and withdraw the arm from the car.
6 Check the inner pivot bushes for wear and deterioration. Check the lower balljoint on the outer end of the arm for excessive wear indicated by up and down movement of the ball in the socket. Check the arm for damage or deterioration. The bushes may be renewed using a simple puller consisting of a metal tube and washers, together with a long bolt and nut. It is not possible to renew the balljoint separately.

Refitting

7 Refitting is a reversal of removal, but delay final tightening of the inner pivot bolt until the full weight of the car is on the suspension.

7 Front anti-roll bar - removal and refitting

Non - GTI models

Removal

1 Remove the lower suspension arm from one side, as described in Section 6.
2 Unscrew the nut securing the remaining end of the anti-roll bar to the other suspension arm and recover the washer.
3 Unbolt the guide bar from the subframe **(see illustration)**.
4 Unscrew the mounting clamp bolts **(see illustration)** and withdraw the anti-roll bar over the subframe.
5 Examine the rubber bearings for damage and deterioration, and renew them if necessary. The bearings in the suspension arms can be prised or driven out.

Refitting

6 Refitting is a reversal of removal, but delay fully tightening the clamp bolts until the full weight of the car is on wheels. The guide bar bolts should also remain loosened until after the bearing clamp bolts have been tightened.

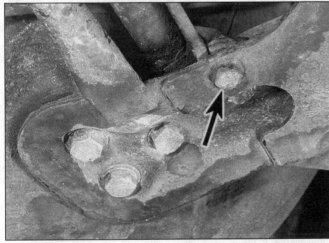

7.3 Anti-roll bar guide bar bolt (arrowed) on non-GTI models

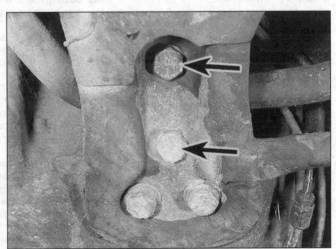

7.4 Anti-roll bar mounting clamp bolts (arrowed)

10

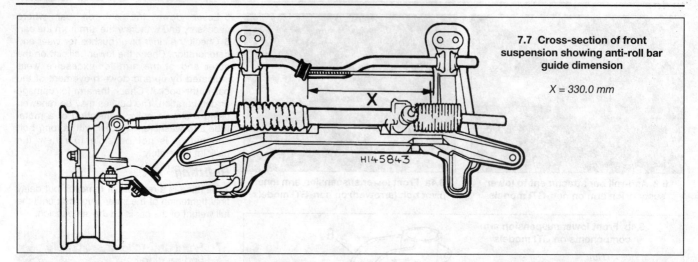

7.7 Cross-section of front suspension showing anti-roll bar guide dimension

X = 330.0 mm

7 The guide bar length must be adjusted to the dimension shown when refitting **(see illustration)**. Note that a full-circle clamp is fitted to early models with a 6.0 mm diameter anti-roll bar, whereas a split clamp is fitted to later models with a 7.0 mm diameter bar. On the later type, position the clamp centrally on the turned-back end of the bar before tightening the bolts.

GTI models

Removal

8 Chock the rear wheels then jack up the front of the car and support it on axle stands (see "Jacking and vehicle support"). Remove the front roadwheels.
9 Unscrew the self-locking nuts from the bottom of the link arms **(see illustration)** and if necessary use a separator tool to release the joints.
10 Unscrew the bearing clamp bolts and withdraw the anti-roll bar over the subframe.
11 Unscrew the self-locking nuts from the tops of the link arms and remove the arms from the suspension struts, again using a separator tool if required.
12 Examine the rubber bearings for damage and deterioration and renew them if necessary. Check the balljoints on the link arms for excessive wear, and the rubber boots for any damage. The balljoints cannot be renewed separately, so if any damage is

7.9 Anti-roll bar link arm bottom mounting on GTI models

evident the complete link arm must be renewed.
13 The left-hand side anti-roll bar bearing incorporates a location ring and therefore the bearings must always be fitted to their correct sides. The left-hand bearing is colour-coded in grey or red and the right-hand bearing in yellow or white.

Refitting

14 Refitting is a reversal of removal, but delay fully tightening the mountings until the weight of the car is on its wheels.

8 Rear hub/drum and bearings - general information

The removal and refitting of the rear hub/drum assembly is described in Chapter 9, together with the inspection of the drum for wear.

On pre-1986 models the hub/drum and bearings are a sealed assembly and it is not possible to renew the bearings separately. If the bearings are worn excessively it will therefore be necessary to renew the complete hub/drum assembly.

If the hub/drum oil seal is worn or damaged it can be renewed by prising it out with a screwdriver and pressing in the new one with a metal tube. Clean and grease the seal contact surface on the trailing arm before refitting the hub/drum.

Models manufactured from early 1986 are fitted with modified rear hub/drum assemblies which does allow separate renewal of the bearings.

Bearing renewal requires the use of a press in conjunction with special tools to remove the old bearing, and this is best entrusted to your Peugeot dealer (once removed, a bearing is rendered unserviceable).

When renewing the oil seal, Peugeot recommend the use of special tool No. 7.052Y to seat the new seal. If unavailable, make a careful note of the position of the original seal before removing it.

9 Rear suspension components - general information

Although it is possible to remove the rear suspension torsion bars, trailing arms and anti-roll bar independently of the complete rear axle assembly, it is essential to have certain special tools available to complete the work successfully.

Due to the complexity of the tasks, and the requirement for special tools to accurately set the suspension geometry and vehicle ride height on refitting, the removal and refitting of individual rear suspension components is considered to be beyond the scope of DIY work, and should be entrusted to a Peugeot dealer.

Procedures for removal and refitting of the rear shock absorbers, and the complete rear suspension assembly are given in Sections 10 and 11 respectively.

10 Rear shock absorber - removal and refitting

Removal

1 Position the rear of the car on ramps or alternatively jack it up and support it beneath the wheels. Apply the handbrake.
2 Unscrew the shock absorber bottom mounting nut and tap the bolt outwards until it clears the shock absorber **(see illustration)**. If the bolt head fouls the handbrake cable bracket, loosen the bracket bolt on the side of the trailing arm and lift the bracket as required. Do not forget to tighten the bolt after refitting the shock absorber.
3 Unscrew the upper mounting nut, remove the washer, and tap out the bolt.
4 Withdraw the shock absorber from under the car.
5 A thorough check of the shock absorber may now be made by gripping the bottom

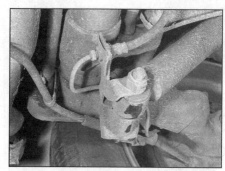

10.2 Rear shock absorber bottom mounting

11.6 Rear suspension cross-tube front clamp and seat belt anchorage

13.2 Steering wheel retaining nut

mounting in a vice and attempting to extend and retract it. If the resistance is not firm and even in both directions, or if there are signs of leakage or damage, the shock absorber must be renewed.

Refitting

6 Refitting is a reversal of removal, but renew the self-locking nuts. The nuts must be tightened when the distance between the mounting bolt centres is 288.0 mm. The Peugeot tool 80911 for this operation consists of a bar and adjustable bolt located beneath the lifting ramp and hooked on the suspension tube; however, loading the rear of the car by trial and error will produce the same result.

11 Rear suspension assembly - removal and refitting

Removal

1 Chock the front wheels then jack up the rear of the car and support it on axle stands (see "Jacking and vehicle support").
2 Remove the handbrake cables, with reference to Chapter 9.
3 Remove the complete exhaust system, with reference to Chapter 4D.
4 Disconnect the flexible brake hoses from the rear suspension assembly, with reference to Chapter 9.
5 Unscrew the left-hand rear mounting nut, remove the exhaust bracket then temporarily refit the nut.

6 Unbolt and remove the front clamp and bracket (see illustration), but do not unscrew the seat belt anchorage (where fitted).
7 Adjust the position of the car on the axle stands so that the rear wheels are just touching the ground, then place additional stands or jacks beneath the suspension tube.
8 Working in the luggage compartment unscrew the front and rear mounting nuts then carefully withdraw the assembly from under the car.

Refitting

9 Refitting is a reversal of removal, but tighten all nuts and bolts to the specified torque. When tightening the front clamp make sure that the ring is centred in the seat belt anchorage bracket. Refer to Chapter 4D and 9 when refitting disturbed exhaust and braking system components and bleed the brake hydraulic system on completion.

12 Vehicle ride height - checking

Checking of the vehicle ride height requires the use of Peugeot special tools to accurately compress the suspension in a suspension checking bay.

The operation should be entrusted to a Peugeot dealer, as it not possible to carry out checking accurately without the use of the appropriate tools.

13 Steering wheel - removal and refitting

Removal

1 Set the front wheels in the straight-ahead position.
2 Prise out the centre pad, then use a socket to unscrew the retaining nut (see illustration).
3 Mark the hub in relation to the inner column then pull off the steering wheel.

HAYNES HINT *If the wheel is tight, tap it up near the centre, using the palm of your hand, or twist it from side to side, whilst pulling upwards to release it from the shaft splines.*

Refitting

4 Refitting is a reversal of removal, but check that the steering wheel is correctly centred with the front wheels straight ahead. Tighten the nut while holding the steering wheel rim.

14 Steering column and lock - removal and refitting

Removal

1 Remove the steering wheel, (Section 13).
2 Remove the lower trim panel from under the steering column (see illustration).
3 Mark the column lower universal joint in relation to the intermediate shaft then unscrew and remove the clamp bolt (see illustration).
4 Remove the combination switches, as described in Chapter 12.
5 Disconnect the ignition switch wiring connectors.
6 Unscrew the mounting nuts and bolts, disconnect the inner column from the intermediate shaft, and withdraw the steering column from the car. Where shear bolts are fitted they must be drilled to remove the heads, then unscrewed after removing the column.

10

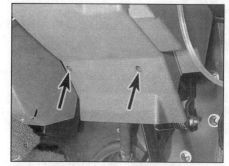

14.2 Steering column lower trim panel screws (arrowed)

14.3 Steering column lower universal joint and clamp bolt (arrowed)

14.7 Steering column intermediate shaft (arrowed)

7 If necessary, the intermediate shaft can be removed after prising out the grommet and unscrewing the bottom clamp bolt **(see illustration)**.

8 To remove the steering lock, unscrew the retaining bolt then, with the ignition key aligned with the small arrow between the 'A' and 'M' positions, depress the plunger in the housing and withdraw the lock **(see illustration)**.

Refitting

9 Refitting is a reversal of removal.

15 Steering gear - removal and refitting

Manual steering gear

Removal

1 Chock the rear wheels then jack up the front of the car and support it on axle stands (see *"Jacking and vehicle support"*). Remove the front roadwheels.

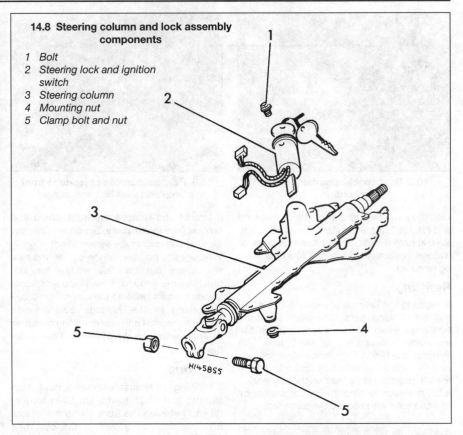

14.8 Steering column and lock assembly components

1 Bolt
2 Steering lock and ignition switch
3 Steering column
4 Mounting nut
5 Clamp bolt and nut

2 Unscrew the track rod end locknuts then use a separator tool to detach the track rod end balljoints from the hub carrier steering arms.

3 Mark the lower column in relation to the pinion on the steering gear.

4 Unscrew and remove the column-to-pinion clamp bolt.

5 Unscrew and remove the two mounting bolts and withdraw the steering gear from one side of the subframe **(see illustration)**.

Refitting

6 Refitting is a reversal of removal, but tighten all nuts and bolts to the specified torque. On completion, have the front wheel toe setting checked (see Section 21).

Power-assisted steering gear

Removal

7 Chock the rear wheels then jack up the front of the car and support it on axle stands (see *"Jacking and vehicle support"*). Remove the front roadwheels.

8 Prepare a suitable container, then disconnect the fluid pipes from the steering gear, and allow the fluid to drain into the container.

9 Unscrew the track rod end balljoint locknuts, then use a separator tool to detach the track rod end balljoints from the hub carrier steering arms.

10 Mark the lower column in relation to the pinion on the steering gear.

11 Unscrew and remove the column-to-pinion clamp bolt.

12 On manual transmission models, disconnect the three gearchange control rods from the levers on the transmission.

13 Extract the spring clip from the gearchange linkage **(see illustration)**, then unclip the transmission selector and

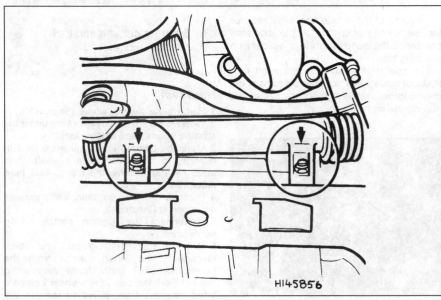

15.5 Steering gear mounting bolt locations (arrowed)

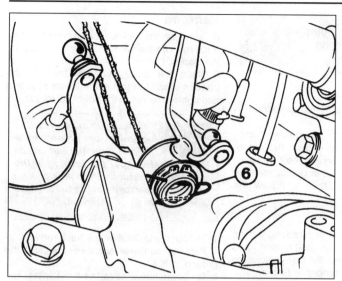

15.13 Extract the spring clip (6) from the gearchange linkage

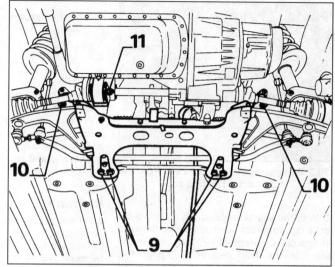

15.16 Front subframe attachments

9 Rear securing bolts
10 Front securing bolts

11 Lower engine mounting nut

engagement rods, and support them in an upright position out of the way, using wire or string.

14 Remove the two steering gear securing bolts, and recover the spacer tubes from the subframe, then disconnect the steering gear pinion from the steering column shaft.

15 Support the front subframe using a trolley jack and interposed block of wood positioned under the subframe crossmember.

16 Remove the four bolts securing the rear of the subframe to the body, and the two nuts or bolts, as applicable, securing the front of the subframe to the body **(see illustration)**. Also remove the nut and bolt from the lower engine mounting.

17 Carefully lower the subframe sufficiently

to enable removal of the steering gear, ensuring that the subframe is adequately supported.

18 Rotate the steering gear towards the rear of the vehicle, and withdraw the assembly over the rear of the subframe, taking care not to damage the rack bellows.

Refitting

19 Refitting is a reversal of removal, bearing in mind the following points:

a) Ensure that the spacer tubes are fitted to the steering gear securing bolts.
b) Tighten all fixings to the specified torque.
c) Ensure that the marks made on the steering gear pinion and the lower column during removal are aligned.

d) When reconnecting the fluid pipes to the steering gear, the high pressure fluid pipe must be vertical **(see illustration)**.
e) Secure the hose to the high-pressure fluid pipe using a cable-tie.
f) Check the gearchange mechanism for correct operation after reconnecting the linkages.
g) On completion, bleed the power steering hydraulic system as described in Section 17, and have the front wheel toe setting checked (see Section 21).

16 Steering gear rubber bellows - renewal

1 Remove the relevant track rod end, as described in Section 19.
2 Release the clips from each end of the bellows then ease the bellows from the steering gear and pull it from the track rod.
3 Clean the track rod and bellows location on the steering gear.
4 Slide the new bellows onto the track rod and steering gear, check that it is not twisted, then fit the clips.
5 Refit the track rod end with reference to Section 19.

17 Power steering system - bleeding

10

1 This procedure will only be necessary when any part of the hydraulic system has been disconnected.
2 Referring to "Weekly checks", remove the fluid reservoir filler cap, and top-up with the specified fluid to the maximum level mark.

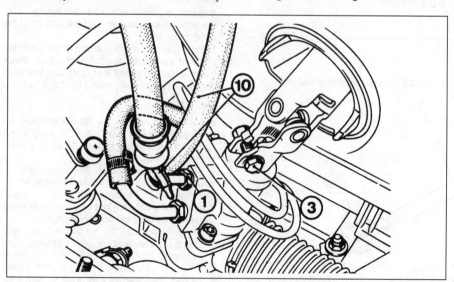

15.19 Correct refitting of power assisted steering gear

1   High-pressure pipe
3   Column-to-pinion clamp bolt

10   Hose secured with cable tie

19.3 Separating the track rod end from the hub carrier steering arm

3 With the engine stopped, slowly move the steering from lock-to-lock several times to purge out the trapped air, then top-up the level in the fluid reservoir. Repeat this procedure until the fluid level in the reservoir does not drop any further.

4 Start the engine, then slowly move the steering from lock-to-lock several times to purge out any remaining air in the system. Repeat this procedure until bubbles cease to appear in the fluid reservoir.

5 If, when turning the steering, an abnormal noise is heard from the fluid lines, it indicates that there is still air in the system. Check this by turning the wheels to the straight-ahead position and switching off the engine. If the fluid level in the reservoir rises, then air is present in the system, and further bleeding is necessary.

6 Once all traces of air have been removed from the power steering hydraulic system, turn the engine off and allow the system to cool. Once cool, check that the fluid level is up to the maximum mark on the power steering fluid reservoir, topping-up if necessary.

18 Power steering pump - removal and refitting

Removal

1 Remove the alternator as described in Chapter 5A.

2 Prepare a suitable container, then disconnect the fluid hoses from the pump, and allow the fluid to drain into the container.

3 Unscrew and remove the power steering pump mounting bolts, then withdraw the pump.

Refitting

4 Refitting is a reversal of removal, but on completion, tension the drivebelt as described in Chapter 1, and bleed the power steering hydraulic system as described in Section 17.

19 Track rod end - removal and refitting

Removal

1 Chock the rear wheels then jack up the front of the car and support it on axle stands (see "Jacking and vehicle support"). Remove the relevant front roadwheel.

2 Loosen the locknut on the track rod end by a quarter of a turn.

3 Unscrew the balljoint locknut and use an extractor tool to separate the balljoint tapered shank from the hub carrier steering arm (see illustration).

4 Unscrew the track rod end from the track rod, noting the number of turns necessary to remove it. Remove the locknut from the track rod end threads.

Refitting

5 Screw on the locknut then screw the new track rod end the same number of turns onto the track rod.

6 Clean the taper surfaces then fit the balljoint shank to the hub carrier steering arm and tighten the nut to the specified torque.

> **HAYNES HINT** *If difficulty is experienced in loosening or tightening a balljoint taper pin nut due to the taper pin turning in the eye, apply pressure with a jack or long lever to the balljoint socket to force the taper pin into its conical seat.*

7 Tighten the locknut on the track rod end.

8 Refit the roadwheel and lower the car to the ground.

9 On completion, have the front wheel toe setting checked (see Section 21).

20 Track rod - removal and refitting

Removal

Note: *A new inner balljoint lockwasher must be used on refitting.*

1 Remove the track rod end as described in Section 19.

2 Release the retaining clips and slide the rubber bellows off the end of the steering gear housing and track rod (see illustration).

3 Unscrew the track rod inner balljoint from the steering rack end, preventing the steering rack from turning by holding the balljoint lockwasher with a pair of grips. Take great care not to mark the surfaces of the rack and balljoint.

4 Remove the track rod assembly, and discard the lockwasher - a new one must be used on refitting.

5 Examine the track rod inner balljoint for signs of slackness or tight spots, and check that the track rod itself is straight and free from damage. If necessary, renew the track rod.

Refitting

6 Locate the new lockwasher assembly on the end of the steering rack, and apply a few drops of locking fluid to the track rod inner balljoint threads.

7 Screw the balljoint into the steering rack, and tighten it to the specified torque whilst retaining the lockwasher with a pair of grips. Again, take great care not to damage or mark the track rod balljoint or steering rack.

8 Carefully slide on the rubber bellows, and locate it on the steering gear housing. Turn the steering fully from lock-to-lock, to check that the gaiter is correctly positioned on the track rod, then secure it in position with new retaining clips.

9 Refit the track rod end as described in Section 19.

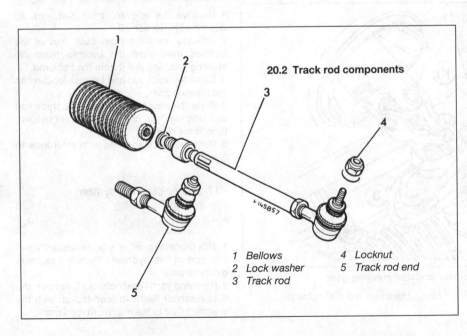

20.2 Track rod components

1 Bellows
2 Lock washer
3 Track rod
4 Locknut
5 Track rod end

21.11 Adjusting the front wheel toe setting

21 Wheel alignment and steering angles - general information

1 A car's steering and suspension geometry is defined in four basic settings - all angles are expressed in degrees (toe settings are also expressed as a measurement); the relevant settings are camber, castor, steering axis inclination, and toe-setting. With the exception of front wheel toe-setting, none of these settings are adjustable.

Front wheel toe setting - checking and adjustment

2 Due to the special measuring equipment necessary to accurately check the wheel alignment, and the skill required to use it properly, checking and adjustment is best left to a Peugeot dealer or similar expert. Note that most tyre-fitting shops now possess sophisticated checking equipment. The following is provided as a guide, should the owner decide to carry out a DIY check.

3 The front wheel toe setting is checked by measuring the distance between the front and rear inside edges of the roadwheel rims. Proprietary toe measurement gauges are available from motor accessory shops. Adjustment is made by screwing the track rod ends in or out of their track rods, to alter the effective length of the track rod assemblies.

4 For **accurate** checking, the vehicle **must** be at the kerb weight, ie unladen and with a full tank of fuel, and the ride height must be correct (see Section 12).

5 Before starting work, check the tyre pressures and tread wear, the condition of the hub bearings, the steering wheel free play, and the condition of the front suspension components (see Chapter 1). Correct any faults found.

6 Park the vehicle on level ground, check that the front roadwheels are in the straight-ahead position, then rock the rear and front ends to settle the suspension. Release the handbrake, and roll the vehicle backwards 1 metre, then forwards again, to relieve any stresses in the steering and suspension components.

7 Measure the distance between the front edges of the wheel rims and the rear edges of the rims. Subtract the rear measurement from the front measurement, and check that the result is within the specified range.

8 If adjustment is necessary, apply the handbrake, then jack up the front of the vehicle and support it securely on axle stands (see *"Jacking and vehicle support"*). Turn the steering wheel onto full-left lock, and record the number of exposed threads on the right-hand track rod end. Now turn the steering onto full-right lock, and record the number of threads on the left-hand side. If there are the same number of threads visible on both sides, then subsequent adjustment should be made equally on both sides. If there are more threads visible on one side than the other, it will be necessary to compensate for this during adjustment. **Note:** *It is most important that after adjustment, the same number of threads are visible on each track rod end.*

9 First clean the track rod end threads; if they are corroded, apply penetrating fluid before starting adjustment. Release the rubber bellows outboard clips (where necessary), and peel back the bellows; apply a smear of grease to the inside of the bellows, so that both are free, and will not be twisted or strained as their respective track rods are rotated.

10 Use a straight-edge and a scriber or similar to mark the relationship of each track rod to its track rod end then, holding each track rod in turn, unscrew its locknut fully.

11 Alter the length of the track rods, bearing in mind the note made in paragraph 8. Screw them into or out of the track rod ends, rotating the track rod using an open-ended spanner fitted to the flats provided on the track rod. Shortening the track rods (screwing them into their track rod ends) will reduce toe-in/increase toe-out **(see illustration)**.

12 When the setting is correct, hold the track rods and securely tighten the track rod end locknuts. Count the exposed threads to check the length of both track rods. If they are not the same, then the adjustment has not been made equally, and problems will be encountered with tyre scrubbing in turns; also, the steering wheel spokes will no longer be horizontal when the wheels are in the straight-ahead position.

13 If the track rod lengths are the same, lower the vehicle to the ground and re-check the toe setting; re-adjust if necessary. When the setting is correct, securely tighten the track rod end locknuts. Ensure that the rubber bellows are seated correctly, and are not twisted or strained, and secure them in position with new retaining clips (where necessary).

10

Chapter 11
Bodywork and fittings

Contents

Degrees of difficulty

Easy, suitable for novice with little experience	Fairly easy, suitable for beginner with some experience	Fairly difficult, suitable for competent DIY mechanic 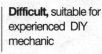	Difficult, suitable for experienced DIY mechanic	Very difficult, suitable for expert DIY or professional

1 General information

The body shell is of one-piece design and safety cell construction, whereby the outer members yield progressively and in a controlled direction in the event of impact, giving maximum protection to the passenger compartment. The body panels are of lightweight high strength steel.

The front wings are bolted to the main body for ease of removal. The complete body is given an extensive anti-corrosion treatment during manufacture; including stone chip protection and wax injection. Peugeot guarantee the body against perforation as a result of corrosion for a period of six years provided the car is given periodic inspections by a Peugeot garage.

2 Maintenance - bodywork and underframe

The general condition of a vehicle's bodywork is the one thing that significantly affects its value. Maintenance is easy but needs to be regular. Neglect, particularly after minor damage, can lead quickly to further deterioration and costly repair bills. It is important also to keep watch on those parts of the vehicle not immediately visible, for instance the underside, inside all the wheel arches and the lower part of the engine compartment.

The basic maintenance routine for the bodywork is washing preferably with a lot of water, from a hose. This will remove all the loose solids which may have stuck to the vehicle. It is important to flush these off in such a way as to prevent grit from scratching the finish. The wheel arches and underframe need washing in the same way to remove any accumulated mud which will retain moisture and tend to encourage rust. Oddly enough, the best time to clean the underframe and wheel arches is in wet weather when the mud is thoroughly wet and soft. In very wet weather the underframe is usually cleaned of large accumulations automatically and this is a good time for inspection.

Periodically, except on vehicles with a wax-based underbody protective coating, it is a good idea to have the whole of the underframe of the vehicle steam cleaned, engine compartment included, so that a thorough inspection can be carried out to see what minor repairs and renovations are necessary. Steam cleaning is available at many garages and is necessary for removal of the accumulation of oily grime which sometimes is allowed to become thick in certain areas. If steam cleaning facilities are not available, there are one or two excellent grease solvents available which can be brush applied; the dirt can then be simply hosed off. Note that these methods should not be used on vehicles with wax-based underbody protective coating or the coating will be removed. Such vehicles should be inspected annually, preferably just prior to winter, when the underbody should be washed down and any damage to the wax coating repaired using underseal. Ideally, a completely fresh coat should be applied. It would also be worth considering the use of such wax-based protection for injection into door panels, sills, box sections, etc, as an additional safeguard against rust damage where such protection is not provided by the vehicle manufacturer.

After washing paintwork, wipe off with a chamois leather to give an unspotted clear finish. A coat of clear protective wax polish will give added protection against chemical pollutants in the air. If the paintwork sheen has dulled or oxidised, use a cleaner/polisher combination to restore the brilliance of the shine. This requires a little effort, but such dulling is usually caused because regular washing has been neglected. Care needs to be taken with metallic paintwork as special non-abrasive cleaner/polisher is required to avoid damage to the finish.

Always check that the door and ventilator opening drain holes and pipes are completely clear so that water can be drained out. Bright work should be treated in the same way as paint work. Windscreens and windows can be kept clear of the smeary film which often appears by the use of a proprietary glass cleaner. Never use any form of wax or other body or chromium polish on glass.

3 Maintenance - upholstery and carpets

Mats and carpets should be brushed or vacuum cleaned regularly to keep them free of grit. If they are badly stained remove them from the vehicle for scrubbing or sponging and make quite sure they are dry before refitting. Seats and interior trim panels can be kept clean by wiping with a damp cloth and a proprietary upholstery cleaner. If they do become stained (which can be more apparent on light coloured upholstery) use a little liquid detergent and a soft nail brush to scour the grime out of the grain of the material. Do not forget to keep the headlining clean in the same way as the upholstery. When using liquid cleaners inside the vehicle do not over-wet the surfaces being cleaned. Excessive damp could get into the seams and padded interior causing stains, offensive odours or even rot. If the inside of the vehicle gets wet accidentally it is worthwhile taking some trouble to dry it out properly, particularly where carpets are involved. Do not leave oil or electric heaters inside the vehicle for this purpose.

4 Minor body damage - repair

Repair of minor scratches in bodywork

If the scratch is very superficial, and does not penetrate to the metal of the bodywork, repair is very simple. Lightly rub the area of the scratch with a paintwork renovator, or a very fine cutting paste, to remove loose paint from the scratch, and to clear the surrounding bodywork of wax polish. Rinse the area with clean water.

Apply touch-up paint to the scratch using a fine paint brush; continue to apply fine layers of paint until the surface of the paint in the scratch is level with the surrounding paintwork. Allow the new paint at least two weeks to harden: then blend it into the surrounding paintwork by rubbing the scratch area with a paintwork renovator or a very fine cutting paste. Finally, apply wax polish.

Where the scratch has penetrated right through to the metal of the bodywork, causing the metal to rust, a different repair technique is required. Remove any loose rust from the bottom of the scratch with a penknife, then apply rust-inhibiting paint, to prevent the formation of rust in the future. Using a rubber or nylon applicator fill the scratch with bodystopper paste. If required, this paste can be mixed with cellulose thinners, to provide a very thin paste which is ideal for filling narrow scratches. Before the stopper-paste in the scratch hardens, wrap a piece of smooth cotton rag around the top of a finger. Dip the finger in cellulose thinners, and then quickly sweep it across the surface of the stopper-paste in the scratch; this will ensure that the surface of the stopper-paste is slightly hollowed. The scratch can now be painted over as described earlier in this Section.

Repair of dents in bodywork

When deep denting of the vehicle's bodywork has taken place, the first task is to pull the dent out, until the affected bodywork almost attains its original shape. There is little point in trying to restore the original shape completely, as the metal in the damaged area will have stretched on impact and cannot be reshaped fully to its original contour. It is better to bring the level of the dent up to a point which is about 3 mm below the level of the surrounding bodywork. In cases where the dent is very shallow anyway, it is not worth trying to pull it out at all. If the underside of the dent is accessible, it can be hammered out gently from behind, using a mallet with a wooden or plastic head. Whilst doing this, hold a suitable block of wood firmly against the outside of the panel to absorb the impact from the hammer blows and thus prevent a large area of the bodywork from being "belled-out".

Should the dent be in a section of the bodywork which has a double skin or some other factor making it inaccessible from behind, a different technique is called for. Drill several small holes through the metal inside the area - particularly in the deeper section. Then screw long self-tapping screws into the holes just sufficiently for them to gain a good purchase in the metal. Now the dent can be pulled out by pulling on the protruding heads of the screws with a pair of pliers.

The next stage of the repair is the removal of the paint from the damaged area, and from an inch or so of the surrounding "sound" bodywork. This is accomplished most easily by using a wire brush or abrasive pad on a power drill, although it can be done just as effectively by hand using sheets of abrasive paper. To complete the preparation for filling, score the surface of the bare metal with a screwdriver or the tang of a file, or alternatively, drill small holes in the affected area. This will provide a really good "key" for the filler paste.

To complete the repair see the Section on filling and re-spraying.

Repair of Rust holes or gashes in bodywork

Remove all paint from the affected area and from an inch or so of the surrounding "sound" bodywork, using an abrasive pad or a wire brush on a power drill. If these are not available a few sheets of abrasive paper will do the job just as effectively. With the paint removed you will be able to gauge the severity of the corrosion and therefore decide whether to renew the whole panel (if this is possible) or to repair the affected area. New body panels are not as expensive as most people think and it is often quicker and more satisfactory to fit a new panel than to attempt to repair large areas of corrosion.

Remove all fittings from the affected area except those which will act as a guide to the original shape of the damaged bodywork (eg headlight shells etc). Then, using tin snips or a hacksaw blade, remove all loose metal and any other metal badly affected by corrosion. Hammer the edges of the hole inwards in order to create a slight depression for the filler paste.

Wire brush the affected area to remove the powdery rust from the surface of the remaining metal. Paint the affected area with rust inhibiting paint; if the back of the rusted area is accessible treat this also.

Before filling can take place it will be necessary to block the hole in some way. This can be achieved by the use of aluminium or plastic mesh, or aluminium tape.

Aluminium or plastic mesh or glass fibre matting is probably the best material to use for a large hole. Cut a piece to the approximate size and shape of the hole to be filled, then position it in the hole so that its edges are below the level of the surrounding bodywork. It can be retained in position by several blobs of filler paste around its periphery.

Aluminium tape should be used for small or very narrow holes. Pull a piece off the roll and trim it to the approximate size and shape required, then pull off the backing paper (if used) and stick the tape over the hole; it can be overlapped if the thickness of one piece is insufficient. Burnish down the edges of the tape with the handle of a screwdriver or similar, to ensure that the tape is securely attached to the metal underneath.

Bodywork repairs - filling and re-spraying

Before using this Section, see the Sections on dent, deep scratch, rust holes and gash repairs.

Many types of bodyfiller are available, but generally speaking those proprietary kits which contain a tin of filler paste and a tube of resin hardener are best for this type of repair; some can be used directly from the tube. A wide, flexible plastic or nylon applicator will be found invaluable for imparting a smooth and well contoured finish to the surface of the filler.

Mix up a little filler on a clean piece of card or board - measure the hardener carefully (follow the maker's instructions on the pack) otherwise the filler will set too rapidly or too slowly. Using the applicator, apply the filler paste to the prepared area; draw the applicator across the surface of the filler to achieve the correct contour and to level the filler surface. As soon as a contour that approximates to the correct one is achieved, stop working the paste - if you carry on too long the paste will become sticky and begin to "pick up" on the applicator. Continue to add thin layers of filler paste at twenty-minute intervals until the level of the filler is just proud of the surrounding bodywork.

Once the filler has hardened, excess can be removed using a metal plane or file. From then on, progressively finer grades of abrasive paper should be used, starting with a 40 grade production paper and finishing with 400 grade wet-and-dry paper. Always wrap the abrasive paper around a flat rubber, cork, or wooden block - otherwise the surface of the filler will not be completely flat. During the smoothing of the filler surface the wet-and-dry paper should be periodically rinsed in water. This will ensure that a very smooth finish is imparted to the filler at the final stage.

At this stage the "dent" should be surrounded by a ring of bare metal, which in turn should be encircled by the finely "feathered" edge of the good paintwork. Rinse the repair area with clean water, until all of the dust produced by the rubbing-down operation has gone.

Spray the whole repair area with a light coat of primer - this will show up any imperfections in the surface of the filler. Repair these imperfections with fresh filler paste or bodystopper, and once more smooth the surface with abrasive paper. If bodystopper is used, it can be mixed with cellulose thinners to form a really thin paste which is ideal for filling

small holes. Repeat this spray and repair procedure until you are satisfied that the surface of the filler, and the feathered edge of the paintwork are perfect. Clean the repair area with clean water and allow to dry fully.

The repair area is now ready for final spraying. Paint spraying must be carried out in a warm, dry, windless and dust free atmosphere. This condition can be created artificially if you have access to a large indoor working area, but if you are forced to work in the open, you will have to pick your day very carefully. If you are working indoors, dousing the floor in the work area with water will help to settle the dust which would otherwise be in the atmosphere. If the repair area is confined to one body panel, mask off the surrounding panels; this will help to minimise the effects of a slight mis-match in paint colours. Bodywork fittings (eg chrome strips, door handles etc) will also need to be masked off. Use genuine masking tape and several thicknesses of newspaper for the masking operations.

Before commencing to spray, agitate the aerosol can thoroughly, then spray a test area (an old tin, or similar) until the technique is mastered. Cover the repair area with a thick coat of primer; the thickness should be built up using several thin layers of paint rather than one thick one. Using 400 grade wet-and-dry paper, rub down the surface of the primer until it is really smooth. While doing this, the work area should be thoroughly doused with water, and the wet-and-dry paper periodically rinsed in water. Allow to dry before spraying on more paint.

Spray on the top coat, again building up the thickness by using several thin layers of paint. Start spraying in the centre of the repair area and then, with a single side-to-side motion, work outwards until the whole repair area and about 50 mm of the surrounding original paintwork is covered. Remove all masking material 10 to 15 minutes after spraying on the final coat of paint.

Allow the new paint at least two weeks to harden, then, using a paintwork renovator or a very fine cutting paste, blend the edges of the paint into the existing paintwork. Finally, apply wax polish.

Plastic components

With the use of more and more plastic body components by the vehicle manufacturers (eg bumpers, spoilers, and in some cases major body panels), rectification of more serious damage to such items has become a matter of either entrusting repair work to a specialist in this field, or renewing complete components. Repair of such damage by the DIY owner is not really feasible owing to the cost of the equipment and materials required for effecting such repairs. The basic technique involves making a groove along the line of the crack in the plastic using a rotary burr in a power drill. The damaged part is then welded back together by using a hot air gun to heat up and fuse a plastic filler rod into the groove.

Any excess plastic is then removed and the area rubbed down to a smooth finish. It is important that a filler rod of the correct plastic is used, as body components can be made of a variety of different types (eg polycarbonate, ABS, polypropylene).

Damage of a less serious nature (abrasions, minor cracks etc) can be repaired by the DIY owner using a two-part epoxy filler repair material. Once mixed in equal proportions, this is used in similar fashion to the bodywork filler used on metal panels. The filler is usually cured in twenty to thirty minutes, ready for sanding and painting.

If the owner is renewing a complete component himself, or if he has repaired it with epoxy filler, he will be left with the problem of finding a suitable paint for finishing which is compatible with the type of plastic used. At one time the use of a universal paint was not possible owing to the complex range of plastics encountered in body component applications. Standard paints, generally speaking, will not bond to plastic or rubber satisfactorily. However, it is now possible to obtain a plastic body parts finishing kit which consists of a pre-primer treatment, a primer and coloured top coat. Full instructions are normally supplied with a kit, but basically the method of use is to first apply the pre-primer to the component concerned and allow it to dry for up to 30 minutes. Then the primer is applied and left to dry for about an hour before finally applying the special coloured top coat. The result is a correctly coloured component where the paint will flex with the plastic or rubber, a property that standard paint does not normally possess.

5 Major body damage - repair

The construction of the body is such that great care must be taken when making cuts, or when renewing major members, to preserve the basic safety characteristics of the structure. In addition, the heating of certain areas is not advisable.

In view of the specialised knowledge necessary for this work, and the alignment jigs and special tools frequently required, the owner is advised to consult a specialist body repairer or Peugeot dealer.

6 Bonnet - removal and refitting

11

Removal

1 Open the bonnet and support with the stay.
2 Using a pencil, mark the position of the hinges on the bonnet (**see illustration**).
3 Unbolt the braided lead and disconnect the windscreen washer tubing (**see illustration**).

6.2 Bonnet hinge

6.3 Braided lead fitted to the bonnet

7.2 Bonnet lock retaining bolts

4 While an assistant supports the bonnet, unscrew the nut and remove the bottom of the stay from the right-hand suspension tower.

5 Place some cloth beneath the rear corners of the bonnet, unscrew the hinge bolts and withdraw it from the car.

Refitting

6 Refitting is a reversal of removal, but check that the bonnet is central within its aperture and flush with the front wings. If necessary loosen the hinge bolts and move it within the elongated holes to reposition it, then adjust the bonnet lock and striker, as described in Section 7.

7 Bonnet lock and remote control cable - removal, refitting and adjustment

Removal

1 Remove the front grille, as described in Section 8.

2 Unbolt the lock from the crossmember and disconnect the control cable **(see illustration)**.

3 Working inside the car, remove the screws from the cable release lever located below the left-hand end of the facia.

4 Unclip the cable and withdraw it from inside the car.

5 If necessary the bonnet striker may be unscrewed from the bonnet and the safety spring unclipped.

Refitting

6 Refitting is a reversal of removal, but check that the striker enters the lock centrally and holds the front of the bonnet level with the front wings. If necessary loosen the lock bolts and move the lock within the elongated holes. Adjust the bonnet height by screwing the striker pin in or out. Adjust the rubber buffers to support the front corners of the bonnet.

8 Front grille - removal and refitting

Removal

1 Open the bonnet and support with the stay.

2 Remove the screws from the top of the grille then lift it upwards from the lower mounting holes **(see illustrations)**.

Refitting

3 Refitting is a reversal of removal.

9 Bumpers - removal and refitting

Removal

Front bumper

1 The bumper is removed complete with the front spoiler.

2 Working under the vehicle, unscrew the two front bumper mounting nuts at the brackets **(see illustration)**.

3 On non-GTI models, unscrew the side mounting nuts beneath the front wheel arches and withdraw the bumper from the car, together with the side mounting rubbers.

4 On GTI models, disconnect the battery negative lead, and disconnect the wiring from the front driving lamps.

5 Remove the clip securing the front wing trim to the bumper.

6 Unscrew the bolts securing the driving lamp brackets to the body, loosen the side bumper mounting nuts beneath the front wheel arches, and withdraw the bumper from the car.

7 The brackets may be removed separately if required.

Rear bumper

8 Unscrew the rear, side and bottom mounting nuts and withdraw the bumper rearwards **(see illustration)**. On certain models, additional fixing clips must also be released and a lower moulding removed before the bumper can be withdrawn.

9 The brackets may be removed separately if required.

Refitting

10 Refitting both the front and rear bumpers is a reversal of removal.

8.2a Remove the screws . . .

8.2b . . . and lift the front grille from the outer . . .

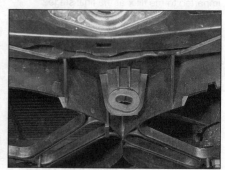

8.2c . . . and inner mounting holes

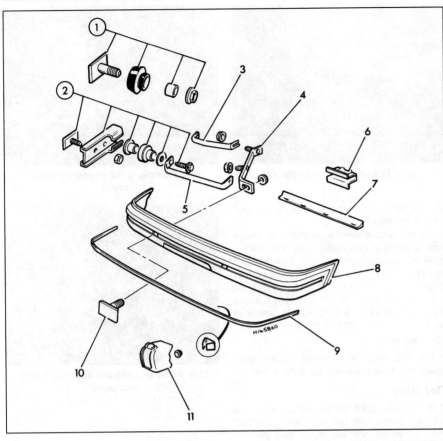

9.2 Front bumper components

1 *Side mounting (non-GTI)*
2 *Side mounting (GTI)*
3 *Side bracket (non-GTI)*
4 *Bracket*
5 *Side bracket (GTI)*
6 *Seal clip*
7 *Seal*
8 *Bumper*
9 *Moulding*
10 *Mounting plate*
11 *Headlight washer bracket*

10 Door - removal and refitting

Removal

1 The door hinges are welded to the body pillar and bolted to the door.
2 Remove the plastic caps from the hinge pivot pins.
3 Drive out the roll pin from the door check strap.
4 Where applicable, remove the trim panel (Section 11) and disconnect the loudspeaker wiring from the door.
5 Support the door in the fully open position by placing blocks, or a jack and a pad of rag, under its lower edge.
6 Drive out the hinge pivot pins and remove the door.

Refitting

7 Refit by reversing the removal operations.
8 Where necessary, the striker on the body pillar may be adjusted to ensure correct closure of the door.

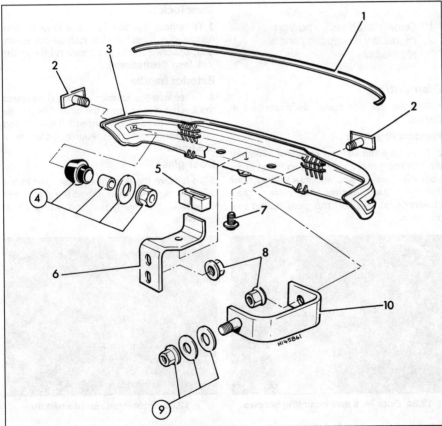

9.8 Rear bumper components

1 *Moulding*
2 *Mounting plates*
3 *Bumper*
4 *Side mounting and nut*
5 *Rubber buffer*
6 *Bracket*
7 *Mounting bolt*
8 *Nuts*
9 *Bracket nut and washers*
10 *Bracket*

11

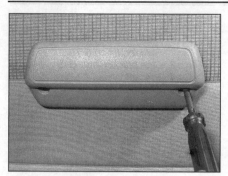

11.2 Removing the armrest

11.3 Removing the side pocket

11.4 Removing the window regulator handle

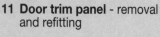

11 Door trim panel - removal and refitting

Removal

Front doors

1 If electric windows are fitted, disconnect the battery negative lead.
2 Remove the two screws and withdraw the armrest **(see illustration)**.
3 Remove the screws and withdraw the side pocket **(see illustration)**.
4 On models with manually operated windows, fully close the window, note the position of the window regulator handle, then pull the handle from the spindle **(see illustration)**.

5 Prise out the interior door handle surround **(see illustration)**.
6 Using a wide-bladed screwdriver, or similar tool, prise the trim panel from the door - working progressively from the bottom upwards and inserting the screwdriver adjacent to each clip. Where applicable, disconnect the electric window switch wiring and door speaker wiring as the panel is withdrawn, on models so equipped.

Rear doors

7 The procedure is as given for the front doors, but there are slight trim differences.

Refitting

8 Refitting the front and rear door panels is a reversal of removal, but first make sure that the clips are correctly located in the panel.

11.5 Removing the interior door handle surround

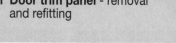

12 Door (Hatchback and Van models) - dismantling and reassembly

Dismantling

1 Remove the trim panel, as described in Section 11.

Window regulator

2 To remove the window regulator, unscrew the mounting nuts, slide the two lifting arms from the channels, and withdraw the regulator through the access aperture **(see illustrations)**. Support the glass during this operation.

Door lock

3 To remove the door lock and inner remote handle, disconnect the link rods as necessary and, unscrew the Torx screws retaining the lock **(see illustrations)**.

Exterior handle

4 To remove the exterior handle, disconnect the link rod and unscrew the bolts. The private lock is removed by disconnecting the link rod and pulling out the retaining clip **(see illustration)**.

Door glass

5 To remove the door glass, first remove the window regulator then unbolt the glass side channels, tilt the glass and withdraw it upwards.

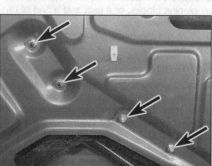

12.2a Window regulator mounting nuts (arrowed)

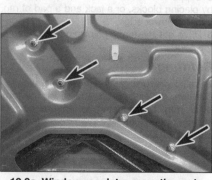

12.2b The window regulator lifting arms and window glass channel

12.3a Door lock and mounting screws

12.3b Door inner remote handle

12.4 Pull out the retaining clip to remove the private lock

12.6a On early models, remove the inner cover . . .

12.6b . . . and remove the exterior mirror mounting screws

Exterior mirror (early models)

6 To remove the early type mirror, prise off the inner cover and use an Allen key to remove the mounting screws **(see illustrations)**.

Exterior mirror (later models)

7 To remove the later type mirror, carefully prise the trim cover from the interior mirror control lever **(see illustration)**.

8 Remove the mounting screws, then feed the rubber grommet through the hole and withdraw the mirror from outside **(see illustration)**.

Reassembly

9 Reassembly of the door is a reversal of the dismantling procedure. However, when refitting the door glass, adjust the position of the side channels so that the glass moves smoothly without excessive play.

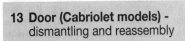

13 Door (Cabriolet models) - dismantling and reassembly

Dismantling

Note: *Refer to Section 12 for door lock, exterior handle and exterior mirror dismantling and reassembly procedures.*

12.7 On later models, prise the trim cover from the control lever . . .

Window regulator

1 Remove the trim panel as described in Section 11.

2 Where applicable, disconnect the battery, then disconnect the wiring from the window regulator motor.

3 Unscrew the nuts and withdraw the regulator from the door.

Door glass

4 Remove the regulator then detach the weatherstrips from the top edge of the door.

5 Raise the glass, and lift it from the door.

6 Unscrew the mounting nuts, and remove the fixed quarterlight glass through the sliding glass location.

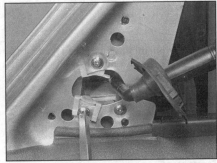

12.8 . . . remove the screws and withdraw the mirror

Reassembly

7 Reassembly is a reversal of dismantling, but carry out the following adjustments. Temporarily refit the window regulator handle, or reconnect the regulator motor wiring, as applicable, then close the window, and if necessary adjust the height of the window by reaching in through the speaker aperture and turning the screw indicated **(see illustration)**. (The illustration shows the regulator part-removed - with the regulator installed, access to the adjustment screw is possible through the speaker aperture.) Close the door, and check that the rear edge of the door glass seals correctly with the hood. If not, remove the cap and turn the screw shown **(see illustration)**.

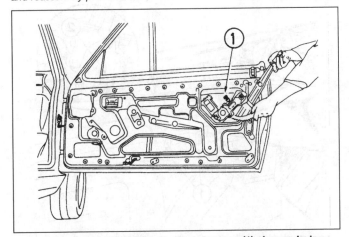

13.7a Door glass height adjustment screw (1) shown during removal of regulator assembly - Cabriolet models

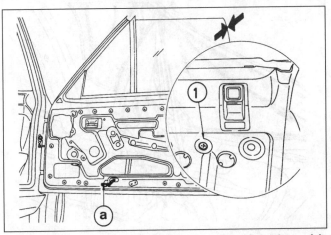

13.7b Door glass rear edge adjustment screw (1) on Cabriolet models
a Switch wiring

11

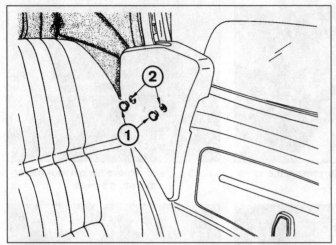

14.2 Prise off the trim caps (1) and unscrew the hinge cover securing screw (2) - Cabriolet models

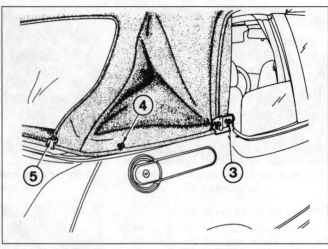

14.3 Hood bracket securing bolt (3) and lower hood securing bolts (4 and 5) - Cabriolet models

14 Hood and rear window (Cabriolet models) - removal and refitting

Removal

1 Open the hood to the point where it is in balance.

2 Working inside the vehicle, prise off the trim caps, and unscrew the hinge cover securing screws **(see illustration)**.

3 Working outside the vehicle, unscrew the brackets and securing bolts **(see illustration)**.

4 Fold down the rear seats and remove the parcel shelf, then slide off the retaining strips and unclip the edges of the hood lining.

5 Release the three press-studs, prise off the rear hood crossmember trim strip, then extract the crossmember securing screws and withdraw the crossmember.

6 Unzip the rear window, and release the

Velcro securing strips from the hood, then withdraw the window from outside the vehicle.

7 Unclip the tensioners, then remove the indicated bracket securing bolts **(see illustration)**.

8 Fold the hood down, remove the remaining hood frame securing bolts, then lift the frame from the vehicle.

Refitting

9 Place the hood in its compartment, and refit the lower frame securing bolts **(see illustration)**. Do not tighten the screws at this stage.

10 Partially unfold the hood, then loosely refit the bracket securing bolts. **Note:** *Ensure that the brackets are not lodged in the hinges, which may cause scratching of the paint on the rear wings.*

11 Fully unfold the hood, and check that the hooks at the front corners of the hood line up with their strikers. If the hooks and strikers are

not aligned, move the hood support brackets (the securing bolt holes are elongated) until satisfactory alignment is obtained.

12 Open and close the hood a number of times to ensure that it operates correctly, then tighten the lower frame securing bolts.

13 The effort required to operate the handle can be adjusted by loosening the locknuts and adjusting the length of the hooks.

14 Partially fold the hood, and refit the rear window and the hood rear crossmember and trim strip.

15 Clip the tensioners to their lugs, then refit the bracket securing bolts.

16 Fold the hood completely flat, and check that the stops are in contact with the rear stretcher. If adjustment is required, loosen the locknuts and adjust the length of the stops as necessary.

17 Partially raise the hood, then clip the edges of the hood lining in place, and refit the retaining strips.

18 Clip the hood lining side strips in place.

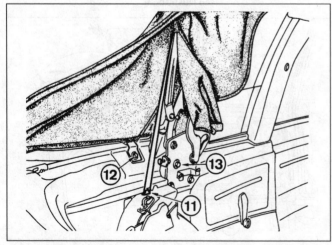

14.7 Unclip the tensioners (11) and remove the bracket securing bolts (12 and 13) - Cabriolet models

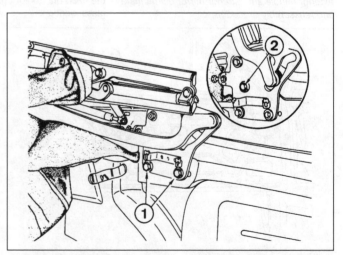

14.9 Refit and lower the frame securing bolts (1), then partially unfold the hood and loosely refit the bolts (2) - Cabriolet models

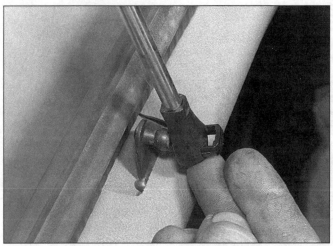

16.2 Disconnecting the tailgate struts

16.4 Tailgate mounting nuts behind the headlining

15 Power-operated hood components (Cabriolet models) - general information

Whenever any work is carried out which involves disconnecting the hood hydraulic fluid pipes, the hydraulic fluid circuit must be bled. At the time of writing, little information was available regarding this procedure, and it is recommended that the task is entrusted to a Peugeot dealer.

16 Tailgate - removal and refitting

Removal

1 Open the tailgate and have an assistant support it.
2 Disconnect the struts from the body by prising out the plastic clips and pulling off the sockets (see illustration).
3 Disconnect the wiring for the heated rear window and tailgate wiper motor. Also disconnect the washer tube.
4 Prise the blanking plates from the rear of the headlining, then unscrew the mounting nuts and lift the tailgate from the car (see illustration).

Refitting

5 Refitting is a reversal of removal, but before fully tightening the mounting nuts check that the tailgate is positioned centrally in the body aperture and make any adjustments to the lock and striker, as described in Section 17.

17 Tailgate lock - removal and refitting

Removal

1 Open the tailgate and prise off the trim panel using a wide-bladed screwdriver (see illustration).
2 Unbolt the latch and disconnect the operating rod.
3 Slide out the spring clip and withdraw the lock barrel and escutcheon (see illustration).

Refitting

4 Refitting is a reversal of removal. Check that the latch engages the striker correctly and, if necessary, adjust the striker position within the elongated bolt holes. Adjust the rubber stops so that the tailgate is supported firmly at the corners when shut.

18 Windscreen and tailgate glass - general information

Both the windscreen and tailgate glass are bonded in position and therefore it is recommended that a professional fitter is employed in the event of breakage. Special equipment and adhesive are required for removal of the old glass and fitting of the new, which may not be readily available to the home mechanic.

19 Rear quarter glass (GTI models) - removal and refitting

Removal

1 Open the quarter window and remove the screw securing the glass to the latch. Remove the special nut from the glass.
2 Open the window further then support it and remove the screws securing the glass to the front hinges. Remove the special nuts.

Refitting

3 Refitting is a reversal of removal.

20 Rear quarter glass and regulator (Cabriolet models) - removal and refitting

Removal

1 Fold down the front and rear seats, then open the hood a little way.
2 Fully close the quarter glass.
3 Unbolt the seat belt lower anchor.
4 Note the position of the regulator handle, then remove it by easing it off from behind using pliers, or an alternative similar tool.
5 Using a wide-bladed screwdriver, release the plastic clips and withdraw the trim panel.
6 Pull off the polythene sheet.

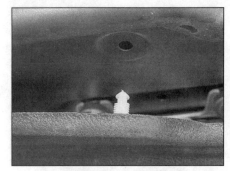

17.1 Tailgate trim panel clip

17.3 Tailgate lock and lock barrel

11

7 Unscrew the five bolts securing the regulator mechanism.

8 Remove the casing from the hood hinge.

9 Remove the pad from the quarter glass lower channel.

10 Push in the regulator mechanism, then tilt it and withdraw it through the aperture, complete with the cable **(see illustration)**. Take care not to damage the seat belt reel.

11 Remove the inner quarter glass weatherstrip and clips.

12 Push the plastic rivet centre pins and remove the stretcher support.

13 Lift the glass and remove it.

Refitting

14 Refitting is a reversal of removal. If a new glass is being fitted, position the lower channel as shown **(see illustration)**. Remove the guide pads from the old glass by drilling out the rivet heads. Fit them to the new glass using the special sleeves and screws obtainable from a Peugeot dealer **(see illustration)**. Apply a little locking fluid to the screw threads before inserting and tightening them. Unlike the door glass, there are no adjustment points.

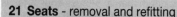
21 Seats - removal and refitting

Removal

Front seat

1 Move the seat fully forward and remove the rear inner mounting bolts **(see illustration)**.

2 Remove the remaining mounting bolts from under the car and from the brackets, then remove the seat from the car.

Rear seat

3 Fold the cushion forwards and unbolt it from the hinges **(see illustration)**.

4 Fold the backrest down, unscrew the nuts from the outer pivot bracket(s) and withdraw the backrest from the inner pivot (where applicable).

Refitting

5 Refitting the front and rear seats is a reversal of removal.

22 Grab handles - removal and refitting

Removal

1 Prise up the cover plates for access to the screws at each end.

2 Remove the screws and the grab handles.

Refitting

3 Refitting is a reversal of removal.

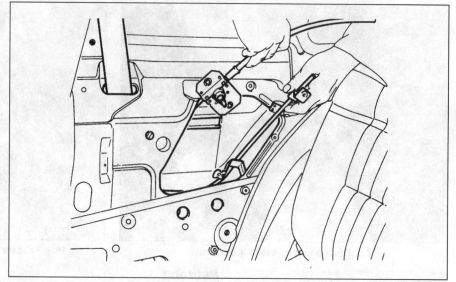

20.10 Removing the rear quarterlight glass regulator mechanism on Cabriolet models

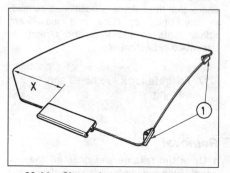

20.14a Channel position on the rear quarterlight glass - Cabriolet models

x = 145.0 mm   *1   Guide pads*

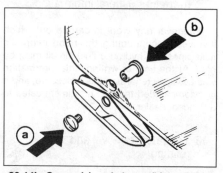

20.14b Screw (a) and sleeve (b) for fitting the guide pads to the rear quarterlight glass on Cabriolet models

23 Sunroof - general information

The sunroof fitted to some models incorporates an outer glass and inner cover. The control handle operates lock latches located at the rear of the sunroof. The handle also operates a vacuum seal system which holds and seals the sunroof in any desired position.

The vacuum seal is operated by engine vacuum. With the handle shut, the vacuum valve is closed and the seal exerts pressure under the periphery of the glass. When the handle is opened, the vacuum valve opens and causes the seal to collapse, enabling the glass to be moved.

21.1 Front seat rear inner mounting bolts

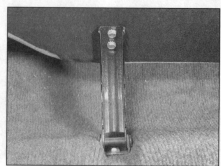

21.3 Rear seat cushion hinge

26.4 Removing the central air vents

26.5 Digital clock and retaining barbs (arrowed)

26.6 Removing the rear of the oddments tray

24 Sunroof glass - removal and refitting

Removal

1 Working inside the car, remove the roof console. Then remove the screws from the sunroof handle and latch.
2 From outside the car, remove the front cover and the corner screws.
3 Slide off the side covers to the rear, while exerting outward pressure.
4 Remove the rear stops, then withdraw the sunroof rearwards. Take care not to damage the top edge of the tailgate.

Refitting

5 Refitting is a reversal of removal, but lightly grease the guide channels. Should resonance

be a problem when the sunroof is open, a modified rubber seal or a wind deflector is available to eliminate the trouble.

25 Glovebox - removal and refitting

Removal

1 Open the glovebox.
2 Remove the pivot retainers from under the facia, disconnect the pivots from the hinge plates and withdraw the glovebox.
3 If necessary the striker can be unbolted and removed.

Refitting

4 Refitting is a reversal of removal.

26 Facia panel - removal and refitting

Removal

Pre-1988 models

1 Disconnect the battery negative lead then remove the steering wheel (Chapter 10) and instrument panel (Chapter 12).
2 Remove the screws and withdraw the steering column lower shroud.
3 Remove the ashtray.
4 Prise out the central air vents (see illustration).
5 Prise out the digital clock which is retained by plastic barbs (see illustration).
6 Using a hooked instrument, withdraw the rear of the oddments recess (see illustration).
7 Remove the radio, as described in Chapter 12, or prise out the blank (as required).
8 Remove the gear lever surround and centre console, noting that the console is held at the top by plastic clips (see illustration).
9 Remove the screw from inside the ashtray recess (see illustration).
10 Unscrew the facia bottom mounting bolts including the one on the bonnet release handle (see illustration).
11 With the glovebox open, remove the mounting screw located near the glovebox lamp (see illustration).
12 Remove the central lower panels (see illustration).

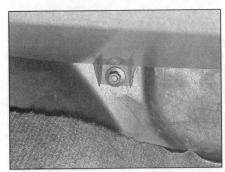

26.8 Centre console upper clip (arrowed)

26.9 Facia mounting screw located in the ashtray recess (arrowed)

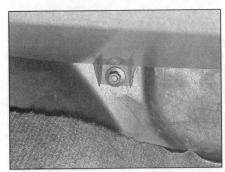

26.10 A facia bottom mounting bolt

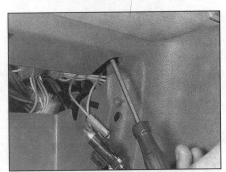

26.11 Removing a facia mounting screw

26.12 Facia central lower panels and bracket

11

26.13 Facia front mounting nut

26.16 Removing a right-hand lower facia panel securing screw

26.19a Prise out the coin box . . .

13 With the bonnet open, remove the plastic grille and unscrew the front facia mounting nuts **(see illustration)**.

14 Withdraw the facia panel at the same time disconnecting the relevant switches and cigar lighter. Reconnect the switch wiring immediately to ensure correct refitting.

1988 models onward

15 Disconnect the battery negative lead.

16 Remove the screws and withdraw the right-hand lower facia panel **(see illustration)**.

17 Prise out the instrument panel rheostat, and disconnect the wires.

18 Remove the screws and withdraw the lower steering column shroud.

19 Prise out the coin box and the triangular cover **(see illustrations)**.

20 Pull off the heater control knobs.

21 Remove the screws in the outer control knob apertures and withdraw the heater control surround **(see illustration)**.

22 Remove the screws and withdraw the central vent assembly **(see illustrations)**.

23 Remove the radio (Chapter 12) or oddments compartment, as applicable.

24 Remove the screws and withdraw the trim quadrants from each side of the facia.

25 Remove the ashtray and disconnect the wiring from the cigar lighter **(see illustration)**. Identify the wiring.

26 Unclip the clock surround **(see illustration)**.

27 Insert lengths of welding rod, or similar, into the holes at the top of the switch surround to release the upper clips, then undo the lower screws and remove the surround **(see illustrations)**.

28 Prise the steering column grommet from the floorpan.

29 Unscrew the mounting nuts and lower the steering column to the floor **(see illustration)**.

30 Prise the small vents from each side of the centre console.

31 Pull back the carpet and remove the screws **(see illustration)**.

26.19b . . . and triangular cover

26.21 . . . Withdraw the heater control surround

26.22a Removing the central vent assembly upper . . .

26.22b . . . and lower screws

26.25 Removing the ashtray

26.26 Removing the clock surround

26.27a Method of releasing the switch surround upper clips

26.27b Remove the lower screws and withdraw the surround

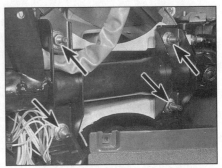

26.29 Steering column mounting nuts (arrowed)

32 Prise the small tray from the centre console **(see illustration)**.

33 Remove the screws, and slide the surround up the gear lever **(see illustration)**.

34 Remove the upper and lower nuts, and withdraw the centre console **(see illustrations)**.

35 Unclip the felt cover from under the facia.

36 Remove the screws and withdraw the front facia panel. Disconnect the wiring from the switches **(see illustration)**.

37 Remove the heater control panel retaining screws.

38 If necessary, remove the side vents.

39 Remove the instrument panel (Chapter 12)

and choke cable, where applicable (Chapter 4A).

40 Remove the left lower facia mounting screw.

41 Unclip the glovebox and remove the lighting switch. Also remove the light.

42 Remove the remaining mounting screws and nuts, and withdraw the facia sufficiently to disconnect the wiring. Access to the front mounting nuts is gained by removing the wiper arms and the plastic guard from the plenum chamber in the engine compartment. Identify each wire for location.

43 Unclip the fuse and relay panel, and withdraw the facia panel from the car.

Refitting

All models

44 Refitting is a reversal of removal, but on completion check the operation of all electrical components.

26.31 Prise out the console vent and remove the screw

26.32 Removing the centre console tray

26.33 Remove the screws and slide the surround up the gear lever

26.34a Removing the centre console upper nuts . . .

26.34b . . . and lower nut

26.36 Front facia panel screws (arrowed)

11

Chapter 12
Body electrical system

Contents

Degrees of difficulty

Easy, suitable for novice with little experience	**Fairly easy,** suitable for beginner with some experience	**Fairly difficult,** suitable for competent DIY mechanic	**Difficult,** suitable for experienced DIY mechanic	**Very difficult,** suitable for expert DIY or professional

Specifications

General

System type . . . . 12-volt negative earth

Fuses (early models)

No	Circuit protected	Rating (amp)
1	Reverse light, cooling fan relay, tachometer (GTI)	10
2	Accessories, indicators, fuel gauge, warning lights, heater blower motor	25
3	Ignition switch, wash/wipe system, stop-lights, tachometer (non-GTI option), radio, heated rear window, electric window relay (option), clock illumination (GTI).	25
4	Central door locking (option)	10
5	Cooling fan	25
6	Hazard warning switch	10
7	Spare	-
8	Cigarette lighter, clock, interior lights, glovebox illumination, radio . .	20
9	Electric front windows	25
10	Heated rear window, horns	20
11	Rear foglight	5
12	Side/tail lights/warning light, instrument panel illumination, number plate lights	5
13	(In-line) fuel pump (GTI)	25

Fuses (1986 to 1988 GTI and CTI models)

No	Circuit protected	Rating (amp)
1	Reversing lights, tachometer	10
2	Direction indicators, heater blower motor, oil pressure gauge, oil temperature gauge, heated seats, fuel gauge, coolant temperature gauge, low battery charge warning, oil pressure warning, brake system warning, coolant temperature warning, low coolant level warning	25
3	Windscreen wiper/washer, stop-lights, headlight washer, radio, accessories	25
4	Spare	-
5	Hazard warning	10
6	Spare	-
7	Cigarette lighter, clock, interior lights, boot light, central door locking, radio	25
8	Horns	25
9	Electrically-operated windows	20
10	Rear foglight	5
11	Tail light (RH), number plate light	5
12	Tail light (LH)	5
13	Instrument panel illumination, side lights	5
14	Fuel pump	15

Fuses (1988 to 1989 models, except GTI and CTI)

No	Circuit protected	Rating (amp)
1	Reversing lights	10
2	Direction indicators, heater blower motor, ignition warning light	25
3	Fuel gauge, stop-lights, front and rear wash/wipe, tachometer, headlight wash, radio, storage tray light, warning lights (coolant temperature, oil pressure, coolant level, handbrake, choke)	25
4	Spare	-
5	Hazard warning	10
6	Spare	-
7	Cigarette lighter, clock, interior lights, boot light, central door locking, radio	25
8	Horns, heated rear window	25
9	Electrically-operated windows	20
10	Rear fog light	5
11	Tail lights, number plate light	5
12	Spare	-
13	Instrument panel illumination, side lights	5
14	Fuel pump	15

Fuses (1988 to 1989 GTI and CTI models)

No	Circuit protected	Rating (amp)
1	Reversing lights, tachometer	10
2	Direction indicators, heater blower motor, oil pressure gauge, oil temperature gauge, heated seats, fuel gauge, coolant temperature gauge, low battery charge warning, oil pressure warning, brake system warning, coolant temperature warning, low coolant level warning	25
3	Front and rear wash/wipe, stop-lights, headlight washer, radio, accessories, storage tray light, map reading light	25
4	Spare	-
5	Hazard warning	10
6	Spare	-
7	Cigarette lighter, clock, interior lights, boot light, central door locking, radio	20
8	Horns, heated rear window	25
9	Electrically-operated windows	20
10	Rear foglight	5
11	Tail light, number plate light	5
12	Spare	5
13	Instrument panel illumination, side lights	5
14	Fuel pump	15

Fuses (1989 to 1991 - all models)

No	Circuit protected	Rating (amp)
1	Reversing lights, tachometer, fuel gauge, warning lights (low battery charge, coolant temperature, oil pressure, low coolant level, brake system, choke)	10
2	Direction indicators, gauges (fuel, oil temperature, ... coolant temperature, oil pressure), heater blower . . .motor, warning lights (low battery charge, coolant temperature, oil pressure, low coolant level, brake system, choke)	25
3	Map reading light, stop-lights, windscreen and tailgate wash/wipe, tachometer, radio, glovebox light, electric windows, heated rear window	25
4	Driving lights	15
5	Hazard warning lights	10
6	Spare	-
7	Cigarette lighter, clock, interior lights, luggage compartment light, central locking, radio, power feed to tow bar	25
8	Horn, heated rear window	25
9	Electric windows	20
10	Rear fog light	5
11	Tail lights, number plate lights	5
12	Spare	-
13	Instrument panel illumination, side lights	5
14	Electric fuel pump	15

Fuses (1991 models onward)

No	Circuit protected	Rating (amp)
1	Reversing lights, tachometer, fuel gauge, warning lights (low battery charge, coolant temperature, oil pressure, low coolant level, brake system, choke)	10
2	Direction indicators, gauges (fuel, oil temperature, coolant temperature, oil pressure), heater blower motor, warning lights (low battery charge, coolant temperature, oil pressure, low coolant level, brake system, choke, ABS)	25
3	Map reading light, stop-lights, windscreen and tailgate wash/wipe, tachometer, radio, glovebox light, heated rear window	25
4	Driving lights	15
5	Hazard warning lights	10
6	Spare	-
7	Clock, interior lights, luggage compartment light, central locking, radio, power feed to tow bar	25
8	Horn, heated rear window, cigarette lighter	30
9	Electric windows	20
10	Rear fog lights	5
11	Tail lights	5
12	Spare	-
13	Instrument panel illumination, side lights	5
14	Electric fuel pump	15

Fuses in engine compartment

Circuit protected	Rating (amp)
ABS	30
Power supply to ABS electronic control unit	15
Cooling fan	30
Oxygen sensor	10

Bulbs

	Wattage
Headlights:	
Non-GTI	45/40
GTI	H4 (60/55)
Front parking lights	5
Direction indicator lights	21
Front driving light (GTI)	H3 (55)
Tail/stop-lights	5/21
Reverse light	21
Rear foglights	21
Interior light	5
Number plate lights	5

12

1 General information and precautions

General information

The electrical system is of 12-volt negative earth type. Power for the lights and all electrical accessories is supplied by a lead/acid battery which is charged by the alternator.

This Chapter covers repair and service procedures for the various electrical components and systems generally not associated with the engine. Information on the battery, ignition system, alternator, and starter motor can be found in the relevant Parts of Chapter 5.

Precautions

Warning: Before carrying out any work on the electrical system, read through the precautions given in "Safety first!" at the beginning of this manual and in Chapter 5.
Caution: Prior to working on any component in the electrical system, the battery negative lead should first be disconnected, to prevent the possibility of electrical short-circuits and/or fires. If a radio/cassette player with anti-theft security code is fitted, refer to the information given in the reference sections of this manual before disconnecting the battery.

2 Electrical fault finding - general information

Note: *Refer to the precautions given in "Safety first!" and in Section 1 of this Chapter before starting work. The following tests relate to testing of the main electrical circuits, and should not be used to test delicate electronic circuits, particularly where an electronic control unit is used.*

General

1 A typical electrical circuit consists of an electrical component, any switches, relays, motors, fuses, fusible links or circuit breakers related to that component, and the wiring and connectors which link the component to both the battery and the chassis. To help to pinpoint a problem in an electrical circuit, wiring diagrams are included at the end of this manual.
2 Before attempting to diagnose an electrical fault, first study the appropriate wiring diagram, to obtain a complete understanding of the components included in the particular circuit concerned. The possible sources of a fault can be narrowed down by noting if other components related to the circuit are operating properly. If several components or

circuits fail at one time, the problem is likely to be related to a shared fuse or earth connection.
3 Electrical problems usually stem from simple causes, such as loose or corroded connections, a faulty earth connection, a blown fuse, a melted fusible link, or a faulty relay. Visually inspect the condition of all fuses, wires and connections in a problem circuit before testing the components. Use the wiring diagrams to determine which terminal connections will need to be checked in order to pinpoint the trouble-spot.
4 The basic tools required for electrical fault-finding include a circuit tester or voltmeter (a 12-volt bulb with a set of test leads can also be used for certain tests); an ohmmeter (to measure resistance and check for continuity); a battery and set of test leads; and a jumper wire, preferably with a circuit breaker or fuse incorporated, which can be used to bypass suspect wires or electrical components. Before attempting to locate a problem with test instruments, use the wiring diagram to determine where to make the connections.
5 To find the source of an intermittent wiring fault (usually due to a poor or dirty connection, or damaged wiring insulation), a "wiggle" test can be performed on the wiring. This involves wiggling the wiring by hand to see if the fault occurs as the wiring is moved. It should be possible to narrow down the source of the fault to a particular section of wiring. This method of testing can be used in conjunction with any of the tests described in the following sub-Sections.
6 Apart from problems due to poor connections, two basic types of fault can occur in an electrical circuit - open-circuit, or short-circuit.
7 Open-circuit faults are caused by a break somewhere in the circuit, which prevents current from flowing. An open-circuit fault will prevent a component from working.
8 Short-circuit faults are caused by a "short" somewhere in the circuit, which allows the current flowing in the circuit to "escape" along an alternative route, usually to earth. Short-circuit faults are normally caused by a breakdown in wiring insulation, which allows a feed wire to touch either another wire, or an earthed component such as the bodyshell. A short-circuit fault will normally cause the relevant circuit fuse to blow.

Finding an open-circuit

9 To check for an open-circuit, connect one lead of a circuit tester or the negative lead of a voltmeter either to the battery negative terminal or to a known good earth.
10 Connect the other lead to a connector in the circuit being tested, preferably nearest the battery or fuse. At this point, battery voltage should be present, unless the lead from the battery or the fuse itself is faulty (bearing in mind that some circuits are live only when the ignition switch is moved to a particular position).

11 Switch on the circuit, then connect the tester lead to the connector nearest the circuit switch on the component side.
12 If voltage is present (indicated either by the tester bulb lighting or a voltmeter reading, as applicable), this means that the section of the circuit between the relevant connector and the switch is problem-free.
13 Continue to check the remainder of the circuit in the same fashion.
14 When a point is reached at which no voltage is present, the problem must lie between that point and the previous test point with voltage. Most problems can be traced to a broken, corroded or loose connection.

Finding a short-circuit

15 To check for a short-circuit, first disconnect the load(s) from the circuit (loads are the components which draw current from a circuit, such as bulbs, motors, heating elements, etc).
16 Remove the relevant fuse from the circuit, and connect a circuit tester or voltmeter to the fuse connections.
17 Switch on the circuit, bearing in mind that some circuits are live only when the ignition switch is moved to a particular position.
18 If voltage is present (indicated either by the tester bulb lighting or a voltmeter reading, as applicable), this means that there is a short-circuit.
19 If no voltage is present during this test, but the fuse still blows with the load(s) reconnected, this indicates an internal fault in the load(s).

Finding an earth fault

20 The battery negative terminal is connected to "earth" - the metal of the engine/transmission and the vehicle body - and many systems are wired so that they only receive a positive feed, the current returning via the metal of the car body. This means that the component mounting and the body form part of that circuit. Loose or corroded mountings can therefore cause a range of electrical faults, ranging from total failure of a circuit, to a puzzling partial failure. In particular, lights may shine dimly (especially when another circuit sharing the same earth point is in operation), motors (eg wiper motors or the radiator cooling fan motor) may run slowly, and the operation of one circuit may have an apparently-unrelated effect on another. Note that on many vehicles, earth straps are used between certain components, such as the engine/transmission and the body, usually where there is no metal-to-metal contact between components, due to flexible rubber mountings, etc.
21 To check whether a component is properly earthed, disconnect the battery and connect one lead of an ohmmeter to a known good earth point. Connect the other lead to the wire or earth connection being tested. The resistance reading should be zero; if not, check the connection as follows.

3.4 Removing a fuse

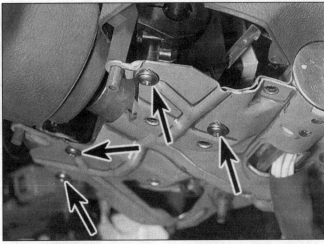

4.4 Combination switch screws (arrowed)

22 If an earth connection is thought to be faulty, dismantle the connection, and clean both the bodyshell and the wire terminal (or the component earth connection mating surface) back to bare metal. Be careful to remove all traces of dirt and corrosion, then use a knife to trim away any paint, so that a clean metal-to-metal joint is made. On reassembly, tighten the joint fasteners securely; if a wire terminal is being refitted, use serrated washers between the terminal and the bodyshell, to ensure a clean and secure connection. When the connection is remade, prevent the onset of corrosion in the future by applying a coat of petroleum jelly or silicone-based grease, or by spraying on (at regular intervals) a proprietary ignition sealer, or a water-dispersant lubricant.

3 Fuses and relays - general information

Fuses

1 The fuse board is located above the glovebox on the left-hand side of the facia.
2 Blade type fuses are used and symbols by the fuses denote the circuit protected.
3 On GTI models an in-line fuse for the fuel pump is located near the rear of the fuse board. The fuse board also incorporates a connector which can be adjusted to supply the radio with negative or positive current according to the polarity of the radio fitted. On later models, additional fuses are located behind the left-hand side of the radiator, on the left-hand side of the bulkhead, and near the horn on 1.9 GTI models.
4 To remove a fuse, first switch off the ignition then open the glovebox. Depress the spring clip and lower the fuse board. Pull the fuse out of its terminals; the wire within the fuse should be visible; if the fuse is blown the wire will be broken or melted (**see illustration**).

5 Always renew a fuse with one of an identical rating; never use a fuse with a different rating from the original or substitute anything else. Never renew a fuse more than once without tracing the source of the trouble. The fuse rating is stamped on top of the fuse; note that fuses are also colour-coded for easy recognition.
6 Persistent blowing of a particular fuse indicates a fault in the circuit(s) protected. Where more than one circuit is involved, switch on one item at a time until the fuse blows, so showing in which circuit the fault lies.
7 Besides a fault in the electrical component concerned, a blown fuse can also be caused by a short-circuit in the wiring to the component. Look for trapped or frayed wires allowing a live wire to touch vehicle metal, and for loose or damaged connectors.
8 The fuse board is retained at the rear by two plastic ball and socket joints which can be snapped apart to remove the assembly.

Relays

9 A relay is an electrically-operated switch, which is used for the following reasons:
  a) A relay can switch a heavy current remotely from the circuit in which the current is flowing, allowing the use of lighter gauge wiring and switch contacts.
  b) A relay can receive more than one control input, unlike a mechanical switch.
  c) A relay can have a timer function - for example an intermittent wiper delay.
10 If a circuit which includes a relay develops a fault, remember that the relay itself could be faulty. Testing is by substitution of a known good relay. Do not assume that relays which look similar are necessarily identical for purposes of substitution.
11 Relays are incorporated in most circuits and are mounted on the fuse board or within the engine compartment.

12 Make sure that the ignition is switched off, then pull the relay from its socket. Push the new relay firmly in to refit. Refer to the wiring diagram key for a list of relays.

4 Switches - removal and refitting

Steering column combination switches

1 Disconnect the battery negative lead.
2 Remove the steering wheel and column shrouds, with reference to Chapter 10.
3 Disconnect the wiring harness plug.
4 Remove the relevant screws and withdraw the switch from the column platform (**see illustration**).
5 Refitting is a reversal of removal.

Facia switches (pre-1988 models)

6 Disconnect the battery negative lead.
7 Carefully prise out the switch against the tension of the plastic retaining tabs (**see illustration**).
8 Disconnect the wiring or multi-plug, noting the fitted location, and remove the switch.
9 Refitting is a reversal of removal.

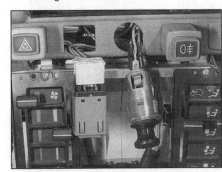

4.7 Heated rear window switch and cigar lighter removed from facia

12

4.13a On later models, remove the switch panel lower screws . . .

4.13b Insert lengths of rod into the special holes . . .

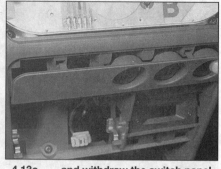

4.13c . . . and withdraw the switch panel surround

Facia switches (1988 models onward)

10 Disconnect the battery negative lead.
11 Open the ashtray.
12 Unclip the bottom of the clock surround (where fitted) and remove it.
13 Remove the screws from the bottom of the switch panel, then insert lengths of welding rod (or similar) into the special holes, and remove the switch panel surround (**see illustrations**).
14 The individual switches may now be removed by inserting two small screwdrivers in the slots on each side of the switch, extracting the switch, and disconnecting the wiring.
15 Refitting is a reversal of removal.

Instrument panel rheostat - removal and refitting

16 Prise the rheostat from the steering column lower shroud, and disconnect the wiring (**see illustration**).
17 Refitting is a reversal of removal.

Reversing light switch - removal and refitting

18 Disconnect the wiring and unscrew the switch from the top or side of the transmission housing (**see illustration**). Remove the washer.
19 Refitting is a reversal of removal, but renew the washer if necessary

Courtesy light switch

20 Disconnect the battery negative lead.

21 The switch is secured to the door pillar by a self-tapping screw. Extract the screw and withdraw the switch and leads (**see illustration**).
22 If the leads are disconnected, tape them to the pillar to prevent them from slipping inside the pillar cavity.
23 It is recommended that the metal contacts of the switch are smeared with petroleum jelly as a precaution against corrosion.
24 Refit by reversing the removal operation.

Glovebox illumination switch

25 Disconnect the battery negative lead.
26 Open the glovebox then reach up and release the switch from the inside of the facia (**see illustration**).
27 Disconnect the wiring.
28 Refitting is a reversal of removal.

Ignition switch/steering column lock

29 Refer to Chapter 10.

Handbrake warning switch

30 Move the front seats fully forward then remove the screw and lift the cover from the handbrake lever.
31 With the handbrake applied, remove the mounting screw, withdraw the switch and disconnect the wiring (**see illustration**).
32 Refitting is a reversal of removal.

Brake stop light switch

33 Disconnect the battery negative lead.
34 Remove the lower facia panel from the steering column.
35 Disconnect the two wires (**see illustration**).

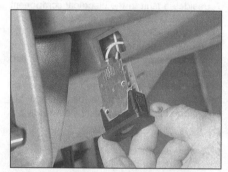

4.16 Instrument illumination rheostat

4.18 Reversing light switch location on the BH3 transmission

4.21 Removing a courtesy light switch

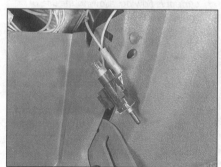

4.26 Glovebox illumination switch

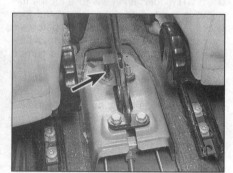

4.31 Handbrake warning light switch (arrowed)

4.35 Brake stop light switch wiring connector (arrowed)

36 Unscrew the locknut nearest the pedal, and withdraw the switch from the bracket.

37 Refitting is a reversal of removal, but adjust the locknuts so that the distance between the end of the switch threaded body and the pedal (fully released) is 3.5 mm.

5 Instrument panel - removal and refitting

Removal

Pre-1988 models

1 Disconnect the battery negative lead.

2 On non-GTI models, using an Allen key, unscrew the two upper retaining screws at each end of the panel surround **(see illustration)**.

3 On GTI models, remove the plastic tray from the top of the panel surround by pushing it towards the windscreen to release the securing clips. Unscrew the now-exposed panel surround securing screw.

4 Unscrew the two lower surround retaining screws located either side of the steering column shroud **(see illustration)**.

5 Withdraw the surround from the facia.

6 Pull out the instrument panel while depressing the lower spring supports, then disconnect the multi-plugs and speedometer cable **(see illustrations)**.

7 If necessary, the individual components can be removed for repair or renewal **(see illustrations)**.

1988 models onward

8 Disconnect the battery negative lead.

9 Remove the trapezium-shaped coin compartment or cover from the top of the facia by lifting the bottom edge.

10 Pull off the heater control knobs, using card or thick cloth and pliers on the central bars.

11 Remove the screws beneath the outer control knobs, and withdraw the upper front panel surround.

12 Remove the screws and withdraw the visor trim from the instrument panel.

5.2 Removing the instrument panel upper . . .

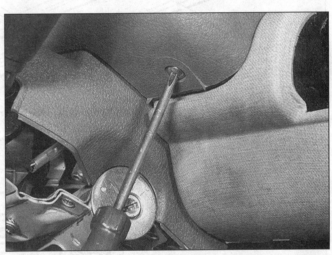

5.4 . . . and lower retaining screws

5.6a Instrument panel spring support

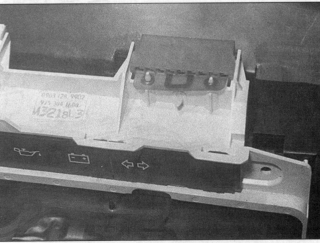

5.6b Instrument panel right-hand upper multiplug

12

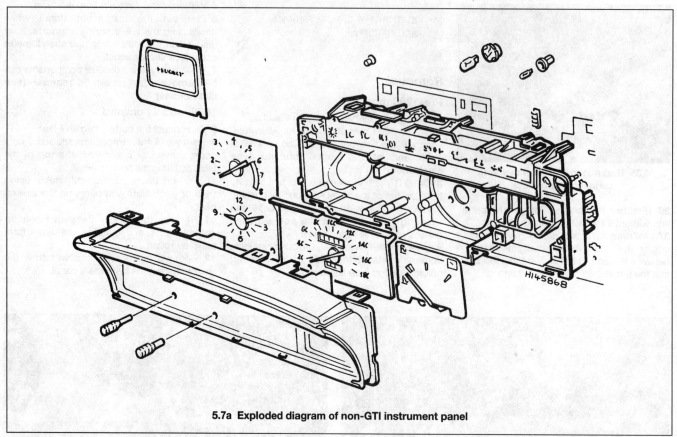

5.7a Exploded diagram of non-GTI instrument panel

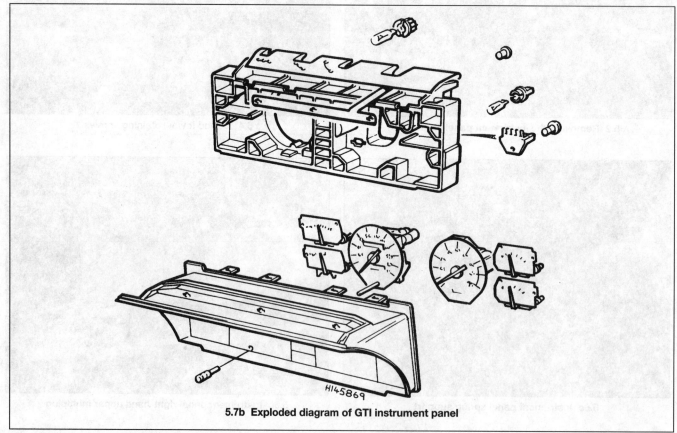

5.7b Exploded diagram of GTI instrument panel

5.16 Removing the instrument panel mounting screws on later models . . .

13 Remove the screws and withdraw the centre vents.

14 Using a screwdriver through the steering column lower shroud, unscrew the visor locating studs.

15 Remove the side screw, then lift away the visor.

16 Remove the mounting screws from each side of the instrument panel **(see illustration)**.

17 Tilt the instrument panel and disconnect the wiring plugs, noting their locations **(see illustration)**.

18 Disconnect the speedometer cable by squeezing the end fitting. Remove the instrument panel. If necessary, the individual components can be removed for repair or renewal.

Refitting

19 On all models, refitting is a reversal of removal.

7.3a Speedometer cable end with instrument panel removed

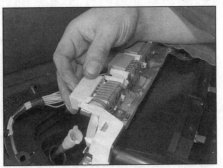

5.17 . . . and disconnecting the wiring plugs

6 Clock - removal and refitting

Removal

Pre-1988 models

1 Disconnect the battery negative lead.

2 Using a small screwdriver, carefully prise the clock from its location in the facia.

3 Disconnect the clock wiring and remove the unit.

1988 models onward

4 Disconnect the battery negative lead.

5 Remove the trapezium-shaped coin compartment or cover from the top of the facia by lifting the bottom edge.

6 Pull off the heater control knobs, using card or thick cloth and pliers on the central bars.

7 Remove the screws beneath the control knobs, and withdraw the upper front panel surround.

8 Open and remove the ashtray.

9 Unclip the bottom of the clock surround and remove it.

10 Remove the oddments tray, or if fitted, the radio, as described in Section 22.

11 Remove the screws and withdraw the lower front panel surround by releasing the bottom edge first.

12 Disconnect the wiring plug from the rear of the clock, then release the clock from the lower front panel surround.

Refitting

13 On all models, refitting is a reversal of removal.

7 Speedometer cable - renewal

1 Disconnect the speedometer cable from the transmission by removing the retaining bolt or rubber plug.

2 Remove the instrument panel, as described in Section 5.

3 Prise the rubber grommet from the bulkhead beneath the facia **(see illustrations)**.

4 Remove the retaining clips, where fitted, and withdraw the speedometer cable.

5 Refitting is a reversal of removal.

8 Bulbs (exterior lights) - renewal

General

1 With all light bulbs, remember that if they have just been in use, they may be very hot. Switch off the power before renewing a bulb.

2 With quartz halogen bulbs (headlights and similar applications), use a tissue or clean cloth when handling the bulb; do not touch the bulb glass with the fingers. Even small quantities of grease from the fingers will cause blackening and premature failure. If a bulb is accidentally touched, clean it with methylated spirit and a clean rag.

3 Unless otherwise stated, fit the new bulb by reversing the removal operations.

Bulb renewal

Headlight

4 Where fitted, remove the cover from the rear of the headlight.

5 Pull the connector from the bulb **(see illustration)**.

6 Remove the rubber cover, noting that the water drain hole is at the bottom **(see illustration)**.

7.3b Speedometer cable grommet on the bulkhead

8.5 Pull off the connector . . .

8.6 . . . remove the rubber cover . . .

12

8.7a . . . release the spring clips . . .

8.7b . . . and withdraw the headlight bulb

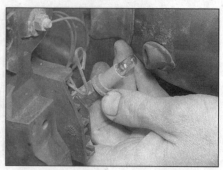

8.9 Removing the front parking light bulbholder

7 Release the spring clips and withdraw the bulb **(see illustrations)**.

8 Fit the new bulb with the locating tab uppermost.

Front parking lights

9 Pull the bulbholder from the rear of the headlight then depress and twist the bulb to remove it **(see illustration)**.

Front direction indicator

10 Turn the bulbholder anti-clockwise and withdraw it from the rear of the light **(see illustration)**.

11 Depress and twist the bulb to remove it **(see illustration)**.

Front direction indicator side repeater

12 On early models, reach up behind the front wing, squeeze the plastic tabs together and push out the light. On later models, turn the light anti-clockwise and withdraw it from the front wing **(see illustration)**.

13 Disconnect the wiring, remove the end cap, and extract the bulb:

14 When refitting the early type, position the

light so that the location peg enters the hole in the front wing.

Front driving light (GTI models)

15 Remove the two lens surround retaining screws and withdraw the surround, lens and reflector **(see illustration)**.

16 Release the spring clips and remove the bulb assembly **(see illustration)**.

17 Detach the bulb feed wire at the connector.

Rear light cluster bulbs

18 Remove the lens upper retaining screws then tilt the lens back and release it from the lower tabs **(see illustrations)**.

19 Depress and twist the bulb to remove it **(see illustration)**.

Rear foglight

20 Remove the screws and withdraw the lens **(see illustration)**.

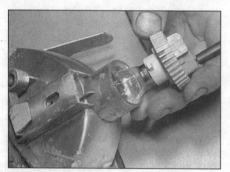

8.10 Remove the front direction indicator light bulbholder . . .

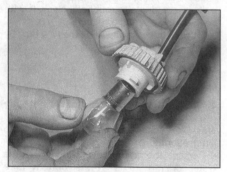

8.11 . . . and extract the bulb

8.12 Removing the front direction indicator side repeater on later models

8.15 On GTI models, remove the driving light lens surround, lens and reflector . . .

8.16 . . . then release the spring clips and remove the bulb assembly

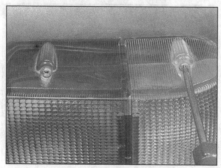

8.18a Remove the rear light cluster screws . . .

8.18b . . . and release the lens from the tabs

8.19 Removing a rear light cluster bulb

8.20 Remove the rear foglight lens . . .

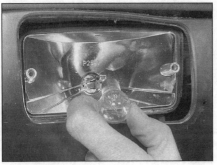

8.21 . . . and extract the bulb

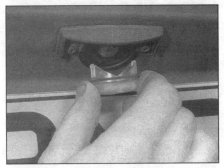

8.22 Remove the rear number plate light lens . . .

8.23 . . . and extract the bulb

21 Depress and twist the bulb to remove it (see illustration).

Number plate light

22 Twist off the lens (see illustration).

9.3 Prise out the interior light for access to the bulb

23 Depress and twist the bulb to remove it (see illustration).

Reversing light (1991 models onward)

24 On later models, a single reversing light is mounted in the rear valance, instead of the twin lights in the rear light clusters fitted to previous models.
25 Bulb renewal is as described previously for the rear foglight bulb.

9 Bulbs (interior lights) - renewal

General

1 See Section 8, paragraphs 1 and 3.
2 Some switch illumination/pilot bulbs are integral with their switches and cannot be renewed separately.

Bulb renewal

Interior light

3 Prise the light from the console (see illustration).
4 Extract the festoon type bulb from within the light unit.

Map reading light

5 Prise the light from the console and extract the festoon type bulb (see illustration).

Instrument panel bulbs

6 Remove the instrument panel, as described in Section 5.
7 Two types of bulb are fitted. Pull out the square type bulbholder and remove the wedge type bulb (see illustration). Twist the round type bulbholder through 90° to remove it, but on this type the bulb cannot be separated from the holder.

Glovebox light

8 On pre-1988 models, remove the switch, with reference to Section 4, then depress and twist the bulb to remove it.
9 On 1988 models onward, open the glovebox and prise out the light. Remove the festoon-type bulb from the terminals.

Clock illumination bulb

10 Remove the clock as described in Section 6.
11 Twist the bulbholder from the rear of the clock, then remove the bulb from the holder (see illustration).

9.5 Removing the map reading light and extract the bulb

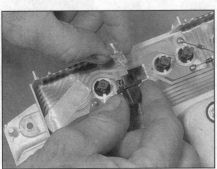

9.7 Removing square type instrument panel bulbholder

9.11 Removing digital clock illumination light bulb

12

9.13 Heater control panel illumination light bulb (arrowed) on early models

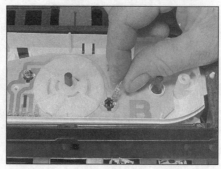

9.18 Removing the heater control panel illumination bulb on later models

Heater control panel illumination bulbs (pre-1988 models)

12 Remove the facia centre air vents, with reference to Chapter 11.
13 Pull the bulbholder from the rear of the panel and extract the bulb **(see illustration)**.

Heater control panel illumination bulbs (1988 models onward)

14 Disconnect the battery negative lead.
15 Remove the trapezium-shaped coin compartment or cover from the top of the facia by lifting the bottom edge.

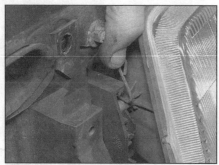

10.3 Releasing the headlight spring clips

16 Pull off the heater control knobs, using card or thick cloth and pliers on the central bars.
17 Remove the screws beneath the control knobs, and withdraw the upper front panel surround.
18 Pull the bulb from the control panel **(see illustration)**.

10 Headlight unit - removal and refitting

Removal

1 Remove the headlight and front parking light bulbs (see Section 8).
2 Remove the front radiator grille as described in Chapter 11.
3 Release the spring clips from the pivot pins on each side of the headlight **(see illustration)**.
4 Press the load level adjustment arm from the lever ball and withdraw the headlight.

Refitting

5 Refitting is a reversal of removal.

11 Front direction indicator light unit - removal and refitting

Removal

1 Remove the headlight, as described in Section 10.
2 Remove the indicator bulb (see Section 8).
3 Remove the screw securing the light to the headlight adjustment assembly and withdraw the light unit **(see illustrations)**.

Refitting

4 Refitting is a reversal of removal.

12 Headlight beam alignment - checking and adjusting

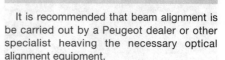

It is recommended that beam alignment is be carried out by a Peugeot dealer or other specialist heaving the necessary optical alignment equipment.

Each headlight incorporates a manual adjustment to compensate for different loads. If this fails to provide the correct beam, emergency adjustment is possible by turning the screw in the top of the manual adjustment for vertical movement, and the knob at the rear of the headlight for horizontal movement.

13 Dim-dip lighting system - general information

All models manufactured from late 1986 are fitted with a dim-dip lighting system, which essentially prevents the vehicle from being driven with the sidelights alone switched on.

11.3a Remove the headlight adjustment assembly screw . . .

11.3b . . . and withdraw the front direction indicator light unit

14.2a Unscrew the nut . . .

14.2b . . . and remove the wiper arm

When the ignition is switched on with the sidelights also switched on, the relay is energised, closing the internal contacts and supplying current to the dipped beam circuit via the resistor. This causes the dip filaments in the headlights to be illuminated at one-sixth dipped beam brightness. The relay winding is earthed through the headlight main beam filaments, so that the relay is de-energised when the main beam is switched on.

14 Wiper arms - removal and refitting

Removal

1 Before removing a wiper arm, stick some masking tape to the screen glass, along the edge of the blade so that its position on the

glass can be restored when the arm is being refitted to its spindle splines.
2 Flip up the plastic cover, unscrew the nut and pull the arm from the spindle **(see illustrations)**.

Refitting

3 Refitting is a reversal of removal, but align the blade with the tape on the glass before pushing the arm home.

15 Windscreen wiper motor and linkage - removal and refitting

Removal

1 Remove the wiper arms, as described in Section 14.
2 Disconnect the battery negative lead.

3 Open the bonnet then remove the air inlet grille by removing the screws and easing the grille from the windscreen weatherstrip **(see illustration)**.
4 Unscrew the nuts from the wiper spindle bodies **(see illustration)**.
5 Disconnect the wiper motor wiring connector.
6 Unscrew the mounting bolt and disengage the wiper motor from the upper location pins.
7 The motor can be separated from the linkage by removing the nut securing the crank to the spindle.

Refitting

8 Refitting is a reversal of removal, but use a screwdriver to lift the weatherstrip as the grille is inserted.

16 Tailgate wiper motor - removal and refitting

Removal

1 Remove the wiper arm, as described in Section 14.
2 Remove the tailgate trim, with reference to Chapter 11.
3 Disconnect the battery negative lead.
4 Disconnect the wiring and the relay wiring connector **(see illustrations)**.
5 Unscrew the spindle nut and remove the spacer and washer.
6 Unscrew the mounting bolts and withdraw the motor assembly, noting the location of the washers and earth wires **(see illustration)**.
7 The relay can be removed by removing the mounting screw.

Refitting

8 Refitting is a reversal of removal.

17 Washer system - general information

The washer fluid reservoir is located in the left-hand front corner of the engine compartment with the bulk of the unit below

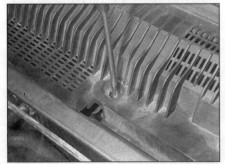

15.3 Removing the air intake grille screws

15.4 Wiper spindle body

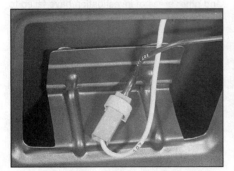

16.4a Tailgate wiper motor wiring connection . . .

16.4b . . . and wiper motor relay

16.6 Tailgate wiper motor and mounting bolts

12

20.3 Horn and mounting nut

22.3 Removing the radio on early models

22.6 Removing the radio side trims on later models

the wheel arch. The reservoir supplies both the windscreen and tailgate jets. On some models a headlight washer system is installed with the reservoir in the right-hand front corner of the engine compartment.

The washer jets are adjustable by inserting a pin into their nozzles and moving them to give an acceptable pattern on the glass.

The use of a good quality screen wash product is recommended. In winter add some methylated spirit to the fluid to prevent freezing. Never use cooling system antifreeze as it will damage the paintwork.

18 Tailgate heated window - general information

Take great care not to scratch the heater elements with carelessly stacked luggage or rings on the fingers.

Avoid sticking labels over the elements, and clean the glass interior surface with warm water and a little detergent, wiping in the same direction as the elements run.

 Small breaks in the heated rear window grid can be repaired using special conductive paint, obtainable from motor accessory shops. Use the paint as directed by the manufacturer.

19 Central door locking system - general information

On models fitted with a central door locking system it is possible to lock all doors, including the tailgate, simply by locking the driver's door.

The system uses electric actuators to move the door lock mechanisms. The actuators can be removed by dismantling the doors, as described in Chapter 11.

20 Horn - removal and refitting

Removal

1 Disconnect the battery negative lead.
2 Remove the relevant headlight, as described in Section 10.
3 Unscrew the mounting nut, remove the horn and disconnect the wiring **(see illustration)**.

Refitting

4 Refitting is a reversal of removal.

21 Air compressor and horn (1.9 GTI models) - removal and refitting

Removal

1 Disconnect the battery negative lead.
2 Remove the left-hand headlight as described in Section 10.
3 Disconnect the air hose and supply wire.
4 Unbolt and remove the compressor or horn as required.

Refitting

5 Refitting is a reversal of removal.

22 Radio - removal and refitting

Removal

Note: *If the radio incorporates an anti-theft system, once the battery has been disconnected, the radio unit cannot be re-activated until the appropriate security code has been entered. Do not remove the unit unless the appropriate code is known.*

Early models

1 A standard radio aperture is provided in the centre console.
2 Disconnect the battery negative lead.
3 Pull off the control knobs and unscrew the mounting nuts. The surround can then be withdrawn and the radio removed after disconnecting the aerial and wiring **(see illustration)**.
4 An in-line fuse is normally fitted to the feed wire behind the radio.

Later models

5 Disconnect the battery negative lead.
6 Remove the radio side trims **(see illustration)**, and insert lengths of welding rod or metal dowel into the exposed holes to release the clips. Special tools are available for this operation from motor accessory shops or Peugeot dealers.
7 Withdraw the radio from the facia, and disconnect the aerial and wiring.

Refitting

8 Refitting is a reversal of removal.

23 Vehicle immobiliser - general information

From 1993, a vehicle immobiliser system is fitted to certain GTI models. The system is activated by locking the car with the PLIP remote control device.

A possible fault with the system should not be overlooked if the car cannot be started, and other areas of investigation have failed to locate the cause. Refer to a Peugeot dealer for additional information.

NOTES:

1. All diagrams are divided into numbered circuits depending on function e.g. Diagram 2: Exterior lighting.
2. Items are arranged in relation to a plan view of the vehicle.
3. Items may appear on more than one diagram so are found using a grid reference e.g. 2/A1 denotes an item on diagram 2 grid location A1.
4. Complex items appear on the diagrams as blocks and are expanded on the internal connections page.
5. Not all items are fitted to all models.
6. For fuse information see specifications.
7. Wire identification is not by colour, but by letters or numbers appearing on the wire at each end.

INTERNAL CONNECTION DETAILS

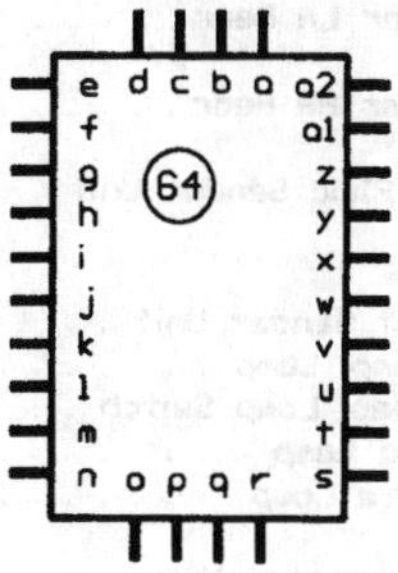

KEY TO SYMBOLS

PLUG-IN CONNECTOR	
EARTH	
BULB	⊗
LINE CONNECTOR	
FUSE/ FUSIBLE LINK	
FUSE/RELAY BOARD CONNECTOR PIN No.	2
EARTH POINT	

P121C

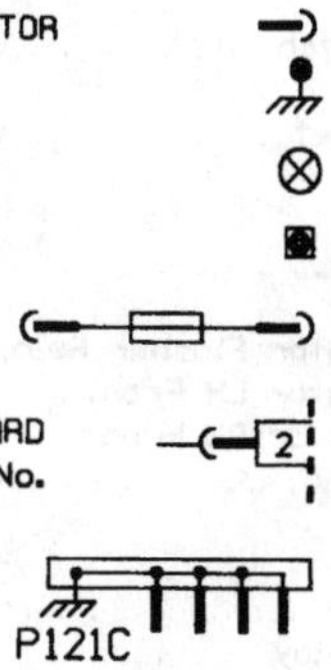

KEY TO INSTRUMENT CLUSTER (ITEM 64)

a = Oil Pressure Warning Lamp
b = Ignition Warning Lamp
c = High Temp. Warning Lamp
d = Brake Warning Lamp
e = Brake Warning Lamp
f = Direction Indicator Lamp
g = Instrument Illumination
h = Earth
i = Main Beam Warning Lamp
j = Dipped Beam Warning Lamp
k = Instrument Illumination
l = Tachometer
m = Clock
n = +VE Supply
o = Choke Warning Lamp
p = Low Fuel Warning Lamp
q = Fuel Gauge
r = Sidelamp Warning Lamp

KEY TO INSTRUMENT CLUSTER (ITEM 64) (ADDITIONAL CONNECTIONS XU/TU MODELS ONLY)

s = Direction Indicator Lamp LH
t = Direction Indicator Lamp RH
u = Oil Level Warning Lamp
v = Oil Temperature Gauge
w = Coolant Temperature Gauge
x = Coolant Level Warning Lamp
y = + VE Supply
z = Earth
a1 = Oil Pressure Gauge
a2 = Injection System Warning Lamp

ITEM	DESCRIPTION	DIAGRAM/ GRID REF.
1	Air Flow Sensor	1b/B5
2	Alternator	1/C3, 1a/C3, 1b/B2, 2/C3
3	Ashtray Illumination	2a/H4
4	Auto. Trans. Inhibitor Relay	1/G4
5	Auto. Trans. Inhibitor Switch	1/D5
6	Auto. Trans. Pump Control Relay	1/G6
7	Battery	1/C7, 1a/C7, 1b/C7, 2/C8, 2a/B7, 3/B7, 3a/B7
8	Brake Pad Wear Sensor	1/D1, 1/D8, 1a/D1, 1a/D8, 1b/C1, 1b/C8
9	Central Locking Control Switch	3a/K1
10	Central Locking Motor LH Front	3a/K8
11	Central Locking Motor LH Rear	3a/M8
12	Central Locking Motor RH Rear	3a/M1
13	Central Locking Motor Tailgate	3a/M5
14	Choke Switch	1/J3, 1a/J3
15	Cigar Lighter	2a/H4

12

Key to wiring diagrams

ITEM	DESCRIPTION	DIAGRAM/ GRID REF.	ITEM	DESCRIPTION	DIAGRAM/ GRID REF.
16	Cigar Lighter Illumination	2a/H4	63	Ignition Switch	1/J1,
17	Clock	2a/J3			1a/J1,
18	Combination Switch – Lighting,	2/J3,			1b/K1,
	Direction Indicators And Horn	2a/G3,			2/F1,
		3/G3			2a/G1,
19	Combination Switch – Wash/Wipe	3/G3			3/E1,
20	Coolant Temp. Gauge Sender Unit	1a/D5,			3a/F1
		1b/G4	64	Instrument Cluster	1/H3,
21	Coolant Temp. Sensor	1b/D5			1a/H3,
22	Coolant Temp. Switch	1/B5,			1b/K3,
		1a/C5,			2/F3,
		1b/G3			2a/F3
23	Cooling Fan Motor	1/A5,	65	Instrument Illumination Control	2a/F3
		1a/B5	66	Interior Lamp	2a/D5
24	Cooling Fan Resistor	1/G8,	67	Interior Lamp Door Switch LH	2a/C8
		1a/A5	68	Interior Lamp Door Switch RH	2a/C1
25	Cooling Fan Switch	1/A3,	69	Lamp Cluster LH Rear	2/M7,
		1a/B3			2a/M7
26	Diagnostic Socket	1/D6,	70	Lamp Cluster RH Rear	2/M1,
		1a/D6,			2a/M1
		1b/D2	71	Low Brake Fluid Sender Unit	1/E2,
27	Dim/Dip Relay	2/E5			1a/E2,
28	Dim/Dip Resistor	2/E7			1b/E2
29	Direction Indicator Flasher Relay	2a/E7	72	Low Coolant Sender Unit	1b/F8
30	Direction Indicator LH Front	2a/A8	73	Luggage Comp. Lamp	2a/L4
31	Direction Indicator RH Front	2a/A1	74	Luggage Comp. Lamp Switch	2a/M4
32	Distributor	1/E6,	75	Map Reading Lamp	2a/E5
		1a/E6,	76	Number Plate Lamp	2/M4,
		1b/E5			2/M5
33	Driving Lamp LH	2/A6	77	Oil Level Indicator Unit	1b/H5
34	Driving Lamp Relay	2/E4	78	Oil Level Sensor	1b/G4
35	Driving Lamp RH	2/A3	79	Oil Pressure Sender Unit	1b/G3
36	Electric Window Motor LH Front	3a/J8	80	Oil Pressure Switch	1/B5,
37	Electric Window Motor RH Front	3a/J1			1a/C5,
38	Electric Window Relay	3a/D6			1b/G4
39	Electric Window Switch LH	3a/H8	81	Oil Temp. Sender Unit	1b/H4
40	Electric Window Switch RH (Drivers)	3a/J1	82	Radio/Cassette Unit	3a/F5
41	Electric Window Switch RH (Passengers)	3a/H1	83	Reversing Lamp Switch	2/D5
42	Foglamp Rear	2/M3	84	Spark Plugs	1/E5,
43	Foglamp Switch	2/G3			1a/E5,
44	Fuel Gauge Sender Unit	1/M5,			1b/E4
		1a/M5,	85	Speaker LH Front	3a/C8
		1b/M5	86	Speaker RH Front	3a/C1
45	Fuel Injection ECU	1b/G6	87	Starter Motor	1/C6,
46	Fuel Injectors	1b/D4			1a/C6,
47	Fuel Pump	1/L6,			1b/B6,
		1b/M6			2/B5
48	Glove Box/Lamp Switch	2a/J7	88	Stop-Lamp Switch	2a/D3
49	Handbrake Warning Switch	1/L5,	89	Supplementary Air Device	1b/D5
		1a/L5,	90	Suppressor	1/C2,
		1b/K5			1b/B2
50	Hazard Warning Lamp/Switch	2a/F4	91	Tachymetric Relay	1b/A7
51	Headlamp Unit LH	2/A7	92	TDC Position Sensor	1/C6,
52	Headlamp Unit RH	2/A2			1a/D6,
53	Heated Rear Window	3/M4			1b/D3
54	Heated Rear Window Relay	3/E6	93	Throttle Switch	1b/B4
55	Heated Rear Window Switch	3/H3	94	Washer Pump Front	3/B8
56	Heater Blower Motor	3/H4	95	Washer Pump Rear	3/M2
57	Heater Blower Motor Control Unit	3/C8	96	Wiper Motor Front	3/C3
58	Heater Blower Motor Speed Control	3/J4	97	Wiper Motor Rear	3/M5
59	Heater/Ventilation Illumination	2a/H3	98	Wiper Relay Front	3/E8,
60	Horn	3/A8			3/J5
61	Ignition Coil	1/E7,	99	Wiper Relay Rear	3/M6
		1a/E7,			
		1b/E6			
62	Ignition Module	1/E7,			
		1a/E6,			
		1b/E6			

Key to wiring diagrams (continued)

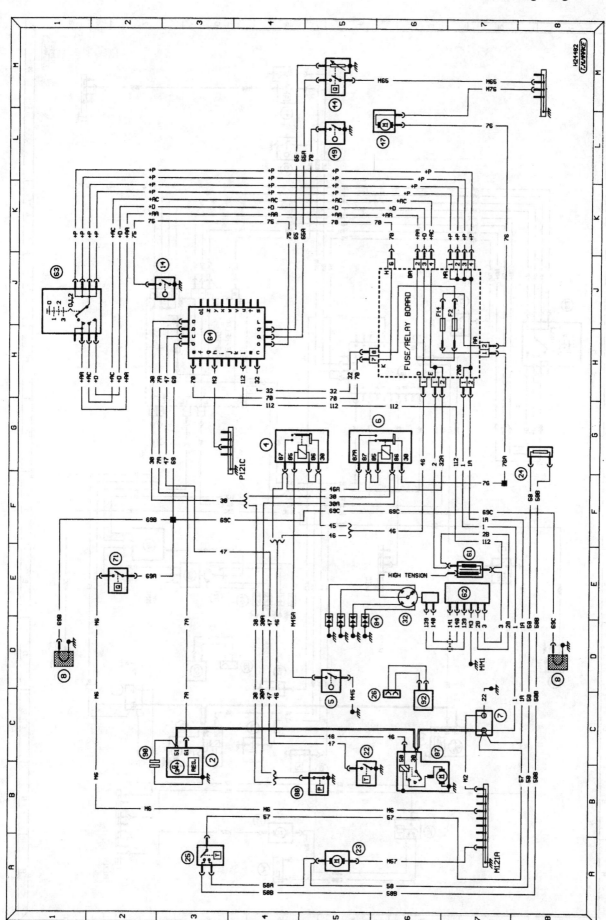

Diagram 1: Typical starting, charging, ignition, cooling fan, warning lamps and gauges (XV8, XW7, XY8 and XU51C engine models)

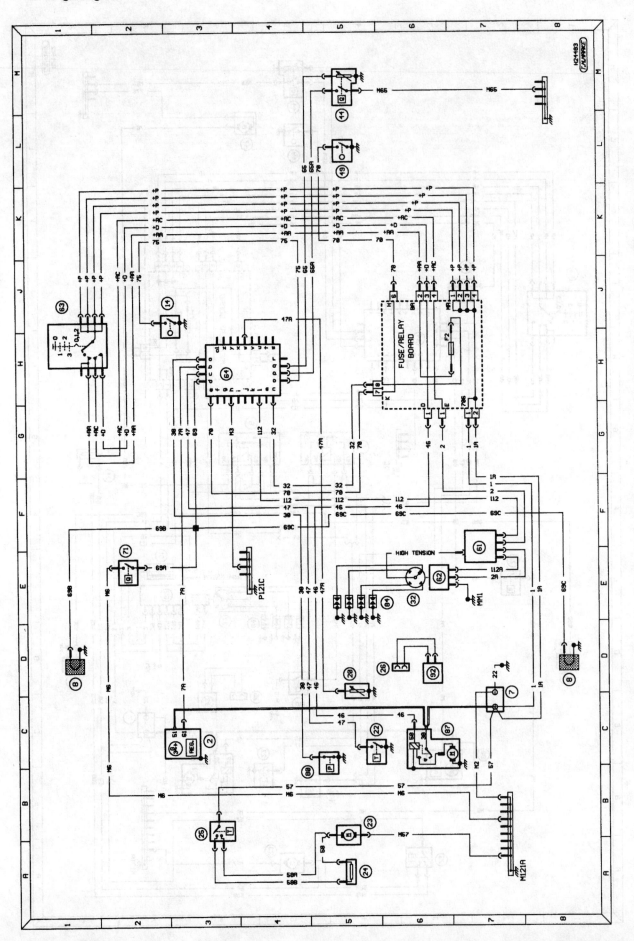

Diagram 1a: Typical starting, charging, ignition, cooling fan, warning lamps and gauges (TU1, TU3 and TU9 engine models)

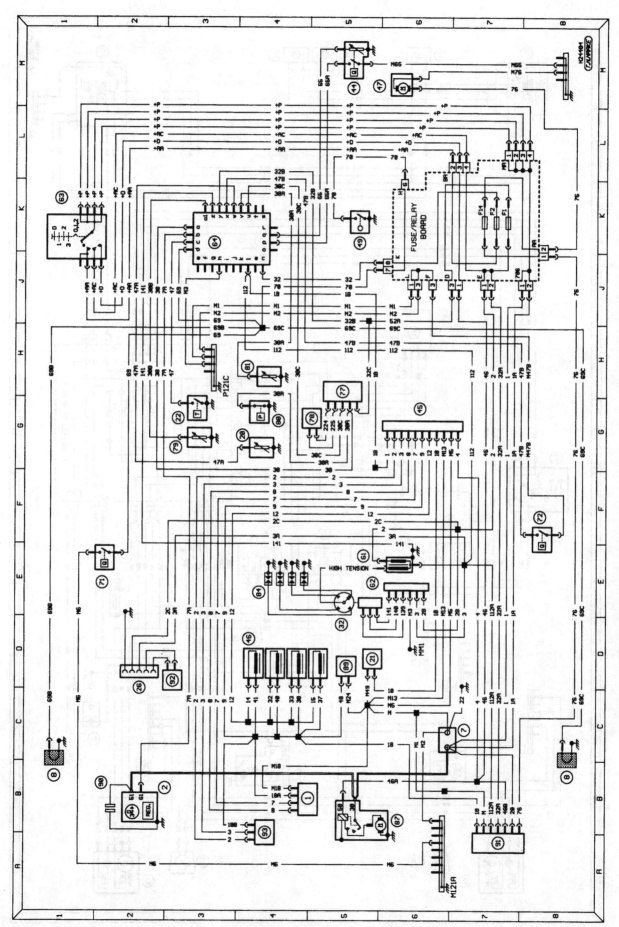

Diagram1b: Typical engine management, warning lamps and gauges (XU5J/JA and XU9JA engine models)

12

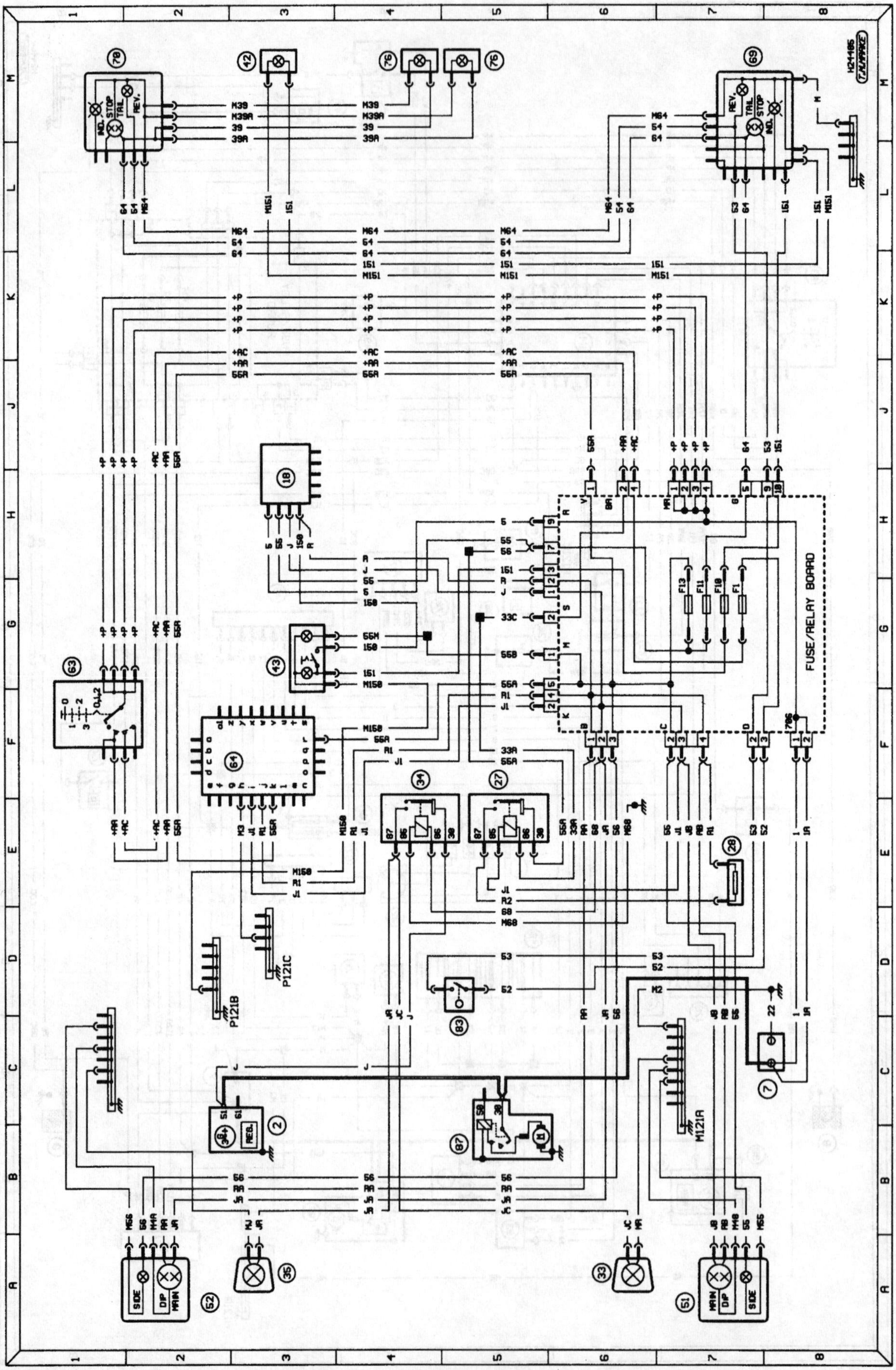

Diagram 2: Typical exterior lighting - reversing lamps, foglamps, sidelamps and headlamps

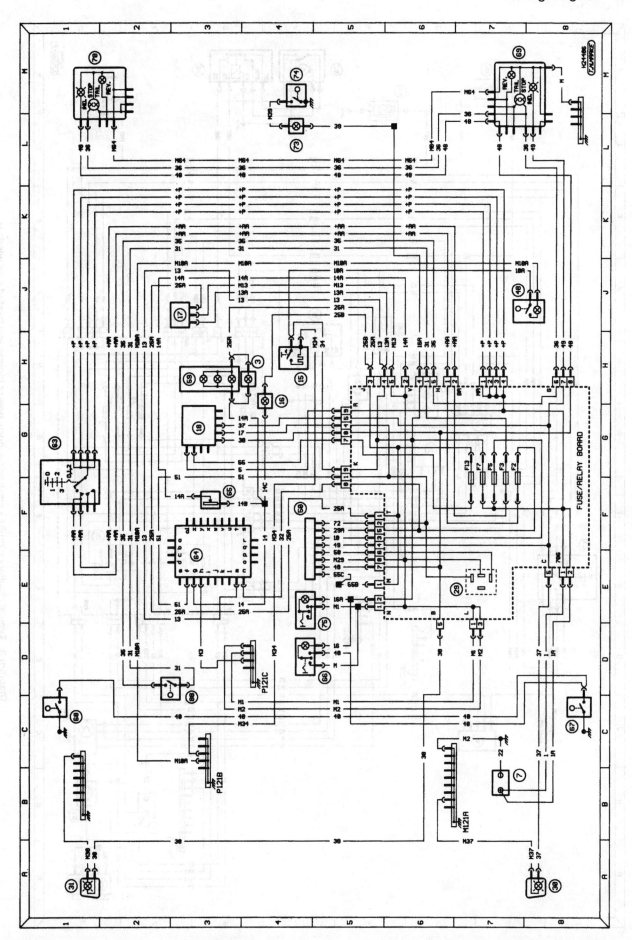

Diagram 2a: Typical exterior lighting - direction indicators and stop-lamps; typical interior lighting and associated circuits

12

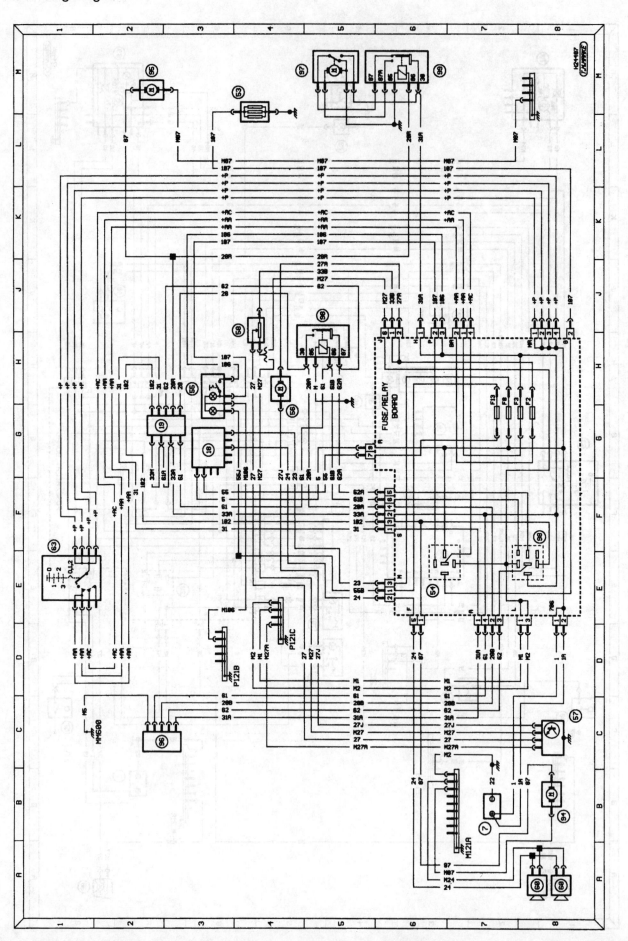

Diagram 3: Typical ancillary circuits - wash/wipe, horn, heater blower and heated rear window

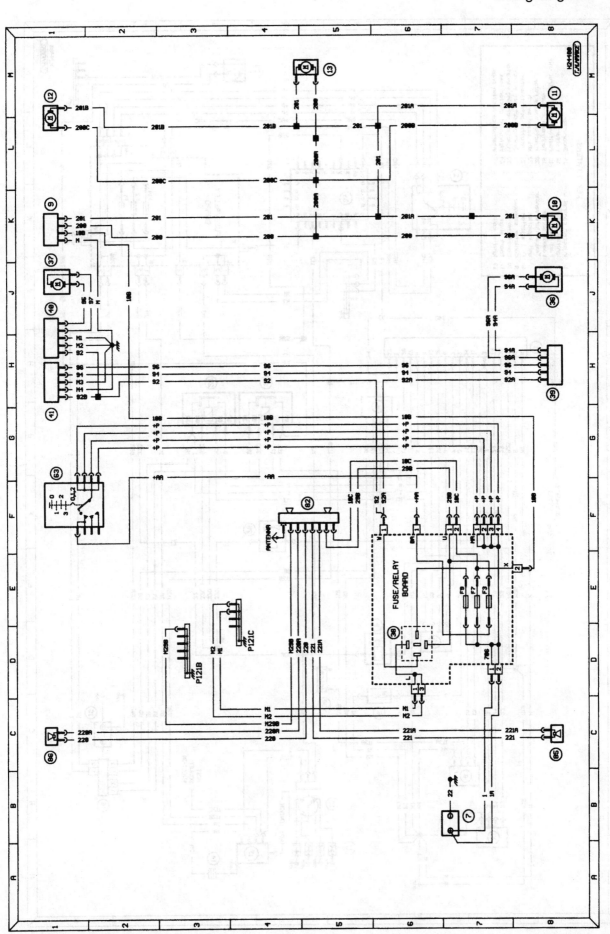

Diagram 3a: Typical ancillary circuits - electric windows, central locking and radio/cassette

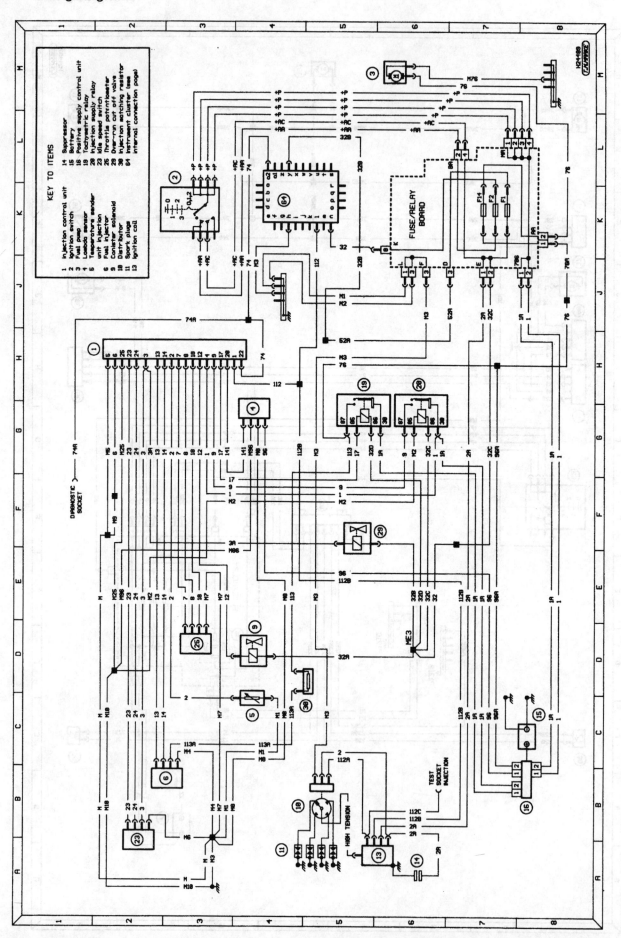

KEY TO ITEMS

1 Injection control unit
2 Ignition switch
3 Fuel pump
4 Lambda sensor
5 Temperature sender
6 Fuel injector
9 Canister solenoid
10 Distributor
11 Spark plugs
13 Ignition coil
14 Suppressor
15 Battery
16 Positive supply control unit
19 Tachymetric relay
20 Injection supply relay
23 Idle speed switch
25 Throttle potentiometer
29 Over-run cut off valve
30 Injection matching resistor
64 Instrument cluster (see internal connection page)

Supplementary diagram A: Typical engine management (TU3M/Z and TU3FM/L engine models)

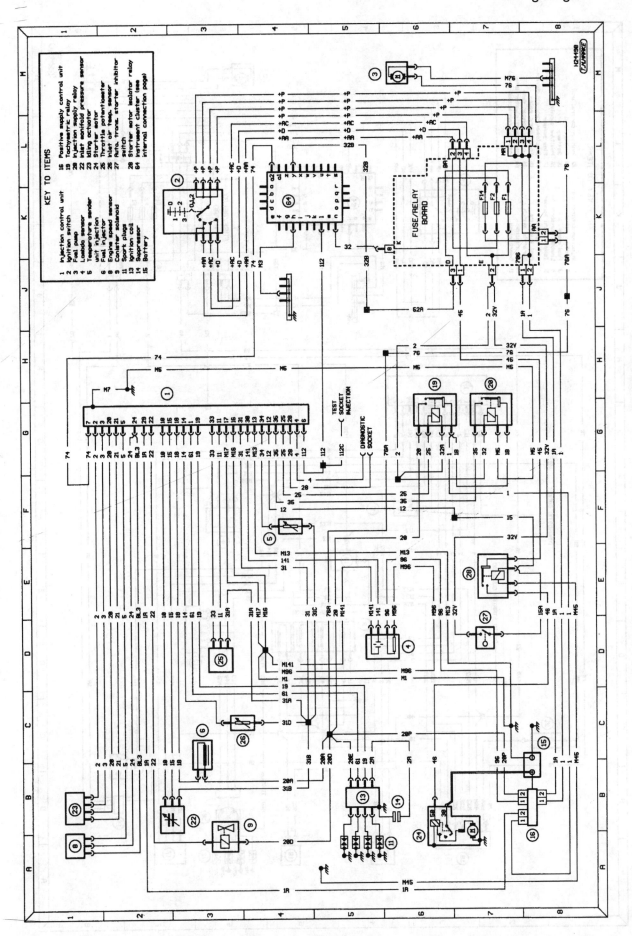

KEY TO ITEMS

1 Injection control unit
2 Ignition switch
3 Fuel pump
4 Loadio sender
5 Temperature sender
6 Fuel injector
8 Engine speed sensor
9 Canister solenoid
11 Spark plugs
13 Ignition coil
14 Suppressor
15 Battery

16 Positive supply control unit
19 Tachymetric relay
20 Injection supply relay
22 Inlet manifold pressure sensor
23 Idling actuator
24 Starter motor
25 Throttle potentiometer
26 Inlet air temp. sensor
27 Auto. trans. starter inhibitor switch
28 Starter motor isolator relay
64 Instrument cluster (see internal connection page)

Supplementary diagram B: Typical engine management (TU1M/L and XU5M3/Z/L engine models)

12

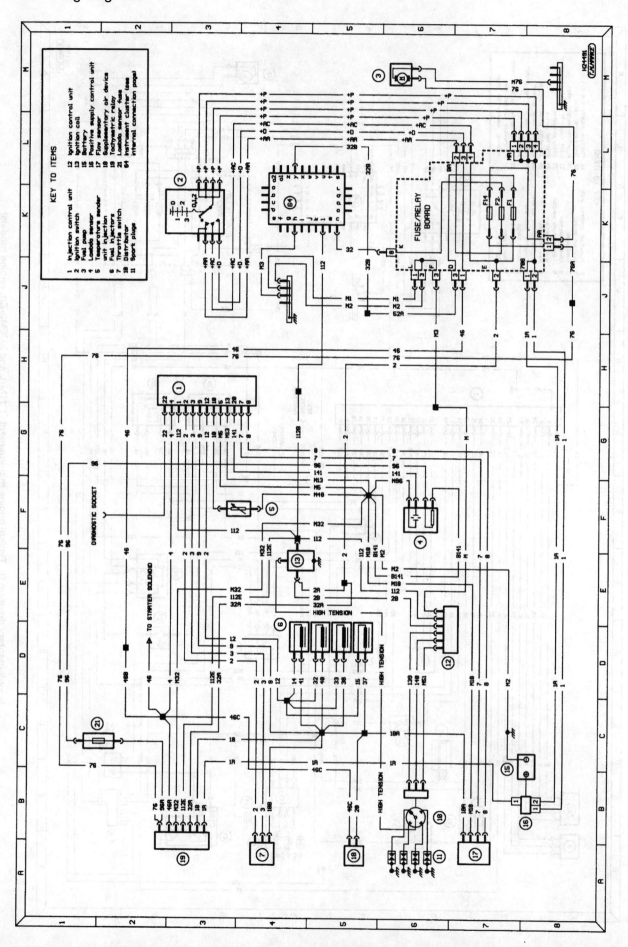

KEY TO ITEMS

1 Injection control unit
2 Ignition switch
4 Fuel pump
5 Temperature sender
6 Fuel injectors
7 Throttle switch
10 Distributor
11 Spark plugs
12 Ignition control unit
13 Ignition coil
15 Battery
17 Positive supply control unit
18 Flow sensor
19 Tachymetric relay
20 Supplementary air device
unit injection
21 Lambda sensor fuse
64 Instrument cluster (see internal connection page)

Supplementary diagram C: Typical engine management (XU9J1/Z/L engine models)

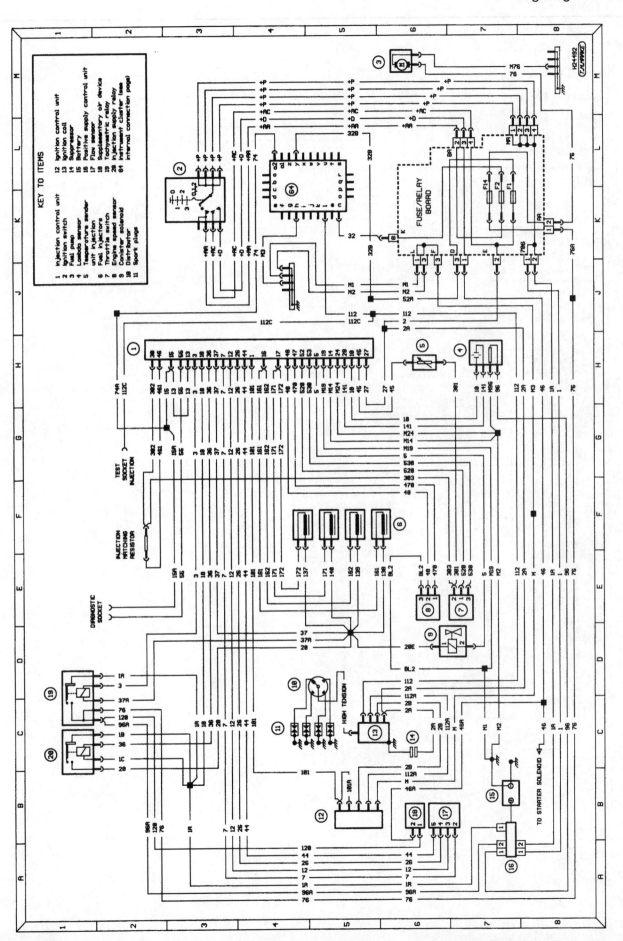

Supplementary diagram D: Typical engine management (XU9JA/L engine models)

KEY TO ITEMS

1 Injection control unit
2 Ignition switch
3 Fuel pump
4 Lambdo sensor
5 Temperature sender
6 Fuel injectors
   unit injection
7 Throttle switch
8 Engine speed sensor
9 Canister solenoid
10 Distributor
11 Spark plugs
12 Ignition control unit
13 Ignition coil
14 Suppressor
15 Battery
16 Positive supply control unit
17 Flow sensor
18 Supplementary air device
19 Tachymetric relay
20 Injection supply relay
64 Instrument cluster (see
   internal connection page)

Dimensions and weights

Note: *All figures are approximate, and may vary according to model. Refer to manufacturer's data for exact figures.*

Dimensions

Overall length	3705 mm
Overall width:	
Basic, GL, GE and Van	1562 mm
All other models except Cabriolet	1572 mm
Cabriolet	1589 mm
Overall height	1372 to 1381 mm
Wheelbase	2420 mm
Front track:	
All models except SR, GT, Cabriolet and GTI	1350 mm
SR and GT models	1364 mm
1.6 GTI and Cabriolet models	1392 mm
1.9 GTI models	1383 mm
Rear track:	
All models except SR, GT, Cabriolet and GTI	1300 mm
SR and GT models	1314 mm
1.6 GTI and Cabriolet models	1328 mm
1.9 GTI models	1344 mm

Weights

Kerb weight*	740 to 935 kg
Maximum towing weight:	
TU9 and TU1 engines	700 kg
All other engines	800 kg
Maximum roof rack load	50 kg

Exact kerb weight varies depending on model - refer to VIN plate for details

Length (distance)

Inches (in)	x 25.4	= Millimetres (mm)	x 0.0394	=	Inches (in)
Feet (ft)	x 0.305	= Metres (m)	x 3.281	=	Feet (ft)
Miles	x 1.609	= Kilometres (km)	x 0.621	=	Miles

Volume (capacity)

Cubic inches (cu in; in³)	x 16.387	= Cubic centimetres (cc; cm³)	x 0.061	=	Cubic inches (cu in; in³)
Imperial pints (Imp pt)	x 0.568	= Litres (l)	x 1.76	=	Imperial pints (Imp pt)
Imperial quarts (Imp qt)	x 1.137	= Litres (l)	x 0.88	=	Imperial quarts (Imp qt)
Imperial quarts (Imp qt)	x 1.201	= US quarts (US qt)	x 0.833	=	Imperial quarts (Imp qt)
US quarts (US qt)	x 0.946	= Litres (l)	x 1.057	=	US quarts (US qt)
Imperial gallons (Imp gal)	x 4.546	= Litres (l)	x 0.22	=	Imperial gallons (Imp gal)
Imperial gallons (Imp gal)	x 1.201	= US gallons (US gal)	x 0.833	=	Imperial gallons (Imp gal)
US gallons (US gal)	x 3.785	= Litres (l)	x 0.264	=	US gallons (US gal)

Mass (weight)

Ounces (oz)	x 28.35	= Grams (g)	x 0.035	=	Ounces (oz)
Pounds (lb)	x 0.454	= Kilograms (kg)	x 2.205	=	Pounds (lb)

Force

Ounces-force (ozf; oz)	x 0.278	= Newtons (N)	x 3.6	=	Ounces-force (ozf; oz)
Pounds-force (lbf; lb)	x 4.448	= Newtons (N)	x 0.225	=	Pounds-force (lbf; lb)
Newtons (N)	x 0.1	= Kilograms-force (kgf; kg)	x 9.81	=	Newtons (N)

Pressure

Pounds-force per square inch (psi; lbf/in²; lb/in²)	x 0.070	= Kilograms-force per square centimetre (kgf/cm²; kg/cm²)	x 14.223	=	Pounds-force per square inch (psi; lbf/in²; lb/in²)
Pounds-force per square inch (psi; lbf/in²; lb/in²)	x 0.068	= Atmospheres (atm)	x 14.696	=	Pounds-force per square inch (psi; lbf/in²; lb/in²)
Pounds-force per square inch (psi; lbf/in²; lb/in²)	x 0.069	= Bars	x 14.5	=	Pounds-force per square inch (psi; lbf/in²; lb/in²)
Pounds-force per square inch (psi; lbf/in²; lb/in²)	x 6.895	= Kilopascals (kPa)	x 0.145	=	Pounds-force per square inch (psi; lbf/in²; lb/in²)
Kilopascals (kPa)	x 0.01	= Kilograms-force per square centimetre (kgf/cm²; kg/cm²)	x 98.1	=	Kilopascals (kPa)
Millibar (mbar)	x 100	= Pascals (Pa)	x 0.01	=	Millibar (mbar)
Millibar (mbar)	x 0.0145	= Pounds-force per square inch (psi; lbf/in²; lb/in²)	x 68.947	=	Millibar (mbar)
Millibar (mbar)	x 0.75	= Millimetres of mercury (mmHg)	x 1.333	=	Millibar (mbar)
Millibar (mbar)	x 0.401	= Inches of water (inH₂O)	x 2.491	=	Millibar (mbar)
Millimetres of mercury (mmHg)	x 0.535	= Inches of water (inH₂O)	x 1.868	=	Millimetres of mercury (mmHg)
Inches of water (inH₂O)	x 0.036	= Pounds-force per square inch (psi; lbf/in²; lb/in²)	x 27.68	=	Inches of water (inH₂O)

Torque (moment of force)

Pounds-force inches (lbf in; lb in)	x 1.152	= Kilograms-force centimetre (kgf cm; kg cm)	x 0.868	=	Pounds-force inches (lbf in; lb in)
Pounds-force inches (lbf in; lb in)	x 0.113	= Newton metres (Nm)	x 8.85	=	Pounds-force inches (lbf in; lb in)
Pounds-force inches (lbf in; lb in)	x 0.083	= Pounds-force feet (lbf ft; lb ft)	x 12	=	Pounds-force inches (lbf in; lb in)
Pounds-force feet (lbf ft; lb ft)	x 0.138	= Kilograms-force metres (kgf m; kg m)	x 7.233	=	Pounds-force feet (lbf ft; lb ft)
Pounds-force feet (lbf ft; lb ft)	x 1.356	= Newton metres (Nm)	x 0.738	=	Pounds-force feet (lbf ft; lb ft)
Newton metres (Nm)	x 0.102	= Kilograms-force metres (kgf m; kg m)	x 9.804	=	Newton metres (Nm)

Power

Horsepower (hp)	x 745.7	= Watts (W)	x 0.0013	=	Horsepower (hp)

Velocity (speed)

Miles per hour (miles/hr; mph)	x 1.609	= Kilometres per hour (km/hr; kph)	x 0.621	=	Miles per hour (miles/hr; mph)

Fuel consumption*

Miles per gallon (mpg)	x 0.354	= Kilometres per litre (km/l)	x 2.825	=	Miles per gallon (mpg)

Temperature

Degrees Fahrenheit = (°C x 1.8) + 32   Degrees Celsius (Degrees Centigrade; °C) = (°F - 32) x 0.56

* It is common practice to convert from miles per gallon (mpg) to litres/100 kilometres (l/100km), where mpg x l/100 km = 282

Buying spare parts

Spare parts are available from many sources, including maker's appointed garages, accessory shops, and motor factors. To be sure of obtaining the correct parts, it will sometimes be necessary to quote the vehicle identification number. If possible, it can also be useful to take the old parts along for positive identification. Items such as starter motors and alternators may be available under a service exchange scheme - any parts returned should always be clean.

Our advice regarding spare part sources is as follows.

Officially-appointed garages

This is the best source of parts which are peculiar to your car, and which are not otherwise generally available (eg badges, interior trim, certain body panels, etc). It is also the only place at which you should buy parts if the vehicle is still under warranty.

Accessory shops

These are very good places to buy materials and components needed for the maintenance of your car (oil, air and fuel filters, spark plugs, light bulbs, drivebelts, oils and greases, brake pads, touch-up paint, etc). Components of this nature sold by a reputable shop are of the same standard as those used by the car manufacturer.

Besides components, these shops also sell tools and general accessories, usually have convenient opening hours, charge lower prices, and can often be found not far from home. Some accessory shops have parts counters where the components needed for almost any repair job can be purchased or ordered.

Motor factors

Good factors will stock all the more important components which wear out comparatively quickly, and can sometimes supply individual components needed for the overhaul of a larger assembly (eg brake seals and hydraulic parts, bearing shells, pistons, valves, alternator brushes). They may also handle work such as cylinder block reboring, crankshaft regrinding and balancing, etc.

Tyre and exhaust specialists

These outlets may be independent, or members of a local or national chain. They frequently offer competitive prices when compared with a main dealer or local garage, but it will pay to obtain several quotes before making a decision. When researching prices, also ask what "extras" may be added - for instance, fitting a new valve and balancing the wheel are both commonly charged on top of the price of a new tyre.

Other sources

Beware of parts or materials obtained from market stalls, car boot sales or similar outlets. Such items are not invariably sub-standard, but there is little chance of compensation if they do prove unsatisfactory. In the case of safety-critical components such as brake pads, there is the risk not only of financial loss but also of an accident causing injury or death.

Second-hand components or assemblies obtained from a car breaker can be a good buy in some circumstances, but this sort of purchase is best made by the experienced DIY mechanic.

Vehicle identification

Modifications are a continuing and unpublicised process in vehicle manufacture. Spare parts manuals and lists are compiled on a numerical basis, the individual vehicle numbers being essential to identify correctly the component required.

The *vehicle identification plate* is located on the right-hand front wing valance in the engine compartment **(see illustration)**.

The *body serial number* is stamped on the scuttle crossmember above the vehicle identification plate.

The *engine number* is situated on the cylinder block. On non-XU engine models with an aluminium cylinder block, the number is stamped on a plate which is riveted to the flywheel end of the block; on later models with a cast-iron block, the number is stamped on a machined surface on the flywheel end of the block. On early XU engine models, the number is stamped on a plate which is riveted to the timing belt end of the front of the cylinder block; on later models, the number is stamped on a machined surface at the flywheel end of the front of the block.

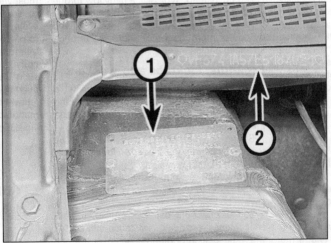

Vehicle identification plate (1) and body serial number (2)

Whenever servicing, repair or overhaul work is carried out on the car or its components, observe the following procedures and instructions. This will assist in carrying out the operation efficiently and to a professional standard of workmanship.

Joint mating faces and gaskets

When separating components at their mating faces, never insert screwdrivers or similar implements into the joint between the faces in order to prise them apart. This can cause severe damage which results in oil leaks, coolant leaks, etc upon reassembly. Separation is usually achieved by tapping along the joint with a soft-faced hammer in order to break the seal. However, note that this method may not be suitable where dowels are used for component location.

Where a gasket is used between the mating faces of two components, a new one must be fitted on reassembly; fit it dry unless otherwise stated in the repair procedure. Make sure that the mating faces are clean and dry, with all traces of old gasket removed. When cleaning a joint face, use a tool which is unlikely to score or damage the face, and remove any burrs or nicks with an oilstone or fine file.

Make sure that tapped holes are cleaned with a pipe cleaner, and keep them free of jointing compound, if this is being used, unless specifically instructed otherwise.

Ensure that all orifices, channels or pipes are clear, and blow through them, preferably using compressed air.

Oil seals

Oil seals can be removed by levering them out with a wide flat-bladed screwdriver or similar implement. Alternatively, a number of self-tapping screws may be screwed into the seal, and these used as a purchase for pliers or some similar device in order to pull the seal free.

Whenever an oil seal is removed from its working location, either individually or as part of an assembly, it should be renewed.

The very fine sealing lip of the seal is easily damaged, and will not seal if the surface it contacts is not completely clean and free from scratches, nicks or grooves. If the original sealing surface of the component cannot be restored, and the manufacturer has not made provision for slight relocation of the seal relative to the sealing surface, the component should be renewed.

Protect the lips of the seal from any surface which may damage them in the course of fitting. Use tape or a conical sleeve where possible. Lubricate the seal lips with oil before fitting and, on dual-lipped seals, fill the space between the lips with grease.

Unless otherwise stated, oil seals must be fitted with their sealing lips toward the lubricant to be sealed.

Use a tubular drift or block of wood of the appropriate size to install the seal and, if the seal housing is shouldered, drive the seal down to the shoulder. If the seal housing is unshouldered, the seal should be fitted with its face flush with the housing top face (unless otherwise instructed).

Screw threads and fastenings

Seized nuts, bolts and screws are quite a common occurrence where corrosion has set in, and the use of penetrating oil or releasing fluid will often overcome this problem if the offending item is soaked for a while before attempting to release it. The use of an impact driver may also provide a means of releasing such stubborn fastening devices, when used in conjunction with the appropriate screwdriver bit or socket. If none of these methods works, it may be necessary to resort to the careful application of heat, or the use of a hacksaw or nut splitter device.

Studs are usually removed by locking two nuts together on the threaded part, and then using a spanner on the lower nut to unscrew the stud. Studs or bolts which have broken off below the surface of the component in which they are mounted can sometimes be removed using a stud extractor. Always ensure that a blind tapped hole is completely free from oil, grease, water or other fluid before installing the bolt or stud. Failure to do this could cause the housing to crack due to the hydraulic action of the bolt or stud as it is screwed in.

When tightening a castellated nut to accept a split pin, tighten the nut to the specified torque, where applicable, and then tighten further to the next split pin hole. Never slacken the nut to align the split pin hole, unless stated in the repair procedure.

When checking or retightening a nut or bolt to a specified torque setting, slacken the nut or bolt by a quarter of a turn, and then retighten to the specified setting. However, this should not be attempted where angular tightening has been used.

For some screw fastenings, notably cylinder head bolts or nuts, torque wrench settings are no longer specified for the latter stages of tightening, "angle-tightening" being called up instead. Typically, a fairly low torque wrench setting will be applied to the bolts/nuts in the correct sequence, followed by one or more stages of tightening through specified angles.

Locknuts, locktabs and washers

Any fastening which will rotate against a component or housing during tightening should always have a washer between it and the relevant component or housing.

Spring or split washers should always be renewed when they are used to lock a critical component such as a big-end bearing retaining bolt or nut. Locktabs which are folded over to retain a nut or bolt should always be renewed.

Self-locking nuts can be re-used in non-critical areas, providing resistance can be felt when the locking portion passes over the bolt or stud thread. However, it should be noted that self-locking stiffnuts tend to lose their effectiveness after long periods of use, and should then be renewed as a matter of course.

Split pins must always be replaced with new ones of the correct size for the hole.

When thread-locking compound is found on the threads of a fastener which is to be re-used, it should be cleaned off with a wire brush and solvent, and fresh compound applied on reassembly.

Special tools

Some repair procedures in this manual entail the use of special tools such as a press, two or three-legged pullers, spring compressors, etc. Wherever possible, suitable readily-available alternatives to the manufacturer's special tools are described, and are shown in use. In some instances, where no alternative is possible, it has been necessary to resort to the use of a manufacturer's tool, and this has been done for reasons of safety as well as the efficient completion of the repair operation. Unless you are highly-skilled and have a thorough understanding of the procedures described, never attempt to bypass the use of any special tool when the procedure described specifies its use. Not only is there a very great risk of personal injury, but expensive damage could be caused to the components involved.

Environmental considerations

When disposing of used engine oil, brake fluid, antifreeze, etc, give due consideration to any detrimental environmental effects. Do not, for instance, pour any of the above liquids down drains into the general sewage system, or onto the ground to soak away. Many local council refuse tips provide a facility for waste oil disposal, as do some garages. If none of these facilities are available, consult your local Environmental Health Department, or the National Rivers Authority, for further advice.

With the universal tightening-up of legislation regarding the emission of environmentally-harmful substances from motor vehicles, most vehicles have tamperproof devices fitted to the main adjustment points of the fuel system. These devices are primarily designed to prevent unqualified persons from adjusting the fuel/air mixture, with the chance of a consequent increase in toxic emissions. If such devices are found during servicing or overhaul, they should, wherever possible, be renewed or refitted in accordance with the manufacturer's requirements or current legislation.

OIL CARE
FOLLOW THE CODE

O I L   B A N K   L I N E
0800 66 33 66

Note: It is antisocial and illegal to dump oil down the drain. To find the location of your local oil recycling bank, call this number free.

The jack supplied with the vehicle tool kit should only be used for changing the roadwheels - see *"Wheel changing"* at the front of this manual. When carrying out any other kind of work, raise the vehicle using a hydraulic (or "trolley") jack, and always supplement the jack with axle stands.

The sill jacking points or their adjacent re-inforced areas should be used as jacking points for raising the car **(see illustration)**. A beam may be placed under the front subframe and the front end jacked up under that. The side-members of the front subframe should be used as axle stand support points.

The rear side-members may be used in a similar way.

Never work under, around, or near a raised vehicle, unless it is adequately supported in at least two places.

Front jacking point

Jack supplied with tool kit (1) shown engaged with front jacking point (2)

Radio/cassette unit anti-theft system

The radio/cassette unit fitted as standard or optional equipment may be equipped with a built-in security code, to deter thieves. If the power source to the unit is cut, the anti-theft system will activate. Even if the power source is immediately reconnected, the radio/cassette unit will not function until the correct security code has been entered. Therefore, if you do not know the correct security code for the radio/cassette unit do not disconnect either of the battery terminals, or remove the radio/cassette unit from the vehicle.

To enter the correct security code, follow the instructions provided with the radio/cassette player or vehicle handbook.

If an incorrect code is entered, the unit will become locked, and cannot be operated.

If this happens, or if the security code is lost or forgotten, seek the advice of your Peugeot dealer.

Introduction

A selection of good tools is a fundamental requirement for anyone contemplating the maintenance and repair of a motor vehicle. For the owner who does not possess any, their purchase will prove a considerable expense, offsetting some of the savings made by doing-it-yourself. However, provided that the tools purchased meet the relevant national safety standards and are of good quality, they will last for many years and prove an extremely worthwhile investment.

To help the average owner to decide which tools are needed to carry out the various tasks detailed in this manual, we have compiled three lists of tools under the following headings: *Maintenance and minor repair*, *Repair and overhaul*, and *Special*. Newcomers to practical mechanics should start off with the *Maintenance and minor repair* tool kit, and confine themselves to the simpler jobs around the vehicle. Then, as confidence and experience grow, more difficult tasks can be undertaken, with extra tools being purchased as, and when, they are needed. In this way, a *Maintenance and minor repair* tool kit can be built up into a *Repair and overhaul* tool kit over a considerable period of time, without any major cash outlays. The experienced do-it-yourselfer will have a tool kit good enough for most repair and overhaul procedures, and will add tools from the *Special* category when it is felt that the expense is justified by the amount of use to which these tools will be put.

Maintenance and minor repair tool kit

The tools given in this list should be considered as a minimum requirement if routine maintenance, servicing and minor repair operations are to be undertaken. We recommend the purchase of combination spanners (ring one end, open-ended the other); although more expensive than open-ended ones, they do give the advantages of both types of spanner.

☐ *Combination spanners:*
Metric - 8 to 19 mm inclusive
☐ *Adjustable spanner - 35 mm jaw (approx.)*
☐ *Spark plug spanner (with rubber insert) - petrol models*
☐ *Spark plug gap adjustment tool - petrol models*
☐ *Set of feeler gauges*
☐ *Brake bleed nipple spanner*
☐ *Screwdrivers:*
Flat blade - 100 mm long x 6 mm dia
Cross blade - 100 mm long x 6 mm dia
☐ *Combination pliers*
☐ *Hacksaw (junior)*
☐ *Tyre pump*
☐ *Tyre pressure gauge*
☐ *Oil can*
☐ *Oil filter removal tool*
☐ *Fine emery cloth*
☐ *Wire brush (small)*
☐ *Funnel (medium size)*

Repair and overhaul tool kit

These tools are virtually essential for anyone undertaking any major repairs to a motor vehicle, and are additional to those given in the *Maintenance and minor repair* list. Included in this list is a comprehensive set of sockets. Although these are expensive, they will be found invaluable as they are so versatile - particularly if various drives are included in the set. We recommend the half-inch square-drive type, as this can be used with most proprietary torque wrenches.

The tools in this list will sometimes need to be supplemented by tools from the *Special* list:

☐ *Sockets (or box spanners) to cover range in previous list (including Torx sockets)*
☐ *Reversible ratchet drive (for use with sockets)*
☐ *Extension piece, 250 mm (for use with sockets)*
☐ *Universal joint (for use with sockets)*
☐ *Torque wrench (for use with sockets)*
☐ *Self-locking grips*
☐ *Ball pein hammer*
☐ *Soft-faced mallet (plastic/aluminium or rubber)*
☐ *Screwdrivers:*
Flat blade - long & sturdy, short (chubby), and narrow (electrician's) types
Cross blade – Long & sturdy, and short (chubby) types
☐ *Pliers:*
Long-nosed
Side cutters (electrician's)
Circlip (internal and external)
☐ *Cold chisel - 25 mm*
☐ *Scriber*
☐ *Scraper*
☐ *Centre-punch*
☐ *Pin punch*
☐ *Hacksaw*
☐ *Brake hose clamp*
☐ *Brake/clutch bleeding kit*
☐ *Selection of twist drills*
☐ *Steel rule/straight-edge*
☐ *Allen keys (inc. splined/Torx type)*
☐ *Selection of files*
☐ *Wire brush*
☐ *Axle stands*
☐ *Jack (strong trolley or hydraulic type)*
☐ *Light with extension lead*

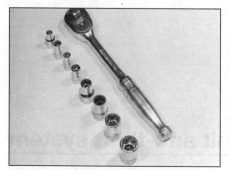

Sockets and reversible ratchet drive

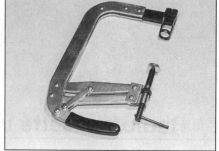

Valve spring compressor

Spline bit set

Piston ring compressor

Clutch plate alignment set

Special tools

The tools in this list are those which are not used regularly, are expensive to buy, or which need to be used in accordance with their manufacturers' instructions. Unless relatively difficult mechanical jobs are undertaken frequently, it will not be economic to buy many of these tools. Where this is the case, you could consider clubbing together with friends (or joining a motorists' club) to make a joint purchase, or borrowing the tools against a deposit from a local garage or tool hire specialist. It is worth noting that many of the larger DIY superstores now carry a large range of special tools for hire at modest rates.

The following list contains only those tools and instruments freely available to the public, and not those special tools produced by the vehicle manufacturer specifically for its dealer network. You will find occasional references to these manufacturers' special tools in the text of this manual. Generally, an alternative method of doing the job without the vehicle manufacturers' special tool is given. However, sometimes there is no alternative to using them. Where this is the case and the relevant tool cannot be bought or borrowed, you will have to entrust the work to a dealer.

- ☐ Valve spring compressor
- ☐ Valve grinding tool
- ☐ Piston ring compressor
- ☐ Piston ring removal/installation tool
- ☐ Cylinder bore hone
- ☐ Balljoint separator
- ☐ Coil spring compressors (where applicable)
- ☐ Two/three-legged hub and bearing puller
- ☐ Impact screwdriver
- ☐ Micrometer and/or vernier calipers
- ☐ Dial gauge
- ☐ Stroboscopic timing light
- ☐ Dwell angle meter/tachometer
- ☐ Universal electrical multi-meter
- ☐ Cylinder compression gauge
- ☐ Hand-operated vacuum pump and gauge
- ☐ Clutch plate alignment set
- ☐ Brake shoe steady spring cup removal tool
- ☐ Bush and bearing removal/installation set
- ☐ Stud extractors
- ☐ Tap and die set
- ☐ Lifting tackle
- ☐ Trolley jack

Buying tools

Reputable motor accessory shops and superstores often offer excellent quality tools at discount prices, so it pays to shop around.

Remember, you don't have to buy the most expensive items on the shelf, but it is always advisable to steer clear of the very cheap tools. Beware of 'bargains' offered on market stalls or at car boot sales. There are plenty of good tools around at reasonable prices, but always aim to purchase items which meet the relevant national safety standards. If in doubt, ask the proprietor or manager of the shop for advice before making a purchase.

Care and maintenance of tools

Having purchased a reasonable tool kit, it is necessary to keep the tools in a clean and serviceable condition. After use, always wipe off any dirt, grease and metal particles using a clean, dry cloth, before putting the tools away. Never leave them lying around after they have been used. A simple tool rack on the garage or workshop wall for items such as screwdrivers and pliers is a good idea. Store all normal spanners and sockets in a metal box. Any measuring instruments, gauges, meters, etc, must be carefully stored where they cannot be damaged or become rusty.

Take a little care when tools are used. Hammer heads inevitably become marked, and screwdrivers lose the keen edge on their blades from time to time. A little timely attention with emery cloth or a file will soon restore items like this to a good finish.

Working facilities

Not to be forgotten when discussing tools is the workshop itself. If anything more than routine maintenance is to be carried out, a suitable working area becomes essential.

It is appreciated that many an owner-mechanic is forced by circumstances to remove an engine or similar item without the benefit of a garage or workshop. Having done this, any repairs should always be done under the cover of a roof.

Wherever possible, any dismantling should be done on a clean, flat workbench or table at a suitable working height.

Any workbench needs a vice; one with a jaw opening of 100 mm is suitable for most jobs. As mentioned previously, some clean dry storage space is also required for tools, as well as for any lubricants, cleaning fluids, touch-up paints etc, which become necessary.

Another item which may be required, and which has a much more general usage, is an electric drill with a chuck capacity of at least 8 mm. This, together with a good range of twist drills, is virtually essential for fitting accessories.

Last, but not least, always keep a supply of old newspapers and clean, lint-free rags available, and try to keep any working area as clean as possible.

Micrometer set

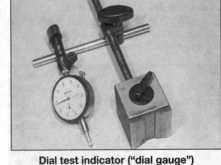

Dial test indicator ("dial gauge")

Stroboscopic timing light

Compression tester

Stud extractor set

This is a guide to getting your vehicle through the MOT test. Obviously it will not be possible to examine the vehicle to the same standard as the professional MOT tester. However, working through the following checks will enable you to identify any problem areas before submitting the vehicle for the test.

Where a testable component is in borderline condition, the tester has discretion in deciding whether to pass or fail it. The basis of such discretion is whether the tester would be happy for a close relative or friend to use the vehicle with the component in that condition. If the vehicle presented is clean and evidently well cared for, the tester may be more inclined to pass a borderline component than if the vehicle is scruffy and apparently neglected.

It has only been possible to summarise the test requirements here, based on the regulations in force at the time of printing. Test standards are becoming increasingly stringent, although there are some exemptions for older vehicles. For full details obtain a copy of the Haynes publication Pass the MOT! (available from stockists of Haynes manuals).

An assistant will be needed to help carry out some of these checks.

The checks have been sub-divided into four categories, as follows:

1 Checks carried out **FROM THE DRIVER'S SEAT**

2 Checks carried out **WITH THE VEHICLE ON THE GROUND**

3 Checks carried out **WITH THE VEHICLE RAISED AND THE WHEELS FREE TO TURN**

4 Checks carried out on **YOUR VEHICLE'S EXHAUST EMISSION SYSTEM**

---

1 Checks carried out **FROM THE DRIVER'S SEAT**

Handbrake

☐ Test the operation of the handbrake. Excessive travel (too many clicks) indicates incorrect brake or cable adjustment.
☐ Check that the handbrake cannot be released by tapping the lever sideways. Check the security of the lever mountings.

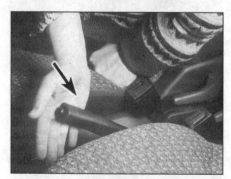

Footbrake

☐ Depress the brake pedal and check that it does not creep down to the floor, indicating a master cylinder fault. Release the pedal, wait a few seconds, then depress it again. If the pedal travels nearly to the floor before firm resistance is felt, brake adjustment or repair is necessary. If the pedal feels spongy, there is air in the hydraulic system which must be removed by bleeding.

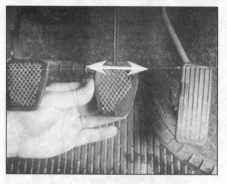

☐ Check that the brake pedal is secure and in good condition. Check also for signs of fluid leaks on the pedal, floor or carpets, which would indicate failed seals in the brake master cylinder.
☐ Check the servo unit (when applicable) by operating the brake pedal several times, then keeping the pedal depressed and starting the engine. As the engine starts, the pedal will move down slightly. If not, the vacuum hose or the servo itself may be faulty.

Steering wheel and column

☐ Examine the steering wheel for fractures or looseness of the hub, spokes or rim.
☐ Move the steering wheel from side to side and then up and down. Check that the steering wheel is not loose on the column, indicating wear or a loose retaining nut. Continue moving the steering wheel as before, but also turn it slightly from left to right.
☐ Check that the steering wheel is not loose on the column, and that there is no abnormal

movement of the steering wheel, indicating wear in the column support bearings or couplings.

Windscreen and mirrors

☐ The windscreen must be free of cracks or other significant damage within the driver's field of view. (Small stone chips are acceptable.) Rear view mirrors must be secure, intact, and capable of being adjusted.

290mm

Seat belts and seats

Note: *The following checks are applicable to all seat belts, front and rear.*

☐ Examine the webbing of all the belts (including rear belts if fitted) for cuts, serious fraying or deterioration. Fasten and unfasten each belt to check the buckles. If applicable, check the retracting mechanism. Check the security of all seat belt mountings accessible from inside the vehicle.

☐ The front seats themselves must be securely attached and the backrests must lock in the upright position.

Doors

☐ Both front doors must be able to be opened and closed from outside and inside, and must latch securely when closed.

2 Checks carried out WITH THE VEHICLE ON THE GROUND

Vehicle identification

☐ Number plates must be in good condition, secure and legible, with letters and numbers correctly spaced – spacing at (A) should be twice that at (B).

☐ The VIN plate and/or homologation plate must be legible.

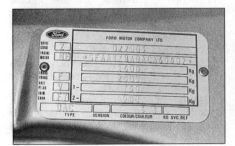

Electrical equipment

☐ Switch on the ignition and check the operation of the horn.

☐ Check the windscreen washers and wipers, examining the wiper blades; renew damaged or perished blades. Also check the operation of the stop-lights.

☐ Check the operation of the sidelights and number plate lights. The lenses and reflectors must be secure, clean and undamaged.

☐ Check the operation and alignment of the headlights. The headlight reflectors must not be tarnished and the lenses must be undamaged.

☐ Switch on the ignition and check the operation of the direction indicators (including the instrument panel tell-tale) and the hazard warning lights. Operation of the sidelights and stop-lights must not affect the indicators - if it does, the cause is usually a bad earth at the rear light cluster.

☐ Check the operation of the rear foglight(s), including the warning light on the instrument panel or in the switch.

Footbrake

☐ Examine the master cylinder, brake pipes and servo unit for leaks, loose mountings, corrosion or other damage.

☐ The fluid reservoir must be secure and the fluid level must be between the upper (**A**) and lower (**B**) markings.

☐ Inspect both front brake flexible hoses for cracks or deterioration of the rubber. Turn the steering from lock to lock, and ensure that the hoses do not contact the wheel, tyre, or any part of the steering or suspension mechanism. With the brake pedal firmly depressed, check the hoses for bulges or leaks under pressure.

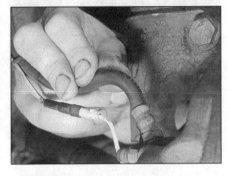

Steering and suspension

☐ Have your assistant turn the steering wheel from side to side slightly, up to the point where the steering gear just begins to transmit this movement to the roadwheels. Check for excessive free play between the steering wheel and the steering gear, indicating wear or insecurity of the steering column joints, the column-to-steering gear coupling, or the steering gear itself.

☐ Have your assistant turn the steering wheel more vigorously in each direction, so that the roadwheels just begin to turn. As this is done, examine all the steering joints, linkages, fittings and attachments. Renew any component that shows signs of wear or damage. On vehicles with power steering, check the security and condition of the steering pump, drivebelt and hoses.

☐ Check that the vehicle is standing level, and at approximately the correct ride height.

Shock absorbers

☐ Depress each corner of the vehicle in turn, then release it. The vehicle should rise and then settle in its normal position. If the vehicle continues to rise and fall, the shock absorber is defective. A shock absorber which has seized will also cause the vehicle to fail.

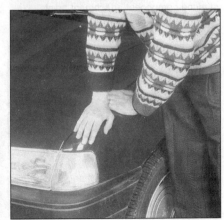

Exhaust system

☐ Start the engine. With your assistant holding a rag over the tailpipe, check the entire system for leaks. Repair or renew leaking sections.

3 Checks carried out
WITH THE VEHICLE RAISED AND THE WHEELS FREE TO TURN

Jack up the front and rear of the vehicle, and securely support it on axle stands. Position the stands clear of the suspension assemblies. Ensure that the wheels are clear of the ground and that the steering can be turned from lock to lock.

Steering mechanism

☐ Have your assistant turn the steering from lock to lock. Check that the steering turns smoothly, and that no part of the steering mechanism, including a wheel or tyre, fouls any brake hose or pipe or any part of the body structure.
☐ Examine the steering rack rubber gaiters for damage or insecurity of the retaining clips. If power steering is fitted, check for signs of damage or leakage of the fluid hoses, pipes or connections. Also check for excessive stiffness or binding of the steering, a missing split pin or locking device, or severe corrosion of the body structure within 30 cm of any steering component attachment point.

Front and rear suspension and wheel bearings

☐ Starting at the front right-hand side, grasp the roadwheel at the 3 o'clock and 9 o'clock positions and shake it vigorously. Check for free play or insecurity at the wheel bearings, suspension balljoints, or suspension mountings, pivots and attachments.
☐ Now grasp the wheel at the 12 o'clock and 6 o'clock positions and repeat the previous inspection. Spin the wheel, and check for roughness or tightness of the front wheel bearing.

☐ If excess free play is suspected at a component pivot point, this can be confirmed by using a large screwdriver or similar tool and levering between the mounting and the component attachment. This will confirm whether the wear is in the pivot bush, its retaining bolt, or in the mounting itself (the bolt holes can often become elongated).

☐ Carry out all the above checks at the other front wheel, and then at both rear wheels.

Springs and shock absorbers

☐ Examine the suspension struts (when applicable) for serious fluid leakage, corrosion, or damage to the casing. Also check the security of the mounting points.
☐ If coil springs are fitted, check that the spring ends locate in their seats, and that the spring is not corroded, cracked or broken.
☐ If leaf springs are fitted, check that all leaves are intact, that the axle is securely attached to each spring, and that there is no deterioration of the spring eye mountings, bushes, and shackles.

☐ The same general checks apply to vehicles fitted with other suspension types, such as torsion bars, hydraulic displacer units, etc. Ensure that all mountings and attachments are secure, that there are no signs of excessive wear, corrosion or damage, and (on hydraulic types) that there are no fluid leaks or damaged pipes.
☐ Inspect the shock absorbers for signs of serious fluid leakage. Check for wear of the mounting bushes or attachments, or damage to the body of the unit.

Driveshafts (fwd vehicles only)

☐ Rotate each front wheel in turn and inspect the constant velocity joint gaiters for splits or damage. Also check that each driveshaft is straight and undamaged.

Braking system

☐ If possible without dismantling, check brake pad wear and disc condition. Ensure that the friction lining material has not worn excessively, (A) and that the discs are not fractured, pitted, scored or badly worn (B).

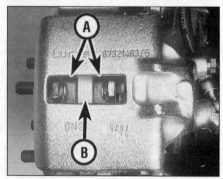

☐ Examine all the rigid brake pipes underneath the vehicle, and the flexible hose(s) at the rear. Look for corrosion, chafing or insecurity of the pipes, and for signs of bulging under pressure, chafing, splits or deterioration of the flexible hoses.
☐ Look for signs of fluid leaks at the brake calipers or on the brake backplates. Repair or renew leaking components.
☐ Slowly spin each wheel, while your assistant depresses and releases the footbrake. Ensure that each brake is operating and does not bind when the pedal is released.

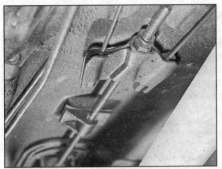

□ Examine the handbrake mechanism, checking for frayed or broken cables, excessive corrosion, or wear or insecurity of the linkage. Check that the mechanism works on each relevant wheel, and releases fully, without binding.

□ It is not possible to test brake efficiency without special equipment, but a road test can be carried out later to check that the vehicle pulls up in a straight line.

Fuel and exhaust systems

□ Inspect the fuel tank (including the filler cap), fuel pipes, hoses and unions. All components must be secure and free from leaks.

□ Examine the exhaust system over its entire length, checking for any damaged, broken or missing mountings, security of the retaining clamps and rust or corrosion.

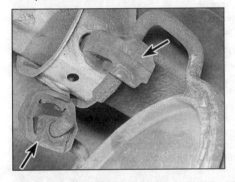

Wheels and tyres

□ Examine the sidewalls and tread area of each tyre in turn. Check for cuts, tears, lumps, bulges, separation of the tread, and exposure of the ply or cord due to wear or damage. Check that the tyre bead is correctly seated on the wheel rim, that the valve is sound and

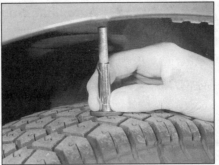

properly seated, and that the wheel is not distorted or damaged.

□ Check that the tyres are of the correct size for the vehicle, that they are of the same size and type on each axle, and that the pressures are correct.

□ Check the tyre tread depth. The legal minimum at the time of writing is 1.6 mm over at least three-quarters of the tread width. Abnormal tread wear may indicate incorrect front wheel alignment.

Body corrosion

□ Check the condition of the entire vehicle structure for signs of corrosion in load-bearing areas. (These include chassis box sections, side sills, cross-members, pillars, and all suspension, steering, braking system and seat belt mountings and anchorages.) Any corrosion which has seriously reduced the thickness of a load-bearing area is likely to cause the vehicle to fail. In this case professional repairs are likely to be needed.

□ Damage or corrosion which causes sharp or otherwise dangerous edges to be exposed will also cause the vehicle to fail.

4 Checks carried out on YOUR VEHICLE'S EXHAUST EMISSION SYSTEM

Petrol models

□ Have the engine at normal operating temperature, and make sure that it is in good tune (ignition system in good order, air filter element clean, etc).

□ Before any measurements are carried out, raise the engine speed to around 2500 rpm, and hold it at this speed for 20 seconds. Allow the engine speed to return to idle, and watch for smoke emissions from the exhaust tailpipe. If the idle speed is obviously much too high, or if dense blue or clearly-visible black smoke comes from the tailpipe for more than 5 seconds, the vehicle will fail. As a rule of thumb, blue smoke signifies oil being burnt (engine wear) while black smoke signifies unburnt fuel (dirty air cleaner element, or other carburettor or fuel system fault).

□ An exhaust gas analyser capable of measuring carbon monoxide (CO) and hydrocarbons (HC) is now needed. If such an instrument cannot be hired or borrowed, a local garage may agree to perform the check for a small fee.

CO emissions (mixture)

□ At the time of writing, the maximum CO level at idle is 3.5% for vehicles first used after August 1986 and 4.5% for older vehicles. From January 1996 a much tighter limit (around 0.5%) applies to catalyst-equipped vehicles first used from August 1992. If the CO level cannot be reduced far enough to pass the test (and the fuel and ignition systems are otherwise in good condition) then the carburettor is badly worn, or there is some problem in the fuel injection system or catalytic converter (as applicable).

HC emissions

□ With the CO emissions within limits, HC emissions must be no more than 1200 ppm (parts per million). If the vehicle fails this test at idle, it can be re-tested at around 2000 rpm; if the HC level is then 1200 ppm or less, this counts as a pass.

□ Excessive HC emissions can be caused by oil being burnt, but they are more likely to be due to unburnt fuel.

Diesel models

□ The only emission test applicable to Diesel engines is the measuring of exhaust smoke density. The test involves accelerating the engine several times to its maximum unloaded speed.

Note: *It is of the utmost importance that the engine timing belt is in good condition before the test is carried out.*

□ Excessive smoke can be caused by a dirty air cleaner element. Otherwise, professional advice may be needed to find the cause.

Engine 1

- [ ] Engine fails to rotate when attempting to start
- [ ] Engine rotates, but will not start
- [ ] Engine difficult to start when cold
- [ ] Engine difficult to start when hot
- [ ] Starter motor noisy or excessively-rough in engagement
- [ ] Engine starts, but stops immediately
- [ ] Engine idles erratically
- [ ] Engine misfires at idle speed
- [ ] Engine misfires throughout the driving speed range
- [ ] Engine hesitates on acceleration
- [ ] Engine stalls
- [ ] Engine lacks power
- [ ] Engine backfires
- [ ] Oil pressure warning light illuminated with engine running
- [ ] Engine runs-on after switching off
- [ ] Engine noises

Cooling system 2

- [ ] Overheating
- [ ] Overcooling
- [ ] External coolant leakage
- [ ] Internal coolant leakage
- [ ] Corrosion

Fuel and exhaust systems 3

- [ ] Excessive fuel consumption
- [ ] Fuel leakage and/or fuel odour
- [ ] Excessive noise or fumes from exhaust system

Clutch 4

- [ ] Pedal travels to floor - no pressure or very little resistance
- [ ] Clutch fails to disengage (unable to select gears)
- [ ] Clutch slips (engine speed increases, with no increase in vehicle speed)
- [ ] Judder as clutch is engaged
- [ ] Noise when depressing or releasing clutch pedal

Manual transmission 5

- [ ] Noisy in neutral with engine running
- [ ] Noisy in one particular gear
- [ ] Difficulty engaging gears
- [ ] Jumps out of gear
- [ ] Vibration
- [ ] Lubricant leaks

Automatic transmission 6

- [ ] Fluid leakage
- [ ] Transmission fluid brown, or has burned smell
- [ ] General gear selection problems
- [ ] Transmission will not downshift (kickdown) with accelerator fully depressed
- [ ] Engine will not start in any gear, or starts in gears other than Park or Neutral
- [ ] Transmission slips, shifts roughly, is noisy, or has no drive in forward or reverse gears

Driveshafts 7

- [ ] Clicking or knocking noise on turns (at slow speed on full-lock)
- [ ] Vibration when accelerating or decelerating

Braking system 8

- [ ] Vehicle pulls to one side under braking
- [ ] Noise (grinding or high-pitched squeal) when brakes applied
- [ ] Excessive brake pedal travel
- [ ] Brake pedal feels spongy when depressed
- [ ] Excessive brake pedal effort required to stop vehicle
- [ ] Judder felt through brake pedal or steering wheel when braking
- [ ] Brakes binding
- [ ] Rear wheels locking under normal braking

Suspension and steering systems 9

- [ ] Vehicle pulls to one side
- [ ] Wheel wobble and vibration
- [ ] Excessive pitching and/or rolling around corners, or during braking
- [ ] Wandering or general instability
- [ ] Excessively-stiff steering
- [ ] Excessive play in steering
- [ ] Lack of power assistance
- [ ] Tyre wear excessive

Electrical system 10

- [ ] Battery will not hold a charge for more than a few days
- [ ] Ignition/no-charge warning light remains illuminated with engine running
- [ ] Ignition/no-charge warning light fails to come on
- [ ] Lights inoperative
- [ ] Instrument readings inaccurate or erratic
- [ ] Horn inoperative, or unsatisfactory in operation
- [ ] Windscreen/tailgate wipers inoperative, or unsatisfactory in operation
- [ ] Windscreen/tailgate washers inoperative, or unsatisfactory in operation
- [ ] Electric windows inoperative, or unsatisfactory in operation
- [ ] Central locking system inoperative, or unsatisfactory in operation

Introduction

The vehicle owner who does his or her own maintenance according to the recommended service schedules should not have to use this section of the manual very often. Modern component reliability is such that, provided those items subject to wear or deterioration are inspected or renewed at the specified intervals, sudden failure is comparatively rare. Faults do not usually just happen as a result of sudden failure, but develop over a period of time. Major mechanical failures in particular are usually preceded by characteristic symptoms over hundreds or even thousands of miles. Those components which do occasionally fail without warning are often small and easily carried in the vehicle.

With any fault-finding, the first step is to decide where to begin investigations. Sometimes this is obvious, but on other occasions, a little detective work will be necessary. The owner who makes half a dozen haphazard adjustments or replacements may be successful in curing a fault (or its symptoms), but will be none the wiser if the fault recurs, and ultimately may have spent more time and money than was necessary. A calm and logical approach will be found to be more satisfactory in the long run. Always take into account any warning signs or abnormalities that may have been noticed in the period preceding the fault - power loss, high or low gauge readings, unusual smells, etc - and remember that failure of components such as fuses or spark plugs may only be pointers to some underlying fault.

The pages which follow provide an easy-reference guide to the more common problems which may occur during the operation of the vehicle. These problems and their possible causes are grouped under headings denoting various components or systems, such as Engine, Cooling system, etc. The Chapter and/or Section which deals with the problem is also shown in brackets. Whatever the fault, certain basic principles apply. These are as follows:

Verify the fault. This is simply a matter of being sure that you know what the symptoms are before starting work. This is particularly important if you are investigating a fault for someone else, who may not have described it very accurately.

Don't overlook the obvious. For example, if the vehicle won't start, is there petrol in the tank? (Don't take anyone else's word on this particular point, and don't trust the fuel gauge either!) If an electrical fault is indicated, look for loose or broken wires before digging out the test gear.

Cure the disease, not the symptom. Substituting a flat battery with a fully-charged one will get you off the hard shoulder, but if the underlying cause is not attended to, the new battery will go the same way. Similarly, changing oil-fouled spark plugs for a new set will get you moving again, but remember that the reason for the fouling (if it wasn't simply an incorrect grade of plug) will have to be established and corrected.

Don't take anything for granted. Particularly, don't forget that a "new" component may itself be defective (especially if it's been rattling around in the boot for months), and don't leave components out of a fault diagnosis sequence just because they are new or recently-fitted. When you do finally diagnose a difficult fault, you'll probably realise that all the evidence was there from the start.

1 Engine

Engine fails to rotate when attempting to start

- [ ] Battery terminal connections loose or corroded (*"Weekly checks"*).
- [ ] Battery discharged or faulty (Chapter 5A).
- [ ] Broken, loose or disconnected wiring in the starting circuit (Chapter 5A).
- [ ] Defective starter solenoid or switch (Chapter 5A).
- [ ] Defective starter motor (Chapter 5A).
- [ ] Starter pinion or flywheel ring gear teeth loose or broken (Chapters 2A, 2B, 2C and 5A).
- [ ] Engine earth strap broken or disconnected (Chapter 5A).

Engine rotates, but will not start

- [ ] Fuel tank empty.
- [ ] Battery discharged (engine rotates slowly) (Chapter 5A).
- [ ] Battery terminal connections loose or corroded (*"Weekly checks"*).
- [ ] Ignition components damp or damaged (Chapters 1 and 5B).
- [ ] Broken, loose or disconnected wiring in the ignition circuit (Chapters 1 and 5B).
- [ ] Worn, faulty or incorrectly-gapped spark plugs (Chapter 1).
- [ ] Choke mechanism incorrectly adjusted, worn or sticking - carburettor models (Chapter 4A).
- [ ] Faulty fuel cut-off solenoid - carburettor models (Chapter 4A).
- [ ] Fuel injection system fault - fuel-injected models (Chapter 4B or 4C).
- [ ] Major mechanical failure (eg camshaft drive) (Chapter 2A, 2B or 2C).

Engine difficult to start when cold

- [ ] Battery discharged (Chapter 5A).
- [ ] Battery terminal connections loose or corroded (Chapter 1).
- [ ] Worn, faulty or incorrectly-gapped spark plugs (Chapter 1).
- [ ] Choke mechanism incorrectly adjusted, worn or sticking - carburettor models (Chapter 4A).
- [ ] Fuel injection system fault - fuel-injected l models (Chapter 4B or 4C).
- [ ] Other ignition system fault (Chapters 1 and 5B).
- [ ] Low cylinder compressions (Chapter 2A, 2B or 2C).

Engine difficult to start when hot

- [ ] Air filter element dirty or clogged (Chapter 1).
- [ ] Choke mechanism incorrectly adjusted, worn or sticking - carburettor models (Chapter 4A).
- [ ] Fuel injection system fault - fuel-injected models (Chapter 4B or 4C).
- [ ] Low cylinder compressions (Chapter 2A, 2B or 2C).

Starter motor noisy or excessively-rough in engagement

- [ ] Starter pinion or flywheel ring gear teeth loose or broken (Chapters 2A, 2B, 2C and 5A).
- [ ] Starter motor mounting bolts loose or missing (Chapter 5A).
- [ ] Starter motor internal components worn or damaged (Chapter 5A).

Engine starts, but stops immediately

- [ ] Loose or faulty electrical connections in the ignition circuit (Chapters 1 and 5B).
- [ ] Vacuum leak at the carburettor/throttle body or inlet manifold (Chapter 4A, 4B or 4C).
- [ ] Blocked carburettor jet(s) or internal passages - carburettor models (Chapter 4A).
- [ ] Blocked injector/fuel injection system fault - fuel-injected models (Chapter 4B or 4C).

Engine idles erratically

- [ ] Air filter element clogged (Chapter 1).
- [ ] Vacuum leak at the carburettor/throttle body, inlet manifold or associated hoses (Chapter 4A, 4B or 4C).
- [ ] Worn, faulty or incorrectly-gapped spark plugs (Chapter 1).
- [ ] Uneven or low cylinder compressions (Chapter 2A, 2B or 2C).
- [ ] Camshaft lobes worn (Chapter 2A, 2B or 2C).
- [ ] Timing belt incorrectly tensioned (Chapter 2A, 2B or 2C).
- [ ] Blocked carburettor jet(s) or internal passages - carburettor models (Chapter 4A).
- [ ] Blocked injector/fuel injection system fault - fuel-injected models (Chapter 4B or 4C).

Engine misfires at idle speed

- [ ] Worn, faulty or incorrectly-gapped spark plugs (Chapter 1).
- [ ] Faulty spark plug HT leads (Chapter 1).
- [ ] Vacuum leak at the carburettor/throttle body, inlet manifold or associated hoses (Chapter 4A, 4B or 4C).
- [ ] Blocked carburettor jet(s) or internal passages - carburettor models (Chapter 4A).
- [ ] Blocked injector/fuel injection system fault - fuel-injected models (Chapter 4B or 4C).
- [ ] Distributor cap cracked or tracking internally (where applicable) (Chapter 1).
- [ ] Uneven or low cylinder compressions (Chapter 2A, 2B or 2C).
- [ ] Disconnected, leaking, or perished crankcase ventilation hoses (Chapter 4D).

Engine (continued)

Engine misfires throughout the driving speed range

- ☐ Fuel filter choked - fuel-injected models (Chapter 1).
- ☐ Fuel pump faulty, or delivery pressure low (Chapter 4A, 4B or 4C).
- ☐ Fuel tank vent blocked, or fuel pipes restricted (Chapter 4A, 4B or 4C).
- ☐ Vacuum leak at the carburettor/throttle body, inlet manifold or associated hoses (Chapter 4A, 4B or 4C).
- ☐ Worn, faulty or incorrectly-gapped spark plugs (Chapter 1).
- ☐ Faulty spark plug HT leads (Chapter 1).
- ☐ Distributor cap cracked or tracking internally (where applicable) (Chapter 1).
- ☐ Faulty ignition coil or ignition module (Chapter 5B).
- ☐ Uneven or low cylinder compressions (Chapter 2A, 2B or 2C).
- ☐ Blocked carburettor jet(s) or internal passages - carburettor models (Chapter 4A).
- ☐ Blocked injector/fuel injection system fault - fuel-injected models (Chapter 4B or 4C).

Engine hesitates on acceleration

- ☐ Worn, faulty or incorrectly-gapped spark plugs (Chapter 1).
- ☐ Vacuum leak at the carburettor/throttle body, inlet manifold or associated hoses (Chapter 4A, 4B or 4C).
- ☐ Blocked carburettor jet(s) or internal passages - carburettor models (Chapter 4A).
- ☐ Blocked injector/fuel injection system fault - fuel-injected (Chapter 4B or 4C).

Engine stalls

- ☐ Vacuum leak at the carburettor/throttle body, inlet manifold or associated hoses (Chapter 4A, 4B or 4C).
- ☐ Fuel filter choked - fuel-injected models (Chapter 1).
- ☐ Fuel pump faulty, or delivery pressure low (Chapter 4A, 4B or 4C).
- ☐ Fuel tank vent blocked, or fuel pipes restricted (Chapter 4A, 4B, 4C or 4D).
- ☐ Blocked carburettor jet(s) or internal passages - carburettor models (Chapter 4A).
- ☐ Blocked injector/fuel injection system fault - fuel-injected models (Chapter 4B or 4C).

Engine lacks power

- ☐ Timing chain or belt incorrectly fitted or tensioned (Chapter 2A, 2B or 2C).
- ☐ Fuel filter choked - fuel-injected models (Chapter 1).
- ☐ Fuel pump faulty, or delivery pressure low (Chapter 4A, 4B, or 4C).
- ☐ Uneven or low cylinder compressions (Chapter 2A, 2B or 2C).
- ☐ Worn, faulty or incorrectly-gapped spark plugs (Chapter 1).
- ☐ Vacuum leak at the carburettor/throttle body, inlet manifold or associated hoses (Chapter 4A, 4B or 4C).
- ☐ Blocked carburettor jet(s) or internal passages - carburettor models (Chapter 4A).
- ☐ Blocked injector/fuel injection system fault - fuel-injected models (Chapter 4B or 4C).
- ☐ Brakes binding (Chapters 1 and 9).
- ☐ Clutch slipping (Chapter 6).

Engine backfires

- ☐ Timing chain or belt incorrectly fitted or tensioned (Chapter 2A, 2B or 2C).
- ☐ Vacuum leak at the carburettor/throttle body, inlet manifold or associated hoses (Chapter 4A, 4B or 4C).
- ☐ Blocked carburettor jet(s) or internal passages - carburettor models (Chapter 4A).
- ☐ Blocked injector/fuel injection system fault - fuel-injected models (Chapter 4B or 4C).

Oil pressure warning light illuminated with engine running

- ☐ Low oil level, or incorrect oil grade (Chapter 1).
- ☐ Faulty oil pressure warning light switch (Chapter 5A).
- ☐ Worn engine bearings and/or oil pump (Chapter 2D).
- ☐ High engine operating temperature (Chapter 3).
- ☐ Oil pressure relief valve defective (Chapter 2A, 2B or 2C).
- ☐ Oil pick-up strainer clogged (Chapter 2A, 2B or 2C).

Engine runs-on after switching off

- ☐ Excessive carbon build-up in engine (Chapter 2D).
- ☐ High engine operating temperature (Chapter 3).
- ☐ Faulty fuel cut-off solenoid - carburettor models (Chapter 4A).
- ☐ Fuel injection system fault - fuel-injected models (Chapter 4B or 4C).

Engine noises

Pre-ignition (pinking) or knocking during acceleration or under load

- ☐ Ignition timing incorrect/ignition system fault (Chapters 1 and 5B).
- ☐ Incorrect grade of spark plug (Chapter 1).
- ☐ Incorrect grade of fuel (Chapter 1).
- ☐ Vacuum leak at the carburettor/throttle body, inlet manifold or associated hoses (Chapter 4A, 4B or 4C).
- ☐ Excessive carbon build-up in engine (Chapter 2D).
- ☐ Blocked carburettor jet(s) or internal passages - carburettor models (Chapter 4A).
- ☐ Blocked injector/fuel injection system fault - fuel-injected models (Chapter 4B or 4C).

Whistling or wheezing noises

- ☐ Leaking inlet manifold or carburettor/throttle body gasket (Chapter 4A, 4B or 4C).
- ☐ Leaking exhaust manifold gasket or pipe-to-manifold joint (Chapter 4A, 4B, 4C or 4D).
- ☐ Leaking vacuum hose (Chapters 4A, 4B, 4C, 4D, 5B and 9).
- ☐ Blowing cylinder head gasket (Chapter 2A, 2B and 2C).

Tapping or rattling noises

- ☐ Worn valve gear or camshaft (Chapter 2A, 2B or 2C).
- ☐ Ancillary component fault (coolant pump, alternator, etc) (Chapters 3, 5A, etc).

Knocking or thumping noises

- ☐ Worn big-end bearings (regular heavy knocking, perhaps less under load) (Chapter 2D).
- ☐ Worn main bearings (rumbling and knocking, perhaps worsening under load) (Chapter 2D).
- ☐ Piston slap (most noticeable when cold) (Chapter 2D).
- ☐ Ancillary component fault (coolant pump, alternator, etc) (Chapters 3, 5A, etc).

2 Cooling system

Overheating

- [ ] Insufficient coolant in system (*"Weekly checks"*).
- [ ] Thermostat faulty (Chapter 3).
- [ ] Radiator core blocked, or grille restricted (Chapter 3).
- [ ] Electric cooling fan or thermoswitch faulty (Chapter 3).
- [ ] Pressure cap faulty (Chapter 3).
- [ ] Ignition timing incorrect/ignition system fault (Chapters 1 and 5B).
- [ ] Inaccurate temperature gauge sender unit (Chapter 3).
- [ ] Airlock in cooling system (Chapter 1).

Overcooling

- [ ] Thermostat faulty (Chapter 3).
- [ ] Inaccurate temperature gauge sender unit (Chapter 3).

External coolant leakage

- [ ] Deteriorated or damaged hoses or hose clips (Chapter 1).
- [ ] Radiator core or heater matrix leaking (Chapter 3).
- [ ] Pressure cap faulty (Chapter 3).
- [ ] Coolant pump seal leaking (Chapter 3).
- [ ] Boiling due to overheating (Chapter 3).
- [ ] Core plug leaking (Chapter 2D).

Internal coolant leakage

- [ ] Leaking cylinder head gasket (Chapter 2A, 2B or 2C).
- [ ] Cracked cylinder head or cylinder bore (Chapter 2A, 2B, 2C or 2D).
- [ ] Leaking cylinder liner base seal (Chapter 2D)

Corrosion

- [ ] Infrequent draining and flushing (Chapter 1).
- [ ] Incorrect coolant mixture or inappropriate coolant type (Chapter 1).

3 Fuel and exhaust systems

Excessive fuel consumption

- [ ] Air filter element dirty or clogged (Chapter 1).
- [ ] Choke cable incorrectly adjusted, or choke sticking - carburettor models (Chapter 4A).
- [ ] Fuel injection system fault - fuel-injected models (Chapter 4B or 4C).
- [ ] Ignition timing incorrect/ignition system fault (Chapters 1 and 5B).
- [ ] Tyres under-inflated (*"Weekly checks"*).

Fuel leakage and/or fuel odour

- [ ] Damaged or corroded fuel tank, pipes or connections (Chapter 4A, 4B, 4C or 4D).
- [ ] Carburettor float chamber flooding (float height incorrect) - carburettor models (Chapter 4A).

Excessive noise or fumes from exhaust system

- [ ] Leaking exhaust system or manifold joints (Chapters 1 and 4D).
- [ ] Leaking, corroded or damaged silencers or pipe (Chapters 1 and 4D).
- [ ] Broken mountings causing body or suspension contact (Chapter 1).

4 Clutch

Pedal travels to floor - no pressure or very little resistance

- [ ] Broken clutch cable (Chapter 6).
- [ ] Incorrect clutch pedal stroke adjustment (Chapter 1).
- [ ] Broken clutch release bearing or fork (Chapter 6).
- [ ] Broken diaphragm spring in clutch pressure plate (Chapter 6).

Clutch fails to disengage (unable to select gears).

- [ ] Incorrect clutch pedal stroke adjustment (Chapter 1).
- [ ] Clutch plate sticking on transmission input shaft splines (Chapter 6).
- [ ] Clutch plate sticking to flywheel or pressure plate (Chapter 6).
- [ ] Faulty pressure plate assembly (Chapter 6).
- [ ] Clutch release mechanism worn or incorrectly assembled (Chapter 6).

Clutch slips (engine speed increases, with no increase in vehicle speed).

- [ ] Incorrect clutch pedal stroke adjustment (Chapter 1).
- [ ] Clutch plate linings excessively worn (Chapter 6).
- [ ] Clutch plate linings contaminated with oil or grease (Chapter 6).
- [ ] Faulty pressure plate or weak diaphragm spring (Chapter 6).

Judder as clutch is engaged

- [ ] Clutch plate linings contaminated with oil or grease (Chapter 6).
- [ ] Clutch plate linings excessively worn (Chapter 6).
- [ ] Clutch cable sticking or frayed (Chapter 6).
- [ ] Faulty or distorted pressure plate or diaphragm spring (Chapter 6).
- [ ] Worn or loose engine or transmission mountings (Chapter 2A, 2B or 2C).
- [ ] Clutch plate hub or transmission input shaft splines worn (Chapter 6).

Noise when depressing or releasing clutch pedal

- [ ] Worn clutch release bearing (Chapter 6).
- [ ] Worn or dry clutch pedal bushes (Chapter 6).
- [ ] Faulty pressure plate assembly (Chapter 6).
- [ ] Pressure plate diaphragm spring broken (Chapter 6).
- [ ] Broken clutch plate cushioning springs (Chapter 6).

5 Manual transmission

Noisy in neutral with engine running

☐ Input shaft bearings worn (noise apparent with clutch pedal released, but not when depressed) (Chapter 7A).*
☐ Clutch release bearing worn (noise apparent with clutch pedal depressed, possibly less when released) (Chapter 6).

Noisy in one particular gear

☐ Worn, damaged or chipped gear teeth (Chapter 7A).*

Difficulty engaging gears

☐ Clutch fault (Chapter 6).
☐ Worn or damaged gear linkage (Chapter 7A).
☐ Incorrectly-adjusted gear linkage (Chapter 7A).
☐ Worn synchroniser units (Chapter 7A).*

Jumps out of gear

☐ Worn or damaged gear linkage (Chapter 7A).
☐ Incorrectly-adjusted gear linkage (Chapter 7A).
☐ Worn synchroniser units (Chapter 7A).*
☐ Worn selector forks (Chapter 7A).*

Vibration

☐ Lack of oil (Chapter 1).
☐ Worn bearings (Chapter 7A).*

Lubricant leaks

☐ Leaking differential output (driveshaft) oil seal (Chapter 7A).
☐ Leaking housing joint (Chapter 7A).*

Although the corrective action necessary to remedy the symptoms described is beyond the scope of the home mechanic, the above information should be helpful in isolating the cause of the condition, so that the owner can communicate clearly with a professional mechanic.

6 Automatic transmission

Note: *Due to the complexity of the automatic transmission, it is difficult for the home mechanic to properly diagnose and service this unit. For problems other than the following, the vehicle should be taken to a dealer service department or automatic transmission specialist. Do not be too hasty in removing the transmission if a fault is suspected, as most of the testing is carried out with the unit still fitted.*

Fluid leakage

☐ Automatic transmission fluid is usually dark in colour. Fluid leaks should not be confused with engine oil, which can easily be blown onto the transmission by airflow.
☐ To determine the source of a leak, first remove all built-up dirt and grime from the transmission housing and surrounding areas using a degreasing agent, or by steam-cleaning. Drive the vehicle at low speed, so airflow will not blow the leak far from its source. Raise and support the vehicle, and determine where the leak is coming from. The following are common areas of leakage:
  a) *Fluid pan or "sump" (Chapter 1 and 7B).*
  b) *Dipstick tube (Chapter 1 and 7B).*
  c) *Transmission-to-fluid cooler pipes/unions (Chapter 7B).*

Transmission fluid brown, or has burned smell

☐ Transmission fluid level low, or fluid in need of renewal (Chapter 1).

General gear selection problems

☐ Chapter 7B deals with checking and adjusting the selector cable

on automatic transmissions. The following are common problems which may be caused by a poorly-adjusted cable:
  a) *Engine starting in gears other than Park or Neutral.*
  b) *Indicator panel indicating a gear other than the one actually being used.*
  c) *Vehicle moves when in Park or Neutral.*
  d) *Poor gear shift quality or erratic gear changes.*
☐ Refer to Chapter 7B for the selector cable adjustment procedure.

Transmission will not downshift (kickdown) with accelerator pedal fully depressed

☐ Low transmission fluid level (Chapter 1).
☐ Incorrect selector cable adjustment (Chapter 7B).

Engine will not start in any gear, or starts in gears other than Park or Neutral

☐ Incorrect starter/inhibitor switch adjustment (Chapter 7B).
☐ Incorrect selector cable adjustment (Chapter 7B).

Transmission slips, shifts roughly, is noisy, or has no drive in forward or reverse gears

☐ There are many probable causes for the above problems, but the home mechanic should be concerned with only one possibility - fluid level. Before taking the vehicle to a dealer or transmission specialist, check the fluid level and condition of the fluid as described in Chapter 1. Correct the fluid level as necessary, or change the fluid and filter if needed. If the problem persists, professional help will be necessary.

7 Driveshafts

Clicking or knocking noise on turns (at slow speed on full-lock)

☐ Lack of constant velocity joint lubricant, possibly due to damaged bellows (Chapter 8).
☐ Worn outer constant velocity joint (Chapter 8).

Vibration when accelerating or decelerating

☐ Worn inner constant velocity joint (Chapter 8).
☐ Bent or distorted driveshaft (Chapter 8).

8 Braking system

Note: *Before assuming that a brake problem exists, make sure that the tyres are in good condition and correctly inflated, that the front wheel alignment is correct, and that the vehicle is not loaded with weight in an unequal manner. Apart from checking the condition of all pipe and hose connections, any faults occurring on the anti-lock braking system should be referred to a Peugeot dealer for diagnosis.*

Vehicle pulls to one side under braking

☐ Worn, defective, damaged or contaminated brake pads/shoes on one side (Chapters 1 and 9).
☐ Seized or partially-seized front brake caliper/wheel cylinder piston (Chapters 1 and 9).
☐ A mixture of brake pad/shoe lining materials fitted between sides (Chapters 1 and 9).
☐ Brake caliper or backplate mounting bolts loose (Chapter 9).
☐ Worn or damaged steering or suspension components (Chapters 1 and 10).

Noise (grinding or high-pitched squeal) when brakes applied

☐ Brake pad or shoe friction lining material worn down to metal backing (Chapters 1 and 9).
☐ Excessive corrosion of brake disc or drum. (May be apparent after the vehicle has been standing for some time (Chapters 1 and 9).
☐ Foreign object (stone chipping, etc) trapped between brake disc and shield (Chapters 1 and 9).

Excessive brake pedal travel

☐ Inoperative rear brake self-adjust mechanism - drum brakes (Chapter 9).
☐ Faulty master cylinder (Chapter 9).
☐ Air in hydraulic system (Chapters 1 and 9).
☐ Faulty vacuum servo unit (Chapter 9).

Brake pedal feels spongy when depressed

☐ Air in hydraulic system (Chapters 1 and 9).
☐ Deteriorated flexible rubber brake hoses (Chapters 1 and 9).
☐ Master cylinder mounting nuts loose (Chapter 9).
☐ Faulty master cylinder (Chapter 9).

Excessive brake pedal effort required to stop vehicle

☐ Faulty vacuum servo unit (Chapter 9).
☐ Disconnected, damaged or insecure brake servo vacuum hose (Chapter 9).
☐ Primary or secondary hydraulic circuit failure (Chapter 9).
☐ Seized brake caliper or wheel cylinder piston(s) (Chapter 9).
☐ Brake pads or brake shoes incorrectly fitted (Chapters 1 and 9).
☐ Incorrect grade of brake pads or brake shoes fitted (Chapters 1 and 9).
☐ Brake pads or brake shoe linings contaminated (Chapters 1 and 9).

Judder felt through brake pedal or steering wheel when braking

☐ Excessive run-out or distortion of discs/drums (Chapters 1 and 9).
☐ Brake pad or brake shoe linings worn (Chapters 1 and 9).
☐ Brake caliper or brake backplate mounting bolts loose (Chapter 9).
☐ Wear in suspension or steering components or mountings (Chapters 1 and 10).

Brakes binding

☐ Seized brake caliper or wheel cylinder piston(s) (Chapter 9).
☐ Incorrectly-adjusted handbrake mechanism (Chapter 9).
☐ Faulty master cylinder (Chapter 9).

Rear wheels locking under normal braking

☐ Rear brake shoe linings contaminated (Chapters 1 and 9).
☐ Faulty brake pressure regulator (Chapter 9).

9 Suspension and steering

Note: *Before diagnosing suspension or steering faults, be sure that the trouble is not due to incorrect tyre pressures, mixtures of tyre types, or binding brakes.*

Vehicle pulls to one side

☐ Defective tyre (*"Weekly checks"*).
☐ Excessive wear in suspension or steering components (Chapters 1 and 10).
☐ Incorrect front wheel alignment (Chapter 10).
☐ Accident damage to steering or suspension components (Chapter 1).

Wheel wobble and vibration

☐ Front roadwheels out of balance (vibration felt mainly through the steering wheel) (Chapters 1 and 10).
☐ Rear roadwheels out of balance (vibration felt throughout the vehicle) (Chapters 1 and 10).
☐ Roadwheels damaged or distorted (Chapters 1 and 10).
☐ Defective tyre (*"Weekly checks"*).
☐ Worn steering or suspension joints, bushes or components (Chapters 1 and 10).
☐ Wheel bolts loose (Chapters 1 and 10).

Excessive pitching and/or rolling around corners, or during braking

☐ Defective shock absorbers (Chapters 1 and 10).
☐ Broken or weak spring and/or suspension component (Chapters 1 and 10).
☐ Worn or damaged anti-roll bar or mountings (Chapter 10).

Wandering or general instability

☐ Incorrect front wheel alignment (Chapter 10).
☐ Worn steering or suspension joints, bushes or components (Chapters 1 and 10).
☐ Roadwheels out of balance (Chapters 1 and 10).
☐ Defective tyre (*"Weekly checks"*).
☐ Wheel bolts loose (Chapters 1 and 10).
☐ Defective shock absorbers (Chapters 1 and 10).

Excessively-stiff steering

☐ Lack of steering gear lubricant (Chapter 10).
☐ Seized track rod end balljoint or suspension balljoint (Chapters 1 and 10).
☐ Broken or incorrectly-adjusted auxiliary drivebelt - power steering (Chapter 1).
☐ Incorrect front wheel alignment (Chapter 10).
☐ Steering rack or column bent or damaged (Chapter 10).

Suspension and steering (continued)

Excessive play in steering

- ☐ Worn steering column intermediate shaft universal joint (Chapter 10).
- ☐ Worn steering track rod end balljoints (Chapters 1 and 10).
- ☐ Worn rack-and-pinion steering gear (Chapter 10).
- ☐ Worn steering or suspension joints, bushes or components (Chapters 1 and 10).

Lack of power assistance

- ☐ Broken or incorrectly-adjusted auxiliary drivebelt (Chapter 1).
- ☐ Incorrect power steering fluid level ("Weekly checks").
- ☐ Restriction in power steering fluid hoses (Chapter 1).
- ☐ Faulty power steering pump (Chapter 10).
- ☐ Faulty rack-and-pinion steering gear (Chapter 10).

Tyre wear excessive

Tyres worn on inside or outside edges

- ☐ Tyres under-inflated (wear on both edges) ("Weekly checks").
- ☐ Incorrect camber or castor angles (wear on one edge only) (Chapter 10).
- ☐ Worn steering or suspension joints, bushes or components (Chapters 1 and 10).
- ☐ Excessively-hard cornering.
- ☐ Accident damage.

Tyre treads exhibit feathered edges

- ☐ Incorrect toe setting (Chapter 10).

Tyres worn in centre of tread

- ☐ Tyres over-inflated ("Weekly checks").

Tyres worn on inside and outside edges

- ☐ Tyres under-inflated ("Weekly checks").

Tyres worn unevenly

- ☐ Tyres/wheels out of balance (Chapter 1).
- ☐ Excessive wheel or tyre run-out (Chapter 1).
- ☐ Worn shock absorbers (Chapters 1 and 10).
- ☐ Defective tyre ("Weekly checks").

10 Electrical system

Note: *For problems associated with the starting system, refer to the faults listed under "Engine" earlier in this Section.*

Battery will not hold a charge for more than a few days

- ☐ Battery defective internally (Chapter 5A).
- ☐ Battery terminal connections loose or corroded("Weekly checks").
- ☐ Auxiliary drivebelt worn or incorrectly adjusted (Chapter 1).
- ☐ Alternator not charging at correct output (Chapter 5A).
- ☐ Alternator or voltage regulator faulty (Chapter 5A).
- ☐ Short-circuit causing continual battery drain (Chapters 5A and 12).

Ignition/no-charge warning light remains illuminated with engine running

- ☐ Auxiliary drivebelt broken, worn, or incorrectly adjusted (Chapter 1).
- ☐ Alternator brushes worn, sticking, or dirty (Chapter 5A).
- ☐ Alternator brush springs weak or broken (Chapter 5A).
- ☐ Internal fault in alternator or voltage regulator (Chapter 5A).
- ☐ Broken, disconnected, or loose wiring in charging circuit (Chapter 5A).

Ignition/no-charge warning light fails to come on

- ☐ Warning light bulb blown (Chapter 12).
- ☐ Broken, disconnected, or loose wiring in warning light circuit (Chapter 12).
- ☐ Alternator faulty (Chapter 5A).

Lights inoperative

- ☐ Bulb blown (Chapter 12).
- ☐ Corrosion of bulb or bulbholder contacts (Chapter 12).
- ☐ Blown fuse (Chapter 12).
- ☐ Faulty relay (Chapter 12).
- ☐ Broken, loose, or disconnected wiring (Chapter 12).
- ☐ Faulty switch (Chapter 12).

Instrument readings inaccurate or erratic

Instrument readings increase with engine speed

- ☐ Faulty voltage regulator (Chapter 12).

Fuel or temperature gauges give no reading

- ☐ Faulty gauge sender unit (Chapters 3 and 4A, 4B, 4C or 4D).
- ☐ Wiring open-circuit (Chapter 12).
- ☐ Faulty gauge (Chapter 12).

Fuel or temperature gauges give continuous maximum reading

- ☐ Faulty gauge sender unit (Chapters 3 and 4A, 4B, 4C and 4D).
- ☐ Wiring short-circuit (Chapter 12).
- ☐ Faulty gauge (Chapter 12).

Horn inoperative, or unsatisfactory in operation

Horn operates all the time

- ☐ Horn push either earthed or stuck down (Chapter 12).
- ☐ Horn cable-to-horn push earthed (Chapter 12).

Horn fails to operate

- ☐ Blown fuse (Chapter 12).
- ☐ Cable or cable connections loose, broken or disconnected (Chapter 12).
- ☐ Faulty horn (Chapter 12).

Horn emits intermittent or unsatisfactory sound

- ☐ Cable connections loose (Chapter 12).
- ☐ Horn mountings loose (Chapter 12).
- ☐ Faulty horn (Chapter 12).

Windscreen/tailgate wipers inoperative, or unsatisfactory in operation

Wipers fail to operate, or operate very slowly

- [ ] Wiper blades stuck to screen, or linkage seized or binding (*"Weekly checks"* and Chapter 12).
- [ ] Blown fuse (Chapter 12).
- [ ] Cable or cable connections loose, broken or disconnected (Chapter 12).
- [ ] Faulty relay (Chapter 12).
- [ ] Faulty wiper motor (Chapter 12).

Wiper blades sweep over too large or too small an area of the glass

- [ ] Wiper arms incorrectly positioned on spindles (Chapter 12).
- [ ] Excessive wear of wiper linkage (Chapter 12).
- [ ] Wiper motor or linkage mountings loose or insecure (Chapter 12).

Wiper blades fail to clean the glass effectively

- [ ] Wiper blade rubbers worn or perished (*"Weekly checks"*).
- [ ] Wiper arm tension springs broken, or arm pivots seized (Chapter 12).
- [ ] Insufficient windscreen washer additive to adequately remove road film (*"Weekly checks"*).

Windscreen/tailgate washers inoperative, or unsatisfactory in operation

One or more washer jets inoperative

- [ ] Blocked washer jet (Chapter 1).
- [ ] Disconnected, kinked or restricted fluid hose (Chapter 12).
- [ ] Insufficient fluid in washer reservoir (Chapter 1).

Washer pump fails to operate

- [ ] Broken or disconnected wiring or connections (Chapter 12).
- [ ] Blown fuse (Chapter 12).
- [ ] Faulty washer switch (Chapter 12).
- [ ] Faulty washer pump (Chapter 12).

Washer pump runs for some time before fluid is emitted from jets

- [ ] Faulty one-way valve in fluid supply hose (Chapter 12).

Electric windows inoperative, or unsatisfactory in operation

Window glass will only move in one direction

- [ ] Faulty switch (Chapter 12).

Window glass slow to move

- [ ] Regulator seized or damaged, or in need of lubrication (Chapter 11).
- [ ] Door internal components or trim fouling regulator (Chapter 11).
- [ ] Faulty motor (Chapter 11).

Window glass fails to move

- [ ] Blown fuse (Chapter 12).
- [ ] Faulty relay (Chapter 12).
- [ ] Broken or disconnected wiring or connections (Chapter 12).
- [ ] Faulty motor (Chapter 11).

Central locking system inoperative, or unsatisfactory in operation

Complete system failure

- [ ] Blown fuse (Chapter 12).
- [ ] Faulty relay (Chapter 12).
- [ ] Broken or disconnected wiring or connections (Chapter 12).
- [ ] Faulty control unit (Chapter 11).

Latch locks but will not unlock, or unlocks but will not lock

- [ ] Faulty master switch (Chapter 12).
- [ ] Broken or disconnected latch operating rods or levers (Chapter 11).
- [ ] Faulty relay (Chapter 12).
- [ ] Faulty control unit (Chapter 11).

One solenoid/motor fails to operate

- [ ] Broken or disconnected wiring or connections (Chapter 12).
- [ ] Faulty solenoid/motor (Chapter 11).
- [ ] Broken, binding or disconnected latch operating rods or levers (Chapter 11).
- [ ] Fault in door latch (Chapter 11).

A

ABS (Anti-lock brake system) A system, usually electronically controlled, that senses incipient wheel lockup during braking and relieves hydraulic pressure at wheels that are about to skid.

Air bag An inflatable bag hidden in the steering wheel (driver's side) or the dash or glovebox (passenger side). In a head-on collision, the bags inflate, preventing the driver and front passenger from being thrown forward into the steering wheel or windscreen.

Air cleaner A metal or plastic housing, containing a filter element, which removes dust and dirt from the air being drawn into the engine.

Air filter element The actual filter in an air cleaner system, usually manufactured from pleated paper and requiring renewal at regular intervals.

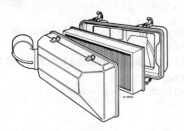
Air filter

Allen key A hexagonal wrench which fits into a recessed hexagonal hole.

Alligator clip A long-nosed spring-loaded metal clip with meshing teeth. Used to make temporary electrical connections.

Alternator A component in the electrical system which converts mechanical energy from a drivebelt into electrical energy to charge the battery and to operate the starting system, ignition system and electrical accessories.

Alternator (exploded view)

Ampere (amp) A unit of measurement for the flow of electric current. One amp is the amount of current produced by one volt acting through a resistance of one ohm.

Anaerobic sealer A substance used to prevent bolts and screws from loosening. Anaerobic means that it does not require oxygen for activation. The Loctite brand is widely used.

Antifreeze A substance (usually ethylene glycol) mixed with water, and added to a vehicle's cooling system, to prevent freezing of the coolant in winter. Antifreeze also contains chemicals to inhibit corrosion and the formation of rust and other deposits that would tend to clog the radiator and coolant passages and reduce cooling efficiency.

Anti-seize compound A coating that reduces the risk of seizing on fasteners that are subjected to high temperatures, such as exhaust manifold bolts and nuts.

Anti-seize compound

Asbestos A natural fibrous mineral with great heat resistance, commonly used in the composition of brake friction materials. Asbestos is a health hazard and the dust created by brake systems should never be inhaled or ingested.

Axle A shaft on which a wheel revolves, or which revolves with a wheel. Also, a solid beam that connects the two wheels at one end of the vehicle. An axle which also transmits power to the wheels is known as a live axle.

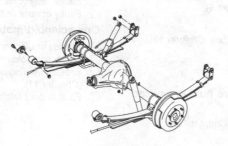
Axle assembly

Axleshaft A single rotating shaft, on either side of the differential, which delivers power from the final drive assembly to the drive wheels. Also called a driveshaft or a halfshaft.

B

Ball bearing An anti-friction bearing consisting of a hardened inner and outer race with hardened steel balls between two races.

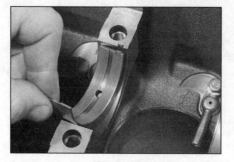
Bearing

Bearing The curved surface on a shaft or in a bore, or the part assembled into either, that permits relative motion between them with minimum wear and friction.

Big-end bearing The bearing in the end of the connecting rod that's attached to the crankshaft.

Bleed nipple A valve on a brake wheel cylinder, caliper or other hydraulic component that is opened to purge the hydraulic system of air. Also called a bleed screw.

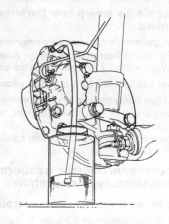
Brake bleeding

Brake bleeding Procedure for removing air from lines of a hydraulic brake system.

Brake disc The component of a disc brake that rotates with the wheels.

Brake drum The component of a drum brake that rotates with the wheels.

Brake linings The friction material which contacts the brake disc or drum to retard the vehicle's speed. The linings are bonded or riveted to the brake pads or shoes.

Brake pads The replaceable friction pads that pinch the brake disc when the brakes are applied. Brake pads consist of a friction material bonded or riveted to a rigid backing plate.

Brake shoe The crescent-shaped carrier to which the brake linings are mounted and which forces the lining against the rotating drum during braking.

Braking systems For more information on braking systems, consult the *Haynes Automotive Brake Manual*.

Breaker bar A long socket wrench handle providing greater leverage.

Bulkhead The insulated partition between the engine and the passenger compartment.

C

Caliper The non-rotating part of a disc-brake assembly that straddles the disc and carries the brake pads. The caliper also contains the hydraulic components that cause the pads to pinch the disc when the brakes are applied. A caliper is also a measuring tool that can be set to measure inside or outside dimensions of an object.

Camshaft A rotating shaft on which a series of cam lobes operate the valve mechanisms. The camshaft may be driven by gears, by sprockets and chain or by sprockets and a belt.

Canister A container in an evaporative emission control system; contains activated charcoal granules to trap vapours from the fuel system.

Canister

Carburettor A device which mixes fuel with air in the proper proportions to provide a desired power output from a spark ignition internal combustion engine.

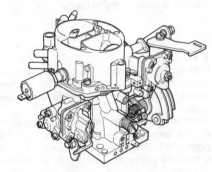

Carburettor

Castellated Resembling the parapets along the top of a castle wall. For example, a castellated balljoint stud nut.

Castellated nut

Castor In wheel alignment, the backward or forward tilt of the steering axis. Castor is positive when the steering axis is inclined rearward at the top.

Catalytic converter A silencer-like device in the exhaust system which converts certain pollutants in the exhaust gases into less harmful substances.

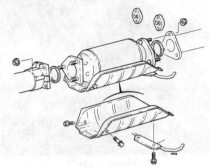

Catalytic converter

Circlip A ring-shaped clip used to prevent endwise movement of cylindrical parts and shafts. An internal circlip is installed in a groove in a housing; an external circlip fits into a groove on the outside of a cylindrical piece such as a shaft.

Clearance The amount of space between two parts. For example, between a piston and a cylinder, between a bearing and a journal, etc.

Coil spring A spiral of elastic steel found in various sizes throughout a vehicle, for example as a springing medium in the suspension and in the valve train.

Compression Reduction in volume, and increase in pressure and temperature, of a gas, caused by squeezing it into a smaller space.

Compression ratio The relationship between cylinder volume when the piston is at top dead centre and cylinder volume when the piston is at bottom dead centre.

Constant velocity (CV) joint A type of universal joint that cancels out vibrations caused by driving power being transmitted through an angle.

Core plug A disc or cup-shaped metal device inserted in a hole in a casting through which core was removed when the casting was formed. Also known as a freeze plug or expansion plug.

Crankcase The lower part of the engine block in which the crankshaft rotates.

Crankshaft The main rotating member, or shaft, running the length of the crankcase, with offset "throws" to which the connecting rods are attached.

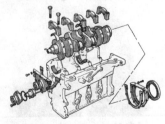

Crankshaft assembly

Crocodile clip See Alligator clip

D

Diagnostic code Code numbers obtained by accessing the diagnostic mode of an engine management computer. This code can be used to determine the area in the system where a malfunction may be located.

Disc brake A brake design incorporating a rotating disc onto which brake pads are squeezed. The resulting friction converts the energy of a moving vehicle into heat.

Double-overhead cam (DOHC) An engine that uses two overhead camshafts, usually one for the intake valves and one for the exhaust valves.

Drivebelt(s) The belt(s) used to drive accessories such as the alternator, water pump, power steering pump, air conditioning compressor, etc. off the crankshaft pulley.

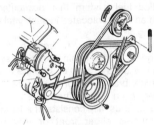

Accessory drivebelts

Driveshaft Any shaft used to transmit motion. Commonly used when referring to the axleshafts on a front wheel drive vehicle.

Driveshaft

Drum brake A type of brake using a drum-shaped metal cylinder attached to the inner surface of the wheel. When the brake pedal is pressed, curved brake shoes with friction linings press against the inside of the drum to slow or stop the vehicle.

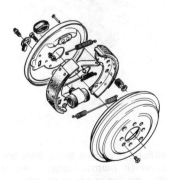

Drum brake assembly

E

EGR valve A valve used to introduce exhaust gases into the intake air stream.

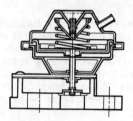

EGR valve

Electronic control unit (ECU) A computer which controls (for instance) ignition and fuel injection systems, or an anti-lock braking system. For more information refer to the *Haynes Automotive Electrical and Electronic Systems Manual*.

Electronic Fuel Injection (EFI) A computer controlled fuel system that distributes fuel through an injector located in each intake port of the engine.

Emergency brake A braking system, independent of the main hydraulic system, that can be used to slow or stop the vehicle if the primary brakes fail, or to hold the vehicle stationary even though the brake pedal isn't depressed. It usually consists of a hand lever that actuates either front or rear brakes mechanically through a series of cables and linkages. Also known as a handbrake or parking brake.

Endfloat The amount of lengthwise movement between two parts. As applied to a crankshaft, the distance that the crankshaft can move forward and back in the cylinder block.

Engine management system (EMS) A computer controlled system which manages the fuel injection and the ignition systems in an integrated fashion.

Exhaust manifold A part with several passages through which exhaust gases leave the engine combustion chambers and enter the exhaust pipe.

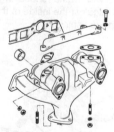

Exhaust manifold

F

Fan clutch A viscous (fluid) drive coupling device which permits variable engine fan speeds in relation to engine speeds.

Feeler blade A thin strip or blade of hardened steel, ground to an exact thickness, used to check or measure clearances between parts.

Feeler blade

Firing order The order in which the engine cylinders fire, or deliver their power strokes, beginning with the number one cylinder.

Flywheel A heavy spinning wheel in which energy is absorbed and stored by means of momentum. On cars, the flywheel is attached to the crankshaft to smooth out firing impulses.

Free play The amount of travel before any action takes place. The "looseness" in a linkage, or an assembly of parts, between the initial application of force and actual movement. For example, the distance the brake pedal moves before the pistons in the master cylinder are actuated.

Fuse An electrical device which protects a circuit against accidental overload. The typical fuse contains a soft piece of metal which is calibrated to melt at a predetermined current flow (expressed as amps) and break the circuit.

Fusible link A circuit protection device consisting of a conductor surrounded by heat-resistant insulation. The conductor is smaller than the wire it protects, so it acts as the weakest link in the circuit. Unlike a blown fuse, a failed fusible link must frequently be cut from the wire for replacement.

G

Gap The distance the spark must travel in jumping from the centre electrode to the side

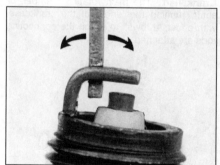

Adjusting spark plug gap

electrode in a spark plug. Also refers to the spacing between the points in a contact breaker assembly in a conventional points-type ignition, or to the distance between the reluctor or rotor and the pickup coil in an electronic ignition.

Gasket Any thin, soft material - usually cork, cardboard, asbestos or soft metal - installed between two metal surfaces to ensure a good seal. For instance, the cylinder head gasket seals the joint between the block and the cylinder head.

Gasket

Gauge An instrument panel display used to monitor engine conditions. A gauge with a movable pointer on a dial or a fixed scale is an analogue gauge. A gauge with a numerical readout is called a digital gauge.

H

Halfshaft A rotating shaft that transmits power from the final drive unit to a drive wheel, usually when referring to a live rear axle.

Harmonic balancer A device designed to reduce torsion or twisting vibration in the crankshaft. May be incorporated in the crankshaft pulley. Also known as a vibration damper.

Hone An abrasive tool for correcting small irregularities or differences in diameter in an engine cylinder, brake cylinder, etc.

Hydraulic tappet A tappet that utilises hydraulic pressure from the engine's lubrication system to maintain zero clearance (constant contact with both camshaft and valve stem). Automatically adjusts to variation in valve stem length. Hydraulic tappets also reduce valve noise.

I

Ignition timing The moment at which the spark plug fires, usually expressed in the number of crankshaft degrees before the piston reaches the top of its stroke.

Inlet manifold A tube or housing with passages through which flows the air-fuel mixture (carburettor vehicles and vehicles with throttle body injection) or air only (port fuel-injected vehicles) to the port openings in the cylinder head.

J

Jump start Starting the engine of a vehicle with a discharged or weak battery by attaching jump leads from the weak battery to a charged or helper battery.

L

Load Sensing Proportioning Valve (LSPV) A brake hydraulic system control valve that works like a proportioning valve, but also takes into consideration the amount of weight carried by the rear axle.

Locknut A nut used to lock an adjustment nut, or other threaded component, in place. For example, a locknut is employed to keep the adjusting nut on the rocker arm in position.

Lockwasher A form of washer designed to prevent an attaching nut from working loose.

M

MacPherson strut A type of front suspension system devised by Earle MacPherson at Ford of England. In its original form, a simple lateral link with the anti-roll bar creates the lower control arm. A long strut - an integral coil spring and shock absorber - is mounted between the body and the steering knuckle. Many modern so-called MacPherson strut systems use a conventional lower A-arm and don't rely on the anti-roll bar for location.

Multimeter An electrical test instrument with the capability to measure voltage, current and resistance.

N

NOx Oxides of Nitrogen. A common toxic pollutant emitted by petrol and diesel engines at higher temperatures.

O

Ohm The unit of electrical resistance. One volt applied to a resistance of one ohm will produce a current of one amp.

Ohmmeter An instrument for measuring electrical resistance.

O-ring A type of sealing ring made of a special rubber-like material; in use, the O-ring is compressed into a groove to provide the sealing action.

O-ring

Overhead cam (ohc) engine An engine with the camshaft(s) located on top of the cylinder head(s).

Overhead valve (ohv) engine An engine with the valves located in the cylinder head, but with the camshaft located in the engine block.

Oxygen sensor A device installed in the engine exhaust manifold, which senses the oxygen content in the exhaust and converts this information into an electric current. Also called a Lambda sensor.

P

Phillips screw A type of screw head having a cross instead of a slot for a corresponding type of screwdriver.

Plastigage A thin strip of plastic thread, available in different sizes, used for measuring clearances. For example, a strip of Plastigage is laid across a bearing journal. The parts are assembled and dismantled; the width of the crushed strip indicates the clearance between journal and bearing.

Plastigage

Propeller shaft The long hollow tube with universal joints at both ends that carries power from the transmission to the differential on front-engined rear wheel drive vehicles.

Proportioning valve A hydraulic control valve which limits the amount of pressure to the rear brakes during panic stops to prevent wheel lock-up.

R

Rack-and-pinion steering A steering system with a pinion gear on the end of the steering shaft that mates with a rack (think of a geared wheel opened up and laid flat). When the steering wheel is turned, the pinion turns, moving the rack to the left or right. This movement is transmitted through the track rods to the steering arms at the wheels.

Radiator A liquid-to-air heat transfer device designed to reduce the temperature of the coolant in an internal combustion engine cooling system.

Refrigerant Any substance used as a heat transfer agent in an air-conditioning system. R-12 has been the principle refrigerant for many years; recently, however, manufacturers have begun using R-134a, a non-CFC substance that is considered less harmful to the ozone in the upper atmosphere.

Rocker arm A lever arm that rocks on a shaft or pivots on a stud. In an overhead valve engine, the rocker arm converts the upward movement of the pushrod into a downward movement to open a valve.

Rotor In a distributor, the rotating device inside the cap that connects the centre electrode and the outer terminals as it turns, distributing the high voltage from the coil secondary winding to the proper spark plug. Also, that part of an alternator which rotates inside the stator. Also, the rotating assembly of a turbocharger, including the compressor wheel, shaft and turbine wheel.

Runout The amount of wobble (in-and-out movement) of a gear or wheel as it's rotated. The amount a shaft rotates "out-of-true." The out-of-round condition of a rotating part.

S

Sealant A liquid or paste used to prevent leakage at a joint. Sometimes used in conjunction with a gasket.

Sealed beam lamp An older headlight design which integrates the reflector, lens and filaments into a hermetically-sealed one-piece unit. When a filament burns out or the lens cracks, the entire unit is simply replaced.

Serpentine drivebelt A single, long, wide accessory drivebelt that's used on some newer vehicles to drive all the accessories, instead of a series of smaller, shorter belts. Serpentine drivebelts are usually tensioned by an automatic tensioner.

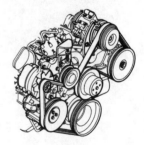

Serpentine drivebelt

Shim Thin spacer, commonly used to adjust the clearance or relative positions between two parts. For example, shims inserted into or under bucket tappets control valve clearances. Clearance is adjusted by changing the thickness of the shim.

Slide hammer A special puller that screws into or hooks onto a component such as a shaft or bearing; a heavy sliding handle on the shaft bottoms against the end of the shaft to knock the component free.

Sprocket A tooth or projection on the periphery of a wheel, shaped to engage with a chain or drivebelt. Commonly used to refer to the sprocket wheel itself.

Starter inhibitor switch On vehicles with an

automatic transmission, a switch that prevents starting if the vehicle is not in Neutral or Park.

Strut See MacPherson strut.

T

Tappet A cylindrical component which transmits motion from the cam to the valve stem, either directly or via a pushrod and rocker arm. Also called a cam follower.

Thermostat A heat-controlled valve that regulates the flow of coolant between the cylinder block and the radiator, so maintaining optimum engine operating temperature. A thermostat is also used in some air cleaners in which the temperature is regulated.

Thrust bearing The bearing in the clutch assembly that is moved in to the release levers by clutch pedal action to disengage the clutch. Also referred to as a release bearing.

Timing belt A toothed belt which drives the camshaft. Serious engine damage may result if it breaks in service.

Timing chain A chain which drives the camshaft.

Toe-in The amount the front wheels are closer together at the front than at the rear. On rear wheel drive vehicles, a slight amount of toe-in is usually specified to keep the front wheels running parallel on the road by offsetting other forces that tend to spread the wheels apart.

Toe-out The amount the front wheels are closer together at the rear than at the front. On

front wheel drive vehicles, a slight amount of toe-out is usually specified.

Tools For full information on choosing and using tools, refer to the *Haynes Automotive Tools Manual*.

Tracer A stripe of a second colour applied to a wire insulator to distinguish that wire from another one with the same colour insulator.

Tune-up A process of accurate and careful adjustments and parts replacement to obtain the best possible engine performance.

Turbocharger A centrifugal device, driven by exhaust gases, that pressurises the intake air. Normally used to increase the power output from a given engine displacement, but can also be used primarily to reduce exhaust emissions (as on VW's "Umwelt" Diesel engine).

U

Universal joint or U-joint A double-pivoted connection for transmitting power from a driving to a driven shaft through an angle. A U-joint consists of two Y-shaped yokes and a cross-shaped member called the spider.

V

Valve A device through which the flow of liquid, gas, vacuum, or loose material in bulk may be started, stopped, or regulated by a movable part that opens, shuts, or partially

obstructs one or more ports or passageways. A valve is also the movable part of such a device.

Valve clearance The clearance between the valve tip (the end of the valve stem) and the rocker arm or tappet. The valve clearance is measured when the valve is closed.

Vernier caliper A precision measuring instrument that measures inside and outside dimensions. Not quite as accurate as a micrometer, but more convenient.

Viscosity The thickness of a liquid or its resistance to flow.

Volt A unit for expressing electrical "pressure" in a circuit. One volt that will produce a current of one ampere through a resistance of one ohm.

W

Welding Various processes used to join metal items by heating the areas to be joined to a molten state and fusing them together. For more information refer to the *Haynes Automotive Welding Manual*.

Wiring diagram A drawing portraying the components and wires in a vehicle's electrical system, using standardised symbols. For more information refer to the *Haynes Automotive Electrical and Electronic Systems Manual*.

Note: *References throughout this index are in the form - "Chapter number" • "page number"*